Introduction to Business

SENIOR CONTRIBUTING AUTHORS

Lawrence J. Gitman, San Diego State University - Emeritus
Carl McDaniel, University of Texas, Arlington
Amit Shah, Frostburg State University
Monique Reece
Linda Koffel, Houston Community College
Bethann Talsma, Davenport University and Grand Rapids Community College
James C. Hyatt, University of The Cumberlands

OpenStax
Rice University
6100 Main Street MS-375
Houston, Texas 77005

To learn more about OpenStax, visit https://openstax.org.
Individual print copies and bulk orders can be purchased through our website.

PRINT BOOK ISBN-10	1-947172-54-9
PRINT BOOK ISBN-13	978-1-947172-54-8
PDF VERSION ISBN-10	1-947172-55-7
PDF VERSION ISBN-13	978-1-947172-55-5
Revision Number	IB-2018-000(09/18)-BKB
Original Publication Year	2018

OpenStax

OpenStax provides free, peer-reviewed, openly licensed textbooks for introductory college and Advanced Placement® courses and low-cost, personalized courseware that helps students learn. A nonprofit ed tech initiative based at Rice University, we're committed to helping students access the tools they need to complete their courses and meet their educational goals.

Rice University

OpenStax, OpenStax CNX, and OpenStax Tutor are initiatives of Rice University. As a leading research university with a distinctive commitment to undergraduate education, Rice University aspires to path-breaking research, unsurpassed teaching, and contributions to the betterment of our world. It seeks to fulfill this mission by cultivating a diverse community of learning and discovery that produces leaders across the spectrum of human endeavor.

Philanthropic Support

OpenStax is grateful for our generous philanthropic partners, who support our vision to improve educational opportunities for all learners.

Laura and John Arnold Foundation	The Maxfield Foundation
Arthur and Carlyse Ciocca Charitable Foundation	Burt and Deedee McMurtry
Ann and John Doerr	Michelson 20MM Foundation
Bill & Melinda Gates Foundation	National Science Foundation
Girard Foundation	The Open Society Foundations
Google Inc.	Jumee Yhu and David E. Park III
The William and Flora Hewlett Foundation	Brian D. Patterson USA-International Foundation
Rusty and John Jaggers	The Bill and Stephanie Sick Fund
The Calvin K. Kazanjian Economics Foundation	Robin and Sandy Stuart Foundation
Charles Koch Foundation	The Stuart Family Foundation
Leon Lowenstein Foundation, Inc.	Tammy and Guillermo Treviño

TABLE OF CONTENTS

Preface

Welcome to *Introduction to Business*, an OpenStax resource. This textbook was written to increase student access to high-quality learning materials, maintaining highest standards of academic rigor at little to no cost.

About OpenStax

OpenStax is a nonprofit based at Rice University, and it's our mission to improve student access to education. Our first openly licensed college textbook was published in 2012, and our library has since scaled to over 25 books for college and AP® courses used by hundreds of thousands of students. OpenStax Tutor, our low-cost personalized learning tool, is being used in college courses throughout the country. Through our partnerships with philanthropic foundations and our alliance with other educational resource organizations, OpenStax is breaking down the most common barriers to learning and empowering students and instructors to succeed.

About OpenStax resources

Customization

Introduction to Business is licensed under a Creative Commons Attribution 4.0 International (CC BY) license, which means that you can distribute, remix, and build upon the content, as long as you provide attribution to OpenStax and its content contributors.

Because our books are openly licensed, you are free to use the entire book or pick and choose the sections that are most relevant to the needs of your course. Feel free to remix the content by assigning your students certain chapters and sections in your syllabus, in the order that you prefer. You can even provide a direct link in your syllabus to the sections in the web view of your book.

Instructors also have the option of creating a customized version of their OpenStax book. The custom version can be made available to students in low-cost print or digital form through their campus bookstore. Visit the Instructor Resources section of your book page on OpenStax.org for more information.

Art attribution in *Introduction to Business*

In *Introduction to Business*, art contains attribution to its title, creator or rights holder, host platform, and license within the caption. Because the art is openly licensed, anyone may reuse the art as long as they provide the same attribution to its original source.

Errata

All OpenStax textbooks undergo a rigorous review process. However, like any professional-grade textbook, errors sometimes occur. Since our books are web based, we can make updates periodically when deemed pedagogically necessary. If you have a correction to suggest, submit it through the link on your book page on OpenStax.org. Subject matter experts review all errata suggestions. OpenStax is committed to remaining transparent about all updates, so you will also find a list of past errata changes on your book page on OpenStax.org.

Format

You can access this textbook for free in web view or PDF through OpenStax.org, and for a low cost in print.

About *Introduction to Business*

Introduction to Business is designed to meet the scope and sequence requirements of foundational business courses. The textbook presents business principles and emerging trends in fields including management, leadership, production, marketing, and finance. Through this content, students will acquire the knowledge, skills, and competencies to prepare for the competitive workplace.

Coverage and scope

Introduction to Business covers the scope and sequence of most introductory business courses. The book provides detailed explanations in the context of core themes such as ethics, entrepreneurship, customer satisfaction, global business, and managing change. Introduction to Business includes hundreds of current business examples from a range of industries, geographic locations, and featuring a variety of individuals. The outcome is a balanced approach to the theory and application of business concepts, with attention to the knowledge and skills necessary for student success in this course and beyond.

Pedagogical foundation

Consistent, integrated learning. Targeted learning outcomes are listed at the beginning of each chapter and then repeated throughout the chapter. The learning outcomes connect to the text and the additional resources that accompany *Introduction to Business*. After reading each section, students can test their retention by answering the questions in the Concept Checks. Every learning goal is further reinforced by a summary.

Hundreds of business examples to bring concepts to life. This book is designed to speak to the typical student. We have done a lot of research about student needs, abilities, experiences, and interests, and then we have shaped the text around them. We have used experiences both inside and outside the classroom to enrich a book that is both readable and enjoyable. We believe that the real business applications found throughout every chapter set the standard for readability and understanding of key concepts.

Learning business terminology, made easy. As students begin to study business, they will explore new words and concepts. To help them learn this language of business, we define each new term in the chapter, display the terms in bold, and offer a complete glossary at the end of the book.

Engaging business themes

Ethics. Business presents outstanding opportunities to do good. Through responsible business practices and the development and distribution of helpful products and services, businesspeople can positively affect their community. A paramount theme of this text is that business must be conducted in an ethical and socially responsible manner. Chapter 2, Making Ethical Decisions and Managing a Socially Responsible Business, is completely devoted to business ethics and social responsibility. We discuss techniques for setting personal ethical standards, how managers influence organizational ethics, tools for creating employee ethical awareness, and the concept of individual and corporate responsibility. *Introduction to Business* also features ethics activities at the end of each chapter. All ethical dilemmas are taken right out of today's business world.

Customer satisfaction and quality. Because customer satisfaction and quality are the foundation of all business principles, these important topics are addressed in most chapters within *Introduction to Business*. Each chapter stresses that satisfied customers who experience high-quality products and services become loyal customers. A box in every chapter called "Customer Satisfaction and Quality" demonstrates how these concepts are applied in actual companies.

Managing change. Change in the business or consumer environment can lead to failures like Kodak's and successes like Apple's. The Managing Change boxed feature describes how companies have recognized and responded to changes in technology, competition, economic forces, demographics, and culture.

Entrepreneurship and small business management. Because many students will either open their own businesses or go to work for small organizations, entrepreneurship and small business principles are covered throughout the text. Chapter 5, Entrepreneurship: Starting and Managing Your Own Business, delivers interesting discussions on starting and managing a small business and the associated advantages and disadvantages. In addition, a feature called "Catching the Entrepreneurial Spirit" offers practical insights into the challenges and rewards of actually owning and managing a small business.

Global business economy. In Chapter 3, Competing in the Global Marketplace, we discuss why global trade is important to the United States, why nations trade, barriers to international trade, how companies enter the global marketplace, and a host of other international concepts and topics. The Trends section of each chapter frequently includes a discussion of how globalization will affect specific business activities. In addition, our Global Business box demonstrates how businesses are expanding their workforce, products, and customer base throughout the world in order to grow.

Features

Rather than provide a dry recitation of facts, we illustrate concepts with contemporary examples. In addition to the in-text examples, we have several boxed features that provide more extensive examples in areas of importance in today's business environment. Each of the boxed features described below includes a series of critical thinking questions to prompt the student to consider the implications of each business strategy.

Ethics in Practice. Ethics in Practice features demonstrate how businesses are responsible not only to the bottom line, but to providing goods and services in a responsible manner.

Customer Satisfaction and Quality. Because customer satisfaction and quality are essential to attracting and keeping customers, the Customer Satisfaction and Quality box addresses how these concepts are illustrated and applied in actual companies.

Expanding Around the Globe. Upon entering today's workplace, you are very likely to conduct business with colleagues, clients, and vendors from around the world. The Expanding Around the Globe feature offers insights into the global economy and highlights the strategies firms take to expand their business and improve their productivity by utilizing global resources.

Managing Change. The turbulent business climate requires companies to adapt their business strategies in response to a variety of economic, social, competitive, and technological forces. The Managing Change feature highlights how businesses have altered their business strategies in response to these forces.

Catching the Entrepreneurial Spirit. This feature highlights the challenges and opportunities available in small businesses and other entrepreneurial ventures.

Activities and cases that put knowledge to work

Introduction to Business helps students develop a solid grounding in the skills that they can apply in the workplace. These skill-building activities and resources help build and polish competencies that future employers will value.

Preparing for tomorrow's workplace skills and team activities. These activities are designed to help build students' business skills and to help them practice teamwork. We have developed assignments focused on five important workplace competencies: using and allocating resources, working with others, acquiring and using information, understanding systems, and working with technology. Team activities in every chapter give students an opportunity to work together, building communication skills and interpersonal skills.

Ethics activities. Ethics activities at the end of each chapter present real-world ethical challenges and prompt students to choose the most ethical course of action.

Working the net activities. These activities guide students through a step-by-step analysis of actual e-business practices and give them opportunities to build online research skills.

Creative thinking cases. The Creative Thinking case in each chapter invites students to explore business strategies of various companies, analyze business decisions, and prepare comments.

Additional resources

Community Hubs

OpenStax partners with the Institute for the Study of Knowledge Management in Education (ISKME) to offer Community Hubs on OER Commons – a platform for instructors to share community-created resources that support OpenStax books, free of charge. Through our Community Hubs, instructors can upload their own materials or download resources to use in their own courses, including additional ancillaries, teaching material, multimedia, and relevant course content. We encourage instructors to join the hubs for the subjects most relevant to your teaching and research as an opportunity both to enrich your courses and to engage with other faculty.

To reach the Community Hubs, visit www.oercommons.org/hubs/OpenStax.

Student and instructor resources

We've compiled additional resources for both students and instructors, including Getting Started Guides, an instructor's manual, test bank, and image slides. Instructor resources require a verified instructor account, which you can apply for when you log in or create your account on OpenStax.org. Take advantage of these resources to supplement your OpenStax book.

Comprehensive instructor's manual. Each component of the instructor's manual is designed to provide maximum guidance for delivering the content in an interesting and dynamic manner. The instructor's manual includes an in-depth lecture outline, which is interspersed with lecture "tidbits" that allow instructors to add timely and interesting enhancements to their lectures. Authored by Linda Hefferin, Elgin Community College.

Test bank. With nearly 2,000 true/false, multiple-choice, fill-in-the-blank, and short answer questions in our test bank, instructors can customize tests to support a variety of course objectives. The test bank is available in Word format. Authored by Amit Shah, Frostburg State University.

PowerPoint lecture slides. The PowerPoint slides provide images and descriptions as a starting place for instructors to build their lectures.

Technology partners

As allies in making high-quality learning materials accessible, our technology partners offer optional low-cost tools that are integrated with OpenStax books. To access the technology options for your text, visit your book page on OpenStax.org.

About the authors

Senior contributing authors

Lawrence J. Gitman, San Diego State University - Emeritus

Lawrence J. Gitman is a prolific author, with over fifty published articles and a number of best-selling college textbooks (some with coauthors). In addition to this book, his works include *Personal Financial Planning, Fourteenth Edition* (2017), *PFIN 6 (2018)*, *Fundamentals of Investing, Thirteenth Edition,* (2017), *Principles of Managerial Finance, Fourteenth Edition* (2015), and *Principles of Managerial Finance, Brief, Seventh Edition* (2015). His books have been used by more than two million college students. Dr. Gitman is a CFP® and has served as a member of the Certified Financial Planner Board of Standards and as an associate editor of several academic journals. He has also served as president of a number of academic organizations, including the Academy of Financial Services, the Midwest Finance Association, and the Financial Management Association National Honor Society. Professor Gitman earned degrees from Purdue University (B.S. in Industrial Management), the University of Dayton (MBA), and the University of Cincinnati (PhD in Finance).

Carl McDaniel, University of Texas, Arlington

Carl McDaniel's career has spanned more than 40 years, during which he was the recipient of several awards for outstanding teaching. He was the chair of the University of Texas at Arlington marketing department for 32 year, and now teaches executive MBA courses locally and in China. McDaniel's research has appeared in such publications as the *Journal of Marketing, Journal of Business Research, Journal of the Academy of Marketing Science*, and *California Management Review*. He has also authored over 50 textbooks in marketing and business. He has a bachelor's degree from the University of Arkansas and a master's degree and doctorate from Arizona State University.

Amit Shah, Frostburg State University

Amit Shah is professor of management and director of the Center for Community Partnerships at Frostburg State University (FSU) in Maryland. He has over 20 years of experience in industry and academia. Dr. Shah has taught a variety of business courses including management, strategic management, and international business. He has published over 60 referreed articles in various journals and published proceedings and has conducted training for various organizations in the area of business and strategy. In his capacity as Center director, he works with various small-to-medium-size organizations — for profit, nonprofit, and government agencies — in organizing management development workshops and training. He has received several awards including Frostburg State University's Outstanding Faculty Service Award, the FSU College of Business's Outstanding Faculty Research Award, and Outstanding SAM Student Chapter Advisor Award. He has also served as president of the Southeastern Chapters of the Decision Sciences Institute and president of the Institute for Operations Research and Management Sciences. When he is not in his classroom or engaged in community service, Dr. Shah enjoys being an entrepreneur serving coffee at Mountain City Coffeehouse and Creamery, which he owns with his wife.

Monique Reece

Monique Reece is the founder and CEO of MarketSmarter, a marketing consulting and training firm that helps companies improve strategy and implement real-time business planning processes to develop a culture of execution. She has more than 20 years of marketing and executive management experience working with both Fortune 100 companies and fast-growing entrepreneurial businesses. Professor Reece formerly served as Executive Vice President at Jones Knowledge and as Director of Global Market Development at Avaya. Monique has served as an Executive Education faculty member at the Daniels College of Business, University of Denver, and as an Adjunct Professor at the Institute for Leadership and Organizational Performance where she taught marketing and customer experience in the Executive MBA program. She has published hundreds of articles and is the author of four books. Monique is also a frequent speaker for industry conferences such as the American Marketing Association and *Inc. Magazine*.

Linda Koffel, Houston Community College

Linda Koffel has been teaching at Houston Community College. She is a winner of the Consortium of Community Colleges for Innovation, a prestigious NISOD award for teaching. She taught in the Goldman Sachs *10,000 Small Businesses* program; is a certified Ice House Entrepreneurial Program professor; and has her own business. Linda Koffel played a key role in the design and development of cutting-edge marketing and entrepreneurial curriculum at Houston Community College.

Bethann Talsma, Davenport University and Grand Rapids Community College

Bethann Talsma is the founder of Platinum Properties, an income property business that provides housing in Grand Rapids, Michigan. She has more than 15 years of experience managing all operations including property procurement, tenant interaction, project management, and administration. Under her leadership the business has experienced steady growth and increased profits. Bethann also serves as an adjunct instructor at both Grand Rapids Community College and Davenport University where she teaches general business courses and Microsoft Office applications, bringing real-life examples to the classroom. In addition, Bethann facilitates corporate trainings for Microsoft Office and Google applications.

James C. Hyatt, University of The Cumberlands

Professor Hyatt serves the University of the Cumberlands teaching graduate courses for the School of Computer and Information Sciences, Executive Programs. He has served as an Assistant Professor at Fort Hays State University and Ashford University, where he taught Business, Technology and Analytics Courses. He has published in Business, Technology and Leadership journals and serves on International Committees. Professor Hyatt has extensive experience in Business, Technology and Analytics consulting. Professor Hyatt received his Ph.D. in Information Systems Management from Walden University and also holds degrees from Fort Hays State University and Southern Utah University.

Reviewers

Maria Zak Aria, Camden County College
Joseph H. Atallah, Devry Institute of Technology
Herm Baine, Broward Community College
Dennis R. Brode, Sinclair Community College
Harvey Bronstein, Oakland Community College
Mark Camma, Atlantic Cape Community College
Bonnie R. Chavez, Santa Barbara City College
M. Bixby Cooper, Michigan State University
Linda Davenport, Klamath Community College
Evelyn Delaney, Daytona Beach Community College
Kathryn E. Dodge, University of Alaska, Fairbanks
Jonas Falik, Queensborough Community College
Janice M. Feldbauer, Austin Community College Northridge
Dennis Foster, Northern Arizona University
James Giles, Bergen Community College
Mary E. Gorman, University of Cincinnati
Gina Hagler
Carnella Hardin, Glendale College
Elizabeth Hastings, Middlesex Community College

Frederic H. Hawkins, Westchester Business Institute
Melvin O. Hawkins, Midlands Technical College
Charlane Bomrad Held, Onondaga Community College
Merrily Joy Hoffman, San Jacinto College
Ralph F. Jagodka, Mount San Antonio College
Andrew Johnson, Bellevue Community College
Connie Johnson, Tampa College
Jerry Kinskey, Sinclair Community College
Raymond T. Lamanna, Berkeley College
Carol Luce, Arizona State University
Tom McFarland, Mt. San Antonio College
Carl Meskimen, Sinclair Community College
Andrew Miller, Hudson Valley Community College
H. Lynn Moretz, Central Piedmont Community College
Linda M. Newell, Saddleback College
Joseph Newton, Bakersfield College
Brandy Nielsen, Great Basin College
David Oliver, Edison College
Teresa Palmer, Illinois State University
Jim Pennypacker
Karli Peterson, Colorado State University
Raymond Pfang, Tarrant County College Connect Campus
Jude A. Rathburn, University of Wisconsin–Milwaukee
Jodell Raymond Monroe Community College
Robert F. Reck, Western Michigan University
Matthew Rivaldi, San Diego City College
Carol Rowey, Community College of Rhode Island
Ann Squire, Blackhawk Technical College
Carolyn Stevenson, Kaplan University
Richard E. T. Strickler, Sr., McLennan Community College
Linda Tancs
Susan Thompson, Palm Beach Community College
David L. Turnipseed, Indiana University-Purdue University Fort Wayne
Maria Vitale, Chaffey College
Valerie Wallingford, Bemidji State University
Ron Weidenfeller, Grand Rapids Community College

Understanding Economic Systems and Business

Exhibit 1.1 (Credit: Marco Verch /flickr / Attribution 2.0 Generic (CC BY 2.0))

Introduction

Learning Outcomes

After reading this chapter, you should be able to answer these questions:

1. How do businesses and not-for-profit organizations help create our standard of living?
2. What are the sectors of the business environment, and how do changes in them influence business decisions?
3. What are the primary features of the world's economic systems, and how are the three sectors of the U.S. economy linked?
4. How do economic growth, full employment, price stability, and inflation indicate a nation's economic health?
5. How does the government use monetary policy and fiscal policy to achieve its macroeconomic goals?
6. What are the basic microeconomic concepts of demand and supply, and how do they establish prices?
7. What are the four types of market structure?
8. Which trends are reshaping the business, microeconomic, and macroeconomic environments and competitive arena?

EXPLORING BUSINESS CAREERS

Team Rubicon: Disaster Relief and a Sense of Purpose

Accounting for a substantial amount of economic activity in the United States, not-for-profits are an undeniable force in the business world, even though their focus on goals other than profit falls outside the traditional model of a for-profit business. But it is this shift away from a focus on profit that allows them to pursue missions of social improvement and contributions to society as a whole. To be truly effective in a not-for-profit organization, a person must share the organization's vision.

The vision for Team Rubicon was shaped by its cofounders, Jake Wood and William McNulty, who saw the devastation caused by the Haiti earthquake in 2010 and sprang into action. Both marines, Wood and McNulty knew they could do something to help in this devastating and chaotic situation. Within 24 hours, they enlisted the help of six other military veterans and first responders, gathered donations and supplies from friends and family, and made their way to Haiti to help with disaster relief, and Team Rubicon was born.

Exhibit 1.2   Team Rubicon (Credit: Bureau of Land Management Oregon and Washington/flickr/ Attribution 2.0 Generic (CC BY 2.0))

The organization gets its name from the Rubicon, a river in northern Italy that Julius Caesar and his troops crossed on their epic march to Rome, with the river marking the point of no return. The name underscores the cofounders' experiences during the Haitian disaster, where despite advice from government officials and other aid organizations not to proceed, their small team crossed into Haiti from the Dominican Republic carrying crucial gear and medical supplies to thousands of earthquake victims.

Seven years later, Team Rubicon's mission is twofold: to pair the skills and experiences of military veterans with first responders to hit the ground running in any type of disaster and to provide a sense of community and accomplishment to veterans who have served their country proudly but may be struggling as a result of their war experiences.

According to the organization's mission statement, Team Rubicon seeks to provide veterans three things they sometimes lose after leaving the military: a purpose, gained through disaster relief; a sense of community, built by serving with others; and a feeling of self-worth from recognizing the impact one individual can make when dealing with natural disasters.

Headquartered in the Los Angeles area, Team Rubicon is staffed by more than 60 employees who work in 10 regions around the country, along with more than 40,000 volunteers ready to deploy within 24 hours. Similar to company operations in for-profit organizations, staff positions at Team Rubicon include regional administrators; field operations (including membership and training); marketing, communications, and social media; fundraising and partnership development; finance and accounting; and people operations.

Team Rubicon's staff members bring professional and/or military experience to their daily jobs, but they all share the organization's vision. Many staff members started as volunteers for Team Rubicon while working in for-profit careers, while others took advantage of the organization's strong internship program to become familiar with its mission and focus on disaster relief.

In 2016, Team Rubicon trained 8,000 military veterans and first responders in disaster relief and responded to 46 disasters, which required more than 85,000 volunteer hours. In addition to donations from individuals and corporations, Team Rubicon relies on its partnerships with other organizations, such as Southwest Airlines, which supplies hundreds of free plane tickets each year to fly volunteers to disaster sites.

Team Rubicon actively engages its nationwide community at every level of the organization, from volunteer to board member, and every step of its operation: from training to planning to implementation to seeking donations and volunteers to help with any type of disaster relief. Over the past several years, Team Rubicon has been recognized as one of the top nonprofits to work for by *The NonProfit Times*, based on employee surveys and business partners' input about the organization's work environment.

The not-for-profit world may not be for everyone, but if its growth is any indication within the overall economy, it does appeal to many. With a resolve to assist those in need, including both disaster victims and returning military personnel, Team Rubicon offers opportunities for those interested in nonprofit careers as well as those passionate about helping others.

Sources: Company website, "Our Mission" and "Staff & Board," https://teamrubiconusa.org, accessed May 29, 2017; Mark Hrywna, "2017 NPT Best Nonprofits to Work," *The NonProfit Times,* http://thenonprofittimes.com, accessed May 27, 2017; Mark Hrywna, "2016 NPT Best Nonprofits to Work," *The NonProfit Times,* http://thenonprofittimes.com, accessed May 27, 2017; Kyle Dickman, "The Future of Disaster Relief Isn't the Red Cross," *Outside,* https://www.outsideonline.com, August 25, 2016.

This module provides the basic structures upon which the business world is built: how it is organized, what outside forces influence it, and where it is heading. It also explores how the world's economies and governments shape economic activity. Each day in the United States, thousands of new businesses are born. Only a rare few will become the next Apple, Google, or Amazon. Unfortunately, many others will never see their first anniversary. The survivors are those that understand that change is the one constant in the business environment. Those organizations pay attention to the business environment in which they operate and the trends that affect all businesses and then successfully adapt to those trends. In this module, we will meet many businesses, both large and small, profit and not-for-profit, that prosper because they track trends and use them to identify potential opportunities. This ability to manage change is a critical factor in separating the success stories from the tales of business failure.

We begin our study of business by introducing you to the primary functions of a business, the relationship between risk and profits, and the importance of not-for-profit organizations. We'll also examine the major components of the business environment and how changing demographic, social, political and legal, and competitive factors affect all business organizations. Next, we'll explore how economies provide jobs for workers and also compete with other businesses to create and deliver products to consumers. You will also learn how governments attempt to influence economic activity through policies such as lowering or raising taxes. Next, we discuss how supply and demand determine prices for goods and services. Finally, we conclude by examining key trends in the business environment, economic systems, and the competitive environment.

1.1 The Nature of Business

1. How do businesses and not-for-profit organizations help create our standard of living?

Take a moment to think about the many different types of businesses you come into contact with on a typical day. As you drive to class, you may stop at a gas station that is part of a major national oil company and grab lunch from a fast food chain such as Taco Bell or McDonald's or the neighborhood pizza place. Need more cash? You can do your banking on a smartphone or other device via mobile apps. You don't even have to visit the store anymore: online shopping brings the stores to you, offering everything from clothes to food, furniture, and concert tickets.

A **business** is an organization that strives for a profit by providing goods and services desired by its customers. Businesses meet the needs of consumers by providing medical care, autos, and countless other goods and services. **Goods** are tangible items manufactured by businesses, such as laptops. **Services** are intangible offerings of businesses that can't be held, touched, or stored. Physicians, lawyers, hairstylists, car washes, and airlines all provide services. Businesses also serve other organizations, such as hospitals, retailers, and governments, by providing machinery, goods for resale, computers, and thousands of other items.

Thus, businesses create the goods and services that are the basis of our standard of living. The **standard of living** of any country is measured by the output of goods and services people can buy with the money they have. The United States has one of the highest standards of living in the world. Although several countries, such as Switzerland and Germany, have higher average wages than the United States, their standards of living aren't higher, because prices are so much higher. As a result, the same amount of money buys less in those countries. For example, in the United States, we can buy an Extra Value Meal at McDonald's for less than $5, while in another country, a similar meal might cost as much as $10.

Businesses play a key role in determining our quality of life by providing jobs and goods and services to society. **Quality of life** refers to the general level of human happiness based on such things as life expectancy, educational standards, health, sanitation, and leisure time. Building a high quality of life is a combined effort of businesses, government, and not-for-profit organizations. In 2017, Vienna, Austria, ranked highest in quality of life, followed by Zurich, Switzerland; Auckland, New Zealand; and Munich, Germany. It may come as a surprise that not one of the world's top cities is in the United States: seven of the top 10 locations are in western Europe, two are in Australia/New Zealand, and one is in Canada. At the other end of the scale, Baghdad, Iraq, is the city scoring the lowest on the annual survey.[1] Creating a quality of life is not without risks, however. **Risk** is the potential to lose time and money or otherwise not be able to accomplish an organization's goals. Without enough blood donors, for example, the American Red Cross faces the risk of not meeting the demand for blood by victims of disaster. Businesses such as Microsoft face the risk of falling short of their revenue and profit goals. **Revenue** is the money a company receives by providing services or selling goods to customers. **Costs** are expenses for rent, salaries, supplies, transportation, and many other items that a company incurs from creating and selling goods and services. For example, some of the costs incurred by Microsoft in developing its software include expenses for salaries, facilities, and advertising. If Microsoft has money left over after it pays all costs, it has a **profit**. A company whose costs are greater than revenues shows a loss.

When a company such as Microsoft uses its resources intelligently, it can often increase sales, hold costs down, and earn a profit. Not all companies earn profits, but that is the risk of being in business. In U.S. business today, there is generally a direct relationship between risks and profit: the greater the risks, the greater the potential for profit (or loss). Companies that take too conservative a stance may lose out to more nimble competitors who react quickly to the changing business environment.

Take Sony, for example. The Japanese electronics giant, once a leader with its Walkman music player and Trinitron televisions, steadily lost ground—and profits—over the past two decades to other companies by not embracing new technologies such as the digital music format and flat-panel TV screens. Sony misjudged what the market wanted and stayed with proprietary technologies rather than create cross-platform options for consumers. Apple, at the time an upstart in personal music devices, quickly grabbed the lion's share of the digital music market with its iPods and iTunes music streaming service. By 2016, Sony restructured its business portfolio and has experienced substantial success with its PlayStation 4 gaming console and original gaming content.[2]

Not-for-Profit Organizations

Not all organizations strive to make a profit. A **not-for-profit organization** is an organization that exists to achieve some goal other than the usual business goal of profit. Charities such as Habitat for Humanity, the United Way, the American Cancer Society, and the World Wildlife Fund are not-for-profit organizations, as are most hospitals, zoos, arts organizations, civic groups, and religious organizations. Over the last 20 years, the number of nonprofit organizations—and the employees and volunteers who work for them—has increased considerably. Government is our largest and most pervasive not-for-profit group. In addition, more than 1.5 million nongovernmental not-for-profit entities operate in the United States today and contribute more than $900 billion annually to the U.S. economy.[3]

Like their for-profit counterparts, these groups set goals and require resources to meet those goals. However, their goals are not focused on profits. For example, a not-for-profit organization's goal might be feeding the poor, preserving the environment, increasing attendance at the ballet, or preventing drunk driving. Not-for-profit organizations do not compete directly with one another in the same manner as, for example, Ford and Honda, but they do compete for talented employees, people's limited volunteer time, and donations.

Exhibit 1.3   Rescue boat Following Hurricane Irma affected The island of Puerto Rico, the Kentucky and Haraii National Guard assisted storm victims by donating to disaster relief efforts. Some not-for-profit charities focused aid toward the people of the region, but others delivered care to a different group of sufferers: animals and pets. Although most animal hospitals are not normally a refuge for displaced animals, many facilities opened their doors to pet owners affected by the torrential rains. *Why are tasks such as animal rescue managed primarily through not-for-profit organizations?* (Credit: Hawaii and Kentucky National Guard /flickr /Attribution 2.0 Generic (CC BY))

The boundaries that formerly separated not-for-profit and for-profit organizations have blurred, leading to a greater exchange of ideas between the sectors. As discussed in detail in the ethics chapter, for-profit businesses are now addressing social issues. Successful not-for-profits apply business principles to operate more effectively. Not-for-profit managers are concerned with the same concepts as their colleagues in for-profit companies: developing strategy, budgeting carefully, measuring performance, encouraging innovation, improving productivity, demonstrating accountability, and fostering an ethical workplace environment.

In addition to pursuing a museum's artistic goals, for example, top executives manage the administrative and business side of the organization: human resources, finance, and legal concerns. Ticket revenues cover a fraction of the museum's operating costs, so the director spends a great deal of time seeking major donations and memberships. Today's museum boards of directors include both art patrons and business executives who want to see sound fiscal decision-making in a not-for-profit setting. Therefore, a museum director must walk a fine line between the institution's artistic mission and financial policies. According to a survey by *The Economist*, over the next several years, major art museums will be looking for new directors, as more than a third of the current ones are approaching retirement.[4]

Factors of Production: The Building Blocks of Business

To provide goods and services, regardless of whether they operate in the for-profit or not-for-profit sector, organizations require inputs in the form of resources called **factors of production**. Four traditional factors of production are common to all productive activity: *natural resources*, *labor (human resources)*, *capital*, and *entrepreneurship*. Many experts now include *knowledge* as a fifth factor, acknowledging its key role in business success. By using the factors of production efficiently, a company can produce more goods and services with the same resources.

Commodities that are useful inputs in their natural state are known as natural resources. They include farmland, forests, mineral and oil deposits, and water. Sometimes natural resources are simply called land, although, as you can see, the term means more than just land. Companies use natural resources in different ways. International Paper Company uses wood pulp to make paper, and Pacific Gas & Electric Company may use water, oil, or coal to produce electricity. Today urban sprawl, pollution, and limited resources have raised questions about resource use. Conservationists, environmentalists, and government bodies are proposing laws to require land-use planning and resource conservation.

Labor, or human resources, refers to the economic contributions of people working with their minds and muscles. This input includes the talents of everyone—from a restaurant cook to a nuclear physicist—who performs the many tasks of manufacturing and selling goods and services.

The tools, machinery, equipment, and buildings used to produce goods and services and get them to the consumer are known as **capital**. Sometimes the term *capital* is also used to mean the money that buys machinery, factories, and other production and distribution facilities. However, because money itself produces nothing, it is not one of the basic inputs. Instead, it is a means of acquiring the inputs. Therefore, in this context, capital does not include money.

Entrepreneurs are the people who combine the inputs of natural resources, labor, and capital to produce goods or services with the intention of making a profit or accomplishing a not-for-profit goal. These people make the decisions that set the course for their businesses; they create products and production processes or develop services. Because they are not guaranteed a profit in return for their time and effort, they must be risk-takers. Of course, if their companies succeed, the rewards may be great.

Today, many individuals want to start their own businesses. They are attracted by the opportunity to be their own boss and reap the financial rewards of a successful firm. Many start their first business from their dorm rooms, such as Mark Zuckerberg of Facebook, or while living at home, so their cost is almost zero. Entrepreneurs include people such as Microsoft cofounder Bill Gates, who was named the richest person in the world in 2017, as well as Google founders Sergey Brin and Larry Page.[5] Many thousands of individuals have started companies that, while remaining small, make a major contribution to the U.S. economy.

CATCHING THE ENTREPRENEURIAL SPIRIT

StickerGiant Embraces Change

Entrepreneurs typically are not afraid to take risks or change the way they do business if it means there is a better path to success. John Fischer of Longmont, Colorado, fits the profile.

The drawn-out U.S. presidential election in 2000 between Bush and Gore inspired Fischer to create a bumper sticker that claimed, "He's Not My President," which became a top seller. As a result of this venture, Fischer started an online retail sticker store, which he viewed as possibly the "Amazon of Stickers." Designing and making stickers in his basement, Fischer's start-up would eventually become a multimillion-dollar company, recognized in 2017 by *Forbes* as one of its top 25 small businesses.

The StickerGiant online store was successful, supplying everything from sports stickers to ones commemorating rock and roll bands and breweries. By 2011, the business was going strong; however, the entrepreneur decided to do away with the retail store, instead focusing the business on custom orders, which became StickerGiant's main product.

As the company became more successful and added more employees, Fischer once again looked to make some changes. In 2012 he decided to introduce a concept called open-book management, in which he shares the company's financials with employees at a weekly meeting. Other topics discussed at the meeting include customer comments and feedback, employee concerns, and colleague appreciation for one another. Fischer believes sharing information about the company's performance (good or bad) not only allows employees to feel part of the operation, but also empowers them to embrace change or suggest ideas that could help the business expand and flourish.

Innovation is also visible in the technology StickerGiant uses to create miles and miles of custom stickers (nearly 800 miles of stickers in 2016). The manufacturing process involves digital printing and laser-finishing equipment. Fischer says only five other companies worldwide have the laser-finishing equipment StickerGiant uses as part of its operations. Because of the investment in this high-tech equipment, the company can make custom stickers in large quantities overnight and ship them to customers the next day.

This small business continues to evolve with an entrepreneur at the helm who is not afraid of making changes or having fun. In 2016, StickerGiant put together Saul the Sticker Ball, a *Guinness World Records* winner that weighed in at a whopping 232 pounds. Fischer and his employees created Saul when they collected more than 170,000 stickers that had been lying around the office and decided to put them to good use. With $10 million in annual sales and nearly 40 employees, StickerGiant continues to be a successful endeavor for John Fischer and his employees almost two decades after Fischer created his first sticker.

Questions for Discussion
1. How does being a risk-taker help Fischer in his business activities?
2. If you were a small business owner, would you consider sharing the company's financial data with employees? Explain your reasoning.

Sources: "All About StickerGiant," https://www.stickergiant.com, accessed May 29, 2017; Bo Burlingham, "Forbes Small Giants 2017: America's Best Small Companies," *Forbes,* http://www.forbes.com, May 9, 2017; Karsten Strauss, "Making Money and Breaking Records in the Sticker Business," *Forbes,* http://www.forbes.com, January 26, 2016; Emilie Rusch, "StickerGiant Does Big Business in Tiny Town of Hygiene," *Denver Post,* April 19, 2016, http://www.denverpost.com; Eric Peterson, "StickerGiant," *Company Week,* https://companyweek.com, September 5, 2016.

A number of outstanding managers and noted academics are beginning to emphasize a fifth factor of production—knowledge. **Knowledge** refers to the combined talents and skills of the workforce and has become a primary driver of economic growth. Today's competitive environment places a premium on knowledge and learning over physical resources. Recent statistics suggest that the number of U.S. **knowledge workers** has doubled over the last 30 years, with an estimated 2 million knowledge job openings annually. Despite the fact that many "routine" jobs have been replaced by automation over the last decade or outsourced to other countries, technology has actually created more jobs that require knowledge and cognitive skills.[6]

1. Explain the concepts of revenue, costs, and profit.
2. What are the five factors of production?
3. What is the role of an entrepreneur in society?

1.2 Understanding the Business Environment

2. What are the sectors of the business environment, and how do changes in them influence business decisions?

Businesses do not operate in a vacuum but rather in a dynamic environment that has a direct influence on how they operate and whether they will achieve their objectives. This external business environment is composed of numerous outside organizations and forces that we can group into seven key subenvironments, as **Exhibit 1.4** illustrates: economic, political and legal, demographic, social, competitive, global, and technological. Each of these sectors creates a unique set of challenges and opportunities for businesses.

Business owners and managers have a great deal of control over the internal environment of business, which covers day-to-day decisions. They choose the supplies they purchase, which employees they hire, the products they sell, and where they sell those products. They use their skills and resources to create goods and services that will satisfy existing and prospective customers. However, the external environmental conditions that affect a business are generally beyond the control of management and change constantly. To compete successfully, business owners and managers must continuously study the environment and adapt their businesses accordingly.

Other forces, such as natural disasters, can also have a major impact on businesses. While still in the rebuilding stage after Hurricane Katrina hit in 2005, the U.S. Gulf Coast suffered another disaster in April 2010 as a result of an explosion on the Deepwater Horizon oil-rig, which killed 11 workers and sent more than 3 million barrels of oil into the Gulf of Mexico. This event, which played out for more than 87 days, severely affected the environment, businesses, tourism, and people's livelihoods. Global oil conglomerate BP, which was responsible for the oil spill, has spent more than $60 billion in response to the disaster and cleanup. Seven years after the explosion, tourism and other businesses are slowly recovering, although scientists are not certain about the long-term environmental consequences of the oil spill.[7]

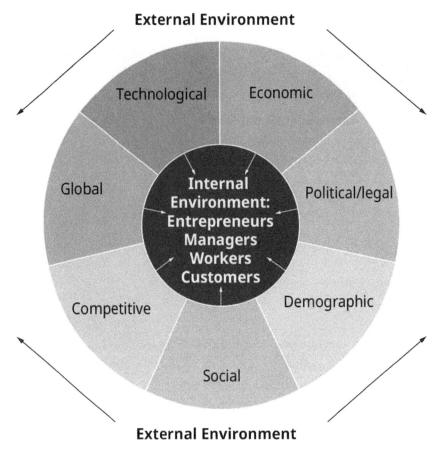

Exhibit 1.4   The Dynamic Business Environment (Attribution: Copyright Rice University, OpenStax, under CC-BY 4.0 license)

No one business is large or powerful enough to create major changes in the external environment. Thus, managers are primarily adapters to, rather than agents of, change. Global competition is basically an uncontrollable element in the external environment. In some situations, however, a firm can influence external events through its strategies. For example, major U.S. pharmaceutical companies have been successful in getting the Food and Drug Administration (FDA) to speed up the approval process for new drugs.[8] In recent years, the five largest companies in the S&P Index—Google, Facebook, Amazon, Microsoft, and Apple—have spent close to $50 million on lobbying activities in the nation's capital in an effort to help policy makers understand the tech industry and the importance of innovation and an "open" internet.[9] Let's now take a brief look at these varied environmental influences.

Economic Influences

This category is one of the most important external influences on businesses. Fluctuations in the level of economic activity create business cycles that affect businesses and individuals in many ways. When the economy is growing, for example, unemployment rates are low, and income levels rise. Inflation and interest rates are other areas that change according to economic activity. Through the policies it sets, such as taxes and interest rate levels, a government attempts to stimulate or curtail the level of economic activity. In addition, the forces of supply and demand determine how prices and quantities of goods and services behave in a free market.

Political and Legal Influences

The political climate of a country is another critical factor for managers to consider in day-to-day business operations. The amount of government activity, the types of laws it passes, and the general political stability of a government are three components of political climate. For example, a multinational company such as General Electric will evaluate the political climate of a country before deciding to locate a plant there. Is the government stable, or might a coup disrupt the country? How restrictive are the regulations for foreign businesses, including foreign ownership of business property and taxation? Import tariffs, quotas, and export restrictions also must be taken into account.

In the United States, laws passed by Congress and the many regulatory agencies cover such areas as competition, minimum wages, environmental protection, worker safety, and copyrights and patents. For example, Congress passed the Telecommunications Act of 1996 to deregulate the telecommunications industry. As a result, competition increased and new opportunities arose as traditional boundaries between service providers blurred. Today the dramatic growth in mobile technology has changed the focus of telecommunications, which now faces challenges related to broadband access and speed, content streaming, and much-needed improvements in network infrastructure to address ever-increasing data transmissions.[10]

Federal agencies play a significant role in business operations. When Pfizer wants to bring a new medication for heart disease to market, it must follow the procedures set by the Food and Drug Administration for testing and clinical trials and secure FDA approval. Before issuing stock, Pfizer must register the securities with the Securities and Exchange Commission. The Federal Trade Commission will penalize Pfizer if its advertisements promoting the drug's benefits are misleading. These are just a few ways the political and legal environment affect business decisions.

States and local governments also exert control over businesses—imposing taxes, issuing corporate charters and business licenses, setting zoning ordinances, and similar regulations. We discuss the legal environment in greater detail in a separate appendix.

Demographic Factors

Demographic factors are an uncontrollable factor in the business environment and extremely important to managers. **Demography** is the study of people's vital statistics, such as their age, gender, race and ethnicity, and location. Demographics help companies define the markets for their products and also determine the size and composition of the workforce. You'll encounter demographics as you continue your study of business.

Demographics are at the heart of many business decisions. Businesses today must deal with the unique shopping preferences of different generations, which each require marketing approaches and goods and services targeted to their needs. For example, the more than 75 million members of the millennial generation were born between 1981 and 1997. In 2017 they surpassed baby boomers as America's largest generation.[11] The marketing impact of millennials continues to be immense. These are technologically savvy and prosperous young people, with hundreds of billions of dollars to spend. And spend they do—freely, even though they haven't yet reached their peak income and spending years.[12] Other age groups, such as Generation X—people born between 1965 and 1980—and the baby boomers—born between 1946 and 1964—have their own spending patterns. Many boomers nearing retirement have money and are willing to spend it on their health, their comforts, leisure pursuits, and cars. As the population ages, businesses are offering more products that appeal to middle-aged and senior markets.[13]

In addition, minorities represent more than 38 percent of the total population, with immigration bringing millions of new residents to the country over the past several decades. By 2060 the U.S. Census Bureau projects the minority population to increase to 56 percent of the total U.S. population.[14] Companies recognize the value of hiring a diverse workforce that reflects our society. Minorities' buying power has increased significantly as well, and companies are developing products and marketing campaigns that target different ethnic groups.

Social Factors

Social factors—our attitudes, values, ethics, and lifestyles—influence what, how, where, and when people purchase products or services. They are difficult to predict, define, and measure because they can be very subjective. They also change as people move through different life stages. People of all ages have a broader range of interests, defying traditional consumer profiles. They also experience a "poverty of time" and seek ways to gain more control over their time. Changing roles have brought more women into the workforce. This development is increasing family incomes, heightening demand for time-saving goods and services, changing family shopping patterns, and impacting individuals' ability to achieve a work-life balance. In addition, a renewed emphasis on ethical behavior within organizations at all levels of the company has managers and employees alike searching for the right approach when it comes to gender inequality, sexual harassment, and other social behaviors that impact the potential for a business's continued success.

MANAGING CHANGE

Balancing Comes Easy at H&R Block

In an industry driven by deadlines and details, it's hard to imagine striking a balance between work and everyday life for full-time employees and seasonal staff. Fortunately, the management team at H&R Block not only believes in maintaining a strong culture, it also tries to offer flexibility to its more than 70,000 employees and seasonal workers in 12,000 retail offices worldwide.

Based in Kansas City, Missouri, and built on a culture of providing exceptional customer service, H&R Block was recently named the top U.S. business with the best work-life balance by online job search site Indeed. Analyzing more than 10 million company reviews by employees, Indeed researchers identified the top 20 firms with the best work-life balance. H&R Block headed the 2017 list, followed by mortgage lender Network Capital Funding Corporation, fast food chain In-N-Out Burger, Texas food retailer H-E-B, and health services company Kaiser Permanente, among others.

According to Paul Wolfe, Indeed's senior vice president of human resources, empathy on the part of organizations is a key factor in helping employees achieve balance. Wolfe says companies that demonstrate empathy and work diligently to provide personal time for all employees tend to take the top spots on the work-life balance list. "Comments we have seen from employee reviews for these companies indicate 'fair' and 'flexible work environments,'" he says. Surprisingly, none of the tech companies known for their generous work perks made the top 20 list in 2017.

In this 24/7 world, when no one is far from a text or tweet, finding time for both family and work can be difficult, especially in the tax services industry, which is so schedule driven for a good part of the year. Making a commitment to help workers achieve a healthy work-life balance not only helps its employees, but it also helps H&R Block retain workers in a tight labor market where individuals continue to have choices when it comes to where and for whom they want to work.

Questions for Discussion

1. How does management's support of employee work-life balance help the company's bottom line?
2. What can other organizations learn from H&R Block when it comes to offering employee perks that encourage personal time for workers even during the busy tax season?

Sources: "Career Opportunities," https://www.hrblock.com, accessed May 25, 2017; "About Us," http://newsroom.hrblock.com, accessed May 25, 2017; Abigail Hess, "The 20 Best Companies for Work-Life Balance," *CNBC,* http://www.cnbc.com, May 4, 2017; Kristen Bahler, "The 20 Best Companies for Work-Life Balance," *Money,* http://time.com, April 20, 2017; Rachel Ritlop, "3 Benefits Companies Can Provide to Boost Work-Life Balance," *Forbes,* http://www.forbes.com, January 30, 2017.

Technology

The application of technology can stimulate growth under capitalism or any other economic system. **Technology** is the application of science and engineering skills and knowledge to solve production and organizational problems. New equipment and software that improve productivity and reduce costs can be among a company's most valuable assets. **Productivity** is the amount of goods and services one worker can produce. Our ability as a nation to maintain and build wealth depends in large part on the speed and effectiveness with which we use technology—to invent and adapt more efficient equipment to improve manufacturing productivity, to develop new products, and to process information and make it instantly available across the organization and to suppliers and customers.

Many U.S. businesses, large and small, use technology to create change, improve efficiencies, and streamline operations. For example, advances in cloud computing provide businesses with the ability to access and store data without running applications or programs housed on a physical computer or server in their offices. Such applications and programs can now be accessed through the internet. Mobile technology allows businesses to communicate with employees, customers, suppliers, and others at the swipe of a tablet or smartphone screen. Robots help businesses automate repetitive tasks that free up workers to focus on more knowledge-based tasks critical to business operations.[15]

CONCEPT CHECK

1. Define the components of the internal and the external business environments.
2. What factors within the economic environment affect businesses?
3. Why do demographic shifts and technological developments create both challenges and new opportunities for business?

1.3   How Business and Economics Work

3. What are the primary features of the world's economic systems, and how are the three sectors of the U.S. economy linked?

A business's success depends in part on the economic systems of the countries where it is located and where its sells its products. A nation's **economic system** is the combination of policies, laws, and choices made by its government to establish the systems that determine what goods and services are produced and how they are allocated. **Economics** is the study of how a society uses scarce resources to produce and distribute goods and services. The resources of a person, a firm, or a nation are limited. Hence, economics is the study of choices—what people, firms, or nations choose from among the available resources. Every economy is concerned with what types and amounts of goods and services should be produced, how they should be produced, and for whom. These decisions are made by the marketplace, the government, or both. In the United States, the government and the free-market system together guide the economy.

You probably know more about economics than you realize. Every day, many news stories deal with economic matters: a union wins wage increases at General Motors, the Federal Reserve Board lowers interest rates, Wall Street has a record day, the president proposes a cut in income taxes, consumer spending rises as the economy grows, or retail prices are on the rise, to mention just a few examples.

Global Economic Systems

Businesses and other organizations operate according to the *economic systems* of their home countries. Today the world's major economic systems fall into two broad categories: free market, or capitalism; and planned economies, which include communism and socialism. However, in reality many countries use a mixed market system that incorporates elements from more than one economic system.

The major differentiator among economic systems is whether the government or individuals decide:

- How to allocate limited resources—the factors of production—to individuals and organizations to best satisfy unlimited societal needs
- What goods and services to produce and in what quantities
- How and by whom these goods and services are produced
- How to distribute goods and services to consumers

Managers must understand and adapt to the economic system or systems in which they operate. Companies that do business internationally may discover that they must make changes in production and selling methods to accommodate the economic system of other countries. Table 1.1 summarizes key factors of the world's economic systems.

The Basic Economic Systems of the World			
	Capitalism	Communism	Socialism	Mixed Economy
Ownership of Business	Businesses are privately owned with minimal government ownership or interference.	Government owns all or most enterprises.	Basic industries such as railroads and utilities are owned by government. Very high taxation as government redistributes income from successful private businesses and entrepreneurs.	Private ownership of land and businesses but government control of some enterprises. The private sector is typically large
Control of Markets	Complete freedom of trade. No or little government control.	Complete government control of markets.	Some markets are controlled, and some are free. Significant central-government planning. State enterprises are managed by bureaucrats. These enterprises are rarely profitable.	Some markets, such as nuclear energy and the post office, are controlled or highly regulated.
Worker Incentives	Strong incentive to work and innovate because profits are retained by owners.	No incentive to work hard or produce quality products.	Private-sector incentives are the same as capitalism, and public-sector incentives are the same as in a planned economy.	Private-sector incentives are the same as capitalism. Limited incentives in the public sector.
Management of Enterprises	Each enterprise is managed by owners or professional managers with little government interference.	Centralized management by the government bureaucracy. Little or no flexibility in decision-making at the factory level.	Significant government planning and regulation. Bureaucrats run government enterprises.	Private-sector management similar to capitalism. Public sector similar to socialism.

Table 1.1

The Basic Economic Systems of the World				
	Capitalism	Communism	Socialism	Mixed Economy
Forecast for 2020	Continued steady growth.	No growth and perhaps disappearance.	Stable with probable slight growth.	Continued growth.
Examples	United States	Cuba, North Korea	Finland, India, Israel	Great Britain, France, Sweden, Canada

Table 1.1

Capitalism

In recent years, more countries have shifted toward free-market economic systems and away from planned economies. Sometimes, as was the case of the former East Germany, the transition to capitalism was painful but fairly quick. In other countries, such as Russia, the movement has been characterized by false starts and backsliding. **Capitalism**, also known as the *private enterprise system*, is based on competition in the marketplace and private ownership of the factors of production (resources). In a competitive economic system, a large number of people and businesses buy and sell products freely in the marketplace. In pure capitalism, all the factors of production are owned privately, and the government does not try to set prices or coordinate economic activity.

A capitalist system guarantees certain economic rights: the right to own property, the right to make a profit, the right to make free choices, and the right to compete. The right to own property is central to capitalism. The main incentive in this system is profit, which encourages entrepreneurship. Profit is also necessary for producing goods and services, building manufacturing plants, paying dividends and taxes, and creating jobs. The freedom to choose whether to become an entrepreneur or to work for someone else means that people have the right to decide what they want to do on the basis of their own drive, interest, and training. The government does not create job quotas for each industry or give people tests to determine what they will do.

Competition is good for both businesses and consumers in a capitalist system. It leads to better and more diverse products, keeps prices stable, and increases the efficiency of producers. Companies try to produce their goods and services at the lowest possible cost and sell them at the highest possible price. But when profits are high, more businesses enter the market to seek a share of those profits. The resulting competition among companies tends to lower prices. Companies must then find new ways of operating more efficiently if they are to keep making a profit—and stay in business.

Exhibit 1.5   McDonald's China Since joining the World Trade Organization in 2001, China has continued to embrace tenets of capitalism and grow its economy. China is the world's largest producer of mobile phones, PCs, and tablets, and the country's over one billion people constitute a gargantuan market. The explosion of McDonald's and KFC franchises epitomizes the success of American-style capitalism in China, and Beijing's bid to host the 2022 Winter Olympics is a symbol of economic openness. This McCafe is an example of changing Western products to suit Chinese tastes. This is an example of changing Western products to suit Chinese tastes. *Do you think China's capitalistic trend can continue to thrive under the ruling Chinese Communist Party that opposes workers' rights, free speech, and democracy?* (Credit: Marku Kudjerski/ flickr/ Attribution 2.0 Generic (CC BY 2.0)

Communism

The complete opposite of capitalism is **communism**. In a communist economic system, the government owns virtually all resources and controls all markets. Economic decision-making is centralized: the government, rather than the competitive forces in the marketplace, decides what will be produced, where it will be produced, how much will be produced, where the raw materials and supplies will come from, who will get the output, and what the prices will be. This form of centralized economic system offers little if any choice to a country's citizens. Early in the 20th century, countries that chose communism, such as the former Soviet Union and China, believed that it would raise their standard of living. In practice, however, the tight controls over most aspects of people's lives, such as what careers they can choose, where they can work, and what they can buy, led to lower productivity. Workers had no reasons to work harder or produce quality goods, because there were no rewards for excellence. Errors in planning and resource allocation led to shortages of even basic items.

These factors were among the reasons for the 1991 collapse of the Soviet Union into multiple independent nations. Recent reforms in Russia, China, and most of the eastern European nations have moved these economies toward more capitalistic, market-oriented systems. North Korea and Cuba are the best remaining examples of communist economic systems. Time will tell whether Cuba takes small steps toward a market economy now that the United States reestablished diplomatic relations with the island country a few years ago.[16]

Socialism

Socialism is an economic system in which the basic industries are owned by the government or by the private sector under strong government control. A socialist state controls critical, large-scale industries such as transportation, communications, and utilities. Smaller businesses and those considered less critical, such as retail, may be privately owned. To varying degrees, the state also determines the goals of businesses, the prices and selection of goods, and the rights of workers. Socialist countries typically provide their citizens with a higher level of services, such as health care and unemployment benefits, than do most capitalist countries. As a result, taxes and unemployment may also be higher in socialist countries. For example, in 2017, the top individual tax rate in France was 45 percent, compared to 39.6 percent in the United States. With both countries electing new presidents in 2017, tax cuts may be a campaign promise that both President Macron and President Trump take on as part of their overall economic agendas in the coming years.[17]

Many countries, including the United Kingdom, Denmark, India, and Israel, have socialist systems, but the systems vary from country to country. In Denmark, for example, most businesses are privately owned and operated, but two-thirds of the population is sustained by the state through government welfare programs.

Mixed Economic Systems

Pure capitalism and communism are extremes; real-world economies fall somewhere between the two. The U.S. economy leans toward pure capitalism, but it uses government policies to promote economic stability and growth. Also, through policies and laws, the government transfers money to the poor, the unemployed, and the elderly or disabled. American capitalism has produced some very powerful organizations in the form of large corporations, such as General Motors and Microsoft. To protect smaller firms and entrepreneurs, the government has passed legislation that requires that the giants compete fairly against weaker competitors.

Canada, Sweden, and the UK, among others, are also called **mixed economies**; that is, they use more than one economic system. Sometimes, the government is basically socialist and owns basic industries. In Canada, for example, the government owns the communications, transportation, and utilities industries, as well as some of the natural-resource industries. It also provides health care to its citizens. But most other activity is carried on by private enterprise, as in a capitalist system. In 2016, UK citizens voted for Britain to leave the European Union, a move that will take two or more years to finalize. It is too early to tell what impact the Brexit decision will have on the UK economy and other economies around the world.[18]

The few factors of production owned by the government in a mixed economy include some public lands, the postal service, and some water resources. But the government is extensively involved in the economic system through taxing, spending, and welfare activities. The economy is also mixed in the sense that the country tries to achieve many social goals—income redistribution and retirement pensions, for example—that may not be attempted in purely capitalist systems.

Macroeconomics and Microeconomics

The state of the economy affects both people and businesses. How you spend your money (or save it) is a personal economic decision. Whether you continue in school and whether you work part-time are also economic decisions. Every business also operates within the economy. Based on their economic expectations, businesses decide what products to produce, how to price them, how many people to employ, how much to pay these employees, how much to expand the business, and so on.

Economics has two main subareas. **Macroeconomics** is the study of the economy as a whole. It looks at *aggregate* data for large groups of people, companies, or products considered as a whole. In contrast, **microeconomics** focuses on individual parts of the economy, such as households or firms.

Both *macroeconomics* and *microeconomics* offer a valuable outlook on the economy. For example, Ford might use both to decide whether to introduce a new line of vehicles. The company would consider such macroeconomic factors as the national level of personal income, the unemployment rate, interest rates, fuel costs, and the national level of sales of new vehicles. From a microeconomic viewpoint, Ford would judge consumer demand for new vehicles versus the existing supply, competing models, labor and material costs and availability, and current prices and sales incentives.

Economics as a Circular Flow

Another way to see how the sectors of the economy interact is to examine the **circular flow** of inputs and outputs among households, businesses, and governments as shown in Exhibit 1.6. Let's review the exchanges by following the red circle around the inside of the diagram. Households provide inputs (natural resources, labor, capital, entrepreneurship, knowledge) to businesses, which convert these inputs into outputs (goods and services) for consumers. In return, households receive income from rent, wages, interest, and ownership profits (blue circle). Businesses receive revenue from consumer purchases of goods and services.

The other important exchange in Exhibit 1.6 takes place between governments (federal, state, and local) and both households and businesses. Governments supply many types of publicly provided goods and services (highways, schools, police, courts, health services, unemployment insurance, social security) that benefit consumers and businesses. Government purchases from businesses also contribute to business revenues. When a construction firm repairs a local stretch of state highway, for example, government pays for the work. As the diagram shows, government receives taxes from households and businesses to complete the flow.

Changes in one flow affect the others. If government raises taxes, households have less to spend on goods and services. Lower consumer spending causes businesses to reduce production, and economic activity declines; unemployment may rise. In contrast, cutting taxes can stimulate economic activity. Keep the circular flow in mind as we continue our study of economics. The way economic sectors interact will become more evident as we explore macroeconomics and microeconomics.

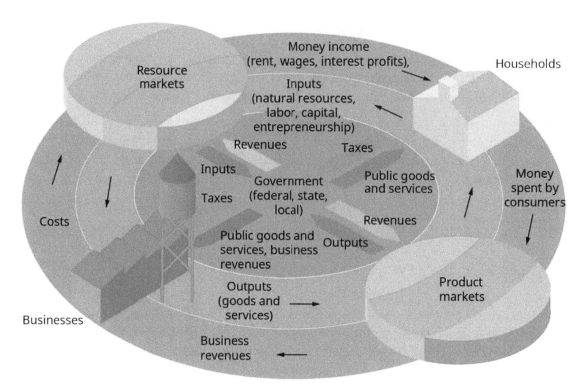

Exhibit 1.6 Economics as a Circular Flow (Attribution: Copyright Rice University, OpenStax, under CC-BY 4.0 license)

CONCEPT CHECK

1. What is economics, and how can you benefit from understanding basic economic concepts?
2. Compare and contrast the world's major economic systems. Why is capitalism growing, communism declining, and socialism still popular?
3. What is the difference between macroeconomics and microeconomics?

1.4 | Macroeconomics: The Big Picture

4. How do economic growth, full employment, price stability, and inflation indicate a nation's economic health?

Have you ever looked at CNN's *Headline News* on a mobile device or turned on the radio and heard something like, "Today the Labor Department reported that for the second straight month unemployment declined"? Statements like this are macroeconomic news. Understanding the national economy and how changes in government policies affect households and businesses is a good place to begin our study of economics.

Let's look first at macroeconomic goals and how they can be met. The United States and most other countries have three main macroeconomic goals: economic growth, full employment, and price stability. A nation's economic well-being depends on carefully defining these goals and choosing the best economic policies for achieving them.

Striving for Economic Growth

Perhaps the most important way to judge a nation's economic health is to look at its production of goods and services. The more the nation produces, the higher its standard of living. An increase in a nation's output of goods and services is **economic growth**.

The most basic measure of economic growth is the **gross domestic product (GDP)**. GDP is the total market value of all final goods and services produced within a nation's borders each year. The Bureau of Labor Statistics publishes quarterly GDP figures that can be used to compare trends in national output. When GDP rises, the economy is growing.

The rate of growth in real GDP (GDP adjusted for inflation) is also important. Recently, the U.S. economy has been growing at a slow but steady rate of between 3 and 4 percent annually. This growth rate has meant a steady increase in the output of goods and services and relatively low unemployment. When the growth rate slides toward zero, the economy begins to stagnate and decline.

One country that continues to grow more rapidly than most is China, whose GDP has been growing at 6 to 7 percent per year. Today few things in the global marketplace are not or cannot be made in China. The primary contributor to China's rapid growth has been technology. For example, most tablets and laptops are manufactured in China.

The level of economic activity is constantly changing. These upward and downward changes are called **business cycles**. Business cycles vary in length, in how high or low the economy moves, and in how much the economy is affected. Changes in GDP trace the patterns as economic activity expands and contracts. An increase in business activity results in rising output, income, employment, and prices. Eventually, these all peak, and output, income, and employment decline. A decline in GDP that lasts for two consecutive quarters (each a three-month period) is called a **recession**. It is followed by a recovery period when economic activity once again increases. The most recent recession began in December 2007 and ended in June 2009.

Businesses must monitor and react to the changing phases of business cycles. When the economy is growing, companies often have a difficult time hiring good employees and finding scarce supplies and raw materials. When a recession hits, many firms find they have more capacity than the demand for their goods and services requires. During the most recent recession, many businesses operated at substantially lower than capacity. When plants use only part of their capacity, they operate inefficiently and have higher costs per unit produced. Let's say that Mars Corp. has a huge plant that can produce one million Milky Way candy bars a day, but because of a recession Mars can sell only half a million candy bars a day. The plant uses large, expensive machines. Producing Milky Ways at 50 percent capacity does not efficiently utilize Mars's investment in its plant and equipment.

Keeping People on the Job

Another macroeconomic goal is **full employment**, or having jobs for all who want to and can work. Full employment doesn't actually mean 100 percent employment. Some people choose not to work for personal reasons (attending school, raising children) or are temporarily unemployed while they wait to start a new job. Thus, the government defines full employment as the situation when about 94 to 96 percent of those available to work actually have jobs. During the 2007–2009 recession in the United States, the unemployment rate peaked at 10 percent in October 2009. Today, that rate hovers at about 4 percent.[19]

Maintaining low unemployment levels is of concern not just to the United States but also to countries around the world. For example, high youth unemployment rates (for workers 25 years of age and younger) in Spain, Italy, and Greece continue to cause protests in these European countries as elected officials struggle with how to turn around their respective economies and put more people, particularly young people, back to work. The UK's impending exit from the European Union may also have an effect on unemployment rates, as global companies move jobs out of Britain to central European countries such as Poland.[20]

Measuring Unemployment

To determine how close we are to full employment, the government measures the **unemployment rate**. This rate indicates the percentage of the total labor force that is not working but is actively looking for work. It excludes "discouraged workers," those not seeking jobs because they think no one will hire them. Each month the U.S. Department of Labor releases statistics on employment. These figures help us understand how well the economy is doing.

Types of Unemployment

Economists classify unemployment into four types: frictional, structural, cyclical, and seasonal. The categories are of small consolation to someone who is unemployed, but they help economists understand the problem of unemployment in our economy.

Frictional unemployment is short-term unemployment that is not related to the business cycle. It includes people who are unemployed while waiting to start a better job, those who are reentering the job market, and those entering for the first time, such as new college graduates. This type of unemployment is always present and has little impact on the economy.

Structural unemployment is also unrelated to the business cycle but is involuntary. It is caused by a mismatch between available jobs and the skills of available workers in an industry or a region. For example, if the birthrate declines, fewer teachers will be needed. Or the available workers in an area may lack the skills that employers want. Retraining and skill-building programs are often required to reduce structural unemployment.

Cyclical unemployment, as the name implies, occurs when a downturn in the business cycle reduces the demand for labor throughout the economy. In a long recession, cyclical unemployment is widespread, and even people with good job skills can't find jobs. The government can partly counteract cyclical unemployment with programs that boost the economy.

In the past, cyclical unemployment affected mainly less-skilled workers and those in heavy manufacturing. Typically, they would be rehired when economic growth increased. Since the 1990s, however, competition has forced many American companies to downsize so they can survive in the global marketplace. These job reductions affected workers in all categories, including middle management and other salaried positions. Firms continue to reevaluate workforce requirements and downsize to stay competitive to compete with Asian, European, and other U.S. firms. After a strong rebound from the global recession of 2007–2009, when the auto industry slashed more than 200,000 hourly and salaried workers from their payrolls, the automakers are now taking another close look at the size of their global workforces. For example, as sales steadily rose after the recession, Ford Motor Company's workforce in North America increased by 25 percent over the past five years. As car sales plateaued in 2017, the company recently announced it would cut approximately 10 percent of its global workforce in an effort to reduce costs, boost profits, and increase its stock value for shareholders.[21]

The last type is **seasonal unemployment**, which occurs during specific times of the year in certain industries.

Employees subject to seasonal unemployment include retail workers hired for the holiday shopping season, lettuce pickers in California, and restaurant employees in ski country during the summer.

Keeping Prices Steady

The third macroeconomic goal is to keep overall prices for goods and services fairly steady. The situation in which the average of all prices of goods and services is rising is called **inflation**. Inflation's higher prices reduce **purchasing power**, the value of what money can buy. Purchasing power is a function of two things: inflation and income. If incomes rise at the same rate as inflation, there is no change in purchasing power. If prices go up but income doesn't rise or rises at a slower rate, a given amount of income buys less, and purchasing power falls. For example, if the price of a basket of groceries rises from $30 to $40 but your salary remains the same, you can buy only 75 percent as many groceries ($30 ÷ $40) for $30. Your purchasing power declines by 25 percent ($10 ÷ $40). If incomes rise at a rate faster than inflation, then purchasing power increases. So you can, in fact, have rising purchasing power even if inflation is increasing. Typically, however, inflation rises faster than incomes, leading to a decrease in purchasing power.

Inflation affects both personal and business decisions. When prices are rising, people tend to spend more—before their purchasing power declines further. Businesses that expect inflation often increase their supplies, and people often speed up planned purchases of cars and major appliances.

From the early 2000s to April 2017, inflation in the United States was very low, in the 0.1 to 3.8 percent range; for 2016 it was 1.3 percent. For comparison, in the 1980s, the United States had periods of inflation in the 12 to 13 percent range.[22] Some nations have had high double- and even triple-digit inflation in recent years. As of early 2017, the monthly inflation rate in Venezuela was an astounding 741 percent, followed by the African country of South Sudan at 273 percent.[23]

Exhibit 1.7   Nespresso Buyers of Nespresso coffee, KitKat chocolate bars, and Purina pet food are paying more for these items as global food giant Nestlé raises prices. Increasing input costs, such as costs of raw materials, have been hard on food businesses, raising the price of production, packaging, and transportation. *How might fluctuations in the producer price index (PPI) affect the consumer price index (CPI) and why?* (Credit: Kārlis Dambrāns/ flickr/ Attribution 2.0 Generic (CC BY 2.0))

Types of Inflation

There are two types of inflation. **Demand-pull inflation** occurs when the demand for goods and services is greater than the supply. Would-be buyers have more money to spend than the amount needed to buy available goods and services. Their demand, which exceeds the supply, tends to pull prices up. This situation is sometimes described as "too much money chasing too few goods." The higher prices lead to greater supply, eventually creating a balance between demand and supply.

Cost-push inflation is triggered by increases in production costs, such as expenses for materials and wages. These increases push up the prices of final goods and services. Wage increases are a major cause of cost-push inflation, creating a "wage-price spiral." For example, assume the United Auto Workers union negotiates a three-year labor agreement that raises wages 3 percent per year and increases overtime pay. Carmakers will then raise car prices to cover their higher labor costs. Also, the higher wages will give autoworkers more money to buy goods and services, and this increased demand may pull up other prices. Workers in other industries will demand higher wages to keep up with the increased prices, and the cycle will push prices even higher.

How Inflation Is Measured

The rate of inflation is most commonly measured by looking at changes in the **consumer price index (CPI)**, an index of the prices of a "market basket" of goods and services purchased by typical urban consumers. It is published monthly by the Department of Labor. Major components of the CPI, which are weighted by importance, are food and beverages, clothing, transportation, housing, medical care, recreation, and education. There are special indexes for food and energy. The Department of Labor collects about 80,000 retail price quotes and 5,000 housing rent figures to calculate the CPI.

The CPI sets prices in a base period at 100. The base period, which now is 1982–1984, is chosen for its price stability. Current prices are then expressed as a percentage of prices in the base period. A rise in the CPI means prices are increasing. For example, the CPI was 244.5 in April 2017, meaning that prices more than doubled since the 1982–1984 base period.

Changes in wholesale prices are another important indicator of inflation. The **producer price index (PPI)** measures the prices paid by producers and wholesalers for various commodities, such as raw materials, partially finished goods, and finished products. The PPI, which uses 1982 as its base year, is actually a family of indexes for many different product categories, including crude goods (raw materials), intermediate goods (which become part of finished goods), and finished goods. For example, the PPI for finished goods was 197.7 in April 2017, a 3.9-point increase, and for chemicals was 106.5, up 3.8 points since April 2016. Examples of other PPI indexes include processed foods, lumber, containers, fuels and lubricants, metals, and construction. Because the PPI measures prices paid by producers for raw materials, energy, and other commodities, it may foreshadow subsequent price changes for businesses and consumers.

The Impact of Inflation

Inflation has several negative effects on people and businesses. For one thing, inflation penalizes people who live on fixed incomes. Let's say that a couple receives $2,000 a month retirement income beginning in 2018. If inflation is 10 percent in 2019, then the couple can buy only about 91 percent (100 ÷ 110) of what they could purchase in 2018. Similarly, inflation hurts savers. As prices rise, the real value, or purchasing power, of a nest egg of savings deteriorates.

CONCEPT CHECK

1. What is a business cycle? How do businesses adapt to periods of contraction and expansion?
2. Why is full employment usually defined as a target percentage below 100 percent?
3. What is the difference between demand-pull and cost-push inflation?

1.5 Achieving Macroeconomic Goals

5. How does the government use monetary policy and fiscal policy to achieve its macroeconomic goals?

To reach macroeconomic goals, countries must often choose among conflicting alternatives. Sometimes political needs override economic needs. For example, bringing inflation under control may call for a politically difficult period of high unemployment and low growth. Or, in an election year, politicians may resist raising taxes to curb inflation. Still, the government must try to guide the economy to a sound balance of growth, employment, and price stability. The two main tools it uses are monetary policy and fiscal policy.

Monetary Policy

Monetary policy refers to a government's programs for controlling the amount of money circulating in the economy and interest rates. Changes in the money supply affect both the level of economic activity and the rate of inflation. The **Federal Reserve System (the Fed)**, the central banking system of the United States, prints money and controls how much of it will be in circulation. The money supply is also controlled by the Fed's regulation of certain bank activities.

When the Fed increases or decreases the amount of money in circulation, it affects interest rates (the cost of borrowing money and the reward for lending it). The Fed can change the interest rate on money it lends to banks to signal the banking system and financial markets that it has changed its monetary policy. These changes have a ripple effect. Banks, in turn, may pass along this change to consumers and businesses that receive loans from the banks. If the cost of borrowing increases, the economy slows because interest rates affect consumer and business decisions to spend or invest. The housing industry, business, and investments react most to changes in interest rates.

As a result of the 2007–2009 recession and the global financial crisis that ensued, the Fed dropped the federal funds rate—the interest rate charged on overnight loans between banks—to 0 percent in December 2008 and kept the rate at zero until December 2015, when it raised the rate to 0.25 percent. This decision marked the first increase in the federal-funds rate since June 2006, when the federal funds rate was 5.25 percent. As the U.S. economy continues to show a slow but steady expansion, the Fed subsequently increased the federal funds rate to a range of 0.75 to 1 percent in March 2017. As expected, this change has a ripple effect: the regional Federal Reserve Banks increase the discount rate they charge commercial banks for short-term loans, many commercial banks raise the interest rates they charge their customers, and credit card companies increase the annual percentage rate (APR) they charge consumers on their credit card balances.[24]

As you can see, the Fed can use monetary policy to contract or expand the economy. With **contractionary policy**, the Fed restricts, or tightens, the money supply by selling government securities or raising interest rates. The result is slower economic growth and higher unemployment. Thus, contractionary policy reduces spending and, ultimately, lowers inflation. With **expansionary policy**, the Fed increases, or loosens, growth in the money supply. An expansionary policy stimulates the economy. Interest rates decline, so business and consumer spending go up. Unemployment rates drop as businesses expand. But increasing the money supply also has a negative side: more spending pushes prices up, increasing the inflation rate.

Exhibit 1.8 **Powell** As chair of the Board of Governors of the Federal Reserve System, Jerome (Jay) Powell is considered the face of U.S. monetary policy. Powell took over the chair in February 2018 from Janet Yellen, the first woman ever to be appointed Fed chair. *What are the responsibilities of the chair of the Board of Governors of the Federal Reserve System?* (Credit: Federalreserve/ flickr/ US Government Works)

Fiscal Policy

The other economic tool used by the government is **fiscal policy**, its program of taxation and spending. By cutting taxes or by increasing spending, the government can stimulate the economy. Look again at Exhibit 1.6. The more government buys from businesses, the greater the business revenues and output. Likewise, if consumers or businesses have to pay less in taxes, they will have more income to spend for goods and services. Tax policies in the United States therefore affect business decisions. High corporate taxes can make it harder for U.S. firms to compete with companies in countries with lower taxes. As a result, companies may choose to locate facilities overseas to reduce their tax burden.

Nobody likes to pay taxes, although we grudgingly accept that we have to. Although most U.S. citizens complain that they are overtaxed, we pay lower taxes per capita (per person) than citizens in many countries similar to ours. In addition, our taxes represent a lower percentage of gross income and GDP compared to most countries.

Taxes are, of course, the major source of revenue for our government. Every year, the president prepares a budget for the coming year based upon estimated revenues and expenditures. Congress receives the president's report and recommendations and then, typically, debates and analyzes the proposed budget for several months. The president's original proposal is always modified in numerous ways. Exhibit 1.9 shows the sources of revenue and expenses for the U.S. budget.

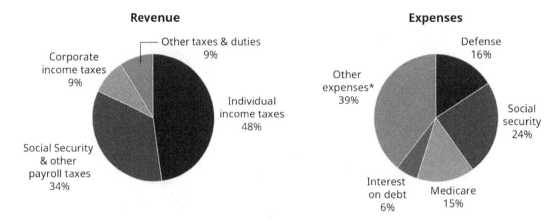

Exhibit 1.9 Revenues and Expenses for the Federal Budget Source: U.S. Treasury, "Final Monthly Treasury Statement of Receipts and Outlays of the United States Government for Fiscal Year 2016," https://www.fiscal.treasury.gov, accessed May 23, 2017.

Whereas fiscal policy has a major impact on business and consumers, continual increases in government spending raises another important issue. When government takes more money from business and consumers (the private sector), a phenomenon known as **crowding out** occurs. Here are three examples of crowding out:

1. The government spends more on public libraries, and individuals buy fewer books at bookstores.
2. The government spends more on public education, and individuals spend less on private education.
3. The government spends more on public transportation, and individuals spend less on private transportation.

In other words, government spending is crowding out private spending.

If the government spends more for programs (social services, education, defense) than it collects in taxes, the result is a **federal budget deficit**. To balance the budget, the government can cut its spending, increase taxes, or do some combination of the two. When it cannot balance the budget, the government must make up any shortfalls by borrowing (just like any business or household).

In 1998, for the first time in a generation, there was a federal budget surplus (revenue exceeding spending) of about $71 billion. That budget surplus was short lived, however. By 2005, the deficit was more than $318 billion. In the fiscal year of 2009, the federal deficit was at an all-time high of more than $1.413 trillion. Six years later, at the end of the 2015 fiscal year, the deficit decreased to $438 billion.[25] The U.S. government has run budget deficits for many years. The accumulated total of these past deficits is the **national debt**, which now amounts to about $19.8 trillion, or about $61,072 for every man, woman, and child in the United States. Total interest on the debt is more than $2.5 trillion a year.[26] To cover the deficit, the U.S. government borrows money from people and businesses in the form of Treasury bills, Treasury notes, and Treasury bonds. These are federal IOUs that pay interest to their owners.

The national debt is an emotional issue debated not only in the halls of Congress, but by the public as well. Some believe that deficits contribute to economic growth, high employment, and price stability. Others have the following reservations about such a high national debt:

- *Not Everyone Holds the Debt:* The government is very conscious of who actually bears the burden of the national debt and keeps track of who holds what bonds. If only the rich were bondholders, then they alone would receive the interest payments and could end up receiving more in interest than they paid in taxes. In the meantime, poorer people, who held no bonds, would end up paying taxes that would be transferred to the rich as interest, making the debt an unfair burden to them. At times, therefore, the government has instructed commercial banks to reduce their total debt by divesting some of their bond holdings. That's also why the Treasury created **savings bonds**. Because these bonds are issued in relatively small denominations, they allow more people to buy and hold government debt.

- *It Crowds Out Private Investment:* The national debt also affects private investment. If the government raises the interest rate on bonds to be able to sell them, it forces private businesses, whose corporate bonds (long-term debt obligations issued by a company) compete with government bonds for investor dollars, to raise rates on their bonds to stay competitive. In other words, selling government debt to finance government spending makes it more costly for private industry to finance its own investment. As a result, government debt may end up crowding out private investment and slowing economic growth in the private sector.

CONCEPT CHECK

1. What are the two kinds of monetary policy?
2. What fiscal policy tools can the government use to achieve its macroeconomic goals?
3. What problems can a large national debt present?

1.6 Microeconomics: Zeroing in on Businesses and Consumers

6. What are the basic microeconomic concepts of demand and supply, and how do they establish prices?

Now let's shift our focus from the whole economy to *microeconomics,* the study of households, businesses, and industries. This field of economics is concerned with how prices and quantities of goods and services behave in a free market. It stands to reason that people, firms, and governments try to get the most from their limited resources. Consumers want to buy the best quality at the lowest price. Businesses want to keep costs down and revenues high to earn larger profits. Governments also want to use their revenues to provide the most effective public goods and services possible. These groups choose among alternatives by focusing on the prices of goods and services.

As consumers in a free market, we influence what is produced. If Mexican food is popular, the high demand attracts entrepreneurs who open more Mexican restaurants. They want to compete for our dollars by supplying Mexican food at a lower price, of better quality, or with different features, such as Santa Fe Mexican food rather than Tex-Mex. This section explains how business and consumer choices influence the price and availability of goods and services.

Exhibit 1.10   Galaxy Note 7 Samsung's strategy to take on Apple's iPhone domination hit a terrible snag in 2016, when its Galaxy Note 7 mobile phone was recalled and the product eliminated. Defective batteries in the Note 7 made them catch fire and cause serious damage. Samsung eventually killed the entire line of Note 7 phones, recalling nearly 3 million phones, which cost the company more than $5 billion. *How do businesses determine the optimum quantity of products or services to make available to consumers?* (Credit: Paul Sullivan/ flickr/ Attribution-NoDerivs 2.0 Generic (CC BY-ND 2.0))

The Nature of Demand

Demand is the quantity of a good or service that people are willing to buy at various prices. The higher the price, the lower the quantity demanded, and vice versa. A graph of this relationship is called a **demand curve**.

Let's assume you own a store that sells jackets for snowboarders. From past experience, you know how many jackets you can sell at different prices. The demand curve in **Exhibit 1.11** depicts this information. The *x*-axis (horizontal axis) shows the quantity of jackets, and the *y*-axis (vertical axis) shows the related price of those jackets. For example, at a price of $100, customers will buy (demand) 600 snowboard jackets.

In the graph, the demand curve slopes downward and to the right because as the price falls, people will want to buy more jackets. Some people who were not going to buy a jacket will purchase one at the lower price. Also, some snowboarders who already have a jacket will buy a second one. The graph also shows that if you put a large number of jackets on the market, you will have to reduce the price to sell all of them.

Understanding demand is critical to businesses. Demand tells you *how much you can sell* and *at what price*—in other words, how much money the firm will take in that can be used to cover costs and hopefully earn a profit. Gauging demand is difficult even for the very largest corporations, but particularly for small firms.

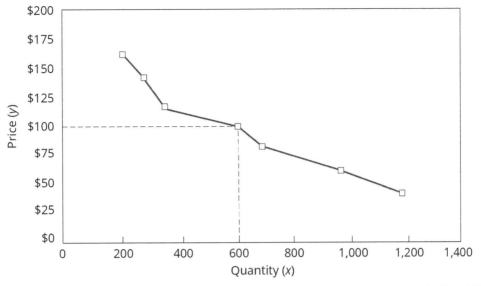

Exhibit 1.11   Demand Curve for Jackets for Snowboarders (Attribution: Copyright Rice University, OpenStax, under CC-BY 4.0 license)

The Nature of Supply

Demand alone is not enough to explain how the market sets prices. We must also look at **supply**, the quantity of a good or service that businesses will make available at various prices. The higher the price, the greater the number of jackets a supplier will supply, and vice versa. A graph of the relationship between various prices and the quantities a business will supply is a **supply curve**.

We can again plot the quantity of jackets on the *x*-axis and the price on the *y*-axis. As Exhibit 1.12 shows, 800 jackets will be available at a price of $100. Note that the supply curve slopes upward and to the right, the opposite of the demand curve. If snowboarders are willing to pay higher prices, suppliers of jackets will buy more inputs (for example, Gore-Tex® fabric, dye, machinery, labor) and produce more jackets. The quantity supplied will be higher at higher prices, because manufacturers can earn higher profits.

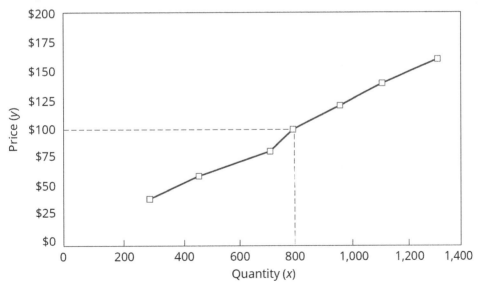

Exhibit 1.12   Supply Curve for Jackets for Snowboarders (Attribution: Copyright Rice University, OpenStax, under CC-BY 4.0 license)

How Demand and Supply Interact to Determine Prices

In a stable economy, the number of jackets that snowboarders demand depends on the jackets' price. Likewise, the number of jackets that suppliers provide depends on price. But at what price will consumer demand for jackets match the quantity suppliers will produce?

To answer this question, we need to look at what happens when demand and supply interact. By plotting both the demand curve and the supply curve on the same graph in **Exhibit 1.13**, we see that they cross at a certain quantity and price. At that point, labeled E, the quantity demanded equals the quantity supplied. This is the point of **equilibrium**. The equilibrium price is $80; the equilibrium quantity is 700 jackets. At that point, there is a balance between the quantity consumers will buy and the quantity suppliers will make available.

Market equilibrium is achieved through a series of quantity and price adjustments that occur automatically. If the price increases to $160, suppliers produce more jackets than consumers are willing to buy, and a surplus results. To sell more jackets, prices will have to fall. Thus, a surplus pushes prices downward until equilibrium is reached. When the price falls to $60, the quantity of jackets demanded rises above the available supply. The resulting shortage forces prices upward until equilibrium is reached at $80.

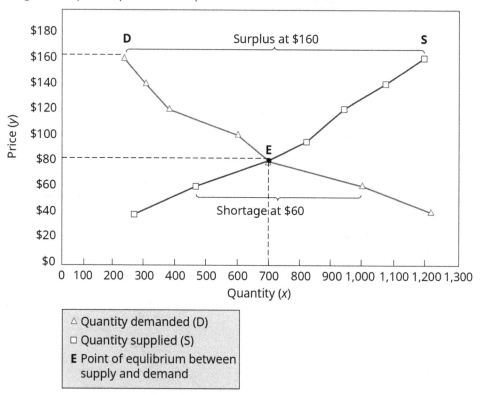

Exhibit 1.13   Equilibrium Price and Quantity for Jackets for Snowboarders (Attribution: Copyright Rice University, OpenStax, under CC-BY 4.0 license)

The number of snowboard jackets supplied and bought at $80 will tend to rest at equilibrium unless there is a shift in either demand or supply. If demand increases, more jackets will be purchased at every price, and the demand curve shifts to the right (as illustrated by line D_2 in **Exhibit 1.14**). If demand decreases, less will be bought at every price, and the demand curve shifts to the left (D_1). When demand decreased, snowboarders bought 500 jackets at $80 instead of 700 jackets. When demand increased, they purchased 800.

Changes in Demand

A number of things can increase or decrease demand. For example, if snowboarders' incomes go up, they may decide to buy a second jacket. If incomes fall, a snowboarder who was planning to purchase a jacket may wear an old one instead. Changes in fashion or tastes can also influence demand. If snowboarding were suddenly to go out of fashion, demand for jackets would decrease quickly. A change in the price of related products can also influence demand. For example, if the average price of a snowboard rises to $1,000, people will quit snowboarding, and jacket demand will fall.

Another factor that can shift demand is expectations about future prices. If you expect jacket prices to increase significantly in the future, you may decide to go ahead and get one today. If you think prices will fall, you will postpone your purchase. Finally, changes in the number of buyers will affect demand. Snowboarding is a young person's sport, and the number of teenagers will increase in the next few years. Therefore, the demand for snowboard jackets should increase.

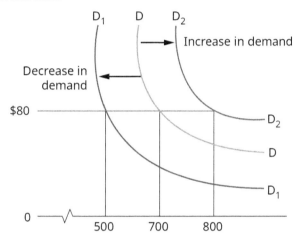

Exhibit 1.14   Shifts in Demand for Jackets for Snowboarders (Attribution: Copyright Rice University, OpenStax, under CC-BY 4.0 license)

Changes in Supply

Other factors influence the supply side of the picture. New technology typically lowers the cost of production. For example, North Face, a supplier of ski and snowboard jackets, purchased laser-guided pattern-cutting equipment and computer-aided pattern-making equipment. Each jacket was cheaper to produce, resulting in a higher profit per jacket. This provided an incentive to supply more jackets at every price. If the price of resources such as labor or fabric goes up, North Face will earn a smaller profit on each jacket, and the amount supplied will decrease at every price. The reverse is also true. Changes in the prices of other goods can also affect supply.

Let's say that snow skiing becomes a really hot sport again. The number of skiers jumps dramatically, and the price of ski jackets soars. North Face can use its machines and fabrics to produce either ski or snowboard jackets. If the company can make more profit from ski jackets, it will produce fewer snowboard jackets at every price. Also, a change in the number of producers will shift the supply curve. If the number of jacket suppliers increases, they will place more jackets on the market at every price. If any suppliers stop making jackets available, the supply will naturally decrease. Taxes can also affect supply. If the government decides, for some reason, to tax the supplier for every snowboard jacket produced, then profits will fall, and fewer jackets will be offered at every price. Table 1.2 summarizes the factors that can shift demand and supply curves.

To better understand the relationship between supply and demand across the economy, consider the impact of 2005's Hurricane Katrina on U.S. energy prices. Oil and gas prices were already at high levels before Hurricane Katrina disrupted production in the Gulf Coast. Most U.S. offshore drilling sites are located in the Gulf of Mexico, and almost 30 percent of U.S. refining capacity is in Gulf States that were hit hard by the storm. Prices rose almost immediately as supplies fell while demand remained at the same levels.

The storm drove home the vulnerability of the U.S. energy supply to not only natural disasters, but also terrorist attacks and price increases from foreign oil producers. Many energy policy experts questioned the wisdom of having such a high concentration of oil facilities—about 25 percent of the oil and natural gas infrastructure—in hurricane-prone states. Refiners were already almost at capacity before Katrina's devastation.[27]

Factors That Cause Demand and Supply Curves to Shift		
	Shift Demand	
Factor	**To the Right If**	**To the Left If**
Buyers' incomes	Increase	Decrease
Buyers' preferences/tastes	Increase	Decrease
Prices of substitute products	Increase	Decrease
Expectations about future prices	Will rise	Will fall
Number of buyers	Increases	Decreases
	Shift Supply	
	To the Right If	**To the Left If**
Technology	Lowers cost	Increases cost
Resource prices	Fall	Rise
Changes in prices of other products that can be produced with the same resources	Profit of other product falls	Profit of other product rises
Number of suppliers	Increases	Decreases
Taxes	Decreases	Increases

Table 1.2

High energy prices affect the economy in many ways. With oil at the time costing $50 to $60 a barrel—more than double the 2003 price—both businesses and consumers across the United States felt the pinch in their wallets. Midwestern agricultural businesses export about 70 percent of their grain production through Gulf of Mexico port facilities. With fewer usable docking spaces, barges couldn't unload and return for more crops. The supply of both transportation services and grain products was inadequate to meet demand, pushing up transportation and grain costs. Higher gas prices also contributed to rising prices, as 80 percent of shipping costs are related to fuel.

More than a decade after Katrina, U.S. gas prices have fluctuated dramatically, with the cost of a gallon of regular gas peaking in 2014 at $3.71, dropping as low as $1.69 in early 2015, and moderating to $2.36 in mid-2017. Recent research by JP Morgan Chase revealed that consumers spend roughly 80 percent of their savings from lower gas prices, which helps the overall economy.[28]

CONCEPT CHECK

1. What is the relationship between prices and demand for a product?
2. How is market equilibrium achieved? Describe the circumstances under which the price for gasoline would have returned to equilibrium in the United States after Hurricane Katrina.
3. Draw a graph that shows an equilibrium point for supply and demand.

1.7 Competing in a Free Market

7. What are the four types of market structure?

One of the characteristics of a free-market system is that suppliers have the right to compete with one another. The number of suppliers in a market defines the **market structure**. Economists identify four types of market structures: (1) perfect competition, (2) pure monopoly, (3) monopolistic competition, and (4) oligopoly. Table 1.3 summarizes the characteristics of each of these market structures.

Perfect Competition

Characteristics of **perfect (pure) competition** include:

- A large number of small firms are in the market.
- The firms sell similar products; that is, each firm's product is very much like the products sold by other firms in the market.
- Buyers and sellers in the market have good information about prices, sources of supply, and so on.
- It is easy to open a new business or close an existing one.

Comparison of Market Structures				
Characteristics	Perfect Competition	Pure Monopoly	Monopolistic Competition	Oligopoly
Number of firms in market	Many	One	Many, but fewer than perfect competition	Few

Table 1.3

Comparison of Market Structures				
Characteristics	Perfect Competition	Pure Monopoly	Monopolistic Competition	Oligopoly
Firm's ability to control price	None	High	Some	Some
Barriers to entry	None	Subject to government regulation	Few	Many
Product differentiation	Very little	No products that compete directly	Emphasis on showing perceived differences in products	Some differences
Examples	Farm products such as wheat and corn	Utilities such as gas, water, cable television	Retail specialty clothing stores	Steel, automobiles, airlines, aircraft manufacturers

Table 1.3

In a perfectly competitive market, firms sell their products at prices determined solely by forces beyond their control. Because the products are very similar and each firm contributes only a small amount to the total quantity supplied by the industry, price is determined by supply and demand. A firm that raised its price even a little above the going rate would lose customers. In the wheat market, for example, the product is essentially the same from one wheat producer to the next. Thus, none of the producers has control over the price of wheat.

Perfect competition is an ideal. No industry shows all its characteristics, but the stock market and some agricultural markets, such as those for wheat and corn, come closest. Farmers, for example, can sell all of their crops through national commodity exchanges at the current market price.

Pure Monopoly

At the other end of the spectrum is **pure monopoly**, the market structure in which a single firm accounts for all industry sales of a particular good or service. The firm *is* the industry. This market structure is characterized by **barriers to entry**—factors that prevent new firms from competing equally with the existing firm. Often the barriers are technological or legal conditions. Polaroid, for example, held major patents on instant photography for years. When Kodak tried to market its own instant camera, Polaroid sued, claiming patent violations. Polaroid collected millions of dollars from Kodak. Another barrier may be one firm's control of a natural resource. DeBeers Consolidated Mines Ltd., for example, controls most of the world's supply of uncut diamonds.

Public utilities, such as gas and water companies, are pure monopolies. Some monopolies are created by a government order that outlaws competition. The U.S. Postal Service is currently one such monopoly.

Monopolistic Competition

Three characteristics define the market structure known as **monopolistic competition**:

- Many firms are in the market.
- The firms offer products that are close substitutes but still differ from one another.
- It is relatively easy to enter the market.

Under monopolistic competition, firms take advantage of product differentiation. Industries where monopolistic competition occurs include clothing, food, and similar consumer products. Firms under monopolistic competition have more control over pricing than do firms under perfect competition because consumers do not view the products as perfect substitutes. Nevertheless, firms must demonstrate product differences to justify their prices to customers. Consequently, companies use advertising to distinguish their products from others. Such distinctions may be significant or superficial. For example, Nike says "Just Do It," and Tylenol is advertised as being easier on the stomach than aspirin.

Oligopoly

An **oligopoly** has two characteristics:

- A few firms produce most or all of the output.
- Large capital requirements or other factors limit the number of firms.

Boeing and Airbus Industries (aircraft manufacturers) and Apple and Google (operating systems for smartphones) are major players in different oligopolistic industries.

With so few firms in an oligopoly, what one firm does has an impact on the other firms. Thus, the firms in an oligopoly watch one another closely for new technologies, product changes and innovations, promotional campaigns, pricing, production, and other developments. Sometimes they go so far as to coordinate their pricing and output decisions, which is illegal. Many antitrust cases—legal challenges arising out of laws designed to control anticompetitive behavior—occur in oligopolies.

The market structure of an industry can change over time. Take, for example, telecommunications. At one time, AT&T had a monopoly on long-distance telephone service nationwide. Then the U.S. government divided the company into seven regional phone companies in 1984, opening the door to greater competition. Other companies such as MCI and Sprint entered the fray and built state-of-the-art fiber-optic networks to win customers from the traditional providers of phone service. The 1996 Telecommunications Act changed the competitive environment yet again by allowing local phone companies to offer long-distance service in exchange for letting competition into their local markets. Today, the broadcasting, computer, telephone, and video industries are converging as companies consolidate through merger and acquisition.

CONCEPT CHECK

1. What is meant by market structure?
2. Compare and contrast perfect competition and pure monopoly. Why is it rare to find perfect competition?
3. How does an oligopoly differ from monopolistic competition?

1.8 | Trends in the Business Environment and Competition

8. Which trends are reshaping the business, microeconomic, and macroeconomic environments and competitive arena?

Trends in the business and economic environment occur in many areas. As noted earlier, today's workforce is more diverse than ever, with increasing numbers of minorities and older workers. Competition has intensified. Technology has accelerated the pace of work and the ease with which we communicate. Let's look at how companies are meeting the challenges of a changing workforce, the growing demand for energy, and how companies are meeting competitive challenges.

Changing Workforce Demographics

As the baby boomer generation ages, so does the U.S. workforce. In 2010, more than 25 percent of all employees were retirement age. Fast forward to the U.S. labor force in 2017, however, and millennials have taken over the top spot in the labor market, with more than 40 percent of the total workforce. Although older workers are now retiring closer to the traditional retirement age of 65, many plan to keep working beyond 65, often into their 70s. No longer is retirement an all-or-nothing proposition, and older workers in the baby boomer generation are taking a more positive attitude toward their later years. A surprising number of Americans expect to work full- or part-time after "retirement," and most would probably work longer if phased retirement programs were available at their companies. Financial reasons motivate most of these older workers, who worry that their longer life expectancies will mean outliving the money they saved for retirement, especially after retirement savings took a hit during the global recession of 2007–2009. For others, however, the satisfaction of working and feeling productive is more important than money alone.[29]

These converging dynamics continue to create several major challenges for companies today. And by 2020, additional generational shifts are projected to occur in the U.S. labor force, which will have an even bigger effect on how companies do business and retain their employees. Today's workforce spans five generations: recent college graduates (Generation Z); people in their 30s and 40s (millennials and Generation X); baby boomers; and traditionalists (people in their 70s). It is not unusual to find a worker who is 50, 60, or even 70 working for a manager who is not yet 30. People in their 50s and 60s offer their vast experience of "what's worked in the past," whereas those in their 20s and 30s tend to be experimental, open to options, and unafraid to take risks. The most effective managers will be the ones who recognize generational differences and use them to the company's advantage.[30]

Many companies have developed programs such as flexible hours and telecommuting to retain older workers and benefit from their practical knowledge and problem-solving skills. In addition, companies should continually track where employees are in their career life cycles, know when they are approaching retirement age or thinking about retirement, and determine how to replace them and their knowledge and job experiences.[31]

Another factor in the changing workforce is the importance of recognizing diversity among workers of all ages and fostering an inclusive organizational culture. According to a recent report by the U.S. Census Bureau, millennials are the largest generation in U.S. history, and more than 44 percent classify themselves as something other than "white." In addition, women continue to make progress on being promoted to management, although their path to CEO seems to be filled with obstacles. Recent statistics suggest that fewer than 5 percent of Fortune 500 companies have female CEOs. The most successful organizations will be the ones that recognize the importance of diversity and inclusion as part of their ongoing corporate strategies.[32]

MANAGING CHANGE

EY Makes Diversity and Inclusion a Top Priority

As older workers continue to leave the U.S. labor force and younger individuals begin work or move to other jobs to further their careers, businesses must recognize the importance of diversity and inclusion as key corporate strategies. This is particularly critical as multicultural millennials become the dominant group in the U.S. workforce. One leader in embracing diversity as an important part of corporate life is EY (formerly Ernst & Young), a global leader in assurance, tax, and advisory services.

EY believes its core values and business strategies are firmly based on diversity and inclusiveness, as evidenced by the company landing in the top spot of DiversityInc's 2017 list of the top companies for diversity. This recognition for EY is no accident; the company has made diversity and inclusion key goals for its more than 214,000 employees around the world. With a diverse workforce becoming the norm, it is no longer acceptable for companies to simply hold a random seminar or two for their managers and employees to discuss diversity and inclusion in the workplace.

Karyn Twaronite, EY's global diversity and inclusion officer, believes that a simple, ongoing approach is the most effective way to address diversity and inclusion in the workplace. The company uses a decision-making strategy called PTR, or preference, tradition, and requirement, to help managers think about diversity and inclusion. The strategy challenges managers to examine preferences toward job candidates who are similar to themselves, asks them whether their decision about hiring a specific candidate is influenced by traditional characteristics of a certain role, and urges them to make their selection based on the requirements of the job rather than on their personal preferences. In other words, the decision-making tool gives people a way to question the status quo without accusing colleagues of being biased.

Another way EY fosters inclusiveness is sponsoring professional network groups within the organization. These groups provide members with opportunities to network across various EY divisions, create informal mentoring relationships, and strengthen leadership skills. Some of the established networks within EY include groups for LGBT employees; blacks, Latinos, and pan-Asians; women; veterans; and employees with disabilities.

As a global company that works with clients in many countries, EY knows the importance of acknowledging different perspectives and cultures as part of its daily business. The company is committed to making sure employees as well as clients respect different viewpoints and individual differences, including background, education, gender, ethnicity, religious background, sexual orientation, ability, and technical skills. According to EY's diversity web page, research shows that a company's diverse teams are more likely to improve market share and have success in new markets and that they demonstrate stronger collaboration and better retention.

Questions for Discussion
1. How does EY's approach to diversity and inclusion translate to additional revenues for the company?
2. Would a company's commitment to diversity make a difference to you when interviewing for a job? Why or why not?

Sources: Company website, "A Diverse and Inclusive Workforce," http://www.ey.com, accessed May 29, 2017; "DiversityInc Top 50: #1—EY: Why They're on the List," http://www.diversityinc.com, accessed May 29, 2017; "Founded on Inclusiveness; Strengthened by Diversity: A Place for Everyone," http://exceptionaley.com, accessed May 29, 2017; Grace Donnelly, "Here's EY's Simple But Effective Strategy for Increasing Diversity," *Fortune,* http://fortune.com, February 10, 2017.

Global Energy Demands

As standards of living improve worldwide, the demand for energy continues to rise. Emerging economies such as China and India need energy to grow. Their demands are placing pressure on the world's supplies and affecting prices, as the laws of supply and demand would predict. For example, in recent years, China and India were responsible for more than half of the growth in oil products consumption worldwide. State-supported energy companies in China, India, Russia, Saudi Arabia, and other countries will place additional competitive pressure on privately owned oil companies such as BP, Chevron, ExxonMobil, and Shell.[33]

Countries worldwide worry about relying too heavily on one source of supply for energy. The United States imports a large percentage of its oil from Canada and Saudi Arabia. Europeans get 39 percent of their natural gas from Russia's state-controlled gas utility OAO Gazprom.[34] This gives foreign governments the power to use energy as a political tool. For example, continuing tensions between Russia and Ukraine in November 2015 caused Russia to stop sending natural gas to Ukraine, which also causes gas disruptions in Europe because Russia uses Ukraine's pipelines to transport some of its gas deliveries to European countries. In 2017, Russia announced plans to build its own pipeline alongside Ukraine's gas line in the Baltic Sea, which would allow Russia to bypass Ukraine's pipelines altogether and deliver gas directly to European countries.[35]

Countries and companies worldwide are seeking additional sources of supply to prevent being held captive to one supplier. For example, the relatively new technology of extracting oil from shale rock formations in the United States (known as fracking) has help create an important resource for the country's oil industry. This innovative approach to finding new sources of energy now accounts for more than half of the country's oil output, which can help reduce U.S. dependence on foreign oil and create new jobs.[36]

Meeting Competitive Challenges

Companies are turning to many different strategies to remain competitive in the global marketplace. One of the most important is **relationship management**, which involves building, maintaining, and enhancing interactions with customers and other parties to develop long-term satisfaction through mutually beneficial partnerships. Relationship management includes both *supply chain management*, which builds strong bonds with suppliers, and *relationship marketing*, which focuses on customers. In general, the longer a customer stays with a company, the more that customer is worth. Long-term customers buy more, take less of a company's time, are less sensitive to price, and bring in new customers. Best of all, they require no acquisition or start-up costs. Good long-standing customers are worth so much that in some industries, reducing customer defections by as little as five points—from, say, 15 percent to 10 percent per year—can double profits.

Another important way companies stay competitive is through **strategic alliances** (also called *strategic partnerships*). The trend toward forming these cooperative agreements between business firms is accelerating rapidly, particularly among high-tech firms. These companies have realized that strategic partnerships are more than just important—they are critical. Strategic alliances can take many forms. Some companies enter into strategic alliances with their suppliers, who take over much of their actual production and manufacturing. For example, Nike, the largest producer of athletic footwear in the world, does not manufacture a single shoe.

Other companies with complementary strengths team up. For example, Harry's Shave Club, an online men's grooming subscription service, recently teamed up with retail giant Target to improve sales and boost its brand presence among Target shoppers. Harry's products are now available in Target's brick-and-mortar stores and on Target's website as part of an exclusive deal that makes Target the only mass retailer to carry Harry's grooming products. The men's shaving industry accounts for more than $2.6 billion in annual sales.[37]

CONCEPT CHECK

1. What steps can companies take to benefit from the aging of their workers and to effectively manage a multigenerational workforce?
2. Why is the increasing demand for energy worldwide a cause for concern?
3. Describe several strategies that companies can use to remain competitive in the global economy.

🔑 Key Terms

barriers to entry Factors, such as technological or legal conditions, that prevent new firms from competing equally with an existing firm.

business An organization that strives for a profit by providing goods and services desired by its customers.

business cycles Upward and downward changes in the level of economic activity.

capital The inputs, such as tools, machinery, equipment, and buildings, used to produce goods and services and get them to the customer.

capitalism An economic system based on competition in the marketplace and private ownership of the factors of production (resources); also known as the *private enterprise system.*

circular flow The movement of inputs and outputs among households, businesses, and governments; a way of showing how the sectors of the economy interact.

communism An economic system characterized by government ownership of virtually all resources, government control of all markets, and economic decision-making by central government planning.

consumer price index (CPI) An index of the prices of a "market basket" of goods and services purchased by typical urban consumers.

contractionary policy The use of monetary policy by the Fed to tighten the money supply by selling government securities or raising interest rates.

cost-push inflation Inflation that occurs when increases in production costs push up the prices of final goods and services.

costs Expenses incurred from creating and selling goods and services.

crowding out The situation that occurs when government spending replaces spending by the private sector.

cyclical unemployment Unemployment that occurs when a downturn in the business cycle reduces the demand for labor throughout the economy.

demand The quantity of a good or service that people are willing to buy at various prices.

demand curve A graph showing the quantity of a good or service that people are willing to buy at various prices.

demand-pull inflation Inflation that occurs when the demand for goods and services is greater than the supply.

demography The study of people's vital statistics, such as their age, gender, race and ethnicity, and location.

economic growth An increase in a nation's output of goods and services.

economic system The combination of policies, laws, and choices made by a nation's government to establish the systems that determine what goods and services are produced and how they are allocated.

economics The study of how a society uses scarce resources to produce and distribute goods and services.

entrepreneurs People who combine the inputs of natural resources, labor, and capital to produce goods or services with the intention of making a profit or accomplishing a not-for-profit goal.

equilibrium The point at which quantity demanded equals quantity supplied.

expansionary policy The use of monetary policy by the Fed to increase, or loosen, the growth of the money supply.

factors of production The resources used to create goods and services.

federal budget deficit The condition that occurs when the federal government spends more for programs than it collects in taxes.

Federal Reserve System (the Fed) The central banking system of the United States.

fiscal policy The government's use of taxation and spending to affect the economy.

frictional unemployment Short-term unemployment that is not related to the business cycle.

full employment The condition when all people who want to work and can work have jobs.

goods Tangible items manufactured by businesses.

gross domestic product (GDP) The total market value of all final goods and services produced within a nation's borders each year.

inflation The situation in which the average of all prices of goods and services is rising.

knowledge The combined talents and skills of the workforce.

knowledge workers Workers who create, distribute, and apply knowledge.

macroeconomics The subarea of economics that focuses on the economy as a whole by looking at aggregate data for large groups of people, companies, or products.

market structure The number of suppliers in a market.

microeconomics The subarea of economics that focuses on individual parts of the economy, such as households or firms.

mixed economies Economies that combine several economic systems; for example, an economy where the government owns certain industries but others are owned by the private sector.

monetary policy A government's programs for controlling the amount of money circulating in the economy and interest rates.

monopolistic competition A market structure in which many firms offer products that are close substitutes and in which entry is relatively easy.

national debt The accumulated total of all of the federal government's annual budget deficits.

not-for-profit organization An organization that exists to achieve some goal other than the usual business goal of profit.

oligopoly A market structure in which a few firms produce most or all of the output and in which large capital requirements or other factors limit the number of firms.

perfect (pure) competition A market structure in which a large number of small firms sell similar products, buyers and sellers have good information, and businesses can be easily opened or closed.

producer price index (PPI) An index of the prices paid by producers and wholesalers for various commodities, such as raw materials, partially finished goods, and finished products.

productivity The amount of goods and services one worker can produce.

profit The money left over after all costs are paid.

purchasing power The value of what money can buy.

pure monopoly A market structure in which a single firm accounts for all industry sales of a particular good or service and in which there are *barriers to entry*.

quality of life The general level of human happiness based on such things as life expectancy, educational standards, health, sanitation, and leisure time.

recession A decline in GDP that lasts for at least two consecutive quarters.

relationship management The practice of building, maintaining, and enhancing interactions with customers and other parties to develop long-term satisfaction through mutually beneficial partnerships.

revenue The money a company receives by providing services or selling goods to customers.

risk The potential to lose time and money or otherwise not be able to accomplish an organization's goals.

savings bonds Government bonds issued in relatively small denominations.

seasonal unemployment Unemployment that occurs during specific seasons in certain industries.

services Intangible offerings of businesses that can't be held, touched, or stored.

socialism An economic system in which the basic industries are owned either by the government itself or by the private sector under strong government control.

standard of living A country's output of goods and services that people can buy with the money they have.

strategic alliance A cooperative agreement between business firms; sometimes called a *strategic partnership*.

structural unemployment Unemployment that is caused by a mismatch between available jobs and the skills of available workers in an industry or region; not related to the business cycle.

supply The quantity of a good or service that businesses will make available at various prices.

supply curve A graph showing the quantity of a good or service that businesses will make available at various prices.

technology The application of science and engineering skills and knowledge to solve production and organizational problems.

unemployment rate The percentage of the total labor force that is not working but is *actively looking for work*.

Summary of Learning Outcomes

1.1 The Nature of Business

1. How do businesses and not-for-profit organizations help create our standard of living?

Businesses attempt to earn a profit by providing goods and services desired by their customers. Not-for-profit organizations, though not striving for a profit, still deliver many needed services for our society. Our standard of living is measured by the output of goods and services. Thus, businesses and not-for-profit organizations help create our standard of living. Our quality of life is not simply the amount of goods and services available for consumers but rather the society's general level of happiness.

Economists refer to the building blocks of a business as the factors of production. To produce anything, one must have natural resources, labor (human resources), capital, and entrepreneurship to assemble the resources and manage the business. Today's competitive business environment is based upon knowledge and learning. The companies that succeed will be those that learn fast, use knowledge efficiently, and develop new insights.

1.2 Understanding the Business Environment

2. What are the sectors of the business environment, and how do changes in them influence business decisions?

The external business environment consists of economic, political and legal, demographic, social, competitive, global, and technological sectors. Managers must understand how the environment is changing and the impact of those changes on the business. When economic activity is strong, unemployment rates are low, and income levels rise. The political environment is shaped by the amount of government intervention in business affairs, the types of laws it passes to regulate both domestic and foreign businesses, and the general political stability of a government. Demographics, or the study of people's vital statistics, are at the heart of many business decisions. Businesses today must deal with the unique preferences of different generations, each of which requires different marketing approaches and different goods and services. The population is becoming increasingly diverse: currently minorities represent more than 38 percent of the total U.S. population, and that number will continue to increase over the next several decades. Minorities' buying power has increased significantly as well, and companies are developing products and marketing campaigns that target different ethnic groups. Social factors—our attitudes, values, and lifestyles—influence what, how, where, and when people purchase products. They are difficult to predict, define, and measure because they can be very subjective. They also change as people move through different life stages.

1.3 How Business and Economics Work

3. What are the primary features of the world's economic systems, and how are the three sectors of the U.S. economy linked?

Economics is the study of how individuals, businesses, and governments use scarce resources to produce and distribute goods and services. Today there is a global trend toward capitalism. Capitalism, also known as the *private enterprise system,* is based upon marketplace competition and private ownership of the factors of production. Competition leads to more diverse goods and services, keeps prices stable, and pushes businesses to become more efficient.

In a communist economy, the government owns virtually all resources, and economic decision-making is done by central government planning. Governments have generally moved away from communism because it is inefficient and delivers a low standard of living. Socialism is another centralized economic system in which the basic industries are owned by the government or by the private sector under strong government control. Other industries may be privately owned. The state is also somewhat influential in determining the goals of business, the prices and selection of products, and the rights of workers. Most national economies today are a mix of socialism and capitalism.

The two major areas in economics are macroeconomics, the study of the economy as a whole, and microeconomics, the study of households and firms. The individual, business, and government sectors of the economy are linked by a series of two-way flows. The government provides public goods and services to the other two sectors and receives income in the form of taxes. Changes in one flow affect the other sectors.

1.4 Macroeconomics: The Big Picture

4. How do economic growth, full employment, price stability, and inflation indicate a nation's economic health?

A nation's economy is growing when the level of business activity, as measured by gross domestic product (GDP) is rising. GDP is the total value of all goods and services produced in a year. The goal of full employment is to have a job for all who can and want to work. How well a nation is meeting its employment goals is measured by the unemployment rate. There are four types of unemployment: frictional, structural, cyclical, and seasonal. With price stability, the overall prices of goods and services are not moving very much either up or down. Inflation is the general upward movement of prices. When prices rise, purchasing power falls. The rate of inflation is measured by changes in the consumer price index (CPI) and the producer price index (PPI). There are two main causes of inflation. If the demand for goods and services exceeds the supply, prices will rise. This is called demand-pull inflation. With cost-push inflation, higher production costs, such as expenses for materials and wages, increase the final prices of goods and services.

1.5 Achieving Macroeconomic Goals

5. How does the government use monetary policy and fiscal policy to achieve its macroeconomic goals?

Monetary policy refers to actions by the Federal Reserve System (the Fed) to control the money supply. When the Fed restricts the money supply, interest rates rise, the inflation rate drops, and economic growth slows. By expanding the money supply, the Fed stimulates economic growth. The government also uses fiscal policy— changes in levels of taxation and spending—to control the economy. Reducing taxes or increasing spending stimulates the economy; raising taxes or decreasing spending does the opposite. When the government spends more than it receives in tax revenues, it must borrow to finance the deficit. Some economists favor deficit spending as a way to stimulate the economy; others worry about our high level of national debt.

1.6 Microeconomics: Zeroing in on Businesses and Consumers

6. What are the basic microeconomic concepts of demand and supply, and how do they establish prices?

Demand is the quantity of a good or service that people will buy at a given price. Supply is the quantity of a good or service that firms will make available at a given price. When the price increases, the quantity demanded falls, but the quantity supplied rises. A price decrease leads to increased demand but a lower supply. At the point where the quantity demanded equals the quantity supplied, demand and supply are in balance. This equilibrium point is achieved by market adjustments of quantity and price.

1.7 Competing in a Free Market
7. What are the four types of market structure?

Market structure is the number of suppliers in a market. Perfect competition is characterized by a large number of buyers and sellers, very similar products, good market information for both buyers and sellers, and ease of entry into and exit from the market. In a pure monopoly, there is a single seller in a market. In monopolistic competition, many firms sell close substitutes in a market that is fairly easy to enter. In an oligopoly, a few firms produce most or all of the industry's output. An oligopoly is also difficult to enter, and what one firm does will influence others.

1.8 Trends in the Business Environment and Competition
8. Which trends are reshaping the business, microeconomic, and macroeconomic environments and competitive arena?

To remain competitive, businesses must identify and respond to trends in the various sectors of the business environment. As the population ages, large numbers of baby boomers are approaching retirement age. Companies must plan for this exodus of employees and find ways to retain the vast amounts of knowledge they represent. Many older workers are choosing to continue working after traditional retirement age, creating a five-generation workforce. Worldwide demand for energy, especially from China and India, is challenging oil companies to increase supplies or to find alternative technologies to produce more oil, such as fracking. U.S. vulnerability to disruptions in energy supply became painfully apparent when Hurricane Katrina put Gulf Coast refineries and offshore drilling rigs out of commission. Companies are using relationship management and strategic alliances to compete effectively in the global economy.

Preparing for Tomorrow's Workplace Skills

1. Select a not-for-profit organization whose mission interests you. What are the organization's objectives? What resources does it need to achieve those goals? Select a for-profit business that provides a similar service, and compare the two organizations. How does each use the factors of production? (Resources, Information, Systems)

2. **Team Activity** Form seven teams. Each team is responsible for one of the sectors of the external business environment discussed in the chapter (economic, political/legal, demographic, social, competitive, global, and technological). Your boss, the company president, has asked each team to report on the changes in that area of the external environment and how they will affect the firm over the next five years. The firm is the Boeing Company. Each team should use the library, the internet, and other data sources to make its projections. Each team member should examine at least one data source. The team should then pool the data and prepare its response. A spokesperson for each team should present the findings to the class. (Interpersonal, Resources, Information)

3. If a friend claimed, "Economics is all theory and not very practical," how might you counter this claim? Share your rationale with the class. (Interpersonal, Information)

4. **Team Activity** Create two teams of four people each. Have one side choose a communist economy and the other capitalism. Debate the proposition that "capitalism/a command economy is good for developing nations." (Interpersonal, Information)

5. What are the latest actions the federal government has taken to manage the economy? Has it used

monetary policy or fiscal policy to achieve its macroeconomic goals? Summarize your findings. Choose one of the following industries, and discuss how the government's actions will affect that industry: airlines, automobile manufacturers, banking, biotechnology, chemical manufacturing, home building, oil and gas, retail stores, and telecommunication services. (Information, Systems)

6. As a manufacturer of wireless headphones, you are questioning your pricing policies. You note that over the past five years, the CPI increased an average of 3 percent per year but that the price of a pair of wireless headphones increased an average of 8 percent per year for the first three years and 2 percent per year for the next two years. What does this information tell you about demand, supply, and other factors influencing the market for these headphones? (Resources, Information)

Ethics Activity

Historically, diesel cars have not been big sellers in the U.S. auto market, mainly because their engines couldn't pass the strict emissions standards set up by the Environmental Protection Agency and the California Air Resources Board. But that all changed in 2005, when German automaker Volkswagen made a decided push to develop "clean diesel" engines, specifically manufactured to meet strict U.S. emissions standards.

By 2010, VW had introduced several models of diesel cars in the United States, and their sales helped propel Volkswagen to the number-two slot in global auto sales, after Toyota and ahead of GM. While VW was receiving major media attention for its clean diesel models, researchers from West Virginia University discovered that these so-called clean engines had been constructed with a "defeat device"—software that could actually tell when the car was being tested off road for emissions and lower the level of emissions that harm the environment.

By December 2014, Volkswagen agreed to voluntarily recall more than a half-million clean diesel cars in the United States to address the emissions issues. But the scandal continued to escalate, with accusations that senior management knew about the rigged engines, and VW's CEO resigned and several other executives were fired.

Class-action lawsuits and other litigation followed, and in April 2017, VW agreed to a $4.3 billion settlement, which included a criminal fine of $2.8 billion, as well as various buyback plans for the affected diesel cars. In addition, over the last several years, VW has experienced a significant decline in U.S. sales and is now trying to win back customers.

Using a web search tool, locate information about this topic, and then write responses to the following questions. Be sure to support your arguments and cite your sources.

Ethical Dilemma: How can VW ensure that its diesel cars now comply with U.S. emissions standards? What can VW do to regain consumers' confidence after this worldwide scandal? Do you agree with the billions of dollars in fines that VW will have to pay to move beyond the emissions debacle?

Sources: "VW Diesel Crisis: Timeline of Events," https://www.cars.com, May 19, 2017; Jack Ewing, "Inside VW's Campaign of Trickery," *The New York Times,* http://www.nytimes.com, May 7, 2017; Christoph Rauwald, "How a Top-Secret Deal Could Have Stopped VW's Diesel Scandal," *Bloomberg,* http://www.bloomberg.com, January 12, 2017; "6 VW Execs Indicted as Carmaker Agrees to $4.3 Billion Diesel Cheat Settlement," *Fortune,* http://fortune.com, January 12, 2017; Geoffrey Smith and Roger Parloff, "Hoaxwagen: Inside Volkswagen's Diesel Fraud," *Fortune,* http://fortune.com, March 7, 2016.

Working the Net

1. The Bureau of Labor Statistics compiles demographic data. Visit **http://www.bls.gov/bls/ demographics.htm**, and describe the different types of information it provides. What kinds of changes are likely to occur in the United States over the next 25 years? Click on Spending & Time Use and select How Americans Spend Time to read about the American Time Use Survey. What trends can you identify?

2. Go to either the Red Herring **(http://www.redherring.com)** or Wired **(http://www.wired.com)** site and research technology trends. Compile a list of three trends that sound most promising to you, and describe them briefly. How will they affect businesses? What impact, if any, will they have on you personally?

3. Use the Bureau of Labor Statistics site (**http://stat.bls.gov**) to determine the current trends in GDP growth, unemployment, and inflation. What do these trends tell you about the level of business activity and the business cycle? If you owned a staffing agency, how would this information affect your decision-making?

4. What's the latest U.S. economic news? Go to the CNBC website, and select the Economy page, which categorizes news about the world economy, the U.S. economy, and other important topics **(http://www.cnbc.com/economy/)**. Read the various articles about the U.S. economy, and then do the same for GDP Outlook. Prepare a summary of what you learned, and use it to discuss where you think the economy is headed for the next 6 to 12 months.

5. How would you spend the national budget if you were president? Here's your chance to find out how your ideas would affect the federal budget. Go online to Committee for a Responsible Federal Budget, at **http://www.crfb.org**, and under Tools, click on Stabilize the Debt, which is an exercise in making difficult decisions and how government officials make trade-offs when they prepare the federal budget. Experiment with your own budget ideas at the site. What are the effects of your decisions?

Critical Thinking Case

Walmart Gets Serious about E-Commerce

As the world's largest retailer, Walmart has built thousands of brick-and-mortar stores in the United States, Mexico, and elsewhere. Although a success story when it comes to traditional retail locations, Walmart has struggled with its e-commerce efforts, with recent online sales accounting for about 3 percent of the company's $300 billion in annual sales. The company has tried several different e-commerce strategies in the past, but none of them was an overwhelming success. Some company insiders objected to the pricing strategy used for online purchases; they were fearful that Walmart's lower prices online would take customers (and sales) away from the retail locations.

Doug McMillon, Walmart's CEO since 2014, believed a significant change was needed in the company's e-commerce business, and he recently made changes in a big way. Over the past two years, Walmart spent billions to acquire several online companies to expand its e-commerce business in an effort to take a small bite out of retail giant Amazon's success. In 2016, Walmart purchased Jet.com, an e-commerce site that sells a little bit of everything (books, clothing, electronics, etc.) at discount prices. Once the $3 billion acquisition was completed, Jet's cofounder and CEO, Marc Lore, who now runs Walmart's e-commerce platform, worked with McMillon to identify other established online companies to add to their e-commerce portfolio, and add they did.

First Walmart purchased footwear e-tailer ShoeBuy for $70 million in January 2017. The following month, Walmart bought outdoor specialty retailer Moosejaw for $51 million. Then in March, Walmart paid $75 million for ModCloth, an eclectic shopping site for women's fashions. Walmart is also said to be in negotiations to buy Bonobos, a hip fashion retailer geared to millennial males.

Reaction to the acquisitions has been mixed, depending on whom you ask. Retail analysts applaud the company's radical move, pointing out that several well-known traditional retailers have closed their doors or filed bankruptcy because they failed to take part in the e-commerce revolution. Fashionistas, on the other hand, are lukewarm about the move. However, McMillon's decision to allow the online retailers to operate independently may help retain loyal customers. The new e-commerce strategy may also lure typical in-store shoppers to take advantage of the expanded offerings available through both Walmart.com and Jet.com.

Critical Thinking Questions
1. What are some advantages of Walmart purchasing established web businesses?
2. What impact is Walmart's acquisition of nontraditional retailers likely to have on the shopping habits of Walmart's customers?
3. How will the aggressive e-commerce plan implemented by Walmart affect operations at its retail locations?

Sources: Brad Stone and Matthew Boyle, "Amazon Won't Know What Hit 'Em!" *Bloomberg Businessweek,* http://www.bloomberg.com, May 8–May 14, 2017; "What an Acquisition of Bonobos Would Signal About Wal-Mart's Strategy," *Forbes,* http://www.forbes.com, May 9, 2017; "Walmart Acquires Niche Online Retailers, to the Dismay of Hipsters," *Denver Post,* http://www.denverpost.com, March 24, 2017; Alana Abramson, "Walmart Acquires Online Women's Retailer ModCloth," *Fortune,* http://fortune.com, March 17, 2017; Phil Wahba, "Walmart's 29% Online Holiday Season Growth Sends Shares Jumping," *Fortune,* http://fortune.com, February 21, 2017; Laura Heller, "Take That Amazon: Walmart Buys Moosejaw for $51 Million," *Forbes,* http://www.forbes.com, February 15, 2017; "Walmart Acquires ShoeBuy for $70 Million," *Business Insider,* http://www.businessinsider.com, January 6, 2017.

Hot Links Address Book

1. What makes a company good to work for or most admired? Find out by checking *Fortune*'s special lists at **http://www.fortune.com**.
2. Which country has the largest GDP? The most people? The answers can be found in The World Factbook at **https://www.cia.gov**.
3. Get the scoop on the latest technology trends affecting our lives from CNET's website at **http://www.cnet.com**. The site also includes product reviews, how-to videos, and smart home features.
4. The Federal Reserve Board issues a variety of statistical information about the state of the U.S. economy. Find it at the Federal Reserve's site by clicking on the Economic Research and Data links: **http://www.federalreserve.gov**.
5. Want to know the current public debt per citizen, or even what it was in 1790? Go to **https://www.transparency.treasury.gov/** and click on National Debt.
6. The U.S. Bureau of Economic Analysis (BEA) tracks national and regional economic statistics, including the GDP. To find the latest GDP statistics, visit the BEA at.
7. How are the job prospects in your area? Your region's unemployment statistics can give you an idea of how hard it will be to find a job. Find the most recent unemployment statistics from the Bureau of Labor

Statistics at **http://www.bls.gov**.

8. How do the PPI and the CPI differ? Get the answers to this and other questions about the PPI by visiting the Bureau of Labor Statistics PPI site at **http://www.bls.gov/ppi**.

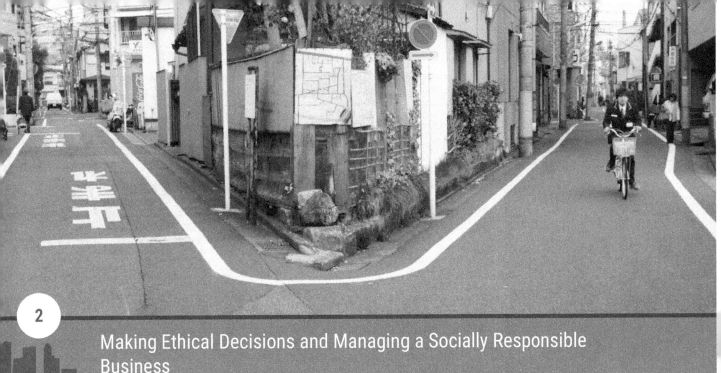

2 | Making Ethical Decisions and Managing a Socially Responsible Business

Exhibit 2.1

 Introduction

Learning Outcomes

After reading this chapter, you should be able to answer these questions:

1. What philosophies and concepts shape personal ethical standards?
2. How can organizations encourage ethical business behavior?
3. What is corporate social responsibility?
4. How do businesses meet their social responsibilities to various stakeholders?
5. What are the trends in ethics and corporate social responsibility?

EXPLORING BUSINESS CAREERS

Playing with a Purpose at Hasbro

Hasbro is a global play and entertainment company that takes corporate social responsibility (CSR) very seriously. Founded nearly a century ago in Rhode Island, Hasbro integrates its CSR efforts throughout the organization with the goal of helping to make the world a better place for children of all ages.

In 2017, the company achieved the number one spot in the "100 Best Corporate Citizens" rankings, published annually by *Corporate Responsibility* magazine. Hasbro is no stranger to this achievement; over the past five years, Hasbro has consistently been in the top five spots on this prestigious list—and that is no accident.

Exhibit 2.2   **Hasbro's Monopoly game**   (Credit: Ben Tsai/ Flickr/ Public Domain)

With more than 5,000 employees, Hasbro relies heavily on its strategic brand blueprint to guide its efforts in CSR, innovation, philanthropy, and product development. With a business portfolio that includes such well-known brands as Nerf, Play-Doh, Transformers, Monopoly, and The Game of Life, the company focuses its CSR efforts on four key areas: product safety, environmental sustainability, human rights and ethical sourcing, and community.

According to the company, product safety is its highest priority. Hasbro uses a five-step quality assurance process that starts with design and then moves to engineering, manufacturing, and packaging. Another key part of product safety at Hasbro is incorporating continuous feedback from both consumers and retailers and insisting that these high standards and quality processes apply to all third-party factories worldwide that manufacture its products.

Hasbro is also committed to finding new ways to reduce its environmental footprint. Over the past several years, the company has reduced energy consumption, cut greenhouse gas emissions, and reduced water consumption and waste production in its production facilities. In addition, Hasbro has totally eliminated the use of wire ties in all of its product packaging, saving more than *34,000* miles of wire ties—more than enough to wrap around the earth's circumference.

Human rights and ethical sourcing remains a key ingredient of Hasbro's CSR success. Treating people fairly is a core company value, as is working diligently to make great strides in diversity and inclusion at all levels of the organization. Company personnel work closely with third-party factories to ensure that the human rights of all workers in the Hasbro global supply chain are recognized and upheld.

Philanthropy, corporate giving, and employee volunteering are key components of the Hasbro community. Through its various charitable programs, Hasbro made close to $15 million in financial contributions and product donations in 2016, which reached close to an estimated 4 million children around the globe. Several years ago the company started an annual Global Day of Joy as a way of engaging its employees worldwide in community service. In a recent year, more than 93 percent of Hasbro's employees participated in service projects in more than 40 countries.

Hasbro is in the business of storytelling, and its CSR efforts tell the story of an ethical, responsible organization whose mission is to create the world's best play experiences. Its ability to be accountable for its actions and to help make the world a better place one experience at time continues to make it a highly successful company.

Sources: Brian Goldner, "Who Are You Really?—Brian Goldner, President & CEO for Hasbro, Inc.," http://insights.ethisphere.com, accessed June 29, 2017; "CSR Fact Sheet," https://csr.hasbro.com, accessed June 23, 2017; "The World's Biggest Public Companies: Hasbro," *Forbes,* https://www.forbes.com, accessed June 23, 2017; "2016 Global Philanthropy & Social Impact," https://csr.hasbro.com, accessed June 23, 2017; Elizabeth Gurdus, "Hasbro CEO Reveals the Magic Behind the Toymaker's Earnings Beat," *CNBC,* http://www.cnbc.com, April 24, 2017; Jade Burke, "Hasbro Reaches Top Spot in CSR Listing," *Toy News,* http://www.toynews-online.biz, April 21, 2017; Kathrin Belliveau, "CSR at Hasbro: What It Means to Play with Purpose," *LinkedIn,* https://www.linkedin.com, April 20, 2017.

Every day, managers and business owners make business decisions based on what they believe to be right and wrong. Through their actions, they demonstrate to their employees what is and is not acceptable behavior and shape the moral standard of the organization. As you will see in this module, personal and professional ethics are important cornerstones of an organization and shape its ultimate contributions to society in the form of corporate social responsibility. First, let's consider how individual business ethics are formed.

2.1 Understanding Business Ethics

1. What philosophies and concepts shape personal ethical standards?

Ethics is a set of moral standards for judging whether something is right or wrong. The first step in understanding business ethics is learning to recognize an **ethical issue**. An ethical issue is a situation where someone must choose between a set of actions that may be ethical or unethical. For example, Martin Shkreli, former CEO of Turing Pharmaceuticals, raised the price of a drug used for newborns and HIV patients by more than *5000* percent, defending the price increase as a "great business decision."[1] Few people would call that ethical behavior. But consider the actions of the stranded, hungry people in New Orleans who lost everything in the aftermath of Hurricane Katrina. They broke into flooded stores, taking food and bottled water without paying for them. Was this unethical behavior? Or what about the small Texas plastics manufacturer that employed over 100 people and specialized in the Latin American market? The president was distraught because he knew the firm would be bankrupt by the end of the year if it didn't receive more contracts. He knew that he was losing business because he refused to pay bribes. Bribes were part of the culture in his major markets. Closing the firm would put many people out of work. Should he start paying bribes in order to stay in business? Would this be unethical? Let's look at the next section to obtain some guidance on recognizing unethical situations.

Recognizing Unethical Business Activities

Researchers from Brigham Young University tell us that all unethical business activities will fall into one of the following categories:

1. *Taking things that don't belong to you.* The unauthorized use of someone else's property or taking property under false pretenses is taking something that does not belong to you. Even the smallest offense, such as using the postage meter at your office for mailing personal letters or exaggerating your travel expenses, belongs in this category of ethical violations.

2. *Saying things you know are not true.* Often, when trying for a promotion and advancement, fellow employees discredit their coworkers. Falsely assigning blame or inaccurately reporting conversations is lying. Although "This is the way the game is played around here" is a common justification, saying things that are untrue is an ethical violation.

3. *Giving or allowing false impressions.* The salesperson who permits a potential customer to believe that cardboard boxes will hold the customer's tomatoes for long-distance shipping when the salesperson knows the boxes are not strong enough has given a false impression. A car dealer who fails to disclose that a car has been in an accident is misleading potential customers.

4. *Buying influence or engaging in a conflict of interest.* A conflict of interest occurs when the official responsibilities of an employee or government official are influenced by the potential for personal gain. Suppose a company awards a construction contract to a firm owned by the father of the state attorney general while the state attorney general's office is investigating that company. If this construction award has the potential to shape the outcome of the investigation, a conflict of interest has occurred.

5. *Hiding or divulging information.* Failing to disclose the results of medical studies that indicate your firm's new drug has significant side effects is the ethical violation of hiding information that the product could be harmful to purchasers. Taking your firm's product development or trade secrets to a new place of employment constitutes the ethical violation of divulging proprietary information.

6. *Taking unfair advantage.* Many current consumer protection laws were passed because so many businesses took unfair advantage of people who were not educated or were unable to discern the nuances of complex contracts. Credit disclosure requirements, truth-in-lending provisions, and new regulations on auto leasing all resulted because businesses misled consumers who could not easily follow the jargon of long, complex agreements.

7. *Committing improper personal behavior.* Although the ethical aspects of an employee's right to privacy are still debated, it has become increasingly clear that personal conduct outside the job can influence performance and company reputation. Thus, a company driver must abstain from substance abuse because of safety issues. Even the traditional company holiday party and summer picnic have come under scrutiny due to the possibility that employees at and following these events might harm others through alcohol-related accidents.

8. *Abusing power and mistreating individuals.* Suppose a manager sexually harasses an employee or subjects employees to humiliating corrections or reprimands in the presence of customers. In some cases, laws protect employees. Many situations, however, are simply interpersonal abuse that constitutes an ethical violation.

9. *Permitting organizational abuse.* Many U.S. firms with operations overseas, such as Apple, Nike, and Levi Strauss, have faced issues of organizational abuse. The unfair treatment of workers in international operations appears in the form of child labor, demeaning wages, and excessive work hours. Although a business cannot change the culture of another country, it can perpetuate—or stop—abuse through its operations there.

10. *Violating rules.* Many organizations use rules and processes to maintain internal controls or respect the authority of managers. Although these rules may seem burdensome to employees trying to serve customers, a violation may be considered an unethical act.

11. *Condoning unethical actions.* What if you witnessed a fellow employee embezzling company funds by forging her signature on a check? Would you report the violation? A winking tolerance of others' unethical behavior is itself unethical.[2]

After recognizing that a situation is unethical, the next question is what do you do? The action that a person takes is partially based upon his or her ethical philosophy. The environment in which we live and work also plays a role in our behavior. This section describes personal philosophies and legal factors that influence the choices we make when confronting an ethical dilemma.

Justice—The Question of Fairness

Another factor influencing individual business ethics is **justice**, or what is fair according to prevailing standards of society. We all expect life to be reasonably fair. You expect your exams to be fair, the grading to be fair, and your wages to be fair, based on the type of work being done.

Today we take justice to mean an equitable distribution of the burdens and rewards that society has to offer. The distributive process varies from society to society. Those in a democratic society believe in the "equal pay for equal work" doctrine, in which individuals are rewarded based on the value the free market places on their services. Because the market places different values on different occupations, the rewards, such as wages, are not necessarily equal. Nevertheless, many regard the rewards as just. A politician who argued that a supermarket clerk should receive the same pay as a physician, for example, would not receive many votes from the American people. At the other extreme, communist theorists have argued that justice would be served by a society in which burdens and rewards were distributed to individuals according to their abilities and their needs, respectively.

Utilitarianism—Seeking the Best for the Majority

One of the philosophies that may influence choices between right and wrong is **utilitarianism**, which focuses on the consequences of an action taken by a person or organization. The notion that people should act so as to generate the greatest good for the greatest number is derived from utilitarianism. When an action affects the majority adversely, it is morally wrong. One problem with this philosophy is that it is nearly impossible to accurately determine how a decision will affect a large number of people.

Another problem is that utilitarianism always involves both winners and losers. If sales are slowing and a manager decides to fire five people rather than putting everyone on a 30-hour workweek, the 20 people who keep their full-time jobs are winners, but the other five are losers.

A final criticism of utilitarianism is that some "costs," although small relative to the potential good, are so negative that some segments of society find them unacceptable. Reportedly, the backs of animals a year are deliberately broken so that scientists can conduct spinal cord research that could someday lead to a cure for spinal cord injuries. To a number of people, however, the "costs" are simply too horrible for this type of research to continue.

Following Our Obligations and Duties

The philosophy that says people should meet their obligations and duties when analyzing an ethical dilemma is called **deontology**. This means that a person will follow his or her obligations to another individual or society because upholding one's duty is what is considered ethically correct. For instance, people who follow this philosophy will always keep their promises to a friend and will follow the law. They will produce very consistent decisions, because they will be based on the individual's set duties. Note that this theory is not necessarily concerned with the welfare of others. Say, for example, a technician for Orkin Pest Control has decided that it's his ethical duty (and is very practical) to always be on time to meetings with homeowners. Today he is running late. How is he supposed to drive? Is the technician supposed to speed, breaking his duty to society to uphold the law, or is he supposed to arrive at the client's home late, breaking his duty to be on time? This scenario of conflicting obligations does not lead us to a clear ethically correct resolution, nor does it protect the welfare of others from the technician's decision.

Individual Rights

In our society, individuals and groups have certain rights that exist under certain conditions regardless of any external circumstances. These rights serve as guides when making individual ethical decisions. The term *human rights* implies that certain rights—to life, to freedom, to the pursuit of happiness—are bestowed at birth and cannot be arbitrarily taken away. Denying the rights of an individual or group is considered to be unethical and illegal in most, though not all, parts of the world. Certain rights are guaranteed by the government and its laws, and these are considered *legal rights*. The U.S. Constitution and its amendments, as well as state and federal statutes, define the rights of American citizens. Those rights can be disregarded only in extreme circumstances, such as during wartime. Legal rights include the freedom of religion, speech, and assembly; protection from improper arrest and searches and seizures; and proper access to counsel, confrontation of witnesses, and cross-examination in criminal prosecutions. Also held to be fundamental is the right to privacy in many matters. Legal rights are to be applied without regard to race, color, creed, gender, or ability.

CONCEPT CHECK

1. How are individual business ethics formed?
2. What is utilitarianism?
3. How can you recognize unethical activities?

2.2 How Organizations Influence Ethical Conduct

2. How can organizations encourage ethical business behavior?

People choose between right and wrong based on their personal code of ethics. They are also influenced by the ethical environment created by their employers. Consider the following headlines:

- Investment advisor Bernard Madoff sentenced to 150 years in prison for swindling clients out of more than $65 billion.
- Former United Airlines CEO Jeff Smisek leaves the company after a federal investigation into whether United tried to influence officials at the Port Authority of New York.
- Renaud Laplanche, the founder of Lending Club, loses his job because of faulty practices and conflicts of interest at the online peer-to-peer lender.
- Wells Fargo CEO John Stumpf fired after company employees opened more than 2 million fake accounts

to meet aggressive sales targets.[3]

As these actual stories illustrate, poor business ethics can create a very negative image for a company, can be expensive for the firm and/or the executives involved, and can result in bankruptcy and jail time for the offenders. Organizations can reduce the potential for these types of liability claims by educating their employees about ethical standards, by leading through example, and through various informal and formal programs.

Leading by Example

Employees often follow the examples set by their managers. That is, leaders and managers establish patterns of behavior that determine what's acceptable and what's not within the organization. While Ben Cohen was president of Ben & Jerry's ice cream, he followed a policy that no one could earn a salary more than seven times that of the lowest-paid worker. He wanted all employees to feel that they were equal. At the time he resigned, company sales were $140 million, and the lowest-paid worker earned $19,000 per year. Ben Cohen's salary was $133,000, based on the "seven times" rule. A typical top executive of a $140 million company might have earned 10 times Cohen's salary. Ben Cohen's actions helped shape the ethical values of Ben & Jerry's.

Offering Ethics Training Programs

In addition to providing a system to resolve ethical dilemmas, organizations also provide formal training to develop an awareness of questionable business activities and practice appropriate responses. Many companies have some type of ethics training program. The ones that are most effective, like those created by Levi Strauss, American Express, and Campbell Soup Company, begin with techniques for solving ethical dilemmas such as those discussed earlier. Next, employees are presented with a series of situations and asked to come up with the "best" ethical solution. One of these ethical dilemmas is shown in Table 2.1. According to a recent survey by the Ethics Resource Center, more than 80 percent of U.S. companies provide some sort of ethics training for employees, which may include online activities, videos, and even games.[4]

An Ethical Dilemma Used for Employee Training
Bill Gannon was a middle manager of a large manufacturer of lighting fixtures in Newark, New Jersey. Bill had moved up the company ladder rather quickly and seemed destined for upper management in a few years. Bill's boss, Dana Johnson, had been pressuring him about the semiannual reviews concerning Robert Talbot, one of Bill's employees. Dana, it seemed, would not accept any negative comments on Robert's evaluation forms. Bill had found out that a previous manager who had given Robert a bad evaluation was no longer with the company. As Bill reviewed Robert's performance for the forthcoming evaluation period, he found many areas of subpar performance. Moreover, a major client had called recently complaining that Robert had filled a large order improperly and then had been rude to the client when she called to complain.

Table 2.1

An Ethical Dilemma Used for Employee Training
Discussion Questions

Discussion Questions
1. What ethical issues does the situation raise?
2. What courses of action could Bill take? Describe the ethics of each course.
3. Should Bill confront Dana? Dana's boss?
4. What would you do in this situation? What are the ethical implications?

Table 2.1

Establishing a Formal Code of Ethics

Most large companies and thousands of smaller ones have created, printed, and distributed codes of ethics. In general, a **code of ethics** provides employees with the knowledge of what their firm expects in terms of their responsibilities and behavior toward fellow employees, customers, and suppliers. Some ethical codes offer a lengthy and detailed set of guidelines for employees. Others are not really codes at all but rather summary statements of goals, policies, and priorities. Some companies have their codes framed and hung on office walls, included as a key component of employee handbooks, and/or posted on their corporate websites.

Examples of company codes of ethics:
Costco http://phx.corporate-ir.net/phoenix.zhtml?c=83830&p=irol-govhighlights
Starbucks https://www.starbucks.com/about-us/company-information/business-ethics-and-compliance
AT&T https://www.att.com/gen/investor-relations?pid=5595

Do codes of ethics make employees behave in a more ethical manner? Some people believe that they do. Others think that they are little more than public relations gimmicks. If senior management abides by the code of ethics and regularly emphasizes the code to employees, then it will likely have a positive influence on behavior.

The "100 Best Corporate Citizens" as ranked by *Corporate Responsibility* magazine are selected based on seven categories, including employee relations, human rights, corporate governance (including code of ethics), philanthropy and community support, financial performance, environment, and climate change.[5] The top corporate citizens in 2017 were:

1. Hasbro, Inc.
2. Intel Corp.
3. Microsoft Corp.
4. Altria Group, Inc.
5. Campbell Soup Company
6. Cisco Systems, Inc.
7. Accenture
8. Hormel Foods Corp.
9. Lockheed Martin Corp.
10. Ecolab, Inc.

CUSTOMER SATISFACTION AND QUALITY

Campbell's Adds CSR to Its Recipe

The Campbell Soup Company is no longer just about traditional cans of processed soup. Under the guidance of its management team, particularly its former CEO Denise Morrison (Morrison retired from Campbell's in July of 2018), Campbell's has undergone a transformation that includes a strong emphasis on organics and fresh food—and a large serving of corporate citizenship.

Named one of the Best Corporate Citizens by *Corporate Responsibility* magazine in 2017, Campbell's is working to make sustainability and transparency part of its business DNA, and this culture shift has had an important influence on the company's business strategies.

Morrison, who took over as CEO in 2011, is a firm believer in the company's central vision: real food that matters for life's moments. "We can make a profit and make a difference, and we are doing both through our business . . . in a way that's authentic, that's transparent, and that truly matters," she explains.

Under Morrison's watch, the company recently acquired several fresh food and organic companies, including Bolthouse Farms, one of the largest suppliers of fresh carrots in the United States, and Garden Fresh Gourmet, which produces a top line of fresh salsa and hummus. Tracking the strong change in consumer preference for healthier food, Campbell's also recently acquired Plum Organics, a line of organic baby food products, which should help solidify the company's reputation for fresh ingredients with millennials and their families.

The company's transformation from a processed food giant to a major competitor in the fresh food business has also had a positive influence on the company's bottom line. Campbell's shareholders have to be pleased with the 20 percent increase in the company's stock price over the past two years, as the markets, competitors, and consumers take notice of the company's strong commitment to sustainability.

Inherent in the company's reinvention is the strong emphasis on corporate citizenship—doing good and giving back seem to be top priorities for Campbell's. In addition to acquiring sustainable and fresh food companies, Campbell's has also made a conscious decision to support the communities where their employees live and work. For example, the company launched a healthy communities initiative in Camden, New Jersey, where Campbell's is headquartered—an urban city that has seen its share of economic and social challenges in the past. In partnership with several local organizations, this initiative has helped fund community gardens, food pantries, nutrition education, and cooking classes that help build healthy communities. The Camden experience has been so successful that the company has expanded the program to other cities where it operates, including Detroit, Michigan, and Norwalk, Connecticut.

The company's ongoing commitment to fresh food, community involvement, and corporate social responsibility has helped change the narrative when it comes to being a sustainable and ethical organization.

Questions for Discussion
1. How does Campbell Soup Company's recent business acquisitions help support its CSR strategies?
2. Provide examples of how the company's transformation from a processed food giant to a purveyor of fresh ingredients can help attract a new group of customers.

Sources: "Corporate Responsibility and Sustainability Are Good for Business," https://www.campbellsoupcompany.com, accessed June 27, 2017; "Campbell Soup Wants to Make You a Personal Eating Plan (video)," *Fortune,* http://fortune.com, May 2, 2017; Don Seiffert, "Campbell Soup CEO Makes 3 Predictions about the Future of Food," *Boston Business Journal,* http://www.bizjournals.com, April 13, 2017; Aaron Hurst, "How Denise Morrison Took Processed Food Icon Campbell's on a Fresh Food Buying Spree," *Fast Company,* https://www.fastcompany.com, March 2, 2017; Abigail Stevenson, "Campbell Soup CEO: Stunning Disruption in the Ecosystem of Food," *CNBC,* http://www.cnbc.com, July 21, 2016.

Making the Right Decision

In many situations, there may be no simple right or wrong answers. Yet there are several questions you can ask yourself, and a couple of self-tests you can do, to help you make the right ethical decision. First, ask yourself, "Are there any legal restrictions or violations that will result from the action?" If so, take a different course of action. If not, ask yourself, "Does it violate my company's code of ethics?" If so, again find a different path to follow. Third, ask, "Does this meet the guidelines of my own ethical philosophy?" If the answer is "yes," then your decision must still pass two important tests.

The Feelings Test

You must now ask, "How does it make me feel?" This enables you to examine your comfort level with a particular decision. Many people find that, after reaching a decision on an issue, they still experience discomfort that may manifest itself in a loss of sleep or appetite. Those feelings of conscience can serve as a future guide in resolving ethical dilemmas.

The Newspaper or Social Media Test

The final test involves the front page of the newspaper or social media posts. The question to be asked is how an objective reporter would describe your decision in a front-page newspaper story, an online media site, or a social media platform such as Twitter or Facebook. Some managers rephrase the test for their employees: How will the headline read if I make this decision, or what will be the reaction of my social media followers? This test is helpful in spotting and resolving potential conflicts of interest.

Exhibit 2.3   Making an ethical decision might come down to how you feel about the decision or to the newspaper or social media post test. The question to ask yourself is how the decision would make you feel if an objective reporter described the decision on the front page of a newspaper or via a social media post on Twitter or Facebook—all of which would be viewed by many, many people. Speaking of social media, it plays a pivotal role in ethical decision-making today, when people use the medium to share critical comments about friends as well as employers, business colleagues, and competitors. *Should companies view employees' social media pages on a regular basis, or is that information off-limits to employers?* (Credit: Mike MacKenzie/ Flickr/ Attribution 2.0 Generic (CC BY 2.0))

CONCEPT CHECK

1. What is the role of top management in organizational ethics?
2. What is a code of ethics?

2.3 Managing a Socially Responsible Business

3. What is corporate social responsibility?

Acting in an ethical manner is one of the four components of the pyramid of **corporate social responsibility (CSR),** which is the concern of businesses for the welfare of society as a whole. It consists of obligations beyond those required by law or union contract. This definition makes two important points. First, CSR is voluntary. Beneficial action required by law, such as cleaning up factories that are polluting air and water, is not voluntary. Second, the obligations of corporate social responsibility are broad. They extend beyond investors in the company to include workers, suppliers, consumers, communities, and society at large.

Exhibit 2.4 portrays economic responsibility as the foundation for the other three responsibilities. At the same time that a business pursues profits (economic responsibility), however, it is expected to obey the law (legal responsibility); to do what is right, just, and fair (ethical responsibility); and to be a good corporate citizen (philanthropic responsibility). These four components are distinct but together constitute the whole. Still, if the company doesn't make a profit, then the other three responsibilities won't matter.

Many companies continue to work hard to make the world a better place to live. Recent data suggests that Fortune 500 companies spend more than $15 billion annually on CSR activities. Consider the following examples:

- Starbucks has donated more than one million meals to local communities via its FoodShare program and alliance with Feeding America, giving 100 percent of leftover food from their seven thousand U.S. company-owned stores.
- Salesforce encourages its employees to volunteer in community activities and pays them for doing so, up to 56 paid hours every year. For employees who participate in seven days of volunteerism in one year, Salesforce also gives them a $1,000 grant to donate to the employee's nonprofit of choice.
- Employees who work for Deloitte, a global audit, consulting, and financial services organization, can get paid for up to 48 hours of volunteer work each year. In a recent year, more than 27,000 Deloitte professionals contributed more than 353,000 volunteer hours to their communities around the world.[6]

Understanding Social Responsibility

Peter Drucker, the late globally respected management expert, said that we should look first at what an organization does *to* society and second at what it can do *for* society. This idea suggests that social responsibility has two basic dimensions: legality and responsibility.

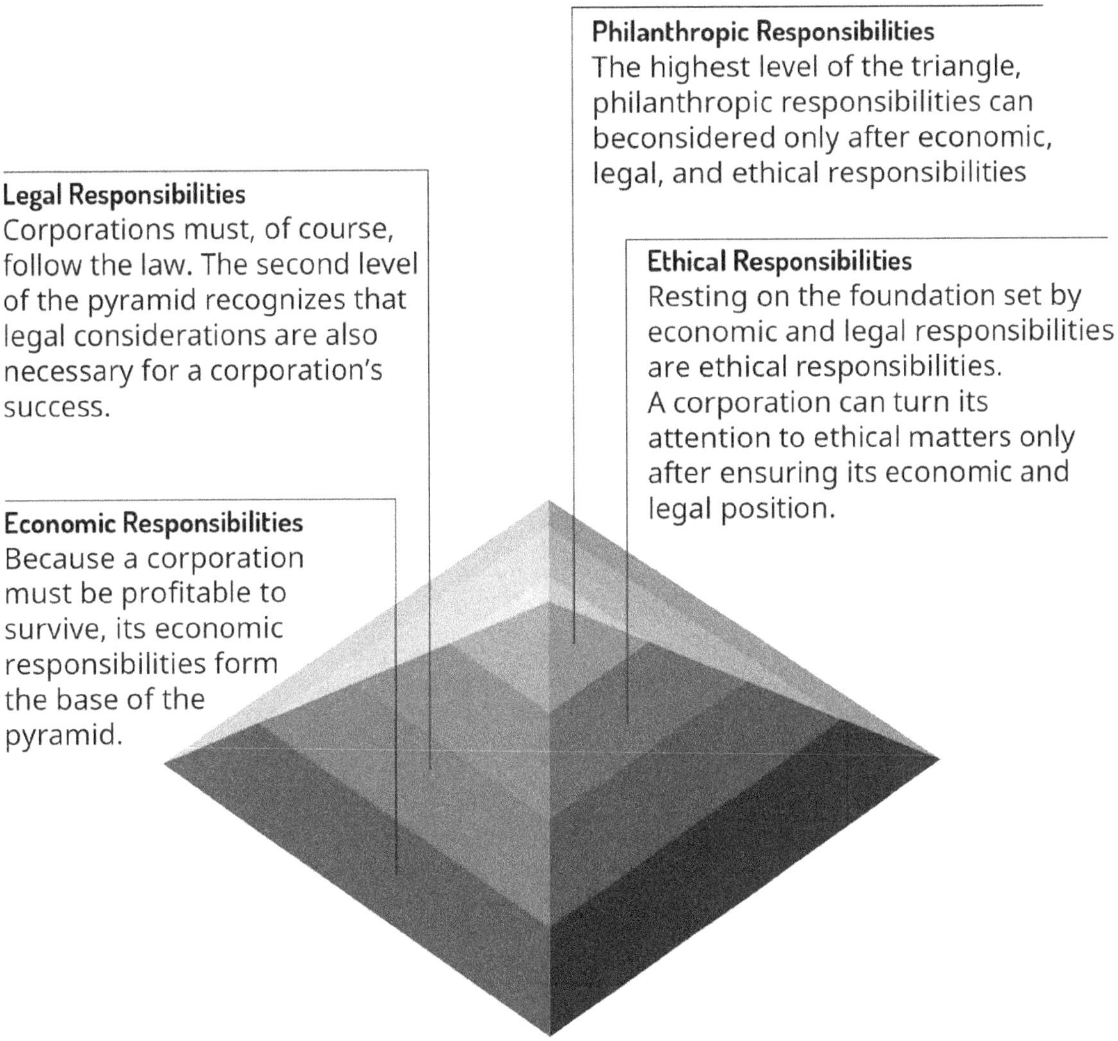

Philanthropic Responsibilities
The highest level of the triangle, philanthropic responsibilities can beconsidered only after economic, legal, and ethical responsibilities

Legal Responsibilities
Corporations must, of course, follow the law. The second level of the pyramid recognizes that legal considerations are also necessary for a corporation's success.

Ethical Responsibilities
Resting on the foundation set by economic and legal responsibilities are ethical responsibilities. A corporation can turn its attention to ethical matters only after ensuring its economic and legal position.

Economic Responsibilities
Because a corporation must be profitable to survive, its economic responsibilities form the base of the pyramid.

Exhibit 2.4   The Pyramid of Corporate Social Responsibility (Attribution: Copyright Rice University, OpenStax, under CC BY 4.0 license.)

Illegal and Irresponsible Behavior

The idea of corporate social responsibility is so widespread today that it is hard to conceive of a company continually acting in illegal and irresponsible ways. Nevertheless, such actions do sometimes occur, which can create financial ruin for organizations, extreme financial hardships for many former employees, and general struggles for the communities in which they operate. Unfortunately, top executives still walk away with millions. Some, however, will ultimately pay large fines and spend time in prison for their actions. Federal, state, and local laws determine whether an activity is legal or not. The laws that regulate business are discussed later in this module.

Irresponsible but Legal Behavior

Sometimes companies act irresponsibly, yet their actions are legal. For example, the Minnesota-based company that makes MyPillow was recently fined $1 million by the state of California for making unsubstantiated claims that the "most comfortable pillow you'll ever own" could help alleviate medical conditions such as snoring, fibromyalgia, migraines, and other disorders. The company's CEO countered that the claims were actually made by customers; these testimonials were posted on the company's website but later removed. In addition to the fine, the company faced several class-action lawsuits, and the Better Business Bureau has revoked MyPillow's accreditation.[7]

CATCHING THE ENTREPRENEURIAL SPIRIT

Badger Company Founder Walks the Walk

As a carpenter, Bill Whyte was always looking for a solution to his dry, cracked hands, especially in the harsh New Hampshire winters. After trying many commercial lotions that didn't really work, Whyte experimented with olive oil and beeswax to come up with a soothing balm to help heal rough hands. Mixing up the concoction at home, Whyte came up with a product that seemed to work and was made from natural ingredients.

Originally called Bear Paw, the lotion became known as Badger Balm after a friend found a competing product already named Bear Paw. Whyte set up a production line at home to fill the tins. Soon he was pounding the pavement in the town of Gilsum, trying to sell the new product to hardware stores, lumber yards, and health food stores.

Fast-forward a little more than 20 years from his early days of experimentation, and Whyte (affectionately known as the "head badger") runs W.S. Badger Company with the same goals and passions he started with back in the mid-1990s. The company uses only organic plant extracts, exotic oils, beeswax, and minerals to make the most effective products to soothe, heal, and protect the body. And the natural ingredients come from all over the world—for example, organic extra virgin olive oil from Spain, organic rose essential oil from Bulgaria, and bergamot oil from southern Italy.

Badger's homey culture is no accident. In fact, in the early days, Whyte made soup every Friday for the small staff. Today, Whyte and family members, including his wife Kathy, chief operating officer; daughter Rebecca, head of sustainability and innovation; and daughter Emily, head of sales and marketing, all embrace the ethical and social principles of this family business that have made the company a success.

To reinforce the commitment of being socially responsible and demonstrating transparency, W.S. Badger Company became a Certified Benefit Corporation, or B Corp for short. This certification requires companies to meet rigorous standards for transparency, accountability, and social and environmental performance. (Benefit Corporations are discussed in more detail later in this module.)

Becoming a B Corp. has helped the company organize how it operates. For example, pay for the highest-paid full-time employee is capped at five times that of the lowest paid, which is now $15 an hour (more than double New Hampshire's minimum wage); a portion of company profits flows to employees via profit sharing, and all employees participate in a bonus plan; and new parents are encouraged to bring their babies to work, a program that has helped foster a new style of teamwork for the entire organization, as well as increase employee morale. In addition, Badger donates 10 percent of its pre-tax profits annually to nonprofit organizations that focus on the health and welfare of children, matches employee contributions to charitable causes (up to $100 per employee), and donates an additional $50 to a nonprofit chosen by each employee on their birthday.

Badger staff, which now number more than 100, enjoy a living wage, great benefits, and a socially responsible work environment thanks to a visionary who found an eco-friendly way to soothe his rough hands and created an ethical business as part of his journey.

Questions for Discussion

1. How does Badger's approach to social responsibility help attract and retain employees?
2. Does the company's certification as a Benefit Corporation provide Badger with a competitive advantage? Explain your reasoning.

Sources: "Badger's History & Legend," "Babies at Work Policy," and "2016 Annual Impact Report," https://www.badgerbalm.com, accessed June 27, 2017; "About Badger," https://www.bcorporation.net, accessed June 27, 2017; "Badger 'Still In' on Climate Action, Asks New Hampshire Businesses, State Officials, and Local Leaders to Join Forces in Honoring Paris Agreement," http://www.prweb.com, June 22, 2017; Amy Feldman, "Badger Balm Creator Once Dismissed Being a B Corp as 'Just Marketing.' Now He's a True Believer," *Forbes,* http://www.forbes.com, May 9, 2017.

Legal and Responsible Behavior

The vast majority of business activities fall into the category of behavior that is both legal and responsible. Most companies act legally, and most try to be socially responsible. Research shows that consumers, especially those under 30, are likely to buy brands that have excellent ethical track records and community involvement. Outdoor specialty retailer REI, for example, recently announced that it gave back nearly 70 percent of its profits to the outdoor community. A member cooperative, the company invested a record $9.3 million in its nonprofit partners in 2016.[8]

CONCEPT CHECK

1. What are the four components of social responsibility?
2. Give an example of legal but irresponsible behavior.

2.4 | Responsibilities to Stakeholders

4. How do businesses meet their social responsibilities to various stakeholders?

What makes a company be admired or perceived as socially responsible? Such a company meets its obligations to its stakeholders. **Stakeholders** are the individuals or groups to whom a business has a responsibility. The stakeholders of a business are its employees, its customers, the general public, and its investors.

Responsibility to Employees

An organization's first responsibility is to provide a job to employees. Keeping people employed and letting them have time to enjoy the fruits of their labor is the finest thing business can do for society. Beyond this fundamental responsibility, employers must provide a clean, safe working environment that is free from all forms of discrimination. Companies should also strive to provide job security whenever possible.

Enlightened firms are also empowering employees to make decisions on their own and suggest solutions to company problems. Empowerment contributes to an employee's self-worth, which, in turn, increases productivity and reduces absenteeism.

Each year, in collaboration with Great Place to Work®, *Fortune* conducts an extensive employee survey of the best places to work in the United States. For 2017, the top companies included Google, Wegmans Food Markets, Edward Jones, Genentech, Salesforce, Acuity, and Quicken Loans. Some companies offer unusual benefits to their employees. For example, biotech company Genentech offers employee compensation for taking alternative methods of transportation to work at its South San Francisco campus. Employees can earn $12 per day for walking or biking to work, and those who drive a carpool or vanpool can earn $8 and $16, respectively. In addition, the company offers free commuter bus service for all employees via 27 routes around the Bay Area.[9]

Responsibility to Customers

To be successful in today's business environment, a company must satisfy its customers. A firm must deliver what it promises, as well as be honest and forthright in everyday interactions with customers, suppliers, and others. Recent research suggests that many consumers, particularly millennials, prefer to do business with companies and brands that communicate socially responsible messages, utilize sustainable manufacturing processes, and practice ethical business standards.[10]

Responsibility to Society

A business must also be responsible to society. A business provides a community with jobs, goods, and services. It also pays taxes that go to support schools, hospitals, and better roads. Some companies have taken an additional step to demonstrate their commitment to stakeholders and society as a whole by becoming Certified Benefit Corporations, or B Corps for short. Verified by B Lab, a global nonprofit organization, B Corps meet the highest standards of social and environmental performance, public transparency, and legal accountability and strive to use the power of business to solve social and environmental problems via an impact assessment that rates each company on a possible score of 200 points. To become certified as a Benefit Corporation, companies need to reach a score of at least 80 and must be recertified every two years. There are more than 2,000 companies worldwide that have been certified as B Corps, including Method, W.S. Badger Company, Fishpeople Seafood, LEAP Organics, New Belgium Brewing Company, Ben & Jerry's, Cabot Creamery Co-op, Comet Skateboards, Etsy, Patagonia, Plum Organics, and Warby Parker.[11]

Environmental Protection

Business is also responsible for protecting and improving the world's fragile environment. The world's forests are being destroyed fast. Every second, an area the size of a football field is laid bare. Plant and animal species are becoming extinct at the rate of 17 per hour. A continent-size hole is opening up in the earth's protective ozone shield. Each year we throw out 80 percent more refuse than we did in 1960; as a result, more than half of the nation's landfills are filled to capacity.

To slow the erosion of the world's natural resources, many companies have become more environmentally responsible. For example, Toyota now uses renewable energy sources such as solar, wind, geothermal, and water power for electricity to run its facilities. When its new $1 billion North American headquarters opened in Plano, Texas, in May 2017, Toyota said the 2.1 million square-foot campus would eventually be powered by 100% clean energy, helping the auto giant move closer to its goal of eliminating carbon emissions in all of its operations.[12]

ETHICS IN PRACTICE

This Fish Story Has a Tasting Ending

Duncan Berry has always been an environmentalist at heart. Brought up on the Oregon coast, he was a sea captain at an early age, spending nearly two decades on the ocean before going on to become a successful entrepreneur in the organic cotton industry. After selling the textile business at the age of 50, he retired back to the Oregon coast to work on a state initiative to preserve marine habitats.

He quickly discovered that the state's commercial fishing industry had gone into major disrepair since his seafaring adventure years earlier. Berry learned the majority of seafood consumed in the United States was being imported from other countries and more than 90 percent of U.S. seafood was being exported. In addition, great harm was being done to the ocean because it was being overfished.

Although several groups were already working to improve the commercial fishing industry, he observed that one key group was not part of the discussion: consumers. Berry decided a key component of change had to be involving consumers in the process. He spent more than a year meeting with everyone involved in the Oregon fishing industry—from fishermen to processors, distributors, truck drivers, chefs, and consumers—to gain perspective on why the industry was failing. His "aha" moment occurred when he realized the majority of fish is consumed in restaurants because consumers think preparing fish at home is too difficult and time-consuming. That's when he co-founded Fishpeople Seafood.

Started in 2012, Fishpeople has a mission of changing the way people think about seafood by being transparent about where the seafood comes from, how it is processed, and how it is handled. Berry believes the company's transparency helps consumers understand how the process translates into sustainable food that tastes good and is good for you. The company makes shelf-stable, ready-to-eat restaurant-quality seafood in the form of soups, meal kits, and fresh and frozen filets, complete with farm-to-table ingredients. On every package there is a code consumers can enter at the company's website that will tell them everything about the seafood's origin, down to the fisherman who caught it. Fishpeople also operates a processing plant in Toledo, Oregon, where workers are paid a livable wage and receive health insurance—benefits typically unheard of in the fishing industry.

Fishpeople's products are available in more than 5,000 stores nationwide, including Walmart, Whole Foods, Costco, Kroger, and other grocery stores and markets. Recently the company announced a merger with Ilwaco Landing Fishermen, which will help further the two groups' shared vision of supporting local fishermen and providing sustainable seafood to consumers.

Questions for Discussion
1. How does Fishpeople's transparency contribute to the company's success?
2. What responsibility, if any, does Fishpeople have to the local fishing industry?

Sources: Company website, https://fishpeopleseafood.com, accessed June 27, 2017; J. David Santen, Jr., "Adding Value to Oregon Seafood," *Built Oregon,* http://builtoregon.com, accessed June 27, 2017; Elizabeth Crawford, "Fishpeople Wants to Fix the 'Fundamentally Broken' Seafood Industry with Increased Transparency," *Food Navigator,* http://www.foodnavigator-usa.com, May 25, 2017; Fishpeople Seafood Announces Merger with Ilwaco Landing Fishermen," *Tillamook County Pioneer,* https://www.tillamookcountypioneer.net, May 22, 2017; Leigh Buchanan, "Why This Entrepreneur Ditched Fashion for the 'Hunting and Gathering' Business," *Inc.,* https://www.inc.com, April 2017 issue; Kate Harrison, "This Former Green Textile Maven Is Making Microwaved Seafood Sustainable," *Forbes,* http://www.forbes.com, August 25, 2015.

Corporate Philanthropy

Companies also display their social responsibility through corporate philanthropy. **Corporate philanthropy** includes cash contributions, donations of equipment and products, and support for the volunteer efforts of company employees. Recent statistics suggest U.S. corporate philanthropy exceeds more than $19 billion annually.[13] American Express is a major supporter of the American Red Cross. The organization relies almost entirely on charitable gifts to carry out its programs and services, which include disaster relief, armed-forces emergency relief, blood and tissue services, and health and safety services. The funds provided by American Express have enabled the Red Cross to deliver humanitarian relief to victims of numerous disasters around the world.[14] When Hurricane Katrina hit the Gulf Coast, Bayer sent 45,000 diabetes blood glucose monitors to the relief effort. Within weeks of the disaster, Abbott, Alcoa, Dell, Disney, Intel, UPS, Walgreens, Walmart, and others contributed more than $550 million for disaster relief.[15]

Exhibit 2.5   Hybrid cars and all-electric vehicles such as Tesla models are turning heads and changing the way the world drives. Electric vehicles are more eco-friendly, but they are also more expensive to own. Analysts project that after charging, insurance, and maintenance costs, electric cars cost thousands of dollars more than conventional vehicles. *Do the environmental benefits associated with electric cars justify the higher cost of ownership?* (Credit: Steve Jurvetson/ Flickr/ Attribution 2.0 Generic (CC BY 2.0))

Responsibilities to Investors

Companies' relationships with investors also entail social responsibility. Although a company's economic responsibility to make a profit might seem to be its main obligation to its shareholders, some investors increasingly are putting more emphasis on other aspects of social responsibility.

Some investors are limiting their investments to securities (e.g., stocks and bonds) that coincide with their beliefs about ethical and social responsibility. This is called **social investing**. For example, a social investment fund might eliminate from consideration the securities of all companies that make tobacco products or liquor, manufacture weapons, or have a history of being environmentally irresponsible. Not all social investment strategies are alike. Some ethical mutual funds will not invest in government securities because they help to fund the military; others freely buy government securities, with managers noting that federal funds also support the arts and pay for AIDS research. Today, assets invested using socially responsible strategies total more than $7 trillion.[16]

Perhaps partly as the result of the global recession of 2007–2009, over the last several years companies have tried to meet responsibilities to their investors as well as to their other stakeholders. Recent research suggests that now more than ever, CEOs are being held to higher standards by boards of directors, investors, governments, media, and even employees when it comes to corporate accountability and ethical behavior. A recent global study by PwC reveals that over the last several years, there has been a large increase in the number of CEOs being forced out due to some sort of ethical lapse in their organizations. Strategies to prevent such missteps should include establishing a culture of integrity to prevent anyone from breaking the rules, making sure company goals and metrics do not create undue pressure on employees to cut corners, and implementing effective processes and controls to minimize the opportunity for unethical behavior.[17]

2.5 | Trends in Ethics and Corporate Social Responsibility

5. What are the trends in ethics and corporate social responsibility?

Three important trends related to ethics and corporate social responsibility are strategic changes in corporate philanthropy, a new social contract between employers and employees, and the growth of global ethics and corporate social responsibility.

Changes in Corporate Philanthropy

Historically, corporate philanthropy has typically involved companies seeking out charitable groups and giving them money or donating company products or services. Today, the focus has shifted to **strategic giving**, which ties philanthropy and corporate social responsibility efforts closely to a company's mission or goals and targets donations to the communities where a company does business. Some of the top businesses recognized for their efforts in giving back to the communities in which they operate include technology giant Salesforce, San Antonio's NuStar Energy, insurance and financial services firm Veterans United, and software leader Intuit.[18]

A Social Contract between Employer and Employee

Another trend in social responsibility is the effort by organizations to redefine their relationship with their employees. Many people have viewed social responsibility as a one-way street that focuses on the obligations of business to society, employees, and others. Now, companies recognize that the social contract between employer and employee is an important aspect of the workplace and that both groups have to be committed to working together in order for the organization to prosper. The social contract can be defined in terms of four important aspects: compensation, management, culture, and learning and development.[19]

When it comes to compensation, companies today must recognize that most employees do not stay with one organization for decades. Thus, companies need to change their compensation structure to acknowledge the importance of short-term performance and to update their methods for determining compensation, including benefits and other nontraditional perks such as increased paid leave and telecommuting options.

In the current workplace environment, where employees are likely to jump to new jobs every couple years, managers need to take a more active and engaged approach to supervising employees and perhaps change the way they think about loyalty, which may be difficult for managers used to supervising the same group of employees for a long period of time. Engaging employees on a regular basis, setting realistic expectations, and identifying specific development paths may help retain key employees.

Thanks to today's tight labor market, some employees feel empowered to demand more from their employer and its overall culture via strategies such as increased flexibility, transparency, and fairness. This increased importance of the employee's role in the company's culture helps workers stay engaged in the mission of the organization and perhaps makes them less likely to look elsewhere for employment.

Finally, rapidly changing technology used in today's workplace continues to shift the learning and development component of the employer-employee contract, causing immense challenges to both companies and workers. It may be more difficult to identify the employee skills that will be critical over the next several years, causing employers either to increase training of current workers or to look outside the organization for other individuals who already possess the technical skills needed to get the job done.

Global Ethics and Social Responsibility

When U.S. businesses expand into global markets, they must take their codes of ethics and policies on corporate social responsibility with them. As a citizen of several countries, a multinational corporation has several responsibilities. These include respecting local practices and customs, ensuring that there is harmony between the organization's staff and the host population, providing management leadership, and developing a solid group of local managers who will be a credit to their community. When a multinational firm makes an investment in a foreign country, it should commit to a long-term relationship. That means involving all stakeholders in the host country in decision-making. Finally, a responsible multinational will implement ethical guidelines within the organization in the host country. By fulfilling these responsibilities, the company will foster respect for both local and international laws.

Multinational corporations often must balance conflicting interests of stakeholders when making decisions regarding social responsibilities, especially in the area of human rights. Questions involving child labor, forced labor, minimum wages, and workplace safety can be particularly difficult. Recently Gap, Inc. decided to publish the list of its global factories in an effort to provide transparency about its suppliers and the efforts the company continues to make to improve working conditions around the world. The company has partnered with Verité, a nongovernmental organization focused on ensuring that people work under safe, fair, and legal conditions. By soliciting feedback from factory workers making its products, Gap is hoping to improve working conditions and help these factories become leaders in their local communities.[20]

CONCEPT CHECK

1. Describe strategic giving.
2. What role do employees have in improving their job security?
3. How do multinational corporations demonstrate social responsibility in a foreign country?

🔑 Key Terms

code of ethics A set of guidelines prepared by a firm to provide its employees with the knowledge of what the firm expects in terms of their responsibilities and behavior toward fellow employees, customers, and suppliers.

corporate philanthropy The practice of charitable giving by corporations; includes contributing cash, donating equipment and products, and supporting the volunteer efforts of company employees.

corporate social responsibility (CSR) The concern of businesses for the welfare of society as a whole; consists of obligations beyond those required by law or contracts.

deontology A philosophy in which a person will follow his or her obligations to an individual or society because upholding one's duty is what is ethically correct.

ethical issue A situation where a person must choose from a set of actions that may be ethical or unethical.

ethics A set of moral standards for judging whether something is right or wrong.

justice What is considered fair according to the prevailing standards of society; an equitable distribution of the burdens and rewards that society has to offer.

social investing The practice of limiting investments to securities of companies that behave in accordance with the investor's beliefs about ethical and social responsibility to encourage businesses to be more socially responsible.

stakeholders Individuals or groups to whom a business has a responsibility; include employees, customers, the general public, and investors.

strategic giving The practice of tying philanthropy and corporate social responsibility efforts closely to a company's mission or goals and targeting donations to the communities where a company does business.

utilitarianism A philosophy that focuses on the consequences of an action to determine whether it is right or wrong; holds that an action that affects the majority adversely is morally wrong.

📖 Summary of Learning Outcomes

2.1 Understanding Business Ethics
  1. What philosophies and concepts shape personal ethical standards?

Ethics is a set of moral standards for judging whether something is right or wrong. A utilitarianism approach to setting personal ethical standards focuses on the consequences of an action taken by a person or organization. According to this approach, people should act so as to generate the greatest good for the greatest number. Every human is entitled to certain rights such as freedom and the pursuit of happiness. Another approach to ethical decision-making is justice, or what is fair according to accepted standards.

2.2 How Organizations Influence Ethical Conduct
  2. How can organizations encourage ethical business behavior?

Top management must shape the ethical culture of the organization. They should lead by example, offer ethics-training programs, and establish a formal code of ethics.

2.3 Managing a Socially Responsible Business
  3. What is corporate social responsibility?

Corporate social responsibility is the concern of businesses for the welfare of society as a whole. It consists of obligations beyond just making a profit and goes beyond what is required by law or union contract.

Companies may engage in illegal and irresponsible behavior, irresponsible but legal behavior, or legal and responsible behavior. The vast majority of organizations act legally and try to be socially responsible.

2.4 Responsibilities to Stakeholders
4. How do businesses meet their social responsibilities to various stakeholders?

Stakeholders are individuals or groups to whom business has a responsibility. Businesses are responsible to employees. They should provide a clean, safe working environment. Organizations can build employees' self-worth through empowerment programs. Businesses also have a responsibility to customers to provide good, safe products and services. Organizations are responsible to the general public to be good corporate citizens. Firms must help protect the environment and provide a good place to work. Companies also engage in corporate philanthropy, which includes contributing cash, donating goods and services, and supporting volunteer efforts of employees. Finally, companies are responsible to investors. They should earn a reasonable profit for company owners.

2.5 Trends in Ethics and Corporate Social Responsibility
5. What are the trends in ethics and corporate social responsibility?

Today, corporate philanthropy is shifting away from simply giving to any needy group and is focusing instead on strategic giving, in which the philanthropy relates more closely to the corporate mission or goals and targets donations to areas where the firm operates.

A second trend is toward a new social contract between employer and employee. Instead of the employer having the sole responsibility for maintaining jobs, now the employee must assume part of the burden and find ways to add value to the organization.

As the world increasingly becomes a global community, multinational corporations are now expected to assume a global set of ethics and responsibility. Global companies must understand local customs. They should also involve local stakeholders in decision-making. Multinationals must also make certain that their suppliers are not engaged in human rights violations.

Preparing for Tomorrow's Workplace Skills

1. Many CEOs have sold shares of their company's stock when prices were near their high points. Even though their actions were legal, it soon became apparent that they knew that the stock was significantly overpriced. Was the CEO ethically obligated to tell the public that this was the case—even knowing that doing so could cause the stock price to plummet, thereby hurting someone who bought the stock earlier that day? (Systems)
2. Jeffrey Immelt, former chairman and CEO of General Electric, one of the world's most-admired companies according to *Fortune* magazine, says that execution, growth, and great people are required to keep the company on top. Immelt said that these are predictable, but a fourth factor is not—virtue, and virtue was at the top of his list. Using a search engine, find articles on what GE is doing to enhance its corporate citizenship. Report your findings to the class. Could GE do more, or are they already doing too much? Why? (Systems, Technology)
3. Boeing Corp. makes business ethics a priority, asking employees to take refresher training every year. It encourages employees to take the Ethics Challenge with their work groups and to discuss the issues with their peers. You can take your own ethics challenge. Go to **http://www.ethics.org** and click on the Ethics Effectiveness Quick Test. Summarize your findings. Were there any answers that surprised you? (Information)

4. Identify the potential ethical and social responsibility issues confronting the following organizations: Microsoft, Pfizer, Nike, American Cancer Society, and R.J. Reynolds. Make recommendations on how these issues should be handled. (Systems)

5. **Team Activity** Divide the class into teams. Debate whether the only social responsibility of the employer to the employee is to provide a job. Include a discussion of the employee's responsibility to bring value to the firm. Also, debate the issue of whether the only social responsibility of a firm is to earn a profit. (Interpersonal)

Ethics Activity

Let's Be Honest

The Honest Company is a consumer-goods business that sells nontoxic, eco-friendly items for baby and personal care, household cleaning, and a healthy lifestyle. Cofounded by actress Jessica Alba a little more than six years ago, Honest Co. is built on the promise of "telling all and doing our best to live up to your expectations."

Over the years the company has received high praise and media buzz about its ethical approach to making products that are not only good for people but good for the environment. On its website, Honest Co. goes to great lengths to share with consumers its guiding principles that products are made without harming people or the planet.

A little over two years ago, however, the company experienced some bad press when *The Wall Street Journal* reported that two independent lab tests found samples of Honest laundry detergent contained a cleaning agent on the list of chemicals the company pledged to avoid. At first, pushback from company officials was loud and clear: they denied their products were anything but eco-friendly and safe for consumers and went as far as calling the report "false" and "junk science."

Unfortunately, the reports about Honest products and their harmful ingredients didn't go away. After the laundry detergent story faded, the company quietly reconfigured the ingredients that went into the detergent as well as other products. But that wasn't the end of the story. Several months later, Honest Co. voluntarily recalled organic baby powder that might cause infections and more recently recalled diaper wipes that appeared discolored.

Despite these recent challenges, Honest Co. continues to be successful and was rumored to be on the short list of possible acquisitions for global conglomerates such as Procter & Gamble, Johnson & Johnson, and Unilever. These consumer-good giants are snapping up smaller, eco-friendly firms that have blossomed into full-fledged ethically and environmentally conscious organizations with strong sales and solid reputations among consumers. Recently, however, Unilever acquired one of Honest Co.'s biggest rivals, Seventh Generation, Inc., leaving Honest Co. to again rethink its business strategies, including hiring a new CEO.

Using a web search tool, locate information about this topic and then write responses to the following questions. Be sure to support your arguments and cite your sources.

Ethical Dilemma: Do you think the company's reaction to reports of hazardous ingredients hurt its reputation for honesty and ethical behavior? Do you think the company's missteps caused Unilever to shy away from acquiring the company? Or, do you take the stance that Alba's entertainment background played a part in the press going after the company? If you were an advisor to the new CEO, what suggestions would you give him for getting the company back on track, especially when it comes to corporate social responsibility?

Sources: "Our Principles," https://www.honest.com, accessed June 27, 2017; Eun Kyung Kim, "Jessica Alba's Honest Company Recalls Diaper Wipes over Mold Concerns," *Today,* http://www.today.com, May 16, 2017; Steve Tobak, "Jessica Alba's 'Honest' Mess," *Entrepreneur,* https://www.entrepreneur.com, March 29, 2017; Jason Del Rey, "Jessica Alba's Honest Company Is Replacing Its CEO after a Sale to Unilever Fell Through," *Recode,* https://www.recode.net, March 16, 2017; Serena Ng, "Jessica Alba's Honest Co. to Drop Use of Disputed Ingredient," *The Wall Street Journal,* http://www.wsj.com, September 30, 2016; Kathryn Vasel, "The Honest Company Gets Sued . . . Again," *CNN Money,* http://money.cnn.com, April 27, 2016.

 # Working the Net

1. You will find the listing for the 100 Best Corporate Citizens at the website for *Corporate Responsibility* magazine (**http://thecro.com).** Review the current list of companies and pay close attention to those marked with a "yellow card" caution and a "red card" caution. These are companies that have either been removed from the list due to unethical behavior or have been warned that some of their actions border on unethical. What surprised you about the companies that have been flagged? Select one of the flagged companies and explain what they can do to improve their CSR profile.

2. Richard S. Scrushy, former CEO of HealthSouth Corporation, was charged with $1.4 billion in fraud. He was acquitted. Bernie Ebbers, former CEO of WorldCom, was found guilty of helping mastermind an $11 billion accounting fraud. Go to the internet and read several articles about the charges against both men. Find articles on why one was guilty on all counts and the other acquitted on all counts. Explain the ethical issues involved with each.

3. Visit the website of People for the Ethical Treatment of Animals (PETA), **http://peta.org**, and under the Issues tab, read about PETA's view of Animals Used for Clothing. Do you agree with this view? Why or why not? How do you think manufacturers of fur clothing would justify their actions to someone from PETA? Would you work for a store that sold fur-trimmed clothing? Explain your answer.

4. Green Money Journal, **http://www.greenmoneyjournal.com**, is a bimonthly online journal that promotes socially responsibility investing. What are the current topics of concern in this area? Visit the archives to find articles on socially responsible investing and two areas of corporate social responsibility. Summarize what you have learned.

5. Double the Donation, **https://doublethedonation.com**, is a website that provides information on top forms of corporate philanthropy and highlights companies with strong giving programs. Research several companies and their philanthropic activities and provide details about what makes these organizations excellent corporate citizens.

 # Critical Thinking Case

Uber Hits a Bumpy Road

Uber Technologies, Inc. is the world's largest technology start-up, valued at close to $70 billion. But that doesn't mean it has been smooth sailing for the ride-hailing company since its start in 2009. Despite disrupting and revolutionizing the transportation industry in a short period of time, Uber's meteoric rise has caused some shortcuts in organizational structure, corporate culture, and effective HR practices that have left the company with self-inflicted wounds that may take a long time to heal.

Uber has experienced several scandals over the past few years, including drivers demanding to be classified as employees (not contractors), a tool called "greyball" that allows data collected from the Uber app to identify and avoid enforcement officers trying to catch Uber drivers in cities where the service was illegal, and recent resignations of top executives, including the company's president and the heads of product development and engineering. But nothing has been quite as damaging as a recent blog post by a former female employee, which detailed the inappropriate behavior that seemed to be commonplace in Uber's workplace culture.

The allegations of sexual harassment put forth by former Uber engineer Susan Fowler were explosive. Detailed in a February 2017 blog post, Fowler says she alerted company HR about her manager's inappropriate behavior, even taking screenshots of his suggestive emails, but Fowler was told her boss would not be fired for sexual harassment because he was a "high performer" for the company. After Fowler's story went public, the company hired former U.S. attorney Eric Holder to investigate the allegations and other workplace issues. Holder's recommendations, which the Uber board of directors unanimously approved, include changes to senior leadership, enhanced oversight by the company's board, changes to the company's internal financial and audit controls, revisions to the company's cultural values, mandatory leadership training for senior executives and other managers, improvements to the overall HR function and complaint process, and the establishment of an employee diversity advisory board. In addition, as the result of a separate investigation, Uber fired more than 20 other people because of harassment claims.

With increasing pressure from the company's board and other investors, CEO Travis Kalanick said he would take a leave of absence while still mourning the unexpected death of his mother in a recent boating accident. However, most board members lost faith that Kalanick would be able to come back after his leave and make things better. At the urging of the board, two venture capitalists were dispatched to Chicago, where Kalanick was interviewing COO candidates, to present him with a letter from five of Uber's major investors demanding his resignation. After hours of discussion, Kalanick agreed to step down. According to an Uber spokesperson, a committee of 14 executives is running the company until a new CEO is hired.

Critical Thinking Questions

1. According to recent data, only 36 percent of Uber's current employees are women. How do you think this situation helped perpetuate a flawed corporate culture?
2. What can Uber do to ensure its competitors are not chipping away at its dominant market share as a result of such bad press?
3. Do you think installing an experienced female CEO would help the company change its culture and workplace environment? Explain your reasoning.

Sources: Marisa Kendall, "Uber: Here's Who's Running the Show Now," *Mercury News*, http://www.mercurynews.com, June 23, 2017; Eric Newcomer, "Uber CEO Travis Kalanick Quits Under Pressure from Investors," *Bloomberg News,* https://www.bloomberg.com, June 21, 2017; Mike Issac, "Inside Travis Kalanick's Resignation as Uber's C.E.O.," *The New York Times,* http://www.nytimes.com, June 21, 2017; "Holder Recommendations on Uber," *The New York Times,* https://www.nytimes.com, June 13, 2017; Eric Newcomer, "Uber Fires More Than 20 Employees in Harassment Probe," *Bloomberg Technology,* https://www.bloomberg.com, June 6, 2017; Erin Griffith, "The Uncomfortable Reality Behind Uber's Culture Meltdown," *Fortune,* http://fortune.com, April 20, 2017; Johana Bhuiyan, "Uber Has Published Its Much Sought After Diversity Numbers for the First Time," *Recode,* https://www.recode.net, March 28, 2017; Marco della Cava, "Uber President Quits as Company Searches for COO," *USA Today,* https://www.usatoday.com, March 20, 2017; Mike Isaac, "How Uber Deceives the Authorities Worldwide," *The New York Times,* http://www.nytimes.com, March 3, 2017; Susan J. Fowler, "Reflecting on One Very, Very Strange Year at Uber," https://www.susanjfowler.com/blog, February 19, 2017.

Hot Links Address Book

1. Find out which companies test their products on animals and which don't in the campaign section of the PETA website, **http://www.peta.org**.

2. How is the International Business Ethics Institute working to promote business ethics worldwide? Find out at **http://www.business-ethics.org**.

3. Ben & Jerry's ice cream has always taken its responsibilities as a corporate good citizen seriously. Learn about the company's positions on various issues and products that support social issues at its website, **http://www.benjerry.com**.

4. Discover what the Texas Instruments employee Ethics Quick Test includes, as well as the company's overall ethics policies, by searching for "Ethics at TI" on the corporate home page, **http://www.ti.com**.

5. What does IBM require from its employees in terms of ethical business conduct? You will find the information on IBM's website under Corporate responsibility, **http://www.ibm.com**.

6. Levi Strauss's unique corporate culture rewards and recognizes employee achievement. To learn about its employee community involvement program, go to the Levi Strauss website at **http://www.levistrauss.com**.

7. Want to see how the global environment is changing and learn the latest about global warming? Check out **http://www.climatehotmap.org**.

8. General Motors is committed to continuous improvement in its environmental performance. Check out GM's Sustainability Report at **http://www.gmsustainability.com**.

9. Before donating to any charity, check out its credentials and overall track record at **http://charitywatch.org**.

10. Learn how U.S. businesses gain competitive advantage through corporate social responsibility programs at the Business for Social Responsibility (BSR) website, **http://www.bsr.org**.

3

Competing in the Global Marketplace

Exhibit 3.1 (Credit: Xiquinho Silva /Flickr/ Attribution 2.0 Generic (CC BY 2.0))

 Introduction

Learning Outcomes

After reading this chapter, you should be able to answer these questions:

1. Why is global trade important to the United States, and how is it measured?
2. Why do nations trade?
3. What are the barriers to international trade?
4. How do governments and institutions foster world trade?
5. What are international economic communities?
6. How do companies enter the global marketplace?
7. What threats and opportunities exist in the global marketplace?
8. What are the advantages of multinational corporations?
9. What are the trends in the global marketplace?

EXPLORING BUSINESS CAREERS

Mike Schlater Domino's Pizza

Domino's Pizza has more than 14,000 stores worldwide. As executive vice president of Domino's Pizza's international division, Mike Schlater is president of Domino's Canada with more than 440 stores. Originally from Ohio, Schlater started his career with Domino's as a pizza delivery driver and worked his way up into management. Schlater saved his earnings, and with some help from his brother, he was able to accept the opportunity to have the first international Domino's franchise in Winnipeg, Manitoba, in

1983. Within weeks, Schlater's store in Canada reached higher sales than his previous store in Ohio had ever attained. However, it was not an easy start. Schlater had to identify the international suppliers and get them approved to sell their products to Domino's. This shows one of the challenges that organizations face when entering new global markets. To meet quality standards designed to protect a brand, companies must undertake an extensive review of potential new suppliers to ensure consistent product quality. By 2007, Schlater and a partner unified all of the franchises under one corporate umbrella, and Schlater is now president of Domino's of Canada, Ltd., which operates more than 440 stores located in every province, as well as the Yukon and Northwest Territories.

Exhibit 3.2   Domino's store. (Credit: Mr. Blue Mau Mau/ Flickr/ Attribution 2.0 Generic (CC BY 2.0))

Such an impressive career path might seem like luck to some, but Schlater achieved his success due to determination and attention to detail. Luck did play a role in a recent event in his live, though. Schlater manages dough in his business but also came into "dough" by winning $250,000 in a lottery. Since Schlater believes in philanthropy, he donated the entire amount to Cardinal Carter High School in his hometown. Over the years, Schlater has donated millions of dollars to foundations and charities, such as The London Health Sciences Foundation, because he now has the ability to indulge after spending decades climbing the corporate ladder at Domino's Pizza. A father of three, he moved to Essex County from Winnipeg after buying the Domino's master franchise for Canada. He wanted to live close to the border because one of his daughters was in a private school in Ohio and another was headed to university there.

The master franchisees of Domino's Pizza's international business are individuals or entities who, under a specific licensing agreement with Domino's, control all operations within a specific country. They operate their own stores, set up a distribution infrastructure to transport materials into and throughout the country, and create subfranchisees. One particular benefit of master franchisees is their local knowledge. As discussed in this chapter, a major challenge when opening a business on foreign soil is negotiating the political, cultural, and economic differences of that country. Master franchisees allow Domino's, and the franchisee, to take advantage of their local expertise in dealing with marketing strategies, political and regulatory issues, and the local labor market. It takes local experience to know, for example, that only 30 percent of the people in Poland have phones, so carryout needs to be the focus of the business; that Turkey has changed its street names three times in the past 30 years, so delivery is much more challenging; or that, in Japanese, there is no word for pepperoni, the most popular topping worldwide. These are just a few of the challenges that Domino's has had to overcome on the road to becoming the worldwide leader in the pizza delivery business. Under the leadership of people like Schlater, and with the help of dedicated, local master franchisees, Domino's has been able to not only compete in but to lead the global pizza delivery market.

Sources: "Domino's Pizza Corporate Facts," http://phx.corporate-ir.net, accessed June 20, 2017; Domino's Canada website, https://www.dominos.ca, accessed June 20, 2017; Trevor Wilhelm, "Domino's CEO, who lives in Leamington, will donate $250K lotto winnings to high school," *Windsor Star*, February 27, 2015.

This chapter examines the business world of the global marketplace. It focuses on the processes of taking a business global, such as licensing agreements and franchisees; the challenges that are encountered; and the regulatory systems governing the world market of the 21st century.

Today, global revolutions are under way in many areas of our lives: management, politics, communications, and technology. The word *global* has assumed a new meaning, referring to a boundless mobility and competition in social, business, and intellectual arenas. The purpose of this chapter is to explain how global trade is conducted. We also discuss the barriers to international trade and the organizations that foster global trade. The chapter concludes with trends in the global marketplace.

3.1 | Global Trade in the United States

1. Why is global trade important to the United States, and how is it measured?

No longer just an option, having a global vision has become a business imperative. Having a **global vision** means recognizing and reacting to international business opportunities, being aware of threats from foreign competitors in all markets, and effectively using international distribution networks to obtain raw materials and move finished products to the customer.

U.S. managers must develop a global vision if they are to recognize and react to international business opportunities, as well as remain competitive at home. Often a U.S. firm's toughest domestic competition comes from foreign companies. Moreover, a global vision enables a manager to understand that customer and distribution networks operate worldwide, blurring geographic and political barriers and making them increasingly irrelevant to business decisions. Over the past three decades, world trade has climbed from $200 billion a year to more than $1.4 trillion.[1] U.S. companies play a major role in this growth in world trade, with 113 of the Fortune 500 companies making over 50 percent of their profits outside the United States. Among these companies are recognizable names such as Apple, Microsoft, Pfizer, Exxon Mobil, and General Electric.[2]

Starbucks Corp. is among the fastest growing global consumer brands and one of the most visible emblems of U.S. commercial culture overseas. Of Starbucks's 24,000 total stores, almost 66 percent are international stores that contribute a substantial amount to the company's revenues, which have grown from $4.1 billion in 2003 to $21.3 billion in 2016.[3]

Go into a Paris McDonald's and you may not recognize where you are. There are no Golden Arches or utilitarian chairs and tables and other plastic features. The restaurants have exposed brick walls, hardwood floors, and armchairs. Some French McDonald's even have faux marble walls. Most restaurants have TVs with continuous music videos. You can even order an espresso, beer, and a chicken on focaccia bread sandwich. It's not America.

Global business is not a one-way street, where only U.S. companies sell their wares and services throughout the world. Foreign competition in the domestic market used to be relatively rare but now occurs in almost every industry. In fact, U.S. makers of electronic goods, cameras, automobiles, fine china, tractors, leather goods, and a host of other consumer and industrial products have struggled to maintain their domestic market shares against foreign competitors. Toyota now has 14 percent of the U.S. auto market, followed by Honda at 9 percent and Nissan with 8 percent.[4] Nevertheless, the global market has created vast new business opportunities for many U.S. firms.

The Importance of Global Business to the United States

Many countries depend more on international commerce than the United States does. For example, France, Great Britain, and Germany all derive more than 55 percent of their gross domestic product (GDP) from world trade, compared to about 28 percent for the United States.[5] Nevertheless, the impact of international business on the U.S. economy is still impressive:

- Trade-dependent jobs have grown at a rate three times the growth of U.S.-dependent jobs.
- Every U.S. state has realized a growth of jobs attributable to trade.
- Trade has an effect on both service and manufacturing jobs.[6]

These statistics might seem to imply that practically every business in the United States is selling its wares throughout the world, but most is accounted for by big business. About 85 percent of all U.S. exports of manufactured goods are shipped by 250 companies. Yet, 98 percent of all exporters are small and medium-size firms.[7]

The Impact of Terrorism on Global Trade

The terrorist attacks on America on September 11, 2001, and the Charlie Hebdo terrorist attacks in Paris in 2015 have changed the way the world conducts business. The immediate impacts of these events have included a short-term shrinkage of global trade. Globalization, however, will continue because the world's major markets are too vitally integrated for globalization to stop. Nevertheless, terrorism has caused the growth to be slower and costlier.[8]

Companies are paying more for insurance and to provide security for overseas staff and property. Heightened border inspections slow movements of cargo, forcing companies to stock more inventory. Tighter immigration policies curtail the liberal inflows of skilled and blue-collar workers that allowed companies to expand while keeping wages in check. The impact of terrorism may lessen over time, but multinational firms will always be on guard.[9]

Measuring Trade between Nations

International trade improves relationships with friends and allies; helps ease tensions among nations; and—economically speaking—bolsters economies, raises people's standard of living, provides jobs, and improves the quality of life. The value of international trade is over $16 trillion a year and growing. This section takes a look at some key measures of international trade: exports and imports, the balance of trade, the balance of payments, and exchange rates.

Exports and Imports

The developed nations (those with mature communication, financial, educational, and distribution systems) are the major players in international trade. They account for about 70 percent of the world's exports and imports. **Exports** are goods and services made in one country and sold to others. **Imports** are goods and services that are bought from other countries. The United States is both the largest exporter and the largest importer in the world.

Each year the United States exports more food, animal feed, and beverages than the year before. A third of U.S. farm acreage is devoted to crops for export. The United States is also a major exporter of engineering products and other high-tech goods, such as computers and telecommunications equipment. For more than 60,000 U.S. companies (the majority of them small), international trade offers exciting and profitable opportunities. Among the largest U.S. exporters are Apple, General Motors Corp., Ford Motor Co., Procter & Gamble, and Cisco Systems.[10]

Despite our impressive list of resources and great variety of products, imports to the United States are also growing. Some of these imports are raw materials that we lack, such as manganese, cobalt, and bauxite, which are used to make airplane parts, exotic metals, and military hardware. More modern factories and lower labor costs in other countries make it cheaper to import industrial supplies (such as steel) and production equipment than to produce them at home. Most of Americans' favorite hot beverages—coffee, tea, and cocoa—are imported. Lower manufacturing costs have resulted in huge increases in imports from China.

Balance of Trade

The difference between the value of a country's exports and the value of its imports during a specific time is the country's **balance of trade**. A country that exports more than it imports is said to have a *favorable* balance of trade, called a **trade surplus**. A country that imports more than it exports is said to have an *unfavorable* balance of trade, or a **trade deficit**. When imports exceed exports, more money from trade flows out of the country than flows into it.

Although U.S. exports have been booming, we still import more than we export. We have had an unfavorable balance of trade throughout the 1990s, 2000s and 2010s. In 2016, our exports totaled $2.2 trillion, yet our imports were $2.7 trillion. Thus, in 2016 the United States had a trade deficit of $500 billion.[11] America's exports continue to grow, but not as fast as our imports: The export of goods, such as computers, trucks, and airplanes, is very strong. The sector that is lagging in significant growth is the export of services. Although America exports many services—ranging from airline trips to education of foreign students to legal advice—part of the problem is due to piracy, which leads companies to restrict the distribution of their services to certain regions. The FBI estimates that the theft of intellectual property from products, books and movies, and pharmaceuticals totals in the billions every year.[12]

Balance of Payments

Another measure of international trade is called the **balance of payments**, which is a summary of a country's international financial transactions showing the difference between the country's total payments to and its total receipts from other countries. The balance of payments includes imports and exports (balance of trade), long-term investments in overseas plants and equipment, government loans to and from other countries, gifts and foreign aid, military expenditures made in other countries, and money transfers in and out of foreign banks.

From 1900 until 1970, the United States had a trade surplus, but in the other areas that make up the balance of payments, U.S. payments exceeded receipts, largely due to the large U.S. military presence abroad. Hence, almost every year since 1950, the United States has had an unfavorable balance of payments. And since 1970, both the balance of payments *and* the balance of trade have been unfavorable. What can a nation do to reduce an unfavorable balance of payments? It can foster exports, reduce its dependence on imports, decrease its military presence abroad, or reduce foreign investment. The U.S. balance of payments deficit was over $504 billion in 2016.[13]

The Changing Value of Currencies

The exchange rate is the price of one country's currency in terms of another country's currency. If a country's currency *appreciates*, less of that country's currency is needed to buy another country's currency. If a country's currency *depreciates*, more of that currency will be needed to buy another country's currency.

How do appreciation and depreciation affect the prices of a country's goods? If, say, the U.S. dollar depreciates relative to the Japanese yen, U.S. residents have to pay more dollars to buy Japanese goods. To illustrate, suppose the dollar price of a yen is $0.012 and that a Toyota is priced at 2 million yen. At this exchange rate, a U.S. resident pays $24,000 for a Toyota ($0.012 × 2 million yen = $24,000). If the dollar depreciates to $0.018 to one yen, then the U.S. resident will have to pay $36,000 for a Toyota.

As the dollar depreciates, the prices of Japanese goods rise for U.S. residents, so they buy fewer Japanese goods—thus, U.S. imports decline. At the same time, as the dollar depreciates relative to the yen, the yen appreciates relative to the dollar. This means prices of U.S. goods fall for the Japanese, so they buy more U.S. goods—and U.S. exports rise.

Currency markets operate under a system called **floating exchange rates**. Prices of currencies "float" up and down based upon the demand for and supply of each currency. Global currency traders create the supply of and demand for a particular currency based on that currency's investment, trade potential, and economic strength. If a country decides that its currency is not properly valued in international currency markets, the government may step in and adjust the currency's value. In a **devaluation**, a nation lowers the value of its currency relative to other currencies. This makes that country's exports cheaper and should, in turn, help the balance of payments.

In other cases, a country's currency may be undervalued, giving its exports an unfair competitive advantage. Many people believe that China's huge trade surplus with the United States is partially because China's currency was undervalued. In 2017, the U.S. Department of Commerce issued a fact sheet detailing how it accused China of dumping steel on the U.S. market as well as providing financial assistance to Chinese companies to produce, manufacture, and export stainless steel to the United States from the People's Republic of China.[14]

CONCEPT CHECK

1. What is global vision, and why is it important?

2. What impact does international trade have on the U.S. economy?
3. Explain the impact of a currency devaluation.

3.2 | Why Nations Trade

2. Why do nations trade?

One might argue that the best way to protect workers and the domestic economy is to stop trade with other nations. Then the whole circular flow of inputs and outputs would stay within our borders. But if we decided to do that, how would we get resources like cobalt and coffee beans? The United States simply can't produce some things, and it can't manufacture some products, such as steel and most clothing, at the low costs we're used to. The fact is that nations—like people—are good at producing different things: you may be better at balancing a ledger than repairing a car. In that case you benefit by "exporting" your bookkeeping services and "importing" the car repairs you need from a good mechanic. Economists refer to specialization like this as *advantage*.

Absolute Advantage

A country has an **absolute advantage** when it can produce and sell a product at a lower cost than any other country or when it is the only country that can provide a product. The United States, for example, has an absolute advantage in reusable spacecraft and other high-tech items.

Suppose that the United States has an absolute advantage in air traffic control systems for busy airports and that Brazil has an absolute advantage in coffee. The United States does not have the proper climate for growing coffee, and Brazil lacks the technology to develop air traffic control systems. Both countries would gain by exchanging air traffic control systems for coffee.

Comparative Advantage

Even if the United States had an absolute advantage in both coffee and air traffic control systems, it should still specialize and engage in trade. Why? The reason is the **principle of comparative advantage**, which says that each country should specialize in the products that it can produce most readily and cheaply and trade those products for goods that foreign countries can produce most readily and cheaply. This specialization ensures greater product availability and lower prices.

For example, India and Vietnam have a comparative advantage in producing clothing because of lower labor costs. Japan has long held a comparative advantage in consumer electronics because of technological expertise. The United States has an advantage in computer software, airplanes, some agricultural products, heavy machinery, and jet engines.

Thus, comparative advantage acts as a stimulus to trade. When nations allow their citizens to trade whatever goods and services they choose without government regulation, free trade exists. **Free trade** is the policy of permitting the people and businesses of a country to buy and sell where they please without restrictions. The opposite of free trade is **protectionism**, in which a nation protects its home industries from outside competition by establishing artificial barriers such as tariffs and quotas. In the next section, we'll look at the various barriers, some natural and some created by governments, that restrict free trade.

The Fear of Trade and Globalization

The continued protests during meetings of the World Trade Organization and the protests during the convocations of the World Bank and the International Monetary Fund (the three organizations are discussed later in the chapter) show that many people fear world trade and globalization. What do they fear? The negatives of global trade are as follows:

- Millions of Americans have lost jobs due to imports or production shifting abroad. Most find new jobs, but often those jobs pay less.
- Millions of others fear losing their jobs, especially at those companies operating under competitive pressure.
- Employers often threaten to export jobs if workers do not accept pay cuts.
- Service and white-collar jobs are increasingly vulnerable to operations moving offshore.

Sending domestic jobs to another country is called **outsourcing**, a topic you can explore in more depth. Many U.S. companies, such as Dell, IBM, and AT&T, have set up call service centers in India, the Philippines, and other countries. Now even engineering and research and development jobs are being outsourced. Outsourcing and "American jobs" were a big part of the 2016 presidential election with Carrier's plan to close a plant in Indianapolis and open a new plant in Mexico. While intervention by President Trump did lead to 800 jobs remaining in Indianapolis, Carrier informed the state of Indiana that it will cut 632 workers from its Indianapolis factory. The manufacturing jobs will move to Monterrey, Mexico, where the minimum wage is $3.90 per day.[15]

Exhibit 3.3   Anti-globalization groups oppose America's free-trade stance, arguing that corporate interests are hurting the U.S. economy and usurping the power of the American people. The recent protests at the G20 meetings in Hamburg, Germany, expressed anti-free-trade sentiment, supporting the idea that multinational corporations wield too much power. *Are fears expressed by anti-globalization activists and nationalists justified?* (Credit: fiction of reality/ Flickr/ Attribution 2.0 Generic (CC BY 2.0))

So is outsourcing good or bad? If you happen to lose your job, it's obviously bad for you. However, some economists say it leads to cheaper goods and services for U.S. consumers because costs are lower. Also, it should stimulate exports to fast-growing countries. No one knows how many jobs will be lost to outsourcing in coming years. According to estimates, almost 2.4 million U.S. jobs were outsourced in 2015.[16]

Benefits of Globalization

A closer look reveals that globalization has been the engine that creates jobs and wealth. Benefits of global trade include the following:

- Productivity grows more quickly when countries produce goods and services in which they have a comparative advantage. Living standards can increase faster. One problem is that big **G20** countries have added more than 1,200 restrictive export and import measures since 2008.
- Global competition and cheap imports keep prices down, so inflation is less likely to stop economic growth. However, in some cases this is not working because countries manipulate their currency to get a price advantage.
- An open economy spurs innovation with fresh ideas from abroad.
- Through infusion of foreign capital and technology, global trade provides poor countries with the chance to develop economically by spreading prosperity.
- More information is shared between two trading partners that may not have much in common initially, including insight into local cultures and customs, which may help the two nations expand their collective knowledge and learn ways to compete globally.[17]

CONCEPT CHECK

1. Describe the policy of free trade and its relationship to comparative advantage.
2. Why do people fear globalization?
3. What are the benefits of globalization?

3.3 Barriers to Trade

3. What are the barriers to international trade?

International trade is carried out by both businesses and governments—as long as no one puts up trade barriers. In general, trade barriers keep firms from selling to one another in foreign markets. The major obstacles to international trade are natural barriers, tariff barriers, and nontariff barriers.

Natural Barriers

Natural barriers to trade can be either physical or cultural. For instance, even though raising beef in the relative warmth of Argentina may cost less than raising beef in the bitter cold of Siberia, the cost of shipping the beef from South America to Siberia might drive the price too high. *Distance* is thus one of the natural barriers to international trade.

Language is another natural trade barrier. People who can't communicate effectively may not be able to negotiate trade agreements or may ship the wrong goods.

Tariff Barriers

A **tariff** is a tax imposed by a nation on imported goods. It may be a charge per unit, such as per barrel of oil or per new car; it may be a percentage of the value of the goods, such as 5 percent of a $500,000 shipment of shoes; or it may be a combination. No matter how it is assessed, any tariff makes imported goods more costly, so they are less able to compete with domestic products.

Protective tariffs make imported products less attractive to buyers than domestic products. The United States, for instance, has protective tariffs on imported poultry, textiles, sugar, and some types of steel and clothing, and in March of 2018 the Trump administration added tariffs on steel and aluminum from most countries. On the other side of the world, Japan imposes a tariff on U.S. cigarettes that makes them cost 60 percent more than Japanese brands. U.S. tobacco firms believe they could get as much as a third of the Japanese market if there were no tariffs on cigarettes. With tariffs, they have under 2 percent of the market.

Arguments for and against Tariffs

Congress has debated the issue of tariffs since 1789. The main arguments *for* tariffs include the following:

- Tariffs protect infant industries. A tariff can give a struggling new domestic industry time to become an effective global competitor.
- Tariffs protect U.S. jobs. Unions and others say tariffs keep foreign labor from taking away U.S. jobs.
- Tariffs aid in military preparedness. Tariffs should protect industries and technology during peacetime that are vital to the military in the event of war.

The main arguments *against* tariffs include the following:

- Tariffs discourage free trade, and free trade lets the principle of competitive advantage work most efficiently.
- Tariffs raise prices, thereby decreasing consumers' purchasing power. In 2017, the United States imposed tariffs of 63.86 percent to 190.71 percent on a wide variety of Chinese steel products. The idea was to give U.S. steel manufacturers a fair market after the Department of Commerce concluded their antidumping and anti-subsidy probes. It is still too early to determine what the effects of these tariffs will be, but higher steel prices are likely. Heavy users of steel, such as construction and automobile industries, will see big increases in their production costs. It is also likely that China may impose tariffs on certain U.S. products and services and that any negotiations on intellectual property and piracy will bog down.[18]

Nontariff Barriers

Governments also use other tools besides tariffs to restrict trade. One type of nontariff barrier is the **import quota**, or limits on the quantity of a certain good that can be imported. The goal of setting quotas is to limit imports to the specific amount of a given product. The United States protects its shrinking textile industry with quotas. A complete list of the commodities and products subject to import quotas is available on line at the U.S. Customs and Border Protection Agency website.[19]

A complete ban against importing or exporting a product is an **embargo**. Often embargoes are set up for defense purposes. For instance, the United States does not allow various high-tech products, such as supercomputers and lasers, to be exported to countries that are not allies. Although this embargo costs U.S. firms billions of dollars each year in lost sales, it keeps enemies from using the latest technology in their military hardware.

Government rules that give special privileges to domestic manufacturers and retailers are called **buy-national regulations**. One such regulation in the United States bans the use of foreign steel in constructing U.S. highways. Many state governments have buy-national rules for supplies and services. In a more subtle move, a country may make it hard for foreign products to enter its markets by establishing customs regulations that are different from generally accepted international standards, such as requiring bottles to be quart size rather than liter size.

Exchange controls are laws that require a company earning foreign exchange (foreign currency) from its exports to sell the foreign exchange to a control agency, usually a central bank. For example, assume that Rolex, a Swiss company, sells 300 watches to Zales Jewelers, a U.S. chain, for US$600,000. If Switzerland had exchange controls, Rolex would have to sell its U.S. dollars to the Swiss central bank and would receive Swiss francs. If Rolex wants to buy goods (supplies to make watches) from abroad, it must go to the central bank and buy foreign exchange (currency). By controlling the amount of foreign exchange sold to companies, the government controls the amount of products that can be imported. Limiting imports and encouraging exports helps a government to create a favorable balance of trade.

CONCEPT CHECK

1. Discuss the concept of natural trade barriers.
2. Describe several tariff and nontariff barriers to trade.

3.4 Fostering Global Trade

4. How do governments and institutions foster world trade?

Antidumping Laws

U.S. firms don't always get to compete on an equal basis with foreign firms in international trade. To level the playing field, Congress has passed antidumping laws. **Dumping** is the practice of charging a lower price for a product (perhaps below cost) in foreign markets than in the firm's home market. The company might be trying to win foreign customers, or it might be seeking to get rid of surplus goods.

When the variation in price can't be explained by differences in the cost of serving the two markets, dumping is suspected. Most industrialized countries have antidumping regulations. They are especially concerned about *predatory dumping,* the attempt to gain control of a foreign market by destroying competitors with impossibly low prices.

The United States recently imposed tariffs on softwood lumber from Canada. Canada was found guilty of pricing softwood lumber at between 7.72 and 4.49 percent below their costs. U.S. customs officers will now levy tariffs on Canadian timber exports with tax rates from 17.41 percent to 30.88 percent, depending on the business.[20]

From our discussion so far, it might seem that governments act only to restrain global trade. On the contrary, governments and international financial organizations work hard to increase it, as this section explains.

Trade Negotiations and the World Trade Organization

The **Uruguay Round** of trade negotiations is an agreement that dramatically lowers trade barriers worldwide. Adopted in 1994, the agreement has been now signed by 148 nations. The most ambitious global trade agreement ever negotiated, the Uruguay Round reduced tariffs by one-third worldwide, a move that is expected to increase global income by $235 billion annually. Perhaps the most notable aspect of the agreement is its recognition of new global realities. For the first time, an agreement covers services, intellectual property rights, and trade-related investment measures such as exchange controls.

As a follow-up to the Uruguay Round, a negotiating round started in the capital of Qatar in 2001 is called the Doha Round. To date, the round has shown little progress in advancing free trade. Developing nations are pushing for the reduction of farm subsidies in the United States, Europe, and Japan. Poor countries say that the subsidies stimulate overproduction, which drives down global agricultural prices. Because developing nations' primary exports are agricultural commodities, low prices mean that they cannot compete in the global marketplace. On the other hand, the United States and Europe are interested in bringing down trade barriers in services and manufacturing. The continuing talks have served as a lightning rod for protesters, who claim that the World Trade Organization (WTO) serves the interests of multinational corporations, promotes trade over preserving the environment, and treats poor nations unfairly.[21]

The **World Trade Organization** replaces the old General Agreement on Tariffs and Trade (GATT), which was created in 1948. The GATT contained extensive loopholes that enabled countries to evade agreements to reduce trade barriers. Today, all WTO members must fully comply with all agreements under the Uruguay Round. The WTO also has an effective dispute settlement procedure with strict time limits to resolve disputes.

The WTO has emerged as the world's most powerful institution for reducing trade barriers and opening markets. The advantage of WTO membership is that member countries lower trade barriers among themselves. Countries that don't belong must negotiate trade agreements individually with all their trading partners. Only a few countries, such as North Korea, Turkmenistan, and Eritrea, are not members of the WTO.[22]

Exhibit 3.4   Headquartered in Toulouse, France, Airbus is one of the world's top commercial aircraft manufacturers, operating design and manufacturing facilities in Europe, Japan, China, and the United States. The airliner's current product lineup of 12 jet-aircraft types ranging from 100 seats to 600 seats is heavy competition for Boeing, a top U.S. airline firm with which Airbus has ongoing subsidy-related disputes. *What is the World Trade Organization's role in settling disputes between competing multinational corporations?* (Credit: Bartlomiej Mostek/ Flickr/ Attribution 2.0 Generic (CC BY 2.0))

The United States has had mixed results in bringing disputes before the WTO. To date, it has won slightly fewer than half of the cases it has presented to the WTO. America has also won about one-third of the cases brought against it by other countries. One of America's recent losses came in a ruling where the U.S. claimed that tuna imported from Mexico was not meeting the "dolphin safe" criteria, meaning that dolphins were not being killed during the process to catching tuna. The WTO ruled in favor of Mexico. Recently, the United States targeted Europe, India, South Korea, Canada, and Argentina to file cases against. The disputes ranged from European aviation practices to Indian trade barriers affecting U.S. automakers.

One of the biggest disputes before the WTO involved the United States and the European Union. The United States claims that Europe has given Airbus $15 billion in aid to develop airplanes. The European Union claims that the U.S. government has provided $23 billion in military research that has benefited Boeing's commercial aircraft business. It also claimed that Washington State (the home of Boeing manufacturing) has given the company $3.2 billion in unfair tax breaks.[23]

The World Bank and International Monetary Fund

Two international financial organizations are instrumental in fostering global trade. The **World Bank** offers low-interest loans to developing nations. Originally, the purpose of the loans was to help these nations build infrastructure such as roads, power plants, schools, drainage projects, and hospitals. Now the World Bank offers loans to help developing nations relieve their debt burdens. To receive the loans, countries must pledge to lower trade barriers and aid private enterprise. In addition to making loans, the World Bank is a major source of advice and information for developing nations. The United States has granted the organization millions to create knowledge databases on nutrition, birth control, software engineering, creating quality products, and basic accounting systems.

The **International Monetary Fund (IMF)** was founded in 1945, one year after the creation of the World Bank, to promote trade through financial cooperation and eliminate trade barriers in the process. The IMF makes short-term loans to member nations that are unable to meet their budgetary expenses. It operates as a lender of last resort for troubled nations. In exchange for these emergency loans, IMF lenders frequently extract significant commitments from the borrowing nations to address the problems that led to the crises. These steps may include curtailing imports or even devaluing the currency.

Some global financial problems do not have a simple solution. One option would be to pump a lot more funds into the IMF, giving it enough resources to bail out troubled countries and put them back on their feet. In effect, the IMF would be turned into a real lender of last resort for the world economy.

The danger of counting on the IMF, though, is the "moral hazard" problem. Investors would assume that the IMF would bail them out and would therefore be encouraged to take bigger and bigger risks in emerging markets, leading to the possibility of even deeper financial crises in the future.

CONCEPT CHECK

1. Describe the purpose and role of the WTO.
2. What are the roles of the World Bank and the IMF in world trade?

3.5 | International Economic Communities

5. What are international economic communities?

Nations that frequently trade with each other may decide to formalize their relationship. The governments meet and work out agreements for a common economic policy. The result is an economic community or, in other cases, a bilateral trade agreement (an agreement between two countries to lower trade barriers). For example, two nations may agree upon a **preferential tariff**, which gives advantages to one nation (or several nations) over others. When members of the British Commonwealth (countries that are former British territories) trade with Great Britain, they pay lower tariffs than do other nations. For example, Canada and Australia are former British territories but still members of the British Commonwealth. You will note that Queen Elizabeth still appears on Canadian currency and the Union Jack is still incorporated into the Australian flag. In other cases, nations may form free-trade associations. In a **free-trade zone**, few duties or rules restrict trade among the partners, but nations outside the zone must pay the tariffs set by the individual members.

North American Free Trade Agreement (NAFTA)

The **North American Free Trade Agreement (NAFTA)** created the world's largest free-trade zone. The agreement was ratified by the U.S. Congress in 1993. It includes Canada, the United States, and Mexico, with a combined population of 450 million and an economy of over $20.8 trillion.[24]

Canada, one of the largest U.S. trading partners, entered a free-trade agreement with the United States in 1988. Thus, most of the new long-run opportunities opened for U.S. business under NAFTA are in Mexico,

America's third-largest trading partner. Before NAFTA, tariffs on Mexican exports to the United States averaged just 4 percent, and most goods entered the United States duty-free, so NAFTA's primary impact was to open the Mexican market to U.S. companies. When the treaty went into effect, tariffs on about half the items traded across the Rio Grande disappeared. Since NAFTA came into effect, U.S.-Mexican trade has increased from $80 billion to $515 billion annually. The pact removed a web of Mexican licensing requirements, quotas, and tariffs that limited transactions in U.S. goods and services. For instance, the pact allows U.S. and Canadian financial-services companies to own subsidiaries in Mexico for the first time in 50 years.

Exhibit 3.5   The softwood lumber dispute between the United States and Canada that has resulted in the U.S. imposing tariffs on Canadian softwood lumber imports is one of the longest trade disputes between the two nations. The dispute is the result of disagreements about Canadian lumber production and imports between the two nations. The main contention in the softwood lumber dispute is the U.S. claim that the Canadian government is unfairly subsidizing Canadian lumber production by providing access to public land while U.S. producers harvest softwood lumber on their own property. *Why do anti-free-trade groups support these tariffs when the result will be higher prices for softwood lumber?* (Credit: Jesse Wagstaff/ Flickr/ Attribution-NoDerivs 2.0 Generic (CC BY 2.0))

The real test of NAFTA will be whether it can deliver rising prosperity on both sides of the Rio Grande. For Mexicans, NAFTA must provide rising wages, better benefits, and an expanding middle class with enough purchasing power to keep buying goods from the United States and Canada. That scenario seems to be working. At the Delphi Corp. auto parts plant in Ciudad Juárez, just across the border from El Paso, Texas, the assembly line is a cross section of working-class Mexico. In the years since NAFTA lowered trade and investment barriers, Delphi has significantly expanded its presence in the country. Today it employs 70,000 Mexicans, who every day receive up to 70 million U.S.-made components to assemble into parts. The wages are modest by U.S. standards—an assembly-line worker with two years' experience earns about $2.30 an hour. But that's triple Mexico's minimum wage, and Delphi jobs are among the most coveted in Juárez. The United States recently notified the Canadian and Mexican governments that it intends to renegotiate aspects of the NAFTA agreement.[25]

The largest new trade agreement is **Mercosur**, which includes Peru, Brazil, Argentina, Uruguay, and Paraguay. The elimination of most tariffs among the trading partners has resulted in trade revenues that currently exceed $16 billion annually. Recent recessions in Mercosur countries have limited economic growth, even though trade among Mercosur countries has continued to grow.

Central America Free Trade Agreement

The newest free trade agreement is the Central America Free Trade Agreement (CAFTA) passed in 2005. Besides the United States, the agreement includes Costa Rica, the Dominican Republic, El Salvador, Guatemala, Honduras, and Nicaragua. The United States is already the principal exporter to these nations, so economists don't think that it will result in a major increase in U.S. exports. It will, however, reduce tariffs on exports to CAFTA countries. Already, some 80 percent of the goods imported into the United States from CAFTA nations are tariff-free. CAFTA countries may benefit from the new permanent trade deal if U.S. multinational firms deepen their investment in the region.

The European Union

In 1993, the member countries of the European Community (EC) ratified the Maastricht Treaty, which proposed to take the EC further toward economic, monetary, and political union. Although the heart of the treaty deals with developing a unified European Market, Maastricht was also intended to increase integration among **European Union (EU)** members.

The EU has helped increase this integration by creating a borderless economy for the 28 European nations, shown on the map in **Exhibit 3.6**.[26]

EU28 Member States:	Candidate Countries:
• Austria	• Albania
• Belgium	• Former Yugoslav Republic of Macedonia
• Bulgaria	• Montenegro
• Croatia	• Serbia
• Cyprus	• Turkey
• Czech Republic	
• Denmark	
• Estonia	
• Finland	
• France	
• Germany	
• Greece	
• Hungary	
• Ireland	
• Italy	
• Latvia	
• Lithuania	
• Luxembourg	
• Malta	
• The Netherlands	
• Poland	
• Portugal	
• Romania	
• Slovakia	
• Slovenia	
• Spain	
• Sweden	
• United Kingdom	

European Union member states have set up common institutions to which they delegate some of their sovereignty so that decisions on specific matters of joint interest can be made democratically at the European level. This pooling of sovereignty is also called **European integration**. In 2016, citizens of the United Kingdom voted to leave the European Union, a plan known as Brexit, which could take several years to occur.[27]

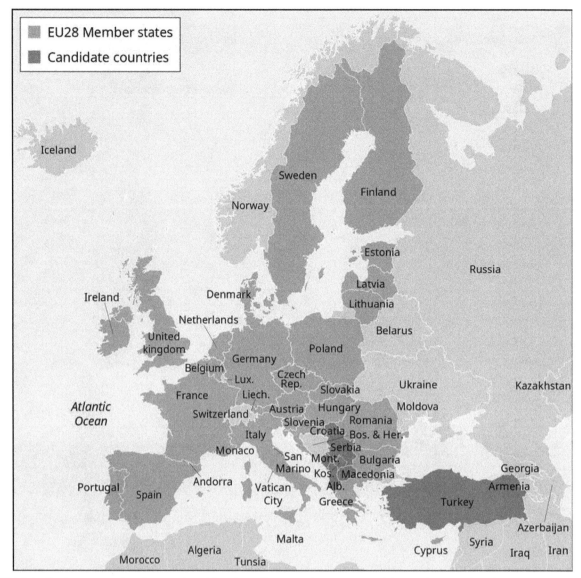

Exhibit 3.6   The European Union Source: Adapted from https://europa.eu/european-union/about-eu/countries/member-countries_en.

One of the principal objectives of the European Union is to promote economic progress of all member countries. The EU has stimulated economic progress by eliminating trade barriers, differences in tax laws, and differences in product standards, and by establishing a common currency. A new European Community Bank was created, along with a common currency called the euro. The European Union's single market has created 2.5 million new jobs since it was founded and generated more than $1 trillion in new wealth.[28] The opening of national EU markets has brought down the price of national telephone calls by 50 percent since 1998. Under pressure of competition, the prices of airfares in Europe have fallen significantly. The removal of national restrictions has enabled more than 15 million Europeans to go to another EU country to work or spend their retirement.

The EU is a very tough antitrust enforcer; some would say it is tougher than the United States. The EU, for example, fined Google $2.7 billion for favoring some of its own services in its search results.[29]Unlike in the United States, the EU can seal off corporate offices for unspecified periods to prevent destruction of evidence and enter the homes, cars, yachts, and other personal property of executives suspected of abusing their companies' market power or conspiring to fix prices.

Microsoft has been fighting the European Court since 2002, with no quick end in sight. The Court fined Microsoft for monopolizing internet access by offering Internet Explorer with its Windows software. The company is also appealing a Court decision requiring it to share code with "open source" companies. Another big U.S. company, Coca-Cola, settled a six-year antitrust dispute with the European Court by agreeing to strict limits on its sales tactics. Coke can't sign exclusive agreements with retailers that would ban competing soft drinks or give retailers rebates based on sales volume. Furthermore, it must give rivals, like Pepsi, 20 percent of the space in Coke coolers so Pepsi can stock its own brands. If Coke violates the terms of the agreement, it will be fined 10 percent of its worldwide revenue (over $2 billion).[30]

An entirely different type of problem facing global businesses is the possibility of a protectionist movement by the EU against outsiders. For example, European automakers have proposed holding Japanese imports at roughly their current 10 percent market share. The Irish, Danes, and Dutch don't make cars and have unrestricted home markets; they are unhappy at the prospect of limited imports of Toyotas and Hondas. Meanwhile, France has a strict quota on Japanese cars to protect its own Renault and Peugeot. These local automakers could be hurt if the quota is raised at all.

Interestingly, a number of big U.S. companies are already considered more "European" than many European companies. Coke and Kellogg's are considered classic European brand names. Ford and General Motors compete for the largest share of auto sales on the continent. Apple, IBM, and Dell dominate their markets. General Electric, AT&T, and Westinghouse are already strong all over Europe and have invested heavily in new manufacturing facilities there.

The European Union proposed a constitution that would centralize powers at the Union level and decrease the powers of individual member countries. It also would create a single voice in world affairs by creating a post of foreign minister. The constitution also gave the EU control over political asylum, immigration, guaranteed freedom of speech, and collective labor bargaining. In order to become law, each EU country had to ratify the constitution. The two most powerful countries in the EU, France and Germany, voted "no" in the summer of 2005. Citizens of both countries were afraid that the constitution would draw jobs away from Western Europe and to the Eastern European EU countries. These new members of the EU have lower wage rates and fewer regulations. Voters were also worried that the constitution would result in free-market reforms along American or British lines over France and Germany's traditional social protections. Concerns over immigration also sparked the referendum vote that is leading to the United Kingdom leaving the European Union.

CONCEPT CHECK

1. Explain the pros and cons of NAFTA.
2. What is the European Union? Will it ever be a United States of Europe?

3.6 Participating in the Global Marketplace

6. How do companies enter the global marketplace?

Companies decide to "go global" for a number of reasons. Perhaps the most urgent reason is to earn additional profits. If a firm has a unique product or technological advantage not available to other international competitors, this advantage should result in major business successes abroad. In other situations, management may have exclusive market information about foreign customers, marketplaces, or market situations. In this case, although exclusivity can provide an initial motivation for going global, managers must realize that competitors will eventually catch up. Finally, saturated domestic markets, excess capacity, and potential for cost savings can also be motivators to expand into international markets. A company can enter global trade in several ways, as this section describes.

Exporting

When a company decides to enter the global market, usually the least complicated and least risky alternative is **exporting**, or selling domestically produced products to buyers in another country. A company, for example, can sell directly to foreign importers or buyers. Exporting is not limited to huge corporations such as General Motors or Apple. Indeed, small companies typically enter the global marketplace by exporting. China is the world's largest exporter, followed by the United States.[31] Many small businesses claim that they lack the money, time, or knowledge of foreign markets that exporting requires. The U.S. Small Business Administration (SBA) now offers the Export Working Capital Program, which helps small and medium-size firms obtain working capital (money) to complete export sales. The SBA also provides counseling and legal assistance for small businesses that wish to enter the global marketplace. Companies such as American Building Restoration Products of Franklin, Wisconsin, have benefited tremendously from becoming exporters. American Building is now selling its chemical products to building restoration companies in Mexico, Israel, Japan, and Korea. Exports account for more than 5 percent of the firm's total sales.

Plenty of governmental help is available when a company decides to begin exporting. Export Assistance Centers (EAC) provide a one-stop resource for help in exporting. Over 700 EACs are placed strategically around the country. Often the SBA is located in the same building as the EAC. The SBA can guarantee loans of $50,000 to $100,000 to help an exporter grow its business. Online help is also available at http://www.ustr.gov. The site lists international trade events, offers international marketing research, and has practical tools to help with every step of the exporting process. Companies considering exporting for the first time can go to http://www.export.gov and get answers to questions such as: What's in it for me? Am I ready for this? What do I have to do? The site also provides a huge list of resources for the first-time exporter.

Licensing and Franchising

Another effective way for a firm to move into the global arena with relatively little risk is to sell a license to manufacture its product to a firm in a foreign country. **Licensing** is the legal process whereby a firm (the *licensor*) agrees to let another firm (the *licensee*) use a manufacturing process, trademark, patent, trade secret, or other proprietary knowledge. The licensee, in turn, agrees to pay the licensor a royalty or fee agreed on by both parties.

International licensing is a multibillion-dollar-a-year industry. Entertainment and character licensing, such as DVD movies and characters such as Batman, is the largest single category. Trademarks are the second-largest source of licensing revenue. Caterpillar licenses its brand for both shoes and clothing, which is very popular in Europe.

U.S. companies have eagerly embraced the licensing concept. For instance, Labatt Brewing Company has a license to produce Miller High Life in Canada. The Spalding Company receives more than $2 million annually from license agreements on its sporting goods. Fruit of the Loom lends its name through licensing to 45 consumer items in Japan alone, for at least 1 percent of the licensee's gross sales.

The licensor must make sure it can exercise sufficient control over the licensee's activities to ensure proper quality, pricing, distribution, and so on. Licensing may also create a new competitor in the long run if the licensee decides to void the license agreement. International law is often ineffective in stopping such actions. Two common ways that a licensor can maintain effective control over its licensees are by shipping one or more critical components from the United States and by locally registering patents and trademarks in its own name.

Franchising is a form of licensing that has grown rapidly in recent years. Many U.S. franchisors operate thousands of outlets in foreign countries. More than half of the international franchises are for fast-food restaurants and business services. McDonald's, however, decided to sell its Chinese stores to a group of outside investors for $1.8 billion, but retained 20 percent of the equity.[32]

Having a big-name franchise doesn't always guarantee success or mean that the job will be easy. In China, Home Depot closed its stores after opening 12 to serve the large Chinese population. Had they done market research, they would have known that the majority of urban dwellers live in recently built apartments and that DIY (Do It Yourself) is viewed with disdain in Chinese society, where it is seen as a sign of poverty.[33] When Subway opened its first sandwich shop in China, locals stood outside and watched for a few days. Patrons were so confused that the franchisee had to print signs explaining how to order. Customers didn't believe the tuna salad was made from a fish because they couldn't see the head or tail. And they didn't like the idea of touching their food, so they would hold the sandwich vertically, peel off the paper wrap, and eat it like a banana. Most of all, the Chinese customers didn't want sandwiches.

It's not unusual for Western food chains to adapt their strategies when selling in China. McDonald's, aware that the Chinese consume more chicken than beef, offered a spicy chicken burger. KFC got rid of coleslaw in favor of seasonal dishes such as shredded carrots or bamboo shoots.

Contract Manufacturing

In **contract manufacturing**, a foreign firm manufactures private-label goods under a domestic firm's brand. Marketing may be handled by either the domestic company or the foreign manufacturer. Levi Strauss, for instance, entered into an agreement with the French fashion house of Cacharel to produce a new Levi's line, Something New, for distribution in Germany.

The advantage of contract manufacturing is that it lets a company test the water in a foreign country. By allowing the foreign firm to produce a certain volume of products to specification and put the domestic firm's brand name on the goods, the domestic firm can broaden its global marketing base without investing in overseas plants and equipment. After establishing a solid base, the domestic firm may switch to a joint venture or direct investment, explained below.

Joint Ventures

Joint ventures are somewhat similar to licensing agreements. In a **joint venture**, the domestic firm buys part of a foreign company or joins with a foreign company to create a new entity. A joint venture is a quick and relatively inexpensive way to enter the global market. It can also be very risky. Many joint ventures fail. Others fall victim to a takeover, in which one partner buys out the other.

Sometimes countries have required local partners in order to establish a business in their country. China, for example, had this requirement in a number of industries until recently. Thus, a joint venture was the only way to enter the market. Joint ventures help reduce risks by sharing costs and technology. Often joint ventures will bring together different strengths from each member. In the General Motors-Suzuki joint venture in Canada, for example, both parties have contributed and gained. The alliance, CAMI Automotive, was formed to manufacture low-end cars for the U.S. market. The plant, which was run by Suzuki management, produces the Chevrolet Equinox and the Pontiac Torrent, as well as the new Suzuki SUV. Through CAMI, Suzuki has gained access to GM's dealer network and an expanded market for parts and components. GM avoided the cost of developing low-end cars and obtained models it needed to revitalize the lower end of its product line and its average fuel economy rating. After the successful joint venture, General Motors gained full control of the operation in 2011. The CAMI factory may be one of the most productive plants in North America. There GM has learned how Japanese automakers use work teams, run flexible assembly lines, and manage quality control.[34]

Direct Foreign Investment

Active ownership of a foreign company or of overseas manufacturing or marketing facilities is **direct foreign investment**. Direct investors have either a controlling interest or a large minority interest in the firm. Thus, they stand to receive the greatest potential reward but also face the greatest potential risk. A firm may make a direct foreign investment by acquiring an interest in an existing company or by building new facilities. It might do so because it has trouble transferring some resources to a foreign operation or obtaining that resource locally. One important resource is personnel, especially managers. If the local labor market is tight, the firm may buy an entire foreign firm and retain all its employees instead of paying higher salaries than competitors.

Sometimes firms make direct investments because they can find no suitable local partners. Also, direct investments avoid the communication problems and conflicts of interest that can arise with joint ventures. IBM, in the past, insisted on total ownership of its foreign investments because it did not want to share control with local partners.

General Motors has done very well by building a $4,400 (RMB 29,800) minivan in China that gets 43 miles per gallon in city driving. The Wuling Sunshine has a quarter the horsepower of U.S. minivans, weak acceleration, and a top speed of 81 miles per hour. The seats are only a third of the thickness of seats in Western models, but look plush compared to similar Chinese cars. The minivans have made GM the largest automotive seller in China, and have made China a large profit center for GM.[35]

Walmart now has over 6,000 stores located outside the United States. In 2016, international sales were over $116 billion. About one-third of all new Walmart stores are opened in global markets.[36]

Not all of Walmart's global investments have been successful. In Germany, Walmart bought the 21-store Wertkauf hypermarket chain and then 74 unprofitable and often decrepit Interspar stores. Problems in integrating and upgrading the stores resulted in at least $200 million in losses. Like all other German stores, Walmart stores were required by law to close at 8 p.m. on weekdays and 4 p.m. on Saturdays, and they could not open at all on Sundays. Costs were astronomical. As a result, Walmart left the German retail market.

Walmart has turned the corner on its international operations. It is pushing operational authority down to country managers in order to respond better to local cultures. Walmart enforces certain core principles such as everyday low prices, but country managers handle their own buying, logistics, building design, and other operational decisions.

Global firms change their strategies as local market conditions evolve. For example, major oil companies like Shell Oil and ExxonMobil had to react to dramatic changes in the price of oil due to technological advances such as more efficient automobiles, fracking, and horizontal drilling.

MANAGING CHANGE

Managing the Drop in Oil Prices

In 2014, crude oil was $90 a barrel, but increased production due to the shale oil boom and the reluctance of OPEC countries to reduce output led to a price drop to $45–$60 throughout the first quarter of 2015. While this is terrific news for consumers, it does provide challenges to managers at both large and small companies connected to the oil industry. Companies such as Chevron, Royal Dutch Shell, and ExxonMobil saw dramatic reductions in their earnings, which were also reflected in lower stock prices.

The action taken by senior executives at Chevron was to trim their planned capital expenditures by $5 billion in 2016, resulting in the elimination of 1,500 jobs, while ExxonMobil executives Jeff Woodbury and CEO Rex Tillerson (now the former U.S. Secretary of State) were less specific; they planned several belt-tightening strategies and forecast several years of low oil prices. Likewise, Ben van Beurden, the CEO of Royal Dutch Shell, announced plans to eliminate 6,500 jobs and also predicted long-range low prices for oil.

In addition to layoffs, actions that oil company managers can employ include mergers for companies that don't have the ability to become fully efficient themselves. They can merge with other companies that can improve overall efficiencies and operations. Contrary to the cost-cutting plans mentioned earlier, some companies might consider increasing their spending plans. Going against the reduced expenditures trend is Encana, a North American oil producer, which plans to increase its overall spending. Some of the factors that allowed Encana to increase spending was its low debt-to-equity ratio and its growth, which exceeded the industry average.

Growth is an important component of a company's strategy, and reactive short-term strategies can often hurt long-term growth. By implementing performance-improvement programs, companies can address problems and inefficiencies within the company and allow them to focus on innovation. Another strategy that companies can use is to review and alter their supply chain by focusing on costs and efficiency. Companies can expand their supplier base, thus increasing competition and reducing costs. This also requires companies to embrace a lean manufacturing mindset.

New technology can also be used as a cost driver. New technologies such as microseismic sensors used to monitor fracking operations in drilling operations miles under the earth can boost production. Adopting new technology can also lead to changes in the workers that companies employ. New technology usually requires higher-skilled workers, while reducing the number of lower-skilled workers.

The drop in oil prices has produced a survival-of-the-fittest competition among energy companies. The companies that employ multiple strategies to improve efficiency are the ones that will survive and prosper.

Critical Thinking Questions
1. Do you think that Royal Dutch Shell and ExxonMobil would have been more successful if they had considered strategies other than cutting spending and eliminating jobs? Why or why not?
2. How should oil companies react if oil prices rise to the $90 to $100 per barrel level? Explain your reasoning.

Sources: Stanley Reed and Clifford Krauss, "Royal Dutch Shell Profits Continue to Fall, Prompting

Layoffs," *The New York Times*, http://www.nytimes.com, July 30, 2015; John Biers, "More Belt-tightening Ahead as Exxon, Chevron Profits Dive," *Yahoo! News*, https://www.yahoo.com, July 31, 2015; Aisha Tejani, "How Oil Companies Are Responding to the Oil Price Drop," http://www.castagra.com, accessed June 30, 2017.

Countertrade

International trade does not always involve cash. Today, countertrade is a fast-growing way to conduct international business. In **countertrade**, part or all of the payment for goods or services is in the form of other goods or services. Countertrade is a form of barter (swapping goods for goods), an age-old practice whose origins have been traced back to cave dwellers. The U.S. Commerce Department says that roughly 30 percent of all international trade involves countertrade. Each year, about 300,000 U.S. firms engage in some form of countertrade. U.S. companies, including General Electric, Pepsi, General Motors, and Boeing, barter billions of goods and services every year. Recently, the Malaysian government bought 20 diesel-powered locomotives from China and paid for them with palm oil.

CONCEPT CHECK

1. Discuss several ways that a company can enter international trade.
2. Explain the concept of countertrade.

3.7 | Threats and Opportunities in the Global Marketplace

7. What threats and opportunities exist in the global marketplace?

To be successful in a foreign market, companies must fully understand the foreign environment in which they plan to operate. Politics, cultural differences, and the economic environment can represent both opportunities and pitfalls in the global marketplace.

Political Considerations

We have already discussed how tariffs, exchange controls, and other governmental actions threaten foreign producers. The political structure of a country may also jeopardize a foreign producer's success in international trade.

Intense nationalism, for example, can lead to difficulties. **Nationalism** is the sense of national consciousness that boosts the culture and interests of one country over those of all other countries. Strongly nationalistic countries, such as Iran and New Guinea, often discourage investment by foreign companies. In other, less radical forms of nationalism, the government may take actions to hinder foreign operations. France, for example, requires pop music stations to play at least 40 percent of their songs in French. This law was enacted because the French love American rock and roll. Without airtime, American music sales suffer. In another example of nationalism, U.S.-based PPG made an unsolicited bid to acquire Netherlands-based AzkoNobel NV. There was a chorus of opposition from Dutch politicians to the idea of a foreign takeover of AzkoNobel, the Dutch paint manufacturer. The government warned that it would move to defend AzkoNobel from a hostile takeover attempt. AzkoNobel played up the sentiment, tweeting about its rejection of the hostile takeover with the hashtag #DutchPride.[37]

In a hostile climate, a government may *expropriate* a foreign company's assets, taking ownership and compensating the former owners. Even worse is *confiscation,* when the owner receives no compensation. This happened during rebellions in several African nations during the 1990s and 2000s.

Cultural Differences

Central to any society is the common set of values shared by its citizens that determine what is socially acceptable. Culture underlies the family, educational system, religion, and social class system. The network of social organizations generates overlapping roles and status positions. These values and roles have a tremendous effect on people's preferences and thus on marketers' options. For example, in China Walmart holds live fishing contests on the premises, and in South Korea the company hosts a food competition with variations on a popular Korean dish, kimchee.

Language is another important aspect of culture. Marketers must take care in selecting product names and translating slogans and promotional messages so as not to convey the wrong meaning. For example, Mitsubishi Motors had to rename its Pajero model in Spanish-speaking countries because the term refers to a sexual activity. Toyota Motor's MR2 model dropped the *2* in France because the combination sounds like a French swear word. The literal translation of Coca-Cola in Chinese characters means "bite the wax tadpole."

Each country has its own customs and traditions that determine business practices and influence negotiations with foreign customers. For example, attempting to do business in Western Europe during the first two weeks in August is virtually impossible. Businesses close, and everyone goes on vacation at the same time. In many countries, personal relationships are more important than financial considerations. For instance, skipping social engagements in Mexico may lead to lost sales. Negotiations in Japan often include long evenings of dining, drinking, and entertaining; only after a close personal relationship has been formed do business negotiations begin. Table 3.1 presents some cultural dos and don'ts.

Cultural Dos and Don'ts Guidelines and Examples	
DO:	DON'T:
• Always present your business card with both hands in Asian countries. It should also be right-side-up and print-side-showing so that the recipient can read it as it is being presented. If you receive a business card, accept it with gratitude and examine it carefully. Don't quickly put it into your pocket. • Use a "soft-sell" and subtle approach when promoting a product in Japan. Japanese people do not feel comfortable with America's traditional hard-selling style. • Understand the role of religion in business transactions. In Muslim countries, Ramadan is a holy month when most people fast. During this time everything slows down, particularly business. • Have a local person available to culturally and linguistically interpret any advertising that you plan to do. When American Airlines wanted to promote its new first-class seats in the Mexican market, it translated the "Fly in Leather" campaign literally, which meant "Fly Naked" in Spanish.	• Glad-hand, back-slap, and use first names on your first business meeting in Asia. If you do, you will be considered a lightweight. • Fill a wine glass to the top if dining with a French businessperson. It is considered completely uncouth. • Begin your first business meeting in Asia talking business. Be patient. Let your clients get to know you first.

Table 3.1

Economic Environment

The level of economic development varies considerably, ranging from countries where everyday survival is a struggle, such as Sudan and Eritrea, to countries that are highly developed, such as Switzerland and Japan. In general, complex, sophisticated industries are found in developed countries, and more basic industries are found in less developed nations. Average family incomes are higher in the more developed countries than in the least-developed markets. Larger incomes mean greater purchasing power and demand, not only for consumer goods and services but also for the machinery and workers required to produce consumer goods. Table 3.2 provides a glimpse of global wealth.

Business opportunities are usually better in countries that have an economic infrastructure in place. **Infrastructure** is the basic institutions and public facilities upon which an economy's development depends. When we think about how our own economy works, we tend to take our infrastructure for granted. It includes the money and banking system that provide the major investment loans to our nation's businesses; the educational system that turns out the incredible varieties of skills and basic research that actually run our nation's production lines; the extensive transportation and communications systems—interstate highways, railroads, airports, canals, telephones, internet sites, postal systems, and television stations—that link almost every piece of our geography into one market; the energy system that powers our factories; and, of course, the market system itself, which brings our nation's goods and services into our homes and businesses.

Where the Money Is	
The Top 20	**Gross National Income Per Capita* US$**
Luxembourg	103,199
Switzerland	79,243
Norway	70,392
Ireland	62,562
Qatar	60,787
Iceland	59,629
United States	57,436
Denmark	53,744
Singapore	52,961
Australia	51,850
Sweden	51,165
San Marino	46,447
Netherlands	45,283
Austria	44,498
Finland	43,169
Canada	42,210
Germany	41,902
Belgium	41,283
United Kingdom	40,096
Japan	38,912
The Bottom Five	
Madagascar	391
Central African Republic	364
Burundi	325
Malawi	295

Where the Money Is	
The Top 20	Gross National Income Per Capita* US$
South Sudan	233

* **Gross National Income** is the value of the final goods and services produced by a country (Gross Domestic Product) together with its income received from other countries (such as interest and dividends) less similar payments made to other countries.

Final goods are the goods ultimately consumed rather than used in the production of another good. For example, a car sold to a consumer is a final good; the components, such as tires sold to the car manufacturer, are not. They are intermediate goods used to make the final good. The same tires, if sold to a consumer, would be a final good.

Sources: Some data refers to IMF staff estimates and some are actual figures for the year 2017, made on April 12, 2017. Adapted from the World Economic Outlook Database—April 2017, International Monetary Fund, accessed on April 18, 2017.

Table 3.2

CONCEPT CHECK

1. Explain how political factors can affect international trade.
2. Describe several cultural factors that a company involved in international trade should consider.
3. How can economic conditions affect trade opportunities?

3.8 | The Impact of Multinational Corporations

8. What are the advantages of multinational corporations?

Corporations that move resources, goods, services, and skills across national boundaries without regard to the country in which their headquarters are located are **multinational corporations**. Some are so rich and have so many employees that they resemble small countries. For example, the sales of both Exxon and Walmart are larger than the GDP of all but a few nations in the world. Multinational companies are heavily engaged in international trade. The successful ones take political and cultural differences into account.

Many global brands sell much more outside the United States than at home. Coca-Cola, Philip Morris's Marlboro brand, Pepsi, Kellogg, Pampers, Nescafe, and Gillette, are examples.

The Fortune 500 made over $1.5 trillion in profit in 2016. In slow-growing, developed economies like Europe and Japan, a weaker dollar helps, because it means cheaper products to sell into those markets, and profits earned in those markets translate into more dollars back home. Meanwhile, emerging markets in Asia, Latin America, and Eastern Europe are growing steadily. General Electric expects 60 percent of its revenue growth to come from emerging markets over the next decade. For Brown-Forman, the spirits company, a fifth of its sales growth of Jack Daniels, the Tennessee whiskey, is coming from developing markets like Mexico and Poland.

IBM had rapid sales growth in emerging markets such as Russia, India, and Brazil.[38]

The largest multinational corporations in the world are shown in Table 3.3.

Despite the success of American multinationals abroad, there is some indication that preference for U.S. brands may be slipping.

Exhibit 3.7   As overseas investment grows, so does the need for global branding. The Wisconsin National Guard picked NBA star Giannis Antetokounmpo to be the face of its recruiting and marketing effort. Recognizable to NBA fans the world over, Antetokounmpo personifies a youthful, dynamic spirit that transcends cultural and geographic boundaries. *Why is it increasingly important that multinational advertisers identify and sign celebrity spokespersons capable of bridging different cultures?* (Credit: Erik Drost/ Flickr/ Attribution-ShareAlike 2.0 Generic (CC BY 2.0))

The Multinational Advantage

Large multinationals have several advantages over other companies. For instance, multinationals can often overcome trade problems. Taiwan and South Korea have long had an embargo against Japanese cars for political reasons and to help domestic automakers. Yet Honda USA, a Japanese-owned company based in the United States, sends Accords to Taiwan and Korea. In another example, when the environmentally conscious Green movement challenged the biotechnology research conducted by BASF, a major German chemical and drug manufacturer, BASF moved its cancer and immune-system research to Cambridge, Massachusetts.

Another advantage for multinationals is their ability to sidestep regulatory problems. U.S. drugmaker SmithKline and Britain's Beecham decided to merge in part so that they could avoid licensing and regulatory hassles in their largest markets. The merged company can say it's an insider in both Europe and the United States. "When we go to Brussels, we're a member state [of the European Union]," one executive explains. "And when we go to Washington, we're an American company."

Exhibit 3.8   South Korea's Samsung is a leading manufacturer of giant high-definition TVs. Samsung produces the largest curved ultra-high-definition (UHD) screens for the worldwide home-theater market. Samsung's monster 110-inch curved UHD screen is among the world's largest such screens. Unfortunately, for most of the world's consumers, the giant Samsung TVs can be too costly, but the 88-inch version can be purchased for under $20,000. *How does being a multinational corporation enable Samsung to succeed in the high-end electronics market?* (Credit: Chris F/ Flickr/ Attribution 2.0 Generic (CC BY 2.0))

Multinationals can also shift production from one plant to another as market conditions change. When European demand for a certain solvent declined, Dow Chemical instructed its German plant to switch to manufacturing a chemical that had been imported from Louisiana and Texas. Computer models help Dow make decisions like these so it can run its plants more efficiently and keep costs down.

The World's Top 11 Largest Multinational Corporations			
RANK	RANK COMPANY	Revenues ($M)	Home Country
1	Walmart	$482,130	United States
2	State Grid	$329,601	China
3	China National Petroleum	$299,271	China
4	Sinopec Group	$294,344	China
5	Royal Dutch Shell	$272,156	Netherlands
6	Exxon Mobil	$246,204	United States
7	Volkswagen	$236,600	Germany
8	Toyota Motor	$236,592	Japan
9	Apple	$233,715	United States

The World's Top 11 Largest Multinational Corporations			
RANK	RANK COMPANY	Revenues ($M)	Home Country
10	BP	$225,982	United Kingdom
11	Berkshire Hathaway	$210,821	United States

Table 3.3 Source: Adapted from "The World's Largest Corporations," *Fortune* http://fortune.com/global500/, accessed June 30, 2017.

EXPANDING AROUND THE GLOBE

U.S. Brands Face Global Competition

America is the cradle of the consumer goods brand. Here, a free-spending and marketing-saturated public nurtured Apple, Google, Coca-Cola, Microsoft, and countless others to maturity. Many of those brands grew up to conquer other societies, as well.

But American brands' domination in the global marketplace is eroding. From Samsung to Toyota to Mercedes Benz to SAP, companies in Europe and Asia are turning out top-quality goods and selling them as such rather than competing on price. "There are longer-term trends toward greater competition. The United States was the only global brand country [but] that's no longer the case," says Earl L. Taylor, chief marketing officer of the Marketing Science Institute. "Consumers prefer brands that they take to be of higher quality" regardless of the country of origin, he notes. "Increasingly, there will be other successful global brands in the U.S. [market]."

Of the brands at the top of Interbrand's recent list of the world's most valuable, four of the top five still originate in the United States; the five most valuable are Apple, Google, Coca-Cola, and Microsoft, while Toyota (Japan) comes in at number five. American companies have lost the most ground in the middle tier of recognizable brand names, says George T. Haley, professor of marketing at the University of New Haven's School of Business.

One area from which U.S. brands are feeling the pressure is the Asia-Pacific region, which harbors the fastest-growing emerging markets today. In the appliance category, two Chinese companies, Haier and Kelon, are becoming top competitors for well-known U.S. brands Whirlpool and Maytag. In fact, Haier bought GE's appliance division in 2016. The Chinese branding trend is not confined only to hard goods. Sporting goods and sportswear brand Li Ning, well known within China, is building its international profile. While the Chinese basketball team wore Nike uniforms at the Athens Olympic Games, the Spanish team wore Li Ning apparel. The threat to U.S. brands is not confined to China, however. South Korean brands, such as Samsung, LG, and Hyundai, have emerged on the global stage in specific categories, such as smartphones, household appliances, and automobiles.

The animosity that many Europeans feel toward the United States is translated into a preference for European or even Asian brands at the expense of U.S. brands. Plus, experts say, European brands are simply becoming stronger and more consistent.

Meanwhile, European brands are gaining momentum in the areas of white goods and consumer goods, putting the pressure on such well-known U.S. brands as Bissell and Hoover, experts say. For instance, Gaggenau is a popular, high-end European kitchen appliance brand, along with Bosch and Dyson. Other European brands maintaining cachet—if not always the allure of luxury—include Absolut, Virgin, Mini (as in Cooper), Red Bull, and Ikea.

Critical Thinking Questions

1. What can U.S. multinational firms do to regain and maintain their leadership in global branding? Are there sectors and product areas where U.S. brands are gaining share?
2. Do you think that the quality of American products and services is declining, or that the rest of the world is just getting better? Explain your answer.

Sources: "Interbrand: Best Global Brands 2016 Rankings," http://interbrand.com, accessed June 30, 2017; Vasileios Davvetas and Adamantios Diamantopoulos (2016), "How Product Category Shapes Preferences toward Global and Local Brands: A Schema Theory Perspective," *Journal of International Marketing*, 24 (4), 61–81; Deborah Vence, "Not Taking Care of Business?" *Marketing News,* March 15, 2005, pp. 19–20.

Multinationals can also tap new technology from around the world. In the United States, Xerox has introduced some 80 different office copiers that were designed and built by Fuji Xerox, its joint venture with a Japanese company. Versions of the super-concentrated detergent that Procter & Gamble first formulated in Japan in response to a rival's product are now being sold under the Ariel brand name in Europe and under the Cheer and Tide labels in the United States. Also, consider Otis Elevator's development of the Elevonic 411, an elevator that is programmed to send more cars to floors where demand is high. It was developed by six research centers in five countries. Otis's group in Farmington, Connecticut, handled the systems integration, a Japanese group designed the special motor drives that make the elevators ride smoothly, a French group perfected the door systems, a German group handled the electronics, and a Spanish group took care of the small-geared components. Otis says the international effort saved more than $10 million in design costs and cut the process from four years to two.

Finally, multinationals can often save a lot in labor costs, even in highly unionized countries. For example, when Xerox started moving copier-rebuilding work to Mexico to take advantage of the lower wages, its union in Rochester, New York, objected because it saw that members' jobs were at risk. Eventually, the union agreed to change work styles and to improve productivity to keep the jobs at home.

CONCEPT CHECK

1. What is a multinational corporation?
2. What are the advantages of multinationals?

3.9 Trends in Global Competition

9. What are the trends in the global marketplace?

In this section, we will examine several underlying trends that will continue to propel the dramatic growth in world trade. These trends are market expansion, resource acquisition, and the emergence of China and India.

Market Expansion

The need for businesses to expand their markets is perhaps the most fundamental reason for the growth in world trade. The limited size of domestic markets often motivates managers to seek markets beyond their national frontiers. The economies of large-scale manufacturing demand big markets. Domestic markets, particularly in smaller countries like Denmark and the Netherlands, simply can't generate enough demand. Nestlé was one of the first businesses to "go global" because its home country, Switzerland, is so small. Nestlé was shipping milk to 16 different countries as early as 1875. Today, hundreds of thousands of businesses are recognizing the potential rich rewards to be found in international markets.

Resource Acquisition

More and more companies are going to the global marketplace to acquire the resources they need to operate efficiently. These resources may be cheap or skilled labor, scarce raw materials, technology, or capital. Nike, for example, has manufacturing facilities in many Asian countries in order to use cheaper labor. Honda opened a design studio in southern California to put that "California flair" into the design of some of its vehicles. Large multinational banks such as Bank of New York and Citigroup have offices in Geneva, Switzerland. Geneva is the private banking center of Europe and attracts capital from around the globe.

The Emergence of China and India

China and India—two of the world's economic powerhouses—are impacting businesses around the globe, in very different ways. The boom in China's worldwide exports has left few sectors unscathed, be they garlic growers in California, jeans makers in Mexico, or plastic-mold manufacturers in South Korea. India's impact has altered how hundreds of service companies from Texas to Ireland compete for billions of dollars in contracts.

The causes and consequences of each nation's growth are somewhat different. China's exports have boomed largely thanks to foreign investment: lured by low labor costs, big manufacturers have surged into China to expand their production base and push down prices globally. Now manufacturers of all sizes, making everything from windshield wipers to washing machines to clothing, are scrambling either to reduce costs at home or to outsource more of what they make in cheaper locales such as China and India.[39]

Indians are playing invaluable roles in the global innovation chain. Hewlett-Packard, Cisco Systems, and other tech giants now rely on their Indian teams to devise software platforms and multimedia features for next-generation devices. Google principal scientist Krishna Bharat set up the Google Bangalore lab complete with colorful furniture, exercise balls, and a Yamaha organ—like Google's Mountain View, California, headquarters—to work on core search-engine technology. Indian engineering houses use 3-D computer simulations to tweak designs of everything from car engines and forklifts to aircraft wings for such clients as General Motors Corp. and Boeing Co. Barring unforeseen circumstances, within five years India should vault over Germany as the world's fourth-biggest economy. By mid-century, China should overtake the United States as number one. By then, China and India could account for half of global output.[40]

ETHICS IN PRACTICE

The United Nations Sustainability Development Goals

Corporations like Albertson's, Unilever, Kimberly Clark, and Siemens are starting to take action on the United Nations Sustainability Development Goals. For many years, through corporate social responsibility (CSR) programs, corporations have donated money and employee time to address various social and environmental problems, both globally and in their own backyards. The Carnegie Foundation and the Bill and Melinda Gates Foundation are examples of this commitment. While these efforts have achieved some progress in environmental protection, ethical business practices, building sustainable positive impacts, and economic development by organizations, they do require deeper and longer engagement. Because the benefits to corporations' profitability are mostly peripheral, short-term impacts such as a drop in demand often mean that attention is drawn away from CSR programs to attending to immediate bottom-line issues.

In 2015, the United Nations member-nations adopted 17 resolutions aimed at ending poverty, ensuring sustainability, and ensuring prosperity for all. The aggressive goals were set to be met over the next 15 years.

1. End poverty in all its forms everywhere.
2. End hunger, achieve food security and improved nutrition, and promote sustainable agriculture.
3. Ensure healthy lives and promote well-being for all at all ages.
4. Ensure inclusive and equitable quality education and promote lifelong learning opportunities for all.
5. Achieve gender equality and empower all women and girls.
6. Ensure availability and sustainable management of water and sanitation for all.
7. Ensure access to affordable, reliable, sustainable, modern energy for all.
8. Promote sustained, inclusive, sustainable economic growth; full and productive employment; and decent work for all.
9. Build resilient infrastructure, promote inclusive and sustainable industrialization, and foster innovation.
10. Reduce inequality within and among countries.
11. Make cities and human settlements inclusive, safe, resilient, and sustainable.
12. Ensure sustainable consumption and production patterns.
13. Take urgent action to combat climate change and its impacts.
14. Conserve and sustainably use the oceans, seas, and marine resources for sustainable development.
15. Protect, restore, and promote sustainable use of terrestrial ecosystems; sustainably manage forests; combat desertification and halt and reverse land degradation; and halt biodiversity loss.
16. Promote peaceful and inclusive societies for sustainable development; provide access to justice for all; and build effective, accountable, inclusive institutions at all levels.
17. Strengthen the means of implementation and revitalize the global partnership for sustainable development.

Companies like Albertson's recognize that a robust CSR program can enhance a corporation's reputation, which can indirectly boost the bottom line. They used number 14 on the United Nations Sustainability Development list in concert with World Oceans Day to announce that they as a company pledged to meet the U.N. goals. "We recognize that the wellbeing of people and the sustainability of our oceans are interdependent. As one of the largest U.S. retailers of seafood, we are committed to protecting the world's oceans so they can remain a bountiful natural resource that contributes to global food security, the livelihoods of hard-working fishermen and the global economy," said Buster Houston, Director of Seafood at Albertson's Companies. The company is also committed to the concept of fair trade and was the first retailer to sell tuna with the fair trade seal.

Siemens, the German-based multinational, also supported the adoption of meeting the United Nations Sustainability Development goals, which they believe is based on their company values—responsible, excellent, innovative. They define sustainable development as the means to achieve profitable and long-term growth. In doing so, they align ourselves with the goals of the UN's 2030 Agenda for Sustainable Development.

Critical Thinking Questions

1. Why would companies pledge to meet the United Nations Sustainability Development goals when their competitors could ignore them in the name of greater, perhaps short-term, profits?

2. Are you as a consumer more likely to purchase products from Albertson's rather than another grocery chain that did not agree to the United Nations sustainability program? If you were working for a company deciding to purchase a large industrial component that was 10% more expensive than a competing product, would Siemens's affirmation of meeting the United Nations Sustainability Development goals sway your decision? How would you explain the rationale for your decision?

Sources: Thane Kreiner, "Corporations and Social Entrepreneurship: A Shift?" https://www.scu.edu, accessed June 30, 2017; United Nations Sustainable Development website: http://www.un.org, accessed June 30, 2017; "Practicing Sustainability—in the Interest of Future Generations," https://www.siemens.com, accessed June 30, 2017; "Albertsons Companies Commits to United Nations Sustainable Development Goals, Joins Influential Seafood Task Force," *Cision PR Newswire*, http://www.prnewswire.com, June 6, 2017; Ingrid Embree, "How 17 Companies Are Tackling Sustainable Development Goals (and Your Company Can, Too)," *Huffington Post,* http://www.huffingtonpost.com, September 14, 2016.

An accelerating trend is that technical and managerial skills in both China and India are becoming more important than cheap assembly labor. China will stay dominant in mass manufacturing and is one of the few nations building multibillion-dollar electronics and heavy industrial plants. India is a rising power in software, design, services, and precision industry.

CONCEPT CHECK

1. What trends will foster continued growth in world trade?
2. Describe some of the ways businesses can take advantage of these trends to "go global."

🔑 Key Terms

absolute advantage The situation when a country can produce and sell a product at a lower cost than any other country or when it is the only country that can provide the product.

balance of payments A summary of a country's international financial transactions showing the difference between the country's total payments to and its total receipts from other countries.

balance of trade The difference between the value of a country's exports and the value of its imports during a specific time.

buy-national regulations Government rules that give special privileges to domestic manufacturers and retailers.

contract manufacturing The practice in which a foreign firm manufactures private-label goods under a domestic firm's brand name.

countertrade A form of international trade in which part or all of the payment for goods or services is in the form of other goods and services.

devaluation A lowering of the value of a nation's currency relative to other currencies.

direct foreign investment Active ownership of a foreign company or of manufacturing or marketing facilities in a foreign country.

dumping The practice of charging a lower price for a product in foreign markets than in the firm's home market.

embargo A total ban on imports or exports of a product.

European integration The delegation of limited sovereignty by European Union member states to the EU so that common laws and policies can be created at the European level.

European Union Trade agreement among 28 European nations.

exchange controls Laws that require a company earning foreign exchange (foreign currency) from its exports to sell the foreign exchange to a control agency, such as a central bank.

exporting The practice of selling domestically produced goods to buyers in another country.

exports Goods and services produced in one country and sold to other countries.

floating exchange rates A system in which prices of currencies move up and down based upon the demand for and supply of the various currencies.

free trade The policy of permitting the people and businesses of a country to buy and sell where they please without restrictions.

free-trade zone An area where the nations allow free, or almost free, trade among each other while imposing tariffs on goods of nations outside the zone.

G20 Informal group that brings together 19 countries and the European Union—the 20 leading economies in the world.

global vision The ability to recognize and react to international business opportunities, be aware of threats from foreign competition, and effectively use international distribution networks to obtain raw materials and move finished products to customers.

import quota A limit on the quantity of a certain good that can be imported.

imports Goods and services that are bought from other countries.

infrastructure The basic institutions and public facilities upon which an economy's development depends.

International Monetary Fund (IMF) An international organization, founded in 1945, that promotes trade, makes short-term loans to member nations, and acts as a lender of last resort for troubled nations.

joint venture An agreement in which a domestic firm buys part of a foreign firm or joins with a foreign firm to create a new entity.

licensing The legal process whereby a firm agrees to allow another firm to use a manufacturing process, trademark, patent, trade secret, or other proprietary knowledge in exchange for the payment of a royalty.

Mercosur Trade agreement between Peru, Brazil, Argentina, Uruguay, and Paraguay.

multinational corporations Corporations that move resources, goods, services, and skills across national boundaries without regard to the country in which their headquarters are located.

nationalism A sense of national consciousness that boosts the culture and interests of one country over those of all other countries.

North American Free Trade Agreement (NAFTA) A 1993 agreement creating a free-trade zone including Canada, Mexico, and the United States.

outsourcing Sending work functions to another country, resulting in domestic workers losing their jobs.

preferential tariff A tariff that is lower for some nations than for others.

principle of comparative advantage The concept that each country should specialize in the products that it can produce most readily and cheaply and trade those products for those that other countries can produce more readily and cheaply.

protectionism The policy of protecting home industries from outside competition by establishing artificial barriers such as tariffs and quotas.

protective tariffs Tariffs that are imposed in order to make imports less attractive to buyers than domestic products are.

tariff A tax imposed on imported goods.

trade deficit An unfavorable balance of trade that occurs when a country imports more than it exports.

trade surplus A favorable balance of trade that occurs when a country exports more than it imports.

Uruguay Round A 1994 agreement originally signed by 117 nations to lower trade barriers worldwide.

World Bank An international bank that offers low-interest loans, as well as advice and information, to developing nations.

World Trade Organization (WTO) An organization established by the Uruguay Round in 1994 to oversee international trade, reduce trade barriers, and resolve disputes among member nations.

Summary of Learning Outcomes

3.1 Global Trade in the United States
1. Why is global trade important to the United States, and how is it measured?

International trade improves relations with friends and allies, eases tensions among nations, helps bolster economies, raises people's standard of living, and improves the quality of life. The United States is still the largest importer and exporter in the world. We export a fifth of our industrial production and about a third of our farm crops.

Two concepts important to global trade are the balance of trade (the difference in value between a country's exports and its imports over some period) and the balance of payments (the difference between a country's total payments to other countries and its total receipts from other countries). The United States now has both a negative balance of trade and a negative balance of payments. Another important concept is the exchange rate, which is the price of one country's currency in terms of another country's currency. Currencies float up and down based upon the supply of and demand for each currency. Sometimes a government steps in and devalues its currency relative to the currencies of other countries.

3.2 Why Nations Trade
2. Why do nations trade?

Nations trade because they gain by doing so. The principle of comparative advantage states that each country should specialize in the goods it can produce most readily and cheaply and trade them for those that other countries can produce most readily and cheaply. The result is more goods at lower prices than if each country produced by itself everything it needed. Free trade allows trade among nations without government restrictions.

3.3 Barriers to Trade

3. What are the barriers to international trade?

The three major barriers to international trade are natural barriers, such as distance and language; tariff barriers, or taxes on imported goods; and nontariff barriers. The nontariff barriers to trade include import quotas, embargoes, buy-national regulations, and exchange controls. The main argument against tariffs is that they discourage free trade and keep the principle of comparative advantage from working efficiently. The main argument for using tariffs is that they help protect domestic companies, industries, and workers.

3.4 Fostering Global Trade

4. How do governments and institutions foster world trade?

The World Trade Organization, established by the Uruguay Round of trade negotiations, has dramatically lowered trade barriers worldwide. For the first time, a trade agreement covers services, intellectual property rights, and exchange controls. The World Bank makes loans to developing nations to help build infrastructures. The International Monetary Fund makes loans to member nations that cannot meet their budgetary expenses. Despite efforts to expand trade, terrorism can have a negative impact on trade growth.

3.5 International Economic Communities

5. What are international economic communities?

International economic communities reduce trade barriers among themselves while often establishing common tariffs and other trade barriers toward nonmember countries. The best-known economic communities are the European Union, NAFTA, CAFTA, and Mercosur.

3.6 Participating in the Global Marketplace

6. How do companies enter the global marketplace?

There are a number of ways to enter the global market. The major ones are exporting, licensing, contract manufacturing, joint ventures, and direct investment.

3.7 Threats and Opportunities in the Global Marketplace

7. What threats and opportunities exist in the global marketplace?

Domestic firms entering the international arena need to consider the politics, economies, and culture of the countries where they plan to do business. For example, government trade policies can be loose or restrictive, countries can be nationalistic, and governments can change. In the area of culture, many products fail because companies don't understand the culture of the country where they are trying to sell their products. Some developing countries also lack an economic infrastructure, which often makes it very difficult to conduct business.

3.8 The Impact of Multinational Corporations

8. What are the advantages of multinational corporations?

Multinational corporations have several advantages. First, they can sidestep restrictive trade and licensing restrictions because they frequently have headquarters in more than one country. Multinationals can also move their operations from one country to the next depending on which location offers more favorable economic conditions. In addition, multinationals can tap into a vast source of technological expertise by drawing upon the knowledge of a global workforce.

3.9 Trends in Global Competition
9.   What are the trends in the global marketplace?

Global business activity will continue to escalate due to several factors. Firms that desire a larger customer base or need additional resources will continue to seek opportunities outside their country's borders. China and India are emerging as global economic powerhouses.

Preparing for Tomorrow's Workplace Skills

1.   How can a country's customs create barriers to trade? Ask foreign students to describe such barriers in their country. American students should give examples of problems that foreign businesspeople might experience with American customs. (Information)
2.   Should the United Kingdom exit the European Union? Why might Britain not wish to exit? (Systems)
3.   Do you think that CAFTA will have a major impact on the U.S. economy? Why? (Systems)
4.   What do you think is the best way for a small company to enter international trade? Why? (Information)
5.   How can the United States compete against China and India in the long run? (Information)
6.   Identify some U.S. multinational companies that have been successful in world markets. How do you think they have achieved their success? (Information)
7.   **Team Activity** Divide the class into teams. Each team should choose a country and research its infrastructure to determine how it will help or hinder trade. Include a variety of countries, ranging from the most highly developed to the least developed. (Resources, Interpersonal, Information, Technology)

Ethics Activity

The executives of a clothing manufacturer want to outsource some of their manufacturing to more cost-efficient locations in Indonesia. After visiting several possible sites, they choose one and begin to negotiate with local officials. They discover that it will take about six months to get the necessary permits. One of the local politicians approaches the executives over dinner and hints that he can speed up the process for an advisory fee of $5,000.

Using a web search tool, locate articles about this topic, and then write responses to the following questions. Be sure to support your arguments and cite your sources.

Ethical Dilemma: Is paying the advisory fee a bribe or an acceptable cost of doing business in that area of the world? What should the executives do before agreeing to pay the fee?

Sources: Eric Markowitz, "The Truth about Bribery and Doing Foreign Business," *Inc.*, https://www.inc.com, accessed March 19, 2018; Roberto A. Ferdman, "How the World's Biggest Companies Bribe Foreign Governments," *The Washington Post,* https://www.washingtonpost.com, accessed March 19, 2018; David Rising, "The 10 Countries Most Likely to Use Bribery in Business," *Huffington Post*, https://www.huffingtonpost.com, accessed March 19, 2018.

Working the Net

1. Go to the Trade Compliance Center site at http://tcc.export.gov. Click on Foreign Trade Barrier Examples, and then search the reports. Pick a country that interests you from the index, and read the most current available reports for that country. Would this country be a good market for a small U.S. motor scooter manufacturer interested in expanding internationally? Why or why not? What are the main barriers to trade the company might face?

2. While still at the Trade Compliance Center site, http://tcc.export.gov, click on Trade Agreements and then List All Agreements. Select one that interests you, and summarize what you learn about it.

3. Review the historical data about exchange rates between the U.S. dollar and the Japanese yen available at http://www.x-rates.com. Pull up charts comparing the yen to the dollar for several years. List any trends you spot. What years would have been best for a U.S. company to enter the Japanese marketplace? Given current exchange rate conditions, do you think Japanese companies are increasing or decreasing their exporting efforts in the United States?

4. Visit Foreign Trade Online, http://www.foreign-trade.com, and browse through the resources of this international business-to-business trade portal. What types of information does the site provide? Which would be most useful to a company looking to begin exporting? To a company who already exports and wants to find new markets? Rate the usefulness of the site and the information it offers.

5. Go to http://www.fita.org, which is the Federation of International Trade Associations. Click on Really Useful Links for International Trade. Follow five of those links, and explain how they would help a U.S. manufacturer that wanted to go global.

6. Go to the World Trade Organization site at http://www.wto.org. Next, click on WTO News. Inform the class about current activities and actions at the WTO.

7. Go to http://www.worldbank.org and then to http://www.imf.org. Compare the types of information available on each website. Pick one example from each site, and report your findings to the class.

Critical Thinking Case

We Want Our MTV (International)

MTV, a division of Viacom International Media Networks and a mainstay of American pop culture, is just as popular in Shanghai as it is in Seattle and Sydney, or in Lagos (Nigeria) as it is in Los Angeles. MTV is a division of Viacom, and their international divisions are called the Viacom International Media Networks. London-based MTV Networks International, the world's largest global network, has taken its winning formula to 167 foreign markets on six continents, including urban and rural areas. It reaches 4 billion homes in 40 languages through locally programmed and locally operated TV channels and websites. While the United States currently generates about 70 percent of MTV's profits, 85 percent of the company's subscriber base lives outside the United States.

The MTV brand has evolved beyond its music television roots into a multimedia lifestyle, entertainment, and culture brand for all ages. In addition to MTV and MTV2, its channel lineup includes Nickelodeon, VH1, Comedy Central, LOGO, TMF (The Music Factory), Game One, and several European music, comedy, and lifestyle channels, as well as Paramount Channel, Spike, and a growing number of flagship local networks such as Channel 5 in the UK, Telefe in Argentina, and COLORS in India. Adding to the complexity is MTV's multimedia and interactive nature, with gaming, texting, and websites, as well as television. Another challenge is integrating acquisitions of local companies such as South American Telefe, which it purchased in 2016.

The company also has an international insights team that gathers the latest consumer insights from around the world. You can get some insight into this initiative at https://insights.viacom.com. The local perspective is invaluable in helping the network understand its markets, whether in terms of musical tastes or what entertainment children like. For example, Alex Okosi, a Nigerian who went to college in the United States, is chief executive for MTV Base, which launched in sub-Saharan Africa in 2005. Okosi recommended that MTV consider each country as an individual market, rather than blending them all together.

One reason for MTVNI's success is "glocalization"—its ability to adapt programs to fit local cultures while still maintaining a consistent, special style. "When we set a channel up, we always provide a set of parameters in terms of standards of things we require," an MTV executive explains. "Obviously an MTV channel that doesn't look good enough is not going to do the business for us, let alone for the audience. There's a higher expectation." Then the local unit can tailor content to its market. MTV India conveys a "sense of the colorful street culture," explains Bill Roedy, former MTV Networks International president, while MTV Japan has "a sense of technology edginess; MTV Italy, style and elegance." In Africa, MTV Base features videos from top African artists as well as from emerging African music talent. According to company executives, the goal is to "provide a unique cultural meeting point for young people in Africa, using the common language of music to connect music fans from different backgrounds and cultures."

Critical Thinking Questions

1. Do you think that MTV's future lies mostly in its international operations? Explain your reasoning.
2. What types of political, economic, and competitive challenges does MTV Networks International face by operating worldwide?
3. How has MTV Networks International overcome cultural differences to create a world brand?

Sources: MTV Viacom Blog, http://blog.viacom.com, accessed June 30, 2017; *MTV International* website, http://www.mtv.com/, accessed June 30, 2017; MTV Consumer Insights website, https://insights.viacom.com, accessed June 30, 2017.

Hot Links Address Book

1. A good starting place for help in doing business in foreign markets is the U.S. government's export portal. Here you will find links to export basics, regulations, exchange rates, country and industry research, and much more. http://www.export.gov
2. For links to a wealth of statistics on world trade, go to the U.S. International Trade Administration's (ITA) Office of Trade and Economic Analysis website, http://www.ita.doc.gov.
3. Check out the current U.S. balance of trade with various countries at http://www.bea.gov.
4. Get up-to-the-minute exchange rates at http://www.xe.com.
5. The World Trade Organization tracks the latest trade developments between countries and regions around the world. For the most recent global trading news, visit the WTO's website at http://www.wto.org.
6. Gain additional insight into the workings of the International Monetary Fund at http://www.imf.org.
7. For the latest information about NAFTA, visit http://www.naftanow.org.
8. Think you'd like to work overseas? For information about jobs in foreign countries, visit http://www.internationaljobs.com.

4 Forms of Business Ownership

Exhibit 4.1 (Credit: pxhere / Attribution CC0 Public Domain)

 Introduction

Learning Outcomes

After reading this chapter, you should be able to answer these questions:

1. What are the advantages and disadvantages of the sole proprietorship form of business organization?
2. What are the advantages of operating as a partnership, and what downside risks should partners consider?
3. How does the corporate structure provide advantages and disadvantages to a company, and what are the major types of corporations?
4. What other options for business organization does a company have in addition to sole proprietorships, partnerships, and corporations?
5. What makes franchising an appropriate form of organization for some types of business, and why does it continue to grow in importance?
6. Why are mergers and acquisitions important to a company's overall growth?
7. What current trends will affect the business organizations of the future?

EXPLORING BUSINESS CAREERS

Jessica MacLean

Sole Proprietor

In most any elementary school classroom, at least one child's answer to the question, "What do you want to do with your life?" will be, "A lawyer." One of the most popular careers, lawyers are powerful figures in society, shaping our laws and ensuring that we adhere to them. Their prominence and power have led to the stereotype of rich, career-driven lawyers, often leaving no room in our minds for those who truly want to bring justice to the world. However, Jessica MacLean, a lawyer focusing primarily on women's rights, is quick to say that, as with many stereotypes, that is only one side of the story. "I know because I lived that—I was on my way to being a successful corporate lawyer. But I realized what I was doing and how different that was from why I'd started practicing. So I walked away from it all to start my own practice."

Nervous about the prospect of private practice, she has chosen to operate as a sole proprietorship for now. Sole proprietorships are easy to set up for people who want to work on their own, prefer direct control of the business, and desire the flexibility to sell the business or close the doors at any time. "For me, it's the best choice because I am not responsible for or to anyone else. I can easily dissolve the business if I find it is not proceeding how I'd planned. More positively, too, if it does succeed, I know that success is due to my hard work.

Indeed MacLean's law career was not always in corporate law. She turned her sights toward law after a gender and communications professor at DePaul University suggested her argumentative style might be an asset in that profession. "She said I needed to tone it down for class—that the other students seemed afraid to speak up—but then asked if I'd ever considered being a lawyer." MacLean, who had always been interested in issues of justice and legality surrounding women, took her professor's advice and made the leap into law.

While in law school, she clerked for the city of Chicago in their department of personnel's sexual harassment office and volunteered for the Cook County state's attorney's office in the domestic violence division. The cases she worked on were emotionally trying. Despite the difficulty of the cases, she was drawn to them, compelled by the people she helped and the change she was able to effect. After school, she continued in related practice, working first for the Cook County state's attorney's office.

After several years with the state's attorney's office, she needed a change. It was then that MacLean decided to work for a corporation, a form of business that you will learn about in this chapter. "Why did I switch to corporate law? I think I was burnt out, to some extent. It's so hard to work on those cases, day after day. I needed to see if I would be better somewhere else."

Having enjoyed the rewards of working with the state's attorney's office and a corporation and being a sole proprietor, in 2014 MacLean joined a limited liability partnership (LLP, a form of business that you will learn about in this chapter) firm in Chicago. As her needs changed, the form and type of business organization she has worked for has changed also.

This chapter discusses sole proprietorships, as well as several other forms of business ownership, including partnerships and corporations, and compares the advantages and disadvantages of each.

With a good idea and some cash in hand, you decide to start a business. But before you get going, you need to ask yourself some questions that will help you decide what form of business organization will best suit your needs.

Would you prefer to go it alone as a *sole proprietorship,* or do you want others to share your burdens and challenges in a *partnership*? Or would the limited liability protection of a *corporation,* or perhaps the flexibility of a *limited liability company (LLC),* make more sense?

There are other questions you need to consider too: Will you need financing? How easy will it be to obtain?

Will you attract employees? How will the business be taxed, and who will be liable for the company's debts? If you choose to share ownership with others, how much operating control would they want, and what costs would be associated with that?

As **Table 4.1** illustrates, sole proprietorships are the most popular form of business ownership, accounting for 72 percent of all businesses, compared with 10 percent for partnerships and 18 percent for corporations. Because most sole proprietorships and partnerships remain small, corporations generate approximately 81 percent of total business revenues and 58 percent of total profits.

Most start-up businesses select one of these major ownership forms. In the following pages, we will discover the advantages and disadvantages of each form of business ownership and the factors that may make it necessary to change from one form of organization to another as the needs of the business change. As a company expands from small to midsize or larger, the form of business structure selected in the beginning may no longer be appropriate.

4.1   Going It Alone: Sole Proprietorships

1. What are the advantages and disadvantages of the sole proprietorship form of business organization?

Jeremy Shepherd was working full-time for an airline when, at the age of 22, he wandered into an exotic pearl market in China, searching for a gift for his girlfriend. The strand of pearls he handpicked by instinct was later valued by a jeweler back in the States at 20 times what he paid for it. Jeremy cashed his next paycheck and hurried back to Asia, buying every pearl he could afford. Founded in 1996, his company Pearl Paradise was brought online in 2000. Shepherd chose the **sole proprietorship** form of business organization—a business that is established, owned, operated, and often financed by one person—because it was the easiest to set up. He did not want partners, and low liability exposure made incorporating unnecessary.

Fluent in Mandarin Chinese, Japanese, and Spanish and immersed in Asian culture, Shepherd believed the internet was the way to market his pearls (**http://www.pearlparadise.com**). Offering a wide range of pearl jewelry through 14 websites worldwide, his company sells as many as 1,000 items per day. The recent addition of an exclusive Los Angeles showroom allows celebrity customers to shop by appointment. With $20 million in sales annually, PearlParadise.com is the industry leader in terms of sales and volume.[1]

Comparison of Forms of Business Organization			
Form	Number	Sales	Profits
Sole Proprietorships	72 percent	4 percent	15 percent
Partnerships	10 percent	15 percent	27 percent
Corporations	18 percent	81 percent	58 percent

Table 4.1 Source: Internal Revenue Service, as reported in Table 746, U.S. Bureau of the Census, *Statistical Abstract of the United States, 2012,* 131st ed. (Washington, DC: U.S. Government Printing Office, 2012), p. 492. Note: US Bureau of Census stopped collecting and publishing this data after 2012.

Advantages of Sole Proprietorships

Sole proprietorships have several advantages that make them popular:

- *Easy and inexpensive to form*. As Jeremy Shepherd discovered, sole proprietorships have few legal requirements (local licenses and permits) and are not expensive to form, making them the business organization of choice for many small companies and start-ups.
- *Profits all go to the owner*. The owner of a sole proprietorship obtains the start-up funds and gets all the profits earned by the business. The more efficiently the firm operates, the higher the company's profitability.
- *Direct control of the business*. All business decisions are made by the sole proprietorship owner without having to consult anyone else.
- *Freedom from government regulation*. Sole proprietorships have more freedom than other forms of business with respect to government controls.
- *No special taxation*. Sole proprietorships do not pay special franchise or corporate taxes. Profits are taxed as personal income as reported on the owner's individual tax return.
- *Ease of dissolution*. With no co-owners or partners, the sole proprietor can sell the business or close the doors at any time, making this form of business organization an ideal way to test a new business idea.

Disadvantages of Sole Proprietorships

Along with the freedom to operate the business as they wish, sole proprietors face several disadvantages:

- *Unlimited liability.* From a legal standpoint, the sole proprietor and the company are one and the same, making the business owner personally responsible for all debts the company incurs, even if they exceed the company's value. The owner may need to sell other personal property—their car, home, or other investments—to satisfy claims against the business.
- *Difficulty raising capital.* Business assets are unprotected against claims of personal creditors, so business lenders view sole proprietorships as high risk due to the owner's unlimited liability. Owners must often use personal funds—borrowing on credit cards, second-mortgaging their homes, or selling investments—to finance their business. Expansion plans can also be affected by an inability to raise additional funding.
- *Limited managerial expertise.* The success of a sole proprietorship rests solely with the skills and talents of the owner, who must wear many different hats and make all decisions. Owners are often not equally skilled in all areas of running a business. A graphic designer may be a wonderful artist but not know bookkeeping, how to manage production, or how to market their work.
- *Trouble finding qualified employees.* Sole proprietors often cannot offer the same pay, fringe benefits, and advancement as larger companies, making them less attractive to employees seeking the most favorable employment opportunities.
- *Personal time commitment.* Running a sole proprietorship business requires personal sacrifices and a huge time commitment, often dominating the owner's life with 12-hour workdays and 7-day workweeks.
- *Unstable business life.* The life span of a sole proprietorship can be uncertain. The owner may lose interest, experience ill health, retire, or die. The business will cease to exist unless the owner makes provisions for it to continue operating or puts it up for sale.
- *Losses are the owner's responsibility.* The sole proprietor is responsible for all losses, although tax laws allow these to be deducted from other personal income.

The sole proprietorship may be a suitable choice for a one-person start-up operation with no employees and little risk of liability exposure. For many sole proprietors, however, this is a temporary choice, and as the business grows, the owner may be unable to operate with limited financial and managerial resources. At this point, the owner may decide to take in one or more partners to ensure that the business continues to flourish.

CATCHING THE ENTREPRENEURIAL SPIRIT

Work-Life Balance Important in Small Business

According to a survey released by the Wells Fargo/Gallup Small Business Index, about two-thirds of small business owners are satisfied with how they balance their personal lives and work schedules, and the New York Enterprise Report survey found that they work twice as much as regular employees. The survey also found that 33 percent of small business owners work more than 50 hours per week, while 25 percent reported working over 60 hours per week. A survey by Gallup finds 39 percent of small business owners working over 60 hours per week.

The 2016 Annual Bank of the West Small Business Growth Survey found that 62 percent of the respondents reported the stress of ownership as worse than what they had originally imagined. At the same time, the same people indicated that being a small business owner puts them in charge of their destiny, offers freedom, and is more rewarding than ever imagined. Over two-thirds of small business owners, according to a survey, said they were satisfied with their personal work-life balance, and almost 90 percent said they were satisfied with being a small business owner in general. Dennis Jacobe, chief economist at Gallup, argues, "People see the benefits more closely tied to them when they're the owner," he says. "Working hard and long is a natural aspect of the kind of people willing to start their own business."

But if employees have trouble balancing work and life, odds are they will have less confidence in you as a leader, a recent study shows. The study, which polled more than 50,000 U.S. workers from various markets including professional services, consumer goods, and financial services, found that employees who strike a positive balance between home and work were 11 percent more likely to praise their leaders' ability to set a clear direction.

The Society for Human Resource Management's (SHRM) research also shows work-life balance has a great impact on how employees feel about their leaders. Jennifer Schramm, a manager in SHRM's workplace trends and forecasting research department, predicts that as companies try to maximize the productivity of each employee, work-life balance and the resulting employee satisfaction will become increasingly more important. And research shows that happy employees can yield happy returns for businesses.

Critical Thinking Questions
1. Many small business owners expect their employees to be as committed and to work as hard as they do. How would you avoid falling into that trap while still demanding the best from your workers?
2. As a small business owner, consider some strategies to ensure an appropriate work-life balance for your employees.

Sources: Brian Sutter, "How Hard Small Business Owners Work," SCORE, https://www.score.org, accessed August 17, 2017; The Hartford Insurance Company, "2015 Small Business Success Study," accessed August 17, 2017; Michelle Di Gangi, "Attitude check: Small business owners say it's all worth it," July 26, 2016, Bank of the West; 2016 Annual Bank of the West Small Business Growth Survey, conducted by Harris Poll, July 26, 2016; Jena Wuu, "Work-Life Not an Issue for Owners," *Inc.*, http://www.inc.com, August 10, 2005; Christina Galoozis, "Employees View Leadership Through Lens of Work-Life Balance,"

Inc., http://www.inc.com, June 8, 2005.

4.2 Partnerships: Sharing the Load

2. What are the advantages of operating as a partnership, and what downside risks should partners consider?

Can **partnerships**, an association of two or more individuals who agree to operate a business together for profit, be hazardous to a business's health? Let's assume partners Ron and Liz own a stylish and successful beauty salon. After a few years of operating the business, they find they have contrasting visions for their company. Liz is happy with the status quo, while Ron wants to expand the business by bringing in investors and opening salons in other locations.

How do they resolve this impasse? By asking themselves some tough questions. Whose view of the future is more realistic? Does the business actually have the expansion potential Ron believes it does? Where will he find investors to make his dream of multiple locations a reality? Is he willing to dissolve the partnership and start over again on his own? And who would have the right to their clients?

Ron realizes that expanding the business in line with his vision would require a large financial risk and that his partnership with Liz offers many advantages he would miss in a sole proprietorship form of business organization. After much consideration, he decides to leave things as they are.

For those individuals who do not like to "go it alone," a partnership is relatively simple to set up. Offering a shared form of business ownership, it is a popular choice for professional-service firms such as lawyers, accountants, architects, stockbrokers, and real estate companies.

The parties agree, *either orally or in writing,* to share in the profits and losses of a joint enterprise. A *written partnership agreement,* spelling out the terms and conditions of the partnership, *is recommended* to prevent later conflicts between the partners. Such agreements typically include the name of the partnership, its purpose, and the contributions of each partner (financial, asset, skill/talent). It also outlines the responsibilities and duties of each partner and their compensation structure (salary, profit sharing, etc.). It should contain provisions for the addition of new partners, the sale of partnership interests, and procedures for resolving conflicts, dissolving the business, and distributing the assets.

There are two basic types of partnerships: *general and limited.* In a **general partnership**, all partners share in the management and profits. They co-own the assets, and each can act on behalf of the firm. Each partner also has unlimited liability for all the business obligations of the firm. A **limited partnership** has two types of partners: one or more **general partners**, who have unlimited liability, and one or more **limited partners**, whose liability is limited to the amount of their investment. In return for limited liability, limited partners agree not to take part in the day-to-day management of the firm. They help to finance the business, but the general partners maintain operational control.

There are also limited liability partnerships (LLP), which are similar to a general partnership except that partners are not held responsible for the business debt and liabilities. Another type is a limited liability limited partnership (LLLP), which is basically a limited partnership with addition of limited liability, hence protecting the general partner from the debt and liabilities of the partnership.

Advantages of Partnerships

Some advantages of partnerships come quickly to mind:

- *Ease of formation.* Like sole proprietorships, partnerships are easy to form. The partners agree to do business together and draw up a *partnership agreement.* For most partnerships, applicable state laws are not complex.
- *Availability of capital.* Because two or more people contribute financial resources, partnerships can raise funds more easily for operating expenses and business expansion. The partners' combined financial strength also increases the firm's ability to raise funds from outside sources.
- *Diversity of skills and expertise.* Partners share the responsibilities of managing and operating the business. Combining partner skills to set goals, manage the overall direction of the firm, and solve problems increases the chances for the partnership's success. To find the right partner, you must examine your own strengths and weaknesses and know what you need from a partner. Ideal partnerships bring together people with complementary backgrounds rather than those with similar experience, skills, and talents. In Table 4.2 you'll find some advice on choosing a partner.
- *Flexibility.* General partners are actively involved in managing their firm and can respond quickly to changes in the business environment.
- *No special taxes.* Partnerships pay no income taxes. A partnership must file a partnership return with the Internal Revenue Service, reporting how profits or losses were divided among the partners. Each partner's profit or loss is then reported on the partner's personal income tax return, with any profits taxed at personal income tax rates.
- *Relative freedom from government control.* Except for state rules for licensing and permits, the government has little control over partnership activities.

Perfect Partners

Picking a partner is both an art and a science. Someone may have all the right credentials on paper, but does that person share your vision and the ideas you have for your company? Are they a straight shooter? Honesty, integrity, and ethics are important, because you may be liable for what your partner does. Be prepared to talk about everything, and trust your intuition and your gut feelings—they're probably right. Ask yourself and your potential partner the following questions—then see how well your answers match up:

1. Why do you want a partner?
2. What characteristics, talents, and skills does each person bring to the partnership?
3. How will you divide responsibilities—from long-range planning to daily operations? Who will handle such tasks as marketing, sales, accounting, and customer service?
4. What is your long-term vision for the business—its size, life span, financial commitment, etc.?
5. What are your personal reasons for forming this company? Are you looking to create a small company or build a large one? Are you seeking a steady paycheck or financial independence?
6. Will all parties put in the same amount of time, or is there an alternative arrangement that is acceptable to everyone?
7. Do you have similar work ethics and values?
8. What requirements will be in the partnership agreement?

Table 4.2

Disadvantages of Partnerships

Business owners must consider the following disadvantages of setting up their company as a partnership:

- *Unlimited liability.* All general partners have unlimited liability for the debts of the business. In fact, any one partner can be held personally liable for all partnership debts and legal judgments (such as malpractice)—regardless of who caused them. As with sole proprietorships, business failure can lead to a loss of the general partners' personal assets. To overcome this problem, many states now allow the formation of *limited liability partnerships (LLPs),* which protect each individual partner from responsibility for the acts of other partners and limit their liability to harm resulting from their own actions.
- *Potential for conflicts between partners.* Partners may have different ideas about how to run their business, which employees to hire, how to allocate responsibilities, and when to expand. Differences in personalities and work styles can cause clashes or breakdowns in communication, sometimes requiring outside intervention to save the business.
- *Complexity of profit sharing.* Dividing the profits is relatively easy if all partners contribute equal amounts of time, expertise, and capital. But if one partner puts in more money and others more time, it might be more difficult to arrive at a fair profit-sharing formula.
- *Difficulty exiting or dissolving a partnership.* As a rule, partnerships are easier to form than to leave. When one partner wants to leave, the value of their share must be calculated. To whom will that share be sold, and will that person be acceptable to the other partners? If a partner who owns more than 50 percent of the entity withdraws, dies, or becomes disabled, the partnership must reorganize or end. To avoid these problems, most partnership agreements include specific guidelines for transferring partnership interests

and buy–sell agreements that make provision for surviving partners to buy a deceased partner's interest. Partners can also purchase special life insurance policies designed to fund such a purchase.

Business partnerships are often compared to marriages. As with a marriage, choosing the right partner is critical. So if you are considering forming a partnership, allow plenty of time to evaluate your and your potential partner's goals, personality, expertise, and working style before joining forces.

CONCEPT CHECK

1. How does a partnership differ from a sole proprietorship?
2. Describe the four main types of partnerships, and explain the difference between a limited partner and a general partner.
3. What are the main advantages and disadvantages of a partnership?

4.3 Corporations: Limiting Your Liability

3. How does the corporate structure provide advantages and disadvantages to a company, and what are the major types of corporations?

When people think of corporations, they typically think of major, well-known companies, such as Apple, Alphabet (parent company of Google), Netflix, IBM, Microsoft, Boeing, and General Electric. But corporations range in size from large multinationals with thousands of employees and billions of dollars in sales to midsize or even smaller firms with few employees and revenues under $25,000.

A **corporation** is a legal entity subject to the laws of the state in which it is formed, where the right to operate as a business is issued by state charter. A corporation can own property, enter into contracts, sue and be sued, and engage in business operations under the terms of its charter. Unlike sole proprietorships and partnerships, corporations are taxable entities with a life separate from their owners, who are not personally liable for its debts.

When launching her company, Executive Property Management Services, Inc., 32-year-old Linda Ravden realized she needed the liability protection of the corporate form of business organization. Her company specialized in providing customized property management services to mid- and upper-level corporate executives on extended work assignments abroad, often for three to five years or longer. Taking care of substantial properties in the million-dollar range and above was no small responsibility for Ravden's company. Therefore, the protection of a corporate business structure, along with carefully detailed contracts outlining the company's obligations, were crucial in providing Ravden with the liability protection she needed—and the peace of mind to focus on running her business without constant worry. Note that an LLC does not provide unlimited protection; you can still get in trouble for such things as mingling personal and business funds.[2]

MANAGING CHANGE

Pacific Sun's Golden Glow

It all started as a little surf shop in 1980 in Newport Beach, California. It wasn't called PacSun then. It wasn't even all that different from other shops carrying surfboards and wax, except for one thing. The founders had a better idea.

During Southern California's wet, cool winters, the beaches got empty, and the surf store business went dry. Where did everyone go? To the mall, of course. Their idea—to be the first surf shop to move into California's popular mall locations—worked. The company soon grew to 21 stores, selling such popular name brands as Billabong, Gotcha, CatchIt, Stussy, and Quiksilver, as well as its own private-label brands.

What began as a little surf shop became a leading mall-based specialty retailer in the fast-growing surf, skate, and hip-hop apparel markets. With close to a thousand stores in the United States and Puerto Rico and sales topping $1 billion, how did the founders make the leap from selling and waxing surfboards to being a major player in the youth apparel market? How has Pacific Sunwear of California, Inc. (**http://www.pacsun.com**) succeeded when thousands of other clothing companies failed?

"We listen and we change," says the CEO of Pacific Sun. "The kids have the answers, so we listen to get the trends, the solutions, and find out what we are doing right." To remain on the cutting edge of teen tastes, the company hosts an open house every Wednesday at its corporate headquarters in Anaheim, California, where vendors present their wares to PacSun's savvy team of buyers. Being able to distinguish between short-lived fads and actual trends is important when making merchandise choices. The company's focus on "active brand management" is what kept its sales climbing.

The founders' philosophy had served their business well. In 1993, the 60-store company sold stock to the public. It had grown to over 1,000 stores in 50 states and Puerto Rico, with 12,000 employees. The company's PacSun stores cater to a completely different customer than its d.e.m.o. hip-hop stores. In April 2006, PacSun launched its third concept, One Thousand Steps, a footwear store.

With changing trends and online shopping challenges facing many brick-and-mortar retailers, companies such as Wet Seal and Quicksilver filed for bankruptcy in 2015, and PacSun filed for bankruptcy in April 2016. At the time of bankruptcy filing, the company had 593 PacSun stores employing approximately 2,000 employees. In September 2016, PacSun emerged from the bankruptcy after it cut debt and closed stores. The company also turned over all of its stock to the private equity firm Golden Gate Capital, its senior lender.

As its business took off, PacSun successfully made the leap from the small sole proprietorship form of business organization to corporate retailing giant. Facing changing trends and technologies, the firm hit a bump in the road and is working hard to reestablish. The company is indeed a thousand steps away from its humble beginnings.

Critical Thinking Questions

1. How did PacSun manage its evolution from a small, local business to a leading mall-based specialty retailer? What could be the reasons for its missteps resulting in the bankruptcy filing?
2. What form of business organization might PacSun have chosen when it started, and what might have prompted it to change as it grew?

Sources: Marie Driscoll, "Pacific Sun's Golden Glow," *Business Week Online*, November 9, 2004, http://www.businessweek.com; Ron Ehlers (VP Information Services, Pacific Sunwear of California, Inc.)

"Pacific Sunwear: Maintain a Fresh Brand by Anticipating Consumer Needs," presentation to the Retail Systems MIX Summit, May 25, 2005, http://www.retailsystems.com; "Corporate Profile," Pacific Sun corporate Web site, http://www.pacsun.com; Samantha Masunaga, "PacSun files for Chapter 11 bankruptcy protection, plans to go private," *Los Angeles Times,* http://www.latimes.com, accessed August 17, 2017; Steven Church, "Pacific Sunwear Has 'Retailer's Dream' as Bankruptcy Wraps Up," *Bloomberg,* https://www.bloomberg.com, accessed August 2017.

Corporations play an important role in the U.S. economy. As Table 4.1 demonstrated, corporations account for only 18 percent of all businesses but generate 81 percent of all revenues and 58 percent of all profits. Company type and size vary; however, when you look at the top companies by revenue in the United States or globally, they include many familiar names that affect our daily lives.

In the United States, according to Fortune magazine, the top three corporations in the 2017 were (1) Walmart Stores (revenue: $485.9 B), (2) Berkshire Hathaway (revenue: $223.6 B), and (3) Apple (revenue: $215.6 B), whereas Forbes magazine found that the top three corporations were (1) Berkshire Hathaway (revenue: $222.9B), (2) Apple (revenue: $217.5B), and (3) JPMorgan Chase (revenue: $102.5B). By comparison, the top three companies in 2017 according to the World Economic Forum were (1) Apple, (2) Alphabet, and (3) Microsoft. These corporations rise and fall on the various lists based on their revenue in a given year and how the organizations measure revenue and the time frames that they use.[3]

The Incorporation Process

Setting up a corporation is more complex than starting a sole proprietorship or partnership. Most states base their laws for chartering corporations on the Model Business Corporation Act of the American Bar Association, although registration procedures, fees, taxes, and laws that regulate corporations vary from state to state.

Exhibit 4.2   Incorporated in 1969, Walmart is one of America's most popular retail stores. Opened as Walmart Discount City by retailer Sam Walton in 1962, the retailer quickly established a strong brand image. Today, Walmart operates in more than 28 countries, and the Walmart icon is among the most recognizable trademarks in all of business. *What steps must companies take to become incorporated?* (Credit: Mike Mozart/ Flickr/ Attribution 2.0 Generic (CC BY 2.0))

A firm does not have to incorporate in the state where it is based and may benefit by comparing the rules of several states before choosing a state of incorporation. Although Delaware is a small state with few corporations actually based there, its procorporate policies make it the state of incorporation for many companies, including about half the Fortune 500. Incorporating a company involves five main steps:

- Selecting the company's name
- Writing the *articles of incorporation* (see **Table 4.3**) and filing them with the appropriate state office, usually the secretary of state
- Paying required fees and taxes
- Holding an organizational meeting
- Adopting bylaws, electing directors, and passing the first operating resolutions

The state issues a corporate charter based on information in the articles of incorporation. Once the corporation has its charter, it holds an organizational meeting to adopt bylaws, elect directors, and pass initial operating resolutions. Bylaws provide legal and managerial guidelines for operating the firm.

Articles of Incorporation
Articles of incorporation are prepared on a form authorized or supplied by the state of incorporation. Although they may vary slightly from state to state, all articles of incorporation include the following key items: • Name of corporation • Company's goals • Types of stock and number of shares of each type to issue • Life of the corporation (usually "perpetual," meaning with no time limit) • Minimum investment by owners • Methods for transferring shares of stock • Address of the corporate office • Names and addresses of the first board of directors

Table 4.3

The Corporate Structure

As **Exhibit 4.4** shows, corporations have their own organizational structure with three important components: stockholders, directors, and officers.

Stockholders (or shareholders) are the owners of a corporation, holding shares of stock that provide them with certain rights. They may receive a portion of the corporation's profits in the form of dividends, and they can sell or transfer their ownership in the corporation (represented by their shares of stock) at any time. Stockholders can attend annual meetings, elect the board of directors, and vote on matters that affect the corporation in accordance with its charter and bylaws. Each share of stock generally carries one vote.

The stockholders elect a **board of directors** to govern and handle the overall management of the corporation. The directors set major corporate goals and policies, hire corporate officers, and oversee the firm's operations and finances. Small firms may have as few as 3 directors, whereas large corporations usually have 10 to 15.

The boards of large corporations typically include both corporate executives and outside directors (not employed by the organization) chosen for their professional and personal expertise. Outside directors often bring a fresh view to the corporation's activities because they are independent of the firm.

Hired by the board, the *officers* of a corporation are its top management and include the president and chief executive officer (CEO), vice presidents, treasurer, and secretary, who are responsible for achieving corporate goals and policies. Officers may also be board members and stockholders.

Exhibit 4.3 When Walt Disney cast his now-famous mouse as Steamboat Willie back in the 1920s, he had little idea that his animation project would turn into one of the largest entertainment companies in the world. The house that Walt built, with its magical theme parks, movie studios, and product lines, is overseen today by visionary directors with accomplished backgrounds in media, technology, and government. *What important tasks and responsibilities are entrusted to Disney's board of directors?* (Marc Levin/ Flickr/ Attribution 2.0 Generic (CC BY 2.0))

Advantages of Corporations

The corporate structure allows companies to merge financial and human resources into enterprises with great potential for growth and profits:

- *Limited liability.* A key advantage of corporations is that they are separate legal entities that exist apart from their owners. Owners' (stockholders') liability for the obligations of the firm is limited to the amount of the stock they own. If the corporation goes bankrupt, creditors can look only to the assets of the corporation for payment.
- *Ease of transferring ownership.* Stockholders of public corporations can sell their shares at any time without affecting the status of the corporation.
- *Unlimited life.* The life of a corporation is unlimited. Although corporate charters specify a life term, they also include rules for renewal. Because the corporation is an entity separate from its owners, the death or withdrawal of an owner does not affect its existence, unlike a sole proprietorship or partnership.
- *Tax deductions.* Corporations are allowed certain tax deductions, such as operating expenses, which reduces their taxable income.
- *Ability to attract financing.* Corporations can raise money by selling new shares of stock. Dividing ownership into smaller units makes it affordable to more investors, who can purchase one or several thousand shares. The large size and stability of corporations also helps them get bank financing. All these financial resources allow corporations to invest in facilities and human resources and expand beyond the scope of sole proprietorships or partnerships. It would be impossible for a sole proprietorship or partnership to make automobiles, provide nationwide telecommunications, or build oil or chemical refineries.

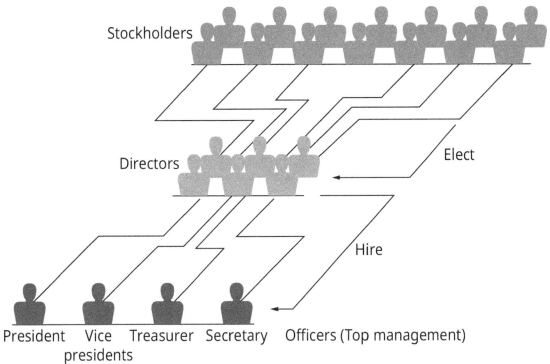

Stockholders

Directors

Elect

Hire

President   Vice   Treasurer   Secretary   Officers (Top management)
             presidents

Exhibit 4.4   Organizational Structure of Corporations Attribution: Copyright Rice University, OpenStax, under CC BY-NC-SA 4.0 license

Disadvantages of Corporations

Although corporations offer companies many benefits, they have some disadvantages:

- *Double taxation of profits.* Corporations must pay federal and state income taxes on their profits. In addition, any profits (dividends) paid to stockholders are taxed as personal income, although at a somewhat reduced rate.
- *Cost and complexity of formation.* As outlined earlier, forming a corporation involves several steps, and costs can run into thousands of dollars, including state filing, registration, and license fees, as well as the cost of attorneys and accountants.
- *More government restrictions.* Unlike sole proprietorships and partnerships, corporations are subject to many regulations and reporting requirements. For example, corporations must register in each state where they do business and must also register with the Securities and Exchange Commission (SEC) before selling stock to the public. Unless it is closely held (owned by a small group of stockholders), a firm must publish financial reports on a regular basis and file other special reports with the SEC and state and federal agencies. These reporting requirements can impose substantial costs, and published information on corporate operations may also give competitors an advantage.

Types of Corporations

Three types of corporate business organization provide limited liability.

The **C corporation** is the conventional or basic form of corporate organization. Small businesses may achieve liability protection through S corporations or limited liability companies (LLCs).

An **S corporation** is a hybrid entity, allowing smaller corporations to avoid double taxation of corporate profits as long as they meet certain size and ownership requirements. Organized like a corporation with stockholders, directors, and officers, an S corporation is taxed like a partnership. Income and losses flow through to the stockholders and are taxed as personal income. S corporations are allowed a maximum of 100 qualifying shareholders and one class of stock. The owners of an S corporation are not personally liable for the debts of the corporation.

A newer type of business entity, the **limited liability company (LLC)**, is also a hybrid organization. Like S corporations, they appeal to small businesses because they are easy to set up and not subject to many restrictions. LLCs offer the same liability protection as corporations as well as the option of being taxed as a partnership or a corporation. First authorized in Wyoming in 1977, LLCs became popular after a 1988 tax ruling that treats them like partnerships for tax purposes. Today all states allow the formation of LLCs.

Table 4.4 summarizes the advantages and disadvantages of each form of business ownership.

Advantages and Disadvantages of Major Types of Business Organization		
Sole Proprietorship	Partnership	Corporation
Advantages		
Owner receives all profits.	More expertise and managerial skill available.	Limited liability protects owners from losing more than they invest.
Low organizational costs.	Relatively low organizational costs.	Can achieve large size due to marketability of stock (ownership).
Income taxed as personal income of proprietor.	Income taxed as personal income of partners.	Receives certain tax advantages.
Independence.	Fundraising ability is enhanced by more owners.	Greater access to financial resources allows growth.
Secrecy.		Can attract employees with specialized skills.
Ease of dissolution.		Ownership is readily transferable.
		Long life of firm (not affected by death of owners).
Disadvantages		
Owner receives all losses.	Owners have unlimited liability; may have to cover debts of other, less financially sound partners.	Double taxation because both corporate profits and dividends paid to owners are taxed, although the dividends are taxed at a reduced rate.

Table 4.4

Advantages and Disadvantages of Major Types of Business Organization		
Sole Proprietorship	Partnership	Corporation
Owner has unlimited liability; total wealth can be taken to satisfy business debts.	Dissolves or must reorganize when partner dies.	More expensive and complex to form.
Limited fundraising ability can inhibit growth.	Difficult to liquidate or terminate.	Subject to more government regulation.
Proprietor may have limited skills and management expertise.	Potential for conflicts between partners.	Financial reporting requirements make operations public.
Few long-range opportunities and benefits for employees.	Difficult to achieve large-scale operations.	
Lacks continuity when owner dies.		

Table 4.4

CONCEPT CHECK

1. What is a corporation? Describe how corporations are formed and structured.
2. Summarize the advantages and disadvantages of corporations. Which features contribute to the dominance of corporations in the business world?
3. Why do S corporations and limited liability companies (LLCs) appeal to small businesses?

4.4   Specialized Forms of Business Organization

4. What other options for business organization does a company have in addition to sole proprietorships, partnerships, and corporations?

In addition to the three main forms, several specialized types of business organization also play an important role in our economy. We will look at cooperatives and joint ventures in this section and take a detailed look at franchising in the following section.

Cooperatives

When you eat a Sunkist orange or spread Land O'Lakes butter on your toast, you are consuming foods produced by cooperatives. A **cooperative** is a legal entity with several *corporate features,* such as limited liability, an unlimited life span, an elected board of directors, and an administrative staff. Member-owners pay annual fees to the cooperative and share in the profits, which are distributed to members in proportion to their contributions. Because they do not retain any profits, cooperatives are not subject to taxes.

There are currently 2.6 million cooperatives with one billion members employing more than 12.5 million employees in more than 145 countries worldwide.[4] Cooperatives operate in every industry, including agriculture, childcare, energy, financial services, food retailing and distribution, health care, insurance, housing, purchasing and shared services, and telecommunications, among others. They range in size from large enterprises such as Fortune 500 companies to small local storefronts and fall into four distinct categories: consumer, producer, worker, and purchasing/shared services.

Cooperatives are autonomous businesses owned and democratically controlled by their members—the people who buy their goods or use their services—not by investors. Unlike investor-owned businesses, cooperatives are organized solely to meet the needs of the member-owners, not to accumulate capital for investors. As democratically controlled businesses, many cooperatives practice the principle of "one member, one vote," providing members with equal control over the cooperative.

There are two types of cooperatives. **Buyer cooperatives** combine members' purchasing power. Pooling buying power and buying in volume increases purchasing power and efficiency, resulting in lower prices. At the end of the year, members get shares of the profits based on how much they bought. Obtaining discounts to lower costs gives the corner Ace Hardware store the chance to survive against retailing giants such as Home Depot Inc. and Lowe's.

Founded in 1924, Ace Hardware is one of the nation's largest cooperatives and is wholly owned by its independent hardware retailer members in stores spanning all 50 states and 70 countries. In August 2017, Ace opened its 5,000th store. In 2017, the company reported its revenues in the second quarter were $1.5 billion, which was an increase of 4.6 percent from 2016's second quarter. The net income for the second quarter of 2017 was $51.1 million.[5]

Seller cooperatives are popular in agriculture, wherein individual producers join to compete more effectively with large producers. Member dues support market development, national advertising, and other business activities. In addition to Sunkist and Land O'Lakes, other familiar cooperatives are Calavo (avocados), Ocean Spray (cranberries and juices), and Blue Diamond (nuts). CHS Inc., the largest cooperative in the United States, sells energy, supply, food, and grain.

Cooperatives empower people to improve their quality of life and enhance their economic opportunities through self-help. Throughout the world, cooperatives are providing members with credit and financial services, energy, consumer goods, affordable housing, telecommunications, and other services that would not otherwise be available to them. There are several principles that cooperatives must follow, according to San Luis Valley REC, International Co-operative Alliance, and Daman Prakash, author of *The Principles of Cooperation.* They include (1) open membership, which means that cooperatives are open to all people to use its services; (2) democratic member control, which means that organizations are controlled by their members; (3) members' economic participation, which means that members contribute equally to the capital of the cooperative; (4) autonomy, which means cooperatives are self-help organizations controlled by their members; and (5) education and training, which means that cooperatives provide education and training for their members while also electing representatives, managers, and employees.[6]

Joint Ventures

In a **joint venture**, two or more companies form an alliance to pursue a specific project, usually for a specified time period. There are many reasons for joint ventures. The project may be too large for one company to handle on its own, and joint ventures also afford companies access to new markets, products, or technology. Both large and small companies can benefit from joint ventures.

In 2005, South Korea's Hyundai Motor Company announced it signed a $1.24 billion deal to form a joint venture with China's Guangzhou Automobile Group. The arrangement gave the South Korean automaker access to the commercial vehicle market in China, where its passenger cars are already the top selling foreign brand. Each side will hold equal stakes in the new entity, named Guangzhou Hyundai Motor Company. The new plant began production in 2007 with an annual capacity of 200,000 units producing small to large trucks and buses as well as commercial vehicles. According to Reuters, Hyundai made plans to build a fifth factory in China. With five factories in operation, Hyundai's annual Chinese production capacity will be 1.65 million vehicles.[7]

CONCEPT CHECK

1. Describe the two types of cooperatives and the advantages of each.
2. What are the benefits of joint ventures?

4.5 Franchising: A Popular Trend

5. What makes franchising an appropriate form of organization for some types of business, and why does it continue to grow in importance?

When Shep Bostin decided to buy a franchise, he researched the usual suspects: Jiffy Lube, McDonald's, and Quiznos Subs. Bostin, then 38, was a top executive at a dying Gaithersburg, Maryland, technology firm, but instead of becoming another McDonald's franchisee, Bostin chose to remain a geek, albeit one who wheeled around in the signature black PT Cruiser of Geeks On Call, a company that provides on-site computer assistance via a large pool of experienced techies. Bostin made residential and commercial "house calls" for more than a decade as a Geeks On Call franchisee. There are approximately 123 independently owned and operated Geeks On Call franchise territories in 50 states serving over 250,000 customers.[8]

Choosing the right franchise can be challenging. Franchises come in all sizes and demand different skills and qualifications. And with somewhere around 2,500 different franchised businesses in the United States, Bostin had a lot to choose from—from cookie-bouquet peddlers and dog trainers to acupuncture specialists. Table 4.5 shows the top franchises for 2017 from various sources. Entrepreneur's rankings utilize among other factors costs/fees, brand strength, support, and financial strength. Franchise Business Review focuses on owner satisfaction, whereas Franchise Gator utilizes a formula with factors such as financial stability and engagement.

Exhibit 4.5 Chance the Rapper was a big winner at the 2017 Grammy Awards. His win was also validation for a new business model. Chance the Rapper does not have a deal with a traditional record label but instead releases his music through streaming services. *How might this approach benefit other aspiring music artists to gain footing and become a force in the music industry?* (Credit: Julio Enriquez/ Flickr/ Attribution 2.0 Generic (CC BY 2.0))

Top 10 Franchises for 2017	
Entrepreneur Top 10	
Franchise	**Initial investment**
1. 7-Eleven Inc.	$37K to $1.6M
2. McDonald's	$1M to $2.2M
3. Dunkin' Donuts	$229K to $1.7M
4. The UPS Store	$178K to $403K
5. Jimmy John's Gourmet Sandwiches	$330K to $558K
6. Dairy Queen	$1.1M to $1.9M
7. Ace Hardware Corp.	$273K to $1.6M
8. Wingstop Restaurant Inc.	$303K to $923K

Table 4.5 Sources: "2017 Franchise 500 Ranking, Franchise 500 2017," *https://www.entrepreneur.com/franchise500* (August 17, 2017); "Top Franchise Opportunities for 2017," Franchise Business Review, https://topfranchises.franchisebusinessreview.com/, (August 17, 2017); "Top 100 Franchises of 2017," Franchise Gator, https://www.franchisegator.com/lists/top-100/, (August 17, 2017).

Top 10 Franchises for 2017	
9. Sport Clips	$189K to $355K
10. RE/MAX LLC	$38K to $224K

Franchise Business Review Top 10

Franchise Name/ Industry	Minimum Investment
Visiting Angels (Senior care)	$77,985
MaidPro (Cleaning and maintenance)	$74,560
Pinot's Palette (Sports and recreation)	$63,400
Christian Brothers Automotive (Automotive)	$146,693
Home Instead Senior Care (Senior care)	$463,698
Our Town America (Advertising and Sales)	$115,000
FASTSIGNS (Business services)	$63,300
Sandler Training (Business services)	$182,329
Soccer Shots ((Child services)	$88,150
Two Men and a Truck (Services)	$36,000

Franchise Gator Top 10

Franchise Name	Minimum Cash Required
Fast Signs	$100,000
Tropical Smoothie Cafe	$100,000
Marco's Pizza	$100,000
Zoup	$100,000
Mathnasium	$100,000
Christian Brothers Automotive	$80,000
Two Men and a Truck	$150,000
Kiddie Academy	$200,000
Wild Birds Unlimited	$40,000

Table 4.5 Sources: "2017 Franchise 500 Ranking, Franchise 500 2017," *https://www.entrepreneur.com/franchise500* (August 17, 2017); "Top Franchise Opportunities for 2017," Franchise Business Review, https://topfranchises.franchisebusinessreview.com/, (August 17, 2017); "Top 100 Franchises of 2017," Franchise Gator, https://www.franchisegator.com/lists/top-100/, (August 17, 2017).

Top 10 Franchises for 2017	
SportClips	$200,000

Table 4.5 Sources: "2017 Franchise 500 Ranking, Franchise 500 2017," *https://www.entrepreneur.com/franchise500* (August 17, 2017); "Top Franchise Opportunities for 2017," Franchise Business Review, https://topfranchises.franchisebusinessreview.com/, (August 17, 2017); "Top 100 Franchises of 2017," Franchise Gator, https://www.franchisegator.com/lists/top-100/, (August 17, 2017).

Chances are you recognize some of the names listed in Table 4.5 and deal with franchise systems in your neighborhood every day. When you have lunch at **Taco Bell** or Jamba Juice, make copies at FedEx Office, change your oil at Jiffy Lube, buy candles at Wicks 'n' Sticks, or mail a package at The UPS Store, you are dealing with a franchised business. These and other familiar name brands mean quality, consistency, and value to consumers. Franchised businesses provided about 8.9 million direct jobs with a $890 billion economic output for the U.S. economy.[9]

Franchising is a form of business organization that involves a **franchisor**, the company supplying the product or service concept, and the **franchisee**, the individual or company selling the goods or services in a certain geographic area. The franchisee buys a package that includes a proven product or service, proven operating methods, and training in managing the business. Offering a way to own a business without starting it from scratch and to expand operations quickly into new geographic areas with limited capital investment, franchising is one of the fastest growing segments of the economy. If you are interested in franchising, food companies represent the largest number of franchises.

A **franchise agreement** is a contract that allows the franchisee to use the franchisor's business name, trademark, and logo. The agreement also outlines rules for running the franchise, services provided by the franchisor, and financial terms. The franchisee agrees to follow the franchisor's operating rules by keeping inventory at certain levels, buying a standard equipment package, keeping up sales and service levels, taking part in franchisor promotions, and maintaining a relationship with the franchisor. In return, the franchisor provides the use of a proven company name and symbols, help in finding a site, building plans, guidance and training, management assistance, managerial and accounting systems and procedures, employee training, wholesale prices for supplies, and financial assistance.

Advantages of Franchises

Like other forms of business organization, franchising offers some distinct advantages:

- *Increased ability for franchisor to expand.* Because franchisees finance their own units, franchisors can grow without making a major investment.
- *Recognized name, product, and operating concept.* Consumers know they can depend on products from franchises such as Pizza Hut, Hertz, and Holiday Inn. As a result, the franchisee's risk is reduced and the opportunity for success increased. The franchisee gets a widely known and accepted business with a proven track record, as well as operating procedures, standard goods and services, and national advertising.
- *Management training and assistance.* The franchisor provides a structured training program that gives the new franchisee a crash course in how to start and operate their business. Ongoing training programs for managers and employees are another plus. In addition, franchisees have a peer group for support and sharing ideas.
- *Financial assistance.* Being linked to a nationally known company can help a franchisee obtain funds from

a lender. Also, the franchisor typically gives the franchisee advice on financial management, referrals to lenders, and help in preparing loan applications. Many franchisors also offer short-term credit for buying supplies, payment plans, and loans to purchase real estate and equipment. Although franchisors give up a share of profits to their franchisees, they receive ongoing revenues in the form of royalty payments.

Exhibit 4.6   Countless franchise opportunities exist for entrepreneurs with access to start-up capital. Despite the broad range of franchise opportunities available, lists of the fastest-growing franchises are heavily weighted with restaurant chains and cleaning services. Start-up costs for a Quiznos franchise can be pricey; expenses associated with opening a Club Pilates franchise or a Visiting Angels adult care service are significantly lower. *How do entrepreneurs evaluate which franchising opportunity is right for them?* (Credit: Mr. Blue Mau Mau/ Flickr/ Attribution 2.0 Generic (CC BY 2.0))

Disadvantages of Franchises

Franchising also has some disadvantages:

- *Loss of control.* The franchisor has to give up some control over operations and has less control over its franchisees than over company employees.
- *Cost of franchising.* Franchising can be a costly form of business. Costs will vary depending on the type of business and may include expensive facilities and equipment. The franchisee also pays fees and/or royalties, which are usually tied to a percentage of sales. Fees for national and local advertising and management advice may add to a franchisee's ongoing costs.
- *Restricted operating freedom.* The franchisee agrees to conform to the franchisor's operating rules and facilities design, as well as inventory and supply standards. Some franchises require franchisees to purchase from only the franchisor or approved suppliers. The franchisor may also restrict the franchisee's territory or site, which could limit growth. Failure to conform to franchisor policies could mean the loss of the franchise.

Franchise Growth

Many of today's major franchise brands, such as McDonald's and KFC, started in the 1950s. Through the 1960s and 1970s, many more types of businesses—clothing, convenience stores, business services, and many others—used franchising to distribute their goods and services. Growth comes from expansion of established franchises—for example, Subway, Pizza Hut, and OrangeTheory Fitness—as well as new entrants such as those identified by Entrepreneur and Franchise Gator among other sources. According to Entrepreneur magazine, the top three new franchises in 2017 are (1) Mosquito Joe, (2) Blaze Fast-Fire'd Pizza, and (3) uBreakiFix, whereas according to Franchise Gator, the top three new franchises in 2017 are (1) Mosquito Joe, (2) Digital Doc, and (3) Nurse Next Door Home Healthcare Services. On both rankings, Mosquito Joe ranks at the top. Mosquito Joe provides mosquito control treatment services for both residential and commercial clients.[10]

Changing demographics drive franchise industry growth, in terms of who, how, and what experiences the most rapid growth. The continuing growth and popularity of technology and personal computing is responsible for the rapidly multiplying number of eBay drop-off stores, and tech consultants such as Geeks on Call are in greater demand than ever. Other growth franchise industries are the specialty coffee market, children's enrichment and tutoring programs, senior care, weight control, and fitness franchises.

The Next Big Thing in Franchising

All around you, people are talking about the next big thing—Subway is the new miracle weight-loss solution, the workout at OrangeTheory Fitness is the answer to America's fitness needs—and you are ready to take the plunge and buy a trendy franchise. But consumers' desires can change with the tide, so how do you plan an entrance—and exit—strategy when purchasing a franchise that's a big hit today but could be old news by tomorrow? Table 4.6 outlines some tips on purchasing a franchise.

International Franchising

Like other forms of business, franchising is part of our global marketplace economy. As international demand for all types of goods and services grows, most franchise systems are already operating internationally or planning to expand overseas. Restaurants, hotels, business services, educational products, car rentals, and nonfood retail stores are popular international franchises.

Franchisors in foreign countries face many of the same problems as other firms doing business abroad. In addition to tracking markets and currency changes, franchisors must understand local culture, language differences, and the political environment. Franchisors in foreign countries also face the challenge of aligning their business operations with the goals of their franchisees, who may be located half a globe away.

Tips for Purchasing a Franchise

1. Take a personality test to determine the traits that will help and hurt you and assess your strengths and weaknesses.
2. Do your research about the franchise company, its services, and your potential location, and study the field.
3. Seek assistance from tax advisors and contract specialists.
4. Focus on financials: count your money, limit liability with appropriate business structure, and look beyond.
5. Beware of franchise consultants.
6. Use the franchise disclosure document to ensure everything is clear.
7. Utilize your instincts, and follow your gut.

Table 4.6 Sources: "12 Things To Do Before You Buy a Franchise," *Forbes*, https://www.forbes.com, June 22, 2016; U.S. Small Business Administration, "6 Franchise Purchasing Tips," https://www.sba.gov, August 19, 2014; "5 Tips for Buying a Franchise," *Small BusinessTrends*, https://smalltrends.com, January 29, 2013.

Is Franchising in Your Future?

Are you ready to be a franchisee? Before taking the plunge, ask yourself some searching questions: Are you excited about a specific franchise concept? Are you willing to work hard and put in long hours? Do you have the necessary financial resources? Do you have prior business experience? Do your expectations and personal goals match the franchisor's?

Qualities that rank high on franchisors' lists are passion about the franchise concept, desire to be your own boss, willingness to make a substantial time commitment, assertiveness, optimism, patience, and integrity. Prior business experience is also a definite plus, and some franchisors prefer or require experience in their field.

EXPANDING AROUND THE GLOBE

Setting Up (Sandwich) Shop in China

Lured by China's fast-food industry, estimated today at $180 billion, Jim Bryant, 50, was not the only entrepreneur to discover it is hard to do business in China. In ten years, Bryant has opened 19 Subway stores in Beijing—only half the number he was supposed to have by now—while other companies such as Chili's and Dunkin' Donuts have given up their Chinese operations altogether.

Subway, or Sai Bei Wei (Mandarin for "tastes better than others"), is now the third-largest U.S. fast-food chain in China, right behind McDonald's and KFC, and all its stores are profitable. Although Bryant had never eaten a Subway sandwich before, Jana Brands, the company Bryant worked for in China, sold $20 million in crab to Subway annually, so he knew it was big business. When Subway founder Fred DeLuca visited Beijing in 1994, Bryant took him to a place not on the official tour: McDonald's. It was Sunday night, and the place was packed. "We could open 20,000 Subways here and not scratch the surface,"

Bryant remembers DeLuca saying.

Two weeks later, Bryant called Subway's headquarters in Milford, Connecticut, and asked to be the company representative in China. He would recruit local entrepreneurs, train them to become franchisees, and act as a liaison between them and the company. He would receive half the initial $10,000 franchise fee and one-third of their 8 percent royalty fees. He could also open his own Subway restaurants. Steve Forman, the founder of Jana Brands, invested $1 million in return for a 75 percent stake.

All foreign businesses in China had to be joint ventures with local partners, so Bryant used the Chinese business practice of relying on local relationships to find a manager for his first restaurant in Beijing. The project ran into problems immediately. Work on the store was delayed, and construction costs soared. It didn't take Bryant long to realize that he and Forman had been swindled out of $200,000.

When it finally opened, the restaurant was a hit among Americans in Beijing, but the locals weren't sure what to make of it. They didn't know how to order and didn't like the idea of touching their food, so they held the sandwich vertically, peeled off the paper, and ate it like a banana. Most of all, the Chinese didn't seem to want sandwiches.

But Subway did little to alter its menu—something that still irks some Chinese franchisees. "Subway should have at least one item tailored to Chinese tastes to show they respect local culture," says Luo Bing Ling, a Beijing franchisee. Bryant thinks that with time, sandwiches will catch on in China. Maybe he's right: Tuna salad, which he couldn't give away at first, is now the number one seller. Today there are nearly 600 Subway stores in China, with China's fast-food industry estimated at over $180 billion.

Critical Thinking Questions
1. What are some of the main problems U.S. franchisors encounter when attempting to expand their business in a country such as China?
2. What steps can franchisors take to ensure a smooth and successful launch of a new franchise business in a foreign country?

Sources: Subway, "Explore Our World," http://www.subway.com, accessed April 2, 2018; "Sales Revenue in Fast Food Restaurants in China 2011–2018," *Statista,* https://www.statista.com, accessed April 2, 2018; Carlye Adler, "How China Eats a Sandwich," *Fortune*, March 21, 2005, p. F210-B; Julie Bennett, "Chinese Market Offers Franchise Challenges," *Startup Journal–The Wall Street Journal Online*, http://www.startupjournal.com.

So what can you do to prepare when considering the purchase of a franchise? When evaluating franchise opportunities, professional guidance can prevent expensive mistakes, so interview advisers to find those that are right for you. Selecting an attorney with franchise experience will hasten the review of your franchise agreement. Getting to know your banker will speed up the loan process if you plan to finance your purchase with a bank loan, so stop by and introduce yourself. The proper real estate is a critical component for a successful retail franchise, so establish a relationship with a commercial real estate broker to begin scouting locations. Doing your homework can spell the difference between success and failure, and some early preparation can help lay the groundwork for the successful launch of your franchised business.

If the franchise route to business ownership seems right for you, begin educating yourself on the franchise process by investigating various franchise opportunities. You should research a franchise company thoroughly before making any financial commitment. Once you've narrowed your choices, ask for the Uniform Franchise

Offering Circular *(UFOC)* for that franchisor, and read it thoroughly. The Federal Trade Commission (FTC) requires franchisors to prepare this document, which provides a wealth of information about the franchisor, including its history, operating style, management, past or pending litigation, the franchisee's financial obligations, and any restrictions on the sale of units. Interviewing current and past franchisees is another essential step. And most franchise systems use computers, so if you are not computer literate, take a class in the basics.

Would-be franchisees should also check recent issues of small-business magazines such as Entrepreneur, Inc., Startups, and Success for industry trends, ideas on promising franchise opportunities, and advice on how to choose and run a franchise. The International Franchise Association website at **http://www.franchise.org** has links to Franchising World and other useful sites. (For other franchise-related sites, see the "Working the Net" questions.)

CONCEPT CHECK

1. Describe franchising and the main parties to the transaction.
2. Summarize the major advantages and disadvantages of franchising.
3. Why has franchising proved so popular?

4.6 Mergers and Acquisitions

6. Why are mergers and acquisitions important to a company's overall growth?

A **merger** occurs when two or more firms combine to form one new company. For example, in 2016, Johnson Controls, a leading provider of building efficiency solutions, agreed to merge with Ireland's Tyco International, a leading provider of fire and security solutions, resulting in a company that will be a leader in products, technologies, and integrated solutions for the building and energy sectors. The merger is valued at $30 billion, with new Johnson Controls PLC to be based in Ireland. Currently, AT&T and Time Warner have an $85.4 billion merger pending. "Once we complete our acquisition of Time Warner Inc., we believe there is an opportunity to build an automated advertising platform that can do for premium video and TV advertising what the search and social media companies have done for digital advertising," AT&T's CEO Randall Stephenson said in a prepared statement. Mergers such as this one, in a well-established industry, can produce winning results in terms of improved efficiency and cost savings.[11]

In an **acquisition**, a corporation or investor group finds a target company and negotiates with its board of directors to purchase it. In Verizon's recent $4.5 billion acquisition of Yahoo, Verizon was the acquirer, and Yahoo the target company.[12]

Worldwide merger activity in the first quarter of 2017 was mixed. The volume of deals was lower but with higher dollar value. The total number of deals fell by 17.9 percent versus the first quarter of 2016; however, the overall deal value was $678.5 billion.[13] We will discuss the increase in international mergers later in this chapter.

Types of Mergers

The three main types of mergers are horizontal, vertical, and conglomerate. In a **horizontal merger**, companies at the same stage in the same industry merge to reduce costs, expand product offerings, or reduce competition. Many of the largest mergers are horizontal mergers to achieve economies of scale. Its $1.25 billion acquisition of trucking company Overnite allowed UPS, the world's largest shipping carrier, to step up expansion of its heavy freight–delivery business, thus expanding its product offerings.[14]

In a **vertical merger**, a company buys a firm in its same industry, often involved in an earlier or later stage of the production or sales process. Buying a supplier of raw materials, a distribution company, or a customer gives the acquiring firm more control. A good example of this is Google's acquisition of Urchin Software Corp., a San Diego–based company that sells web analytics software and services that help companies track the effectiveness of their websites and online advertising. The move enables Google to bolster the software tools it provides to its advertisers.[15]

A **conglomerate merger** brings together companies in unrelated businesses to reduce risk. Combining companies whose products have different seasonal patterns or respond differently to business cycles can result in more stable sales. The Philip Morris Company, now called Altria Group, started out in the tobacco industry but diversified as early as the 1960s with the acquisition of Miller Brewing Company. It diversified into the food industry with its subsequent purchase of General Foods, Kraft Foods, and Nabisco, among others. Later spinning off many businesses, current product categories include cigarettes, smokeless tobacco such as Copenhagen and Skoal, cigars, e-vapor products such as MarkTen, and wines.

A specialized, financially motivated type of merger, the **leveraged buyout (LBO)** became popular in the 1980s but is less common today. LBOs are corporate takeovers financed by large amounts of borrowed money—as much as 90 percent of the purchase price. LBOs can be started by outside investors or the corporation's management. For example, the private equity firm Apollo Global Management LLC agreed to buy U.S. security company ADT Corp. in the largest leveraged buyout (LBO) of 2016.[16]

Often a belief that a company is worth more than the value of all its stock is what drives an LBO. They buy the stock and take the company private, expecting to increase cash flow by improving operating efficiency or selling off units for cash to pay off debt. Although some LBOs do improve efficiency, many do not live up to investor expectations or generate enough cash to pay their debt.

Merger Motives

Although headlines tend to focus on mega-mergers, "merger mania" affects small companies too, and motives for mergers and acquisitions tend to be similar regardless of the company's size. The goal is often strategic: to improve overall performance of the merged firms through cost savings, elimination of overlapping operations, improved purchasing power, increased market share, or reduced competition. Oracle Corp. paid $5.85 billion to acquire Siebel Systems, its largest competitor in the sales automation programs market.[17]

Company growth, broadening product lines, acquiring technology or management skills, and the ability to quickly acquire new markets are other motives for acquiring a company. Yahoo Inc.'s $1 billion cash purchase of a 40 percent stake in China's biggest e-commerce firm, Alibaba.com, instantly strengthened its ties to the world's second largest internet market.[18]

Purchasing a company can also offer a faster, less risky, less costly option than developing products or markets in-house or expanding internationally. Amazon's 2017 purchase of Whole Foods Market, an upscale grocery chain, for $13.7 billion was a move to enter the retail grocery sector. In addition to the new product market, this move offers Amazon opportunity to sell Amazon tech products in the grocery stores as well as access to an entirely new set of data on consumers.[19]

Another motive for acquisitions is financial restructuring—cutting costs, selling off units, laying off employees, and refinancing the company to increase its value to stockholders. Financially motivated mergers are based not on the potential to achieve economies of scale, but rather on the acquirer's belief that the target has hidden value to be unlocked through restructuring. Most financially motivated mergers involve larger companies. In January 2018, Brookfield Business Partners, a subsidiary of Canada's Brookfield Asset Management, announced that it plans to acquire Westinghouse Electric Co LLC, the bankrupt nuclear services company owned by Toshiba Corp., for $4.6 billion. Brookfield has a history of turning around distressed businesses.[20]

Emerging Truths

Along with the technology boom of the late 1990s, merger activity also soared. Total annual transactions averaged $1.6 trillion a year. Companies were using their stock, which had been pushed to unrealistically high levels, to buy each other. When the technology bubble burst in 2000, the level of merger activity dropped as well. It fell even further after the United States was attacked on September 11, 2001. Then massive corporate wrongdoing began to surface. Stocks plummeted in reaction to these events, and merger transactions, which generally track stock market movements, fell as a result.

Today, merger activity is once again on the rise. Propelled by a solid economy, low interest rates, good credit, rising stock prices, and stockpiles of cash, 2016's $3.84 trillion of global M&A was historically a very strong year, with several blockbuster deals.[21]

Size is definitely an advantage when competing in the global marketplace, but bigger does not always mean better in the merger business. Study results show that heady mega-mergers can, in fact, be a bust for investors who own those shares. So companies are wise to consider their options before stuffing their dollars in the biggest merger slot machine they can find. In their eagerness to snare a deal, many buyers pay a premium that wipes out the merger's entire potential economic gain. Often managers envision grand synergies that prove illusory or unworkable or buy a company that isn't what it seems—not fully understanding what they are getting.

Integrating acquisitions is both an art and a science. Acquirers often underestimate the costs and logistical nightmare of consolidating the operations of merged companies with very different cultures. As a result, they may fail to keep key employees aboard, sales forces selling, and customers happy.

Companies will always continue to seek out acquisition candidates, but the fundamental business case for merging will have to be strong. So what should companies look for to identify mergers with a better-than-even chance of turning out well?

- A purchase price that is low enough—a 10 percent premium over market as opposed to 50 percent—so the buyer doesn't need heroic synergies to make the deal work.
- A target that is significantly smaller than the buyer—and in a business the buyer understands. The more "transformational" the deal, such as entering a new business arena, the bigger the risk.
- A buyer who pays in cash and not overinflated stock.
- Evidence that the deal makes both business and financial sense and isn't purely the brainchild of an empire-building CEO. Mergers are tough—culturally, commercially, and logistically. The most important

quality a company can bring to a merger may be humility.

4.7 Trends in Business Ownership

7. What current trends will affect the business organizations of the future?

As we learned earlier, an awareness of trends in the business environment is critical to business success. Many social, demographic, and economic factors affect how businesses organize. When reviewing options for starting or organizing a business or choosing a career path, consider the following trends.

"Baby Boomers" and "Millennials" Drive Franchise Trends

We all hear and read a great deal about the "graying of America," which refers to the "baby boomer" generation heading toward retirement age. This unprecedented demographic phenomenon—in 2006 the first of 78 million members of the baby boomer generation turned 60—is driving the ongoing battle to stay young, slim, and healthy. Every day, 10,000 boomers are turning 65, and the trend is likely to continue until 2030. Boomers have transformed every life stage they've touched so far, and their demographic weight means that business opportunities are created wherever they go.

With their interest in staying fit, Boomers are contributing to the growth of fitness and weight-loss franchises. In just the past year, this category in *Entrepreneur's* Franchise 500 has grown to over 50 franchisors. And according to the IHRSA, 52.9 million Americans belong to a health club—up from 39.4 million 10 years ago—so there are plenty of consumers feeding this growing trend.[22]

Another area of boomer-driven franchise growth is eldercare. Founded in 1994, Home Instead Senior Care is recognized as one of the world's fastest growing franchise companies in the eldercare market, with a network of over 1,000 independently owned and operated franchises in 12 countries. And as the world's population continues to age, the need for its unique services will continue to increase.

Home Instead Senior Care provides a meaningful solution for the elderly who prefer to remain at home. Compared with the annual cost for a nursing home placement ($72,000–$92,000), home care at around $45,000–$60,000 a year is somewhat more affordable. Elder quality of life is enhanced by Home Instead Senior Care's part-time, full-time, and around-the-clock services, designed for people who are capable of managing their physical needs but require some assistance and supervision. Home Instead Senior Care provides meal preparation, companionship, light housekeeping, medication reminders, incidental transportation, and errands. These services make it possible for the elderly to remain in the familiar comfort of their own homes for a longer period of time.[23]

But the best deal yet may be adult day services, one of the fastest-growing franchises and "still one of the best-kept secrets around" according to Entrepreneur magazine. Based on the concept of day care services for children, Sarah Adult Day Services, Inc. offers a franchising opportunity that meets the two criteria for a successful and socially responsible business: a booming demographic market with great potential for growth, and excellent elder care. Programs such as SarahCare centers are highly affordable for its clients, costing around $17,900 a year. The SarahCare franchise allows entrepreneurs to become part of an expanding industry while restoring a sense of dignity and vibrancy to the lives of older adults.[24]

Millennials—individuals born between 1980 and 2000—are the largest living generation in the United States, according to Pew Research. Millennials spend more money in restaurants per capita than any previous generation. They have been recognized as changing the restaurant scene by looking for brands that offer customized food choices, quality ingredients, freshness, authenticity, transparency, and environmental and social responsibility. According to the U.S. Chamber of Commerce Foundation's report, two out of three millennials are interested in entrepreneurship. According to Forbes magazine, 72 percent of millennials would like to be their own boss, 74 percent want flexible work schedules, and 88 percent want "work–life integration." When it comes to owning a franchise, growth potential and meeting a flexible, fulfilling lifestyle are both something that attracts Millennials. A survey by the CT Corporation found that 60 percent of college graduates wanted to start a business after graduation, 67 percent lacked the know-how, 45 percent didn't think they could come up with a name, and 30 percent were not knowledgeable about how to market the business. Franchising is the perfect solution to these issues. For example, Chicago area native and millennial Sal Rehman grew up working in his family's diner. Sal had a dream of operating his own restaurant, and he decided to take the franchising path. In 2015, at the age of 27, Sal opened his first Wing Zone store in suburban Glendale Heights, Illinois. He currently owns five Wing Zones.[25]

Boomers Rewrite the Rules of Retirement

At age 64, Bob Drucker could be the poster child for retirement except that the concept makes him recoil. Drucker is living his dream. He and his wife have a large house on Long Island where Drucker kicks back by floating in his pool when he's not spoiling his granddaughters with trips to Disneyland.

"The only way you can get me out of here is to carry me out," Drucker says, referring to RxUSA, the online pharmacy he founded and runs in Port Washington, New York. "I love my work, and I cannot imagine sitting home and doing nothing."

Drucker is not alone. Today's boomers are working longer at their jobs and embracing postretirement second careers, which often means starting their own small business.[26] As retirees opt to go into business for themselves, they are choosing different forms of business organizations depending on their needs and goals. Some may start small consulting businesses using the simple sole proprietorship form of business organization, while couples or friends might choose to become partners in a retail or franchise venture.

The more healthy and energetic the baby boomer generation remains, the more interested it is in staying active and engaged—and that may mean postponing retirement or not retiring at all. The annual retirement survey by Transamerica Center for Retirement Studies found that as this record number of Americans approaches retirement age, many are not slowing down. In fact, 51 percent of boomers plan to work in some capacity during their retirement years, and 82 percent indicated that they will not retire at or before age 65.[27]

Mergers and Foreign Investment Boom, Too

After shunning big deals for more than three years, corporate America has launched a new merger wave. In 2016, North American companies announced deals totaling almost $2.0 trillion. Many of these deals were large ones, with the largest deal, announced in 2016, AT&T's merger with Time Warner for over $85 billion. In addition, foreign merger activity has reached a new high. Worldwide deal volume in 2015 was 44,000 transactions totaling $4.5 trillion. In 2016, the number of transactions increased to over 48,000, one of the most active periods of merger activity to date. Non-U.S. companies accounted for about two-thirds of the transactions. European companies' cross-border transactions led the way, with deals totaling more than one trillion dollars. The increase is the result of improving economic growth and better stock prices.[28]

This current boom in mergers feels different from earlier merger mania, however. New players are entering the arena, and the number of U.S. and foreign companies making cross-border acquisitions has increased. Whether these new mergers will be good for the global economy remains to be seen. Transactions that lead to cost savings, streamlined operations, and more funding for research and capital investment in new facilities will have positive effects on profitability. Many deals, however, may fail to live up to the acquirers' expectations.

Foreign investment in U.S. companies has also increased dramatically. Annual foreign direct investment reached $373.4 billion in 2016.[29] The jump is the result of a worldwide boom in mergers and acquisitions and the need to finance America's growing trade deficit, as well as the continued attraction of the U.S. economy to investors worldwide.

And what about American investment in foreign economies? It is skyrocketing as U.S. businesses seek out opportunities in developing countries. According to the Congressional Research Service Reports, the outflows from the United States into foreign countries now exceeds $6.4 trillion a year.[30] In addition to the attraction of cheap labor and resources, U.S. companies of all sizes continue to tap the intellectual capital of developing economies such as China and India, outsourcing such functions as payroll, information technology (IT), web/email hosting, customer relationship management (CRM), and human resources (HR) to keep costs under control and enhance profitability.

CONCEPT CHECK

1. What are some of the demographic trends currently impacting American business?
2. As a prospective business owner, what could you do to capitalize on these trends?
3. What other economic trends are influencing today's business organizations?

🔑 Key Terms

acquisition The purchase of a target company by another corporation or by an investor group typically negotiated with the target company board of directors.

board of directors A group of people elected by the stockholders to handle the overall management of a corporation, such as setting major corporate goals and policies, hiring corporate officers, and overseeing the firm's operations and finances.

buyer cooperative A group of cooperative members who unite for combined purchasing power.

C corporation A conventional or basic form of corporate organization.

conglomerate merger A merger of companies in unrelated businesses; done to reduce risk.

cooperative A legal entity typically formed by people with similar interests, such as suppliers or customers, to reduce costs and gain economic power. A cooperative has limited liability, an unlimited life span, an elected board of directors, and an administrative staff; all profits are distributed to the member-owners in proportion to their contributions.

corporation A legal entity with an existence and life separate from its owners, who are not personally liable for the entity's debts. A corporation is chartered by the state in which it is formed and can own property, enter into contracts, sue and be sued, and engage in business operations under the terms of its charter.

franchise agreement A contract setting out the terms of a franchising arrangement, including the rules for running the franchise, the services provided by the franchisor, and the financial terms. Under the contract, the franchisee is allowed to use the franchisor's business name, trademark, and logo.

franchisee In a franchising arrangement, the individual or company that sells the goods or services of the *franchisor* in a certain geographic area.

franchising A form of business organization based on a business arrangement between a *franchisor,* which supplies the product or service concept, and the *franchisee,* who sells the goods or services of the franchisor in a certain geographic area.

franchisor In a franchising arrangement, the company that supplies the product or service concept to the *franchisee.*

general partners Partners who have unlimited liability for all of the firm's business obligations and who control its operations.

general partnership A partnership in which all partners share in the management and profits. Each partner can act on behalf of the firm and has unlimited liability for all its business obligations.

horizontal merger A merger of companies at the same stage in the same industry; done to reduce costs, expand product offerings, or reduce competition.

joint venture Two or more companies that form an alliance to pursue a specific project, usually for a specified time period.

leveraged buyout (LBO) A corporate takeover financed by large amounts of borrowed money; can be started by outside investors or the corporation's management.

limited liability company (LLC) A hybrid organization that offers the same liability protection as a corporation but may be taxed as either a partnership or a corporation.

limited partners Partners whose liability for the firm's business obligations is limited to the amount of their investment. They help to finance the business but do not participate in the firm's operations.

limited partnership A partnership with one or more *general partners*, who have unlimited liability, and one or more *limited partners*, whose liability is limited to the amount of their investment in the company.

merger The combination of two or more firms to form one new company.

partnership An association of two or more individuals who agree to operate a business together for profit.

S corporation A hybrid entity that is organized like a corporation, with stockholders, directors, and officers, but taxed like a partnership, with income and losses flowing through to the stockholders and taxed as their personal income.

seller cooperative Individual producers who join together to compete more effectively with large producers.

sole proprietorship A business that is established, owned, operated, and often financed by one person.

stockholders (or shareholders) The owners of a corporation who hold shares of stock that carry certain rights.

vertical merger A merger of companies at different stages in the same industry; done to gain control over supplies of resources or to gain access to different markets.

Summary of Learning Outcomes

4.1 Going It Alone: Sole Proprietorships

1. What are the advantages and disadvantages of the sole proprietorship form of business organization?

The advantages of sole proprietorships include ease and low cost of formation, the owner's rights to all profits, the owner's control of the business, relative freedom from government regulation, absence of special taxes, and ease of dissolution. Disadvantages include owner's unlimited liability for debts and personal absorption of all losses, difficulty in raising capital, limited managerial expertise, difficulty in finding qualified employees, large personal time commitment, and unstable business life.

4.2 Partnerships: Sharing the Load

2. What are the advantages of operating as a partnership, and what downside risks should partners consider?

The advantages of partnerships include ease of formation, availability of capital, diversity of managerial skills and expertise, flexibility to respond to changing business conditions, no special taxes, and relative freedom from government control. Disadvantages include unlimited liability for general partners, potential for conflict between partners, sharing of profits, and difficulty exiting or dissolving the partnership. Partnerships can be formed as either general or limited partnerships. In a general partnership, the operations of the business are controlled by one or more general partners with unlimited liability. The partners co-own the assets and share the profits. Each partner is individually liable for all debts and contracts of the partnership. In a limited partnership, the limited partners are financial partners whose liability is limited to their investment; they do not participate in the firm's operations.

4.3 Corporations: Limiting Your Liability

3. How does the corporate structure provide advantages and disadvantages to a company, and what are the major types of corporations?

A corporation is a legal entity chartered by a state. Its organizational structure includes stockholders who own the corporation, a board of directors elected by the stockholders to govern the firm, and officers who carry out the goals and policies set by the board. Stockholders can sell or transfer their shares at any time and are entitled to receive profits in the form of dividends. Advantages of corporations include limited liability, ease of transferring ownership, unlimited life tax deductions, and the ability to attract financing. Disadvantages include double taxation of profits, the cost and complexity of formation, and government restrictions.

4.4 Specialized Forms of Business Organization

4. What other options for business organization does a company have in addition to sole proprietorships, partnerships, and corporations?

Businesses can also organize as limited liability companies, cooperatives, joint ventures, and franchises. A limited liability company (LLC) provides limited liability for its owners but is taxed like a partnership. These two features make it an attractive form of business organization for many small firms. Cooperatives are collectively owned by individuals or businesses with similar interests that combine to achieve more economic power. Cooperatives distribute all profits to their members. Two types of cooperatives are buyer and seller cooperatives. A joint venture is an alliance of two or more companies formed to undertake a special project. Joint ventures can be set up in various ways, through partnerships or special-purpose corporations. By sharing management expertise, technology, products, and financial and operational resources, companies can reduce the risk of new enterprises.

4.5 Franchising: A Popular Trend

5. What makes franchising an appropriate form of organization for some types of business, and why does it continue to grow in importance?

Franchising is one of the fastest-growing forms of business ownership. It involves an agreement between a franchisor, the supplier of goods or services, and a franchisee, an individual or company that buys the right to sell the franchisor's products in a specific area. With a franchise, the business owner does not have to start from scratch but buys a business concept with a proven product or service and operating methods. The franchisor provides use of a recognized brand-name product and operating concept, as well as management training and financial assistance. Franchises can be costly to start, and operating freedom is restricted because the franchisee must conform to the franchisor's standard procedures. The growth in franchising is attributed to its ability to expand business operations quickly into new geographic areas with limited capital investment.

4.6 Mergers and Acquisitions

6. Why are mergers and acquisitions important to a company's overall growth?

In a merger, two companies combine to form one company. In an acquisition, one company or investor group buys another. Companies merge for strategic reasons to improve overall performance of the merged firm through cost savings, eliminating overlapping operations, improving purchasing power, increasing market share, or reducing competition. Desired company growth, broadened product lines, and the rapid acquisition of new markets, technology, or management skills are other motives. Another motive for merging is financial restructuring—cutting costs, selling off units, laying off employees, and refinancing the company to increase its value to stockholders.

There are three types of mergers. In a horizontal merger, companies at the same stage in the same industry combine for more economic power, to diversify, or to win greater market share. A vertical merger involves the acquisition of a firm that serves an earlier or later stage of the production or sales process, such as a supplier or sales outlet. In a conglomerate merger, unrelated businesses come together to reduce risk through diversification.

4.7 Trends in Business Ownership

7. What current trends will affect the business organizations of the future?

Americans are getting older but continue to open new businesses, from sole proprietorships to partnerships, corporations to franchise operations. The service sector is booming in efforts to meet the demand for fitness, health, and eldercare.

Other key trends include an escalation of worldwide foreign investment through the number of mergers taking place. All forms of business organization can benefit from outsourcing, tapping into the intellectual capital of developing countries.

Preparing for Tomorrow's Workplace Skills

1. Suppose you are considering two job offers for a computer programming position, one at a two-year-old consulting firm with 10 employees owned by a sole proprietor and one at a publicly traded software developer with sales of $500 million. In addition to comparing the specific job responsibilities, consider the following:

    - Which company offers better training? Do you prefer the on-the-job training you'll get at the small company, or do you want formal training programs as well?
    - Which position offers the chance to work on a variety of assignments?
    - What are the opportunities for advancement? Employee benefits?
    - What happens if the owner of the young company gets sick or decides to sell the company?
    - Which company offers a better working environment for you?

    Answering these and similar questions will help you decide which job meets your particular needs. (Resources, Information)

2. Before starting your own company, you should know the legal requirements in your area. Call the appropriate city or county departments, such as licensing, health, and zoning, to find out what licenses and permits you need and any other requirements you must meet. Do the requirements vary depending on the type of company? Are there restrictions on starting a home-based business? Contact your secretary of state or other agency that handles corporations to get information on how to incorporate. (Information)

3. Bridget Jones wants to open her own business selling her handmade chocolates over the internet. Although she has some money saved and could start the business on her own, she is concerned about her lack of bookkeeping and management experience. A friend mentions he knows an experienced businessperson seeking involvement with a start-up company. As Bridget's business consultant, prepare recommendations for Bridget regarding an appropriate form of business organization, outlining the issues she should consider and the risks involved, supported by reasons for your suggestions. (Interpersonal, Information)

4. You and a partner co-own Swim-Clean, a successful pool supply and cleaning service. Because sales have tapered off, you want to expand your operations to another town 10 miles away. Given the high costs of expanding, you decide to sell Swim-Clean franchises. The idea takes off, and soon you have 25 units throughout the region. Your success results in an invitation to speak at a local Rotary Club luncheon. Prepare a brief presentation describing how you evaluated the benefits and risks of becoming a franchisor, the problems you encountered, and how you established good working relationships with your franchisees. (Information)

5. Do you have what it takes to be a successful franchisee? Start by making a list of your interests and skills, and do a self-assessment using some of the suggestions in this chapter. Next you need to narrow the field of thousands of different franchise systems. At Franchise Handbook Online (**http://www.franchisehandbook.com**) , you'll find articles with checklists to help you thoroughly research a franchise and its industry, as well as a directory of franchise opportunities. Armed with this information, develop a questionnaire to evaluate a prospective franchise. (Resources, Interpersonal, Information)

6. Find news of a recent merger using an online search or a business periodical such as *Bloomberg Businessweek, Fortune,* or *The Wall Street Journal*. Research the merger using a variety of sources including the company's website and news articles. Discover the motives behind the merger, the problems facing the new entity, and the company's progress toward achieving its objectives. (Information)

7. **Team Activity** After pulling one too many all-nighters, you realize your college needs an on-campus

coffee/food delivery service and decide this might be a good business opportunity for you and some friends. Split the class into small groups. Start by outlining the management, technical, and financial resources that are needed to start this company. Then evaluate what resources your group brings to the table and what you will need from partners. Using Exhibit 4.3 as a guide, develop a list of questions for potential partners. After each group presents its findings to the class, it should pair up with another group that seems to offer additional resources. Interview the other group's members using your questions to decide if the teams could work together and if you would proceed with this venture. (Resources, Interpersonal)

Ethics Activity

After seeing a Quiznos franchise recruitment infomercial to recruit franchisees, you are tempted to apply to open your own Quiznos sub shop. However, your research on the company turns up some disturbing information. Many current franchisees are unhappy with the company's management and practices, among them excessive food costs, lack of promised support, and selling new franchise locations that are too close to existing stores. A group of New Jersey franchisees sued Quiznos for selling them franchises but not providing locations 18 months after taking their franchise fees. Some franchise owners question Quiznos's purchasing tactics, choosing food and beverage suppliers based on the referral fees it receives instead of the lowest-cost provider. Other franchisees have suffered major financial losses.

Quiznos, which owned or operated more than 5,000 sub shops at one time and now has less than 1,500 locations worldwide with less than 900 in the United States, disputes the various claims. The president of the company points out that in a franchise operation, there will always be unhappy franchisees and those who can't make a success of their units. Besides, Quiznos's franchise offering materials clearly state that the company may open stores in any locations it selects.

Using a web search tool, locate articles about this topic, and then write responses to the following questions. Be sure to support your arguments and cite your sources.

Ethical Dilemma: What are Quiznos's obligations to its franchisees? Is it ethical for the company to open new franchises very close to existing units and to choose vendors based on fees to the parent company rather than the cost to franchisees?

Sources: The Franchise King, "What Happened to Quiznos?" https://www.thefranchiseking.com, accessed September 14, 2017; Karsten Strauss, "Is Quiznos Toast?" *Forbes,* https://www.forbes.com, June 17, 2015; Venessa Wong, "Can Quiznos Be Saved?" *BuzzFeed News,* https://www.buzzfeed.com, December 8, 2015; Kristi Arellano, "Quiznos' Success Not without Problems," *Denver Post,* June 19, 2005, p. K1; Dina Berta, "Quiznos Denies Franchisees' Charges of Cost Gouging, Encroachment Problems," *Nation's Restaurant News,* June 20, 2005, P. 1+; "Quiznos Denies Fraud Suit Charges by 17 Franchisees," *Nation's Restaurant News,* May 16, 2005, p. 102.

Working the Net

1. Consult *Entrepreneur* at **http://www.entrepreneur.com**. Search for "business legal structures" to read articles about S corporations and LLCs. If you were starting a company, which would you choose and why?

2. Research how to form a corporation and LLC in your state using search engines to find relevant sites.

Here are two to get you started: **http://www.incorporate.com** and **http://www.usa-corporate.com**. Find out what steps are necessary to set up a corporation in your state. How do the fees compare with other states? If you were incorporating a business, what state would you choose and why?

3. The Federal Trade Commission is the government agency that monitors and regulates franchises. Visit the FTC site (**http://www.ftc.gov**), and explore the links to its resources on franchising, including details on the legal responsibilities of franchisors and franchisees. What kinds of problems should a prospective franchisee look out for when considering a franchise? What kinds of scams are typical in the franchise industry?

4. Select three franchises that interest you. Research them at sites such as the Franchise Handbook Online (**http://www.franchisehandbook.com**), *Entrepreneur* magazine's Franchise 500 (**http://www.entrepreneur.com**), and Be the Boss (**www.betheboss.com**). Prepare a chart comparing your selections, including history, number and location of units, financial requirements (initial franchise fee, other start-up costs, royalty and advertising fees), and any other information that would help you evaluate the franchises.

5. *Inc.* magazine (**http://www.inc.com**) has many franchising articles in its section on Startup. It offers insights into how franchisors and franchisees can better manage their businesses. Using the site's resources, discuss ways the owner of a franchise can motivate employees. What specific revenue items and expenses should you monitor daily in a franchise restaurant business to ensure that you are profitable?

 ## Critical Thinking Case

I'm an Owner of a Professional Sports Team!

Many of the richest individuals have added professional sports teams to their ownership portfolios. Paul Allen owns the Seattle Seahawks after founding Microsoft, and another Microsoft alumnus, Steve Balmer, now owns the Los Angeles Clippers. They, like most other owners of sports teams, including Shahid Khan (Jacksonville Jaguars), Jerry Jones (Dallas Cowboys), the Rickets family (Chicago Cubs of Major League Baseball), and Geoff Molson (Montreal Canadiens of the National Hockey League), all have corporate structures that operate as for-profit organizations. There is one exception to the corporate structure, however.

The Green Bay Packers are unique among North American sports teams in that they are a community-owned not-for-profit. They do have shareholders, but the shareholders have limited rights and most shares are bought so that fans can claim ownership and use the stock certificate as a piece of pride of ownership in a unique community treasure. The shares do not pay dividends, and any proceeds from any possible sale or liquidation of the team go to a charity, not the shareholders. This system, plus transfer restrictions and a cap on the number of shares that any single individual can own, ensures that the team remains in public hands and will never leave the city of Green Bay.

Every shareholder in the Green Bay Packers received a ballot for electing the team's board of directors, who then select an executive committee of seven individuals who will meet with chief executive officer Mark Murphy, a former NFL player who also served as the athletic director at Northwestern University prior to joining the Packers. Murphy is charged with hiring other leadership positions, such as the general manager, who then hires the head coach, who is charged with hiring the assistant coaches.

So, what are the negatives to what seems like a perfect organizational structure? Many owners in other cities are able to price their tickets to the market and also able to create revenue streams from corporate advertising in the stadium as well as stadium-naming rights. The Packers have some of the lowest-priced tickets in the league despite 80,000 requests on their season ticket waiting list. Also, teams in other cities can negotiate with city, county, and other government agencies for subsidies and tax breaks for building new stadiums and use the threat of a move to another city as a bargaining chip. For instance, the St. Louis Rams and San Diego Chargers recently moved to Los Angeles while the Oakland Raiders will soon call Las Vegas home.

Another potential drawback is that the organizational structure of the Packers restricts the ability to make organizational changes such as changing the general manager or head coach quickly if things are going badly. Luckily for the Packers, this has not been much of a problem lately having had success with star quarterbacks such as Brett Favre and Aaron Rodgers!

Critical Thinking Questions

1. Is the not-for-profit form of business organization appropriate for the Green Bay Packers? Why or why not?
2. Why has this form of ownership not been replicated in other cities?
3. What are the limitations and constraints that this form of business has on the operations of the Green Bay Packers?

Sources: "Ted Thompson Has No Obligation to Communicate," *Total Packers*, https://www.totalpackers.com, August 8, 2017; Green Bay Packers website, "Packers Hall of Fame to Host Shareholders: A Story of Resilience, Community and Pride," http://www.packers.com, June 23, 2017; Mike Florio, "Packers Ownership Structure Works Well, Until It Doesn't," *NBC Sports*, http://profootballtalk.nbcsports.com, November 26, 2016; "Green Bay Packers Shareholder on What It's Like to Own an NFL Team," *Sporting News,* http://www.sportingnews.com, September 30, 2014; Ken Reed, "Green Bay Packers' Ownership Structure Remains Ideal," *League of Fans*, http://www.leagueoffans, April 6, 2012; Karl Taro Greenfeld, "The Green Bay Packers Have the Best Owners in Sports," *Bloomberg Businessweek,* https://www.bloomberg.com, October 20, 2011.

Hot Links Address Book

1. Which Fortune 500 company had the biggest revenue increase? The highest profits? The highest return to investors? What is the largest entertainment company? Get all the details on U.S. companies at **http://www.fortune.com/fortune500**.
2. Confused about the differences between regular corporations, S corporations, and LLCs? Compare these three business structures at **http://www.4inc.com**.
3. Did you know U.S. cooperatives serve some 120 million members, or 4 in 10 Americans? For more co-op statistics, check the National Cooperative Business Association website at **http://www.ncba.coop/**.
4. Combine your sweet tooth with your good business sense by owning a candy franchise. Indulge yourself by finding out the requirements for owning a Rocky Mountain Chocolate Factory franchise at **http://www.rmcf.com**.
5. Want to know what's hot and what's not in franchising? Improve your chances for success at **http://www.entrepreneur.com/franchises**.

Entrepreneurship: Starting and Managing Your Own Business

Exhibit 5.1 (Credit: Christian Heilmann / flickr / Attribution 2.0 Generic (CC BY 2.0))

 Introduction

Learning Outcomes

After reading this chapter, you should be able to answer these questions:

1. Why do people become entrepreneurs, and what are the different types of entrepreneurs?
2. What characteristics do successful entrepreneurs share?
3. How do small businesses contribute to the U.S. economy?
4. What are the first steps to take if you are starting your own business?
5. Why does managing a small business present special challenges for the owner?
6. What are the advantages and disadvantages facing owners of small businesses?
7. How does the Small Business Administration help small businesses?
8. What trends are shaping entrepreneurship and small-business ownership?

EXPLORING BUSINESS CAREERS

Natalie Tessler, Spa Space

Natalie Tessler has always had an entrepreneurial spirit. After she graduated from New York University's law school, she began working as a tax attorney for a large firm in Chicago. But Tessler soon realized that this left her feeling unfulfilled. She didn't want to practice law, and she didn't want to work for someone else. "I wanted to wake up and be excited for my day," Tessler said. Not until one night, though, when she was having dinner with a friend who recently had begun a writing career, did she realize it was time. "I was listening to her talk about how much she loved her job. Her passion and excitement—I wanted that. I wanted something that grabbed me and propelled me through the day—and being a lawyer wasn't it."

She began searching for what "it" was. She had a tremendous passion and talent for hospitality, entertaining others, and presentation. Seeking an outlet for that flair, she found the spa industry, and the idea for Spa Space was born.

"People think that, owning a spa, I'm able to live this glamorous lifestyle," she laughs. "Owning a spa is nothing like going to one—my nails always are broken from fixing equipment; my back is usually in pain from sitting hunched over a computer trying to figure out the budget or our next marketing promotion." Tessler is a true entrepreneur, embodying the spirit and drive necessary to see her vision become a reality.

Tessler wanted to design a spa that focused on something new: creating a comfortable, personalized environment of indulgence while not neglecting the medical technology of proper skin care. "My father's a dermatologist, so we discussed the importance of making this more than a spa where you can get a frou-frou, smell-good treatment that might actually harm your skin. We both thought it was important to create an experience that is as beneficial for people's skin as it is for their emotional well-being." To address this need, Spa Space has a medical advisory board that helps with product selection, treatment design, and staff training.

Armed with a vision and a plan, Tessler turned her sights toward making it a reality. Spa Space opened in 2001 and has received a great deal of national recognition for its service excellence, unique treatments and products, and its fresh approach to appealing to both men and women. But it hasn't always been smooth sailing for Spa Space. Tessler had to steer the business through several obstacles, including the 9/11 tragedy just three months after the spa's grand opening, and then the Great Recession. Tessler learned to adapt her strategy by refining her target market and the services Spa Space offered. Her resiliency enabled the company to not only survive difficult economic periods, but to thrive and grow 17 years later into what the press recognizes as Chicago's best spa.

Tessler recently turned the reins over to Ilana Alberico, another entrepreneur and founder of Innovative Spa Management, a company that has been named twice to *Inc.* magazine's list of fastest growing companies. When Alberico met Natalie Tessler and learned about her vision, she was inspired to invest in Spa Space. "Natalie's vision still resonates . . . I'm inspired to champion her vision into the future."

Sources: "Our Team," https://spaspace.com, accessed February 1, 2018; Jennifer Keishin Armstrong, "Spa Reviews: Spa Space in Chicago," *Day Spa* magazine, http://www.dayspamagazine.com, accessed February 1, 2018; "About Us," https://ismspa.com, accessed February 1, 2018.

Typical of many who catch the entrepreneurial bug, Natalie Tessler had a vision and pursued it single-mindedly. She is just one of thousands of entrepreneurs from all age groups and backgrounds. Even kids are starting businesses and high-tech firms. College graduates are shunning the corporate world to head out on their own. Downsized employees, midcareer executives, and retirees who have worked for others all their lives are forming the companies they have always wanted to own.

Companies started by entrepreneurs and small-business owners make significant contributions to the U.S. and global economies. Hotbeds of innovation, these small businesses take leadership roles in technological change and the development of new goods and services. Just how important are small businesses to our economy? Table 5.1 provides insight into the role of small business in today's economy.

You may be one of the millions of Americans who's considering joining the ranks of business owners. As you read this chapter, you'll learn why entrepreneurship continues to be one of the hottest areas of business activity. Then you'll get the information and tools you need to help you decide whether owning your own company is the right career path for you. Next you'll discover what characteristics you'll need to become a successful entrepreneur. Then we'll look at the importance of small businesses in the economy, guidelines for starting and managing a small business, the many reasons small businesses continue to thrive in the United States, and the role of the Small Business Administration. Finally, the chapter explores the trends that shape entrepreneurship and small-business ownership today.

5.1   Entrepreneurship Today

1. Why do people become entrepreneurs, and what are the different types of entrepreneurs?

Brothers Fernando and Santiago Aguerre exhibited entrepreneurial tendencies at an early age. At 8 and 9 years old respectively, they sold strawberries and radishes from a vacant lot near their parents' home in Plata del Mar on the Atlantic coast of Argentina. At 11 and 12, they provided a surfboard repair service from their garage. As teenagers, Fer and Santi, as they call each other, opened Argentina's first surf shop, which led to their most ambitious entrepreneurial venture of all.

The flat-footed brothers found that traipsing across hot sand in flip-flops was uncomfortable, so in 1984 they sank their $4,000 savings into manufacturing their own line of beach sandals. Now offering sandals and footwear for women, men, and children, as well as clothing for men, Reef sandals have become the world's hottest beach footwear, with a presence in nearly every surf shop in the United States.[1]

The Economic Impact of Small Business

Most U.S. Businesses Are Small:

- 80% (approximately 23.8 million) of the nearly 29.7 million businesses have no employees (businesses run by individuals or small groups of partners, such as married couples).
- 89% (approximately 5.2 million) of the nearly 5.8 million businesses with employees have fewer than 20 employees.
- 99.6% (approximately 5.7 million) of all businesses have 0–99 employees—98% have 0–20 workers.
- Approximately 5.8 million businesses have fewer than 500 employees.
- Only about 19,000 businesses in the United States have more than 500 employees.
- Companies with fewer than 50 employees pay more than 20% of America's payroll.
- Companies with fewer than 500 employees pay more than 41% of America's payroll.
- 32.5 million people (1 employee in 4) work for businesses with fewer than 50 employees.
- These businesses also pay tens of millions of owners, not included in employment statistics.

Table 5.1 Source: "Firm Size Data: 2014," https://www.sba.gov, accessed February 1, 2018.

CATCHING THE ENTREPRENEURIAL SPIRIT

Young Entrepreneur Living the Dream

Jack Bonneau is the quintessential entrepreneur. In the three years he has been in business, he has expanded his product line, opened multiple locations, established strategic partnerships, and secured sponsorship from several national brands. His business has garnered publicity from *The New York Times, The Denver Post, The Today Show, Good Morning America*, and numerous other media. He has shared his business success on several stages, speaking at TechStars and the Aspen Ideas Festival, and recently delivered the closing keynote speech at a national STEM conference. He even landed a gig on *Shark Tank*.

Jack Bonneau is smart, charismatic, an excellent spokesperson, and persistent in his mission. And he is only 11 years old—which also makes him very adorable.

Jack's business was born from a need that most kids have: a desire for toys. He asked his dad, Steve Bonneau, for a LEGO Star Wars Death Star. The problem was that it cost $400. Jack's dad said he could have it but only if he paid for it himself. This led Jack to do what a lot of kids do to earn some extra cash. He opened a lemonade stand. But he quickly learned that this would never help him realize his dream, so, with the advice and help of his father, he decided to open a lemonade stand at a local farmers market. "There were lots of people who wanted to buy great lemonade from an eight-year-old," says Jack. In no time, Jack had earned enough to buy his LEGO Death Star. "I had sales of around $2,000, and my total profit was $900," Jack said.

Jack realized that he was on to something. Adults love to buy things from cute kids. What if he could make even more money by opening more locations? Jack developed an expansion plan to open three new "Jack Stands" the following spring. Realizing that he would need more working capital, he secured a $5,000 loan from Young Americas Bank, a bank in Denver that specializes in loans to children. Jack made $25,000 in 2015.

The following year, Jack wanted to expand operations, so he secured a second loan for $12,000. He opened stands in several more locations, including shopping malls during the holiday season, selling apple cider and hot chocolate instead of lemonade. He also added additional shop space and recruited other young entrepreneurial kids to sell their products in his space, changing the name to Jack's Stands and Marketplace. One of his first partnerships was Sweet Bee Sisters, a lip balm and lotion company founded by Lily, Chloe, and Sophie Warren. He also worked with 18 other young entrepreneurs who sell a range of products from organic dog treats to scarves and headbands.

Jack's strategy worked, and the business brought in more than $100,000 last year. This year, he became the spokesperson for Santa Cruz Organic Lemonade, and he's now looking at expanding into other cities such as Detroit and New Orleans.

Even though Jack is only 11 years old, he has already mastered financial literacy, customer service, marketing and sales, social skills, and other sound business practices—all the qualities of a successful entrepreneur.

Critical Thinking Questions
1. What do you think enabled Jack Bonneau to start and grow a successful business at such a young age?
2. What personal characteristics and values will Jack need to continue running his business while also attending school full-time?

Sources: "About Jack's Stands & Marketplaces," https://www.jackstands.com, accessed February 1, 2018; Peter Gasca, "This 11-Year-Old Founder's Advice Is As Profound as Any You Could Receive," *Inc.*, https://www.inc.com, July 27, 2017; Claire Martin, "Some Kids Sell Lemonade. He Starts a Chain," *The New York Times,* https://www.nytimes.com, February 26, 2016.

Christy Glass Lowe, who monitors surf apparel for USBX Advisory Services LLC, notes, "They [Reef] built a brand from nothing and now they're the dominant market share leader."

The Aguerres, who currently live two blocks from each other in La Jolla, California, sold Reef to VF Corporation for more than $100 million in 2005. In selling Reef, "We've finally found our freedom," Fernando says. "We traded money for time," adds Santiago. Fernando remains active with surfing organizations, serving as president of the International Surfing Association, where he became known as "Ambassador of the Wave" for his efforts in getting all 90 worldwide members of the International Olympic Committee to unanimously vote in favor of including surfing in the 2020 Olympic Games.[2] He has also been named "Waterman of the Year" by the Surf Industry Manufacturers Association two times in 24 years.[3] Santi raises funds for his favorite not-for-profit, SurfAid. Both brothers are enjoying serving an industry that has served them so well.

The United States is blessed with a wealth of entrepreneurs such as the Aguerres who want to start a **small business**. According to research by the Small Business Administration, two-thirds of college students intend to be entrepreneurs at some point in their careers, aspiring to become the next Bill Gates or Jeff Bezos, founder of Amazon.com. But before you put out any money or expend energy and time, you'd be wise to check out Table 5.2 for some preliminary advice.

The desire to be one's own boss cuts across all age, gender, and ethnic lines. Results of a recent U.S. Census Bureau survey of business owners show that minority groups and women are becoming business owners at a much higher rate than the national average. Table 5.3 illustrates these minority-owned business demographics.

Why has entrepreneurship remained such a strong part of the foundation of the U.S. business system for so many years? Because today's global economy rewards innovative, flexible companies that can respond quickly to changes in the business environment. Such companies are started by **entrepreneurs**, people with vision, drive, and creativity, who are willing to take the risk of starting and managing a business to make a profit.

Are You Ready to Be an Entrepreneur?

Here are some questions would-be entrepreneurs should ask themselves:

1. What is new and novel about your idea? Are you solving a problem or unmet need?
2. Are there similar products/services out there? If so, what makes yours better?
3. Who is your target market? How many people would use your product or service?
4. Have you talked with potential customers to get their feedback? Would they buy your product/service?
5. What about production costs? How much do you think the market will pay?
6. How defensible is the concept? Is there good intellectual property?
7. Is this innovation strategic to my business?
8. Is the innovation easy to communicate?
9. How might this product evolve over time? Would it be possible to expand it into a product line? Can it be updated/enhanced in future versions?
10. Where would someone buy this product/service?
11. How will the product/service be marketed? What are the costs to sell and market it?
12. What are the challenges involved in developing this product/service?

Table 5.2 Sources: Jess Ekstrom, "5 Questions to Ask Yourself Before You Start a Business," *Entrepreneur,* https://www.entrepreneur.com, accessed February 1, 2018; "Resources," http://www.marketsmarter.com, accessed February 1, 2018; Monique Reece, *Real-Time Marketing for Business Growth: How to Use Social Media, Measure Marketing, and Create a Culture of Execution* (Upper Saddle River, NJ: FT Press/Pearson, 2010); Mike Collins, "Before You Start–Innovator's Inventory," *The Wall Street Journal,* May 9, 2005, p. R4.

Statistics for Minority-Owned Businesses

- The number of Hispanic-owned businesses almost tripled between 1997 (1.2 million) and 2012 (3.3 million).
- The percentage of U.S. businesses with 1 to 50 employees owned by African Americans increased by 50% between 1996 and 2015.
- Almost a million firms with employees are minority owned: 53% are Asian American owned, 11% are African American owned, and almost a third are Hispanic owned.
- 19% of all companies with employees are owned by women.

Table 5.3 Sources: Robert Bernstein, "Hispanic-Owned Businesses on the Upswing," International Trade Management Division, U.S. Census, https://www.census.gov, December 1, 2016; The Kauffman Index of Main Street Entrepreneurship, https://www.kauffman.org, November 2016.

Entrepreneur or Small-Business Owner?

The term *entrepreneur* is often used in a broad sense to include most small-business owners. The two groups share some of the same characteristics, and we'll see that some of the reasons for becoming an entrepreneur or a small-business owner are very similar. But there is a difference between entrepreneurship and small-business management. Entrepreneurship involves taking a risk, either to create a new business or to greatly change the scope and direction of an existing one. Entrepreneurs typically are innovators who start companies to pursue their ideas for a new product or service. They are visionaries who spot trends.

Although entrepreneurs may be small-business owners, not all small-business owners are entrepreneurs. Small-business owners are managers or people with technical expertise who started a business or bought an existing business and made a conscious decision to stay small. For example, the proprietor of your local independent bookstore is a small-business owner. Jeff Bezos, founder of Amazon.com, also sells books. But Bezos is an entrepreneur: He developed a new model—web-based book retailing—that revolutionized the bookselling world and then moved on to change retailing in general. Entrepreneurs are less likely to accept the status quo, and they generally take a longer-term view than the small-business owner.

Types of Entrepreneurs

Entrepreneurs fall into several categories: classic entrepreneurs, multipreneurs, and intrapreneurs.

Classic Entrepreneurs

Classic entrepreneurs are risk-takers who start their own companies based on innovative ideas. Some classic entrepreneurs are *micropreneurs* who start small and plan to stay small. They often start businesses just for personal satisfaction and the lifestyle. Miho Inagi is a good example of a micropreneur. On a visit to New York with college friends in 1998, Inagi fell in love with the city's bagels. "I just didn't think anything like a bagel could taste so good," she said. Her passion for bagels led the young office assistant to quit her job and pursue her dream of one day opening her own bagel shop in Tokyo. Although her parents tried to talk her out of it, and bagels were virtually unknown in Japan, nothing deterred her. Other trips to New York followed, including an unpaid six-month apprenticeship at Ess-a-Bagel, where Inagi took orders, cleared trays, and swept floors. On weekends, owner Florence Wilpon let her make dough.

In August 2004, using $20,000 of her own savings and a $30,000 loan from her parents, Inagi finally opened tiny Maruichi Bagel. The timing was fortuitous, as Japan was about to experience a bagel boom. After a slow start, a favorable review on a local bagel website brought customers flocking for what are considered the best bagels in Tokyo. Inagi earns only about $2,300 a month after expenses, the same amount she was making as a company employee. "Before I opened this store I had no goals," she says, "but now I feel so satisfied."[4]

In contrast, *growth-oriented entrepreneurs* want their business to grow into a major corporation. Most high-tech companies are formed by growth-oriented entrepreneurs. Jeff Bezos recognized that with Internet technology he could compete with large chains of traditional book retailers. Bezos's goal was to build his company into a high-growth enterprise—and he chose a name that reflected his strategy: Amazon.com. Once his company succeeded in the book sector, Bezos applied his online retailing model to other product lines, from toys and house and garden items to tools, apparel, music, and services. In partnership with other retailers, Bezos is well on his way to making Amazon's vision "to be Earth's most customer-centric company; to build a place where people can come to find and discover anything they might want to buy online."—a reality.[5]

Multipreneurs

Then there are *multipreneurs,* entrepreneurs who start a series of companies. They thrive on the challenge of building a business and watching it grow. In fact, over half of the chief executives at *Inc.* 500 companies say they would start another company if they sold their current one. Brothers Jeff and Rich Sloan are a good example of multipreneurs, having turned numerous improbable ideas into successful companies. Over the past 20-plus years, they have renovated houses, owned a horse breeding and marketing business, invented a device to prevent car batteries from dying, and so on. Their latest venture, a multimedia company called

StartupNation, helps individuals realize their entrepreneurial dreams. And the brothers know what company they want to start next: yours.[6]

Exhibit 5.2   If there is one person responsible for the mainstream success of solar energy and electric vehicles in the past 10 years, it's Elon Musk, founder and CEO of Tesla. Since the 2000s when he founded Tesla, launching innovation in solar technology, and commercial space exploration with SpaceX, Musk has pioneered countless innovations and has challenged traditional automobile, trucking, and energy companies to challenge and rethink their businesses. *What entrepreneurial type best describes Elon Musk?* (Credit: Steve Jurvetson/ Flickr/ Attribution 2.0 Generic (CC BY 2.0))

Intrapreneurs

Some entrepreneurs don't own their own companies but apply their creativity, vision, and risk-taking within a large corporation. Called **intrapreneurs**, these employees enjoy the freedom to nurture their ideas and develop new products, while their employers provide regular salaries and financial backing. Intrapreneurs have a high degree of autonomy to run their own minicompanies within the larger enterprise. They share many of the same personality traits as classic entrepreneurs, but they take less personal risk. According to Gifford Pinchot, who coined the term *intrapreneur* in his book of the same name, large companies provide seed funds that finance in-house entrepreneurial efforts. These include Intel, IBM, Texas Instruments (a pioneering intrapreneurial company), Salesforce.com, and Xerox.

Why Become an Entrepreneur?

As the examples in this chapter show, entrepreneurs are found in all industries and have different motives for starting companies. The most common reason cited by CEOs of the *Inc.* 500, the magazine's annual list of fastest-growing private companies, is the challenge of building a business, followed by the desire to control their own destiny. Other reasons include financial independence and the frustration of working for someone else. Two important motives mentioned in other surveys are a feeling of personal satisfaction with their work, and creating the lifestyle that they want. Do entrepreneurs feel that going into business for themselves was worth it? The answer is a resounding yes. Most say they would do it again.

CONCEPT CHECK

1. Describe several types of entrepreneurs.
2. What differentiates an entrepreneur from a small-business owner?
3. What are some major factors that motivate entrepreneurs to start businesses?

5.2 | Characteristics of Successful Entrepreneurs

2. What characteristics do successful entrepreneurs share?

Do you have what it takes to become an entrepreneur? Having a great concept is not enough. An entrepreneur must be able to develop and manage the company that implements his or her idea. Being an entrepreneur requires special drive, perseverance, passion, and a spirit of adventure, in addition to managerial and technical ability. Entrepreneurs *are* the company; they tend to work longer hours, take fewer vacations, and cannot leave problems at the office at the end of the day. They also share other common characteristics as described in the next section.

The Entrepreneurial Personality

Studies of the entrepreneurial personality find that entrepreneurs share certain key traits. Most entrepreneurs are

- *Ambitious:* They are competitive and have a high need for achievement.
- *Independent:* They are individualists and self-starters who prefer to lead rather than follow.
- *Self-confident:* They understand the challenges of starting and operating a business and are decisive and confident in their ability to solve problems.
- *Risk-takers:* Although they are not averse to risk, most successful entrepreneurs favor business opportunities that carry a moderate degree of risk where they can better control the outcome over highly risky ventures where luck plays a large role.
- *Visionary:* Their ability to spot trends and act on them sets entrepreneurs apart from small-business owners and managers.
- *Creative:* To compete with larger firms, entrepreneurs need to have creative product designs, bold marketing strategies, and innovative solutions to managerial problems.
- *Energetic:* Starting and operating a business takes long hours. Even so, some entrepreneurs start their companies while still employed full-time elsewhere.
- *Passionate.* Entrepreneurs love their work, as Miho Inagi demonstrated by opening a bagel shop in Tokyo despite the odds against it being a success.
- *Committed.* Because they are so committed to their companies, entrepreneurs are willing to make

personal sacrifices to achieve their goals.

CUSTOMER SATISFACTION AND QUALITY

Ethical Choices Transform Family Business into International Brand

Ever since Apollonia Poilâne was a young girl growing up in Paris, she always knew what she wanted to do when she grew up: take over the family business. But she didn't anticipate how quickly this would happen. When her father—Lionel Poilâne—and her mother died in a helicopter crash in 2002, France lost its most celebrated baker, and Apollonia stepped into the role. She was just 18 years old at the time with plans to matriculate to Harvard in the fall, but the moment her parents had prepared her for had come. As her Harvard admissions essay said, "The work of several generations is at stake."

With organization and determination, Apollonia managed one of the best French bakeries in the world—based in Paris—from her apartment in Cambridge, Massachusetts. She would usually wake up an extra two hours before classes to make sure she would get all the phone calls done for work. "After classes I check on any business regarding the company and then do my homework," she says. "Before I go to bed I call my production manager in Paris to check the quality of the bread." Because the name Poilâne has earned a place with a very small group of prestige bakers, the 18-year-old was determined to continue the tradition of customer satisfaction and quality her grandfather established in 1932. When her grandfather suffered a stroke in 1973, his 28-year-old son, Lionel, poured his heart into the business and made the family bread into the global brand it is today. Lionel opened two more bakeries in Paris and another in London. He developed and nurtured a worldwide network of retailers and celebrities where bread is shipped daily via FedEx to upscale restaurants and wealthy clients around the world.

Experimenting with sourdough is what distinguished Poilâne's products from bread produced by Paris's other bakers, and it has remained the company's signature product. It is baked with a "P" carved into the crust, a throwback to the days when the use of communal ovens forced bakers to identify their loaves, and it also ensures that the loaf doesn't burst while it's baking. Today, Poilâne also sells croissants, pastries, and a few specialty breads, but the company's signature item is still the four-pound *miche*, a wheel of sourdough, a country bread, *pain Poilâne*.

"Apollonia is definitely passionate about her job," says Juliette Sarrazin, manager of the successful Poilâne Bakery in London. "She really believes in the work of her father and the company, and she is looking at the future, which is very good."

Apollonia's work ethic and passion fueled her drive even when she was a student. Each day presented a juggling act of new problems to solve in Paris while other Harvard students slept. As Apollonia told a student reporter from *The Harvard Crimson* writing a story about her, "The one or two hours you spend procrastinating I spend working. It's nothing demanding at all. It was always my dream to run the company."

Her dedication paid off, and Apollonia retained control of important decisions, strategy, and business goals, describing herself as the "commander of the ship," determining the company's overall direction. Today, Poilâne is an $18 million business that employs 160 people. Poilâne runs three restaurants called Cuisine de Bar in Paris and in London, serving casual meals such as soups, salads, and open-faced *tartines*. The company ships more than 200,000 loaves a year to clients in 20 countries, including the United States, Japan, and Saudi Arabia. "More people understand what makes the quality of the bread, what my father spent years studying, so I am thrilled about that," says Apollonia.

Critical Thinking Questions

1. What type of entrepreneur is Apollonia Poilâne?
2. What personal ethics drove Apollonia's decision to take over the family business?

Sources: "About Us," https://www.poilane.com, accessed February 1, 2018; Meg Bortin, "Apollonia Poilâne Builds on Her Family's Legacy," *The New York Times,* https://www.nytimes.com, accessed February 1, 2018; Lauren Collins, "Bread Winner: A Daughter Upholds the Traditions of France's Premier Baking Dynasty," *The New Yorker,* https://www.newyorker.com, December 3, 2012; Gregory Katz, "Her Daily Bread," *American Way* magazine, July 15, 2005, p. 34; Clarel Antoine, "No Time to Loaf Around," *Harvard Crimson,* http://www.thecrimson.com, October 16, 2003.

Most entrepreneurs combine many of the above characteristics. Sarah Levy, 23, loved her job as a restaurant pastry chef but not the low pay, high stress, and long hours of a commercial kitchen. So she found a new one—in her parents' home—and launched Sarah's Pastries and Candies. Part-time staffers help her fill pastry and candy orders to the soothing sounds of music videos playing in the background. Cornell University graduate Conor McDonough started his own web design firm, OffThePathMedia.com, after becoming disillusioned with the rigid structure of his job. "There wasn't enough room for my own expression," he says. "Freelancing keeps me on my toes," says busy graphic artist Ana Sanchez. "It forces me to do my best work because I know my next job depends on my performance."[7]

Exhibit 5.3   Celebrity Ashton Kutcher is more than just a pretty face. The actor-mogul is an active investor in technology-based start-ups such as Airbnb, Skype, and Foursquare with an empire estimated at $200 million dollars. *What personality traits are common to successful young entrepreneurs such as Kutcher?* (Credit: TechCrunch/ Flickr/ Attribution 2.0 Generic (CC BY 2.0))

Managerial Ability and Technical Knowledge

A person with all the characteristics of an entrepreneur might still lack the necessary business skills to run a successful company. Entrepreneurs need the technical knowledge to carry out their ideas and the managerial ability to organize a company, develop operating strategies, obtain financing, and supervise day-to-day activities. Jim Crane, who built Eagle Global Logistics from a start-up into a $250 million company, addressed a group at a meeting saying, "I have never run a $250 million company before so you guys are going to have to start running this business."[8]

Good interpersonal and communication skills are important in dealing with employees, customers, and other business associates such as bankers, accountants, and attorneys. As we will discuss later in the chapter, entrepreneurs believe they can learn these much-needed skills. When Jim Steiner started his toner cartridge remanufacturing business, Quality Imaging Products, his initial investment was $400. He spent $200 on a consultant to teach him the business and $200 on materials to rebuild his first printer cartridges. He made sales calls from 8.00 a.m. to noon and made deliveries to customers from noon until 5:00 p.m. After a quick dinner, he moved to the garage, where he filled copier cartridges until midnight, when he collapsed into bed, sometimes covered with carbon soot. And this was not something he did for a couple of months until he got the business off the ground—this was his life for 18 months.[9] But entrepreneurs usually soon learn that they can't do it all themselves. Often they choose to focus on what they do best and hire others to do the rest.

CONCEPT CHECK

1. Describe the personality traits and skills characteristic of successful entrepreneurs.
2. What does it mean when we say that an entrepreneur should work on the business, not in it?

5.3 Small Business: Driving America's Growth

3. How do small businesses contribute to the U.S. economy?

Although large corporations dominated the business scene for many decades, in recent years small businesses have once again come to the forefront. Downsizings that accompany economic downturns have caused many people to look toward smaller companies for employment, and they have plenty to choose from. Small businesses play an important role in the U.S. economy, representing about half of U.S. economic output, employing about half the private sector workforce, and giving individuals from all walks of life a chance to succeed.

What Is a Small Business?

How many small businesses are there in the United States? Estimates range from 5 million to over 22 million, depending on the size limits government agencies and other groups use to define a small business or the number of businesses with or without employees. The Small Business Administration (SBA) established size standards to define whether a business entity is small and therefore eligible for government programs and preferences that are reserved for "small businesses." Size standards are based on the types of economic activity or industry, generally matched to the North American Industry Classification System (NAICS).[10]

Small businesses are defined in many ways. Statistics for small businesses vary based on criteria such as new/start-up businesses, the number of employees, total revenue, length of time in business, nonemployees, businesses with employees, geographic location, and so on. Due to the complexity and need for consistent statistics and reporting for small businesses, several organizations are now working together to combine comprehensive data sources to get a clear and accurate picture of small businesses in the United States. Table 5.4 provides a more detailed look at small-business owners.

Snapshot of Small-Business Owners

- Start-up activity has risen sharply over the last three years, from an all-time low of minus 0.87% in 2013 to positive 0.48% in 2016.
- Between 1996 and 2011, the rate of business ownership dropped for both men and women; however, business ownership has increased every year since 2014.
- The Kauffman Index of Startup Activity, an early indicator of new entrepreneurship in the United States, rose again slightly in 2016 following sharp increases two years in a row.
- New entrepreneurs who started businesses to pursue opportunity rather than from necessity reached 86.3%, more than 12 percentage points higher than in 2009 at the height of the Great Recession.
- For the first time, Main Street entrepreneurship activity was higher in 2016 than before the onset of the Great Recession. This increase was driven by a jump in business survival rates, which reached a three-decade high of 48.7%. Nearly half of new businesses are making it to their fifth year of operation.
- 47% of U.S. businesses have been in business for 11 or more years.
- In 2016, about 25% of all employing firms had revenues over $1 million, but 2% had revenues under $10,000.

Table 5.4 Sources: "The Kauffman Index: Main Street Entrepreneurship: National Trends," http://www.kauffman.org, November 2016; "Kauffman Index of Startup Activity, 2016 (calculations based from CPS, BDS, and BED)," http://www.kauffman.org; "America's Entrepreneurs: September 2016," https://www.census.gov; "Nearly 1 in 10 Businesses with Employees Are New, According to Inaugural Annual Survey of Entrepreneurs," https://www.census.gov, September 1, 2016.

One of the best sources to track U.S. entrepreneurial growth activity is the Ewing Marion Kauffman Foundation. The Kauffman Foundation is among the largest private foundations in the country, with an asset base of approximately $2 billion, and focuses on projects that encourage entrepreneurship and support education through grants and research activities. They distributed over $17 million in grants in 2013.[11]

The Kauffman Foundation supports new business creation in the United States through two research programs. The annual Kauffman Index of Entrepreneurship series measures and interprets indicators of U.S. entrepreneurial activity at the national, state, and metropolitan level. The foundation also contributes to the cost of the Annual Survey of Entrepreneurs (ASE), which is a public–private partnership between the foundation, the U.S. Census Bureau, and the Minority Business Development Agency. The ASE provides annual data on select economic and demographic characteristics of employer businesses and their owners by gender, ethnicity, race, and veteran status.[12] The Kauffman Index of Entrepreneurship series is an umbrella of annual reports that measures how people and businesses contribute to America's overall economy. What is unique about the Kauffman reports is that the indexes don't focus on only inputs (as most small-business reporting has been done in the past); it reports primarily on entrepreneurial outputs—the actual results of entrepreneurial activity, such as new companies, business density, and growth rates. The reports also include comprehensive, interactive data visualizations that enable users to slice and dice a myriad of data nationally, at the state level, and for the 40 largest metropolitan areas.[13]

The Kauffman Index series consists of three in-depth studies—Start-up Activity, Main Street Entrepreneurship, and Growth Entrepreneurship.

- The Kauffman Index of Startup Activity is an early indicator of new entrepreneurship in the United States. It focuses on new business creation activity and people engaging in business start-up activity, using three components: the rate of new entrepreneurs, the opportunity share of new entrepreneurs, and start-up density.
- The Kauffman Index of Main Street Entrepreneurship measures established small-business activity—focusing on U.S. businesses more than five years old with less than 50 employees from 1997 to 2016. Established in 2015, it takes into account three components of local, small-business activity: the rate of businesses owners in the economy, the five-year survival rate of businesses, and the established small-business density.
- The Kauffman Growth Entrepreneurship Index is a composite measure of entrepreneurial business growth in the United States that captures growth entrepreneurship in all industries and measures business growth from both revenue and job perspectives. Established in 2016, it includes three component measures of business growth: rate of start-up growth, share of scale-ups, and high-growth company density.

Data sources for the Kauffman Index calculations are based on Current Population Survey (CPS), with sample sizes of more than 900,000 observations, and the Business Dynamics Statistics (BDS), which covers approximately 5 million businesses. The Growth Entrepreneurship Index also includes *Inc.* 500/5000 data).

Small businesses in the United States can be found in almost every industry, including services, retail, construction, wholesale, manufacturing, finance and insurance, agriculture and mining, transportation, and warehousing. Established small businesses are defined as companies that have been in business at least five years and employ at least one, but less than 50, employees. Table 5.5 provides the number of employees by the size of established business. More than half of small businesses have between one and four employees.

Number of Employees, by Percentage of Established Small Businesses	
Established small businesses are defined as businesses over the age of five employing at least one, but less than 50, employees.	
Number of Employees	Percentage of Businesses
1–4 employees	53.07%
5–9 employees	23.23%
10–19 employees	14.36%
20–49 employees	9.33%

Table 5.5 Source: Kauffman Foundation calculations from Business Dynamics Statistics, yearly measures. November 2016.

CONCEPT CHECK

1. What are three ways small businesses can be defined?

2.   What social and economic factors have prompted the rise in small business?

5.4 Ready, Set, Start Your Own Business

4.   What are the first steps to take if you are starting your own business?

You have decided that you'd like to go into business for yourself. What is the best way to go about it? Start from scratch? Buy an existing business? Or buy a franchise? About 75 percent of business start-ups involve brand-new organizations, with the remaining 25 percent representing purchased companies or franchises. Franchising may have been discussed elsewhere in your course, so we'll cover the other two options in this section.

Getting Started

The first step in starting your own business is a self-assessment to determine whether you have the personal traits you need to succeed and, if so, what type of business would be best for you. Table 5.6 provides a checklist to consider before starting your business.

Finding the Idea

Entrepreneurs get ideas for their businesses from many sources. It is not surprising that about 80 percent of *Inc.* 500 executives got the idea for their company while working in the same or a related industry. Starting a firm in a field where you have experience improves your chances of success. Other sources of inspiration are personal experiences as a consumer; hobbies and personal interests; suggestions from customers, family, and friends; industry conferences; and college courses or other education.

Checklist for Starting a Business
Before you start your own small business, consider the following checklist: • Identify your reasons • Self-analysis • Personal skills and experience • Finding a niche • Conduct market research • Plan your start-up: write a business plan • Finances: how to fund your business

Table 5.6 Source: "10 Steps to Start Your Business," https://www.sba.gov, accessed February 2, 2018.

An excellent way to keep up with small-business trends is by reading entrepreneurship and small-business magazines and visiting their websites. With articles on everything from idea generation to selling a business, they provide an invaluable resource and profile some of the young entrepreneurs and their successful business ventures (**Table 5.7**).[14]

Successful Entrepreneurs	
Name and Age	Company and Description
Philip Kimmey, 27	Kimmey's dog-sitting and dog-walking network, Rover.com, raised almost $100 million in venture capital and was valued at $300 million in 2017.
Max Mankin, 27	Mankin cofounded Modern Electron and raised $10 million in venture capital to create "advanced thermionic energy converters" that will generate "cheap, scalable, and reliable electricity." Modern Electron will turn every home into a power station.
Alexandra Cristin White, 28	In her early 20s, White founded Glam Seamless, which sells tape-in hair extensions. In 2016, her self-funded company grossed $2.5 million.
Steph Korey, 29; Jen Rubio, 29	Korey and Rubio founded Away, selling "first-class luggage at a coach price" in 2015. They raised $31 million in funding and grossed $12 million in sales in 2016.
Allen Gannet, 26	Gannet founded TrackMaven, a web-marketing analytics company, in 2012; by 2016, his company was grossing $6.7 million a year.
Jake Kassan, 25; Kramer LaPlante, 25	Kassan and Kramer launched their company, MVMT, through Indiegogo, raising $300,000, and in 2016 grossed $60 million, selling primarily watches and sunglasses.
Brian Streem, 29	Streem's company, Aerobo, provides drone services to the film industry, selling "professional aerial filming and drone cinematography." Aerobo grossed $1 million in 2016, its first full year of business.
Natalya Bailey, 30; Louis Perna, 29	Accion Systems began in 2014, raised $10 million in venture funding, and grossed $4.5 million in 2016, making tiny propulsion systems for satellites.
Jessy Dover, 29	Dover is the cofounder of Dagne Dover, a company making storage-efficient handbags for professional women. She and her cofounders grossed $4.5 million in 2016 and debuted on Nordstrom.com in 2017.

These dynamic individuals, who are already so successful in their 20s and 30s, came up with unique ideas and concepts and found the right niche for their businesses.

Interesting ideas are all around you. Many successful businesses get started because someone identifies a need and then finds a way to fill it. Do you have a problem that you need to solve? Or a product that doesn't work as well as you'd like? Raising questions about the way things are done and seeing opportunity in adversity are great ways to generate ideas.

Choosing a Form of Business Organization

A key decision for a person starting a new business is whether it will be a sole proprietorship, partnership, corporation, or limited liability company. As discussed earlier, each type of business organization has advantages and disadvantages. The choice depends on the type of business, number of employees, capital requirements, tax considerations, and level of risk involved.

Developing the Business Plan

Once you have the basic concept for a product or service, you must develop a plan to create the business. This planning process, culminating in a sound **business plan**, is one of the most important steps in starting a business. It can help to attract appropriate loan financing, minimize the risks involved, and be a critical determinant in whether a firm succeeds or fails. Many people do not venture out on their own because they are overwhelmed with doubts and concerns. A comprehensive business plan lets you run various "what if" analyses and evaluate your business without any financial outlay or risk. You can also develop strategies to overcome problems well before starting the business.

Taking the time to develop a good business plan pays off. A venture that seems sound at the idea stage may not look so good on paper. A well-prepared, comprehensive, written business plan forces entrepreneurs to take an objective and critical look at their business venture and analyze their concept carefully; make decisions about marketing, sales, operations, production, staffing, budgeting and financing; and set goals that will help them manage and monitor its growth and performance.

Exhibit 5.4 Each year, a variety of organizations hold business plan competitions to engage the growing number of college students starting their own businesses. The University of Essex and the iLearn entrepreneurship curriculum developed by the University of Texas in Austin, which partnered with Trisakti University in Jakarta, Indonesia, and the U.S. embassy to help run an entrepreneurship course and competition are examples of such competitions. Seven students from "iLearn: Entrepreneurship" were selected as finalists to pitch their business plans to a panel of Indonesian business leaders and embassy representatives. The winning business plan, which was an ecotourism concept, earned $1,000 in seed money. *What research goes into a winning business plan?* (Credit: University of Essex /flickr/ Attribution 2.0 Generic (CC BY 2.0))

The business plan also serves as the initial operating plan for the business. Writing a good business plan takes time. But many businesspeople neglect this critical planning tool in their eagerness to begin doing business, getting caught up in the day-to-day operations instead.

The key features of a business plan are a general description of the company, the qualifications of the owner(s), a description of the products or services, an analysis of the market (demand, customers, competition), sales and distribution channels, and a financial plan. The sections should work together to demonstrate why the business will be successful, while focusing on the uniqueness of the business and why it will attract customers. Table 5.8 describes the essential elements of a business plan.

A common use of a business plan is to persuade lenders and investors to finance the venture. The detailed information in the plan helps them assess whether to invest. Even though a business plan may take months to write, it must capture potential investors' interest within minutes. For that reason, the basic business plan should be written with a particular reader in mind. Then you can fine-tune and tailor it to fit the investment goals of the investor(s) you plan to approach.

Key Elements of a Business Plan
Executive summary provides an overview of the total business plan. Written after the other sections are completed, it highlights significant points and, ideally, creates enough excitement to motivate the reader to continue reading.
Vision and mission statement concisely describe the intended strategy and business philosophy for making the vision happen. Company values can also be included in this section.
Company overview explains the type of company, such as manufacturing, retail, or service; provides background information on the company if it already exists; and describes the proposed form of organization—sole proprietorship, partnership, or corporation. This section should include company name and location, company objectives, nature and primary product or service of the business, current status (start-up, buyout, or expansion) and history (if applicable), and legal form of organization.
Product and/or service plan describes the product and/or service and points out any unique features, as well as explains why people will buy the product or service. This section should offer the following descriptions: product and/or service; features and benefits of the product or service that provide a competitive advantage; available legal protection—patents, copyrights, and trademarks.
Marketing plan shows who the firm's customers will be and what type of competition it will face; outlines the marketing strategy and specifies the firm's competitive edge; and describes the strengths, weaknesses, opportunities, and threats of the business. This section should offer the following descriptions: analysis of target market and profile of target customer; methods of identifying, attracting, and retaining customers; a concise description of the value proposition; selling approach, type of sales force, and distribution channels; types of marketing and sales promotions, advertising, and projected marketing budget; product and/or service pricing strategy; and credit and pricing policies.
Management plan identifies the key players—active investors, management team, board members, and advisors— citing the experience and competence they possess. This section should offer the following descriptions: management team, outside investors and/or directors and their qualifications, outside resource people and their qualifications, and plans for recruiting and training employees.

Table 5.8 Sources: "7 Elements of a Business Plan," https://quickbooks.intuit.com, accessed February 2, 2018; David Ciccarelli, "Write a Winning Business Plan with These 8 Key Elements," *Entrepreneur,* https://www.entrepreneur.com, accessed February 2, 2018; Patrick Hull, "10 Essential Business Plan Components," *Forbes,* https://www.forbes.com, accessed February 2, 2018; Justin G. Longenecker, J. William Petty, Leslie E. Palich, and Frank Hoy, *Small Business Management: Launching & Growing Entrepreneurial Ventures,* 18th edition (Mason, OH: Cengage, 2017); Monique Reece, *Real-Time Marketing for Business Growth: How to Use Social Media, Measure Marketing, and Create a Culture of Execution* (Upper Saddle River, NJ: FT Press/Pearson, 2010).

Key Elements of a Business Plan

Operating plan explains the type of manufacturing or operating system to be used and describes the facilities, labor, raw materials, and product-processing requirements. This section should offer the following descriptions: operating or manufacturing methods, operating facilities (location, space, and equipment), quality-control methods, procedures to control inventory and operations, sources of supply, and purchasing procedures.

Financial plan specifies financial needs and contemplated sources of financing, as well as presents projections of revenues, costs, and profits. This section should offer the following descriptions: historical financial statements for the last 3–5 years or as available; pro forma financial statements for 3–5 years, including income statements, balance sheets, cash flow statements, and cash budgets (monthly for first year and quarterly for second year); financial assumptions; breakeven analysis of profits and cash flows; and planned sources of financing.

Appendix of supporting documents provides materials supplementary to the plan. This section should offer the following descriptions: management team biographies; the company's values; information about the company culture (if it's unique and contributes to employee retention); and any other important data that support the information in the business plan, such as detailed competitive analysis, customer testimonials, and research summaries.

Table 5.8 Sources: "7 Elements of a Business Plan," https://quickbooks.intuit.com, accessed February 2, 2018; David Ciccarelli, "Write a Winning Business Plan with These 8 Key Elements," *Entrepreneur,* https://www.entrepreneur.com, accessed February 2, 2018; Patrick Hull, "10 Essential Business Plan Components," *Forbes,* https://www.forbes.com, accessed February 2, 2018; Justin G. Longenecker, J. William Petty, Leslie E. Palich, and Frank Hoy, *Small Business Management: Launching & Growing Entrepreneurial Ventures,* 18th edition (Mason, OH: Cengage, 2017); Monique Reece, *Real-Time Marketing for Business Growth: How to Use Social Media, Measure Marketing, and Create a Culture of Execution* (Upper Saddle River, NJ: FT Press/Pearson, 2010).

But don't think you can set aside your business plan once you obtain financing and begin operating your company. Entrepreneurs who think their business plan is only for raising money make a big mistake. Business plans should be dynamic documents, reviewed and updated on a regular basis—monthly, quarterly, or annually, depending on how the business progresses and the particular industry changes.

Owners should adjust their sales and profit projections up or down as they analyze their markets and operating results. Reviewing your plan on a constant basis will help you identify strengths and weaknesses in your marketing and management strategies and help you evaluate possible opportunities for expansion in light of both your original mission and goals, current market trends, and business results. The Small Business Administration (SBA) offers sample business plans and online guidance for business plan preparation under the "Business Guide" tab at https://www.sba.gov.

Financing the Business

Once the business plan is complete, the next step is to obtain financing to set up your company. The funding required depends on the type of business and the entrepreneur's own investment. Businesses started by lifestyle entrepreneurs require less financing than growth-oriented businesses, and manufacturing and high-tech companies generally require a large initial investment.

Who provides start-up funding for small companies? Like Miho Inagi and her Tokyo bagel shop, 94 percent of business owners raise start-up funds from personal accounts, family, and friends. Personal assets and money from family and friends are important for new firms, whereas funding from financial institutions may become more important as companies grow. Three-quarters of *Inc.* 500 companies have been funded on $100,000 or less.[15]

The two forms of business financing are **debt**, borrowed funds that must be repaid with interest over a stated time period, and **equity**, funds raised through the sale of stock (i.e., ownership) in the business. Those who provide equity funds get a share of the business's profits. Because lenders usually limit debt financing to no more than a quarter to a third of the firm's total needs, equity financing often amounts to about 65 to 75 percent of total start-up financing.

Exhibit 5.5   FUBU started when a young entrepreneur from Hollis, Queens, began making tie-top skullcaps at home with some friends. With funding from a $100,000 mortgage and a later investment from the Samsung Corporation, CEO Daymond John, turned his home into a successful sportswear company. The FUBU brand tops the list for today's fashionistas who don everything from FUBU's classic Fat Albert line to swanky FUBU suits and tuxedos. *How do start-ups obtain funding?* (Credit: U.S. Embasy Nairobi/ flickr/ Attribution 2.0 Generic (CC BY 2.0))

One way to finance a start-up company is bootstrapping, which is basically funding the operation with your own resources. If the resources needed are not available to an individual, there are other options. Two sources of equity financing for young companies are angel investors and venture-capital firms. **Angel investors** are individual investors or groups of experienced investors who provide financing for start-up businesses by investing their own money, often referred to as "seed capital." This gives the investors more flexibility on what they can and will invest in, but because it is their own money, angels are careful. Angel investors often invest early in a company's development, and they want to see an idea they understand and can have confidence in. Table 5.9 offers some guidelines on how to attract angel financing.

Making a Heavenly Deal

You need financing for your start-up business. How do you get angels interested in investing in your business venture?

- Show them something they understand, ideally a business from an industry they've been associated with.
- Know your business details: Information important to potential investors includes annual sales, gross profit, profit margin, and expenses.
- Be able to describe your business—what it does and who it sells to—in less than a minute. Limit PowerPoint presentations to 10 slides.
- Angels can always leave their money in the bank, so an investment must interest them. It should be something they're passionate about. And timing is important—knowing when to reach out to an angel can make a huge difference.
- They need to see management they trust, respect, and like. Present a competent management team with a strong, experienced leader who can explain the business and answer questions from potential investors with specifics.
- Angels prefer something they can bring added value to. Those who invest could be involved with your company for a long time or perhaps take a seat on your board of directors.
- They are more partial to deals that don't require huge sums of money or additional infusions of angel cash.
- Emphasize the likely exits for investors and know who the competition is, why your solution is better, and how you are going to gain market share with an infusion of cash.

Table 5.9 Sources: Guy Kawasaki, "The Art of Raising Angel Capital," https://guykawasaki.com, accessed February 2, 2018; Murray Newlands, "How to Raise an Angel Funding Round," *Forbes,* https://www.forbes.com, March 16, 2017; Melinda Emerson, "5 Tips for Attracting Angel Investors," *Small Business Trends,* https://smallbiztrends.com, July 26, 2016; Nicole Fallon, "5 Tips for Attracting Angel Investors," *Business News Daily,* https://www.businessnewsdaily.com, January 2, 2014; Stacy Zhao, "9 Tips for Winning over Angels," *Inc.,* https://www.inc.com, June 15, 2005; Rhonda Abrams, "What Does It Take to Impress an Angel Investor?" *Inc.,* https://www.inc.com, March 29, 2001.

Venture capital is financing obtained from *venture capitalists,* investment firms that specialize in financing small, high-growth companies. Venture capitalists receive an ownership interest and a voice in management in return for their money. They typically invest at a later stage than angel investors. We'll discuss venture capital in greater detail when discussing financing the enterprise.

Buying a Small Business

Another route to small-business ownership is buying an existing business. Although this approach is less risky, many of the same steps for starting a business from scratch apply to buying an existing company. It still requires careful and thorough analysis. The potential buyer must answer several important questions: Why is the owner selling? Does he or she want to retire or move on to a new challenge, or are there problems with the business? Is the business operating at a profit? If not, can this be corrected? On what basis has the owner valued the company, and is it a fair price? What are the owner's plans after selling the company? Will he or she be available to provide assistance through the change of ownership of the business? And depending on the type of business it is, will customers be more loyal to the owner than to the product or service being offered? Customers could leave the firm if the current owner decides to open a similar business. To protect against this, many purchasers include a *noncompete clause* in the contract of sale, which generally means that the owner of the company being sold may not be allowed to compete in the same industry of the acquired business for a specific amount of time.

You should prepare a business plan that thoroughly analyzes all aspects of the business. Get answers to all your questions, and determine, via the business plan, whether the business is a sound one. Then you must negotiate the price and other terms of purchase and obtain appropriate financing. This can be a complicated process and may require the use of a consultant or business broker.

Risky Business

Running your own business may not be as easy as it sounds. Despite the many advantages of being your own boss, the risks are great as well. Over a period of five years, nearly 50% percent of small businesses fail according to the Kauffman Foundation.[16]

Businesses close down for many reasons—and not all are failures. Some businesses that close are financially successful and close for nonfinancial reasons. But the causes of business failure can be interrelated. For example, low sales and high expenses are often directly related to poor management. Some common causes of business closure are:

- Economic factors—business downturns and high interest rates
- Financial causes—inadequate capital, low cash balances, and high expenses
- Lack of experience—inadequate business knowledge, management experience, and technical expertise
- Personal reasons—the owners may decide to sell the business or move on to other opportunities

Inadequate early planning is often at the core of later business problems. As described earlier, a thorough feasibility analysis, from market assessment to financing, is critical to business success. Yet even with the best plans, business conditions change and unexpected challenges arise. An entrepreneur may start a company based on a terrific new product only to find that a larger firm with more marketing, financing, and distribution clout introduces a similar item.

The stress of managing a business can also take its toll. The business can consume your whole life. Owners may find themselves in over their heads and unable to cope with the pressures of business operations, from the long hours to being the main decision maker. Even successful businesses have to deal with ongoing challenges. Growing too quickly can cause as many problems as sluggish sales. Growth can strain a company's finances when additional capital is required to fund expanding operations, from hiring additional staff to purchasing more raw material or equipment. Successful business owners must respond quickly and develop plans to manage its growth.

So, how do you know when it is time to quit? "Never give up" may be a good motivational catchphrase, but it is not always good advice for a small-business owner. Yet, some small-business owners keep going no matter what the cost. For example, Ian White's company was trying to market a new kind of city map. White maxed out 11 credit cards and ran up more than $100,000 in debt after starting his company. He ultimately declared personal bankruptcy and was forced to find a job so that he could pay his bills. Maria Martz didn't realize her small business would become a casualty until she saw her tax return showing her company's losses in black and white—for the second year in a row. It convinced her that enough was enough and she gave up her gift-basket business to become a full-time homemaker. But once the decision is made, it may be tough to stick to. "I got calls from people asking how come I wasn't in business anymore. It was tempting to say I'd make their basket but I had to tell myself it is finished now."[17]

CONCEPT CHECK

1. How can potential business owners find new business ideas?
2. Why is it important to develop a business plan? What should such a plan include?
3. What financing options do small-business owners have? What risks do they face?

| 5.5 | ## Managing a Small Business

5. Why does managing a small business present special challenges for the owner?

Managing a small business is quite a challenge. Whether you start a business from scratch or buy an existing one, you must be able to keep it going. The small-business owner must be ready to solve problems as they arise and move quickly if market conditions change.

MANAGING CHANGE

Learning How to Pivot

Most small business owners either use, or at least know of, the iconic email service MailChimp, a company that is growing by more than $120 million every year and is on track to bring in $525 million over the coming year. But Ben Chestnut, the CEO and cofounder, says it took MailChimp several years to figure out what it did well.

When Chestnut was laid off from his job at the Cox Media Group in Atlanta, he founded Rocket Science Group, a web design firm. Cofounder Dan Kurzius (who taught himself to code) joined Chestnut, and they began to focus their sales efforts on tech companies. But when the tech bubble burst, they pivoted to focus on selling to airline and travel companies. Then 9/11 hit, and they needed to change focus again, this time on the real estate market. However, both Chestnut and Kurzius discovered they didn't enjoy sales (and they weren't very good at it), nor did they like the bureaucracy of working with large companies. "The only companies we could relate to were small businesses, and they always asked for email marketing."

This insight helped Chestnut to recall a product feature the Rocket Science Group had previously developed for an email greeting card project. So Chestnut and Kurzius evaluated the marketing software and began to test it with small businesses. "Our day jobs felt like going to these big organizations and pitching to them, and it was miserable," Chestnut says. "But we really loved our nighttime jobs, which were helping the small businesses use this email marketing app." Their passion, along with market feedback, led to their decision to completely focus on email marketing for small businesses. But it wasn't until almost 2009 that MailChimp found its sweet spot. The founders initially wanted to give away one product that collected subscribers and then charge for another, which was sending emails, but it would have been very difficult to divide the product into two pieces. That's when they landed on the Freemium idea. "Let's just make the whole thing free," said Chestnut.

The idea was that if they made it cheap and easy for small businesses to try MailChimp, their business would grow and they would be happy to pay for MailChimp services. MailChimp allows customers to send an email for free to 1,999 people at once but charges for emails sent to over 2,000 people and for premium features. MailChimp charges a monthly recurring fee starting at $10 for sending more than 12,000 emails a month.

The idea quickly proved to be a huge success. MailChimp went from a few hundred thousand users to 1 million users in a year. The next year they added another million users.

The MailChimp founders learned a lot of lessons during their 17 years in business. One of their most important lessons is knowing when to change. When you see an opportunity, don't be afraid to pivot and change course, especially if it means focusing on a market you're passionate about. Listening to market feedback and following their passion earned MailChimp's founders \recognition as "2017 Business of the Year" by *Inc.* magazine.

Critical Thinking Questions
1. What led MailChimp's founders to change its focus on the customers they were selling to?
2. What was MailChimp's "big idea" that changed the business, and why was it so successful?

Sources: Maria Aspan, "Want Proof That Patience Pays Off? Ask the Founders of This 17-Year-Old $525 Million Email Empire," *Inc.*, https://www.inc.com, Winter 2017/January 2018 issue; "MailChimp: From Startup to Inc. Magazine's Top Company," *CNBC,* https://www.cnbc.com, December 12, 2017; Farhad Manjoo, "MailChimp and the Un-Silicon Valley Way to Make It as a Start-Up," *The New York Times,* https://www.nytimes.com, October 5, 2016.

A sound business plan is key to keeping the small-business owner in touch with all areas of his or her business. Hiring, training, and managing employees is another important responsibility because the owner's role may change over time. As the company grows, others will make many of the day-to-day decisions while the owner focuses on managing employees and planning for the firm's long-term success. The owner must constantly evaluate company performance and policies in light of changing market and economic conditions and develop new policies as required. He or she must also nurture a continual flow of ideas to keep the business growing. The types of employees needed may change too as the firm grows. For instance, a larger firm may need more managerial talent and technical expertise.

Using Outside Consultants

One way to ease the burden of managing a business is to hire outside consultants. Nearly all small businesses need a good certified public accountant (CPA) who can help with financial record keeping, decision-making, and tax planning. An accountant who works closely with the owner to help the business grow is a valuable asset. An attorney who knows about small-business law can provide legal advice and draw up essential contracts and documents. Consultants in areas such as marketing, employee benefits, and insurance can be used on an as-needed basis. Outside directors with business experience are another way for small companies to get advice. Resources such as these free the small-business owner to concentrate on medium- and long-range planning and day-to-day operations.

Some aspects of business can be outsourced or contracted out to specialists. Among the more common departments that use outsourcing are information technology, marketing, customer service, order fulfillment, payroll, and human resources. Hiring an outside company—in many cases another small business—can save money because the purchasing firm buys just the services it needs and makes no investment in expensive technology. Management should review outsourced functions as the business grows because at some point it may be more cost-effective to bring them in-house.

Hiring and Retaining Employees

It is important to identify all the costs involved in hiring an employee to make sure your business can afford it. Recruiting, help-wanted ads, extra space, and taxes will easily add about 10–15 percent to their salary, and employee benefits will add even more. Hiring an employee may also mean more work for you in terms of training and management. It's a catch-22: To grow you need to hire more people, but making the shift from solo worker to boss can be stressful.

Attracting good employees is more difficult for a small firm, which may not be able to match the higher salaries, better benefits, and advancement potential offered by larger firms. Small companies need to be creative to attract the right employees and convince applicants to join their firm. Once they hire an employee, small-business owners must make employee satisfaction a top priority in order to retain good people. A company culture that nurtures a comfortable environment for workers, flexible hours, employee benefit programs, opportunities to help make decisions, and a share in profits and ownership are some ways to do this.

Duane Ruh figured out how to build a $1.2 million business in a town with just 650 residents. It's all about treating employees right. The log birdhouse and bird feeder manufacturer, Little Log Co., located in Sargent, Nebraska, boasts employee-friendly policies you read about but rarely see put into practice. Ruh offers his employees a flexible schedule that gives them plenty of time for their personal lives. During a slow period last summer, Ruh cut back on hours rather than lay anyone off. There just aren't that many jobs in that part of Nebraska that his employees could go to, so when he received a buyout offer that would have closed his facility but kept him in place with an enviable salary, he turned it down. Ruh also encourages his employees to pursue side or summer jobs if they need to make extra money, assuring them that their Little Log jobs are safe.[18]

Going Global with Exporting

More and more small businesses are discovering the benefits of looking beyond the United States for market opportunities. The global marketplace represents a huge opportunity for U.S. businesses, both large and small. Small businesses' decision to export is driven by many factors, one of which is the desire for increased sales and higher profits. U.S. goods are less expensive for overseas buyers when the value of the U.S. dollar declines against foreign currencies, and this creates opportunities for U.S. companies to sell globally. In addition, economic conditions such as a domestic recession, foreign competition within the United States, or new markets opening up in foreign countries may also encourage U.S. companies to export.

Like any major business decision, exporting requires careful planning. Small businesses may hire international-trade consultants or distributors to get started selling overseas. These specialists have the time, knowledge, and resources that most small businesses lack. Export trading companies (ETCs) buy goods at a discount from small businesses and resell them abroad. Export management companies (EMCs) act on a company's behalf. For fees of 5–15 percent of gross sales and multiyear contracts, they handle all aspects of exporting, including finding customers, billing, shipping, and helping the company comply with foreign regulations.

Many online resources are also available to identify potential markets for your goods and services, as well as to decipher the complexities involved in preparing to sell in a foreign country. The Small Business Association's Office of International Trade has links to many valuable sites. The Department of Commerce offers services for small businesses that want to sell abroad. Contact its Trade Information Center, 1-800-USA-TRADE, or its Export Center (**http://www.export.gov**).

CONCEPT CHECK

1. How does the small-business owner's role change over time?
2. How does managing a small business contribute to its growth?
3. What are the benefits to small firms of doing business internationally, and what steps can small businesses take to explore their options?

5.6 | Small Business, Large Impact

6. What are the advantages and disadvantages facing owners of small businesses?

An uncertain economy has not stopped people from starting new companies. The National Federation of Independent Businesses reports that 85 percent of Americans view small businesses as a positive influence on American life. This is not surprising when you consider the many reasons why small businesses continue to thrive in the United States:

- *Independence and a better lifestyle:* Large corporations no longer represent job security or offer the fast-track career opportunities they once did. Mid-career employees leave the corporate world—either voluntarily or as a result of downsizing—in search of the new opportunities that self-employment provides. Many new college and business school graduates shun the corporate world altogether to start their own companies or look for work in smaller firms.
- *Personal satisfaction from work:* Many small-business owners cite this as one of the primary reasons for starting their companies. They love what they do.
- *Best route to success:* Business ownership provides greater advancement opportunities for women and minorities, as we will discuss later in this chapter. It also offers small-business owners the potential for profit.
- *Rapidly changing technology:* Technology advances and decreased costs provide individuals and small companies with the power to compete in industries that were formerly closed to them.
- *Major corporate restructuring and downsizing:* These force many employees to look for other jobs or careers. They may also provide the opportunity to buy a business unit that a company no longer wants.
- *Outsourcing:* As a result of downsizing, corporations may contract with outside firms for services they used to provide in-house. Outsourcing creates opportunities for smaller companies that offer these specialized goods and services.
- *Small businesses are resilient:* They are able to respond fairly quickly to changing economic conditions by refocusing their operations.

There are several cities and regions that are regarded as the best locations for start-up businesses and entrepreneurs. Among them are Tulsa, Oklahoma; Tampa, Florida; Atlanta, Georgia; Raleigh, North Carolina; Oklahoma City, Oklahoma; Seattle, Washington; Minneapolis, Minnesota; and Austin, Texas.[19]

Why Stay Small?

Owners of small businesses recognize that being small offers special advantages. Greater flexibility and an uncomplicated company structure allow small businesses to react more quickly to changing market forces. Innovative product ideas can be developed and brought to market more quickly, using fewer financial resources and personnel than would be needed in a larger company. And operating more efficiently keeps costs down as well. Small companies can also serve specialized markets that may not be cost-effective for large companies. Another feature is the opportunity to provide a higher level of personal service. Such attention brings many customers back to small businesses such as gourmet restaurants, health clubs, spas, fashion boutiques, and travel agencies.

Steve Niewulis played in baseball's minor leagues before an injury to his rotator cuff cut short his career. Niewulis decided to combine his love of the game with a clever idea that has elevated him to the big leagues. The fact that players had trouble keeping their hands dry while batting inspired his big idea: a sweat-busting rosin bag attached to a wristband so that a player can dry the bat handle between pitches. In less than two years, Niewulis's Fort Lauderdale, Florida, company, Tap It! Inc., sold thousands of Just Tap It! wristbands. The product, which retails for $12.95, is used by baseball players, basketball players, tennis players, golfers, and even rock climbers. His secret to success? Find a small distribution network that allows small companies, with just one product line, to succeed.[20]

On the other hand, being small is not always an asset. The founders may have limited managerial skills or encounter difficulties obtaining adequate financing, potential obstacles to growing a company. Complying with federal regulations is also more expensive for small firms. Those with fewer than 20 employees spend about twice as much per employee on compliance than do larger firms. In addition, starting and managing a small business requires a major commitment by the owner. Long hours, the need for owners to do much of the work themselves, and the stress of being personally responsible for the success of the business can take a toll.

But managing your company's growing pains doesn't need to be a one-person job. Four years after he started DrinkWorks (now Whirley DrinkWorks), a company that makes custom drinking cups, Richard Humphrey was logging 100-hour weeks. "I was concerned that if I wasn't there every minute, the company would fall apart." Humphrey got sick, lost weight, and had his engagement fall apart. When forced by a family emergency to leave the company in the hands of his five employees, Humphrey was amazed at how well they managed in his absence. "They stepped up to the plate and it worked out," he says. "After that the whole company balanced out."[21]

CONCEPT CHECK

1. Why are small businesses becoming so popular?
2. Discuss the major advantages and disadvantages of small businesses.

5.7 | The Small Business Administration

7. How does the Small Business Administration help small businesses?

Many small-business owners turn to the **Small Business Administration (SBA)** for assistance. The SBA's mission is to speak on behalf of small business, and through its national network of local offices it helps people start and manage small businesses, advises them in the areas of finance and management, and helps them win federal contracts. Its toll-free number—1-800-U-ASK-SBA (1-800-827-5722)—provides general information, and its website at **http://www.sba.gov** offers details on all its programs.[22]

Financial Assistance Programs

The SBA offers financial assistance to qualified small businesses that cannot obtain financing on reasonable terms through normal lending channels. This assistance takes the form of guarantees on loans made by private lenders. (The SBA no longer provides direct loans.) These loans can be used for most business purposes, including purchasing real estate, equipment, and materials. The SBA has been responsible for a significant amount of small-business financing in the United States. In the fiscal year ending on September 30, 2017, the SBA backed more than $25 billion in loans to almost 68,000 small businesses, including about $9 billion to minority-owned firms and $7.5 billion in loans to businesses owned by women. It also provided more than $1.7 billion in home and business disaster loans.[23]

Other SBA programs include the New Markets Venture Capital Program, which promotes economic development and job opportunities in low-income geographic areas, while other programs offer export financing and assistance to firms that suffer economic harm after natural or other disasters.

More than 300 SBA-licensed **Small Business Investment Companies (SBICs)** provide about $6 billion each year in long-term financing for small businesses. The SBA's website suggests seeking angel investors and using SBA-guaranteed loans as a way to fund the start-up. These privately owned and managed investment companies hope to earn a substantial return on their investments as the small businesses grow.

SCORE-ing with Management Assistance Programs

The SBA also provides a wide range of management advice. Its Business Development Library has publications on most business topics. Its "Starting Out" series offers brochures on how to start a wide variety of businesses—from ice-cream stores to fish farms.

Business development officers at the Office of Business Development and local Small Business Development Centers counsel many thousands of small-business owners each year, offering advice, training, and educational programs. The SBA also offers free management consulting through two volunteer groups: the Service Corps of Retired Executives (SCORE), and the Active Corps of Executives (ACE). Executives in these programs use their own business backgrounds to help small-business owners. SCORE has expanded its outreach into new markets by offering email counseling through its website (**http://www.score.org**). The SBA also offers free online resources and courses for small-business owners and aspiring entrepreneurs in its Learning Center, located on the SBA website under the "Learning Center" tab.

Assistance for Women and Minorities

The SBA is committed to helping women and minorities increase their business participation. It offers a minority small-business program, microloans, and the publication of Spanish-language informational materials. It has increased its responsiveness to small businesses by giving regional offices more decision authority and creating high-tech tools for grants, loan transactions, and eligibility reviews.

The SBA offers special programs and support services for socially and economically disadvantaged persons, including women, Native Americans, and Hispanics through its Minority Business Development Agency. It also makes a special effort to help veterans go into business for themselves.

CONCEPT CHECK

1. What is the Small Business Administration (SBA)?
2. Describe the financial and management assistance programs offered by the SBA.

5.8 Trends in Entrepreneurship and Small-Business Ownership

8. What trends are shaping entrepreneurship and small-business ownership?

Entrepreneurship has changed since the heady days of the late 1990s, when starting a dot-com while still in college seemed a quick route to riches and stock options. Much entrepreneurial opportunity comes from major changes in demographics, society, and technology, and at present there is a confluence of all three. A major demographic group is moving into a significantly different stage in life, and minorities are increasing their business ownership in remarkable numbers. We have created a society in which we expect to have our problems taken care of, and the technological revolution stands ready with already-developed solutions. Evolving social and demographic trends, combined with the challenge of operating in a fast-paced technology-dominated business climate, are changing the face of entrepreneurship and small-business ownership.

Into the Future: Start-ups Drive the Economy

Did new business ventures drive the economic recovery from the 2001–2002 and 2007–2009 to recessions, and are they continuing to make significant contributions to the U.S. economy? The economists who review Department of Labor employment surveys and SBA statistics think so. "Small business drives the American economy," says Dr. Chad Moutray, former chief economist for the SBA's Office of Advocacy. "Main Street provides the jobs and spurs our economic growth. American entrepreneurs are creative and productive." Numbers alone do not tell the whole story, however. Are these newly self-employed workers profiting from their ventures, or are they just biding their time during a period of unemployment?

U.S. small businesses employed 57.9 million people in 2016, representing nearly 48 percent of the workforce. The number of net new jobs added to the economy was 1.4 million.[24]

The highest rate of growth is coming from women-owned firms, which continues to rise at rates higher than the national average—and with even stronger growth rates since the recession. There were an estimated 11.6 million women-owned businesses employing nearly 9 million people in 2016, generating more than $1.7 trillion in revenue.[25]

Between 2007 and 2017, women-owned firms increased by 114 percent, compared to a 44 percent increase among all businesses. This means that growth rates for women-owned businesses are 2.5 times faster than the national average. Employment growth was also stronger than national rates. Women-owned businesses increased 27 percent over the past 20 years, while overall business employment has increased by 13 percent since 2007.[26]

These trends show that more workers are striking out on their own and earning money doing it. It has become very clear that encouraging small-business activity leads to continued strong overall economic growth.

Changing Demographics Create Entrepreneurial Diversity

The mantra, "60 is the new 40," describes today's Baby Boomers who indulge in much less knitting and golf in their retirement years. The AARP predicts that silver-haired entrepreneurs will continue to rise in the coming years. According to a recent study by the Kauffman Foundation, Baby Boomers are twice as likely as Millennials to start a new business. In fact, close to 25 percent of all new entrepreneurs fall between the ages of 55 and 64.[27] This has created a ripple effect in the way we work. Boomers have accelerated the growing acceptance of working from home, adding to the millions of U.S. workers already showing up to work in their slippers. In addition, the ongoing corporate brain drain could mean that small businesses will be able to tap into the expertise of seasoned free agents at less-than-corporate prices—and that seniors themselves will become independent consultants to businesses of all sizes.[28]

The growing numbers of Baby Boomer entrepreneurs has prompted some forward-thinking companies to recognize business opportunities in technology. At one time there was a concern that the aging of the population would create a drag on the economy. Conventional wisdom says that the early parenthood years are the big spending years. As we age, we spend less and, because Boomers are such a big demographic group, this was going to create a long-term economic decline. Not true, it now appears. The Boomer generation has built sizable wealth, and they are not afraid to spend it to make their lives more comfortable.

Minorities are also adding to the entrepreneurial mix. As we saw in Table 5.3, minority groups and women are increasing business ownership at a much faster rate than the national average, reflecting their confidence in the U.S. economy. These overwhelming increases in minority business ownership paralleled the demand for U.S. Small Business Administration loan products. Loans to minority business owners in fiscal year 2017 set a record—more than $9.5 billion, or 31 percent, of SBA's total loan portfolio.[29]

The latest Kauffman Foundation Index of Startup Activity found that immigrants and Latinos have swelled the growing numbers of self-employed Americans in recent years, increasing the diversity of the country's entrepreneurial class. Overall, minority-owned businesses increased 38 percent. The SBA notes that the number of Hispanic-owned businesses has increased more than 46 percent between 2007 and 2012.[30]

Exhibit 5.6   The popularity of home businesses such as Rodan+Fields, eBay, and other e-commerce sites has given rise to a new kind of entrepreneur: the "mompreneur." Typically ex-corporate professionals, these web-driven women launch home businesses specializing in the sale of antiques, jewelry, thrift-store fashions, and other items. Aided by digital photography, wireless technology, and friendly postal workers, these savvy moms are one of the fastest-growing segments of entrepreneurs building successful businesses on the web. *Why are many professional women leaving the workplace to start entrepreneurial ventures online?* (Credit: Amanda nobles/ Flickr/ Attribution 2.0 Generic (CC BY 2.0))

How Far Will You Go to Get Rich?

With enough intelligence and determination, people can get rich almost anywhere in the United States. Whether you own chains of dry cleaners in Queens, car dealerships in Chicago, or oil wells in West Texas, fortunes have been made in every state in the Union. There are some places, however, where the chances of creating wealth are much greater than others. That is the reason why people who hope to strike it rich move to places such as Manhattan or Palo Alto. It's not because the cost of living is low or the quality of life as a struggling entrepreneur is fun. Whether starting a software or soft-drink company, entrepreneurs tend to follow the money

But not all companies follow the herd. Guild Education, founded in 2015 by Rachel Carlson and Brittany Stich at Stanford University, left San Francisco due to the high cost of living that could slow down the company's growth. "We have a lot of women who are executives and department heads here, starting with myself and my cofounder," CEO Rachel Carlson said. "So when we left, we deliberately chose a place where you can have a family."[31] Guild Education's mission is to help large employers offer college education and tuition reimbursement as a benefit to the 64 million working-age adults who lack a college degree.

Since moving to Denver, Guild Education has raised another $21 million in venture capital, bringing the total funding to $31.5 million with a company valuation of $125 million.[32] The company headquarters in Denver is next door to a Montessori school and employs 58 employees. "We were joking that we're the polar opposite of Apple," said Carlson. "Remember when the new 'mothership' came out? Every single parent noticed that it had a huge gym but not a day care."

According to PwC's quarterly venture capital study, "MoneyTree Report," the top regions in the United States for venture-backed deals in the third quarter of 2017 were San Francisco ($4.1 billion), New York Metro ($4.2 billion), Silicon Valley (Bay Area $2.2 billion), and New England ($1.8 billion).[33]

In 2017, equity financing in U.S. start-ups rose for the third straight quarter, reaching $19 billion, according to the PwC/CB Insights "MoneyTree Report Q3 2017." "Financing was boosted by a large number of mega-rounds," says Tom Ciccolella, Partner, U.S. Ventures Leader at PwC.[34] Twenty-six mega-rounds of $100 million in companies such as WeWork, 23andMe, Fanatics, and NAUTO contributed to the strong activity levels in the first three quarters of 2017. The top five U.S. industry sectors with the most deals and funding were Internet, Healthcare, Mobile and Telecommunications, Software (Non-Internet/Mobile), and Consumer Products.

CONCEPT CHECK

1. What significant trends are occurring in the small-business arena?
2. How is entrepreneurial diversity impacting small business and the economy?
3. How do ethics impact decision-making with small-business owners?

🔑 Key Terms

angel investors Individual investors or groups of experienced investors who provide financing for start-up businesses by investing their own funds.

business plan A formal written statement that describes in detail the idea for a new business and how it will be carried out; includes a general description of the company, the qualifications of the owner(s), a description of the product or service, an analysis of the market, and a financial plan.

debt A form of business financing consisting of borrowed funds that must be repaid with interest over a stated time period.

entrepreneurs People with vision, drive, and creativity who are willing to take the risk of starting and managing a business to make a profit, or greatly changing the scope and direction of an existing firm.

equity A form of business financing consisting of funds raised through the sale of stock (i.e., ownership) in a business.

intrapreneurs Entrepreneurs who apply their creativity, vision, and risk-taking within a large corporation, rather than starting a company of their own.

small business A business with under 500 employees that is independently managed, is owned by an individual or a small group of investors, is based locally, and is not a dominant company in its industry.

Small Business Administration (SBA) A government agency that speaks on behalf of small business; specifically it helps people start and manage small businesses, advises them in the areas of finance and management, and helps them win federal contracts.

Small Business Investment Company (SBIC) Privately owned and managed investment companies that are licensed by the Small Business Administration and provide long-term financing for small businesses.

venture capital Financing obtained from venture capitalists, investment firms that specialize in financing small, high-growth companies and receive an ownership interest and a voice in management in return for their money.

📑 Summary of Learning Outcomes

5.1 Entrepreneurship Today
1. Why do people become entrepreneurs, and what are the different types of entrepreneurs?

Entrepreneurs are innovators who take the risk of starting and managing a business to make a profit. Most want to develop a company that will grow into a major corporation. People become entrepreneurs for four main reasons: the opportunity for profit, independence, personal satisfaction, and lifestyle. Classic entrepreneurs may be micropreneurs, who plan to keep their businesses small, or growth-oriented entrepreneurs. Multipreneurs start multiple companies, while intrapreneurs work within large corporations.

5.2 Characteristics of Successful Entrepreneurs
2. What characteristics do successful entrepreneurs share?

Successful entrepreneurs are ambitious, independent, self-confident, creative, energetic, passionate, and committed. They have a high need for achievement and a willingness to take moderate risks. Good managerial, interpersonal, and communication skills, as well as technical knowledge are important for entrepreneurial success.

5.3 Small Business: Driving America's Growth
3. How do small businesses contribute to the U.S. economy?

Small businesses play an important role in the economy. They account for over 99 percent of all employer firms and produce about half of U.S. economic output. Most new private-sector jobs created in the United States over the past decade were in small firms. The Small Business Administration defines a small business as independently owned and operated, with a local base of operations, and not dominant in its field. It also defines small business by size, according to its industry. Small businesses are found in every field, but they dominate the service, construction, wholesale, and retail categories.

5.4 Ready, Set, Start Your Own Business

4.   What are the first steps to take if you are starting your own business?

After finding an idea that satisfies a market need, the small-business owner should choose a form of business organization. Preparing a formal business plan helps the business owner analyze the feasibility of his or her idea. The written plan describes in detail the idea for the business and how it will be implemented and operated. The plan also helps the owner obtain both debt and equity financing for the new business.

5.5 Managing a Small Business

5.   Why does managing a small business present special challenges for the owner?

At first, small-business owners are involved in all aspects of the firm's operations. Hiring and retaining key employees and the wise use of outside consultants can free up an owner's time to focus on planning, strategizing, and monitoring market conditions, in addition to overseeing day-to-day operations. Expanding into global markets can be a profitable growth strategy for a small business.

5.6 Small Business, Large Impact

6.   What are the advantages and disadvantages facing owners of small businesses?

Because of their streamlined staffing and structure, small businesses can be efficiently operated. They have the flexibility to respond to changing market conditions. Small firms can serve specialized markets more profitably than large firms, and they provide a higher level of personal service. Disadvantages include limited managerial skill, difficulty in raising capital needed for start-up or expansion, the burden of complying with increasing levels of government regulation, and the major personal commitment that is required by the owner.

5.7 The Small Business Administration

7.   How does the Small Business Administration help small businesses?

The Small Business Administration is the main federal agency serving small businesses. It provides guarantees of private-lender loans for small businesses. The SBA also offers a wide range of management assistance services, including courses, publications, and consulting. It has special programs for women, minorities, and veterans.

5.8 Trends in Entrepreneurship and Small-Business Ownership

8.   What trends are shaping entrepreneurship and small-business ownership?

Changes in demographics, society, and technology are shaping the future of entrepreneurship and small business in America. More than ever, opportunities exist for entrepreneurs of all ages and backgrounds. The numbers of women and minority business owners continues to rise, and older entrepreneurs are changing the small-business landscape. Catering to the needs of an older population and a surge in web-based companies fuel continues technology growth. Entrepreneurs typically follow the money and set up shop in places where there is venture capital money easily available.

▣ Preparing for Tomorrow's Workplace Skills

1. After working in software development with a major food company for 12 years, you are becoming impatient with corporate "red tape" (regulations and routines). You have an idea for a new snack product for nutrition-conscious consumers and are thinking of starting your own company. What entrepreneurial characteristics do you need to succeed? What other factors should you consider before quitting your job? Working with a partner, choose one to be the entrepreneurial employee and one to play the role of his or her current boss. Develop notes for a script. The employee will focus on why this is a good idea—reasons he or she will succeed—and the employer will play devil's advocate to convince him or her that staying on at the large company is a better idea. Then switch roles and repeat the discussion. (Information, Interpersonal)

2. What does it really take to become an entrepreneur? Find out by interviewing a local entrepreneur or researching an entrepreneur you've read about in this chapter or in the business press. Get answers to the following questions, as well as any others you'd like to ask:

   - How did you research the feasibility of your idea?
   - How did you develop your vision for the company?
   - How long did it take you to prepare your business plan?
   - Where did you obtain financing for the company?
   - Where did you learn the business skills you needed to run and grow the company?
   - What are the most important entrepreneurial characteristics that helped you succeed?
   - What were the biggest challenges you had to overcome?
   - What are the most important lessons you learned by starting this company?
   - What advice do you have for would-be entrepreneurs?

   (Information, Interpersonal, Systems)

3. A small catering business in your city is for sale for $250,000. The company specializes in business luncheons and small social events. The owner has been running the business for four years from her home but is expecting her first child and wants to sell. You will need outside investors to help you purchase the business. Develop questions to ask the owner about the business and its prospects, as well as a list of documents you want to see. What other types of information would you need before making a decision to buy this company? Summarize your findings in a memo to a potential investor that explains the appeal of the business for you and how you plan to investigate the feasibility of the purchase. (Information, Interpersonal)

4. Research various types of assistance available to women and minority business owners. Call or visit the nearest SBA office to find out what services and resources it offers. Contact trade associations such as the National Foundation for Women Business Owners (NFWBO), the National Alliance of Black Entrepreneurs, the U.S. Hispanic Chamber of Commerce, and the U.S. Department of Commerce Minority Business Development Agency (MBDA). Call these groups or use the internet to develop a list of their resources and how a small-business owner could use them. (Information, Interpersonal, Technology)

5. Do you have what it takes to be an entrepreneur or small-business owner? You can find many online quizzes to help you figure this out. The Success website offers a quiz to determine whether you have an entrepreneurial mindset at **https://www.success.com.** What did your results tell you, and were you surprised by what you learned? (Information, Technology)

6. **Team Activity** Your class decides to participate in a local business plan competition. Divide the class into small groups, and choose one of the following ideas:

   - A new computer game based on the stock market
   - A company with an innovative design for a skateboard

◦ Travel services for college and high school students

Prepare a detailed outline for the business plan, including the objectives for the business and the types of information you would need to develop product, marketing, and financing strategies. Each group will then present its outline for the class to critique. (Information, Interpersonal, Systems)

Ethics Activity

As the owner of a small factory that makes plastic sheeting, you are constantly seeking ways to increase profits. As the new year begins, one of your goals is to find additional funds to offer annual productivity and/or merit bonuses to your loyal, hardworking employees.

Then a letter from a large national manufacturer of shower curtains seems to provide an answer. As part of a new "supplier diversity" program it is putting in place, the manufacturer is offering substantial purchase contracts to minority-owned suppliers. Even though the letter clearly states that the business must be *minority owned* to qualify for the program, you convince yourself to apply for it based on the fact that all your employees are Latino. You justify your decision by deciding they will benefit from the increased revenue a larger contract will bring, some of which you plan to pass on to them in the form of bonuses later in the year.

Using a web search tool, locate articles about this topic, and then write responses to the following questions. Be sure to support your arguments and cite your sources.

Ethical Dilemma: Is it wrong for this business owner to apply for this program even though it will end up benefiting his employees as well as his business?

Working the Net

1. Visit Sample Business Plans at **http://www.bplans.com** to review examples of all types of business plans. Select an idea for a company in a field that interests you and, using information from the site, prepare an outline for its business plan.
2. Find a business idea you like or dislike by searching the web. Explain why you think this is a good business idea or not. List additional information the entrepreneur should have to consider for this business, and research the industry on the web using a search engine.
3. Evaluate the export potential of your product idea at the Small Business Exporters Network website. Explore three information areas, including market research, export readiness, and financing. Select a trade link site from government, university, or private categories. Compare them in terms of the information offered to small businesses that want to venture into overseas markets. Which is the most useful, and why?
4. Explore the SBA website at **http://www.sba.gov**. What resources are available to you locally? What classes does the Learning Center offer? What about financing assistance? Do you think the website lives up to the SBA's goal of being a one-stop shopping resource for the small-business owner? Why or why not?
5. You want to buy a business but don't know much about valuing small companies. Using the "Business for Sale" column available online at **http://www.inc.com**, develop a checklist of questions to ask when buying a business. Also summarize several ways that businesses arrive at their sale price ("Business for Sale" includes the price rationale for each profiled business).

Critical Thinking Case

Fostering Entrepreneurship in Unlikely Places

Vic Ahmed is no stranger to business start-ups; he's been involved in at least 15 or 20. But his latest venture is a start-up ... for start-ups. Ahmed founded Innovation Pavilion, a business incubator in Centennial, Colorado (Denver's Tech Center), in 2011. A typical business incubator provides start-up companies with workspace, mentoring, training, and sometimes a path to funding, but Innovation Pavilion goes further.

Innovation Pavilion (IP) is an 80,000 square foot "entrepreneurial ecosystem," housing dozens of start-ups and renting out desks, office space, and event space. But it also hosts meetups, educational workshops, and a Toastmasters group designed specifically for entrepreneurs. It contains a makerspace (a workspace providing shared tools and manufacturing equipment for prototyping products) and encourages the growth of niche entrepreneurial communities based on specific industries. For example, IP has a space for IoT (the Internet of Things), one for health care, and another for aerospace. These communities bring together people in an industry to learn from and collaborate with each other.

While IP has a traditional incubator program, with companies housed within the IP campus, it has a semi-virtual hypergrowth accelerator program for more mature firms, too, which is open to companies around the country. It also seeks out educational partnerships, working with the Highland's Ranch STEM program, for instance, and has its own educational spin-off, Xuno Innovative Learning, designed to help companies train their staff and find new employees with the skills they need. IP operates its own streaming TV service, filming educational events and interviews with entrepreneurs.

Innovation Pavilion has national expansion plans—and several signed agreements with specific cities—targeting not the giant metropolitan areas but also second tier and "ring" cities across the country, such as Joliet, Illinois, and Olathe, Kansas, smaller cities that don't get the attention of the larger cities yet have plenty of educated and creative people.

IP is in discussions with 20 cities around the nation, with the goal of building 200,000-square-foot campuses providing incubator services, office space, makerspace, education and training, outreach to young entrepreneurs, conference centers, retail space, and even housing. Entrepreneurs will be able to live and work in a space with everything they need, providing a complete entrepreneurial ecosystem in smaller cities across the nation.

Steve Case, the cofounder of America Online (AOL), shares Vic Ahmed's vision for entrepreneurship in mid-America. His "Rise of the Rest" bus tour has traveled 8,000 miles over the last three years, investing in local start-ups in 33 cities across the country. Case hosts a pitch competition with the best start-ups in each city, and one lucky winner receives a $100,000 investment from Case.

Media attention has focused on the entrepreneurial engines of America's coastal cities, but Ahmed and Case have a more expansive entrepreneurial vision, in which smaller cities throughout the nation rise up alongside larger, start-up hot spots.

Critical Thinking Questions
1. What characteristics made Vic Ahmed a successful entrepreneurs?
2. How did their Ahmed and Steven Case's partnership and shared vision of "Rise of the Rest" serve their business goals?
3. Is focusing on smaller cities rather than areas like silicon valley a good strategy, why?

Sources: Innovation Pavilion website http://www.innovationpavilion.com/ accessed February, 13, 2018; Tamara

Chuang, Centennial incubator plans coworking office expansion to Illinois, complete with STEM school, housing," *Denver Post,* August 1, 2017, https://www.denverpost.com/2017/08/01/innovation-pavilion-illinois-expansion/; Jan Wondra, Innovation Pavilion Expands Base," *The Villager*, November 29, 2017, https://villagerpublishing.com/innovation-pavilion-expands-geographic-base/.

🔲 Hot Links Address Book

1. Do you have a great business idea? Taking the quiz at **http://www.edwardlowe.org**, the Edward Lowe Foundation's website, will help you determine how feasible the idea is.
2. Do you have what it takes to become an entrepreneur? Take the quiz at **https://www.entrepreneur.com/article/247560** to find out.
3. Before your business travels to foreign shores, pay a visit to the SBA's Office of International Trade to learn the best ways to enter global markets at **https://www.sba.gov/offices/headquarters/oit/ resources**.
4. How can you find qualified overseas companies to buy your products? Find out how BuyUSA.com can help you become part of an e-marketplace at **http://www.buyusa.com**.
5. If you are considering starting a business at home, you'll find tips and advice at the American Association of Home-Based Businesses website at **http://www.aahbb.org**.
6. To learn about the services the U.S. Department of Commerce's Minority Business Development Agency provides for small-business owners, check out **http://www.mbda.gov**.

Exhibit 6.1 (Credit: Urs Rüegsegger / flickr / Public Domain Mark 1.0)

 Introduction

Learning Outcomes

After reading this chapter, you should be able to answer these questions:

1. What is the role of management?
2. What are the four types of planning?
3. What are the primary functions of managers in organizing activities?
4. How do leadership styles influence a corporate culture?
5. How do organizations control activities?
6. What roles do managers take on in different organizational settings?
7. What set of managerial skills is necessary for managerial success?
8. What trends will affect management in the future?

EXPLORING BUSINESS CAREERS

Jalem Getz

BuyCostumes.com/Wantable, Inc.

You might ask, "How does one come to work in the world of online costume retail?" A passion for holiday make-believe and dress-up? A keen eye for business potential? The drive to capitalize on a competitive advantage? If you're Jalem Getz, the answer is: all of these. Getz is the founder of BuyCostumes.com, an online costume and accessories retailer and, most recently, founder of Wantable, Inc.

As with most businesses, BuyCostumes.com and Wantable, Inc., are the result of careful planning. BuyCostumes.com was a response to what Getz saw as inherent flaws of resource allocation with the business model of brick-and-mortar costume retailers. "As a brick-and-mortar business, we were the gypsies of retail, which caused scale problems since we started over every year. Because we only were in a mall four or five months a year, locations we had one year often were rented the next. So we had to find new stores to rent each year. Then we had to find management to run the stores, and train employees to staff them. We also had to shuffle the inventory around each year to stock them. It's almost impossible to grow a business like that." By turning to the internet, however, Getz was able to bypass all of those issues. The virtual "space" was available year-round, and inventory and staff were centralized in a single warehouse location.

Getz grew BuyCostumes.com to a multimillion-dollar business before selling it, with a staff of about 600 employees during its peak season. Before Getz sold the business, it carried over 10,000 Halloween items and had upwards of 20 million visitors each holiday season. In one year, it shipped over 1 million costumes across the world, including 45 countries outside the United States. "We say that our goal is to ensure that anytime anyone buys a costume anywhere in the world, it will be from BuyCostumes.com. And, although to some extent we're kidding, we're also very serious."

To keep track of all this action, Getz mixed ideals of a strong work ethic, a willingness to take risks, and an interest in having fun while making a profit. Given the size of the company, BuyCostumes.com organized its management to help keep the company focused on the corporate goal of continued growth. For Getz, his role in the management hierarchy was to "hire excellent people who have similar goals and who are motivated the same way I am and then put them in a position where they can succeed." Beyond that? "Inspect what you expect." This maxim is a concise way to say that, although he does not believe in constantly watching over his employees' shoulders, he does believe in periodically checking in with them to ensure that both he and they are on the same page. By considering the process of management a conversation between himself and his employees, he exhibits a strong participative leadership style.

Getz will joke that he wishes he could say that he spent his childhood dreaming of the day he could work with costumes. The truth, though, is that he saw an opportunity, grabbed it, and hasn't let go since. And sometimes, especially during Halloween, truth can be even more satisfying than fiction.

After selling BuyCostumes.com, Getz experimented with other digital start-ups but quickly realized he worked best with retail. In 2012, he launched Wantable, Inc., an online personal shopping service. In its first four years, Getz led the company to exceed 28,000% annual revenue growth and to hire more than 100 employees. It became profitable in 2016 and looked to double its income the following year.

Sources: "About Wantable," http://blog.wantable.com, accessed October 27, 2017; "Wantable Surpasses 100 Employees," http://www.prweb.com, April 3, 2017; Jeff Engel, "Jalem Getz's Latest Retail Startup Wantable Targets Women, Fast Growth," https://www.xconomy.com, April 21, 2014.

Today's companies rely on managers to guide daily operations using human, technological, financial, and other resources to create a competitive advantage. For many beginning business students, being in "management" is an attractive but somewhat vague future goal. This vagueness is due in part to an incomplete understanding of what managers do and how they contribute to organizational success or failure. This chapter introduces the basic functions of management and the skills managers need to drive an organization toward its goals. We will also discuss how leadership styles influence a corporate culture and highlight the trends that are shaping the future role of managers.

6.1 The Role of Management

1. What is the role of management?

Management is the process of guiding the development, maintenance, and allocation of resources to attain organizational goals. Managers are the people in the organization responsible for developing and carrying out this management process. Management is dynamic by nature and evolves to meet needs and constraints in the organization's internal and external environments. In a global marketplace where the rate of change is rapidly increasing, flexibility and adaptability are crucial to the managerial process. This process is based in four key functional areas of the organization: planning, organizing, leading, and controlling. Although these activities are discussed separately in the chapter, they actually form a tightly integrated cycle of thoughts and actions.

From this perspective, the managerial process can be described as (1) anticipating potential problems or opportunities and designing plans to deal with them, (2) coordinating and allocating the resources needed to implement plans, (3) guiding personnel through the implementation process, and (4) reviewing results and making any necessary changes. This last stage provides information to be used in ongoing planning efforts, and thus the cycle starts over again. The four functions are highly interdependent, with managers often performing more than one of them at a time and each of them many times over the course of a normal workday.

Exhibit 6.2   To encourage greater collaboration between employees, Apple is investing $5 billion in the construction of its new Cupertino, CA, headquarters, which is replacing several buildings the company had outgrown. Most headquarters-based employees of Apple now share not only the same office space, but also the same technology tools and corporate culture. *How do Apple's planning and organizing decisions increase organizational efficiency and effectiveness?* (Credit: Tom Pavel / flickr/ Attribution 2.0 Generic (CC BY 2.0))

The four management functions can help managers increase organizational efficiency and effectiveness.

Efficiency is using the least possible amount of resources to get work done, whereas **effectiveness** is the ability to produce a desired result. Managers need to be both efficient and effective in order to achieve organizational goals. For example in 2016, Delta, one of the most efficient network U.S. airlines, operated at revenue of 12.15 cents per seat-mile, which is the revenue the company makes on one seat (occupied or not) the distance of one mile. No other airline came close to operating this efficiently except Southwest, which flew seats that produced 12.51 cents a mile, the best performance of all U.S. airlines.[1] There are many ways that airlines can manage to produce higher revenue per seat-mile. For instance, they can raise ticket prices, fill more of their seats, operate more efficient aircraft that utilize less fuel, or negotiate favorable salaries with their employees. While efficiency and effectiveness are sometimes lauded by investors, airlines also need to account for customer satisfaction, which can mean extra costs.[2]

To meet the demands of rapid growth, Skechers hired a new chief financial officer, John Vandemore, which allowed their existing CFO (David Weinberg) to concentrate on international expansion. Skechers CEO Robert Greenberg commented: "As international now represents more than 50 percent of our total business, we must continue to ramp up operations and infrastructure to meet the demand. David (Weinberg) understands how to do it the right way at the right speed to maintain our forward momentum. With John (Vandemore) handling CFO responsibilities, David will now have the bandwidth to travel and find opportunities to maximize our efficiencies around the globe."[3]

As these examples and Table 6.1 show, good management uses the four management functions to increase a company's efficiency and effectiveness, which leads to the accomplishment of organizational goals and objectives. Let's look more closely at what each of the management functions entails.

What Managers Do and Why			
Good management consists of these four activities:		Which results in	And leads to
Planning • Set objectives and state mission • Examine alternatives • Determine needed resources • Create strategies to reach objectives	**Leading** • Lead and motivate employees to accomplish organizational goals • Communicate with employees • Resolve conflicts • Manage change		

Table 6.1

What Managers Do and Why					
Good management consists of these four activities:			Which results in		And leads to
Organizing • Design jobs and specify tasks • Create organizational structure • Staff positions • Coordinate work activities • Set policies and procedures • Allocate resources	**Controlling** • Measure performance • Compare performance to standards • Take necessary action to improve performance	Leads to	Organizational efficiency and effectiveness	Leads to	Achievement of organizational mission and objectives

Table 6.1

CONCEPT CHECK

1. Define the term *management*.
2. What are the four key functions of managers?
3. What is the difference between efficiency and effectiveness?

6.2 Planning

2. What are the four types of planning?

Planning begins by anticipating potential problems or opportunities the organization may encounter. Managers then design strategies to solve current problems, prevent future problems, or take advantage of opportunities. These strategies serve as the foundation for goals, objectives, policies, and procedures. Put simply, planning is deciding what needs to be done to achieve organizational objectives, identifying when and how it will be done, and determining who should do it. Effective planning requires extensive information about the external business environment in which the firm competes, as well as its internal environment.

There are four basic types of planning: strategic, tactical, operational, and contingency. Most of us use these different types of planning in our own lives. Some plans are very broad and long term (more strategic in nature), such as planning to attend graduate school after earning a bachelor's degree. Some plans are much more specific and short term (more operational in nature), such as planning to spend a few hours in the library this weekend. Your short-term plans support your long-term plans. If you study now, you have a better chance of achieving some future goal, such as getting a job interview or attending graduate school. Like you, organizations tailor their plans to meet the requirements of future situations or events. A summary of the four types of planning appears in Table 6.2.

Strategic planning involves creating long-range (one to five years), broad goals for the organization and determining what resources will be needed to accomplish those goals. An evaluation of external environmental factors such as economic, technological, and social issues is critical to successful strategic planning. Strategic plans, such as the organization's long-term mission, are formulated by top-level managers and put into action at lower levels in the organization. For example, when Mickey Drexler took over as CEO of J.Crew, the company was floundering and had been recently purchased by a private equity group. One of Drexler's first moves was to change the strategic direction of the company by moving it out of the crowded trend-following retail segment, where it was competing with stores such as Gap, American Eagle, and Abercrombie and back into the preppie, luxury segment where it began. Rather than trying to sell abundant inventory to a mass market, J.Crew cultivated scarcity, making sure items sold out early rather than hit the sale rack later in the season. The company also limited the number of new stores it opened during a two-year span but planned to double the number of stores in the next five to six years. Drexler led the company through public offerings and back to private ownership before bringing on a new CEO in 2017. He remained chairman with ownership in the company.[4]

Types of Planning						
Type of Planning	Time Frame	Level of Management	Extent of coverage	Purpose and Goal	Breadth of Content	Accuracy and Predictability
Strategic	1–5 years	Top management (CEO, vice presidents, directors, division heads)	External environment and entire organization	Establish mission and long-term goals	Broad and general	High degree of uncertainty
Tactical	Less than 1 year	Middle management	Strategic business units	Establish mid-range goals for implementation	More specific	Moderate degree of certainty
Operational	Current	Supervisory management	Geographic and functional divisions	Implement and activate specific objectives	Specific and concrete	Reasonable degree of certainty

Table 6.2

Types of Planning						
Type of Planning	Time Frame	Level of Management	Extent of coverage	Purpose and Goal	Breadth of Content	Accuracy and Predictability
Contingency	When an event occurs or a situation demands	Top and middle management	External environment and entire organization	Meet unforeseen challenges and opportunities	Both broad and detailed	Reasonable degree of certainty once event or situation occurs

Table 6.2

CATCHING THE ENTREPRENEURIAL SPIRIT

Changing Strategy Can Change Your Opportunities

Since 1949, Gordon Bernard, a printing company in Milford, Ohio, focused exclusively on printing fundraising calendars for a variety of clients, such as cities, schools, scout troops, and fire departments. The company's approximately 4,000 clients nationwide, 10 percent of which have been with the company for over 50 years, generated $4 million in revenue in 2006. In order to better serve customers, company president Bob Sherman invested $650,000 in the purchase of a Xerox iGEN3 digital color press so that the company could produce in-house a part of its calendar product that had been outsourced. The high-tech press did more for the company than simply reduce costs, however.

The new press gave the company four-color printing capability for the first time in its history, and that led the management of Gordon Bernard to rethink the company's strategy. The machine excels at short runs, which means that small batches of an item can be printed at a much lower cost than on a traditional press. The press also has the capability to customize every piece that rolls off the machine. For example, if a pet store wants to print 3,000 direct mail pieces, every single postcard can have a personalized greeting and text. Pieces targeted to bird owners can feature pictures of birds, whereas the dog owners' brochure will contain dog pictures. Text and pictures can be personalized for owners of show dogs or overweight cats or iguanas.

Bob Sherman created a new division to oversee the implementation, training, marketing, and creative aspects of the new production process. The company even changed how it thinks of itself. No longer does Gordon Bernard consider itself a printing firm, but as a marketing services company with printing capabilities. That change in strategy prompted the company to seek more commercial work. For example, Gordon Bernard will help clients of its new services develop customer databases from their existing information and identify additional customer information they might want to collect. Even though calendar sales accounted for 97 percent of the firm's revenues, that business is seasonal and leaves large amounts of unused capacity in the off-peak periods. Managers' goals for the new division were to contribute 10 percent of total revenue within a couple years of purchase.

Critical Thinking Questions

1. What type of planning do you think Gordon Bernard is doing?
2. Because Gordon Bernard's strategy changed only after it purchased the iGEN3, does the shift constitute strategic planning? Why or why not?

Sources: GBC Fundraising Calendars, http://www.gordonbernard.com/, accessed September 15, 2017; Gordon Bernard Co Inc., https://www.manta.com, accessed September 15, 2017; Karen Bells, "Hot Off the Press; Milford Printer Spends Big to Fill New Niche," *Cincinnati Business Courier,* July 15, 2005, pp. 17–18.

An organization's **mission** is formalized in its **mission statement**, a document that states the purpose of the organization and its reason for existing. For example, Twitter's mission statement formalizes both concepts while staying within its self-imposed character limit; see **Table 6.3**.

Twitter's Mission, Values, and Strategy
Mission: Give everyone the power to create and share ideas and information instantly, without barriers.
Values: We believe in free expression and think every voice has the power to impact the world.
Strategy: Reach the largest daily audience in the world by connecting everyone to their world via our information sharing and distribution platform products and be one of the top revenue generating Internet companies in the world.
Twitter combines its mission and values to bring together a diverse workforce worldwide to fulfill its strategy.
The 3 Parts of a Company Mission Statement: • Purpose • Value • Action

Table 6.3 Sources: "About" and "Our Values," https://about.twitter.com, accessed October 30, 2017; Justin Fox, "Why Twitter's Mission Statement Matters," *Harvard Business Review*, https://hbr.org, accessed October 30, 2017; Jeff Bercovici, "Mission Critical: Twitter's New 'Strategy Statement' Reflects Shifting Priorities," *Inc.,* https://www.inc.com, accessed October 30, 2017.

In all organizations, plans and goals at the tactical and operational levels should clearly support the organization's mission statement.

Tactical planning begins the implementation of strategic plans. Tactical plans have a shorter (less than one year) time frame than strategic plans and more specific objectives designed to support the broader strategic goals. Tactical plans begin to address issues of coordinating and allocating resources to different parts of the organization.

Under Mickey Drexler, many new tactical plans were implemented to support J.Crew's new strategic direction. For example, he severely limited the number of stores opened each year, with only nine new openings in the first two years of his tenure (he closed seven). Instead, he invested the company's resources in developing a product line that communicated J.Crew's new strategic direction. Drexler dumped trend-driven apparel because it did not meet the company's new image. He even cut some million-dollar volume items. In their place, he created limited editions of a handful of garments that he thought would be popular, many of which fell into his new luxury strategy. For example, J.Crew now buys shoes directly from the same shoe manufacturers that produce footwear for designers such as Prada and Gucci. In general, J.Crew drastically tightened inventories, a move designed to keep reams of clothes from ending up on sale racks and to break its shoppers' habit of waiting for discounts.

This part of the plan generated great results. Prior to Drexler's change in strategy, half of J.Crew's clothing sold at a discount. After implementing tactical plans aimed to change that situation, only a small percentage does. The shift to limited editions and tighter inventory controls has not reduced the amount of new merchandise, however. On the contrary, Drexler created a J.Crew bridal collection, a jewelry line, and Crew Cuts, a line of kids' clothing. The results of Drexler's tactical plans were impressive. J.Crew saw same-store sales rise 17 percent in one year.[5]

Operational planning creates specific standards, methods, policies, and procedures that are used in specific functional areas of the organization. Operational objectives are current, narrow, and resource focused. They are designed to help guide and control the implementation of tactical plans. In an industry where new versions of software have widely varying development cycles, Autodesk, maker of software tools for designers and engineers, implemented new operational plans that dramatically increased profits. Former CEO Carol Bartz shifted the company away from the erratic release schedule it had been keeping to regular, annual software releases. By releasing upgrades on a defined and predictable schedule, the company is able to use annual subscription pricing, which is more affordable for small and midsize companies. The new schedule keeps Autodesk customers on the most recent versions of popular software and has resulted in an overall increase in profitability.[6]

The key to effective planning is anticipating future situations and events. Yet even the best-prepared organization must sometimes cope with unforeseen circumstances, such as a natural disaster, an act of terrorism, or a radical new technology. Therefore, many companies have developed **contingency plans** that identify alternative courses of action for very unusual or crisis situations. The contingency plan typically stipulates the chain of command, standard operating procedures, and communication channels the organization will use during an emergency.

An effective contingency plan can make or break a company. Consider the example of Marriott Hotels in Puerto Rico. Anticipating Hurricane Maria in 2017, workers at the San Juan Marriott had to shift from their regular duties to handling the needs of not only customers, but everyone who needed assistance in the wake of the hurricane that devastated the island. A contingency plan and training for events such as this were a key part of managing this crisis.[7] The company achieved its goal of being able to cater to guest and general needs due to planning and training while having a contingency plan in place. One guest commented on TripAdvisor, "Could not believe how friendly, helpful & responsive staff were even during height of hurricane. Special thanks to Eydie, Juan, Jock, Ashley and security Luis. They kept us safe & were exemplary. Will always stay at Marriott from now on."[8] Within one month after Hurricane Maria hit, operations were back to normal at the San Juan Marriott.[9]

MANAGING CHANGE

Boeing Takes Off in New Direction

Boeing and Airbus have been locked in fierce competition for the world's airplane business for decades. What characterized most of that time period was a focus on designing larger and larger airplanes. Since its development in the 1970s, Boeing revamped its pioneering B747 numerous times and at one time boasted over 1,300 of the jumbo jets in operation around the world. As part of this head-to-head competition for bragging rights to the largest jet in the air, Boeing was working on a 747X, a super-jumbo jet designed to hold 525 passengers. In what seemed to be an abrupt change of strategy, Boeing conceded the super-jumbo segment of the market to its rival and killed plans for the 747X. Instead of trying to create a plane with more seats, Boeing engineers began developing planes to fly fewer people at higher speeds. Then, as the rising price of jet fuel surpassed the airlines' ability to easily absorb its increasing cost, Boeing again changed its strategy, this time focusing on developing jets that use less fuel. In the end, Boeing's strategy changed from plane capacity to jet efficiency.

The new strategy required new plans. Boeing managers identified gaps in Airbus's product line and immediately set out to develop planes to fill them. Boeing announced a new 787 "Dreamliner," which boasted better fuel efficiency thanks to lightweight composite materials and next-generation engine design. Even though the 787 has less than half the seating of the Airbus A380, Boeing's Dreamliner is a hit in the market. Orders for the new plane have been stronger than anticipated, forcing Boeing to change its production plans to meet demand. The company decided to accelerate its planned 787 production rate buildup, rolling out a new jet every two days or so.

Airbus was not so lucky. The company spent so much time and energy on its super-jumbo that its A350 (the plane designed to compete with Boeing's 787) suffered. The 787 uses 15 percent less fuel than the A350, can fly nonstop from Beijing to New York, and is one of the fastest-selling commercial planes ever.

The battle for airline supremacy continues to switch between the two global giants. In 2017, Boeing beat Airbus on commercial jet orders at the Paris Air Show and continues to push forward. A spokesperson has hinted at a hybrid fuselage for midrange planes, which could carry passengers farther at lower costs. If successful, Boeing will regain market share lost to the Airbus A321.

Critical Thinking Questions
1. What seems to be the difference in how Boeing and Airbus have approached planning?
2. Do you think Airbus should change its strategic plans to meet Boeing's or stick with its current plans? Explain.

Sources: Gillian Rich, "Why Boeing's Paris Air Show Orders Are 'Staggering'," http://www.investors.com, June 22, 2017; Jon Ostrower, "Boeing vs. Airbus: A New Winner Emerges at the Paris Air Show," *CNN*, http://money.cnn.com, June 22, 2017; Gillian Rich, "'Hybrid' Design for New Boeing Midrange Jet Could Hit This Sweet Spot," http://www.investors.com, June 20, 2017; Alex Taylor, III, "Boeing Finally Has a Flight Plan," *Fortune*, June 13, 2005, pp. 27–28; J. Lynn Lundsford and Rod Stone, "Boeing Net Falls, but Outlook Is Rosy," *The Wall Street Journal*, July 28, 2005, p. A3; Carol Matlack and Stanley Holmes, "Why Airbus Is Losing Altitude," *Business Week*, June 20, 2005, p. 20; J. Lynn Lunsford, "UPS to Buy 8 Boeing 747s, Lifting Jet's Prospects," *The Wall Street Journal*, September 18, 2005, p. A2; "Airbus to Launch A350 Jet in October," *Xinhua News Agency*, September 14, 2005, online; "Boeing Plans Major Change," *Performance Materials*, April 30, 2001, p. 5.

CONCEPT CHECK

1. What is the purpose of planning, and what is needed to do it effectively?
2. Identify the unique characteristics of each type of planning.

6.3 | Organizing

3. What are the primary functions of managers in organizing activities?

A second key function of managers is **organizing**, which is the process of coordinating and allocating a firm's resources in order to carry out its plans. Organizing includes developing a structure for the people, positions, departments, and activities within the firm. Managers can arrange the structural elements of the firm to maximize the flow of information and the efficiency of work processes. They accomplish this by doing the following:

- Dividing up tasks *(division of labor)*
- Grouping jobs and employees *(departmentalization)*
- Assigning authority and responsibilities *(delegation)*

These and other elements of organizational structure are discussed in detail elsewhere. In this chapter, however, you should understand the three levels of a managerial hierarchy. This hierarchy is often depicted as a pyramid, as in **Exhibit 6.3**. The fewest managers are found at the highest level of the pyramid. Called **top management**, they are the small group of people at the head of the organization (such as the CEO, president, and vice president). Top-level managers develop *strategic plans* and address long-range issues such as which industries to compete in, how to capture market share, and what to do with profits. These managers design and approve the firm's basic policies and represent the firm to other organizations. They also define the company's values and ethics and thus set the tone for employee standards of behavior. For example, Jack Welch, the former CEO of General Electric, was a role model for his managers and executives. Admirers say that he had an extraordinary capacity to inspire hundreds of thousands of people in many countries and he could change the direction of a huge organization like General Electric as if it were a small firm. Following his leadership, General Electric's executives turned in impressive results. During his tenure, General Electric's average annual shareholder return was 25 percent.[10]

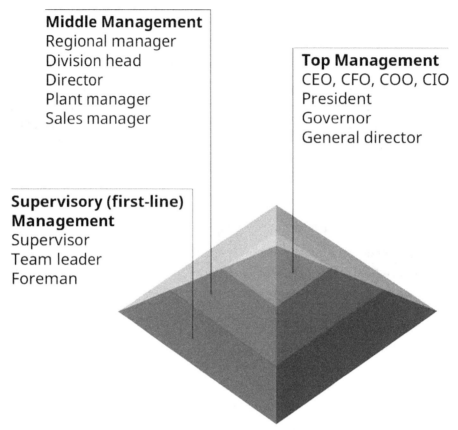

Exhibit 6.3   The Managerial Pyramid (Attribution: Copyright Rice University, OpenStax, under CC BY 4.0 license.)

The second and third tiers of the hierarchy are called **middle management** and **supervisory (first-line) management**, respectively. Middle managers (such as division heads, departmental managers, and regional sales managers) are responsible for beginning the implementation of strategic plans. They design and carry out *tactical plans* in specific areas of the company. They begin the process of allocating resources to meet organizational goals, and they oversee supervisory managers throughout the firm. Supervisors, the most numerous of the managers, are at the bottom of the managerial pyramid. These managers design and carry out *operational plans* for the ongoing daily activities of the firm. They spend a great deal of their time guiding and motivating the employees who actually produce the goods and services.

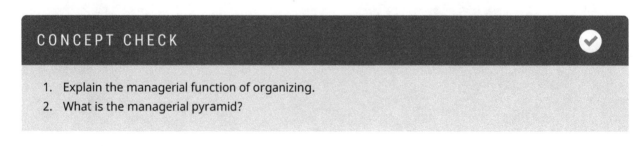

CONCEPT CHECK

1. Explain the managerial function of organizing.
2. What is the managerial pyramid?

6.4 | Leading, Guiding, and Motivating Others

4. How do leadership styles influence a corporate culture?

Leadership, the third key management function, is the process of guiding and motivating others toward the achievement of organizational goals. A leader can be anyone in an organization, regardless of position, able to influence others to act or follow, often by their own choice. Managers are designated leaders according to the organizational structure but may need to use negative consequences or coercion to achieve change. In the organization structure, top managers use leadership skills to set, share, and gain support for the company's direction and strategy—mission, vision, and values, such as Jeff Bezos does at Amazon. Middle and supervisory management use leadership skills in the process of directing employees on a daily basis as the employees carry out the plans and work within the structure created by management. Top-level leadership demonstrated by Bezos was also exhibited by Jack Welch while leading General Electric and led to many studies of his approach to leadership. Organizations, however, need strong effective leadership at all levels in order to meet goals and remain competitive.

To be effective leaders, managers must be able to influence others' behaviors. This ability to influence others to behave in a particular way is called **power**. Researchers have identified five primary sources, or bases, of power:

- **Legitimate power**, which is derived from an individual's position in an organization
- **Reward power**, which is derived from an individual's control over rewards
- **Coercive power**, which is derived from an individual's ability to threaten negative outcomes
- **Expert power**, which is derived from an individual's extensive knowledge in one or more areas
- **Referent power**, which is derived from an individual's personal charisma and the respect and/or admiration the individual inspires

Many leaders use a combination of all of these sources of power to influence individuals toward goal achievement. While CEO of Procter & Gamble, A. G. Lafley got his legitimate power from his position. His reward power came from reviving the company and making the stock more valuable. Also, raises and bonus for managers who met their goals was another form of reward power. Lafley also was not hesitant to use his coercive power. He eliminated thousands of jobs, sold underperforming brands, and killed weak product lines. With nearly 40 years of service to the company, Lafley had a unique authority when it came to P&G's products, markets, innovations, and customers. The company's sales doubled during his nine years as CEO, and its portfolio of brands increased from 10 to 23. He captained the purchase of Clairol, Wella AG, and IAMS, as well as the multibillion-dollar merger with Gillette. As a result, Lafley had a substantial amount of referent power. Lafley is also widely respected, not only by people at P&G, but by the general business community as well. Ann Gillin Lefever, a managing director at Lehman Brothers, said, "Lafley is a leader who is liked. His directives are very simple. He sets a strategy that everybody understands, and that is more difficult than he gets credit for."[11]

Leadership Styles

Individuals in leadership positions tend to be relatively consistent in the way they attempt to influence the behavior of others, meaning that each individual has a tendency to react to people and situations in a particular way. This pattern of behavior is referred to as **leadership style**. As Table 6.4 shows, leadership styles can be placed on a continuum that encompasses three distinct styles: autocratic, participative, and free rein.

Autocratic leaders are directive leaders, allowing for very little input from subordinates. These leaders prefer to make decisions and solve problems on their own and expect subordinates to implement solutions according to very specific and detailed instructions. In this leadership style, information typically flows in one direction, from manager to subordinate. The military, by necessity, is generally autocratic. When autocratic leaders treat employees with fairness and respect, they may be considered knowledgeable and decisive. But often autocrats are perceived as narrow-minded and heavy-handed in their unwillingness to share power, information, and decision-making in the organization. The trend in organizations today is away from the directive, controlling style of the autocratic leader.

Exhibit 6.4   Recently ranking near the top of the *Forbes* list of the world's most powerful women was Sheryl Sandberg, the COO at Facebook. As Facebook's chief operating officer since 2008, Sandberg has helped dramatically boost revenues at the social network. Sandberg also founded Lean In, a nonprofit named after her bestselling book, to support women's empowerment. *What are Sheryl Sandberg's primary sources of power?* (Credit: JD Lasica/ Flickr/ Attribution 2.0 Generic (CC BY 2.0))

Instead, U.S. businesses are looking more and more for **participative leaders**, meaning leaders who share decision-making with group members and encourage discussion of issues and alternatives. Participative leaders use a democratic, consensual, consultative style. One CEO known for her participative leadership style is Meg Whitman, former CEO at Hewlett Packard. When Whitman worked at eBay, a team in the German-based operation began a promotional "treasure hunt," launching registration pages, clues, and an hourly countdown clock. Trouble was, the launch violated eBay's well-established corporate project-development processes. When the treasure hunt began, 10 million contestants logged on, crashing the local servers. Rather than shut the project down, the VP in charge of the German operation allowed the promotion to be fixed and fly under the radar of corporate headquarters. Successful innovations emerged, such as an Easy Lister feature and separate registration processes for private and business sellers. When the VP shared this experience with Meg Whitman, she fostered the idea of rapid prototyping throughout the organization, which "breaks rules to get something done," and modeled such behavior for the entire organization.[12]

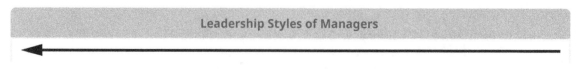

Leadership Styles of Managers

Table 6.4

Leadership Styles of Managers		
Amount of authority held by the leader		
Autocratic Style	**Participative Style (Democratic, Consensual, Consultative)**	**Free-Rein (Laissez-Faire) Style**
Manager makes most decisions and acts in authoritative manner. Manager is usually unconcerned about subordinates' attitudes toward decisions. Emphasis is on getting task accomplished. Approach is used mostly by military officers and some production line supervisors.	Manager shares decision-making with group members and encourages teamwork. Manager encourages discussion of issues and alternatives. Manager is concerned about subordinates' ideas and attitudes. Manager coaches subordinates and helps coordinate efforts. Approach is found in many successful organizations.	Manager turns over virtually all authority and control to group. Members of group are presented with task and given freedom to accomplish it. Approach works well with highly motivated, experienced, educated personnel. Approach is found in high-tech firms, labs, and colleges.

Amount of authority held by group members

Table 6.4

ETHICS IN PRACTICE

Scott Stephenson: Balancing the Duality of Ethics

Whether it's Bernie Madoff defrauding investors, Wells Fargo having to respond to creating fake accounts in the names of real customers, or Mylan N.V. imposing huge price increases on its life-saving EpiPen, it seems like there is never a shortage of ethical issues being an important aspect of business. As shown by these examples, unethical decisions permeate different parts of the business and occur for different reasons.

In the case of Bernie Madoff, it was the greed of one person using a Ponzi scheme to defraud thousands of customers. In the case of Wells Fargo, the culprits were managers putting excessive pressure on workers to meet new account quotas. The case of Mylan included the dramatic rise in the price of the EpiPen in a short time span and reports that CEO Heather Bresch and other executives received compensation that increased over 700 percent during the same time frame. Adding to the Mylan case was the fact that Bresch is the daughter of West Virginia Senator Joseph Manchin, and prior to being appointed CEO at Mylan, Bresch served as Mylan's chief lobbyist and helped craft the Generic Drug User Fee Amendments and the School Access to Emergency Epinephrine Act.

Where does the responsibility of managing ethical behavior in organizations reside? The answer is *everyone* in the organization is responsible to act in an ethical manner. The primary responsibility resides, however, with the CEO and also with the chief financial officer, who has the responsibility to oversee financial compliance with laws and regulations. Scott Stephenson, the CEO of Verisk Analytics, recently commented on how he approaches the duality of what he terms a "loose–tight" approach to leadership where he provides his employees with the discretion and responsibility to make critical decisions in crisis situations where ethics might be involved. That's the loose part. He also works on communicating and building trust in his employees so that he has the confidence they will act responsibly and make the correct decisions in crisis situations. That's the tight part of his leadership duality.

Critical Thinking Questions

1. Do you think Verisk Analytics, a technology company that needs innovation breakthroughs, benefits from Stephenson's "loose–tight" approach? What if Stepheson had been an autocratic leader? Explain your reasoning.

2. What kind of participative leader (described below) does Stephenson seem to be? Explain your choice.

Sources: Scott Stephenson, "The Duality of Balanced Leadership," *Forbes*, https://www.forbes.com, November 29, 2017; Matt Egan, "Wells Fargo Uncovers Up to 1.4 Million More Fake Accounts," *CNN Money,* http://money.cnn.com, August 31, 2017; Jesse Heitz, "The EpiPen Scandal and the Perception of the Washington Establishment," *The Hill,* http://thehill.com, September 1, 2016; "Decade's Top 10 Ethics Scandals," *The Wall Street Journal*, https://www.wsj.com, August 9, 2010.

Participative leadership has three types: democratic, consensual, and consultative. **Democratic leaders** solicit input from all members of the group and then allow the group members to make the final decision through a voting process. This approach works well with highly trained professionals. The president of a physicians' clinic might use the democratic approach. **Consensual leaders** encourage discussion about issues and then require that all parties involved agree to the final decision. This is the general style used by labor mediators. **Consultative leaders** confer with subordinates before making a decision but retain the final decision-making authority. This technique has been used to dramatically increase the productivity of assembly-line workers.

The third leadership style, at the opposite end of the continuum from the autocratic style, is **free-rein** or **laissez-faire** (French for "leave it alone") **leadership**. Managers who use this style turn over all authority and control to subordinates. Employees are assigned a task and then given free rein to figure out the best way to accomplish it. The manager doesn't get involved unless asked. Under this approach, subordinates have unlimited freedom as long as they do not violate existing company policies. This approach is also sometimes used with highly trained professionals as in a research laboratory.

Although one might at first assume that subordinates would prefer the free-rein style, this approach can have several drawbacks. If free-rein leadership is accompanied by unclear expectations and lack of feedback from the manager, the experience can be frustrating for an employee. Employees may perceive the manager as being uninvolved and indifferent to what is happening or as unwilling or unable to provide the necessary structure, information, and expertise.

No leadership style is effective all the time. Effective leaders recognize employee growth and use **situational leadership**, selecting a leadership style that matches the maturity and competency levels of those completing the tasks. Newly hired employees may respond well to authoritative leadership until they understand the job requirements and show the ability to handle routine decisions. Once established, however, those same employees may start to feel undervalued and perform better under a participative or free-rein leadership style. Using situational leadership empowers employees as discussed next.

Employee Empowerment

Participative and free-rein leaders use a technique called empowerment to share decision-making authority with subordinates. **Empowerment** means giving employees increased autonomy and discretion to make their own decisions, as well as control over the resources needed to implement those decisions. When decision-making power is shared at all levels of the organization, employees feel a greater sense of ownership in, and responsibility for, organizational outcomes.

Management use of employee empowerment is on the rise. This increased level of involvement comes from the realization that people at all levels in the organization possess unique knowledge, skills, and abilities that can be of great value to the company. For example, when Hurricane Katrina hit the Gulf Coast, five miles of railroad tracks were ripped off a bridge connecting New Orleans to Slidell, Louisiana. Without the tracks, which fell into Lake Pontchartrain, Norfolk Southern Railroad couldn't transport products between the East and West Coasts. Before the storm hit, however, Jeff McCracken, a chief engineer at the company, traveled to Birmingham with equipment he thought he might need and then to Slidell with 100 employees. After conferring with dozens of company engineers and three bridge companies, McCracken decided to try to rescue the miles of track from the lake. (Building new tracks would have taken several weeks at the least.) To do so, he gathered 365 engineers, machine operators, and other workers, who lined up eight huge cranes and, over the course of several hours, lifted the five miles of sunken tracks in one piece out of the lake and bolted it back on the bridge.[13] By giving employees the autonomy to make decisions and access to required resources, Norfolk Southern was able to avoid serious interruptions in its nationwide service.

Exhibit 6.5   Management thought leader Peter Drucker (1909–2005) was the author of more than three dozen books, translated into almost as many languages. Most management scholars have remarked that although he was firmly associated with the human relations school of management—along with Douglas McGregor and Warren Bennis, for example—the thought leader Drucker most admired was Frederick Winslow Taylor, the father of "scientific" management. *Should any one "school" of management predominate thinking, or should all approaches be considered?* (Credit: IsaacMao/ Flickr/ Attribution 2.0 Generic (CC BY 2.0))

Corporate Culture

The leadership style of managers in an organization is usually indicative of the underlying philosophy, or values, of the organization. The set of *attitudes, values,* and *standards of behavior* that distinguishes one organization from another is called **corporate culture**. A corporate culture evolves over time and is based on the accumulated history of the organization, including the vision of the founders. It is also influenced by the dominant leadership style within the organization. Evidence of a company's culture is seen in its heroes (e.g., the late Andy Grove of Intel[14], myths (stories about the company passed from employee to employee), symbols (e.g., the Nike swoosh), and ceremonies. The culture at Google, working in teams and fostering innovation, sometimes is overlooked while its employee perks are drooled over. But both are important to the company's corporate culture. Since 2007 Google has been at or near the top of *Fortune*'s list of the "100 Best Companies to Work For," an annual list based on employee survey results tabulated by an independent company: Great Place to Work®. [15] "We have never forgotten since our startup days that great things happen more frequently within the right culture and environment," a company spokesperson said in response to the company first taking over the top spot.[16]

Culture may be intangible, but it has a tremendous impact on employee morale and a company's success. Google approaches morale analytically. When it found that mothers were leaving the company in higher rates than other employee groups, the company improved its parental-leave policies. The result was a 50 percent reduction in attrition for working moms. An analytical approach along with culture-building activities such as town halls led by black employees and allies, support for transgender employees, and unconscious-bias workshops are why employees say Google is a safe and inclusive place to work.[17] Clearly Google leaders recognize culture is critical to the company's overall success.

CONCEPT CHECK

1. How do leaders influence other people's behavior?
2. How can managers empower employees?

3. What is corporate culture?

6.5 Controlling

5. How do organizations control activities?

The fourth key function that managers perform is **controlling**. Controlling is the process of assessing the organization's progress toward accomplishing its goals. It includes monitoring the implementation of a plan and correcting deviations from that plan. As Exhibit 6.6 shows, controlling can be visualized as a cyclical process made up of five stages:

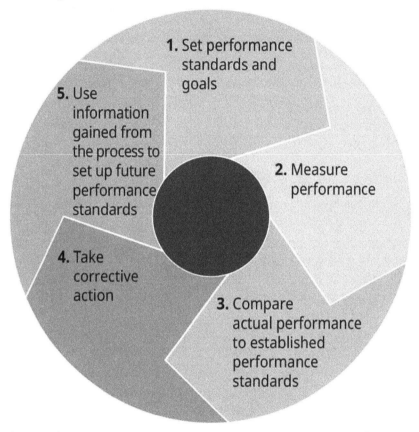

Exhibit 6.6   The Control Process (Attribution: Copyright Rice University, OpenStax, under CC BY 4.0 license.)

Performance standards are the levels of performance the company wants to attain. These goals are based on its strategic, tactical, and operational plans. The most effective performance standards state a measurable behavioral objective that can be achieved in a specified time frame. For example, the performance objective for the sales division of a company could be stated as "$200,000 in gross sales for the month of January." Each individual employee in that division would also have a specified performance goal. Actual firm, division, or individual performance can be measured against desired performance standards to see if a gap exists between the desired level of performance and the actual level of performance. If a performance gap does exist, the reason for it must be determined and corrective action taken.

Feedback is essential to the process of control. Most companies have a reporting system that identifies areas where performance standards are not being met. A feedback system helps managers detect problems before they get out of hand. If a problem exists, the managers take corrective action. Toyota uses a simple but effective control system on its automobile assembly lines. Each worker serves as the customer for the process just before his or hers. Each worker is empowered to act as a quality control inspector. If a part is defective or not installed properly, the next worker won't accept it. Any worker can alert the supervisor to a problem by tugging on a rope that turns on a warning light (i.e., feedback). If the problem isn't corrected, the worker can stop the entire assembly line.

Why is controlling such an important part of a manager's job? First, it helps managers to determine the success of the other three functions: planning, organizing, and leading. Second, control systems direct employee behavior toward achieving organizational goals. Third, control systems provide a means of coordinating employee activities and integrating resources throughout the organization.

CONCEPT CHECK

1. Describe the control process.
2. Why is the control process important to the success of the organization?

6.6 | Managerial Roles

6. What roles do managers take on in different organizational settings?

In carrying out the responsibilities of planning, organizing, leading, and controlling, managers take on many different roles. A role is a set of behavioral expectations, or a set of activities that a person is expected to perform. Managers' roles fall into three basic categories: *informational roles, interpersonal roles,* and *decisional roles.* These roles are summarized in **Table 6.5**. In an **informational role**, the manager may act as an information gatherer, an information distributor, or a spokesperson for the company. A manager's **interpersonal roles** are based on various interactions with other people. Depending on the situation, a manager may need to act as a figurehead, a company leader, or a liaison. When acting in a **decisional role**, a manager may have to think like an entrepreneur, make decisions about resource allocation, help resolve conflicts, or negotiate compromises.

Managerial Decision Making

In every function performed, role taken on, and set of skills applied, a manager is a decision maker. Decision-making means choosing among alternatives. Decision-making occurs in response to the identification of a problem or an opportunity. The decisions managers make fall into two basic categories: programmed and nonprogrammed. **Programmed decisions** are made in response to routine situations that occur frequently in a variety of settings throughout an organization. For example, the need to hire new personnel is a common situation for most organizations. Therefore, standard procedures for recruitment and selection are developed and followed in most companies.

The Many Roles Managers Play in an Organization		
Role	Description	Example
Information Roles		
Monitor	• Seeks out and gathers information relevant to the organization	• Finding out about legal restrictions on new product technology
Disseminator	• Provides information where it is needed in the organization	• Providing current production figures to workers on the assembly line
Spokesperson	• Transmits information to people outside the organization	• Representing the company at a shareholders' meeting
Interpersonal Roles		
Figurehead	• Represents the company in a symbolic way	• Cutting the ribbon at ceremony for the opening of a new building
Leader	• Guides and motivates employees to achieve organizational goals	• Helping subordinates to set monthly performance goals
Liaison	• Acts as a go-between among individuals inside and outside the organization	• Representing the retail sales division of the company at a regional sales meeting
Decisional Roles		
Entrepreneur	• Searches out new opportunities and initiates change	• Implementing a new production process using new technology
Disturbance handler	• Handles unexpected events and crises	• Handling a crisis situation such as a fire
Resource allocator	• Designates the use of financial, human, and other organizational resources	• Approving the funds necessary to purchase computer equipment and hire personnel

Table 6.5

The Many Roles Managers Play in an Organization		
Role	Description	Example
Negotiator	• Represents the company at negotiating processes	• Participating in salary negotiations with union representatives

Table 6.5

Infrequent, unforeseen, or very unusual problems and opportunities require **nonprogrammed decisions** by managers. Because these situations are unique and complex, the manager rarely has a precedent to follow. The earlier example of the Norfolk Southern employee, who had to decide the best way to salvage a five-mile-long piece of railroad track from the bottom of Lake Pontchartrain, is an example of a nonprogrammed decision. Likewise, when Hurricane Katrina was forecast to make landfall, Thomas Oreck, then CEO of the vacuum manufacturer that bears his name, had to make a series of nonprogrammed decisions. Oreck's corporate headquarters were in New Orleans, and its primary manufacturing facility was in Long Beach, Mississippi. Before the storm hit, Oreck transferred its computer systems and call-center operations to backup locations in Colorado and planned to move headquarters to Long Beach. The storm, however, brutally hit both locations. Oreck executives began searching for lost employees, tracking down generators, assembling temporary housing for workers, and making deals with UPS to begin distributing its product (UPS brought food and water to Oreck from Atlanta and took vacuums back to the company's distribution center there). All of these decisions were made in the middle of a very challenging crisis environment.

Whether a decision is programmed or nonprogrammed, managers typically follow five steps in the decision-making process, as illustrated in Exhibit 6.7:

1. Recognize or define the problem or opportunity. Although it is more common to focus on problems because of their obvious negative effects, managers who do not take advantage of new opportunities may lose competitive advantage to other firms.
2. Gather information so as to identify alternative solutions or actions.
3. Select one or more alternatives after evaluating the strengths and weaknesses of each possibility.
4. Put the chosen alternative into action.
5. Gather information to obtain feedback on the effectiveness of the chosen plan.

It can be easy (and dangerous) for managers to get stuck at any stage of the decision-making process. For example, entrepreneurs can become paralyzed evaluating the options. For the Gabby Slome, the cofounder of natural pet food maker Ollie, the idea for starting the company came after her rescue dog began having trouble digesting store-bought pet food after living on scraps. Slome decided that the pet food industry, a $30 billion a year business, was ripe for a natural food alternative. She laments, however, that she let perfect be the enemy of the very good by indulging in "analysis paralysis."[18]

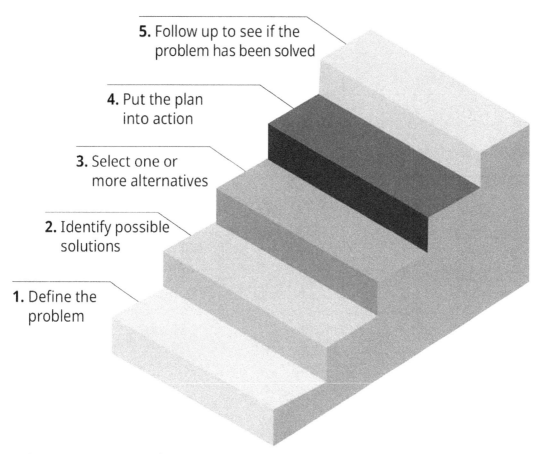

5. Follow up to see if the problem has been solved

4. Put the plan into action

3. Select one or more alternatives

2. Identify possible solutions

1. Define the problem

Exhibit 6.7   The Decision-Making Process (Attribution: Copyright Rice University, OpenStax, under CC BY 4.0 license.)

CONCEPT CHECK

1. What are the three types of managerial roles?
2. Give examples of things managers might do when acting in each of the different types of roles.
3. List the five steps in the decision-making process.

6.7 Managerial Skills

7. What set of managerial skills is necessary for managerial success?

In order to be successful in planning, organizing, leading, and controlling, managers must use a wide variety of skills. A *skill* is the ability to do something proficiently. Managerial skills fall into three basic categories: technical, human relations, and conceptual skills. The degree to which each type of skill is used depends upon the level of the manager's position as seen in **Exhibit 6.8**. Additionally, in an increasingly global marketplace, it pays for managers to develop a special set of skills to deal with global management issues.

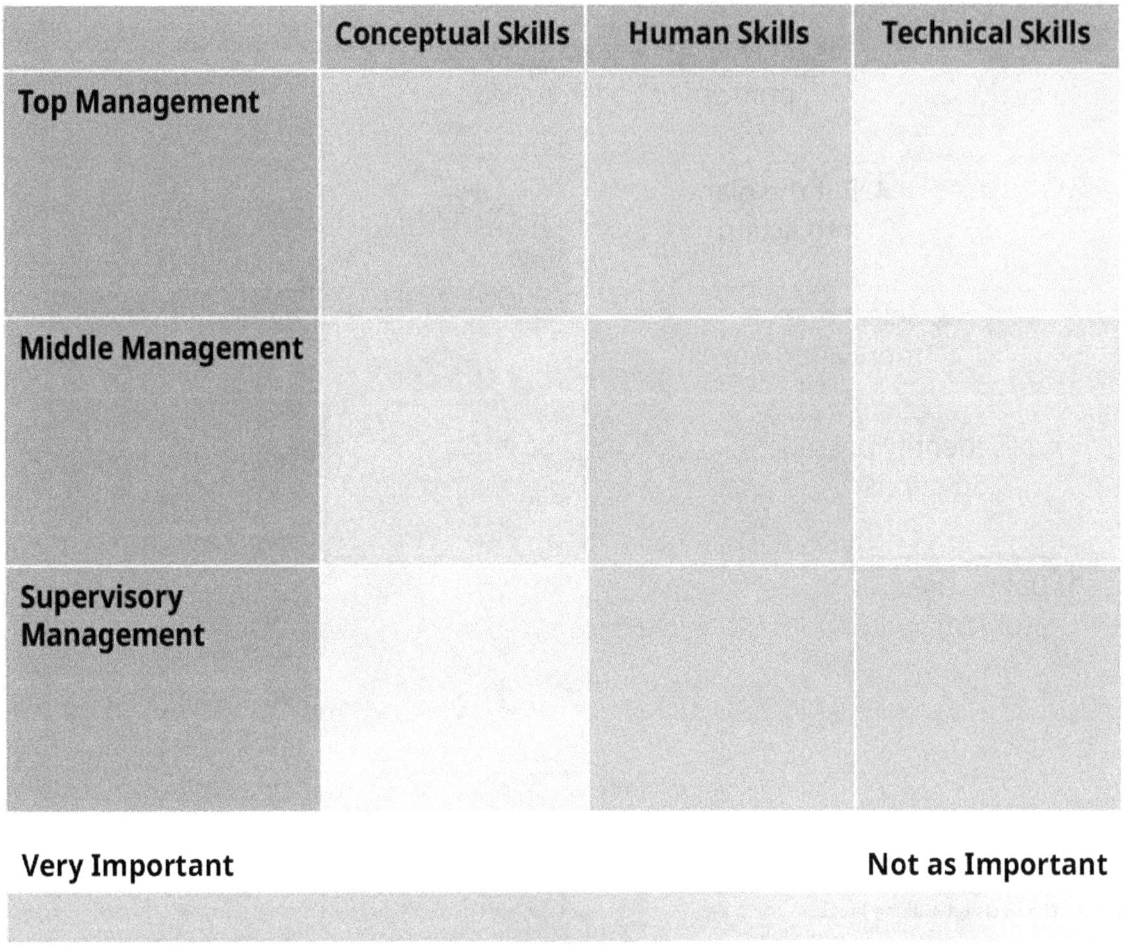

	Conceptual Skills	Human Skills	Technical Skills
Top Management			
Middle Management			
Supervisory Management			

Very Important   **Not as Important**

Exhibit 6.8   The Importance of Managerial Skills at Different Management Levels (Attribution: Copyright Rice University, OpenStax, under CC BY 4.0 license.)

Technical Skills

Specialized areas of knowledge and expertise and the ability to apply that knowledge make up a manager's **technical skills**. Preparing a financial statement, programming a computer, designing an office building, and analyzing market research are all examples of technical skills. These types of skills are especially important for supervisory managers because they work closely with employees who are producing the goods and/or services of the firm.

Human Relations Skills

Human relations skills are the interpersonal skills managers use to accomplish goals through the use of human resources. This set of skills includes the ability to understand human behavior, to communicate effectively with others, and to motivate individuals to accomplish their objectives. Giving positive feedback to employees, being sensitive to their individual needs, and showing a willingness to empower subordinates are all examples of good human relations skills. Identifying and promoting managers with human relations skills are important for companies. A manager with little or no people skills can end up using an authoritarian leadership style and alienating employees.

Conceptual Skills

Conceptual skills include the ability to view the organization as a whole, understand how the various parts are interdependent, and assess how the organization relates to its external environment. These skills allow managers to evaluate situations and develop alternative courses of action. Good conceptual skills are especially necessary for managers at the top of the management pyramid, where strategic planning takes place.

CONCEPT CHECK

1. Define the basic managerial skills.
2. How important is each of these skill sets at the different levels of the management pyramid?

6.8 Trends in Management and Leadership

8. What trends will affect management in the future?

Four important trends in management today are crisis management, outside directors, the growing use of information technology, and the increasing need for global management skills.

Crisis Management

Crises, both internal and external, can hit even the best-managed organization. Sometimes organizations can anticipate crises, in which case managers develop contingency plans, and sometimes they can't. Take, for example, the sudden death of McDonald's CEO Jim Cantalupo. The company had a solid succession plan in place and immediately named Charlie Bell as new CEO. Only a few months later, Bell announced that he had terminal cancer. Even though the company had prepared for the event of its leader's untimely death, surely it couldn't have anticipated that his successor would also be stricken by a terminal illness at almost the same time. Likewise, consider the devastation caused by Hurricanes Harvey, Irma, Maria, and Nate in 2017. Part of Marriott Hotels' crisis management plan included relaxing its "no pets" policy and allowing patrons fleeing the storm to check in with their pets because it was the right thing to do.[19]

Crises cannot be fully anticipated, but managers can develop contingency plans to help navigate through the aftermath of a disaster. For example, consider the challenges that faced Rajiv Joseph, the author of several plays including *Bengal Tiger at the Baghdad Zoo*, who was in Houston preparing to open his new play, *Describe the Night*, at the Alley Theater when Hurricane Harvey hit and flooded the theater a few weeks prior to opening night. The six New York–based actors, the director, the stage manager, and Joseph decided to help in the relief efforts and made their way to the George Brown Convention Center, which had become the central location for relief efforts. When they arrived and the staffers discovered they were theater artists, they were deployed to handle the writing and deployment of public address announcements and manage the incoming crowds. What made the relief efforts successful was planning—matching the skill sets of volunteers with tasks they are best able to perform.[20] Even though those in charge of the relief efforts had contingency plans, they still needed to make dozens of nonprogrammed decisions to effectively manage the ever-changing situation.[21]

No manager or executive can be completely prepared for these types of unexpected crises. However, how a manager handles the situation could mean the difference between disaster, survival, and even financial gain. No matter the crisis, there are some basic guidelines managers should follow to minimize negative outcomes. Managers should not become immobilized by the problem or ignore it. Managers should face the problem head on. Managers should always tell the truth about the situation and then put the best people on the job to correct the problem. Managers should ask for help if they need it, and finally, managers must learn from the experience to avoid the same problem in the future.[22] **Table 6.6** describes what CEOs and other leaders learned about crisis management.

Managers and Information Technology

The second trend having a major impact on managers is the proliferation of data and analytics in information technology. An increasing number of organizations are selling technology, and an increasing number are looking for cutting-edge technology to make and market the products and services they sell. One particularly useful type of technology is dashboard software. Much like the dashboard in a car, dashboard software gives managers a quick look into the relevant information they need to manage their companies. Most large companies are organized in divisions, and often each division relies on a particular type of application or database software. Dashboard software allows employees to access information from software they don't routinely use, for example, from an application used by a different division from their own. More important, however, is the ability of a dashboard to show up-to-the-minute information and to allow employees to see all the information they need—such as financial and performance data—on a single screen.

Lessons Leaders Learned about Managing Crises	
Howard Schultz Chairman, Starbucks	Learn from one crisis at a time. After the Seattle earthquake of 2001, the company invested in a notification system that could handle text messaging. The night before Hurricane Katrina hit, Starbucks sent out 2,300 phone calls to associates in the region, telling them about available resources.
Gary Loveman CEO, Harrah's	Make life easier for your employees. Before the storm hit, management announced that in the event of total entertainment disaster, employees would be paid for at least 90 days. The decision was meant to provide employees with some certainty during a very uncertain time.
J. W. Marriott CEO, Marriott	Communicate for safety. Marriott moved its email system out of New Orleans before Katrina hit. As a result, employees were able to communicate with each other and vendors to get food and water to affected areas. A massive publicity campaign (Dial 1-800-Marriott) helped the company find 2,500 of its 2,800 people in the region.

Table 6.6 Sources: Danny Gavin, "Customer Service Lessons Learned in the Wake of Hurricane Harvey," *Forbes*, September 26, 2017; Jay Steinfeld, "5 Lessons Learned from Hurricane Harvey," *Inc.*, September 21, 2017; Susan Burns and David Hackett, "Business Lessons from Hurricane Irma," 941CEO, November-December 2017; "New Lessons to Learn," Fortune, October 3, 2005, pp. 87–88; AZQuotes, Accessed February 25, 2018, http://www.azquotes.com/quote/863856.

Lessons Leaders Learned about Managing Crises	
Geno Auriemma University of Connecticut Basketball Coach	It's about doing it in a way that it can't be done any better. That is the goal every day.
Danny Gavin VP, Brian Gavin Diamonds	"Create an unforgettable customer experience" may sound like a cliché, but this is our golden rule. Despite waist-high water and treacherous conditions, we had several international orders that needed to be shipped the Wednesday after Hurricane Harvey hit. FedEx and UPS had ceased operations around the Houston area during the storm, but our CEO Brian Gavin was determined to deliver an outstanding customer service experience. That's why he drove with the packages in hand to the nearest FedEx store that was open: College Station. The standard three-hour round trip ended up taking five hours.
Bob Nardelli CEO, Home Depot	Prepare for the next big one. After each catastrophic event, Home Depot does a postmortem on its response efforts so that employees and managers can become more experienced and better prepared. Before Katrina hit, the company prestaged extra supplies and generators, sent 1,000 relief associates to work in the stores in the Gulf Region, and made sure that area stores were overstocked with first-response items such as insecticides, water, and home generators.
Scott Ford CEO, Alltel	Take care of everybody. When Katrina hit, Alltel was missing 35 employees. When the company had found all but one, managers used the company's network infrastructure to track her phone activity, contact the last person she had called, and work with the army to find her.
Paul Pressler CEO, Gap	Empower the workforce. Gap had 1,300 employees affected by Katrina, and one of the biggest problems the company faced was getting people their paychecks. The company, which had extended payroll by 30 days to affected employees, now encourages all employees to use direct deposit as a means to ensure access to their pay.
Jim Skinner CEO, McDonald's	Be flexible with company assets. McDonald's had 280 restaurants close in the immediate aftermath of the storm, but shortly afterward, 201 were already open. During the crisis, McDonald's converted its human resource service center into a crisis command center. The quickly formed help center fielded 3,800 calls.

Table 6.6 Sources: Danny Gavin, "Customer Service Lessons Learned in the Wake of Hurricane Harvey," *Forbes,* September 26, 2017; Jay Steinfeld, "5 Lessons Learned from Hurricane Harvey," *Inc.,* September 21, 2017; Susan Burns and David Hackett, "Business Lessons from Hurricane Irma," 941CEO, November-December 2017; "New Lessons to Learn," Fortune, October 3, 2005, pp. 87–88; AZQuotes, Accessed February 25, 2018, http://www.azquotes.com/quote/863856.

Lessons Leaders Learned about Managing Crises	
Robert Baugh COO, Chiles Restaurants	With Hurricane Irma approaching, Baugh communicated with staff for several days before the storm to prepare and to find out which employees would be evacuating, which would be staying, and which had special needs. The Chiles Group used Hot Schedules, a platform all employees log into, to create a timeline to secure all three restaurants (since these restaurants have lots of outdoor seating and outdoor bars, it was a huge chore) and to broadcast when the restaurants would reopen. Team leaders were responsible for communicating with their members. Vendors and chefs were told earlier in the week to reduce food orders to minimize loss. Freezers and refrigerators were packed with hundreds of bags of ice.

Table 6.6 Sources: Danny Gavin, "Customer Service Lessons Learned in the Wake of Hurricane Harvey," *Forbes,* September 26, 2017; Jay Steinfeld, "5 Lessons Learned from Hurricane Harvey," *Inc.,* September 21, 2017; Susan Burns and David Hackett, "Business Lessons from Hurricane Irma," 941CEO, November-December 2017; "New Lessons to Learn," Fortune, October 3, 2005, pp. 87–88; AZQuotes, Accessed February 25, 2018, http://www.azquotes.com/quote/863856.

Such integrated functionality made dashboards extremely popular. A Gartner commentary suggests that companies put data and analytics at the heart of every company business decision.[23] Despite the increasing popularity of dashboard technology, the control tool has some drawbacks, such as focusing too intently on short-term results and ignoring the overall progress toward long-term goals. And some employees might bristle at being monitored as closely as dashboard tools allow.

Nonetheless, companies are seeing real results from implementing dashboard software. Robert Romanoff, a partner at the law firm of Levenfeld Romanoff in Chicago, uses dashboards that aggregate data from clients, strategic partners, and internal staff from the mailroom to the boardroom to improve what he calls the 3 *P*s. The 3 *P*s are process efficiency, project management, and strategic pricing.[24]

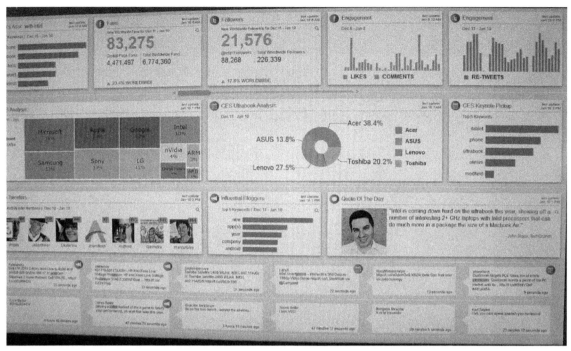

Exhibit 6.9   Marketing and sales professionals are increasingly turning to advanced software programs called "dashboards" to monitor business and evaluate performance. These computer tools use analytics and big data to help managers identify valuable customers, track sales, and align plans with company objectives—all in real time. A typical dashboard might include sales and bookings forecasts, monthly close data, customer satisfaction data, and employee training schedules. This example tracks customers attending the Consumer Electronics Show so that the buzz created by influencers can be measured. *How does information technology affect managerial decision-making?* (Credit: Intel Free Press/ flickr/ Attribution 2.0 Generic (CC BY 2.0))

Managing Multinational Cultures

The increasing globalization of the world market has created a need for managers who have **global management skills**, that is, the ability to operate in diverse cultural environments. With more and more companies choosing to do business in multiple locations around the world, employees are often required to learn the geography, language, and social customs of other cultures. It is expensive to train employees for foreign assignments and pay their relocation costs; therefore, choosing the right person for the job is especially important. Individuals who are open minded, flexible, willing to try new things, and comfortable in a multicultural setting are good candidates for international management positions.

As companies expand around the globe, managers will continue to face the challenges of directing the behavior of employees around the world. They must recognize that because of cultural differences, people respond to similar situations in very different ways. The burden, therefore, falls on the manager to produce results while adapting to the differences among the employees he or she manages.

How a manager gets results, wins respect, and leads employees varies greatly among countries, cultures, and individuals. For example, different cultures have different approaches to time. American, German, and Swiss cultures, among others, take a linear view of time, whereas southern European counties such as Italy take a multi-active time approach, and many Eastern cultures, such as China, take a cyclic approach. An American manager with a linear view of time will approach scheduling planning with a different approach than colleagues with a multi-active or cyclic approach.[25] Despite differences such as these (examples of which can be cited for every country in the world), managing within a different culture is only an extension of what managers do every day: working with differences in employees, processes, and projects.

CONCEPT CHECK

1. How can information technology aid in decision-making?
2. What are three principles of managing multinational cultures?
3. Describe several guidelines for crisis management.

🔑 Key Terms

autocratic leaders Directive leaders who prefer to make decisions and solve problems on their own with little input from subordinates

coercive power Power that is derived from an individual's ability to threaten negative outcomes.

conceptual skills A manager's ability to view the organization as a whole, understand how the various parts are interdependent, and assess how the organization relates to its external environment.

consensual leaders Leaders who encourage discussion about issues and then require that all parties involved agree to the final decision.

consultative leaders Leaders who confer with subordinates before making a decision but who retain the final decision-making authority.

contingency plans Plans that identify alternative courses of action for very unusual or crisis situations; typically stipulate the chain of command, standard operating procedures, and communication channels the organization will use during an emergency.

controlling The process of assessing the organization's progress toward accomplishing its goals; includes monitoring the implementation of a plan and correcting deviations from the plan.

corporate culture The set of attitudes, values, and standards that distinguishes one organization from another.

decisional roles A manager's activities as an entrepreneur, resource allocator, conflict resolver, or negotiator.

democratic leaders Leaders who solicit input from all members of the group and then allow the members to make the final decision through a vote.

effectiveness The ability to produce the desired result or good.

efficiency Using the least amount of resources to accomplish the organization's goals.

empowerment The process of giving employees increased autonomy and discretion to make decisions, as well as control over the resources needed to implement those decisions.

expert power Power that is derived from an individual's extensive knowledge in one or more areas.

free-rein (laissez-faire) leadership A leadership style in which the leader turns over all authority and control to subordinates.

global management skills A manager's ability to operate in diverse cultural environments.

human relations skills A manager's interpersonal skills that are used to accomplish goals through the use of human resources.

informational roles A manager's activities as an information gatherer, an information disseminator, or a spokesperson for the company.

interpersonal roles A manager's activities as a figurehead, company leader, or liaison.

leadership The process of guiding and motivating others toward the achievement of organizational goals.

leadership style The relatively consistent way that individuals in leadership positions attempt to influence the behavior of others.

legitimate power Power that is derived from an individual's position in an organization.

management The process of guiding the development, maintenance, and allocation of resources to attain organizational goals.

middle management Managers who design and carry out tactical plans in specific areas of the company.

mission An organization's purpose and reason for existing; its long-term goals.

mission statement A formal document that states an organization's purpose and reason for existing and describes its basic philosophy.

nonprogrammed decisions Responses to infrequent, unforeseen, or very unusual problems and opportunities where the manager does not have a precedent to follow in decision-making.

operational planning The process of creating specific standards, methods, policies, and procedures that are used in specific functional areas of the organization; helps guide and control the implementation of tactical plans.

organizing The process of coordinating and allocating a firm's resources in order to carry out its plans.

participative leaders Leaders who share decision-making with group members and encourage discussion of issues and alternatives; includes democratic, consensual, and consultative styles.

planning The process of deciding what needs to be done to achieve organizational objectives; identifying when and how it will be done; and determining who should do it.

power The ability to influence others to behave in a particular way.

programmed decisions Decisions made in response to frequently occurring routine situations.

referent power Power that is derived from an individual's personal charisma and the respect and/or admiration the individual inspires.

reward power Power that is derived from an individual's control over rewards.

situational leadership Selecting a leadership style based on the maturity and competency level of those who will complete the task.

strategic planning The process of creating long-range (one to five years), broad goals for the organization and determining what resources will be needed to accomplish those goals.

supervisory (first-line) management Managers who design and carry out operation plans for the ongoing daily activities of the firm.

tactical planning The process of beginning to implement a strategic plan by addressing issues of coordination and allocating resources to different parts of the organization; has a shorter time frame (less than one year) and more specific objectives than strategic planning.

technical skills A manager's specialized areas of knowledge and expertise, as well as the ability to apply that knowledge.

top management The highest level of managers; includes CEOs, presidents, and vice presidents, who develop strategic plans.

Summary of Learning Outcomes

6.1 The Role of Management

1. What is the role of management?

Management is the process of guiding the development, maintenance, and allocation of resources to attain organizational goals. Managers are the people in the organization responsible for developing and carrying out this management process. The four primary functions of managers are planning, organizing, leading, and controlling. By using the four functions, managers work to increase the efficiency and effectiveness of their employees, processes, projects, and organizations as a whole.

6.2 Planning

2. What are the four types of planning?

Planning is deciding what needs to be done, identifying when and how it will be done, and determining who should do it. Managers use four different types of planning: strategic, tactical, operational, and contingency planning. Strategic planning involves creating long-range (one to five years), broad goals and determining the necessary resources to accomplish those goals. Tactical planning has a shorter time frame (less than one year) and more specific objectives that support the broader strategic goals. Operational planning creates specific standards, methods, policies, and procedures that are used in specific functional areas of the organization. Contingency plans identify alternative courses of action for very unusual or crisis situations.

6.3 Organizing

3. What are the primary functions of managers in organizing activities?

Organizing involves coordinating and allocating a firm's resources in order to carry out its plans. It includes developing a structure for the people, positions, departments, and activities within the firm. This is accomplished by dividing up tasks (division of labor), grouping jobs and employees (departmentalization), and assigning authority and responsibilities (delegation).

6.4 Leading, Guiding, and Motivating Others

4. How do leadership styles influence a corporate culture?

Leading is the process of guiding and motivating others toward the achievement of organizational goals. Managers have unique leadership styles that range from autocratic to free-rein. The set of attitudes, values, and standards of behavior that distinguishes one organization from another is called corporate culture. A corporate culture evolves over time and is based on the accumulated history of the organization, including the vision of the founders.

6.5 Controlling

5. How do organizations control activities?

Controlling is the process of assessing the organization's progress toward accomplishing its goals. The control process is as follows: (1) set performance standards (goals), (2) measure performance, (3) compare actual performance to established performance standards, (4) take corrective action (if necessary), and (5) use information gained from the process to set future performance standards.

6.6 Managerial Roles

6. What roles do managers take on in different organizational settings?

In an informational role, the manager may act as an information gatherer, an information distributor, or a spokesperson for the company. A manager's interpersonal roles are based on various interactions with other people. Depending on the situation, a manager may need to act as a figurehead, a company leader, or a liaison.

6.7 Managerial Skills

7. What set of managerial skills is necessary for managerial success?

Managerial skills fall into three basic categories: technical, human relations, and conceptual skills. Specialized areas of knowledge and expertise and the ability to apply that knowledge make up a manager's technical skills. Human relations skills include the ability to understand human behavior, to communicate effectively with others, and to motivate individuals to accomplish their objectives. Conceptual skills include the ability to view the organization as a whole, understand how the various parts are interdependent, and assess how the organization relates to its external environment.

6.8 Trends in Management and Leadership

8. What trends will affect management in the future?

Three important trends in management today are preparing for crises management, the increasing use of information technology, and the need to manage multinational cultures. Crisis management requires quick action, telling the truth about the situation, and putting the best people on the task to correct the situation. Finally, management must learn from the crisis in order to prevent it from happening again. Using the latest information technology, such as dashboard software, managers can make quicker, better-informed decisions. As more companies "go global," the need for multinational cultural management skills is growing. Managers must set a good example, create personal involvement for all employees, and develop a culture of trust.

Preparing for Tomorrow's Workplace Skills

1. Would you be a good manager? Do a self-assessment that includes your current technical, human relations, and conceptual skills. What skills do you already possess, and which do you need to add? Where do your strengths lie? Based on this exercise, develop a description of an effective manager. (Resources, Information)

2. Successful managers map out what they want to do with their time (planning), determine the activities and tasks they need to accomplish in that time frame (organizing), and make sure they stay on track (controlling). How well do you manage your time? Do you think ahead, or do you tend to procrastinate? Examine how you use your time, and identify at least three areas where you can improve your time management skills. (Resources)

3. Often researchers cast leadership in an inspirational role in a company and management in more of an administrative role. That tendency seems to put leadership and management in a hierarchy. Do you think one is more important than the other? Do you think a company can succeed if it has bad managers and good leaders? What about if it has good managers and bad leaders? Are managers and leaders actually the same? (Systems)

4. Today's managers must be comfortable using all kinds of technology. Do an inventory of your computer skills, and identify any gaps. After listing your areas of weakness, make a plan to increase your computer competency by enrolling in a computer class on or off campus. You may want to practice using common business applications such as Microsoft Excel by building a spreadsheet to track your budget, Microsoft PowerPoint by creating slides for your next class project, and Microsoft Outlook by uploading your semester schedule. (Information, Technology)

5. **Team Activity** One of the most common types of planning that managers do is operational planning, or the creation of policies, procedures, and rules and regulations. Assemble a team of three classmates, and work together to draft an operational plan that addresses employee attendance (or absenteeism). (Interpersonal, Systems)

Ethics Activity

Are top executives paid too much? A study of CEO compensation revealed that CEO bonuses rose considerably—from 20 percent to 30 percent—even at companies whose revenues or profits dropped or those that reported significant employee layoffs. Such high pay for CEOs at underperforming companies, as well as CEO compensation at companies with stellar results, has raised many questions from investors and others. The highest gap in pay was in 2000. CEO pay at the largest U.S. firms was 376 times higher than that of average workers. The gap has shrunk to only 271 times higher in 2016, but that is still a lot higher than the 59-to-1 ratio in 1989. The Securities and Exchange Commission (SEC) now requires public companies to disclose full details of executive compensation, including salaries, bonuses, pensions, benefits, stock options, and severance and retirement packages.

Even some CEOs question the high levels of CEO pay. Edgar Woolard, Jr., former CEO and chairman of DuPont, thinks so. "CEO pay is driven today primarily by outside consultant surveys," he says. Companies all want their

CEOs to be in the top half, and preferably the top quarter, of all CEOs. This leads to annual increases. He also criticizes the enormous severance packages that company boards give to CEOs that fail. For example, Carly Fiorina of Hewlett-Packard received $20 million when she was fired.

Using a web search tool, locate articles about this topic, and then write responses to the questions in the Ethical Dilemma section below. Be sure to support your arguments and cite your sources.

Ethical Dilemma: Are CEOs entitled to increases in compensation when their company's financial situation worsens, because their job becomes more challenging? If they fail, are they entitled to huge severance packages for their efforts? Should companies be required to divulge all details of compensation for their highest top managers, and what effect is such disclosure likely to have on executive pay?

Sources: U.S. Securities and Exchange Commission, "SEC Adopts Rule for Pay Ratio Disclosure," https://www.sec.gov, accessed September 21, 2017; Jeff Cox, "CEOs Make 271 Times the Pay of Most Workers," *CNBC,* https://www.cnbc.com, July 20, 2017; Irv Becker, "Why CEOs Aren't Overpaid," *Fortune,* http://fortune.com, June 11, 2017; "CEOs are Overpaid, Says Former DuPont CEO Edgar Woolard Jr.," *PR Newswire*, February 9, 2006, http://proquest.umi.com; Elizabeth Souder, "Firm Questions Exxon CEO's Pay," *Dallas Morning News*, December 15, 2005, http://galenet.thomsonlearning.com; "Weaker Company Performance Does Not Seem to Slow CEO Pay Increases," *Corporate Board*, September-October 2005, p. 27, http://galenet.thomsonlearning.com; "What Price CEO Pay?" *The Blade* (Toledo, Ohio), January 20, 2006, http://www.toledoblade.com.

Working the Net

1. Are you leadership material? See how you measure up at Your Leadership Legacy, http://www.yourleadershiplegacy.com/assessment.html. Read the commentary, and take the test. Study the outcome, and provide an example of how you would put each item into action.

2. Strategic Advantage, http://www.balancedscorecard.org/, offers many reasons why companies should develop strategic plans, as well as a strategy tip of the month, assessment tools, planning exercises, and resource links. Explore the site to learn the effect of strategic planning on financial performance, and present your evidence to the class. Then select a planning exercise, and with a group of classmates, perform it as it applies to your school.

3. Congratulations! You've just been promoted to your first supervisory position. However, you are at a loss as to how to actually manage your staff. This guide to general management, https://www.thebalance.com/management-4073997, brings together a variety of materials to help you. Check out Management Skills, as well as other resources. Develop a plan for yourself to follow.

4. How do entrepreneurs develop the corporate culture of their companies? Do a search of the term "corporate culture" on *Inc.* (https://www.inc.com), *Entrepreneur* (https://www.entrepreneur.com), or *Fast Company* (https://www.fastcompany.com). Prepare a short presentation for your class that explains the importance of corporate culture and how it is developed in young firms.

5. Good managers and leaders know how to empower their employees. The Business e-Coach at http://www.1000ventures.com explains why employee empowerment is so important in today's knowledge economy. After reviewing the information at this site, prepare a brief report on the benefits of employee empowerment. Include several ideas you would like a manager to use to empower you.

6. Get some leadership tips from 7 Steps to Closure at the Learning Center, http://www.learningcenter.net. Complete the Closure Planning Form to develop your own personal Success-Oriented Action Plan.

⬚ Critical Thinking Case

Managing an Extreme Makeover

During a tour of a Toyota Corolla assembly plant located near their headquarters in Bangalore, India, executives of Wipro Ltd. hit on a revolutionary idea—why not apply Toyota's successful manufacturing techniques to managing their software development and clients' back-office operations business?

"Toyota preaches continuous improvement, respect for employees, learning, and embracing change," says T. K. Kurien, 45, former head of Wipro's 13,600-person business-process outsourcing unit. "What we do is apply people, technology, and processes to solve a business problem."

Among the problems spotted early on by Kurien? Cubicles. They're normal for programmers but interrupt the flow for business-process employees. Deciding to position people side by side at long tables assembly-line style "was a roaring disaster," admits Kurien. "The factory idea concerned people." So based on feedback from his middle managers, Kurien arranged classes to explain his concepts and how they would ultimately make life easier for employees.

Wipro also adopted Toyota's *kaizen* system of soliciting employee suggestions. Priya, who has worked for Wipro for years, submitted several *kaizen* and was delighted when her bosses responded promptly to her suggestions. "Even though it's something small, it feels good. You're being considered," she says. Empowerment in the workplace washed over into her private life. As the first woman in her family to attend college, she told her parents they may arrange her marriage only to a man who will not interfere with her career.

Kurien and his managers work hard at boosting employee morale, offering rewards—pens, caps, or shirts—to employees who submit suggestions to *kaizen* boxes. And each week, a top-performing employee receives a cake. Murthy, an accountant who hopes to be Wipro's chief financial officer someday, spearheaded an effort to cut government import approval times from 30 to 15 days. He got a cake with his name written on it in honey. "I was surprised management knew what I was doing," he says. "Now I want to do more projects."

With multibillions in revenues, thousands of employees, and a U.S.-traded stock that advanced 230 percent in a two-year period, Wipro is a star of India's burgeoning information technology industry. The company's paperwork processing operations bear a clear resemblance to a Toyota plant. Two shifts of young people line long rows of tables. At the start of each shift, team leaders discuss the day's goals and divide up tasks. And just like in a Toyota factory, electronic displays mounted on the walls shift from green to red if things get bogged down.

This obsession with management efficiency has helped India become the back-office operation for hundreds of Western companies, resulting in the transfer of many thousands of jobs offshore. "If the Indians get this right, in addition to their low labor rates, they can become deadly competition," says Jeffrey K. Liker, a business professor at the University of Michigan and author of *The Toyota Way*, a book about Toyota's lean manufacturing techniques. If Kurien's management initiatives succeed, experts may soon be extolling the Wipro way.

Critical Thinking Questions

1. What type of manager is T. K. Kurien? How would you characterize his leadership style?
2. What managerial role does T. K. Kurien assume in his approach to attaining his division's goal of improved customer service?
3. What management skill sets does he exhibit?

Sources: Steve Hamm, "Taking a Page from Toyota's Playbook," *Bloomberg Businessweek*, https://www.bloomberg.com, accessed November 17, 2017; Shilpa Phadnis, "T K Kurien to Leave Wipro This Month," *The Times of India*, https://timesofindia.indiatimes.com, January 23, 2017; Toyota Resumes Efficiency Drive," *BBC News*, http://www.bbc.com, March 26, 2015.

Hot Links Address Book

1. Visit the International Business Leaders Forum (IBLF) at http://www.iblfglobal.org to discover what today's international business leaders are focusing on.
2. To learn more about how firms develop contingency plans for all sorts of crises, visit Mind Tools at https://www.mindtools.com.
3. Who are the leaders of this year's *Inc*. 500, and what do they have to say about their success? Find out at the *Inc*. 500 site at https://www.inc.com.
4. Want to learn more about Bill Gates's management style? Go to his personal website, https://www.gatesnotes.com/Bio, to read his official biography, books, and other information.
5. Most successful managers work hard at continually updating their managerial skills. One organization that offers many ongoing training and education programs is the American Management Association. Visit its site at http://www.amanet.org.
6. Search Questia's online library at https://www.questia.com for leadership resources. You'll be able to preview a wide variety of books, journals, and other materials.

7

Designing Organizational Structures

Exhibit 7.1 (Credit: CDC/ Dawn Arlotta / US Government Works)

 Introduction

Learning Outcomes

After reading this chapter, you should be able to answer these questions:

1. What are the traditional forms of organizational structure?
2. What contemporary organizational structures are companies using?
3. Why are companies using team-based organizational structures?
4. What tools do companies use to establish relationships within their organizations?
5. How can the degree of centralization/decentralization be altered to make an organization more successful?
6. How do mechanistic and organic organizations differ?
7. How does the informal organization affect the performance of the company?
8. What trends are influencing the way businesses organize?

EXPLORING BUSINESS CAREERS

Elise Eberwein

EVP of People and Communications, American Airlines

As executive vice president of people and communications at American Airlines, Elise Eberwein's role within the structure of the organization might not be readily apparent. After all, you might ask, doesn't corporate communications typically involve marketing? And what does that have to do with organizational structure? As it turns out, quite a bit at the world's largest airline.

When American Airlines and US Airways finally got the U.S. government's approval to merge in late 2013, it was no longer business as usual for Eberwein and her colleagues at the "new" airline. Until the merger, which basically produced the world's largest airline with more than 6,000 daily flights and 102,900 employees, Eberwein was head of communications at US Airways—a position she held for nine years after various other jobs in the airline industry.

Exhibit 7.2   American Airlines jet. (Credit: Joao Carlos Medau/ flickr/ Attribution 2.0 Generic (CC BY 2.0))

Communications and aviation are in Eberwein's DNA. She worked as a flight attendant at TWA before moving on to manage communications at Denver-based Frontier Airlines. Her next communications experience was at America West, which then merged with US Airways, where Eberwein served as executive vice president of people, communications, and public affairs before she took over the chief communications job at American Airlines.

Corporation communications is no longer just about marketing. The importance of an effective communications strategy cannot be understated in today's 24/7 business environment. Corporate communication executives have taken on an expanded role in many organizations, according to a recent survey by the Korn Ferry Institute. Of the senior communications executives from Fortune 500 companies who responded to the survey, nearly 40 percent said chief communications officers report directly to the CEO. In addition, more than two-thirds of respondents believe the most important leadership characteristic for communications professionals is having a strategic mindset that goes beyond day-to-day communications activities and looks ahead to future possibilities that can be translated into achievable corporate strategies at all levels of the organization.

In a company as large as American Airlines, even after the initial two-year integration plan, there are many departments, unions, and other employees to communicate with on a daily basis, not to mention the millions of customers they serve every day. For example, American's social media hub consists of 30 or so team members, divided into three groups: social customer service, social engagement, and social insights. The customer service group, the largest of the three, operates around the clock to address customers' issues, including missed flight connections and lost luggage, as well as quirky questions like why American airplanes have a specific number of stripes on their tails. Reporting to Eberwein, the social media group is empowered to reach out to any company department directly to get answers for any customer.

Eberwein believes her role includes working closely with the CEO and other managers across the globe to provide consistent, detailed information to all of its stakeholders. To accomplish this feat, Eberwein and other senior managers hold a weekly Monday morning meeting to review the previous week's operations data, revenue results, and people engagement activities. Eberwein believes establishing this regular contact with colleagues across the organization helps reinforce American's commitment to engagement and transparent communications, which ultimately shapes the customer's experience as well as the entire company.

Sources: "Leadership Bios: Elise Eberwein," https://www.aa.com, accessed July 24, 2017; "By the Numbers: Snapshot of the Airline," http://news.aa.com, accessed July 24, 2017; Richard Marshall, Beth Fowler, and Nels Olson, "The Chief Communications Officer: Survey and Findings among the Fortune 500," https://www.kornferry.com, accessed July 24, 2017; Elise Eberwein, "Why the Chief Communications Officer Is Pivotal to the CEO, Especially a New One," *Chief Executive*, http://chiefexecutive.net, September 11, 2016; Michael Slattery, "A Visit to American Airlines Social Media Hub," *Airways* magazine, https://airwaysmag.com, June 10, 2016; Diana Bradley, "American Airlines CEO Discusses Comms Strategy behind US Airways Merger," *PR Week,* http://www.prweek.com, May 27, 2015.

This module focuses on the different types of organizational structure, the reasons an organization might prefer one structure over another, and how the choice of an organizational structure ultimately can impact that organization's success.

In today's dynamic business environment, organizational structures need to be designed so that the organization can quickly respond to new competitive threats and changing customer needs. Future success for companies will depend on their ability to be flexible and respond to the needs of customers. In this chapter, we'll look first at how companies build organizational structures by implementing traditional, contemporary, and team-based models. Then, we'll explore how managers establish the relationships within the structures they have designed, including determining lines of communication, authority, and power. Finally, we'll examine what managers need to consider when designing organizational structures and the trends that are changing the choices companies make about organizational design.

7.1 | Building Organizational Structures

1. What are the traditional forms of organizational structure?

The key functions that managers perform include planning, organizing, leading, and controlling. This module focuses specifically on the organizing function. *Organizing* involves coordinating and allocating a firm's resources so that the firm can carry out its plans and achieve its goals. This organizing, or structuring, process is accomplished by:

- Determining work activities and dividing up tasks *(division of labor)*
- Grouping jobs and employees *(departmentalization)*

- Assigning authority and responsibilities *(delegation)*

The result of the organizing process is a formal structure within an organization. An **organization** is the order and design of relationships within a company or firm. It consists of two or more people working together with a common objective and clarity of purpose. Formal organizations also have well-defined lines of authority, channels for information flow, and means of control. Human, material, financial, and information resources are deliberately connected to form the business organization. Some connections are long-lasting, such as the links among people in the finance or marketing department. Others can be changed at almost any time—for example, when a committee is formed to study a problem.

Every organization has some kind of underlying structure. Typically, organizations base their frameworks on traditional, contemporary, or team-based approaches. Traditional structures are more rigid and group employees by function, products, processes, customers, or regions. Contemporary and team-based structures are more flexible and assemble employees to respond quickly to dynamic business environments. Regardless of the structural framework a company chooses to implement, all managers must first consider what kind of work needs to be done within the firm.

Exhibit 7.3   Founded in 1943, Sweden retailer IKEA has grown from a small mail-order operation to a global force in home furnishings with more than 390 stores throughout Europe, North America, Africa, Australia, and Asia. Best known for its contemporary furniture designs, highly trafficked store openings, and quirky advertising, the IKEA Group consists of multiple divisions corresponding to the company's retail, supply chain, sales, and design and manufacturing functions. *What factors likely influenced the development of IKEA's organizational structure as the company expanded over the years?* (Credit: JJBers/ flickr/ Attribution 2.0 Generic (CC BY 2.0))

Division of Labor

The process of dividing work into separate jobs and assigning tasks to workers is called **division of labor**. In a fast-food restaurant, for example, some employees take or fill orders, others prepare food, a few clean and maintain equipment, and at least one supervises all the others. In an auto assembly plant, some workers install rearview mirrors, while others mount bumpers on bumper brackets. The degree to which the tasks are subdivided into smaller jobs is called **specialization**. Employees who work at highly specialized jobs, such as assembly-line workers, perform a limited number and variety of tasks. Employees who become specialists at one task, or a small number of tasks, develop greater skill in doing that particular job. This can lead to greater efficiency and consistency in production and other work activities. However, a high degree of specialization can also result in employees who are disinterested or bored due to the lack of variety and challenge.

Traditional Structures

After a company divides the work it needs to do into specific jobs, managers then group the jobs together so that similar or associated tasks and activities can be coordinated. This grouping of people, tasks, and resources into organizational units is called **departmentalization**. It facilitates the planning, leading, and control processes.

An **organization chart** is a visual representation of the structured relationships among tasks and the people given the authority to do those tasks. In the organization chart in Exhibit 7.4, each figure represents a job, and each job includes several tasks. The sales manager, for instance, must hire salespeople, establish sales territories, motivate and train the salespeople, and control sales operations. The chart also indicates the general type of work done in each position. As Exhibit 7.5 shows, five basic types of departmentalization are commonly used in organizations:

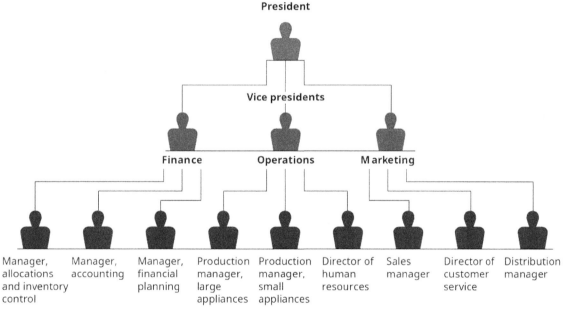

Exhibit 7.4   Organization Chart for a Typical Appliance Manufacturer Attribution: Copyright Rice University, OpenStax, under CC BY-NC-SA 4.0 license

1. *Functional departmentalization*, which is based on the primary functions performed within an organizational unit (marketing, finance, production, sales, and so on). Ethan Allen Interiors, a vertically integrated home furnishings manufacturer, continues its successful departmentalization by function, including retail, manufacturing and sourcing, product design, logistics, and operations, which includes tight financial controls.[1]

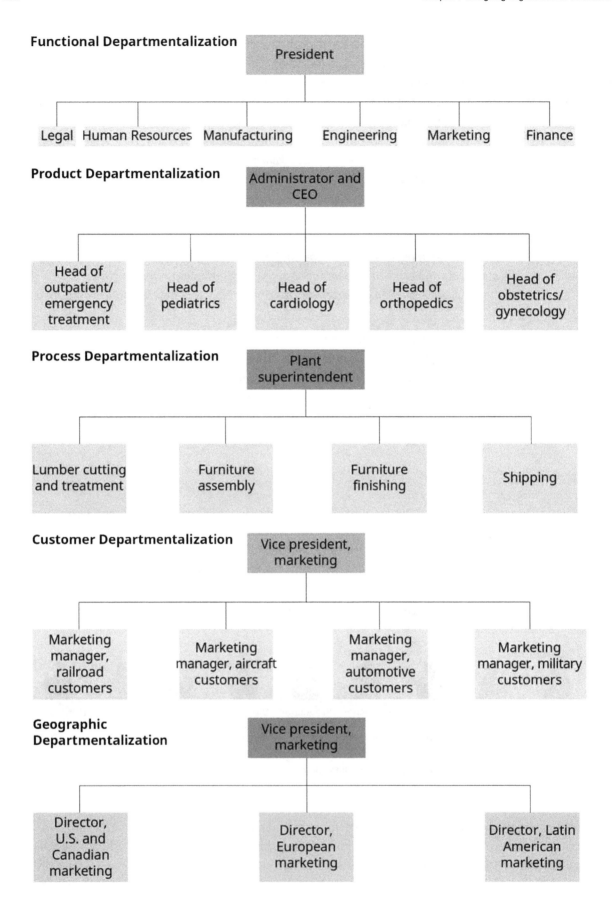

Functional Departmentalization

President

Legal | Human Resources | Manufacturing | Engineering | Marketing | Finance

Product Departmentalization

Administrator and CEO

Head of outpatient/ emergency treatment | Head of pediatrics | Head of cardiology | Head of orthopedics | Head of obstetrics/ gynecology

Process Departmentalization

Plant superintendent

Lumber cutting and treatment | Furniture assembly | Furniture finishing | Shipping

Customer Departmentalization

Vice president, marketing

Marketing manager, railroad customers | Marketing manager, aircraft customers | Marketing manager, automotive customers | Marketing manager, military customers

Geographic Departmentalization

Vice president, marketing

Director, U.S. and Canadian marketing | Director, European marketing | Director, Latin American marketing

Exhibit 7.5   Five Traditional Ways to Organize (Attribution: Copyright Rice University, OpenStax, under CC BY 4.0 license.)

2. **Product departmentalization**, which is based on the goods or services produced or sold by the organizational unit (such as outpatient/emergency services, pediatrics, cardiology, and orthopedics). For example, ITT is a diversified leading manufacturer of highly engineered components and customized technology solutions for the transportation, industrial, and oil and gas markets. The company is organized into four product divisions: Industrial Process (pumps, valves, and wastewater treatment equipment), Control Technologies (motion control and vibration isolation products), Motion Technologies (shock absorbers, brake pads, and friction materials), and Interconnect Solutions (connectors for a variety of markets).[2]

3. **Process departmentalization**, which is based on the production process used by the organizational unit (such as lumber cutting and treatment, furniture finishing, and shipping). For example, the organization of Gazprom Neft, a Russian oil company, reflects the activities the company needs to perform to extract oil from the ground and turn it into a final product: exploration and research, production (drilling), refining, and marketing and distribution.[3] Pixar, the animated-movie company now part of Disney, is divided into three parallel yet interactive process-based groups: technology development, which delivers computer-graphics tools; creative development, which creates stories and characters and animates them; and production, which coordinates the film-making process.[4]

4. **Customer departmentalization**, which is based on the primary type of customer served by the organizational unit (such as wholesale or retail purchasers). The PNC Financial Services Group offers a wide range of services for all of its customers and is structured by the type of consumer it serves: retail banking for consumers; the asset management group, with specific focus on individuals as well as corporations, unions, municipalities, and others; and corporate and institutional banking for middle-market companies nationwide.[5]

ETHICS IN PRACTICE

Ethics in Practice

Panera's Menu Comes Clean

Making a strategic change to a company's overall philosophy and the way it does business affects every part of the organizational structure. And when that change pertains to sustainability and "clean food," Panera Bread Company took on the challenge more than a decade ago and now has a menu free of man-made preservatives, sweeteners, colors, and flavors.

In 2015, Ron Shaich, company founder and CEO, announced Panera's "no-no" list of nearly 100 ingredients, which he vowed would be eliminated or never used again in menu items. Two years later, the company announced that its menu was "100 percent clean," but the process was not an easy one.

Panera used thousands of labor hours to review the 450 ingredients used in menu items, eventually reformulating more than 120 of them to eliminate artificial ingredients. Once the team identified the ingredients that were not "clean," they worked with the company's 300 vendors—and in some instances, a vendor's supplier—to reformulate an ingredient to make it preservative-free. For example, the recipe for the company's popular broccoli cheddar soup had to be revised 60 times to remove artificial ingredients without losing the soup's taste and texture. According to Shaich, the trial-and-error approach was about finding the right balance of milk, cream, and emulsifiers, like Dijon mustard, to replace sodium phosphate (a no-no item) while keeping the soup's texture creamy. Panera also created a new cheddar cheese to use in the soup and used a Dijon mustard that contained unpreserved vinegar as a substitute for the banned sodium phosphate.

Sara Burnett, Panera's director of wellness and food policy, believes that the company's responsibility goes beyond just serving its customers. She believes that Panera can make a difference by using its voice and purchasing power to have a positive impact on the overall food system. In addition, the company's Herculean effort to remove artificial ingredients from its menu items also helped it take a close look at its supply chain and other processes that Panera could simplify by using better ingredients.

Panera is not yet satisfied with its commitment to clean food. The food chain recently announced its goal of sourcing 100 percent cage-free eggs for all of its U.S. Panera bakery-cafés by 2020.

Critical Thinking Questions

1. How does Panera's approach to clean eating provide the company with a competitive advantage?
2. What kind of impact does this commitment to preservative-free food have on the company's organizational structure?
3. Does "clean food" put additional pressure on Panera and its vendors? Explain your reasoning.

Sources: "Our Food Policy," https://www.panerabread.com, accessed July 24, 2017; Emily Payne, "Panera Bread's Sara Burnett on Shifting Demand for a Better Food System," *Food Tank,* http://foodtank.com, accessed July 18, 2017; Julie Jargon, "What Panera Had to Change to Make Its Menu 'Clean,'" *The Wall Street Journal,* https://www.wsj.com, February 20, 2017; John Kell, "Panera Says Its Food Menu Is Now 100% 'Clean Eating,'" *Fortune,* http://fortune.com, January 13, 2017; Lani Furbank, "Seven Questions with Sara Burnett, Director of Wellness and Food Policy at Panera Bread," *Food Tank,* https://foodtank.com, April 12, 2016.

5. *Geographic departmentalization*, which is based on the geographic segmentation of organizational units (such as U.S. and Canadian marketing, European marketing, and Latin American marketing).

People are assigned to a particular organizational unit because they perform similar or related tasks, or because they are jointly responsible for a product, client, or market. Decisions about how to departmentalize affect the way management assigns authority, distributes resources, rewards performance, and sets up lines of communication. Many large organizations use several types of departmentalization. For example, Procter & Gamble (P&G), the multibillion-dollar consumer-products company, integrates four different types of departmentalization, which the company refers to as "four pillars." First, the Global Business Units (GBU) divide the company according to products (baby, feminine, and family care; beauty; fabric and home care; and health and grooming). Then, P&G uses a geographical approach, creating business units to market its products around the world. There are Selling and Market Operations (SMO) groups for North America; Latin America; Europe; Asia Pacific; Greater China; and India, the Middle East, and Africa. P&G's third pillar is Global Business Services division (GBS), which also uses geographic departmentalization. GBS provides technology processes and standard data tools to enable the GBUs and SMOs to better understand the business and to serve consumers and customers better. It supports P&G business units in areas such as accounting and financial reporting, information technology, purchases, payroll and benefits administration, and facilities management. Finally, the divisions of the Corporate Functions pillar provide a safety net to all the other pillars. These divisions are comprised of functional specialties such as customer business development; external relations; human resources; legal, marketing, consumer, and market knowledge; research and development;

and workplace services.[6]

Line-and-Staff Organization

The **line organization** is designed with direct, clear lines of authority and communication flowing from the top managers downward. Managers have direct control over all activities, including administrative duties. An organization chart for this type of structure would show that all positions in the firm are directly connected via an imaginary line extending from the highest position in the organization to the lowest (where production of goods and services takes place). This structure, with its simple design and broad managerial control, is often well-suited to small, entrepreneurial firms.

As an organization grows and becomes more complex, the line organization can be enhanced by adding staff positions to the design. Staff positions provide specialized advisory and support services to line managers in the **line-and-staff organization**, shown in Exhibit 7.6. In daily operations, individuals in **line positions** are directly involved in the processes used to create goods and services. Individuals in **staff positions** provide the administrative and support services that line employees need to achieve the firm's goals. Line positions in organizations are typically in areas such as production, marketing, and finance. Staff positions are found in areas such as legal counseling, managerial consulting, public relations, and human resource management.

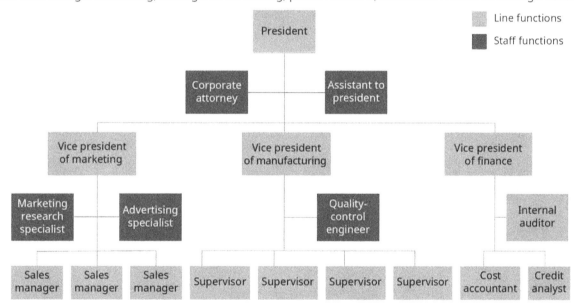

Exhibit 7.6 Line-and-Staff Organization (Attribution: Copyright Rice University, OpenStax, under CC BY 4.0 license.)

CONCEPT CHECK

1. How does specialization lead to greater efficiency and consistency in production?
2. What are the five types of departmentalization?

7.2 Contemporary Structures

2. What contemporary organizational structures are companies using?

Although traditional forms of departmentalization still represent how many companies organize their work, newer, more flexible organizational structures are in use at many firms. Let's look at matrix and committee structures and how those two types of organizations are helping companies better leverage the diverse skills of their employees.

Matrix Structure

The **matrix structure** (also called the *project management* approach) is sometimes used in conjunction with the traditional line-and-staff structure in an organization. Essentially, this structure combines two different forms of departmentalization, functional and product, that have complementary strengths and weaknesses. The matrix structure brings together people from different functional areas of the organization (such as manufacturing, finance, and marketing) to work on a special project. Each employee has two direct supervisors: the line manager from her or his specific functional area and the project manager. **Exhibit 7.7** shows a matrix organization with four special project groups (A, B, C, D), each with its own project manager. Because of the dual chain of command, the matrix structure presents some unique challenges for both managers and subordinates.

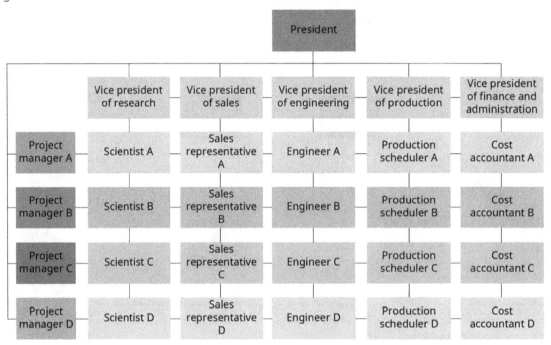

Exhibit 7.7   Matrix Organization (Attribution: Copyright Rice University, OpenStax, under CC BY 4.0 license.)

Advantages of the matrix structure include:

- *Teamwork.* By pooling the skills and abilities of various specialists, the company can increase creativity and innovation and tackle more complex tasks.
- *Efficient use of resources.* Project managers use only the specialized staff they need to get the job done, instead of building large groups of underused personnel.
- *Flexibility.* The project structure is flexible and can adapt quickly to changes in the environment; the group can be disbanded quickly when it is no longer needed.
- *Ability to balance conflicting objectives.* The customer wants a quality product and predictable costs. The organization wants high profits and the development of technical capability for the future. These

competing goals serve as a focal point for directing activities and overcoming conflict. The marketing representative can represent the customer, the finance representative can advocate high profits, and the engineers can push for technical capabilities.

- *Higher performance.* Employees working on special project teams may experience increased feelings of ownership, commitment, and motivation.
- *Opportunities for personal and professional development.* The project structure gives individuals the opportunity to develop and strengthen technical and interpersonal skills.

Disadvantages of the matrix structure include:

- *Power struggles.* Functional and product managers may have different goals and management styles.
- *Confusion among team members.* Reporting relationships and job responsibilities may be unclear.
- *Lack of cohesiveness.* Team members from different functional areas may have difficulty communicating effectively and working together as a team.

Although project-based matrix organizations can improve a company's flexibility and teamwork, some companies are trying to unravel complex matrix structures that create limited accountability and complicate day-to-day operations. Some CEOs and other top managers suggest that matrix structures make it easier to blame others when things don't go as planned.[7]

Committee Structure

In **committee structure**, authority and responsibility are held by a group rather than an individual. Committees are typically part of a larger line-and-staff organization. Often the committee's role is only advisory, but in some situations the committee has the power to make and implement decisions. Committees can make the coordination of tasks in the organization much easier. For example, Novartis, the huge Swiss pharmaceutical company, has a committee structure, which reports to its board of directors. The company's executive committee is responsible for overseeing the business operations of group companies within the global organization and consists of the CEO, CFO, head of HR, general counsel, president of operations, head of biomedical research, global head of drug development, CEOs of the pharmaceutical and oncology units, and CEOs of Sandoz and Alcon, other Novartis companies. Members of the executive committee are selected by the company's board of directors.[8]

Committees bring diverse viewpoints to a problem and expand the range of possible solutions, but there are some drawbacks. Committees can be slow to reach a decision and are sometimes dominated by a single individual. It is also more difficult to hold any one individual accountable for a decision made by a group. Committee meetings can sometimes go on for long periods of time with seemingly little being accomplished.

CONCEPT CHECK

1. Why does the matrix structure have a dual chain of command?
2. How does a matrix structure increase power struggles or reduce accountability?
3. What are advantages of a committee structure? Disadvantages?

7.3 | Using Teams to Enhance Motivation and Performance

3. Why are companies using team-based organizational structures?

One of the most apparent trends in business today is the use of teams to accomplish organizational goals. Using a team-based structure can increase individual and group motivation and performance. This section gives a brief overview of group behavior, defines work teams as specific types of groups, and provides suggestions for creating high-performing teams.

Understanding Group Behavior

Teams are a specific type of organizational group. Every organization contains *groups,* social units of two or more people who share the same goals and cooperate to achieve those goals. Understanding some fundamental concepts related to group behavior and group processes provides a good foundation for understanding concepts about work teams. Groups can be formal or informal in nature. Formal groups are designated and sanctioned by the organization; their behavior is directed toward accomplishing organizational goals. Informal groups are based on social relationships and are not determined or sanctioned by the organization.

Formal organizational groups, like the sales department at Apple, must operate within the larger Apple organizational system. To some degree, elements of the larger Apple system, such as organizational strategy, company policies and procedures, available resources, and the highly motivated employee corporate culture, determine the behavior of smaller groups, such as the sales department, within the company. Other factors that affect the behavior of organizational groups are individual member characteristics (e.g., ability, training, personality), the roles and norms of group members, and the size and cohesiveness of the group. Norms are the implicit behavioral guidelines of the group, or the standards for acceptable and nonacceptable behavior. For example, an Apple sales manager may be expected to work at least two Saturdays per month without extra pay. Although this isn't written anywhere, it is the expected norm.

Group cohesiveness refers to the degree to which group members want to stay in the group and tend to resist outside influences (such as a change in company policies). When group performance norms are high, group cohesiveness will have a positive impact on productivity. Cohesiveness tends to increase when the size of the group is small, individual and group goals are similar, the group has high status in the organization, rewards are group-based rather than individual-based, and the group competes with other groups within the organization. Work group cohesiveness can benefit the organization in several ways, including increased productivity, enhanced worker self-image because of group success, increased company loyalty, reduced employee turnover, and reduced absenteeism. Southwest Airlines is known for its work group cohesiveness. On the other hand, cohesiveness can also lead to restricted output, resistance to change, and conflict with other work groups in the organization.

The opportunity to turn the decision-making process over to a group with diverse skills and abilities is one of the arguments for using work groups (and teams) in organizational settings. For group decision-making to be most effective, however, both managers and group members must understand its strengths and weaknesses (see **Table 7.1**).

Work Groups versus Work Teams

We have already noted that teams are a special type of organizational group, but we also need to differentiate between work groups and work teams. **Work groups** share resources and coordinate efforts to help members better perform their individual duties and responsibilities. The performance of the group can be evaluated by adding up the contributions of the individual group members. **Work teams** require not only coordination but also *collaboration,* the pooling of knowledge, skills, abilities, and resources in a collective effort to attain a common goal. A work team creates *synergy,* causing the performance of the team as a whole to be greater than the sum of team members' individual contributions. Simply assigning employees to groups and labeling them a team does not guarantee a positive outcome. Managers and team members must be committed to creating, developing, and maintaining high-performance work teams. Factors that contribute to their success are discussed later in this section.

Strengths and Weaknesses of Group Decision Making	
Strengths	Weaknesses
• Groups bring more information and knowledge to the decision-making process. • Groups offer a diversity of perspectives and, therefore, generate a greater number of disagreements. • Group decision-making results in a higher-quality decision than does individual decision-making. • Participation of group members increases the likelihood that a decision will be accepted.	• Groups typically take a longer time to reach a solution than an individual takes. • Group members may pressure others to conform, reducing the likelihood of alternatives. • The process may be dominated by one or a small number of participants. • Groups lack accountability, because it is difficult to assign responsibility for outcomes to any one individual.

Table 7.1

Types of Teams

The evolution of the team concept in organizations can be seen in three basic types of work teams: problem-solving, self-managed, and cross-functional. **Problem-solving teams** are typically made up of employees from the same department or area of expertise and from the same level of the organizational hierarchy. They meet on a regular basis to share information and discuss ways to improve processes and procedures in specific functional areas. Problem-solving teams generate ideas and alternatives and may recommend a specific course of action, but they typically do not make final decisions, allocate resources, or implement change.

Many organizations that experienced success using problem-solving teams were willing to expand the team concept to allow team members greater responsibility in making decisions, implementing solutions, and monitoring outcomes. These highly autonomous groups are called **self-managed work teams**. They manage themselves without any formal supervision, taking responsibility for setting goals, planning and scheduling work activities, selecting team members, and evaluating team performance.

Today, approximately 80 percent of Fortune 1000 companies use some sort of self-managed teams.[9] One example is Zappos's shift to self-managed work teams in 2013, where the traditional organizational structure and bosses were eliminated, according to a system called holacracy.[10] Another version of self-managing teams can be found at W. L. Gore, the company that invented Gore-Tex fabric and Glide dental floss. The three employees who invented Elixir guitar strings contributed their spare time to the effort and persuaded a handful of colleagues to help them improve the design. After working three years *entirely* on their own—without asking for any supervisory or top management permission or being subjected to any kind of oversight—the team finally sought the support of the larger company, which they needed to take the strings to market. Today, W. L. Gore's Elixir is the number one selling string brand for acoustic guitar players.[11]

An adaptation of the team concept is called a **cross-functional team**. These teams are made up of employees from about the same hierarchical level but different functional areas of the organization. Many task forces, organizational committees, and project teams are cross-functional. Often the team members work together only until they solve a given problem or complete a specific project. Cross-functional teams allow people with various levels and areas of expertise to pool their resources, develop new ideas, solve problems, and coordinate complex projects. Both problem-solving teams and self-managed teams may also be cross-functional teams.

CUSTOMER SATISFACTION AND QUALITY

Team Approach Flies High at GE Aviation

"Teaming" is the term used at GE Aviation manufacturing plants to describe how self-managed groups of employees are working together to make decisions to help them do their work efficiently, maintain quality, and meet critical deadlines in the global aviation supply chain.

This management concept is not new to GE Aviation; its manufacturing plants in Durham, North Carolina, and Bromont, Quebec, Canada, have been using self-managed teams for more than 30 years. This approach to business operations continues to be successful and is now used at most of its 77 manufacturing facilities worldwide.

The goal of teaming is to move decision-making and authority as close to the end-product as possible, which means front-line employees are accountable for meeting performance goals on a daily basis. For example, if there is some sort of delay in the manufacturing process, it is up to the team to figure out how to keep things moving—even if that means skipping breaks or changing their work schedules to overcome obstacles.

At the Bromont plant, workers do not have supervisors who give them direction. Rather, they have coaches who give them specific goals. The typical functions performed by supervisors, such as planning, developing manufacturing processes, and monitoring vacation and overtime, are managed by the teams themselves. In addition, members from each team sit on a joint council with management and HR representatives to make decisions that will affect overall plant operations, such as when to eliminate overtime and who gets promoted or fired.

This hands-on approach helps workers gain confidence and motivation to fix problems directly rather than sending a question up the chain of command and waiting for a directive. In addition, teaming allows the people who do the work on a daily basis to come up with the best ideas to resolve issues and perform various jobs tasks in the most efficient way possible.

For GE Aviation, implementing the teaming approach has been a successful venture, and the company finds the strategy easiest to implement when starting up a new manufacturing facility. The company recently opened several new plants, and the teaming concept has had an interesting effect on the hiring process. A new plant in Welland, Ontario, Canada, opens soon, and the hiring process, which may seem more rigorous than most job hiring experiences, is well under way. With the team concept in mind, job candidates need to demonstrate not only required technical skills but also soft skills—for example, the ability to communicate clearly, accept feedback, and participate in discussions in a respectful manner.

Critical Thinking Questions

1. What challenges do you think HR recruiters face when hiring job candidates who need to have both technical and soft skills?
2. How can experienced team members help new employees be successful in the teaming structure? Provide some examples.

Sources: GE Reports Canada, "The Meaning of Teaming: Empowering New Hires at GE's Welland Brilliant Factory," https://gereports.ca, July 17, 2017; Sarah Kessler, "GE Has a Version of Self-Management That Is Much Like Zappos' Holacracy—and It Works," *Quartz,* https://qz.com, June 6, 2017; Gareth Phillips, "Look No Managers! Self-Managed Teams," *LinkedIn,* https://www.linkedin.com, June 9, 2016; Amy Alexander, "Step by Step: Train Employees to Take Charge," *Investor's Business Daily,* http://www.investors.com, June 18, 2014; Rasheedah Jones, "Teaming at GE Aviation," *Management Innovation eXchange,* http://www.managementexchange.com, July 14, 2013.

Building High-Performance Teams

A great team must possess certain characteristics, so selecting the appropriate employees for the team is vital. Employees who are more willing to work together to accomplish a common goal should be selected, rather than employees who are more interested in their own personal achievement. Team members should also possess a variety of skills. Diverse skills strengthen the overall effectiveness of the team, so teams should consciously recruit members to fill gaps in the collective skill set. To be effective, teams must also have clearly defined goals. Vague or unclear goals will not provide the necessary direction or allow employees to measure their performance against expectations.

Next, high-performing teams need to practice good communication. Team members need to communicate messages and give appropriate feedback that seeks to correct any misunderstandings. Feedback should also be detached; that is, team members should be careful to critique ideas rather than criticize the person who suggests them. Nothing can degrade the effectiveness of a team like personal attacks. Lastly, great teams have great leaders. Skilled team leaders divide work so that tasks are not repeated, help members set and track goals, monitor their team's performance, communicate openly, and remain flexible to adapt to changing goals or management demands.

CONCEPT CHECK

1. What is the difference between a work team and a work group?

2. Identify and describe three types of work teams.
3. What are some ways to build a high-performance team?

7.4 | Authority—Establishing Organizational Relationships

4. What tools do companies use to establish relationships within their organizations?

Once companies choose a method of departmentalization, they must then establish the relationships within that structure. In other words, the company must decide how many layers of management it needs and who will report to whom. The company must also decide how much control to invest in each of its managers and where in the organization decisions will be made and implemented.

Managerial Hierarchy

Managerial hierarchy (also called the *management pyramid*) is defined by the levels of management within an organization. Generally, the management structure has three levels: top, middle, and supervisory management. In a managerial hierarchy, each organizational unit is controlled and supervised by a manager in a higher unit. The person with the most formal authority is at the top of the hierarchy. The higher a manager, the more power he or she has. Thus, the amount of power decreases as you move down the management pyramid. At the same time, the number of employees increases as you move down the hierarchy.

Not all companies today are using this traditional configuration. One company that has eliminated hierarchy altogether is The Morning Star Company, the largest tomato processor in the world. Based in Woodland, California, the company employs 600 permanent "colleagues" and an additional 4,000 workers during harvest season. Founder and sole owner Chris Rufer started the company and based its vision on the philosophy of self-management, in which professionals initiate communication and coordination of their activities with colleagues, customers, suppliers, and others, and take personal responsibility for helping the company achieve its corporate goals.[12]

An organization with a well-defined hierarchy has a clear **chain of command**, which is the line of authority that extends from one level of the organization to the next, from top to bottom, and makes clear who reports to whom. The chain of command is shown in the organization chart and can be traced from the CEO all the way down to the employees producing goods and services. Under the *unity of command* principle, everyone reports to and gets instructions from only one boss. Unity of command guarantees that everyone will have a direct supervisor and will not be taking orders from a number of different supervisors. Unity of command and chain of command give everyone in the organization clear directions and help coordinate people doing different jobs.

Matrix organizations automatically violate the unity of command principle because employees report to more than one boss, if only for the duration of a project. For example, Unilever, the consumer-products company that makes Dove soap, Ben & Jerry's ice cream, and Hellmann's mayonnaise, used to have a matrix structure with one CEO for North America and another for Europe. But employees in divisions that operated in both locations were unsure about which CEO's decisions took precedence. Today, the company uses a product departmentalization structure.[13] Companies like Unilever tend to abandon matrix structures because of problems associated with unclear or duplicate reporting relationships, in other words, with a lack of unity of command.

Individuals who are part of the chain of command have authority over other persons in the organization. **Authority** is legitimate power, granted by the organization and acknowledged by employees, that allows an individual to request action and expect compliance. Exercising authority means making decisions and seeing that they are carried out. Most managers *delegate*, or assign, some degree of authority and responsibility to others below them in the chain of command. The **delegation of authority** makes the employees accountable to their supervisor. *Accountability* means responsibility for outcomes. Typically, authority and responsibility move downward through the organization as managers assign activities to, and share decision-making with, their subordinates. Accountability moves upward in the organization as managers in each successively higher level are held accountable for the actions of their subordinates.

Span of Control

Each firm must decide how many managers are needed at each level of the management hierarchy to effectively supervise the work performed within organizational units. A manager's **span of control** (sometimes called *span of management*) is the number of employees the manager directly supervises. It can be as narrow as two or three employees or as wide as 50 or more. In general, the larger the span of control, the more efficient the organization. As Table 7.2 shows, however, both narrow and wide spans of control have benefits and drawbacks.

Narrow and Wide Spans of Control		
	Advantages	Disadvantages
Narrow span of control	• This approach allows a high degree of control. • Fewer subordinates may mean the manager is more familiar with each individual. • Close supervision can provide immediate feedback.	• More levels of management mean that it is more expensive. • Decision-making is slower due to vertical layers. • Top management are isolated. • This approach discourages employee autonomy.
Wide span of control	• Fewer levels of management means increased efficiency and reduced costs. • Increased subordinate autonomy leads to quicker decision-making. • This approach allows for greater organizational flexibility. • This approach creates higher levels of job satisfaction due to employee empowerment.	• This approach allows for less control. • Managers may lack familiarity with their subordinates due to the large number. • Managers can be spread so thin that they can't provide necessary leadership or support. • There may be a lack of coordination or synchronization.

Table 7.2

If hundreds of employees perform the same job, one supervisor may be able to manage a very large number of employees. Such might be the case at a clothing plant, where hundreds of sewing machine operators work from identical patterns. But if employees perform complex and dissimilar tasks, a manager can effectively supervise only a much smaller number. For instance, a supervisor in the research and development area of a pharmaceutical company might oversee just a few research chemists due to the highly complex nature of their jobs.

CONCEPT CHECK

1. How does the chain of command clarify reporting relationships?
2. What is the role of a staff position in a line-and-staff organization?
3. What factors determine the optimal span of control?

7.5 Degree of Centralization

5. How can the degree of centralization/decentralization be altered to make an organization more successful?

The optimal span of control is determined by the following five factors:

1. *Nature of the task*. The more complex the task, the narrower the span of control.
2. *Location of the workers*. The more locations, the narrower the span of control.
3. *Ability of the manager to delegate responsibility*. The greater the ability to delegate, the wider the span of control.
4. *Amount of interaction and feedback between the workers and the manager*. The more feedback and interaction required, the narrower the span of control.
5. *Level of skill and motivation of the workers*. The higher the skill level and motivation, the wider the span of control.

The final component in building an effective organizational structure is deciding at what level in the organization decisions should be made. **Centralization** is the degree to which formal authority is concentrated in one area or level of the organization. In a highly centralized structure, top management makes most of the key decisions in the organization, with very little input from lower-level employees. Centralization lets top managers develop a broad view of operations and exercise tight financial controls. It can also help to reduce costs by eliminating redundancy in the organization. But centralization may also mean that lower-level personnel don't get a chance to develop their decision-making and leadership skills and that the organization is less able to respond quickly to customer demands.

Decentralization is the process of pushing decision-making authority down the organizational hierarchy, giving lower-level personnel more responsibility and power to make and implement decisions. Benefits of decentralization can include quicker decision-making, increased levels of innovation and creativity, greater organizational flexibility, faster development of lower-level managers, and increased levels of job satisfaction and employee commitment. But decentralization can also be risky. If lower-level personnel don't have the necessary skills and training to perform effectively, they may make costly mistakes. Additionally, decentralization may increase the likelihood of inefficient lines of communication, competing objectives, and duplication of effort.

Several factors must be considered when deciding how much decision-making authority to delegate throughout the organization. These factors include the size of the organization, the speed of change in its environment, managers' willingness to give up authority, employees' willingness to accept more authority, and the organization's geographic dispersion.

Decentralization is usually desirable when the following conditions are met:

- The organization is very large, like ExxonMobil, Ford, or General Electric.
- The firm is in a dynamic environment where quick, local decisions must be made, as in many high-tech industries.
- Managers are willing to share power with their subordinates.
- Employees are willing and able to take more responsibility.
- The company is spread out geographically, such as Nordstrom, Caterpillar, or Ford.

As organizations grow and change, they continually reevaluate their structure to determine whether it is helping the company to achieve its goals.

CONCEPT CHECK

1. What are the characteristics of a centralized organization?
2. What are the benefits of a decentralized organization?
3. What factors should be considered when choosing the degree of centralization?

7.6 Organizational Design Considerations

6. How do mechanistic and organic organizations differ?

You are now familiar with the different ways to structure an organization, but as a manager, how do you decide which design will work the best for your business? What works for one company may not work for another. In this section, we'll look at two generic models of organizational design and briefly examine a set of contingency factors that favors each.

Exhibit 7.8   The Walt Disney Company expanded its entertainment empire more than a decade ago by acquiring Pixar Studios, the animation powerhouse behind such blockbusters as *Toy Story, Finding Dory, Cars,* and *Up*. The $7.4 billion purchase absorbed Pixar into the Disney Studio Entertainment division, one of the company's four operating units, alongside Parks and Resorts, Media Networks, and Consumer Products and Interactive Media. *Why do some analysts believe that Disney's gigantic organizational structure could engulf the smaller Pixar operation and stifle its creative output?* (Credit: Poi Beltran/ Flicker/ Attribution 2.0 Generic (CC BY 2.0))

Mechanistic versus Organic Structures

Structural design generally follows one of the two basic models described in Table 7.3: mechanistic or organic. A **mechanistic organization** is characterized by a relatively high degree of job specialization, rigid departmentalization, many layers of management (particularly middle management), narrow spans of control, centralized decision-making, and a long chain of command. This combination of elements results in what is called a tall organizational structure. The U.S. Army and the United Nations are typical mechanistic organizations.

In contrast, an **organic organization** is characterized by a relatively low degree of job specialization, loose departmentalization, few levels of management, wide spans of control, decentralized decision-making, and a short chain of command. This combination of elements results in what is called a flat organizational structure. Colleges and universities tend to have flat organizational structures, with only two or three levels of administration between the faculty and the president. Exhibit 7.9 shows examples of flat and tall organizational structures.

Factors Influencing the Choice between Mechanistic and Organic Structures

Although few organizations are purely mechanistic or purely organic, most organizations tend more toward one type or the other. The decision to create a more mechanistic or a more organic structural design is based on factors such as the firm's overall strategy, the size of the organization, and the stability of its external environment, among others.

A company's organizational structure should enable it to achieve its goals, and because setting corporate goals is part of a firm's overall strategy-making process, it follows that a company's structure depends on its *strategy*. That alignment can be challenging for struggling companies trying to accomplish multiple goals. For example, a company with an innovation strategy will need the flexibility and fluid movement of information that an organic organization provides. But a company using a cost-control strategy will require the efficiency and tight control of a mechanistic organization. Often, struggling companies try to simultaneously increase innovation and rein in costs, which can be organizational challenges for managers. Such is the case at Microsoft, where CEO Satya Nadella cut more than 18,000 jobs in 2014 after taking the helm at the technology giant. Most of the cuts were the result of the company's failed acquisition of Nokia's mobile phone business. More recently, the company eliminated additional jobs in sales and marketing (mostly overseas) as Microsoft shifts from a software developer to a cloud computing software delivery service. At the same time, Nadella is also trying to encourage employees and managers to break down barriers between divisions and increase the pace of innovation across the organization.[14]

Mechanistic versus Organic Structure		
Structural Characteristic	Mechanistic	Organic
Job specialization	High	Low
Departmentalization	Rigid	Loose
Managerial hierarchy (levels of management)	Tall (many levels)	Flat (few levels)
Span of control	Narrow	Wide
Decision-making authority	Centralized	Decentralization
Chain of command	Long	Short

Table 7.3

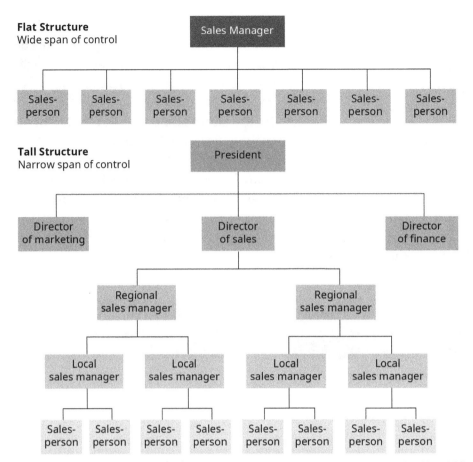

Exhibit 7.9   Flat versus Tall Organizational Structures (Attribution: Copyright Rice University, OpenStax, under CC BY 4.0 license.)

Size is another factor that affects how mechanistic or organic a company's organizational structure is. Much research has been conducted that shows a company's size has a significant impact on its organizational structure. Smaller companies tend to follow the more organic model, in part because they can. It's much easier to be successful with decentralized decision-making, for example, if you have only 50 employees. A company with that few employees is also more likely, by virtue of its size, to have a lesser degree of employee specialization. That's because, when there are fewer people to do the work, those people tend to know more about the entire process. As a company grows, it becomes more mechanistic, as systems are put in place to manage the greater number of employees. Procedures, rules, and regulations replace flexibility, innovation, and independence. That isn't always the case, however. W. L. Gore has nearly 10,000 employees and more than $3 billion in annual revenues, but, as noted earlier, uses an extremely organic organizational structure. Employees have no bosses, participate on teams, and often create roles for themselves to fill functional gaps within the company.[15]

Lastly, the business in which a company operates has a significant impact on its organizational structure. In complex, dynamic, and unstable environments, companies need to organize for flexibility and agility. That is, their organizational structures need to respond to rapid and unexpected changes in the business environment. For companies operating in stable environments, however, the demands for flexibility and agility are not so great. The environment is predictable. In a simple, stable environment, therefore, companies benefit from the efficiencies created by a mechanistic organizational structure.

MANAGING CHANGE

Google Learns the Alphabet

A little less than 20 years ago, Larry Page and Sergey Brin built a search engine that used links to determine the importance of individual pages on the web. Today, Google has grown from two founders to more than 60,000 employees in 50 different countries. While the company is routinely high on the lists of best places to work and companies with the best employee perks, its meteoric growth has not been without challenges.

Much has been written about Google's informal organizational structure, which has fueled a creative environment second to none. At one point, the founders shared an office that looked like a college dorm room, complete with skateboards, beanbag chairs, and remote-controlled airplanes. The company's offices around the world are designed to be the most productive workspaces imaginable, sometimes with meeting rooms designed as camping vans (Amsterdam) or hallways decorated with subway grates and fire hydrants (New York City).

As this creative environment expanded, Google relied on its innovative and competitive culture to produce some of the most-used products around the world, including YouTube, the Android operating system, Gmail, and, of course, Google Search. As Google grew, so did the strain on its informal structure. In the early days, while adding employees on a daily basis, the company needed to find the right balance between maintaining creativity and running a rapidly growing organization.

In 2001, Brin and Page hired an outside CEO, Eric Schmidt, who hired an HR manager and then divided employees into teams based on product or function. This structure seemed to work well until Google started to acquire companies or develop new products to add to its portfolio of business ventures, including Double Click and Nest. At the same time, Page and Brin never lost sight of their "moonshot" projects, potentially game-changing innovations that could change the world, such as a self-driving car, which may or may not become a profitable venture.

Fast-forward to 2015, when the founders decided Google was getting too big to contain in one company. They created Alphabet, which is now a holding company that includes Google as well as several other business ventures. Their decision to refocus Google and pull out other activities under the Alphabet umbrella has provided transparency and an organizational structure that has been simplified. Sundar Pichai, who was quite successful managing Google Search, became the new Google CEO, while Page became the Alphabet CEO and Brin the Alphabet President. (Former Google CEO Schmidt is Alphabet's executive chairman.)

This reorganization allows both Brin and Page to focus on projects they are passionate about, such as Project Loon, a network of balloons flying high above commercial airspace that provides web connectivity to remote areas, while leaving Google and its many successful endeavors to be managed independently by Pichai and his team. Alphabet's recent CFO hire, Ruth Porat, former CFO at Morgan Stanley, has received praise for her guidance in helping company executives take a closer look at costs while still encouraging the innovation and creativity the Google founders seemingly invented. Although not as simple as *A-B-C*, the new organizational structure seems to streamline processes while allowing the various businesses room to grow on their own.

Critical Thinking Questions

1. If you were a long-time "Googler," how would feel about the change in organizational structure at the company?
2. Do you think the creative work environment fostered by company founders has taken a hit with the new Alphabet organizational structure? Why or why not?
3. What are some advantages and disadvantages of creating separate businesses for the company's moonshot projects?

Sources: "Our History," https://www.google.com, accessed July 24, 2017; "Project Loon: Balloon-Powered Internet for Everyone," https://x.company, accessed July 24, 2017; Catherine Clifford, "Google Billionaire Eric Schmidt: These 2 Qualities Are the Best Predictors of Success," *CNBC,* http://www.cnbc.com, June 26, 2017; Dave Smith, "Read Larry Page's New Letter about the Current Status of Alphabet, Google's Parent Company," *Business Insider,* http://www.businessinsider.com, April 27, 2017; Avery Hartmans, "Here Are All the Companies and Divisions within Alphabet, Google's Parent Company," *Business Insider,* http://www.businessinsider.com, October 6, 2016; Leena Rao, "CFO Ruth Porat Is Pushing Google 'Creatives' to Bring Their Costs under Control," *Fortune,* http://fortune.com, September 12, 2016; Adam Lashinsky, "How Alphabet's Structure Shows Off Google's True Value," *Fortune,* http://fortune.com, February 2, 2016; Carey Dunne, "8 of Google's Craziest Offices," *Fast Company Design,* https://www.fastcodesign.com, April 10, 2014.

CONCEPT CHECK

1. Compare and contrast mechanistic and organic organizations.
2. What factors determine whether an organization should be mechanistic or organic?

7.7 The Informal Organization

7. How does the informal organization affect the performance of the company?

Up to this point, we have focused on formal organizational structures that can be seen in the boxes and lines of the organization chart. Yet many important relationships within an organization do not show up on an organization chart. Nevertheless, these relationships can affect the decisions and performance of employees at all levels of the organization.

The network of connections and channels of communication based on the informal relationships of individuals inside the organization is known as the **informal organization**. Informal relationships can be between people at the same hierarchical level or between people at different levels and in different departments. Some connections are work-related, such as those formed among people who carpool or ride the same train to work. Others are based on nonwork commonalties such as belonging to the same church or health club or having children who attend the same school.

Functions of the Informal Organization

The informal organization has several important functions. First, it provides a source of friendships and social contact for organization members. Second, the interpersonal relationships and informal groups help employees feel better-informed about and connected with what is going on in their firm, thus giving them some sense of control over their work environment. Third, the informal organization can provide status and recognition that the formal organization cannot or will not provide employees. Fourth, the network of relationships can aid the socialization of new employees by informally passing along rules, responsibilities, basic objectives, and job expectations. Finally, the organizational grapevine helps employees to be more aware of what is happening in their workplace by transmitting information quickly and conveying it to places that the formal system does not reach.

Informal Communication Channels

The informal channels of communication used by the informal organization are often referred to as the *grapevine* or the *rumor mill.* Managers need to pay attention to the grapevines in their organization, because their employees increasingly put a great deal of stock in the information that travels along it, especially in this era of social media. A recent survey found that many business leaders have their work cut out for them in the speeches and presentations they give employees. Survey participants were asked if they would believe a message delivered in a speech by a company leader or one that they heard over the grapevine. Forty-seven percent of those responding said they would put more credibility in the grapevine. Only 42 percent said they would believe senior leadership, and another 11 percent indicated they would believe a blend of elements from both messages. Perhaps even more interesting is how accurate employees perceive their company grapevine to be: 57 percent gave it favorable ratings. "The grapevine may not be wholly accurate, but it is a very reliable indicator that something is going on," said one survey respondent.[16]

With this in mind, managers need to learn to use the existing informal organization as a tool that can potentially benefit the **formal organization**. An excellent way of putting the informal organization to work for the good of the company is to bring informal leaders into the decision-making process. That way, at least the people who use and nurture the grapevine will have more accurate information to send it.

Exhibit 7.10   Smart managers understand that not all of a company's influential relationships appear as part of the organization chart. A web of informal, personal connections exists between workers, and vital information and knowledge pass through this web constantly. Using social media analysis software and other tracking tools, managers can map and quantify the normally invisible relationships that form between employees at all levels of an organization. *How might identifying a company's informal organization help managers foster teamwork, motivate employees, and boost productivity?* (Credit: University of Exeter /flickr / Attribution 2.0 Generic (CC BY 2.0))

CONCEPT CHECK

1. What is the informal organization?
2. How can informal channels of communication be used to improve operational efficiency?

7.8 | Trends in Organizational Structure

8. What trends are influencing the way businesses organize?

To improve organizational performance and achieve long-term objectives, some organizations seek to reengineer their business processes or adopt new technologies that open up a variety of organizational design options, such as virtual corporations and virtual teams. Other trends that have strong footholds in today's organizations include outsourcing and managing global businesses.

Reengineering Organizational Structure

Periodically, all businesses must reevaluate the way they do business. This includes assessing the effectiveness of the organizational structure. To meet the formidable challenges of the future, companies are increasingly turning to **reengineering**—the complete redesign of business structures and processes in order to improve operations. An even simpler definition of reengineering is "starting over." In effect, top management asks, "If we were a new company, how would we run this place?" The purpose of reengineering is to identify and abandon the outdated rules and fundamental assumptions that guide current business operations. Every company has many formal and informal rules, based on assumptions about technology, people, and organizational goals, that no longer hold. Thus, the goal of reengineering is to redesign business processes to achieve improvements in cost control, product quality, customer service, and speed. The reengineering process should result in a more efficient and effective organizational structure that is better suited to the current (and future) competitive climate of the industry.

The Virtual Corporation

One of the biggest challenges for companies today is adapting to the technological changes that are affecting all industries. Organizations are struggling to find new organizational structures that will help them transform information technology into a competitive advantage. One alternative that is becoming increasingly prevalent is the **virtual corporation**, which is a network of independent companies (suppliers, customers, even competitors) linked by information technology to share skills, costs, and access to one another's markets. This network structure allows companies to come together quickly to exploit rapidly changing opportunities. The key attributes of a virtual corporation are:

- *Technology.* Information technology helps geographically distant companies form alliances and work together.
- *Opportunism.* Alliances are less permanent, less formal, and more opportunistic than in traditional partnerships.
- *Excellence.* Each partner brings its core competencies to the alliance, so it is possible to create an organization with higher quality in every functional area and increase competitive advantage.
- *Trust.* The network structure makes companies more reliant on each other and forces them to strengthen relationships with partners.
- *No borders.* This structure expands the traditional boundaries of an organization.

In the concept's purest form, each company that links up with others to create a virtual corporation is stripped to its essence. Ideally, the virtual corporation has neither a central office nor an organization chart, no hierarchy, and no vertical integration. It contributes to an alliance only its core competencies, or key capabilities. It mixes and matches what it does best with the core competencies of other companies and entrepreneurs. For example, a manufacturer would only manufacture, while relying on a product design firm to decide what to make and a marketing company to sell the end result.

Although firms that are purely virtual organizations are still relatively scarce, many companies are embracing several characteristics of the virtual structure. One example is Cisco Systems. Cisco uses many manufacturing plants to produce its products, but the company owns none of them. In fact, Cisco now relies on contract manufacturers for all of its manufacturing needs. Human hands probably touch fewer than 10 percent of all customer orders, with fewer than half of all orders processed by a Cisco employee. To the average customer, the interdependency of Cisco's suppliers and inventory systems makes it look like one huge, seamless company.

Virtual Teams

Technology is also enabling corporations to create virtual work teams. Geography is no longer a limitation when employees are considered for a work team. Virtual teams mean reduced travel time and costs, reduced relocation expenses, and utilization of specialized talent regardless of an employee's location.

When managers need to staff a project, all they need to do is make a list of required skills and a general list of employees who possess those skills. When the pool of employees is known, the manager simply chooses the best mix of people and creates the virtual team. Special challenges of virtual teams include keeping team members focused, motivated, and communicating positively despite their locations. If feasible, at least one face-to-face meeting during the early stages of team formation will help with these potential problems.

Exhibit 7.11   In today's high-tech world, teams can exist any place where there is access to the internet. With globalization and outsourcing being common strategies in business operations today, companies of all shapes and sizes utilize virtual teams to coordinate people and projects halfway around the world. Unlike coworkers in traditional teams, virtual team members rarely meet in person, working from different locations and continents. *What practical benefits do virtual teams offer to businesses, employees, and other members?* (Credit: ThoroughlyReviewed/ Flickr/ Attribution 2.0 Generic (CC BY 2.0))

Outsourcing

Another organizational trend that continues to influence today's managers is outsourcing. For decades, companies have outsourced various functions. For example, payroll functions such as recording hours, managing benefits and wage rates, and issuing paychecks have been handled for years by third-party providers. Today, however, outsourcing includes a much wider array of business functions: customer service, production, engineering, information technology, sales and marketing, and more.

Historically, companies have outsourced for two main reasons: cost reduction and labor needs. Often, to satisfy both requirements, companies outsource work to firms in foreign countries. In 2017, outsourcing remains a key component of many businesses' operations but is not strictly limited to low-level jobs. Some of the insights highlighted in Deloitte's recent Global Outsourcing Survey bear this out. According to survey respondents from 280 global organizations, outsourcing continues to be successful because it is adapting to changing business environments. According to the survey, outsourcing continues to grow across mature functions such as HR and IT, but it has successfully moved to nontraditional business functions such as facilities management, purchasing, and real estate. In addition, some businesses view outsourcing as a way of infusing their operations with innovation and using it to maintain a competitive advantage—not just as a way to cut costs. As companies increasingly view outsourcing as more than a cost-cutting strategy, they will be expecting more of their vendors in terms of supplying innovation and other benefits.[17]

Another form of outsourcing has become prevalent over the last several years, in part as the result of the slow economic recovery from the global recession of 2007–2009. As many U.S. businesses hesitated to hire full-time workers even as they began to experience gradual growth, some companies began to offer contract work to freelancers, who were not considered full-time employees eligible for company benefits. Known as the *gig economy,* this work approach has advantages and disadvantages. Some gig workers like the independence of being self-employed, while others acknowledge that they are taking on multiple small projects because they can't find full-time work as company employees. Another group of individuals work as full-time employees but may sign up for gigs such as driving for Uber or Lyft to supplement their income. Recent estimates suggest that the gig economy may impact more than one-third of the U.S. workforce over the next few years.[18]

Despite the challenges, outsourcing programs can be effective. To be successful in outsourcing efforts, managers must do the following:

- Identify a specific business problem.
- Consider all possible solutions.
- Decide whether outsourcing the work is the appropriate answer to the problem.
- Develop a strategic outsourcing partnership with vendors and a solid framework that promotes seamless collaboration and communication.
- Engage with outsourcing partners on a regular basis to instill trust between the two entities.
- Remain flexible when it comes to working with outsourcing providers in terms of accommodating requests or adjusting needs when necessary in an effort to build a long-term strategic partnership beneficial to both parties.[19]

Structuring for Global Mergers

Recent mergers creating mega-firms (such as Microsoft and LinkedIn, Amazon and Whole Foods, and Verizon and Yahoo) raise some important questions regarding corporate structure. How can managers hope to organize the global pieces of these huge, complex new firms into a cohesive, successful whole? Should decision-making be centralized or decentralized? Should the firm be organized around geographic markets or product lines? And how can managers consolidate distinctly different corporate cultures? These issues and many more must be resolved if mergers of global companies are to succeed.

Beyond designing a new organizational structure, one of the most difficult challenges when merging two large companies is uniting the cultures and creating a single business. The merger between Pfizer and Pharmacia, makers of Dramamine and Rogaine, is no exception. Failure to effectively merge cultures can have serious effects on organizational efficiency.

As part of its strategic plan for the giant merger, Pfizer put together 14 groups that would make recommendations concerning finances, human resources, operation support, capital improvements, warehousing, logistics, quality control, and information technology. An outside consultant was hired to facilitate the process. One of the first tasks for the groups was to deal with the conqueror (Pfizer) versus conquered (Pharmacia) attitudes. Company executives wanted to make sure all employees knew that their ideas were valuable and that senior management was listening.

As more and more global mergers take place, sometimes between the most unlikely suitors, companies must ensure that the integration plan includes strategies for dealing with cultural differences, establishing a logical leadership structure, implementing a strong two-way communications channel at all levels of the organization, and redefining the "new" organization's vision, mission, values, and culture.[20]

CONCEPT CHECK

1. How does technology enable firms to organize as virtual corporations?
2. What effect could the gig economy have on a company's decision to outsource?
3. What are some organizational issues that must be addressed when two firms merge?

🔑 Key Terms

authority Legitimate power, granted by the organization and acknowledged by employees, that allows an individual to request action and expect compliance.

centralization The degree to which formal authority is concentrated in one area or level of an organization. Top management makes most of the decisions.

chain of command The line of authority that extends from one level of an organization's hierarchy to the next, from top to bottom, and makes clear who reports to whom.

committee structure An organizational structure in which authority and responsibility are held by a group rather than an individual.

cross-functional team Members from the same organizational level but from different functional areas.

customer departmentalization Departmentalization that is based on the primary type of customer served by the organizational unit.

decentralization The process of pushing decision-making authority down the organizational hierarchy.

delegation of authority The assignment of some degree of authority and responsibility to persons lower in the chain of command.

departmentalization The process of grouping jobs together so that similar or associated tasks and activities can be coordinated.

division of labor The process of dividing work into separate jobs and assigning tasks to workers.

formal organization The order and design of relationships within a firm; consists of two or more people working together with a common objective and clarity of purpose.

functional departmentalization Departmentalization that is based on the primary functions performed within an organizational unit.

geographic departmentalization Departmentalization that is based on the geographic segmentation of the organizational units.

group cohesiveness The degree to which group members want to stay in the group and tend to resist outside influences.

informal organization The network of connections and channels of communication based on the informal relationships of individuals inside an organization.

line organization An organizational structure with direct, clear lines of authority and communication flowing from the top managers downward.

line positions All positions in the organization directly concerned with producing goods and services and that are directly connected from top to bottom.

line-and-staff organization An organizational structure that includes both line and staff positions.

managerial hierarchy The levels of management within an organization; typically includes top, middle, and supervisory management.

matrix structure (project management) An organizational structure that combines functional and product departmentalization by bringing together people from different functional areas of the organization to work on a special project.

mechanistic organization An organizational structure that is characterized by a relatively high degree of job specialization, rigid departmentalization, many layers of management, narrow spans of control, centralized decision-making, and a long chain of command.

organic organization An organizational structure that is characterized by a relatively low degree of job specialization, loose departmentalization, few levels of management, wide spans of control, decentralized decision-making, and a short chain of command.

organization The order and design of relationships within a firm; consists of two or more people working together with a common objective and clarity of purpose.

organization chart A visual representation of the structured relationships among tasks and the people given the authority to do those tasks.

problem-solving teams Usually members of the same department who meet regularly to suggest ways to improve operations and solve specific problems.

process departmentalization Departmentalization that is based on the production process used by the organizational unit.

product departmentalization Departmentalization that is based on the goods or services produced or sold by the organizational unit.

reengineering The complete redesign of business structures and processes in order to improve operations.

self-managed work teams Teams without formal supervision that plan, select alternatives, and evaluate their own performance.

span of control The number of employees a manager directly supervises; also called span of management.

specialization The degree to which tasks are subdivided into smaller jobs.

staff positions Positions in an organization held by individuals who provide the administrative and support services that line employees need to achieve the firm's goals.

virtual corporation A network of independent companies linked by information technology to share skills, costs, and access to one another's markets; allows the companies to come together quickly to exploit rapidly changing opportunities.

work groups The groups that share resources and coordinate efforts to help members better perform their individual jobs.

work teams Like a work group but also requires the pooling of knowledge, skills, abilities, and resources to achieve a common goal.

Summary of Learning Outcomes

7.1 Building Organizational Structures
1. What are the traditional forms of organizational structure?

Firms typically use traditional, contemporary, or team-based approaches when designing their organizational structure. In the traditional approach, companies first divide the work into separate jobs and tasks. Managers then group related jobs and tasks together into departments. Five basic types of departmentalization are commonly used in organizations:

- *Functional:* Based on the primary functions performed within an organizational unit
- *Product:* Based on the goods or services produced or sold by the organizational unit
- *Process:* Based on the production process used by the organizational unit
- *Customer:* Based on the primary type of customer served by the organizational unit
- *Geographic:* Based on the geographic segmentation of organizational units

7.2 Contemporary Structures
2. What contemporary organizational structures are companies using?

In recent decades, companies have begun to expand beyond traditional departmentalization methods and use matrix, committee, and team-based structures. Matrix structures combine two types of traditional organizational structures (for example, geographic and functional). Matrix structures bring together people from different functional areas of the organization to work on a special project. As such, matrix organizations are more flexible, but because employees report to two direct supervisors, managing matrix structures can be extremely challenging. Committee structures give authority and responsibility to a group rather than to an individual. Committees are part of a line-and-staff organization and often fulfill only an advisory role. Team-based structures also involve assigning authority and responsibility to groups rather than individuals, but, different from committees, team-based structures give these groups autonomy to carry out their work.

7.3 Using Teams to Enhance Motivation and Performance
3. Why are companies using team-based organizational structures?

Work groups share resources and coordinate efforts to help members better perform their individual duties and responsibilities. The performance of the group can be evaluated by adding up the contributions of the individual group members. Work teams require not only coordination but also *collaboration,* the pooling of knowledge, skills, abilities, and resources in a collective effort to attain a common goal. Four types of work teams are used: problem solving, self-managed, cross-functional, and virtual teams. Companies are using teams to improve individual and group motivation and performance.

7.4 Authority—Establishing Organizational Relationships
4. What tools do companies use to establish relationships within their organizations?

The managerial hierarchy (or the *management pyramid*) comprises the levels of management within the organization, and the managerial span of control is the number of employees the manager directly supervises. In daily operations, individuals in line positions are directly involved in the processes used to create goods and services. Individuals in staff positions provide the administrative and support services that line employees need to achieve the firm's goals. Line positions in organizations are typically in areas such as production, marketing, and finance. Staff positions are found in areas such as legal counseling, managerial consulting, public relations, and human resource management.

7.5 Degree of Centralization
5. How can the degree of centralization/decentralization be altered to make an organization more successful?

In a highly centralized structure, top management makes most of the key decisions in the organization, with very little input from lower-level employees. Centralization lets top managers develop a broad view of operations and exercise tight financial controls. In a highly decentralized organization, decision-making authority is pushed down the organizational hierarchy, giving lower-level personnel more responsibility and power to make and implement decisions. Decentralization can result in faster decision-making and increased innovation and responsiveness to customer preferences.

7.6 Organizational Design Considerations
6. How do mechanistic and organic organizations differ?

A mechanistic organization is characterized by a relatively high degree of work specialization, rigid departmentalization, many layers of management (particularly middle management), narrow spans of control, centralized decision-making, and a long chain of command. This combination of elements results in a tall organizational structure. In contrast, an organic organization is characterized by a relatively low degree of work specialization, loose departmentalization, few levels of management, wide spans of control, decentralized decision-making, and a short chain of command. This combination of elements results in a flat organizational structure.

7.7 The Informal Organization
7. How does the informal organization affect the performance of a company?

The informal organization is the network of connections and channels of communication based on the informal relationships of individuals inside the organization. Informal relationships can be between people at the same hierarchical level or between people at different levels and in different departments. Informal organizations give employees more control over their work environment by delivering a continuous stream of company information throughout the organization, thereby helping employees stay informed.

7.8 Trends in Organizational Structure

8. What trends are influencing the way businesses organize?

Reengineering is a complete redesign of business structures and processes in order to improve operations. The goal of reengineering is to redesign business processes to achieve improvements in cost control, product quality, customer service, and speed.

The virtual corporation is a network of independent companies (suppliers, customers, even competitors) linked by information technology to share skills, costs, and access to one another's markets. This network structure allows companies to come together quickly to exploit rapidly changing opportunities.

Many companies are now using technology to create virtual teams. Team members may be down the hall or across the ocean. Virtual teams mean that travel time and expenses are eliminated and the best people can be placed on the team regardless of where they live. Sometimes, however, it may be difficult to keep virtual team members focused and motivated.

Outsourcing business functions—both globally and domestically—continues to be a regular business practice for companies large and small. Companies choose to outsource either as a cost-saving measure or as a way to gain access to needed human resource talent and innovation. To be successful, outsourcing must solve a clearly articulated business problem. In addition, managers must use outsourcing providers that fit their company's actual needs and strive to engage these providers as strategic partners for the long term. A recent phenomenon known as the gig economy has taken on more importance as it pertains to the U.S. labor force and outsourcing. More people are working as freelancers on a per-project basis, either because they can't get hired as full-time employees or because they prefer to work as self-employed individuals.

Global mergers raise important issues in organizational structure and culture. The ultimate challenge for management is to take two organizations and create a single, successful, cohesive organization.

Preparing for Tomorrow's Workplace Skills

1. When people talk of climbing the corporate ladder, they are referring to moving vertically upward through the organizational structure. Many employees plot career paths that will take them to increasingly higher levels of management. Do you think you would be more interested in climbing higher in an organization, or being a middle-management bridge between the employees who do the work and the executives who set the strategy? Explain the reasons for your choice. (Resources, Interpersonal)

2. Teams are an increasingly popular method of organizing corporations, but not all people are suited for teamwork. As a manager, what do you do with employees who are talented but unapproachable? Can you think of a way to involve people who are uncomfortable in team settings so that your teams have the perspective of these employees as well? (Interpersonal)

3. Think about how gossip and rumors travel through a grapevine. Draw as many grapevines as you can think of that reflect the different ways rumors move through an organization. Can you think of information that a manager would want to disseminate through the grapevine? Is there information that is inappropriate to disseminate through informal channels? Provide examples. (Information)

4. Do you think companies that outsource will inevitably become virtual corporations? Why or why not?

(Resources, Systems)

5. It used to be that only high-level executives and CEOs were able to work out of the office. Mobile computing, however, is trickling down the organizational chart. In your opinion, is there a point in the organizational structure at which working remotely (at home, on the road) should stop? Should all employees in the hierarchy be allowed to work in a virtual environment, or should there be limits? Explain your reasoning. (Technology, Systems)

6. **Team Activity** Have you ever worked on a team with an underperforming member, such as a slacker, a complainer, or a critic? Assemble a team of three to five students and brainstorm a list of "bad" team members you have experience working with. Once you have a list of types, discuss how that person affected the work of the team and the outcome the team produced. Brainstorm ways to better manage and mitigate the negative effects of "bad" team members. Share your results with the class. (Interpersonal, Systems)

Ethics Activity

Training IT Replacements

Recently the University of California at San Francisco (UCSF) announced it would lay off more than 80 IT workers and outsource their jobs to India. This change is part of a larger plan by UCSF to increase its technology outsourcing, which over time could save the organization more than $30 million. A large part of UCSF's IT work focuses on its hospital services, and many other health care facilities have already outsourced these types of "back-end" jobs to foreign countries.

Working through a multinational contractor that will manage the outsourcing process, UCSF has also asked workers who will soon be out of a job to train their overseas replacements via videoconferencing calls to India. One such worker remarked, "I'm speechless. How can they do this to us?"

A UCSF spokesperson explained that the organization provides millions of dollars in charity care for the poor, and that to continue providing those services, the school has to focus on more specialized tech work related to patients and medical research and send other IT work overseas.

UCSF is not alone in sending IT jobs overseas and making the laid-off workers train their Indian replacements. Recently ManpowerGroup, a staffing and workforce services firm with more than 3,000 offices worldwide, issued pink slips to 150 workers in Milwaukee whose jobs were outsourced to India.

Using a web search tool, locate articles about this topic and then write responses to the following questions. Be sure to support your arguments and cite your sources.

Ethical Dilemma: Are UCSF and other companies justified in outsourcing technology jobs to India? Do they have any obligation to find other jobs or provide training for displaced workers? Should organizations ask employees who are being laid off to train their replacements?

Sources: Sam Harnett, "Outsourced: In a Twist, Some San Francisco IT Jobs Are Moving to India," *All Tech Considered,* http://www.npr.org, accessed July 19, 2017; Dan Shafer, "Exclusive: ManpowerGroup HQ Workers Being Laid Off Required to Train Overseas Replacements," *Milwaukee Business Journal,* https://www.bizjournals.com, March 30, 2017; Bill Whitaker, "Are U.S. Jobs Vulnerable to Workers with H-1B Visas?" *60 Minutes,* http://www.cbsnews.com, March 19, 2017; Louis Hansen, "After Pink Slips, USCF Tech Workers Train Their Foreign Replacements," *The Mercury News,* http://www.mercurynews.com, November 3, 2016.

⊕ Working the Net

1. Using a search engine, look for the term "company organizational charts," and find at least three examples of organizational charts for corporations, not-for-profits, or government agencies. Analyze each entity's organizational structure. Is it organized by function, product/service, process, customer type, or geographic location?

2. Search the archives at the *Bloomberg Businessweek* (**https://www.bloomberg.com**), *Fortune* (**http://fortune.com**), or *Forbes* (**http://www.forbes.com**) website for stories about companies that have reorganized. Pick two examples, and prepare a summary of their reorganization efforts, including the underlying reasons the company chose to reorganize, the key elements of the reorganization plan, and if possible, how successful it has been.

3. Visit the *Inc.* magazine website, **http://www.inc.com**, and use the search engine to find articles about virtual corporations. Using a search engine, find the website of at least one virtual corporation, and look for information about how the company uses span of control, informal organization, and other concepts from this module.

4. FlexJobs (**http://www.flexjobs.com**) is an online company devoted to matching job hunters with flexible job experiences, whether they are telecommuting jobs, contract work, or part-time gigs. Read more on how the company started and the void its services have filled over the past decade for people looking for a flexible job situation. Share your findings with classmates, and lead a discussion on the pros and cons of the flexible job movement.

5. Managing change in an organization is no easy task, as you've discovered in your new job with a consulting firm that specializes in change management. To get up to speed, go to Bpubs.com, the Business Publications Search Engine (**http://www.bpubs.com**), and navigate to the Change Management section of the Management Science category. Select three articles that discuss how companies approached the change process, and summarize their experiences.

6. After managing your first project team, you think you might enjoy a career in project management. The Project Management Institute is a professional organization for project managers. Its website, **http://www.pmi.org**, has many resources about this field. Start at the Professional Practices section to learn what project management is, then go to the professional Development and Careers pages. What are the requirements to earn the Project Management Professional designation? Explore other free areas of the site to learn more about the job of project manager. Prepare a brief report on the career and its opportunities. Does what you've learned make you want to follow this career path?

7. Many companies are outsourcing portions of their IT departments. Should they, and why? Develop a position on this issue by researching outsourcing trends on *Information Week,* (**http://www.informationweek.com**), or an IT website of your choosing. Then divide the class into two groups, those that support outsourcing and those that oppose it, and have a debate on this subject.

Critical Thinking Case

Gore's Flat Structure Works Well

Imagine an organization with more than 10,000 employees working in 30 countries around the world—with no hierarchy structure. W. L. Gore & Associates, headquartered in Newark, Delaware, is a model of unusual business practices. Wilbert Gore, who left Dupont to explore new uses for Teflon, started the company in 1958. Best known for its breathable, weatherproof Gore-Tex fabric, Glide dental floss, and Elixir guitar strings, the company has no bosses, no titles, no departments, and no formal job descriptions. There is no managerial hierarchy at Gore, and top management treats employees, called associates, as peers.

In 2005, the company named 22-year associate Terri Kelly as its new chief executive officer. Unlike large public corporations, Gore's announcement was made without much fanfare. Today, more than 12 years later, Kelly continues as chief executive but is the first to admit that it's not about the CEO at Gore—it's about the people who work there and their relationships with one another.

The company focuses on its products and company values rather than on individuals. Committees, comprised of employees, make major decisions such as hiring, firing, and compensation. They even set top executives' compensation. Employees work on teams, which are switched around every few years. In fact, all employees are expected to make minor decisions instead of relying on the "boss" to make them. "We're committed to how we get things done," Kelly says. "That puts a tremendous burden on leaders because it's easier to say 'Just do it' than to explain the rationale. But in the long run, you'll get much better results because people are making a commitment."

Because no formal lines of authority exist, employees can speak to anyone in the company at any time. This arrangement also forces employees to spend considerable time developing relationships. As one employee described it, instead of trying to please just one "boss," you have to please everyone. Several years ago the company underwent a "strategy refresh," conducting surveys and discussions with employees about how they fit into the organization's culture. Not surprisingly, there was a cultural divide based on multiple generations of workers and length of service stature, which Kelly and her associates have worked hard to overcome. She realizes that not everyone will become a "lifer" at Gore, but recognizes the importance of younger employees who have helped the company become more tech-savvy in communications and stay well-connected in a fast-moving business world.

The informal organizational structure continues to work well. With revenues of $3 billion, the company produces thousands of advanced technology products for the electronics, industrial, fabrics, and medical markets. Its corporate structure fosters innovation and has been a significant contributor to associate satisfaction. Employee turnover is a low 3 percent a year, and the company can choose new associates from the thousands of job applications it receives annually. In 2017, Gore was named one of the 12 legends on *Fortune's* "100 Best Companies to Work For." These companies have made *Fortune's* list for all 20 years the magazine has published its annual "Best" rankings.

Critical Thinking Questions
1. Given the lack of formal structure, how important do you think Gore's informal structure becomes?
2. Is W. L. Gore a mechanistic or an organic organization? Support your answer with examples from the case.
3. How do you think Gore's flat organizational structure affects innovation at the company?

Sources: "Our Story," https://www.gore.com, accessed July 18, 2017; Jeremy Hobson, "What It's Like to Lead a Non-Hierarchical Workplace," http://www.wbur.org, accessed July 18, 2017; Alan Deutschman, "The Un-CEO," *Fast Company,* https://www.fastcompany.com, accessed July 18, 2017; Claire Zillman, "Secrets from Best Companies All Stars," *Fortune,* http://fortune.com, March 9, 2017; Daniel Roberts, "At W.L. Gore, 57 Years of Authentic Culture," *Fortune,* http://fortune.com, March 5, 2015.

 Hot Links Address Book

1. Like corporations, government agencies have organization charts, too. Learn how the Department of Health and Human Services is structured at **http://www.hhs.gov/about/orgchart.html**.
2. Find team-building resources galore, from team-building activities and training exercises to guidance in solving team problems, at Team Builders Plus website, **http://teambuildersplus.com**.
3. To read articles on current best practices in outsourcing for both buyers and providers and find other outsourcing resources, visit **http://outsourcing.com**.
4. What benefits can a company gain by using web-based organizational charting software? Check out the features Organimi offers companies at **http://www.organimi.com**.
5. How can your organization develop better group skills? A good place to start is Management Help's Group Skills page. Go to **http://managementhelp.org** and click on Group/Team Skills for links to resources on many topics, including self-directed and self-managed work teams and virtual teams.

8

Managing Human Resources and Labor Relations

Exhibit 8.1 (Credit: Ludovic Bertron /flickr / Attribution 2.0 Generic (CC BY 2.0))

 Introduction

Learning Outcomes

After reading this chapter, you should be able to answer these questions:

1. What is the human resource management process, and how are human resource needs determined?
2. How do firms recruit applicants?
3. How do firms select qualified applicants?
4. What types of training and development do organizations offer their employees?
5. How are performance appraisals used to evaluate employee performance?
6. What are the types of compensation and methods for paying workers?
7. What is a labor union and how is it organized, what is collective bargaining, and what are some of the key negotiation issues?
8. How are grievances between management and labor resolved, and what tactics are used to force a contract settlement?
9. What are the key laws and federal agencies affecting human resource management and labor relations?
10. What trends and issues are affecting human resource management and labor relations?

EXPLORING BUSINESS CAREERS

Andrea Herran, Human Resources Consultant

In college, Andrea Herran studied business administration and minored in psychology. Always interested in a business career, she initially took psychology simply because it was interesting. Little did she know how applicable that minor would become. As a human resources (HR) consultant, she often benefits from her psychology background. "Studying human behavior really gave me the background necessary to put myself in the position of others, to see things from their point of view, which has definitely been helpful in my career in human resources."

Herran started out as an administrative assistant in the HR department of a hotel, and her career has run the gamut of human resources over the 25 years since she graduated from college. She has been an employment coordinator, focusing on employee recruitment and selection, and a personnel manager, where she learned the skills necessary to maintain and evaluate employees. As a training manager, she sharpened her talent for developing, coordinating, and even administering staff training. Eventually, she became the director of human resources for companies both in the United States and abroad. Indeed, beyond the United States, she has worked in Mexico, Argentina, and South Africa.

Andrea worked her way up in the corporate world, but entrepreneurship was more consistent with her desire for a fast-paced, changing environment, both in terms of what she does and who she works with, so she made the move to consulting. "Consulting allows me to draw upon all my human resources skills. I have opened five HR departments in my career, so I bring my full experience to bear on the challenges each company has."

Today, Andrea's passion is working with small businesses, entrepreneurs, managers, and owners as an advisor to "uncomplicate the people side of your business." As the principal of Focus HR Consulting, she advises firms how to set up human resource programs and ensure legal compliance. She also provides leadership coaching and training and mentors employees. She has worked in several industries, including hospitality (hotels and restaurants), advertising, professional services, logistics, technology, and manufacturing.

When Andrea was hired by Aquion Water Treatment Products, she was tasked with updating the company's HR policies and procedures. The company's performance reviews were very task-oriented versus behavior-oriented. Instead of determining whether a task was completed, behavior-oriented reviews seek to evaluate not only whether the person completed the task but also how he or she did so, especially examining the interactions involved in the task. Is an employee punctual at returning consumer request calls? How does he or she relate to customers? As a manager, does he or she express thoughts clearly? "By evaluating specific behaviors, you create an environment with clearly set qualifications for advancement and opportunities for targeted employee development. Without this, the *human* aspect of human resources can be overlooked."

Andrea has never looked back on her choice to become an entrepreneur, and she believes her varied employment history was a key to her success. "Anyone interested in this field should experience as many possibilities within human resources as possible. You leave school with the theory, but only through experience do you really get to see what the potential of such a career is."

Sources: "About Us," http://focushr.biz, accessed February 8, 2018; "Member Spotlight: Andrea Herran," http://www.centerforguiltfreesuccess.com, accessed February 8, 2018; Insureon blog, "5 HR Pros Reveal the Secret to Hiring the Right Employees the First Time," http://www.insureon.com, June 3, 2016.

This chapter looks at the role of human resources within an organization, from the general processes of developing and planning to the more specific tasks of employee evaluation and compensation.

Human resource management and labor relations involve acquisition, development, use, and maintenance of a human resource mix (people and positions) to achieve strategic organizational goals and objectives.

Successful human resource management is based on a company's ability to attract and hire the best employees, equip them with the knowledge and skills they need to excel, compensate them fairly, and motivate them to reach their full potential and perform at high levels. Today's business environment presents numerous challenges to effectively managing employees:

- Technology continues to advance, which places great importance on knowledge workers, especially when demand outstrips the supply of high-talent individuals.
- Global business operations involve rapid data transfer and necessitate accelerated decision-making by executive and technical employees.
- The workforce is increasingly more diversified and multicultural, which places increased emphasis on communication and cultural understanding.
- Work, life, and family priorities are more difficult to balance as dual-worker families populate the labor force.
- Employment and labor laws continue to greatly influence employee recruitment and hiring, compensation decisions, and employee retention and turnover in both union and nonunion organizations.

Each day, human resource experts and front-line supervisors deal with these challenges while sharing responsibility for attracting and retaining skilled, motivated employees. Whether faced with a large or small human resources problem, supervisors need some understanding of difficult employee-relations issues, especially if there are legal implications.

In this chapter, you will learn about the elements of the human resource management process, including human resource planning and job analysis and design, employee recruitment and selection, training and development of employees, performance planning and evaluation, and compensation of the workforce. The chapter also describes labor unions and their representation of millions of American workers in construction, manufacturing, transportation, and service-based industries.

8.1 Achieving High Performance through Human Resources Management

1. What is the human resource management process, and how are human resource needs determined?

Human resource (HR) management is the process of hiring, developing, motivating, and evaluating employees to achieve organizational goals. The goals and strategies of the firm's business model form the basis for making human resource management decisions. HR practices and systems comprise the firm's human resource decision support system that is intended to make employees a key element for gaining competitive advantage. To this end, the HR management process contains the following sequenced activities:

- Job analysis and design
- Human resource planning and forecasting
- Employee recruitment
- Employee selection
- Training and development
- Performance planning and evaluation
- Compensation and benefits

The human resource management process shown in **Exhibit 8.3** encourages the development of high-performance employees. The process is sequential because employees can't be trained and paid until selected and placed in jobs, which follows recruitment, which is preceded by human resource planning and job analysis and design. Good HR practices used along this sequence foster performance improvement, knowledge and skill development, and loyal employees who desire to remain with the organization.

Exhibit 8.2   A job fair, career fair or career expo, are events in which employers, recruiters, and schools give information to potential employees and job seekers attend hoping to make a good impression to potential employers. They also interact with potential coworkers by speaking face-to-face, exchanging résumés, and asking questions in attempt to get a good feel on the work needed. Likewise, online job fairs are held, giving job seekers another way to get in contact with probable employers using the internet. *How do you plan on using events like this in seeking your job? How can utilize the courses that you are taking to illustrate your skills that you can discuss at job fairs.* (Credit: Taavi Burns/ flickr/ Attribution 2.0 Generic (CC BY 2.0))

HR Planning and Job Analysis and Design

Two important, and somewhat parallel, aspects of the human resource management process are determining employee needs of the firm and the jobs to be filled. When Alcon Labs gained approval from the Food and Drug Administration for sales of a new contact lens disinfectant solution in its Opti-Free product line, it had to determine if additional sales representatives were needed and whether new sales positions with different knowledge and skill requirements should be established.[1] **Human resource planning** at Alcon means having the right number of people, with the right training, in the right jobs, to meet its sales goals for the new product. Once the need for sales representatives is determined, human resource specialists assess the skills of the firm's existing employees to see whether new people must be hired or current people can be trained. See Exhibit 8.3 for a representation of the human resource management process.

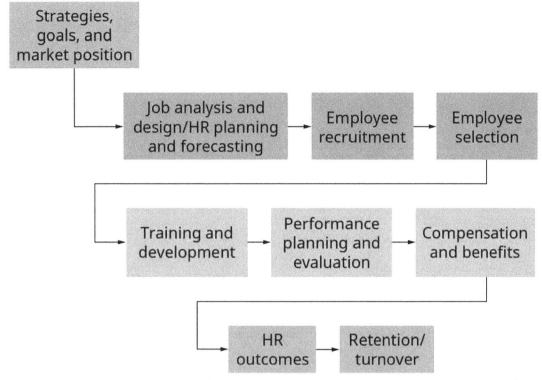

Exhibit 8.3   Human Resource Management Process (Attribution: Copyright Rice University, OpenStax, under CC BY 4.0 license.)

Human resource planners must know what skills different jobs require. Information about a specific job typically begins with a **job analysis**, which is a study of the tasks required to do a job well. This information is used to specify the essential skills, knowledge, and abilities required for the job. When Hubert Joly started as the CEO at Best Buy, the retailer was facing serious financial pressures. The threat of online competition from Amazon was real. Joly was also facing a staffing issue with a lot of turnover. He and his team instituted a plan to keep and promote staff as a core competency that would differentiate Best Buy from online retailers.[2] Also, a key HR responsibility is that jobs are examined to make any changes in job duty and task responsibilities. The tasks and responsibilities of a job are listed in a **job description**. The skills, knowledge, and abilities a person must have to fill a job are spelled out in a **job specification**. These two documents help human resource planners find the right people for specific jobs. A sample job description and specification is shown in Table 8.1.

HR Planning and Forecasting

Forecasting an organization's human resource needs, known as an HR *demand forecast,* is an essential aspect of HR planning. This process involves two forecasts: (1) determining the number of people needed by some future time (in one year, for example) and (2) estimating the number of people currently employed by the organization who will be available to fill various jobs at some future time; this is an *internal supply forecast.*

Job Description and Specification	
Position: College Recruiter Reports to: Vice President of Human	Location: Corporate Offices Resources Classification: Salaried/ Exempt

Job Summary:

Member of HR corporate team. Interacts with managers and department heads to determine hiring needs for college graduates. Visits 20 to 30 college and university campuses each year to conduct preliminary interviews of graduating students in all academic disciplines. Following initial interviews, works with corporate staffing specialists to determine persons who will be interviewed a second time. Makes recommendations to hiring managers concerning best-qualified applicants.

Job Duties and Responsibilities:

Estimated time spent and importance:

15%	Working with managers and department heads, determines college recruiting needs.
10%	Determines colleges and universities with degree programs appropriate to hiring needs to be visited.
15%	Performs college relations activities with numerous colleges and universities.
25%	Visits campuses to conduct interviews of graduating seniors.
15%	Develops applicant files and performs initial applicant evaluations.
10%	Assists staffing specialists and line managers in determining who to schedule for second interviews.
5%	Prepares annual college recruiting report containing information and data about campuses, number interviewed, number hired, and related information.
5%	Participates in tracking college graduates who are hired to aid in determining campuses that provide the most outstanding employees.

Job Specification (Qualifications):

Bachelor's degree in human resource management or a related field. Minimum of two years of work experience in HR or department that annually hires college graduates. Ability to perform in a team environment, especially with line managers and department heads. Very effective oral and written communication skills. Reasonably proficient in Excel, Word, and Windows computer environment and familiar with PeopleSoft software.

The Advancement Planning process at Best Buy involved reducing the turnover that occurs in most retail environments. The company has achieved a second-place ranking, behind only Costco, and its general managers' tenure at a store averages five years. The performance of managers at Best Buy is reviewed to identify people who can fill vacancies and be promoted, a process known as **succession planning**.[3] If Best Buy has a temporary shortage of sales professionals, at the holiday shopping season, for example, they can hire an experienced contractor or interim executive as a temporary or **contingent worker**, someone who wants to work but not on a permanent, continuous basis. **Exhibit 8.4** summarizes the process of planning and forecasting an organization's personnel needs.

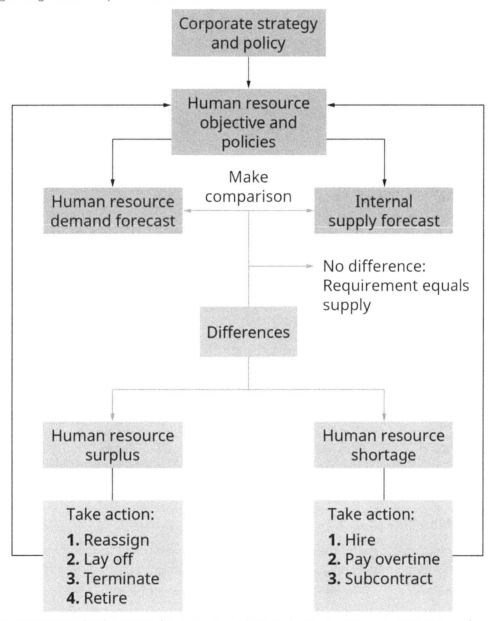

Exhibit 8.4 Human Resource Planning Process (Attribution: Copyright Rice University, OpenStax, under CC BY 4.0 license.)

CONCEPT CHECK

1. Define human resource management.
2. Distinguish between job analysis, job description, and the job specification.
3. Describe the human resource management process.

8.2 | Employee Recruitment

2. How do firms recruit applicants?

When a firm creates a new position or an existing one becomes vacant, the firm starts looking for people with qualifications that meet the requirements of the job. Two sources of job applicants are the internal and external labor markets. The internal labor market consists of employees currently employed by the firm; the external labor market is the pool of potential applicants outside the firm.

Exhibit 8.5   Online recruiting is among the top internet success stories of the past decade. LinkedIn, Monster, and CareerBuilder are hot spots for job hunters and recruiters seeking to establish a working relationship. *What are the advantages and disadvantages of online recruiting compared to traditional forms of recruitment?* (Credit: Bill Gates LinkedIn Profile screen capture, 3/23/2018)

Internal Labor Market

Internal recruitment can be greatly facilitated by using a human resource information system that contains an employee database with information about each employee's previous work experience, skills, education and certifications, job and career preferences, performance, and attendance. Promotions and job transfers are the most common results of internal recruiting. BNSF Railway, Walmart, Boeing, Ritz-Carlton Hotels, and most other firms, large and small, promote from within and manage the upward mobility of their employees.

External Labor Market

The external labor market consists of prospects to fill positions that cannot be filled from within the organization. **Recruitment** is the process of attracting qualified people to form an applicant pool. Numerous methods are used to attract applicants, including print, radio, web, and television advertising. Hospitality and entertainment firms, such as Ritz-Carlton Hotels and Six Flags, frequently use job fairs to attract applicants. A **job fair**, or *corporate open house*, is usually a one- or two-day event at which applicants are briefed about job opportunities, given tours, and encouraged to apply for jobs. For firms needing accountants, engineers, sales managers, and others for professional and scientific positions, college recruiting is very common. These firms (Deloitte, Cisco Systems, Salesforce.com, and thousands of others) schedule job fairs and on-campus interviews with graduating seniors.

Online Recruiting and Job Search

The internet, social media, and specialized software have completely changed the employee recruitment process. Dozens of companies such as Monster.com, Indeed, StartWire, and Glassdoor enable applicants to search for job openings, post their résumés, and apply for jobs that companies have posted. Most companies provide links to their company website and to the career page on their site so applicants can learn about the company culture, listen to or read testimonials from employees about what it is like to work for the company, and search for additional openings that may interest them.

Large firms may receive thousands of online applications per month. To review and evaluate thousands of online résumés and job applications, firms depend on software to scan and track applicant materials using key words to match skills or other requirements for a particular job. Social media has also changed how companies search for applicants and verify applicant information.

MANAGING CHANGE

Social Networking and Employee Recruitment

Referrals and professional networking are commonly used methods of identifying job prospects, particularity for managerial, professional, and technical positions. Several software applications and social networks facilitate employee referrals, reference checking, and hiring based on networks of personal relationships. ExecuNet and ExecRank are just two of the many career sites that allow members to search for contacts and network with other professionals in their fields.

LinkedIn is the most popular social network for professionals. It is a giant database of contacts with profiles that provide an overview of a person's past and present professional experience, skills, professional referrals, and affiliations with business and professional associations. A member can search through an extended network of contacts based on his or her professional acquaintances. The basis for a search can be job, job title, company, geography, zip code, or membership in a professional organization. LinkedIn uses the concept that there are no more than six degrees of separation between two people, or one person can be linked to any other individual through no more than six other people. With more than 530 million members worldwide, LinkedIn's extensive platform is an ideal network for both recruiters and those looking to make their next career move.

LinkedIn, like other social networks, is based on voluntary participation, and members consent to being networked. Nevertheless, important questions can be raised regarding privacy concerns and use of one's social network.

Critical Thinking Questions

1. Social networks can easily generate a name for an HR recruiting target, but how can the hiring firm convert the target into a candidate who is interested in the job?
2. A social network like LinkedIn is an excellent tool that can be used to build a personal brand and find a new job. In what ways could a job seeker potentially *harm* their career opportunities on a social networking site?

Sources: "About ExecuNet," https://www.execunet.com, accessed February 8, 2018; "LinkedIn Statistics," https://expandedramblings.com, accessed February 8, 2018; "Social Recruiting Tips," https://www.betterteam.com, January 24, 2018; Susan M. Heathfield, "Use LinkedIn for Recruiting Employees," *The Balance,* https://www.thebalance.com, April 7, 2017.

Recruitment Branding

Recruitment branding involves presenting an accurate and positive image of the firm to those being recruited. Carbone Smolan Agency (CSA) is a New York–based image consulting firm that assists in developing a recruitment branding strategy.[4] The materials developed by CSA comprise a *realistic job preview*, which informs job candidates about organizational realities of the job and the firm so they can more accurately evaluate jobs and firm expectations concerning work assignments, performance standards, promotional opportunities, company culture, and many other characteristics of the job.

CONCEPT CHECK

1. What are the two sources of job applicants?
2. What are some methods firms use to recruit applicants?
3. What is meant by recruitment branding?

8.3 Employee Selection

3. How do firms select qualified applicants?

After a firm has attracted enough job applicants, employment specialists begin the selection process. **Selection** is the process of determining which people in the applicant pool possess the qualifications necessary to be successful on the job. The steps in the employee selection process are shown in **Exhibit 8.6**. An applicant who can jump over each step, or hurdle, will very likely receive a job offer; thus, this is known as the successive hurdles approach to applicant screening. Alternatively, an applicant can be rejected at any step or hurdle. Selection steps or hurdles are described below:

1. *Initial screening.* During initial screening, an applicant completes an application form and/or submits a résumé, and has a brief interview of 30 minutes or less. The job application includes information about educational background, previous work experience, and job duties performed.
2. *Employment testing.* Following initial screening, the applicant may be asked to take one or more tests, such as the Wonderlic Personnel Tests. Wonderlic offers a suite of pre-employment tests for each phase of the hiring process. Used individually or together, the tests can assess cognitive ability (ability to learn, adapt,

and solve problems), motivation potential (attitude, behavior performance, and productivity), and knowledge and skills (math, verbal, data entry, software proficiency).[5]

HR Senior Vice President Martha LaCroix of the Yankee Candle Company uses personality assessments to make sure that prospective employees will fit the firm's culture. LaCroix was helped by Predictive Index (PI) Worldwide in determining Yankee Candle's best- and worst-performing store managers for developing a best practice behavioral profile of a top-performing store manager.[6] The profile was used for personality testing and to develop interview questions that reveal how an applicant may behave in certain work situations.

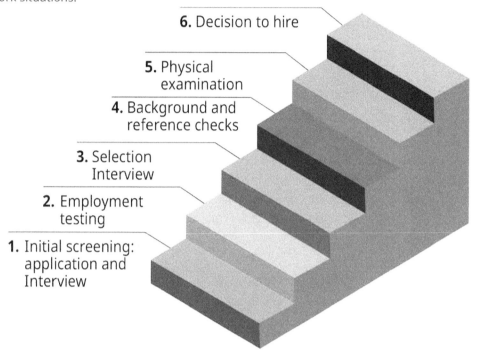

6. Decision to hire

5. Physical examination

4. Background and reference checks

3. Selection Interview

2. Employment testing

1. Initial screening: application and Interview

Exhibit 8.6   Steps of the Employee Selection Process (Attribution: Copyright Rice University, OpenStax, under CC BY 4.0 license.)

3. *Selection interview.* The tool most widely used in making hiring decisions is the **selection interview**, an in-depth discussion of an applicant's work experience, skills and abilities, education, and career interests. For managerial and professional positions, an applicant may be interviewed by several persons, including the line manager for the position to be filled. This interview is designed to determine a person's communication skills and motivation. During the interview, the applicant may be presented with realistic job situations, such as dealing with a disgruntled customer, and asked to describe how he or she would handle the problem. Carolyn Murray of W.L. Gore & Associates (maker of Gore-Tex, among other products) listens for casual remarks that may reveal the reality behind applicant answers to her questions. Using a baseball analogy, Murray gives examples of how three job candidates struck out with her questions. See **Table 8.2**.[7]

Striking Out at the Interview Game		
The Pitch (Question to Applicant)	The Swing (Applicant's Response)	The Miss (Interviewer's Reaction to Response)
"Give me an example of a time when you had a conflict with a team member."	"Our leader asked me to handle all of the FedExing for our team. I did it, but I thought that FedExing was a waste of my time."	"At Gore, we work from a team concept. Her answer shows that she won't exactly jump when one of her teammates needs help."
"Tell me how you solved a problem that was impeding your project."	"One of the engineers on my team wasn't pulling his weight, and we were closing in on a deadline. So I took on some of his work."	"The candidate may have resolved the issue for this particular deadline, but he did nothing to prevent the problem from happening again."
"What's the one thing that you would change about your current position?"	"My job as a salesman has become boring. Now I want the responsibility of managing people."	"He's probably not maximizing his current territory, and he is complaining. Will he find his next role 'boring' and complain about that role, too?"

Table 8.2

4. *Background and reference check.* If applicants pass the selection interview, most firms examine their background and check their references. In recent years, an increasing number of employers, such as American Airlines, Disney, and Microsoft, are carefully researching applicants' backgrounds, particularly their legal history, reasons for leaving previous jobs, and even creditworthiness.

5. *Physical exams and drug testing.* A firm may require an applicant to have a medical checkup to ensure he or she is physically able to perform job tasks. Drug testing is common in the transportation and health care industries. Southwest Airlines, BNSF Railway, Texas Health Resources, and the U.S. Postal Service use drug testing for reasons of workplace safety, productivity, and employee health.

6. *Decision to hire.* If an applicant progresses satisfactorily through all the selection steps (or jumps all of the selection hurdles), a decision to hire the person is made; however, the job offer may be contingent on passing a physical exam and/or drug test. The decision to hire is nearly always made by the manager of the new employee.

An important aspect of employee recruitment and selection involves treating job applicants as valued customers; in fact, some applicants may be customers of the firm.

CUSTOMER SATISFACTION AND QUALITY

Puttin' on the Ritz—For Potential Employees

Your meeting with a human resource representative is often your first exposure to the company you are applying to work for, and firms must provide good customer service to applicants if they expect to hire the most qualified employees.

Companies have several opportunities to create a positive impression of their organization during these key points in the employee selection process. These include a variety of communication channels, such as:

- In-person greetings at a job fair or at the interview itself
- Phone calls to a prospective employee from a human resource professional to set up the interview and any follow-up conversations between human resources and the applicant
- E-mail correspondence to acknowledge receipt of an application and to thank applicants for submitting their job application
- A thank-you note from the employer following the second interview

A firm that is recognized for treating prospective employees especially well is Ritz-Carlton Hotels, a subsidiary of Marriott International. When the Washington D.C. Ritz-Carlton was recruiting employees to staff a new hotel, the goal was to provide applicants with a personal demonstration of the famous Ritz-Carlton service-oriented culture.

As applicants arrived, they experienced the Ritz-Carlton "warm welcome" from several employees who greeted them, wished them luck, and escorted them past a violinist and piano player to the waiting room, where beverages and snacks were available. Applicants went through a standardized screening questionnaire, and those who passed went on to a professionally developed structured interview. Individuals were then personally escorted to the "fond farewell," where they were thanked, given Ritz-Carlton chocolates, and escorted out of the hotel. The goal of Ritz-Carlton managers is to give applicants the same experience they would expect to receive as a customer staying in the hotel. Every applicant receives a personal, formal thank-you note for coming to the job fair, and those who are considered for positions but later rejected receive another note. Ritz-Carlton wants to make a good impression because an applicant could be a future Ritz-Carlton hotel guest, or the son or daughter of a guest.

Ritz-Carlton continues to show exemplary service during the employee orientation process. Every employee must go through seven days of training before ever working in a Ritz-Carlton. Two full days of the orientation are indoctrination in the Ritz-Carlton values and philosophy. The goal is to create a significant emotional experience for new employees during their first few days. This happens the moment new employees arrive for training at 6:00 a.m. and see senior leaders lined up outside the doors of the hotel, clapping and cheering as they greet them. The message is clear: *You are important and we will treat you exactly as we want you to treat customers.*

The leadership team is involved in facilitating the program, sending a powerful message about the importance of consensual commitment. "For these next few days, we will orient you to who we are—our heart, our soul, our goals, our vision, our dreams—so you can join us, and not just work for us."

Horst Schultz, former president and COO of the Ritz-Carlton, first implemented the motto "We Are Ladies and Gentlemen Serving Ladies and Gentlemen" in the mid-1980s, and the motto is still at the heart of the company's values today. In an address to employees, Schultz said, "You are not servants. We are not servants. Our profession is service. We are Ladies and Gentlemen, just as the guests are, who we respect as Ladies and Gentlemen. We are Ladies and Gentlemen and should be respected as such."

Critical Thinking Questions

1. What are the benefits of an employer treating a job applicant like a customer? Are there costs associated with treating applicants poorly?
2. What is the Ritz-Carlton motto? How does it teach both applicants and employees about the

company's values?

Sources: "Gold Standards," http://www.ritzcarlton.com, accessed February 8, 2018; "Lifetime Learning Opportunities," http://www.marriott.com, accessed February 8, 2018; Justin Hoffman, "Secrets of the Ritz-Carlton's 'Legendary' Customer Service," https://www.psafinancial.com, May 8, 2014; Sandra J. Sucher and Stacy McManus, "The Ritz-Carlton Hotel Company," Harvard Business School Case #601-163, March 2001; revised September 2005.

CONCEPT CHECK

1. Describe the employee selection process.
2. What are some of the ways that prospective employees are tested?

8.4 | Employee Training and Development

4. What types of training and development do organizations offer their employees?

To ensure that both new and experienced employees have the knowledge and skills to perform their jobs successfully, organizations invest in training and development activities. **Training and development** involves learning situations in which the employee acquires additional knowledge or skills to increase job performance. Training objectives specify performance improvements, reductions in errors, job knowledge to be gained, and/or other positive organizational results. The process of creating and implementing training and development activities is shown in Exhibit 8.8. Training is done either on the job or off the job.

Exhibit 8.7 Here is the final assembly process on an Airbus 787-10 for Singapore Airlines. This plant is one of Airbus's largest and most technologically advanced manufacturing facilities. *How is technology helping companies develop skilled workers both on and off the job?* (Credit: airbus777/Flickr/ Attribution 2.0 Generic (CC BY 2.0))

On-the-Job Training

New-employee training is essential and usually begins with **orientation**, which entails getting the new employee ready to perform on the job. Formal orientation (often a half-day classroom program) provides information about the company history, company values and expectations, policies, and the customers the company serves, as well as an overview of products and services. More important, however, is the specific job orientation by the new employee's supervisor concerning work rules, equipment, and performance expectations. This second briefing tends to be more informal and may last for several days or even weeks.

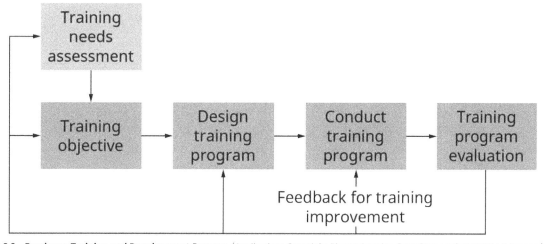

Exhibit 8.8 **Employee Training and Development Process** (Attribution: Copyright Rice University, OpenStax, under CC BY 4.0 license.)

Beyond employee orientation, job training takes place at the job site or workstation and is directly related to the job. This training involves specific job instruction, coaching (guidance given to new employees by experienced ones), special project assignments, or job rotation. **Job rotation** is the reassignment of workers to several different jobs over time. At Walmart, management trainees rotate through three or more merchandising departments, customer service, credit, and even the human resource department during the first year or two on the job.

Two other forms of on-the-job training are apprenticeship and mentoring. An **apprenticeship** usually combines specific on-the-job instruction with classroom training. It may last as long as four years and can be found in the skilled trades of carpentry, plumbing, and electrical work. **Mentoring** involves a senior manager or other experienced employee providing job- and career-related information to a mentee. Inexpensive and providing instantaneous feedback, mentoring is becoming increasingly popular with many firms, including FedEx, Merrill Lynch, Dow Chemical, and Bank of America. Whereas mentoring is typically conducted through ongoing face-to-face interactions between mentor and mentee, technology now allows for a long-distance mentoring relationship. Dow Chemical uses e-mail and video conferencing to facilitate long-distance mentoring between persons who are working in different countries. For a mentee whose second language is English, writing e-mail messages in English helps the individual become fluent in English, which is a requirement of all Dow Chemical employees regardless of location and country of origin.[8]

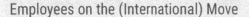

EXPANDING AROUND THE GLOBE

Employees on the (International) Move

Working abroad at one of the thousands of American or foreign multinational firms can be exciting and look good on your résumé. But is an international job assignment a step up the ladder to a more rewarding career path or a potential minefield of professional and family risk? The answer depends as much on an employee's family situation as his or her ambition, as well as how well the company supports and handles a transfer to an international location.

International job experience is increasingly seen as an essential leadership competency; therefore, many companies have developed robust rotational programs designed to give individuals critical global experience. According to the BGRS 2016 Global Mobility Trends Survey, providing high levels of service to relocating employees and their families is a fundamental expectation.

Brookfield Global Relocation Services (BGRS) is a talent mobility and relocation services firm that manages more than 60,000 relocations in 140 countries each year for its corporate and government clients. With 15 offices around the world, the company's staff (that speaks 40 languages) can tap into their network of 1,900 trusted suppliers to help employees and families acclimate to their new work and home environments.

Increasing numbers of recent college graduates and experienced professionals are offered opportunities for overseas work assignments ranging from a few days to 24 months or longer. But acclimating to a new country and culture, as well as a new work environment, can be daunting and involves some unique challenges.

Challenges face expatriates aside from the demands of work include:

- Choosing schools for children
- Securing housing
- Finding medical facilities
- Opening bank accounts
- Finding transportation and obtaining a driver's license
- Completing government forms
- Locating food stores
- Learning about community and entertainment offerings

With 189,000 worldwide staff and partners, KPMG International is one of the world's largest professional services and accounting firms, with a presence in 152 countries. Through programs like the KPMG Global Opportunities (GO) program, the professionals at KPMG can explore job rotation assignments, transfer to a new location, or change to a new job function or group. The company's Career Mobility Connection tool allows employees to evaluate opportunities based on their interests and to seek guidance from a transition advisor on potential career opportunities.

KPMG has developed several programs and standards to guide employees and establish consistency, whether they work in the United States or abroad. One of the most important is the KPMG Code of Conduct, which defines the values and standards by which KPMG conducts business and is intended to help guide actions and behaviors of its global workforce.

Every year, all KPMG employees and partners are required to affirm their agreement to comply with the Code of Conduct. In addition, all partners and employees are required to complete mandatory training that reinforces the principles of the Code and further builds understanding of the firm's expectations.

Critical Thinking Questions

1. How is KPMG's Global Code of Conduct intended to influence and guide the personal values and behaviors of its employees and partners?
2. Why must the Code of Conduct be affirmed by employees and partners every year? Why does KPMG include their partners in this program?
3. What are the top four or five job qualifications an employee should have to be considered for an overseas assignment?

Sources: Corrine Purtill, "Expat Couples Do Best When They've Moved for the Woman's Job," *Quartz at Work*, December 6, 2017; https://work.qz.com/1134685/expat-couples-do-best-when-theyve-moved-for-the-womans-job/; Donald Murray, "The 7 Greatest Challenges of Moving Overseas and How to Resolve Them," *International Living*, March 15, 2018, https://internationalliving.com/the-7-greatest-challenges-of-moving-overseas-and-how-to-resolve-them/; "KPMG's Code of Conduct," Accessed March 15, 2018, https://home.kpmg.com/us/en/home/about/kpmgs-code-of-conduct.html.

Off-the-Job Training

Even with the advantages of on-the-job training, many firms recognize that it is often necessary to train employees away from the workplace. With off-the-job training, employees learn the job away from the job. There are numerous popular methods of off-the-job training. It frequently takes place in a classroom, where cases, role-play exercises, films, videos, lectures, and computer demonstrations are used to develop workplace skills.

Web-based technology is increasingly being used along with more traditional off-the-job training methods. E-learning and e-training involve online computer presentation of information for learning new job tasks. Union Pacific Railroad has tens of thousands of its employees widely dispersed across much of the United States, so it delivers training materials online to save time and travel costs. Technical and safety training at Union Pacific are made available as **programmed instruction**, an online, self-paced, and highly structured training method that presents trainees with concepts and problems using a modular format. Software provided can make sure that employees receive, undergo, and complete, as well as sign off on, various training modules.[9]

Web-based training can also be done using a **simulation**, for example, a scaled-down version of a manufacturing process or even a mock cockpit of a jet airplane. American Airlines uses a training simulator for pilots to practice hazardous flight maneuvers or learn the controls of a new aircraft in a safe, controlled environment with no passengers. The simulator allows for more direct transfer of learning to the job.

CONCEPT CHECK

1. Describe several types of on-the-job training.
2. What are the advantages of simulation training?
3. How is technology impacting off-the-job training?

8.5 Performance Planning and Evaluation

5. How are performance appraisals used to evaluate employee performance?

Along with employee orientation and training, new employees learn about performance expectations through performance planning and evaluation. Managers provide employees with expectations about the job. These are communicated as job objectives, schedules, deadlines, and product and/or service quality requirements. As an employee performs job tasks, the supervisor periodically evaluates the employee's efforts. A **performance appraisal** is a comparison of actual performance with expected performance to determine an employee's contributions to the organization and to make decisions about training, compensation, promotion, and other job changes. The performance planning and appraisal process is shown in **Exhibit 8.9** and described below.

1. The manager establishes performance standards.
2. The employee works to meet the standards and expectations.
3. The employee's supervisor evaluates the employee's work in terms of quality and quantity of output and various characteristics such as job knowledge, initiative, relationships with others, and attendance and punctuality.
4. Following the performance evaluation, reward (pay raise) and job change (promotion) decisions can be made. If work is unsatisfactory, the employee may be put on a performance improvement plan, which outlines the behaviors or performance that must be improved, the milestones and time periods to improve performance, and what will occur if performance is not improved.
5. Rewards are positive feedback and provide reinforcement, or encouragement, for the employee to continue improving their performance.

It was once common practice for performance approvals to be conducted on an annual basis, but most companies have moved away from that standard. Instead, managers are encouraged to provide employees with continuous real-time feedback so that skill development and job performance can be improved more rapidly.

Information for performance appraisals can be assembled using rating scales, supervisor logs of employee job incidents, and reports of sales and production statistics. Regardless of the source, performance information should be accurate and a record of the employee's job behavior and efforts. Table 8.3 illustrates a rating scale for one aspect of a college recruiter's job. A rating of "9" is considered outstanding job behavior and performance; a rating of "1" is viewed as very poor to unacceptable.

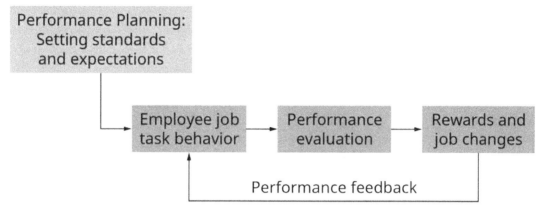

Exhibit 8.9   Performance Planning and Evaluation

Example of Behavior-Based Rating Scale for Performance Appraisal		
Position: College Recruiter		
Job Description: Visits campuses and conducts interviews of graduating seniors		
Explanation of Rating	Performance Rating	Explanation of Rating
This recruiter plans and organizes spring-semester college-recruiting schedule to minimize travel expenses and maximize the number of colleges visited and students interviewed.	9	
	8	Even with tight travel schedules between campuses, this recruiter completes each campus report before arrival at next campus.
	7	In making plans to visit a new campus, this recruiter might not have identified two or three faculty

Table 8.3

Explanation of Rating	Performance Rating	Explanation of Rating
	6	members for obtaining pre-visit information about degree programs.
This recruiter occasionally does not check with college placement office to request student résumés two days before arrival.	5	
	4	Sometimes this recruiter's notes are incomplete concerning a student's response to interview questions.
	3	This recruiter is often several minutes late in starting interviews.
This recruiter is frequently late in sending thank-you letters to students interviewed.	2	
	1	This recruiter is always late completing campus-recruiting reports.

Example of Behavior-Based Rating Scale for Performance Appraisal

Position: College Recruiter

Job Description: Visits campuses and conducts interviews of graduating seniors

Table 8.3

CONCEPT CHECK

1. What are the steps in the performance planning and appraisal process?
2. What purposes do performance appraisals serve?
3. Describe some sources of information for the performance appraisal.

8.6 Employee Compensation and Benefits

6. What are the types of compensation and methods for paying workers?

Compensation, which includes both pay and benefits, is closely connected to performance appraisals. Employees who perform better tend to get bigger pay raises. Several factors affect an employee's pay:

1. *Pay structure and internal influences.* Wages, salaries, and benefits are based on skills, experience, and the level of the job. The most important high-level positions, such as president, chief information officer, and chief financial officer, are compensated at the highest rates. Likewise, different jobs of equal importance to the firm are compensated at similar rates. As the level of management responsibility increases, so does pay. For instance, if a drill-press operator and a lathe operator are considered of equal importance, they may both be paid $21 per hour.

2. *Pay level and external influences.* In deciding how much to pay workers, the firm must also be concerned with the salaries paid by competitors. If competitors are paying higher wages, a firm may lose its best employees. HR professionals regularly evaluate salaries by geography, job position, and competitor and market wages. Wage and salary surveys conducted by the U.S. Chamber of Commerce and the U.S. Department of Labor can also be useful. There are also several websites such as Glassdoor that post salaries for jobs by company.

An employer can decide to pay at, above, or below the going rate. Most firms try to offer competitive wages and salaries within a geographic area or an industry. If a company pays below-market wages, it may not be able to hire skilled people. The level of a firm's compensation is determined by the firm's financial condition (or profitability), efficiency, and employee productivity, as well as the going rates paid by competitors. For example, MillerCoors Brewing Co. is considered a high-paying firm ($29–$33 per hour for production employees).[10]

Types of Compensation or Pay

There are two basic types of compensation: direct and indirect. Direct pay is the wage or salary received by the employee; indirect pay consists of various employee benefits and services. Employees are usually paid directly on the basis of the amount of time they work, the amount they produce, the type of work performed, or some combination of skill, time, and output. An hourly rate of pay or a monthly salary is considered base pay, or an amount of pay received by the employee regardless of output level. In many jobs, such as sales and manufacturing, an employee can earn additional pay as a result of a commission or an **incentive pay** arrangement. The accelerated commission schedule for a salesperson shown below indicates that as sales increase the incentive becomes increasingly more attractive and rewarding; therefore, pay can function as a powerful motivator. In this example, a salesperson receives a base monthly salary of $1,000, then earns 3 percent on the first $50,000 of product sold, 4 percent on the next $30,000, and 5 percent on any sales beyond $80,000.

Base pay	$1,000 per month
3% of 50,000	1,500
4% of 30,000	1,200
5% of 20,000	1,000
	$4,700

Two other incentive pay arrangements are bonuses and profit-sharing. Employees may be paid bonuses for reaching certain monthly or annual performance goals or achieving a specific cost-saving objective. In this instance, employees are rewarded based on achieving certain goals.

In a profit-sharing plan, employees may receive some portion of the firm's profit. Employee profit shares are usually based on annual company financial performance and therefore are paid once a year. With either a bonus or a profit share, an important incentive pay consideration is whether the bonus or profit share is the same for all employees or whether it is differentiated by level in the organization, base pay, or some other criterion. Choice Homes, a large-scale builder of starter homes, pays an annual incentive share that is the same for everyone; the president receives the same profit share or bonus as the lowest-paid employee.

Indirect pay includes pensions, health insurance, vacation time, and many others. Some forms of indirect pay are required by law: unemployment compensation, worker's compensation, and Social Security, which are all paid in part by employers. **Unemployment compensation** provides former employees with money for a certain period while they are unemployed. To be eligible, the employee must have worked a minimum number of weeks, be without a job, and be willing to accept a suitable position offered by the state Unemployment Compensation Commission. Some state laws permit payments to strikers. **Worker's compensation** pays employees for lost work time caused by work-related injuries and may also cover rehabilitation after a serious injury. Social Security is mainly a government pension plan, but it also provides disability and survivor benefits and benefits for people undergoing kidney dialysis and transplants. Medicare (health care for seniors) and Medicaid (health care for the poor) are also part of Social Security.

Many employers also offer benefits not required by law. Among these are paid time off (vacations, holidays, sick days, even pay for jury duty), health insurance (including dental and vision), supplemental benefits (disability, life, pet insurance, legal benefits), 401K contributions, pensions and retirement savings accounts, and stock purchase options.

Some firms with numerous benefits allow employees to mix and match benefit items or select items based on individual needs. A younger employee with a family may desire to purchase medical, disability, and life insurance, whereas an older employee may want to put more benefit dollars into a retirement savings plan. Pay and benefits are obviously important elements of human resource management and are frequently studied as aspects of employee job satisfaction. Pay can be perceived as very satisfactory, or it can be a point of job dissatisfaction. In a study of job satisfaction conducted by SAP, direct compensation was the most important element of job satisfaction by employees from various companies.[11] As the cost of health insurance and other benefits has risen sharply over the past few years, benefits have become increasingly important to workers.

CATCHING THE ENTREPRENEURIAL SPIRIT

Starbucks Perks More Than Coffee

At Starbucks, CEO Howard Schultz understood that the single most important aspect of creating an enduring brand is its people. Schultz wanted to set Starbucks apart from other coffee shops and service businesses, and he did this by offering health benefits and stock ownership for people who work part-time. It had never been done before, and it came with a cost.

In addition to employee benefits, funding to build the brand was funneled into operations to create an experience that would enable the brand to endure and be sold profitably for many years to come. So instead of expensive marketing and advertising campaigns, the company focused on experiential marketing.

Scott Bedbury, the president of marketing of Starbucks at the time, explains. "The stores were once four white walls. There was no comfortable furniture or fireplaces or music. So we set out to create an experience in the stores and a level of brand equity that most traditionally marketed brands couldn't touch. That meant constant creative development of products, and the look and feel in the stores. It wasn't cheap. The first year, we spent $100 million building out stores, which is a significant marketing budget for anyone."

But the defining moment for the brand was the stock option and employee benefit plan. This laid the foundation for the company's internal brand, and was Schultz's mission from the very beginning, explains Bedbury. "When Howard took over the company, he was not a rich man and he didn't own a house or even a car. Howard grew up poor in Brooklyn and was influenced strongly by his dad, who never got health benefits from any of his employers. This fueled Howard's drive to create a company that put employees first. He is passionate that when it comes to customers versus employees, employees will always come first."

But it wasn't easy, and it took a lot of courage to present this idea to investors. Bedbury said, "When Howard tried to raise $2.8 million to buy the company from the three founders, he made 220 presentations and he got shut down in all but 12 of them. He was seen as an idealist who was going to put an unnecessary burden on the bottom line by offering benefits to part-time employees who viewed this as a temporary job. But Howard convinced them that turnover would drop, which it did. Store manager attrition was 15 percent, part-time hourly employees was 65 percent, compared to McDonalds and Taco Bell, which were about 200–300 percent a year. That's turning over your work force every four months, and when you do that, your service suffers and there are all kinds of problems. I don't know why more people don't do it. If you give up some equity to employees, they'll reward you for that."

Critical Thinking Questions
1. How can a company like Starbucks sustain its strong employee culture while continuing to grow rapidly?
2. Can a firm give its employees too much in terms of benefits and services? Explain.

Sources: Blog, MarketSmarter, http://www.marketsmarter.com/blog, accessed March 12, 2018; Carmine Gallo, "How Starbucks CEO Howard Schultz Inspired Us to Dream Bigger," *Forbes,* https://www.forbes.com, December 2, 2016; Tanza Loudenback, "The Story Behind the Rise of Starbucks' Howard Shultz, Who Just Gave a Raise to Every US Employee of His $82 Billion Coffee Company," *Business Insider,* http://www.businessinsider.com, July 11, 2016; Monique Reece, *Real-Time Marketing for Business Growth* (Upper Saddle River, NJ: FT Press/Pearson, 2010).

CONCEPT CHECK

1. How does a firm establish a pay scale for its employees?
2. What is the difference between direct and indirect pay?

3. Why are health insurance and benefits so important to employees?

8.7 | The Labor Relations Process

7. What is a labor union and how is it organized, what is collective bargaining, and what are some of the key negotiation issues?

Tens of thousands of American firms are unionized, and millions of U.S. workers belong to unions. Historically, the mining, manufacturing, construction, and transportation industries have been significantly unionized, but in recent years, service-based firms, including health care organizations, have been unionized.

A **labor union**, such as the International Brotherhood of Teamsters, is an organization that represents workers in dealing with management over disputes involving wages, hours, and working conditions. The labor relations process that produces a union-management relationship consists of three phases: union organizing, negotiating a labor agreement, and administering the agreement. In phase one, a group of employees within a firm may form a union on their own, or an established union (United Auto Workers, for example) may target an employer and organize many of the firm's workers into a local labor union. The second phase constitutes **collective bargaining**, which is the process of negotiating a labor agreement that provides for compensation and working arrangements mutually acceptable to the union and to management. Finally, the third phase of the labor relations process involves the daily administering of the labor agreement. This is done primarily through handling worker grievances and other workforce management problems that require interaction between managers and labor union officials.

The Modern Labor Movement

The basic structure of the modern labor movement consists of three parts: local unions, national and international unions, and union federations. There are approximately 60,000 local unions, 75 national and international unions, and two federations. Union membership has been declining over the past three decades and is now half what it once was. The number of employed union members has declined by 2.9 million since 1983, the first year union statistics were reported. In 1983, union membership was 20.1 percent of workers, with 17.7 million union workers. In 2017, membership declined to 10.7 percent of workers, with 14.8 million members.[12]

A **local union** is a branch or unit of a national union that represents workers at a specific plant or over a specific geographic area. Local 276 of the United Auto Workers represents assembly employees at the General Motors plant in Arlington, Texas. A local union (in conformance with its national union rules) determines the number of local union officers, procedures for electing officers, the schedule of local meetings, financial arrangements with the national organization, and the local's role in negotiating labor agreements.

The three main functions of the local union are collective bargaining, worker relations and membership services, and community and political activities. Collective bargaining takes place every three or four years. Local union officers and shop stewards in the plant oversee labor relations on a day-to-day basis. A **shop steward** is an elected union official who represents union members to management when workers have complaints. For most union members, his or her primary contact with the union is through union officials at the local level.

A national union can range in size from a few thousand members (Screen Actors Guild) to more than a million members (Teamsters). A national union may have a few to as many as several hundred local unions. The number of national unions has steadily declined since the early twentieth century. Much of this decline has resulted from union mergers. In 1999, for example, the United Papermakers International Union (UPICU) and the Oil, Chemical and Atomic Workers Union (OCAW) agreed to merge under the new name of PACE, or Paper, Allied-Industrial, Chemical and Energy International Union. PACE has about 245,000 members.

For 50 years, one union federation (the American Federation of Labor-Congress of Industrial Organization, or AFL-CIO) dominated the American labor movement. A **federation** is a collection of unions banded together to further organizing, public relations, political, and other mutually-agreed-upon purposes of the member unions. In the summer of 2005, several unions (Teamsters, Service Employees International Union, Laborers' International Union, United Farm Workers, Carpenters and Joiners, Unite Here, and the United Food and Commercial Workers Union) split from the AFL-CIO and formed a new federation named the Change to Win Coalition.[13] The new federation and its member unions represent more than 5.5 million union members. Change to Win Coalition member unions left the AFL-CIO over leadership disagreements and ineffective organizing strategies of the AFL-CIO; one of its primary goals is to strengthen union-organizing drives and reverse the decline in union membership.[14]

Union Organizing

A nonunion employer becomes unionized through an organizing campaign. The campaign is started either from within, by unhappy employees, or from outside, by a union that has picked the employer for an organizing drive. Once workers and the union have made contact, a union organizer tries to convince all the workers to sign authorization cards. These cards prove the worker's interest in having the union represent them. In most cases, employers resist this card-signing campaign by speaking out against unions in letters, posters, and employee assemblies. However, it is illegal for employers to interfere directly with the card-signing campaign or to coerce employees into not joining the union.

Once the union gets signed authorization cards from at least 30 percent of the employees, it can ask National Labor Relations Board (NLRB) for a union certification election. This election, by secret ballot, determines whether the workers want to be represented by the union. The NLRB posts an election notice and defines the bargaining unit—employees who are eligible to vote and who will be represented by the particular union if it is certified. Supervisors and managers cannot vote. The union and the employer then engage in a pre-election campaign conducted through speeches, memos, and meetings. Both try to convince workers to vote in their favor. Table 8.4 lists benefits usually emphasized by the union during a campaign and common arguments employers make to convince employees a union is unnecessary.

The election itself is conducted by the NLRB. If a majority vote for the union, the NLRB certifies the union as the exclusive bargaining agent for all employees who had been designated as eligible voters. The employer then has to bargain with the union over wages, hours, and other terms of employment. The complete organizing process is summarized in Exhibit 8.10.

In some situations, after one year, if the union and employer don't reach an agreement, the workers petition for a decertification election, which is similar to the certification election but allows workers to vote out the union. Decertification elections are also held when workers become dissatisfied with a union that has represented them for a longer time. In recent years, the number of decertification elections has increased to several hundred per year.

Benefits Stressed by Unions in Organizing Campaigns and Common Arguments Against Unions		
Almost Always Stressed	Often Stressed	Seldom Stressed
Grievance procedures	More influence in decision-making	Higher-quality products
Job security	Better working conditions	Technical training
Improved benefits	Lobbying opportunities	More job satisfaction
Higher pay		Increased production

Employer Arguments Against Unionization:

- An employee can always come directly to management with a problem; a third party (the union) isn't necessary.
- As a union member, you will pay monthly union dues of $15 to $40.
- Merit-based decisions (promotions) are better than seniority-based decisions.
- Pay and benefits are very similar to the leading firms in the industry.
- We meet all health and safety standards of the Federal Occupational Safety and Health Administration.
- Performance and productivity are more important than union representation in determining pay raises.

Table 8.4

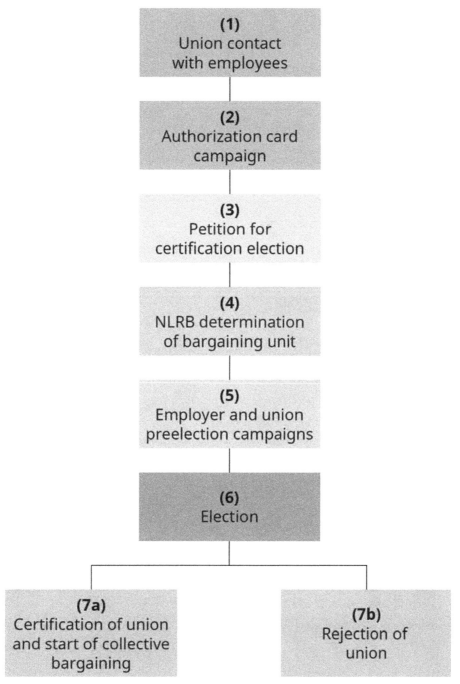

Exhibit 8.10 Union Organizing Process and Election (Attribution: Copyright Rice University, OpenStax, under CC BY 4.0 license.)

Negotiating Union Contracts through Collective Bargaining

A labor agreement, or union contract, is created through *collective bargaining*. Typically, both management and union negotiation teams are made up of a few people. One person on each side is the chief spokesperson. Bargaining begins with union and management negotiators setting a list of contract issues that will be discussed. Much of the bargaining over specific details takes place through face-to-face meetings and the exchange of written proposals. Demands, proposals, and counterproposals are exchanged during several rounds of bargaining. The resulting contract must be approved by top management and ratified by the union members. Once both sides approve, the contract is a legally binding agreement that typically covers such issues as union security, management rights, wages, benefits, and job security. The collective bargaining process is shown in **Exhibit 8.11**. We will now explore some of the bargaining issues.

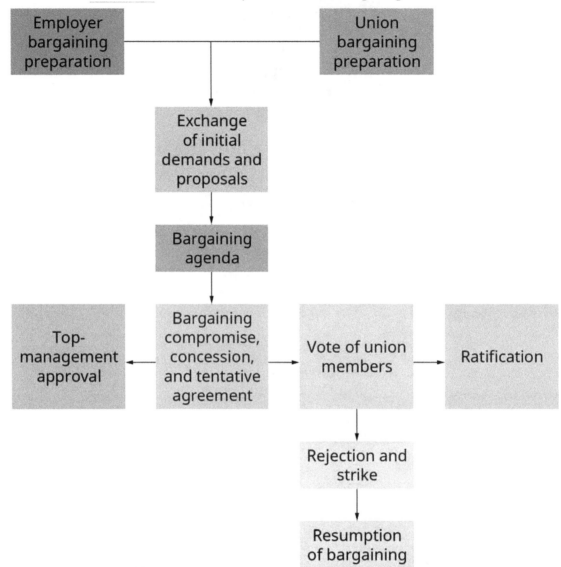

Exhibit 8.11   The Process of Negotiating Labor Agreements (Attribution: Copyright Rice University, OpenStax, under CC BY 4.0 license.)

Union Security

A union wants all employees to be union members. This can be accomplished by negotiating a union security clause. The most common union security arrangement is the **union shop**, whereby nonunion workers can be hired by the firm, but then they must join the union, normally within 30 to 60 days. An **agency shop** does not require employees to join the union, but to remain employees, workers must pay the union a fee (known as the agency fee) to cover the union's expenses in representing them. The union must fairly represent all workers, including those in the bargaining unit who do not become members.

Under the Taft-Hartley Act of 1947, a state can make any and all forms of union security illegal by enacting a **right-to-work law**. In the 28 states that have these laws, employees can work at a unionized company without having to join the union. This arrangement is commonly known as an **open shop**. Workers don't have to join the union or pay dues or fees to the union.

Management Rights

When a company becomes unionized, management loses some of its decision-making abilities. But management still has certain rights that can be negotiated in collective bargaining. One way to resist union involvement in management matters is to put a **management rights clause** in the labor agreement. Most union contracts have one. A typical clause gives the employer all rights to manage the business except as specified in the contract. For instance, if the contract does not specify the criteria for promotions, with a management rights clause, managers will have the right to use any criteria they wish. Another way to preserve management rights is to list areas that are not subject to collective bargaining. This list might secure management's right to schedule work hours; hire and fire workers; set production standards; determine the number of supervisors in each department; and promote, demote, and transfer workers.

Wage and Benefits

Much bargaining effort focuses on wage adjustments and changes in benefits. Once agreed to, they remain in effect for the length of the contract. For example, in 2015, the United Auto Workers negotiated a four-year contract containing modest hourly wage increases with U.S. car manufacturers; pay hikes were about 3 percent for first and third years and 4 percent in year four.[15] Hourly rates of pay can also increase under some agreements when the cost of living increases above a certain level each year, say 4 percent. No cost-of-living adjustment is made when annual living cost increases are under 4 percent, which has been the case for the early years of the twenty-first century.

In addition to requests for wage increases, unions usually want better benefits. In some industries, such as steel and auto manufacturing, benefits are 40 percent of the total cost of compensation. Benefits may include higher wages for overtime work, holiday work, and less desirable shifts; insurance programs (life, health and hospitalization, dental care); payment for certain nonwork time (rest periods, vacations, holiday, sick time); pensions; and income-maintenance plans. Supplementary unemployment benefits (income-maintenance) found in the auto industry are provided by the employer and are in addition to state unemployment compensation given to laid-off workers. The unemployment compensation from the state and supplementary unemployment pay from the employer together maintain as much as 80 percent of an employee's normal pay.

Job Security and Seniority

Wage adjustments, cost-of-living increases, supplementary unemployment pay, and certain other benefits give employees under union contracts some financial security. But most financial security is directly related to job security—the assurance, to some degree, that workers will keep their jobs. Of course, job security depends primarily on the continued success and financial well-being of the company. For example, thousands of airline employees lost their jobs after the 9/11 terrorist attack in 2001; these were employees with the least seniority.

Seniority, the length of an employee's continuous service with a firm, is discussed in about 90 percent of all labor contracts. Seniority is a factor in job security; usually, unions want the workers with the most seniority to have the most job security.

8.8 Managing Grievances and Conflicts

8. How are grievances between management and labor resolved, and what tactics are used to force a contract settlement?

In a unionized work environment, employees follow a step-by-step process for handling grievances or disputes between management and labor. Conflicts over contracts, however, are far more challenging to resolve and may result in the union or employer imposing economic pressure, as described in this section.

Grievance Handling and Arbitration

The union's main way of policing the contract is the grievance procedure. A **grievance** is a formal complaint by an employee or the union that management has violated some part of the contract. Under a typical contract, the employee starts by presenting the grievance to the supervisor, either in person or in writing. The typical grievance procedure is illustrated in **Exhibit 8.13**. An example grievance is a situation in which an employee is disciplined with a one-day suspension (and loss of pay) for being late for work several times in one month.

Exhibit 8.12   Ezekiel Elliott is a star running back for the Dallas Cowboys who was suspended by NFL commissioner Roger Goodell for six games in the 2017 season. The controversial NFL running back, with the support of the NFL Players Association (NFLPA), appealed the decision several times and was able to delay the suspension, but eventually lost a highly publicized case in federal court. U.S. District Judge Katherine Polk Failla ruled that the NFL's decision to suspend Elliott did not violate the labor agreement. *What options did Elliott and the NFLPA have after losing this court case?* (Credit: grantlairdjr/ flickr/ Attribution 2.0 Generic (CC BY 2.0))

If the problem isn't solved, the grievance is put in writing. The employee, one or more union officials, the supervisor, and perhaps the plant manager then discuss the grievance. If the matter still can't be resolved, another meeting takes place with higher-level representatives of both parties present. If top management and the local union president can't resolve the grievance, it goes to arbitration.

Arbitration is the process of settling a labor-management dispute by having a third party—a single arbitrator or a panel—make a decision. The decision is final and binding on the union and employer. The arbitrator reviews the grievance at a hearing and then makes the decision, which is presented in a document called the award. In the one-day suspension mentioned above, the arbitrator might rule that the discipline was improperly made because the employee's attendance record for the month was not accurately maintained by the firm.

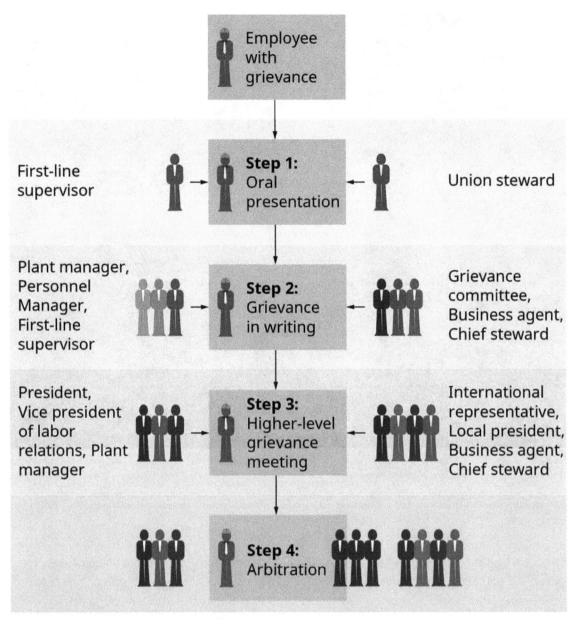

Exhibit 8.13 Typical Grievance Procedure (Attribution: Copyright Rice University, OpenStax, under CC BY 4.0 license.)

Tactics for Pressuring a Contract Settlement

Virtually all labor agreements specify peaceful resolution of conflicts, usually through arbitration. However, when a contract expires and a new agreement has not been reached, the union is free to strike or engage in other efforts to exert economic pressure on the employer. A *strike* occurs when employees refuse to work. The United Auto Workers union used a **selective strike strategy**, a strategy of conducting a strike at a critical plant that supplies parts to other plants, against General Motors. The union conducted its strike at a stamping and parts facility in Flint, Michigan, that supplied critical parts to other plants. The 54-day strike caused the company to stop production at many of its assembly plants because parts were not available from the Flint plant. General Motors lost approximately $2.2 billion during that dispute. Likewise, the employer can put pressure on the union through a lockout or by hiring strike replacements if the union has called a strike. For example, in 2018 aluminum producer Alcoa locked out more than 1,000 union workers from its smelter facility in Quebec, Canada, after union members went on strike.[16] **Table 8.5** provides a summary of union and employer pressure strategies for forcing a contract settlement.

Strategies of Unions and Employers			
Union Strategies		**Employer Strategies**	
Strike:	Employees refuse to work.	**Lockout:**	Employer refuses to let employees enter plant to work.
Boycott:	Employees try to keep customers and others from doing business with employer.	**Strike replacements:**	Employer uses nonunion employees to do jobs of striking union employees.
Picketing:	Employees march near entrance of firm to publicize their view of dispute and discourage customers.	**Mutual-aid pact:**	Employer receives money from other companies in industry to cover some of income lost because of strikes.
Corporate campaign:	Union disrupts stockholder meetings or buys company stock to have more influence over management.	**Shift production:**	Employer moves production to nonunion plant or out of country.

Table 8.5

CONCEPT CHECK

1. Describe the grievance procedure.
2. In what ways do arbitrators act like judges?
3. What are some tactics for pressuring for a contract settlement?

8.9 Legal Environment of Human Resources and Labor Relations

9. What are the key laws and federal agencies affecting human resource management and labor relations?

Federal laws help ensure that job applicants and employees are treated fairly and not discriminated against. Hiring, training, and job placement must be unbiased. Promotion and compensation decisions must be based on performance. These laws help all Americans who have talent, training, and the desire to get ahead. The key laws that currently impact human resource management and labor relations are listed in Table 8.6.

Several laws govern wages, pensions, and unemployment compensation. For instance, the Fair Labor Standards Act sets the federal minimum wage, which is periodically raised by Congress. Many minimum-wage jobs are found in service firms, such as fast-food chains and retail stores. The Pension Reform Act protects the retirement income of employees and retirees. Federal tax laws also affect compensation, including employee profit-sharing and stock purchase plans. When John F. Kennedy signed the Equal Pay Act into law in 1963, the goal was to stop the practice of paying women lower wages for the same job based on their gender. At the time, women with full-time jobs earned between 59 and 64 cents for every dollar their male counterparts earned in the same jobs. Although this law has been in place for several decades, progress has been slow. On April 17, 2012, President Barack Obama proclaimed National Equal Pay Day, noting that women who work full time earn only 77 cents for every dollar their male counterparts make. In 2016, the wage gap changed slightly, with women making 80.5 percent of what men earn.[17]

Laws Impacting Human Resource Management		
Law	Purpose	Agency of Enforcement
Social Security Act (1935)	Provides for retirement income and old-age health care	Social Security Administration
Wagner Act (1935)	Gives workers the right to unionize and prohibits employer unfair labor practices	National Labor Relations Board
Fair Labor Standards Act (1938)	Sets minimum wage, restricts child labor, sets overtime pay	Wage and Hour Division, Department of Labor
Taft-Hartley Act (1947)	Obligates the union to bargain in good faith and prohibits union unfair labor practices	Federal Mediation and Conciliation Service
Equal Pay Act (1963)	Eliminates pay differentials based on gender	Equal Employment Opportunity Commission
Civil Rights Act (1964), Title VII	Prohibits employment discrimination based on race, color, religion, gender, or national origin	Equal Employment Opportunity Commission
Age Discrimination Act (1967)	Prohibits age discrimination against those over 40 years of age	Equal Employment Opportunity Commission
Occupational Safety and Health Act (1970)	Protects worker health and safety, provides for hazard-free workplace	Occupational Safety and Health Administration
Vietnam Veterans' Readjustment Act (1974)	Requires affirmative employment of Vietnam War veterans	Veterans Employment Service, Department of Labor

Table 8.6

Laws Impacting Human Resource Management		
Law	Purpose	Agency of Enforcement
Employee Retirement Income Security Act (1974)—also called Pension Reform Act	Establishes minimum requirements for private pension plans	Internal Revenue Service, Department of Labor, and Pension Benefit Guaranty Corporation
Pregnancy Discrimination Act (1978)	Treats pregnancy as a disability, prevents employment discrimination based on pregnancy	Equal Employment Opportunity Commission
Immigration Reform and Control Act (1986)	Verifies employment eligibility, prevents employment of illegal aliens	Employment Verification Systems, Immigration and Naturalization Service
Americans with Disabilities Act (1990)	Prohibits employment discrimination based on mental or physical disabilities	Department of Labor
Family and Medical Leave Act (1993)	Requires employers to provide unpaid leave for childbirth, adoption, or illness	Equal Employment Opportunity Commission

Table 8.6

Employers must also be aware of changes to laws concerning employee safety, health, and privacy. The Occupational Safety and Health Act (OSH Act) requires employers to provide a workplace free of health and safety hazards. For instance, manufacturers must require their employees working on loading docks to wear steel-toed shoes so their feet won't be injured if materials are dropped. Drug and AIDS testing are also governed by federal laws.

Another employee law that continues to affect the workplace is the Americans with Disabilities Act. To be considered disabled, a person must have a physical or mental impairment that greatly limits one or more major life activities. More than 40 million Americans, 12.6 percent of the population, were disabled in 2015, according to the U.S. Census Bureau.[18] Employers may not discriminate against disabled persons. They must make "reasonable accommodations" so that qualified employees can perform the job, unless doing so would cause "undue hardship" for the business. Altering work schedules, modifying equipment so a wheelchair-bound person can use it, and making buildings accessible by ramps and elevators are considered reasonable. Two companies often praised for their efforts to hire the disabled are McDonald's and DuPont.

The Family and Medical Leave Act went into effect in 1993. The law guarantees continuation of paid health benefits, plus a return to the same or equivalent job, and applies to employers with 50 or more employees. It requires these employers to provide unpaid leave of up to 12 weeks during any 12-month period to workers who have been employed for at least a year and worked at least 1,250 hours during the past year. The reasons for the leave include the birth or adoption of a child; the serious illness of a child, spouse, or parent; or a serious illness that prevents the worker from doing the job.

According to the Bureau of Labor Statistics, only 11 percent of all private industry workers have access to paid family leave. Low-wage earners fare even worse. Only 5 percent of low-wage earners get any paid maternity leave, and nearly half will not take time off because they cannot afford to go without income. The United States continues to be one of only four countries in the world (along with Liberia, Suriname, and Papua New Guinea) that do not guarantee paid parental leave.[19]

The Wagner and Taft-Hartley Acts govern the relationship between an employer and union. Employees have the right to unionize and bargain collectively with the company. The employer must deal with the union fairly, bargain in good faith, and not discriminate against an employee who belongs to the union. The union must also represent all employees covered by a labor agreement fairly and deal with the employer in good faith.

Several federal agencies oversee employment, safety, compensation, and related areas. The **Occupational Safety and Health Administration** (OSHA) sets workplace safety and health standards, provides safety training, and inspects places of work (assembly plants, construction sites, and warehouse facilities, for example) to determine employer compliance with safety regulations.

Exhibit 8.14   For some occupations, danger is part of the job description. Tallies of work-related casualties routinely identify miners, loggers, pilots, commercial fishermen, and steel workers as holding the most deadly jobs. Job fatalities are often linked to the use of heavy or outdated equipment. However, many work-related deaths also happen in common highway accidents or as homicides. Pictured here are miners at the Coal Miner's Memorial and Pennsylvania Welcome Center. *What laws and agencies are designated to improve occupational safety?* (Credit: Mike Steele/ Flickr/ Attribution 2.0 Generic (CC BY 2.0))

The Wage and Hour division of the Department of Labor enforces the federal minimum-wage law and overtime provisions of the Fair Labor Standards Act. Employers covered by this law must pay certain employees a premium rate of pay (or time and one-half) for all hours worked beyond 40 in one week.

The **Equal Employment Opportunity Commission** (EEOC) was created by the 1964 Civil Rights Act. It is one of the most influential agencies responsible for enforcing employment laws. The EEOC has three basic functions: processing discrimination complaints, issuing written regulations, and gathering and disseminating information. An employment discrimination complaint can be filed by an individual or a group of employees who work for a company. The group may comprise a **protected class**, such as women, African Americans, or Hispanic Americans. The protected group may pursue a class-action complaint that may eventually become a lawsuit. As a measure to prevent employment discrimination, many employers set up **affirmative action programs** to expand job opportunities for women and minorities

Even with affirmative action and other company efforts to follow the law, each year the EEOC receives tens of thousands of complaints from current or former employees. The monetary benefits that the EEOC wins for employees has grown substantially during the past 10 years. Large monetary settlements often occur when the EEOC files a class-action suit against an employer. For example, the Ford Motor Company settled sexual and racial harassment claims by more than 30 women for more than $10 million at two Chicago-area manufacturing plants in 2017.[20] Also, Sears, Motorola, and AT&T have had to make large back-pay awards and to offer special training to minority employees after the court found they had been discriminated against.

The NLRB was established to enforce the Wagner Act. Its five members are appointed by the president; the agency's main office is in Washington, DC, and regional and field offices are scattered throughout the United States. NLRB field agents investigate charges of employer and union wrongdoing (or unfair labor practices) and supervise elections held to decide union representation. Judges conduct hearings to determine whether employers and unions have violated the law.

The Federal Mediation and Conciliation Service helps unions and employers negotiate labor agreements. Agency specialists, who serve as impartial third parties between the union and company, use two processes: conciliation and mediation, both of which require expert communication and persuasion. In **conciliation**, the specialist assists management and the union with focusing on the issues in dispute and acts as a go-between, or communication channel through which the union and employer send messages to and share information with each other. The specialist takes a stronger role in **mediation** by suggesting compromises to the disputing organizations.

CONCEPT CHECK

1. Discuss the laws that govern wages, pensions, and employee compensation.
2. Describe the Americans with Disabilities Act.
3. How do the Wagner and Taft-Hartley Acts impact labor-management relations?

8.10 | Trends in Human Resource Management and Labor Relations

10. What trends and issues are affecting human resource management and labor relations?

Some of today's most important trends in human resource management are using employee diversity as a competitive advantage, improving efficiency through outsourcing and technology, and hiring employees who fit the organizational culture. Although overall labor union enrollment continues to decline, a possible surge in membership in service unions is anticipated.

Employee Diversity and Competitive Advantage

American society and its workforce are becoming increasingly more diverse in terms of racial and ethnic status, age, educational background, work experience, and gender. A company with a demographic employee profile that looks like its customers may be in a position to gain a **competitive advantage**, which is a set of unique features of a company and its product or service that are perceived by the target market as superior to those of the competition. Competitive advantage is the factor that causes customers to patronize a firm and not the competition. Many things can be a source of competitive advantage: for Southwest Airlines it is route structure and high asset utilization; for Ritz-Carlton hotels it is very high-quality guest services; for Toyota it is manufacturing efficiency and product durability; and for Starbucks it is location, service, and outstanding coffee products. For these firms, a competitive advantage is also created by their HR practices. Many firms are successful because of employee diversity, which can produce more effective problem-solving, a stronger reputation for hiring women and minorities, greater employee diversity, quicker adaptation to change, and more robust product solutions because a diverse team can generate more options for improvement.[21]

In order for an organization to use employee diversity for competitive advantage, top management must be fully committed to hiring and developing women and minority individuals. An organization that highly values employee diversity is the United States Postal Service (USPS). In 1992 the Postal Service launched a diversity development program to serve as the organization's "social conscience and to increase employees' awareness of and appreciation for ethnic and cultural diversity both in the postal workplace and among customers." Twenty-five years later, 39 percent of postal service employees are minority persons: 21 percent African-American, 8 percent Hispanic, and more than 8.0 percent other minorities. In addition, women make up 40 percent of the organization's workforce.[22]

Outsourcing HR and Technology

The role of the HR professional has changed noticeably over the past 20 years. One significant change has been the use of technology in handling relatively routine HR tasks, such as payroll processing, initial screening of applicants, and benefits enrollments. Large firms such as Nokia and Lockheed Martin purchase specialized software (SAP and Oracle/PeopleSoft) to perform the information-processing aspects of many HR tasks. Other firms, such as Jacobs Engineering Group (a large professional services firm), outsource—or contract out—these tasks to HR service providers such as Aon Hewitt and Workforce Solutions.

HR outsourcing is done when another firm can perform a task better and more efficiently, thus saving costs. Sometimes HR activities are outsourced because HR requirements are extraordinary and too overwhelming to execute in-house in a timely fashion. Frequently, HR activities are outsourced simply because a provider has greater expertise. For example, media conglomerate CBS Corp. recently announced that it hired Fidelity Investments to manage its 401(k) plan, which has more than $4 billion in assets.[23]

Organizational Culture and Hiring for Fit

Regardless of general business and economic conditions, many firms are expanding operations and hiring additional employees. For many growing firms, corporate culture can be a key aspect of developing employees into a competitive advantage for the firm. Corporate culture refers to the core values and beliefs that support the mission and business model of the firm and guide employee behavior. Companies such as JetBlue, Ritz-Carlton, and Cypress frequently hire for fit with their corporate cultures. This necessitates recruitment and selection of employees who exhibit the values of the firm. Ritz-Carlton and Cypress use carefully crafted applicant questionnaires to screen for values and behaviors that support the corporate culture. JetBlue uses behavioral-based interview questions derived from its corporate values of safety, integrity, caring, fun, and passion. Southwest Airlines has non-HR employees (flight attendants, gate agents, and pilots) and even frequent flyer passengers interview applicants to screen for cultural fit as well as strong customer-service orientation.

In addition to cultural fit, firms are increasingly hiring for technical knowledge and skills fit to the job. Tech companies such as IBM, Amazon, and Microsoft receive thousands of résumés and job applications each year and continue to look for the best and the brightest when it comes to technical knowledge and skills. For example, IBM is now focusing on a skills-based approach rather than a candidate's education level and number of academic degrees. Amazon is all about the customer and looks for employees who continue to be "relentlessly curious." Microsoft continues to raise the talent bar by embracing job applicants who have demonstrated leadership, achieved concrete results, and can prove that they love to learn.[24]

More Service Workers Joining Labor Unions

Organized labor has faced tumultuous times during the last several decades due to declining union membership, loss of factory jobs, dwindling political clout, and the shifting of jobs outside the United States. With union membership now down to a little more than 10 percent of the U.S. workforce, some wonder if labor unions, who organize as a united front against poor working conditions, still have a place in the country. Mary Kay Henry, international president of Service Employees International Union (SEIU), is optimistic that unions are capable of resurgence by organizing the growing number of service workers into labor unions. The SEIU is the fastest-growing union in the nation, having jumped to 2 million members from 1.1 million a decade ago.[25]

Henry's goal is to focus on recruiting the country's millions of low-wage service workers, positions that are primarily filled by the working poor. These workers are disproportionately women, immigrants, and members of minority groups, which have all been traditionally more open to unionization. If these workers are successfully recruited into the SEIU, Henry believes that their wages and benefits would increase in much the same way unions brought factory workers into the middle class in the 1930s.

The SEIU believes that the service industry provides a target of opportunity, with the largest expected employment growth through 2026 in low-paid local services:

Job	Projected Growth[26]
Home health aides	47%
Personal care aides	39%
Food preparation	17%
Janitorial	10%

Many believe that the future of labor lies primarily in the success of recruitment efforts and in enrolling the massive numbers of employees who are in fast-growing, low-wage service jobs. For example, the SEIU was successful recently in unionizing hundreds of workers who provide services to people with disabilities in California, with an eye toward raising standards for their work and increasing hourly wages and benefits. Reversing labor's decline will be challenging, but the SEIU looks positively toward the future.[27]

CONCEPT CHECK

1. How can employee diversity give a company a competitive advantage?
2. Explain the concept of hiring for fit.
3. Why does the service industry provide an opportunity for labor union growth?

🔑 Key Terms

affirmative action programs Programs established by organizations to expand job opportunities for women and minorities.

agency shop Workers don't have to join a union but must pay union dues.

apprenticeship A form of on-the-job training that combines specific job instruction with classroom instruction.

arbitration Settling labor-management disputes through a third party. The decision is final and binding.

collective bargaining Negotiating a labor agreement.

competitive advantage A set of unique features of an organization that are perceived by customers and potential customers as significant and superior to the competition.

conciliation Negotiation process in which a specialist in labor-management negotiations acts as a go-between for management and the unions and helps focus on the problems.

contingent worker Person who prefers temporary employment, either part-time or full-time.

Equal Employment Opportunity Commission (EEOC) Processes discrimination complaints, issues regulations regarding discrimination, and disseminates information.

federation A collection of unions banded together to achieve common goals.

grievance A formal complaint by a union worker that management has violated the contract.

human resource (HR) management The process of hiring, developing, motivating, and evaluating employees to achieve organizational goals.

human resource planning Creating a strategy for meeting current and future human resource needs.

incentive pay Additional pay for attaining a specific goal.

job analysis A study of the tasks required to do a particular job well.

job description The tasks and responsibilities of a job.

job fair An event, typically one or two days, held at a convention center to bring together job seekers and firms that are searching for employees.

job rotation Reassignment of workers to several different jobs over time so that they can learn the basics of each job.

job specification A list of the skills, knowledge, and abilities a person must have to fill a job.

labor union An organization that represents workers in dealing with management.

local union Branch of a national union that represents workers in a specific plant or geographic area.

management rights clause Clause in a labor agreement that gives management the right to manage the business except as specified in the contract.

mediation Negotiation process in which a specialist facilitates labor-management contract discussions and suggests compromises.

mentoring A form of on-the-job training in which a senior manager or other experienced employee provides job- and career-related information to a mentee.

Occupational Safety and Health Administration (OSHA) Sets workplace safety and health standards and assures compliance.

open shop Workers do not have to join the union or pay union dues.

orientation Presentation to get the new employee ready to perform his or her job.

performance appraisal A comparison of actual performance with expected performance to assess an employee's contributions to the organization.

programmed instruction A form of computer-assisted off-the-job training.

protected classes The specific groups who have legal protection against employment discrimination;

include women, African-Americans, Native Americans, and others.

recruitment The attempt to find and attract qualified applicants in the external labor market.

recruitment branding Presenting an accurate and positive image of the firm to those being recruited.

right-to-work law State laws that an employee does not have to join a union.

selection The process of determining which persons in the applicant pool possess the qualifications necessary to be successful on the job.

selection interview An in-depth discussion of an applicant's work experience, skills and abilities, education, and career interests.

selective strike strategy Strike at a critical plant that typically stops operations system-wide.

shop steward An elected union official that represents union members to management when workers have complaints.

simulation A scaled-down version or mock-up of equipment, processes, or a work environment.

succession planning Examination of current employees to identify people who can fill vacancies and be promoted.

training and development Activities that provide learning situations in which an employee acquires additional knowledge or skills to increase job performance.

unemployment compensation Government payment to unemployed former workers.

union shop Nonunion workers can be hired but must join the union later.

worker's compensation Pay for lost work time due to employment-related injuries.

Summary of Learning Outcomes

8.1 Achieving High Performance through Human Resources Management

1. What is the human resource management process, and how are human resource needs determined?

The human resource management process consists of a sequence of activities that begins with the job analysis and HR planning; progresses to employee recruitment and selection; then focuses on employee training, performance appraisal, and compensation; and ends when the employee leaves the organization.

Creating a strategy for meeting human resource needs is called human resource planning, which begins with the job analysis. Job analysis is a process of studying a job to determine its tasks and duties for setting pay, determining employee job performance, specifying hiring requirements, and designing training programs. Information from the job analysis is used to prepare a job description, which lists the tasks and responsibilities of the job. A job specification describes the skills, knowledge, and abilities a person needs to fill the job described in the job description. By examining the human resource demand forecast and the internal supply forecast, human resource professionals can determine if the company faces a personnel surplus or shortage.

8.2 Employee Recruitment

2. How do firms recruit applicants?

When a job vacancy occurs, most firms begin by trying to fill the job from within the ranks of their own employees, known as the internal labor market. If a suitable internal candidate is not available, the firm turns to the external labor market. Firms use local media to recruit nontechnical, unskilled, and nonsupervisory workers. To locate highly trained recruits, employers use college recruiters, executive search firms, job fairs, and company websites to promote job openings. During the job search process, firms present an accurate and positive image of the company to those being recruited, called recruitment branding.

8.3 Employee Selection

3. How do firms select qualified applicants?

The selection process helps identify the candidates in the applicant pool who possess the best qualifications for the open position. Typically, an applicant submits an application or résumé and then receives a short, structured interview. If an applicant makes it past the initial screening, he or she may be asked to take an aptitude, personality, or skills test. The next step is the selection interview, which is an in-depth discussion of the applicant's work experience, skills and abilities, education, and career interests. If the applicant passes the selection interview, most firms conduct background checks and talk with their references. Physical exams and drug testing may also be part of the selection process.

8.4 Employee Training and Development

4.   What types of training and development do organizations offer their employees?

Training and development programs are designed to increase employees' knowledge, skills, and abilities in order to foster job performance improvements. Formal training (usually classroom in nature and off-the-job) takes place shortly after being hired. Development programs prepare employees to assume positions of increasing authority and responsibility. Job rotation, executive education programs, mentoring, and special-project assignments are examples of employee development programs.

8.5 Performance Planning and Evaluation

5.   How are performance appraisals used to evaluate employee performance?

A performance appraisal compares an employee's actual performance with the expected performance. Performance appraisals serve several purposes, but are typically used to determine an employee's compensation, training needs, and advancement opportunities.

8.6 Employee Compensation and Benefits

6.   What are the types of compensation and methods for paying workers?

Direct pay is the hourly wage or monthly salary paid to an employee. In addition to the base wage or salary, direct pay may include bonuses and profit shares. Indirect pay consists of various benefits and services. Some benefits are required by law and include unemployment compensation, worker's compensation, and Social Security. Many employers also offer benefits not required by law. These include paid vacations and holidays, pensions, health and other insurance, employee wellness programs, and college tuition reimbursement.

8.7 The Labor Relations Process

7.   What is a labor union and how is it organized, what is collective bargaining, and what are some of the key negotiation issues?

A labor union is an organization that represents workers in dealing with management over disputes involving wages, hours, and working conditions. A company is unionized through an organizing drive that begins either inside, with a small group of existing employees, or outside, with an established union that targets the employer. When the union gets signed authorization cards from 30 percent of the firm's employees, the NLRB conducts a union certification election. A majority vote is needed to certify the union as the exclusive bargaining agent. The union and the employer then begin collective bargaining and have one year in which to reach an agreement.

Collective bargaining is the process of negotiating, administering, and interpreting labor agreements. Both union and management negotiators prepare a bargaining proposal. The two sides meet and exchange demands and ideas. Bargaining consists of compromises and concessions that lead to a tentative agreement. Top management then approves or disapproves the agreement for the management team. Union members vote to either approve or reject the contract. The key issues included in a union contract are wage increases, fringe benefits, and job security.

8.8 Managing Grievances and Conflicts

8. How are grievances between management and labor resolved, and what tactics are used to force a contract settlement?

In most labor agreements, the grievance procedure consists of three or four steps. In the initial step, the employee files a grievance; this is an oral and/or written presentation to the supervisor and may involve a union steward as representative of the grievant. Steps two and three involve meetings of the employee, one or more union officials, the appropriate supervisor, and one or more management officials. If the grievance is not resolved at step three, either party (union or management) can request that an arbitrator, or neutral third party, hear and decide the grievance. The arbitrator reviews the grievance at a hearing and then makes the decision, which is presented in a document called the award.

When a union contract expires and a new agreement has not been reached, the union may impose economic pressure on the firm. These tactics may take the form of strikes, boycotts, picketing, or corporate campaigns. Similarly, employers may implement lockouts, hire replacements, or move production to another facility to place pressure on a union to accept a new contract.

8.9 Legal Environment of Human Resources and Labor Relations

9. What are the key laws and federal agencies affecting human resource management and labor relations?

A number of federal laws (listed in Table 8.6) affect human resource management. Federal law prohibits discrimination based on age, race, gender, color, national origin, religion, or disability. The Americans with Disabilities Act bans discrimination against disabled workers and requires employers to change the work environment to accommodate the disabled. The Family and Medical Leave Act requires employers, with certain exceptions, to provide employees up to 12 weeks of unpaid leave a year. The leave can be for the birth or adoption of a child or due to serious illness of the worker or a family member.

Federal agencies that deal with human resource administration are the EEOC, OSHA, the Office of Federal Contract Compliance Programs (OFCCP), and the Wage and Hour Division of the Department of Labor. The EEOC and OFCCP are primary agencies for the enforcement of employment discrimination laws, OSHA enforces safety regulations, and the Wage and Hour Division enforces the minimum wage and related laws. Many companies employ affirmative action and safety officers to ensure compliance with antidiscrimination and workplace safety laws. The Wagner and Taft-Hartley Acts govern the union-management relationship, in part through the functions performed by the National Labor Relations Board. The law gives workers the right to form and join labor unions and obligates the employer to deal with the union fairly.

8.10 Trends in Human Resource Management and Labor Relations

10. What trends and issues are affecting human resource management and labor relations?

Human resource managers recognize that diverse workforces create an environment that nurtures creative decision-making, effective problem-solving, more agility in adapting to change, and a strong competitive advantage. Therefore, firms are becoming committed to recruiting and hiring a diverse workforce. To maximize efficiency, many firms are outsourcing HR functions and using technology to reduce costs and improve efficiency. Firms are also striving to hire employees who possess qualities that match those of the corporate culture. Although labor unions have faced declining membership in the last several decades, enrollment of service workers into labor unions may increase as low-wage earners seek improved working conditions, pay, and health benefits.

 Preparing for Tomorrow's Workplace Skills

1. Would an overseas job assignment be good for your career development? If you think so, what country would you prefer to live and work in for two or three years, and what type of job would you like to have in that country? (Resources)

2. The benefits package of many employers includes numerous items such as health insurance, life insurance, 401(k) plan, paid vacations, tuition reimbursement, employee price discounts on products of the firm, and paid sick leave. At your age, what are the three or four most important benefits? Why? Twenty years from now, what do you think will be your three or four most important benefits? Why? (Resources)

3. Assume you have been asked to speak at a local meeting of human resource and labor relations professionals. The topic is whether union membership will increase or decline in the next 50 years. Take either the increase or the decline position and outline your presentation. (Information)

4. Go to the government documents section in your college or university library, and inspect publications of the Department of Labor (DOL), including *Employment and Earnings, Compensation and Working Conditions, Monthly Labor Review, Occupational Outlook Handbook,* and *Career Guide to Industries.* Alternatively, go to the DOL Bureau of Labor Statistics website at **http://stats.bls.gov**. Access the most recent DOL publications and locate the following information. (Information)
    - Number of persons in the American workforce
    - Unemployment rate for last year
    - Demographic characteristics of the American workforce: race, ethnic status, age, marital status, and gender
    - Occupations where there are projected shortages for the next five or 10 years
    - Union membership by major industry category: manufacturing, banking and finance, health care, business and personal services, sports and entertainment, and any other area of interest to you

5. Assume you are a director of labor relations for a firm faced with a union certification election in 30 days. Draft a letter to be sent to your employees in which you urge them to vote "no union"; be persuasive in presenting your arguments against the union. (Information)

6. Using the internet, research articles featuring a recent strike or a labor contract settlement. Report to your class the specifics of the strike or settlement. (Technology, Resources)

7. **Team Activity** Select two teams of five. One team will take the position that employees are simply a business expense to be managed. The second team will argue that employees are an asset to be developed to enable the firm to gain a competitive advantage. The remainder of the class will judge which team provided the stronger argument. (Interpersonal)

8. Have you or a family member ever been a union member? If so, name the union and describe it in terms of membership size, membership characteristics, strike history, recent bargaining issues, and employers under union contracts. (Information)

9. **Team Activity** Divide the class into two groups. One group will take the position that workers should be required to join unions and pay dues. The other group will take the position that workers should not be required to join unions. Hold a debate in which a spokesperson from each group is given 10 minutes to present the group's arguments. (Interpersonal)

Ethics Activity

Tracking employee information through global positioning systems (GPS)—in particular, on company vehicles driven by employees—is becoming commonplace. Location information is transmitted to a server via the cell phone network (and sometimes via satellite phone service) and is then available to the company through the web or mobile apps.

As the cost of GPS drops and the number of mobile workers rises—by some accounts, to as much as 75 percent of the workforce by 2020—companies are depending on GPS to monitor the movement of personnel and products to improve customer service and help with time management. "I wanted to see how much time was spent on each job," says one small business owner with a fleet of seven service vehicles. "We've had a few problems in the past—people weren't where they said they'd be. With GPS, we can defend ourselves to the customers. We know how fast the drivers drove, what route they took, and how long they spent on each job." Late in 2017, four wastewater plant mechanics employed by the city of Modesto, California, were fired after GPS showed they used "work hours to socialize at the lift stations with [each other], go home, shop, sleep and drive around in the City utility vehicle."

Companies are not only tracking vehicles, but many now track employees through their mobile phones. Understandably, many employees don't like the idea of Big Brother following their every move; most states allow employers to track their employees' location even in off hours. Many employees take their company vehicles home after their shifts, but even employees with company-owned phones may be tracked after hours, too.

Surveys show that many GPS-tracked employees have serious concerns about after-hours tracking, micromanagement, and privacy [https://www.tsheets.com/gps-survey]. In 2015, a woman in California sued her employer, claiming that she was tracked 24 hours a day through her company-issued iPhone. And when she uninstalled the tracking app, she was fired.

Using a web search tool, locate articles about this topic, and then write responses to the following questions. Be sure to support your arguments and cite your sources.

Ethical Dilemma: Do GPS devices constitute an invasion of employee privacy? Are there guidelines companies can develop for appropriate GPS use?

Sources: Kevin Valine, "Modesto Disciplines Sewer Workers for Goofing Off," *The Modesto Bee,* http://www.modbee.com, January 1, 2018; Kaveh Waddell, "Why Bosses Can Track Their Employees 24/7," *The Atlantic,* https://www.theatlantic.com, January 6, 2017; Andrew Burger, "IDC: Mobile Workers Will Make Up Nearly 75 Percent of U.S. Workforce," http://www.telecompetitor.com, June 23, 2015; David Kravets, "Worker Fired for Disabling GPS App That Tracked Her 24 Hours a Day," *Ars Technica,* https://arstechnica.com, May 11, 2015.

⊕ Working the Net

1. Go to the blog page of the College Recruiter website at **https://www.collegerecruiter.com/blog**, and read the relevant articles to learn how to prepare a résumé that will get results. Develop a list of rules for creating effective résumés. What tips were the most useful to you?

2. Working as a contingent employee can help you explore your career options. Visit the Manpower website at **http://www.manpower.com**, and use the Job Search feature to look for several types of jobs that interest you. Choose your current city and one where you would like to live, either in the United States or abroad. What are the advantages of being a temporary worker? What other services does Manpower offer job seekers?

3. As a corporate recruiter, you must know how to screen prospective employees. The Integrity Center

website at **http://www.integctr.com** offers a brief tutorial on pre-employment screening, a glossary of key words and phrases, and related information. Prepare a short report that tells your assistant how to go about this process.

4. You've been asked to give a speech about the current status of affirmative action and equal employment to your company's managers. Starting with the website of the American Association for Access Equity and Diversity (**https://www.aaaed.org**) and its links to related sites, research the topic and prepare an outline for your talk. Include current legislation and recent court cases.

5. Web-based training is popular at many companies as a way to bring a wider variety of courses to more people at lower costs. The Web-Based Training Information Center site at **http://www.webbasedtraining.com** provides a good introduction. Learn about the basics of online training at its Primer page. Then link to the Resources section, try a demo, and explore other areas that interest you. Prepare a brief report on your findings, including the pros and cons of using the web for training, to present to your class.

6. What are the key issues facing labor unions today? Visit the AFL-CIO website, **http://www.aflcio.org**, and Labornet, **http://www.labornet.org**. Select three current topics and summarize the key points for the class.

7. Not everyone believes that unions are good for workers. The National Right to Work Legal Defense Foundation offers free legal aid to employees whose "human and civil rights have been violated by compulsory unionism abuses." Read the materials on its site (**http://www.nrtw.org**), and prepare a short report on its position regarding the disadvantages of labor unions.

8. Although we tend to think of labor unions as representing manufacturing employees, many office and service-industry employees, teachers, and professional belong to unions. Visit the websites of two of the following nonmanufacturing unions and discuss how they help their members: the Office and Professional Employees International Union (**http://www.opeiu.org**), the American Federation of State, County, and Municipal Employees (**http://www.afscme.org**), the National Education Association (**http://www.nea.org**), the Actor's Equity Association (**http://www.actorsequity.org**), and the American Federation of Musicians (**http://www.afm.org**). What are the differences, if any, between these unions and those in other industries?

Critical Thinking Case

Discrimination in the Workplace Continues

Although we live in enlightened times, a recent Gallup Poll found that 15 percent of American workers still experienced some form of workplace discrimination. The study was conducted to mark the anniversary of the Civil Rights Act of 1964 and the creation of the EEOC.

The poll found that the two most frequently cited types of discrimination are sexual discrimination (31 percent) and discrimination based on race or ethnicity (36 percent). Also mentioned were age, disability, sexual orientation, and religion. The work areas found to be most susceptible to discrimination are promotion and pay. Being selected for a job and treatment in the workplace were also cited. Wage discrimination and sexual harassment are two big battles women continue to fight. Both topics were in the headlines in 2017; one took center stage and the other was brushed under the covers (at least for now).

Thanks to Harvey Weinstein, the topic of sexual harassment was in the spotlight, setting off a tsunami as women around the world reacted with their #MeToo stories. As the movement progressed from Hollywood, to media companies, to Capitol Hill, and finally into corporate America, the topic had a platform. From the boardroom to the factory floor, women who had been sexually harassed shared their stories.

As companies rushed to put zero-tolerance policies into place and issue new training requirements, lawsuits and class-action cases were settled more quickly, some very publicly. In August 2017, the EEOC reached a $10 million settlement with Ford motor company for sexual and racial harassment at two Chicago plants.

In contrast, little was reported on the reversal of the new regulation designed to combat the wage gap between men and women. The revised EEO-1 would have gone into effect March 31, 2018, and required companies with 100 or more employees and federal contractors with 50 or more employees to report W-2 wage information and total hours worked for all employees. The EEO-1 form already requires employers to report data on race/ethnicity and gender.

The Office of Management and Budget (OMB) initiated a review and immediate stay to the U.S. EEOC "in accordance with its authority under the Paperwork Reduction Act (PRA)," reversing the regulation that had been revised on September 29, 2016.

Pay equity advocates who had supported expanded pay-data reporting were critical of the suspension. "We see through the Trump administration's call to halt the equal pay rule that requires employers to collect and submit pay data by gender, race, and ethnicity to the government," said Fatima Goss Graves, president and CEO of the National Women's Law Center in Washington, D.C. "Make no mistake—it's an all-out attack on equal pay. [It] sends a clear message to employers: if you want to ignore pay inequities and sweep them under the rug, this administration has your back."

How important is equal pay? According to the analyses of the 2014–2016 Annual Social and Economic supplement published by the Institute for Women's Policy Research, the United States economy would have produced additional income of $512.6 billion if women received equal pay; this represents 2.8 percent of 2016 gross domestic product (GDP).

In addition, poverty rates would drop from 10.8 percent to 4.4 percent, and the number of children with working mothers living in poverty would be nearly cut in half, dropping from 5.6 million to 3.1 million.

Critical Thinking Questions
1. Why is workplace diversity so important in today's business environment?
2. What are the major sources of workplace discrimination? Cite specific examples from the case.
3. What steps are companies taking to ensure that employees are not discriminated against?

Sources: Susan Chira and Catrin Einhorn, "How Tough Is It to Change a Culture of Harassment? Ask Women at Ford," *The New York Times,* https://www.nytimes.com, December 19, 2017; "Statement of Acting Chair Victoria A. Lipnic about OMB Decision on EEO-1 Pay Data Collection," https://www.eeoc.gov, August 29, 2017; Stephen Miller, "White House Suspends Pay-Data Reporting on Revised EEO-1 Form," https://www.shrm.org, August 31, 2017; Heidi Hartmann, Jeff Hayes, and Jennifer Clark, "How Equal Pay for Working Women Would Reduce Poverty and Grow the American Economy," http://www.iwpr.org, January 13, 2014; "Gallup Poll on Employment Discrimination Shows Progress, Problems, 40 Years after Founding of EEOC" (press release), https://www.eeoc.gov, December 8, 2005.

Hot Links Address Book

1. Search the extensive job database of CareerBuilder.com (**http://www.careerbuilder.com**) for a job in a new city.
2. Get advice for brushing up your interview skills at the Job Hunting Advice page of *The Wall Street Journal's*

career site, **http://careers.wsj.com**.

3. How does the Equal Employment Opportunity Commission promote equal opportunity in employment? Visit **http://www.eeoc.gov** to learn what the agency does.

4. For the latest news in the human resources field, visit the website of the Society for Human Resource Management at **http://www.shrm.org**.

5. Many companies are using the web to help manage employees. Visit ADP, **http://www.adp.com**, to learn how online services can streamline their HR tasks.

6. At the NLRB website, **http://www.nlrb.gov**, you'll learn about the agency's many activities and how it protects workers' rights.

7. Visit the Social Security Administration site to track the latest cost-of-living adjustment at **http://www.ssa.gov**. You'll find it in the Publications section.

9

Motivating Employees

Exhibit 9.1 (Credit: Jeff Turner /flickr / Attribution 2.0 Generic (CC BY 2.0))

 Introduction

Learning Outcomes

After reading this chapter, you should be able to answer these questions:

1. What are the basic principles of Frederick Taylor's concept of scientific management?
2. What did Elton Mayo's Hawthorne studies reveal about worker motivation?
3. What is Maslow's hierarchy of needs, and how do these needs relate to employee motivation?
4. How are McGregor's Theories X and Y and Ouchi's Theory Z used to explain worker motivation?
5. What are the basic components of Herzberg's motivator-hygiene theory?
6. What four contemporary theories on employee motivation offer insights into improving employee performance?
7. How can managers redesign existing jobs to increase employee motivation and performance?
8. What initiatives are organizations using today to motivate and retain employees?

EXPLORING BUSINESS CAREERS

Chuck Kaplan, Ciena Corporation

Chuck Kaplan loves music and playing in a band, but he does not work in the music industry. He works for Ciena Corporation, a global supplier of telecommunications networking equipment, software, and services. Kaplan spends his days leading a team to help customers solve business problems by updating and creating revenue through their networks—the process of modernizing and monetizing networks. He also plays music with OTN Speedwagon, Ciena's all-employee band.

OTN Speedwagon was created after Kaplan thought the entertainment at a corporate function was "cheesy." He and three others took the idea of creating an employee band to their boss, and OTN Speedwagon was born. Its name comes from the networking technology Ciena implements, Optical Transport Network, and the rock band REO Speedwagon; its members are from all over the globe.

The band is made up of employees from multiple departments, time zones, and countries. Members include an executive administrative assistant in London, England; a CTO in Dallas, Texas; sales system engineers in Dallas, Texas, and St. Louis, Missouri; an account manager in Denver, Colorado; senior managers in Baltimore, Maryland, and New York, New York; a sales consultant in Atlanta, Georgia; vice presidents in Atlanta, Georgia, and Dallas, Texas; and a materials management leader in Ottawa, Canada. When playing with the band, they set aside their job titles and focus on producing award-winning music.

OTN Speedwagon performs songs in a variety of styles and enjoys performing whenever and wherever opportunity exists. A highlight is the opportunity to compete at the *Fortune* Battle of the Corporate Band, a competition for all-employee bands. OTN Speedwagon won the event one year, beating seven other corporate bands. Two members also walked away with individual awards: best guitarist and best horns.

Producing great music together is not easy. Everyone knows one person being off-tempo or off-key can ruin a song. Because the band members have different job responsibilities and live in separate countries, they are rarely together. Scheduling live rehearsals is a major challenge, and they often happen only the day of or day before an event. The band is up to the challenge, though, and harnesses technology to solve the problem. The members discuss songs to sing (enough for a multi-hour show!) and pick a key for each song that fits the lead vocalist. One member makes an MP3 soundtrack for each song and shares it and lyrics with the others through a secure file-sharing system. Everyone spends hours practicing to the soundtracks—alone. But hard work and dedication pay off. When the band finally is together, often one time through is enough to perfect each song.

Opportunities and benefits such as being part of the band pay dividends for Ciena, certified as a "great place to work." Band members say trust in each other to do each person's part makes the band a success. Everyone knows what to do and does it, and that level of trust transfers back to the workplace. Members have built trust in coworkers, knocked down walls, and become more collaborative. The experience has brought the employees together, some meeting for the first time at rehearsal, and made the company seem more like a family. Bonus benefit? Corporate events are much more entertaining.

Sources: "About Chuck Kaplan," http://www.ciena.com, accessed January 19, 2018; "What Is Network Monetization?" http://www.ciena.com, accessed January 19, 2018; "OTN Speedwagon," http://www.ciena.com, accessed January 19, 2018; Great Place to Work, "Ciena Corporation," http://reviews.greatplacetowork.com, November 27, 2017; Jessica Stillman, "What This Remote Company Rock Band Can Teach You About Collaboration," *Inc.*, https://www.inc.com, March 10, 2017; Molly Winans, "Ciena's OTN Speedwagon Gears Up to Rock Out at OFC," https://www.ofcconference.org, March 17, 2017; Jane Hobbs, "Being a Great Place to Work Shouldn't Be a Mystery," http://www.ciena.com, October 24, 2016; "Ciena Takes Home National Title at 13th Annual FORTUNE Battle of the Corporate Bands," http://www.ciena.com, October 6, 2013; Bo Gowan, "Behind the Scenes with Ciena's Corporate Rock Band," http://www.ciena.com, September 16, 2013.

This chapter details motivational theory, both historically and currently, and applies that theory to the business world, where motivation, whether in the form of a rock band or not, is a key to success.

People can be a firm's most important resource. They can also be the most challenging resource to manage well. Employees who are motivated and work hard to achieve personal and organizational goals can become a crucial competitive advantage for a firm. The key then is understanding the process of motivation, *what* motivates individuals, and *how* an organization can create a workplace that allows people to perform to the best of their abilities.

Exhibit 9.2   LeBron James is on a roll. The U.S. basketball player began receiving national attention as a high school player in Ohio. By the time he was graduating from high school, he was touted as the consensus first pick in the NBA draft. James was determined to make it in professional basketball. After successful stints in Cleveland and Miami, James is a perennial all-star and has won three NBA championships. *What motivates people to achieve their personal best?* (Credit: Erik Drost/ flickr/ Attribution 2.0 Generic (CC BY 2.0))

9.1 Early Theories of Motivation

1.   What are the basic principles of Frederick Taylor's concept of scientific management?

Motivation is the set of forces that prompt a person to release energy in a certain direction. As such, motivation is essentially a need- and want-satisfying process. A **need** is best defined as the gap between what is and what is *required*. Similarly, a **want** is the gap between what is and what is *desired*. Unsatisfied needs and wants create a state of tension that pushes (motivates) individuals to practice behavior that will result in the need being met or the want being fulfilled. That is, motivation is what pushes us to move from where we are to where we want to be, because expending that effort will result in some kind of reward.

Rewards can be divided into two basic categories: intrinsic and extrinsic. Intrinsic rewards come from within the individual—things like satisfaction, contentment, sense of accomplishment, confidence, and pride. By contrast, extrinsic rewards come from outside the individual and include things like pay raises, promotions, bonuses, prestigious assignments, and so forth. Exhibit 9.3 illustrates the motivation process.

Successful managers are able to marshal the forces to motivate employees to achieve organizational goals. And just as there are many types of gaps between where organizations are and where they want to be, there are many motivational theories from which managers can draw to inspire employees to bridge those gaps. In this chapter, we will first examine motivational theories that grew out of the industrial revolution and early ideas of organizational psychology. Then we will examine needs-based theories and more contemporary ideas about employee motivation like equity, expectancy, goals, and reinforcement theories. Finally, we will show you how managers are applying these theories in real-world situations.

How can managers and organizations promote enthusiastic job performance, high productivity, and job satisfaction? Many studies of human behavior in organizations have contributed to our current understanding of these issues. A look at the evolution of management theory and research shows how managers have arrived at the practices used today to manage human behavior in the workplace. A sampling of the most influential of these theorists and research studies are discussed in this section.

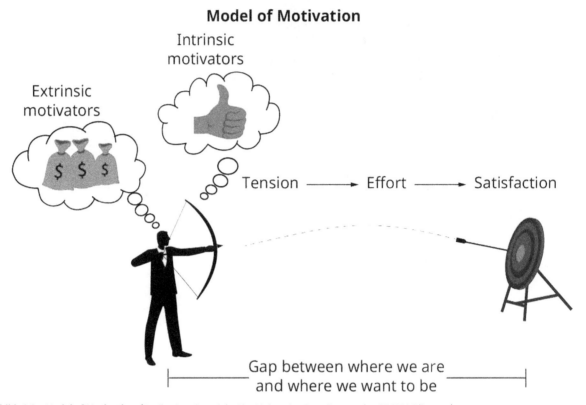

Exhibit 9.3 **Model of Motivation** (Attribution: Copyright Rice University, OpenStax, under CC BY 4.0 license.)

Frederick Taylor's Scientific Management

One of the most influential figures of the *classical era* of management, which lasted from about 1900 to the mid-1930s, was Frederick W. Taylor, a mechanical engineer sometimes called the "father of **scientific management**." Taylor's approach to improved performance was based on economic incentives and the premise that there is "one best way" to perform any job. As a manager at the Midvale and Bethlehem Steel companies in Philadelphia in the early 1900s, Taylor was frustrated at the inefficiency of the laborers working in the mills.

Convinced that productivity could be improved, Taylor studied the individual jobs in the mill and redesigned the equipment and the methods used by workers. Taylor timed each job with a stopwatch and broke down every task into separate movements. He then prepared an instruction sheet telling exactly how each job should be done, how much time it should take, and what motions and tools should be used. Taylor's ideas led to dramatic increases in productivity in the steel mills and resulted in the development of four basic principles of scientific management:

1. Develop a scientific approach for each element of a person's job.
2. Scientifically select, train, teach, and develop workers.
3. Encourage cooperation between workers and managers so that each job can be accomplished in a standard, scientifically determined way.
4. Divide work and responsibility between management and workers according to who is better suited to each task.

Taylor published his ideas in *The Principles of Scientific Management.* His pioneering work vastly increased production efficiency and contributed to the specialization of labor and the assembly-line method of production. Taylor's approach is still being used nearly a century later in companies such as UPS, where industrial engineers maximize efficiency by carefully studying every step of the delivery process looking for the quickest possible way to deliver packages to customers. Though Taylor's work was a giant step forward in the evolution of management, it had a fundamental flaw in that it assumed that all people are primarily motivated by economic means. Taylor's successors in the study of management found that motivation is much more complex than he envisioned.

CONCEPT CHECK

1. How did Frederic Taylor's studies contribute to the early understanding of human motivation?
2. How are Taylor's insights still seen in today's management practices?

9.2 The Hawthorne Studies

2. What did Elton Mayo's Hawthorne studies reveal about worker motivation?

The classical era of management was followed by the *human relations era,* which began in the 1930s and focused primarily on how human behavior and relations affect organizational performance. The new era was ushered in by the Hawthorne studies, which changed the way many managers thought about motivation, job productivity, and employee satisfaction. The studies began when engineers at the Hawthorne Western Electric plant decided to examine the effects of varying levels of light on worker productivity—an experiment that might have interested Frederick Taylor. The engineers expected brighter light to lead to increased productivity, but the results showed that varying the level of light in either direction (brighter or dimmer) led to increased output from the experimental group. In 1927, the Hawthorne engineers asked Harvard professor Elton Mayo and a team of researchers to join them in their investigation.

From 1927 to 1932, Mayo and his colleagues conducted experiments on job redesign, length of workday and workweek, length of break times, and incentive plans. The results of the studies indicated that increases in performance were tied to a complex set of employee attitudes. Mayo claimed that both experimental and control groups from the plant had developed a sense of group pride because they had been selected to participate in the studies. The pride that came from this special attention motivated the workers to increase their productivity. Supervisors who allowed the employees to have some control over their situation appeared to further increase the workers' motivation. These findings gave rise to what is now known as the **Hawthorne effect**, which suggests that employees will perform better when they feel singled out for special attention or feel that management is concerned about employee welfare. The studies also provided evidence that informal work groups (the social relationships of employees) and the resulting group pressure have positive effects on group productivity. The results of the Hawthorne studies enhanced our understanding of what motivates individuals in the workplace. They indicate that in addition to the personal economic needs emphasized in the classical era, social needs play an important role in influencing work-related attitudes and behaviors.

CONCEPT CHECK

1. How did Mayo's studies at the Hawthorne plant contribute to the understanding of human motivation?
2. What is the Hawthorne effect?
3. Was the practice of dimming and brightening the lights ethical?

9.3 | Maslow's Hierarchy of Needs

3. What is Maslow's hierarchy of needs, and how do these needs relate to employee motivation?

Another well-known theorist from the behavioral era of management history, psychologist Abraham Maslow, proposed a theory of motivation based on universal human needs. Maslow believed that each individual has a hierarchy of needs, consisting of physiological, safety, social, esteem, and self-actualization needs, as shown in **Exhibit 9.4**.

Maslow's theory of motivation contends that people act to satisfy their unmet needs. When you're hungry, for instance, you look for and eat food, thus satisfying a basic physiological need. Once a need is satisfied, its importance to the individual diminishes, and a higher-level need is more likely to motivate the person.

According to **Maslow's hierarchy of needs**, the most basic human needs are physiological needs, that is, the needs for food, shelter, and clothing. In large part, it is the physiological needs that motivate a person to find a job. People need to earn money to provide food, shelter, and clothing for themselves and their families. Once people have met these basic needs, they reach the second level in Maslow's hierarchy, which is safety needs. People need to feel secure, to be protected from physical harm, and to avoid the unexpected. In work terms, they need job security and protection from work hazards.

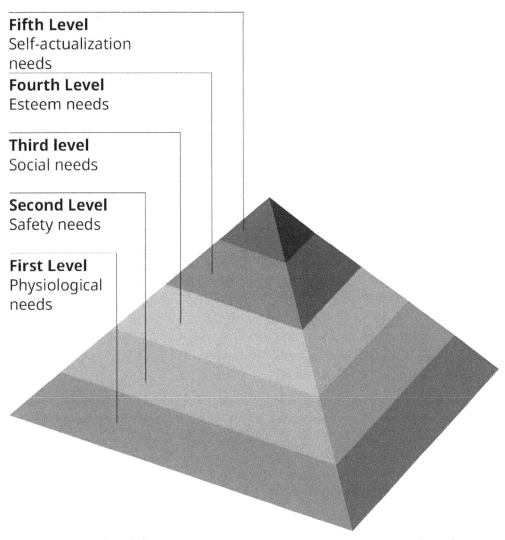

Fifth Level
Self-actualization
needs

Fourth Level
Esteem needs

Third level
Social needs

Second Level
Safety needs

First Level
Physiological
needs

Exhibit 9.4   Maslow's Hierarchy of Needs (Attribution: Copyright Rice University, OpenStax, under CC BY 4.0 license.)

Physiological needs and safety are physical needs. Once these are satisfied, individuals focus on needs that involve relationships with other people. At Maslow's third level are social needs, or needs for belonging (acceptance by others) and for giving and receiving friendship and love. Informal social groups on and off the job help people satisfy these needs. At the fourth level in Maslow's hierarchy are esteem needs, which are needs for the respect of others and for a sense of accomplishment and achievement. Satisfaction of these needs is reflected in feelings of self-worth. Praise and recognition from managers and others in the firm contribute to the sense of self-worth. Finally, at the highest level in Maslow's hierarchy are self-actualization needs, or needs for fulfillment, for living up to one's potential, and for using one's abilities to the utmost. In order to give you a better understanding of how Maslow's hierarchy applies in the real business world, let's look at a detailed example about Wegmans supermarkets. When you think of your first-choice job, you probably aren't thinking about working in a supermarket. With grueling hours, low pay, and annual turnover often approaching 100 percent, supermarkets are generally not considered the best places to work—unless you work at Wegmans, which has been on Fortune's "Best Company to Work For" every year since the list started, earning Wegmans a spot on Fortune's "Great Place to Work Legends" list.

Part of what makes Wegmans successful is the company's attention to its employees' needs at all levels of Maslow's hierarchy. The company pays above-market wages (the sous chef at a Pittsburgh store used to work for Thomas Keller's French Laundry in Napa Valley, and talent like that doesn't come cheap), and until 2003,

Wegmans paid 100 percent of its employees' medical insurance premiums (*physiological needs*). Wegmans' most comparable competitor has a turnover rate of about 19 percent, which doesn't even come close to Wegmans' 5 percent. More than half of Wegmans' store managers began working there in their teens (*safety needs*).

Because employees stay so long, the Wegmans culture has become stronger and more ingrained over time. Edward McLaughlin, director of Cornell's Food Industry Management Program, says, "When you're a 16-year-old kid, the last thing you want to do is wear a geeky shirt and work for a supermarket. But at Wegmans, it's a badge of honor. You are not a geeky cashier. You are part of the social fabric," (*social needs*).[1] Sara Goggins, a 19-year-old college student, was recently complimented on the display she helped prepare for the store's French-inspired patisserie—by Danny Wegman himself (*esteem needs*). Sara keeps a photo of her and Danny Wegman behind the counter. Maria Benjamin used to bake "chocolate meatball cookies" to celebrate coworkers' birthdays. They were so popular that she asked Danny Wegman if the store would sell them in the bakery department. He said yes, and it did. Employees like Sara and Maria are routinely recognized for their contributions to the company (*esteem needs*). Wegmans has spent over $54 million for college scholarships to more than 17,500 full- and part-time employees over the past 20 years. Top management thinks nothing of sending store department managers on training expeditions. A cheese manager might take a 10-day trip to visit and study cheesemakers in London, Paris, and Italy; a wine manager might take a company-sponsored trip through the Napa Valley (*self-actualization needs*).[2] As you can see from this extended example, Wegmans works hard to meet its employees' needs at all levels.

Maslow's theory is not without criticism, however. Maslow claimed that a higher-level need was not activated until a lower-level need was met. He also claimed that a satisfied need is not a motivator. A farmer who has plenty to eat is not motivated by more food (the physiological hunger need). Research has not verified these principles in any strict sense. The theory also concentrates on moving up the hierarchy without fully addressing moving back down the hierarchy. Despite these limitations, Maslow's ideas are very helpful for understanding the needs of people at work and for determining what can be done to satisfy them.

CONCEPT CHECK

1. What is Maslow's hierarchy of needs, and how does it help in understanding human motivation?
2. What are some criticisms of Maslow's hierarchy?

9.4 McGregor's Theories X and Y

4. How are McGregor's Theories X and Y and Ouchi's Theory Z used to explain worker motivation?

Douglas McGregor, one of Maslow's students, influenced the study of motivation with his formulation of two contrasting sets of assumptions about human nature—Theory X and Theory Y.

The **Theory X** management style is based on a pessimistic view of human nature and assumes the following:

- The average person dislikes work and will avoid it if possible.
- Because people don't like to work, they must be controlled, directed, or threatened with punishment to get them to make an effort.
- The average person prefers to be directed, avoids responsibility, is relatively unambitious, and wants security above all else.

This view of people suggests that managers must constantly prod workers to perform and must closely control their on-the-job behavior. Theory X managers tell people what to do, are very directive, like to be in control, and show little confidence in employees. They often foster dependent, passive, and resentful subordinates.

In contrast, a **Theory Y** management style is based on a more optimistic view of human nature and assumes the following:

- Work is as natural as play or rest. People want to and can be self-directed and self-controlled and will try to achieve organizational goals they believe in.
- Workers can be motivated using positive incentives and will try hard to accomplish organizational goals if they believe they will be rewarded for doing so.
- Under proper conditions, the average person not only accepts responsibility but seeks it out. Most workers have a relatively high degree of imagination and creativity and are willing to help solve problems.

Managers who operate on Theory Y assumptions recognize individual differences and encourage workers to learn and develop their skills. An administrative assistant might be given the responsibility for generating a monthly report. The reward for doing so might be recognition at a meeting, a special training class to enhance computer skills, or a pay increase. In short, the Theory Y approach builds on the idea that worker and organizational interests are the same. It is not difficult to find companies that have created successful corporate cultures based on Theory Y assumptions. In fact, *Fortune*'s list of "100 Best Companies to Work For" and the Society for Human Resource Management's list of "Great Places to Work" are full of companies that operate using a Theory Y management style. Starbucks, J. M. Smucker, SAS Institute, Whole Foods Market, and Wegmans are all examples of companies that encourage and support their workers. Genencor, a biotechnology firm listed on America's Best Places to Work five times, has a culture that celebrates success in all aspects of its business. Employees can reward colleagues with on-the-spot awards for extraordinary effort. According to the company's former CEO, Robert Mayer, "Genencor is truly unique among U.S. companies of any size. It is a model for innovation, teamwork, and productivity—and a direct result of our 'work hard, play hard, change the world' philosophy. Investing in our employees has always been good business for Genencor."[3]

Theory Z

William Ouchi (pronounced O Chee), a management scholar at the University of California, Los Angeles, has proposed a theory that combines U.S. and Japanese business practices. He calls it **Theory Z**. Table 9.1 compares the traditional U.S. and Japanese management styles with the Theory Z approach. Theory Z emphasizes long-term employment, slow career development, moderate specialization, group decision-making, individual responsibility, relatively informal control over the employee, and concern for workers. Theory Z has many Japanese elements. But it reflects U.S. cultural values.

In the past decade, admiration for Japanese management philosophy that centers on creating long-term relationships has declined. The cultural beliefs of groupthink, not taking risks, and employees not thinking for themselves are passé. Such conformity has limited Japanese competitiveness in the global marketplace. Today there is a realization that Japanese firms need to be more proactive and nimble in order to prosper. It was that realization that led Japanese icon Sony to name a foreigner as the CEO of Japan's most famous company. Over the years, Sony's performance has declined, until in April 2005, the company posted its biggest loss ever. Nobuki Idei, the former CEO who inherited Sony's massive debts and stagnant product lines, realized his strategy wasn't working, so he became determined to appoint a successor who would be able to transform Sony from the lumbering giant it had become back into the forward-thinking company it had been. Idei tapped Sir Howard Stringer, a Welsh-born American who had been running Sony's U.S. operations. In doing so, Idei hoped to shock company insiders and industry analysts alike. "It's funny, 100 percent of the people around here agree we need to change, but 90 percent of them don't really want to change themselves," he says. "So I finally concluded that we needed our top management to quite literally speak another language." After seven years as CEO, Stringer assumed the position of Chairman and appointed Kazuro Hirai as President and Chief Executive Officer.[4]

Differences in Management Approaches			
Factor	Traditional U.S. Management	Japanese Management	Theory Z (Combination of U.S. and Japanese Management)
Length of employment	Relatively short-term; workers subject to layoffs if business is bad	Lifetime; layoffs never used to reduce costs	Long-term but not necessarily lifetime; layoffs "inappropriate"; stable, loyal workforce; improved business conditions don't require new hiring and training
Rate of evaluation and promotion	Relatively rapid	Relatively slow	Slow by design; managers thoroughly trained and evaluated
Specialization in a functional area	Considerable; worker acquires expertise in single functional area	Minimal; worker acquires expertise in organization instead of functional areas	Moderate; all experience various functions of the organization and have a sense of what's good for the firm rather than for a single area
Decision-making	On individual basis	Input from all concerned parties	Group decision-making for better decisions and easier implementation
Responsibility for success or failure	Assigned to individual	Shared by group	Assigned to individual
Control by manager	Very explicit and formal	More implicit and informal	Relatively informal but with explicit performance measures

Table 9.1 Sources: Comparison of traditional U.S. and Japanese management styles with the Theory Z approach. Based on information from Jerry D. Johnson, Austin College. Dr. Johnson was a research assistant for William Ouchi. William Ouchi, *Theory Z*, Avon, 1982.

Differences in Management Approaches			
Factor	Traditional U.S. Management	Japanese Management	Theory Z (Combination of U.S. and Japanese Management)
Concern for workers	Focuses on work-related aspects of worker's life	Extends to whole life of worker	Is relatively concerned with worker's whole life, including the family

Table 9.1 Sources: Comparison of traditional U.S. and Japanese management styles with the Theory Z approach. Based on information from Jerry D. Johnson, Austin College. Dr. Johnson was a research assistant for William Ouchi. William Ouchi, *Theory Z*, Avon, 1982.

CONCEPT CHECK

1. How do the Theory X, Theory Y, and Theory Z management styles differ?

9.5 Herzberg's Motivator-Hygiene Theory

5. What are the basic components of Herzberg's motivator-hygiene theory?

Another important contribution to our understanding of individual motivation came from Frederick Herzberg's studies, which addressed the question, "What do people really want from their work experience?" In the late 1950s, Herzberg surveyed numerous employees to find out what particular work elements made them feel exceptionally good or bad about their jobs. The results indicated that certain job factors are consistently related to employee job satisfaction, while others can create job dissatisfaction. According to Herzberg, **motivating factors** (also called *job satisfiers*) are primarily intrinsic job elements that lead to satisfaction. **Hygiene factors** (also called *job dissatisfiers*) are extrinsic elements of the work environment. A summary of motivating and hygiene factors appears in Table 9.2.

One of the most interesting results of Herzberg's studies was the implication that the opposite of satisfaction is not dissatisfaction. Herzberg believed that proper management of hygiene factors could prevent employee dissatisfaction, but that these factors could not serve as a source of satisfaction or motivation. Good working conditions, for instance, will keep employees at a job but won't make them work harder. But poor working conditions, which are job dissatisfiers, may make employees quit. According to Herzberg, a manager who wants to increase employee satisfaction needs to focus on the motivating factors, or satisfiers. A job with many satisfiers will usually motivate workers, provide job satisfaction, and prompt effective performance. But a lack of job satisfiers doesn't always lead to dissatisfaction and poor performance; instead, a lack of job satisfiers may merely lead to workers doing an adequate job, rather than their best.

Exhibit 9.5   Flexibility has been a competitive advantage for ride-sharing companies like Uber and Lyft. Companies' flexible work hours have been appealing to many workers who appreciate the flexibility that these jobs provide, either as a full-time job or a way to make supplemental income. *According to Herzberg's motivator-hygiene theory, what effect might Uber and Lyft's work environment have on employee?* (Credit: Alfredo Mendez/ flickr/ Attribution 2.0 Generic (CC BY 2.0))

Although Herzberg's ideas have been widely read and his recommendations implemented at numerous companies over the years, there are some very legitimate concerns about Herzberg's work. Although his findings have been used to explain employee motivation, in fact his studies focused on job satisfaction, a different (though related) concept from motivation. Other criticisms focus on the unreliability of Herzberg's methodology, the fact that the theory ignores the impact of situational variables, and the assumed relationship between satisfaction and productivity. Nevertheless, the questions raised by Herzberg about the nature of job satisfaction and the effects of intrinsic and extrinsic factors on employee behavior have proved a valuable contribution to the evolution of theories of motivation and job satisfaction.

Herzberg's Motivating and Hygiene Factors	
Motivating Factors	**Hygiene Factors**
Achievement	Company policy
Recognition	Supervision
Work itself	Working conditions
Responsibility	Interpersonal relationships at work

Table 9.2

Herzberg's Motivating and Hygiene Factors	
Motivating Factors	Hygiene Factors
Advancement	Salary and benefits
Growth	Job security

Table 9.2

CONCEPT CHECK

1. What is Herzberg's theory, and how does it relate to an understanding of motivation?
2. How can a manager use an understanding of Herzberg's theory to motivate employees?
3. What are the limitations of Herzberg's theory?

9.6 Contemporary Views on Motivation

6. What four contemporary theories on employee motivation offer insights into improving employee performance?

The early management scholars laid a foundation that enabled managers to better understand their workers and how best to motivate them. Since then, new theories have given us an even better understanding of worker motivation. Four of these theories are explained in this section: the expectancy theory, the equity theory, the goal-setting theory, and reinforcement theory.

Expectancy Theory

One of the best-supported and most widely accepted theories of motivation is expectancy theory, which focuses on the link between motivation and behavior. According to **expectancy theory**, the probability of an individual acting in a particular way depends on the strength of that individual's belief that the act will have a particular outcome and on whether the individual values that outcome. The degree to which an employee is motivated depends on three important relationships, shown in Exhibit 9.6.

1. The link between *effort and performance,* or the strength of the individual's expectation that a certain amount of effort will lead to a certain level of performance
2. The link between *performance and outcome,* or the strength of the expectation that a certain level of performance will lead to a particular outcome
3. The link between *outcomes and individual needs,* or the degree to which the individual expects the anticipated outcome to satisfy personal needs. Some outcomes have more valence, or value, for individuals than others do.

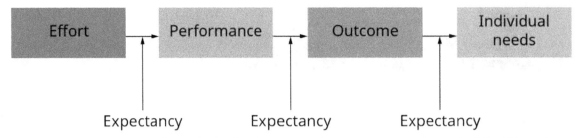

Exhibit 9.6   How Expectations Can Lead to Motivation (Attribution: Copyright Rice University, OpenStax, under CC BY 4.0 license.)

Equity Theory

Another contemporary explanation of motivation, **equity theory** is based on individuals' perceptions about how fairly they are treated compared with their coworkers. Equity means justice or fairness, and in the workplace it refers to employees' perceived fairness of the way they are treated and the rewards they earn. For example, imagine that after graduation you were offered a job that paid $55,000 a year and had great benefits. You'd probably be ecstatic, even more so if you discovered that the coworker in the next cubicle was making $45,000 for the same job. But what if that same colleague were making $59,000 for the same job? You'd probably think it unfair, particularly if the coworker had the same qualifications and started at the same time as you did. Your determination of the fairness of the situation would depend on how you felt you compared to the other person, or referent. Employees evaluate their own *outcomes* (e.g., salary, benefits) in relation to their *inputs* (e.g., number of hours worked, education, and training) and then compare the outcomes-to-inputs ratio to one of the following: (1) the employee's own past experience in a different position in the current organization, (2) the employee's own past experience in a different organization, (3) another employee's experience inside the current organization, or (4) another employee's experience outside the organization.

According to equity theory, if employees perceive that an inequity exists, they will make one of the following choices:

- *Change their work habits* (exert less effort on the job)
- *Change their job benefits and income* (ask for a raise, steal from the employer)
- *Distort their perception of themselves* ("I always thought I was smart, but now I realize I'm a lot smarter than my coworkers.")
- *Distort their perceptions of others* ("Joe's position is really much less flexible than mine.")
- *Look at the situation from a different perspective* ("I don't make as much as the other department heads, but I make a lot more than most graphic artists.")
- *Leave the situation* (quit the job)

Managers can use equity theory to improve worker satisfaction. Knowing that every employee seeks equitable and fair treatment, managers can make an effort to understand an employee's perceptions of fairness and take steps to reduce concerns about inequity.

Exhibit 9.7   Ben & Jerry's founders Ben Cohen and Jerry Greenfield firmly believe the maxim that companies "do well by doing good." This idealism led the founders to once famously swear that no Ben & Jerry's executive would ever make more than seven times the lowliest worker's wage. But when growth required attracting exceptional top-level management, the company eventually abandoned its self-imposed ratio between its lowest and highest compensation rates. *How might perceived inequities in pay affect worker satisfaction and motivation?* (Credit: Mike Mozart/ flickr/ Attribution 2.0 Generic (CC BY 2.0))

Goal-Setting Theory

Goal-setting theory is based on the premise that an individual's intention to work toward a goal is a primary source of motivation. Once set, the goal clarifies for the employee what needs to be accomplished and how much effort will be required for completion. The theory has three main components: (1) specific goals lead to a higher level of performance than do more generalized goals ("do your best"); (2) more difficult goals lead to better performance than do easy goals (provided the individual accepts the goal); and (3) feedback on progress toward the goal enhances performance. Feedback is particularly important because it helps the individual identify the gap between the *real* (the actual performance) and the *ideal* (the desired outcome defined by the goal). Given the trend toward employee empowerment in the workplace, more and more employees are participating in the goal-setting process.

To help employees during the peak 2017 holiday delivery season, UPS, FedEx, and the U.S. Postal Service paid additional overtime to help achieve their goals. UPS even deployed some office personnel to help deliver packages and created team goals to ensure there was cooperation and shared reward with employees from different departments within the organization. The strategy seems to have worked, with UPS reporting an on-time delivery rate of 99.1% for the week before Christmas.[5]

Reinforcement Theory

Reinforcement theory says that behavior is a function of its consequences. In other words, people do things because they know other things will follow. So, depending on what type of consequences follows, people will either practice a behavior or refrain from it. There are three basic types of consequences: positive, negative, and none. In general, we think of positive consequences as rewards, but a **reward** is anything that increases the particular behavior. By contrast, **punishment** is anything that decreases the behavior.

Motivating with the reinforcement theory can be tricky because the theory is functional. All of its components are defined by their function rather than their structure. That is, consequences can operate differently for different people and in different situations. What is considered a punishment by one person may, in fact, be a reward for another. Nonetheless, managers can successfully use reinforcement theory to motivate workers to practice certain behaviors and avoid others. Often, managers use both rewards and punishment to achieve the desired results.

For example, retailers have long needed additional help during peak selling days like Black Friday and Cyber Monday. To help meet these needs, Urban Outfitters recruited salaried workers for a six-hour shift at its new fulfillment facility to help out some of their colleagues and sold the idea to salaried employees as a team-building activity. The workers were offered transportation and paid lunches and asked to wear comfortable shoes. Although it was not mandatory, an Urban Outfitters spokesperson commented: "After successfully opening our new fulfillment center in June, we asked salaried employees at our home office to volunteer for shifts that would help support the new center through a busy month of October. Unsurprisingly, we received a tremendous response, including many of our senior management."[6]

EXPANDING AROUND THE GLOBE

Motivation Is Culture Bound

Most motivation theories in use today were developed in the United States by Americans and about Americans. Of those that were not, many have been strongly influenced by American theories. But several motivation theories do not apply to all cultures. For example, Maslow's theory does not often hold outside the United States. In countries higher on uncertainty avoidance (such as Greece and Japan) as compared with those lower on uncertainty avoidance (such as the United States), security motivates employees more strongly than does self-actualization. Employees in high-uncertainty-avoidance countries often consider job security and lifetime employment more important than holding a more interesting or challenging job. Also contrasting with the American pattern, social needs often dominate the motivation of workers in countries such as Denmark, Norway, and Sweden that stress the quality of life over materialism and productivity.

When researchers tested Herzberg's theory outside the United States, they encountered different results. In New Zealand, for example, supervision and interpersonal relationships appear to contribute significantly to satisfaction and not merely to reducing dissatisfaction. Similarly, researchers found that citizens of Asia, Canada, Europe, Latin America, the Republic of Panama, and the West Indies cited certain extrinsic factors as satisfiers with greater frequency than did their American counterparts. In other words, the factors that motivate U.S. employees may not spark the same motivation in employees in other cultures. Some of the major differences among the cultural groups include the following:

1. English-speaking countries such as England and the United States rank higher on individual achievement and lower on the desire for security.
2. French-speaking countries and areas such as France and the province of Quebec in Canada, although similar to the English-speaking countries, give greater importance to security and somewhat less to challenging work.
3. Northern European countries such as Sweden have less interest in getting ahead and work towards recognition goals and place more emphasis on job accomplishment. In addition, they have more concern for people and less for the organization as a whole (it is important that their jobs not interfere with their personal lives).
4. Latin American and Southern European countries find individual achievement somewhat less important; Southern Europeans place the highest emphasis on job security, whereas both groups of countries emphasize fringe benefits.
5. Germany ranks high on security and fringe benefits and among the highest on getting ahead.
6. Japan, although low on advancement, also ranks second-highest on challenge and lowest on autonomy, with a strong emphasis on good working conditions and a friendly working environment.

Critical Thinking Questions
1. In today's global business environment, with its diversity of perspectives, can a manager ever successfully use equity theory? Why or why not?
2. What impact, if any, do these cultural differences have on managers managing an entirely American workforce? Explain.

Sources: Adapted from Nancy J. Adler and Allison Gunderson, *International Dimensions of Organizational Behavior*, 5th ed. (Cengage Learning, 2008), pp. 174–181; "Motivation across Cultures: Same Value-Different Approach," *Authentic Journeys*, http://blog.authenticjourneys.info, July 10, 2014.

CONCEPT CHECK

1. Discuss the three relationships central to expectancy theory.
2. Explain the comparison process that is a part of equity theory.
3. How does goal-setting theory contribute to our understanding of motivation?
4. What are the main elements of reinforcement theory?

9.7 | From Motivation Theory to Application

7. How can managers redesign existing jobs to increase employee motivation and performance?

The material presented thus far in this chapter demonstrates the wide variety of theorists and research studies that have contributed to our current understanding of employee motivation. Now we turn our attention to more practical matters, to ways that these concepts can be applied in the workplace to meet organizational goals and improve individual performance.

Motivational Job Design

How might managers redesign or modify existing jobs to increase employee motivation and performance? The following three options have been used extensively in the workplace:

- *Job enlargement*. The horizontal expansion of a job, increasing the number and variety of tasks that a person performs, is called **job enlargement**. Increasing task diversity can enhance job satisfaction, particularly when the job is mundane and repetitive in nature. A potential drawback to job enlargement is that employees may perceive that they are being asked to work harder and do more with no change in their level of responsibility or compensation. This can cause resentment and lead to dissatisfaction.
- *Job enrichment*. **Job enrichment** is the vertical expansion of an employee's job. Whereas job enlargement addresses the breadth or scope of a job, enrichment attempts to increase job depth by providing the employee with more autonomy, responsibility, and decision-making authority. In an enriched job, the employee can use a variety of talents and skills and has more control over the planning, execution, and evaluation of the required tasks. In general, job enrichment has been found to increase job satisfaction and reduce absenteeism and turnover.
- *Job rotation*. Also called *cross-training,* **job rotation** is the shifting of workers from one job to another. This may be done to broaden an employee's skill base or because an employee has ceased to be interested in or challenged by a particular job. The organization may benefit from job rotation because it increases flexibility in scheduling and production and because employees can be shifted to cover for absent workers or changes in production or operations. It is also a valuable tool for training lower-level managers in a variety of functional areas. Drawbacks of job rotation include an increase in training costs and decreased productivity while employees are getting "up to speed" in new task areas.

Work-Scheduling Options

As companies try to meet the needs of a diverse workforce and retain quality employees while remaining competitive and financially prosperous, managers are challenged to find new ways to keep workers motivated and satisfied. Increasingly popular are alternatives to the traditional work schedule, such as flextime, compressed workweek, four-day workweek, telecommuting, and job sharing.

One option for employees who want an adjustable schedule is *flextime*, in use at 57 percent of U.S. companies.[7] Flextime allows employees to decide what their work hours will be. Employees are generally expected to work a certain number of hours per week but have some discretion as to when they arrive at work and when they leave for the day.

Another option for employees who want to maximize their leisure hours, indulge in three-day weekends, and avoid commuting during morning and evening rush hours is the *compressed workweek*. Employees work the traditional 40 hours, but fit those hours into a shorter workweek. Most common is the 4-40 schedule, where employees work four 10-hour days a week. Organizations that offer this option claim benefits ranging from increased motivation and productivity to reduced absenteeism and turnover. According to the Society for Human Resource Management, 29 percent of U.S. companies offered employees a compressed workweek in 2017, down from 35 percent in 2013. One of the reasons for the downward trend may be the increasing popularity of a four-day workweek.[8]

In 2017 the Society for Human Resource Management began tracking the popularity of a *four-day workweek*, offered in 13 percent of U.S. companies. In this option, employees work only four days a week, the same as a compressed workweek, but work 32 hours or less. The year before, Amazon announced a pilot project that allows some tech teams in their human resources department to work fewer hours for 75 percent of pay but retain the same benefits as full-time employees. In contrast, Tower Paddle Boards made permanent its pilot of reducing the workday to only five hours for the entire company. Employees retain the same pay and obligations as before so are challenged to be more productive in less time. In addition, the company started a 5 percent profit-sharing plan. Founder Stephan Aarstol says he expected to lose some revenue for a bit, but that didn't happen. Revenue the first year was up 40 percent.[9]

Telecommuting is a work-scheduling option that allows employees to work from home via a computer that is linked with their office, headquarters, or colleagues. Often employers will use a mix of these scheduling options depending on the situation. Jacqueline Pawela-Crew was a group leader in Intel's management engineering unit who worked a compressed schedule. She worked Monday through Thursday, and on two of those days she telecommuted from her home. On the other two days, she worked a flexible schedule, sometimes getting to the office at 6 a.m., so she could be home when her children came home from school. Her former manager, Dan Enloe, was a U.S. Navy reservist and divorced dad, so he also used Intel's flexible schedule to meet his military and family needs.[10] He sees the flexible scheduling as a key motivator for Intel's employees. "I've had workers tell me flat out, they were going to leave Intel if they didn't have the option of some flexibility with their schedules," he says.[11] Ricardo Semler, CEO of Semco, a Brazilian conglomerate with 3,000 employees, sums up flexible work schedules this way: "The essence to us [at Semco] was that people who are free people, who [can act] based on self-interest, who can balance their own lives, are much happier, more productive people. If you take a business call on a Sunday afternoon, for instance, why not go to the movies on a Monday?" Semco's employees not only choose their own schedules, they often choose which part of the business to work for and even how much they'll be paid.[12]

Job sharing is a scheduling option that allows two individuals to split the tasks, responsibilities, and work hours of one 40-hour-per-week job. Though used less frequently than flextime and the compressed workweek, this option can also provide employees with job flexibility. The primary benefit to the company is that it gets "two for the price of one"—the company can draw on two sets of skills and abilities to accomplish one set of job objectives. Mary Kaye Stuart is an account executive at a broadcasting company is Austin, Texas. After her doctor warned her that the stress of her 100-mile commute could shorten her life, she pursued job sharing. She teamed up with a former coworker, and each works three days a week, working together on Wednesdays. "Job sharing is a great solution to keeping people from burning out and preventing turnover," says Melissa Nicholson. She believes in the power of job sharing so much that, after years of doing it herself, she founded Work Muse to help companies set up job-share arrangements. Not all partnerships have been successful, she admits, but when they are, she loves having the ability to be flexible and for the workers to cover each other and support each other. "I'm able to just not think about email or work for four days a week," she said. "That's just an impossibility for most people."[13]

Although each of these work-scheduling options may have some drawbacks for the sponsoring organizations, the benefits far outweigh the problems. The number of companies offering flexible work options has grown, and the trend is expected to continue.

Recognition and Empowerment

All employees have unique needs that they seek to fulfill through their jobs. Organizations must devise a wide array of incentives to ensure that a broad spectrum of employee needs can be addressed in the work environment, thus increasing the likelihood of motivated employees. A sampling of these motivational tools is discussed here.

Formal recognition of superior effort by individuals or groups in the workplace is one way to enhance employee motivation. Recognition serves as positive feedback and reinforcement, letting employees know what they have done well and that their contribution is valued by the organization. Recognition can take many forms, both formal and informal. Some companies use formal awards ceremonies to acknowledge and celebrate their employees' accomplishments. Others take advantage of informal interaction to congratulate employees on a job well done and offer encouragement for the future. Recognition can take the form of a monetary reward, a day off, a congratulatory e-mail, or a verbal "pat on the back." Recognition does not have to come from superiors to be meaningful, however. At The Motley Fool, a financial services company dedicated to helping people invest better, employees use the app YouEarnedIt to recognize the contributions of coworkers. In the app, employees are given "gold" to spend by thanking or complimenting one other along with a statement of what the recipient did to earn it. The recipients cash in the gold for real prizes or gift cards. Employees say this type of recognition may be better than management recognition.[14]

Employee empowerment, sometimes called employee involvement or participative management, involves delegating decision-making authority to employees at all levels of the organization, trusting employees to make the right decision. Employees are given greater responsibility for planning, implementing, and evaluating the results of decisions. Empowerment is based on the premise that human resources, especially at lower levels in the firm, are an underutilized asset. Employees are capable of contributing much more of their skills and abilities to organizational success if they are allowed to participate in the decision-making process and are given access to the resources needed to implement their decisions. Netflix removes obstacles from employees' paths to success by eliminating policies and procedures to show its trust in employee decision-making, including in decisions about expenses and vacations. Netflix hires "fully formed adults" and tells them to use their best judgment to act in the company's best interest. The company believes employees will be more productive if not bound by processes. As a result of following these practices, Netflix is noted among companies 40 percent more productive than others.[15]

Economic Incentives

Any discussion of motivation has to include the use of monetary incentives to enhance performance. Currently, companies are using a variety of variable-pay programs such as piece-rate plans, profit sharing, gain sharing, stock options, and bonuses to encourage employees to be more productive. Unlike the standard salary or hourly wage, variable pay means that a portion of an employee's pay is directly linked to an individual or organizational performance measure. In *piece-rate pay plans,* for example, employees are paid a given amount for each unit they produce, directly linking the amount they earn to their productivity. *Profit-sharing plans* are based on overall company profitability. Using an established formula, management distributes some portion of company profits to all employees. *Gain-sharing plans* are incentive programs based on group productivity. Employees share in the financial gains attributed to the increased productivity of their group. This encourages employees to increase productivity within their specific work area regardless of the overall profit picture for the organization as a whole.

One well-known approach to monetary incentives is the award of *stock options*, or giving employees the right to purchase a given amount of stock at below-market prices. Stock can be a strong motivator because those who receive the options have the chance to make a lot of money. Government tax incentive changes have affected how much equity (stock) companies offer each year, indicating that stock options are declining in popularity.[16]

One popular incentive is the bonus. A *bonus* is simply a one-time lump-sum monetary award. In many cases, employees receive bonuses for achieving a particular performance level, such as meeting or exceeding a sales quota, and it is not uncommon for bonuses to be substantial. Google created a Founders' Award and once gave $12 million in restricted stock to the winners, a huge spot bonus for great work on a project. For line and staff employees, bonuses can add up to 3 to 5 percent of their annual pay; for middle managers, that figure rises to the low double-digit percentage range. For executives, specifically senior executives, bonuses can constitute up to 50 percent of their annual compensation.

That's not to say that small bonuses aren't good motivators. Google discovered the large range in values for the award created jealousy instead of fostering better teamwork. Based on employee input, Google changed from monetary awards to experiential awards, such as gifts and trips, and everyone was happier.[17] "Spot" bonuses allow companies to target employees that impact the bottom line and can help motivate average employees. Sarah Clausen received her first bonus from Dallas-based Associa, a property management company, for overseeing the rollout of video-based town halls. "It really creates a feeling that your work is being valued and appreciated," she says. "It definitely leads me to want to stay here and do a good job."[18]

Regardless of their size, bonuses are replacing the raise as the way companies compensate employees for a job well done and motivate them to perform at even higher levels. That is because bonuses can vary according to outcomes. Financial incentives that allow variability in compensation to reflect an individual employee's contribution are generally known as *pay-for-performance* programs. One of the many companies that use pay-for-performance programs is Allstate, which assigns employees' individual performance one of five grades. The size of an employee's bonus depends on his or her grade. For example, one worker may receive a bonus of 5.5 percent of her annual pay, but the worker in the next cubicle doing the exact same job—though less efficiently or productively—may receive only 2 percent. The pay-for-performance approach can also be used for CEOs. Tesla announced that CEO Elon Musk's compensation could be worth up to $55.8 billion over the next ten years, or nothing. Musk's compensation is tied to the market capitalization of the company.[19] The percentage of annual payroll companies commit for pay-for-performance bonuses has fluctuated slightly in recent years but remains above 12 percent and is expected to continue.[20]

CONCEPT CHECK

1. Explain the difference between job enlargement and job enrichment.
2. What are the four work-scheduling options that can enhance employee performance?
3. Are all employees motivated by the same economic incentives? Explain.

9.8 | Trends in Employee Motivation

8. What initiatives are organizations using today to motivate and retain employees?

This chapter has focused on understanding what motivates people and how employee motivation and satisfaction affect productivity and organizational performance. Organizations can improve performance by investing in people. In reviewing the ways companies are currently choosing to invest in their human resources, we can spot four positive trends: (1) education and training, (2) employee ownership, (3) work-life benefits, and (4) nurturing knowledge workers. All of the companies making *Fortune*'s annual list of the "100 Best Companies to Work For" know the importance of treating employees right. They all have programs that allow them to invest in their employees through programs such as these and many more. Today's businesses also face the challenge of increased costs of absenteeism. This section discusses each of these trends in motivating employees.

Education and Training

Companies that provide educational and training opportunities for their employees reap the benefits of a more motivated, as well as a more skilled, workforce. Employees who are properly trained in new technologies are more productive and less resistant to job change. Education and training provide additional benefits by increasing employees' feelings of competence and self-worth. When companies spend money to upgrade employee knowledge and skills, they convey the message "we value you and are committed to your growth and development as an employee."

CATCHING THE ENTREPRENEURIAL SPIRIT

Everyone's a CFO

Andrew Levine, president of DCI, a New York public relations firm, wanted to implement a more open management style at his company, so he added a financial segment to monthly staff meetings, during which he would share results and trends with his employees. Much to his surprise, employees seemed bored. During one staff meeting he asked his employees how to calculate a profit, and only the receptionist, Sergio Barrios, knew how. Levine was astounded, both at his employees' general deficit in math concepts and at Barrios' knack for figures. Levine then decided to require employees to present the financial reports themselves.

For the next staff meeting, Levine appointed Barrios the chief financial officer (CFO) of the day. Barrios explained the terminology in ways laymen could understand. Since then, Levine has watched his employees become financial whizzes. Each CFO of the day meets with DCI's real CFO for only one day before the meeting. They review income, expenses, and all manner of financial ratios and statements. They discuss revenue projections and general financial trends. The CFO of the day then presents this information at the monthly staff meeting. Maria Mantz, a junior employee, thinks the training is extremely beneficial. "I'm a new, young employee, and I'm being trained not only as a PR executive, but also as a business executive." When Mantz's turn came around, she stood before 30 of her colleagues and began detailing accounts and asking her audience to refer to the revenue table in their handouts. She asked if anyone know what the five clients who showed an increase in activity had in common, and awarded the coworker who knew the answer (they were all performance-based accounts) with a gift card to a local sandwich shop. Then she opened the floor for debate by asking, "Is that a good thing or a bad thing?"

"CFO of the day" has definitely been a good thing for DCI, which has been profitable ever since Levine instituted the program. Employees stay an average of five years, up from two-and-a-half years before the program. And customers are also sticking around longer—the length of the client relationship has doubled to over four years.

Levine has embraced the lessons of open management, or participative management, pioneered by Jack Stack and Springfield Remanufacturing Corporation. Whether the term is CFO for a day, participative or open-book management, or great game of business, the goal is to teach employees about business, thereby engaging them in the business. Companies that embrace these practices believe employees will be more productive if they understand financials and feel like owners. And in the example of DCI, employees are no longer bored during the financial review section of the monthly meeting.

Sources: Peter Carbonara, "Small Business Guide: What Owners Need to Know about Open-Book Management," *Forbes*, https://www.forbes.com, accessed January 19, 2018; Peter Carbonara, "Gaming the System: How a Traditional Manufacturer Opened Its Books and Turned Employees into Millionaires," *Forbes*, https://www.forbes.com, accessed January 19, 2018; Nadine Heintz, "Everyone's a CFO," *Inc.*, https://www.inc.com, accessed January 15, 2018; Bill Fotsch and John Case, "The Business Case for Open-Book Management," *Forbes*, https://www.forbes.com, accessed January 19, 2018; Louis Mosca, "The Dangers of Opening Your Books to Employees," *Forbes*, https://www.forbes.com, accessed January 19, 2018.

Critical Thinking Questions
1. Do you think a CFO-of-the-day program is a good idea for all companies? Why or why not?
2. How comfortable would you be leading the financial discussion at a monthly staff meeting? What could you do to improve your skills in this area?

Employee Ownership

A trend that seems to have leveled off is employee ownership, most commonly implemented as employee stock ownership plans, or *ESOPs*. ESOPs are not the same as stock options, however. In an ESOP, employees receive compensation in the form of company stock. Recall that stock options give employees the opportunity to purchase company stock at a set price, even if the market price of the stock increases above that point. Because ESOP employees are compensated with stock, over time they can become the owners of the company, an attractive exit strategy for current owners seeking a smooth transition. Behind employee ownership programs is the belief that employees who think like owners are more motivated to take care of customers' needs, reduce unnecessary expenses, make operations smoother, and stay with the company longer.

Exhibit 9.8   Companies sometimes create unusual perks to help attract and retain talented workers. Timberland employees receive a $3,000 subsidy to buy a hybrid automobile. Worthington Industries offers workers on-site haircuts for just $4. And at SC Johnson, retirees receive a lifetime membership to the company fitness center. One company even has a beer tap that it offers after 3 p.m. every Friday to get workers off to a relaxing weekend. *What trends are emerging in the ways companies seek to motivate workers and keep them happy on the job?* (Credit: nyuhuhuu/ flickr/ Attribution 2.0 Generic (CC BY 2.0))

According to the National Center for Employee Ownership, there are roughly 6,717 ESOPs in the United States, with a total of 14 million participants.[21] Despite changes in tax laws that resulted in a decrease in the number of publicly traded companies with ESOPs and the closure of dubious plans, the amount of stock held by ESOPs continues to increase.[22] Multiple studies over 30 years conclude definitively that employee ownership results in a powerful competitive tool when combined with participative management.[23]

ESOPs, however, also have drawbacks. The biggest concern is that some employees have so much of their nest eggs tied to their company's ESOP. If the company's performance starts to decline, they risk losing a significant portion of their wealth. This is what happened at Piggly Wiggly Carolina, a chain of grocery stores. Business started to decline. Employee and retirees watched as senior management made decisions to raise prices and then sell stores. The share value started declining each year, losing 90 percent of its value, until employees received notice the company did not have enough value to pay distributions that year. The notice stated that trustees planned to continue selling assets in the hope of making future payments. Former employees filed a lawsuit alleging senior management decisions resulted in lining their own pockets at the cost of the company's value.[24]

Still, many companies successfully implement ESOPs. Axia Home Loans, a national residential mortgage lender based in Seattle, experienced record-breaking production and was able to attract top talent in the first year after creating its ESOP. After taking questions from non-managing shareholders about exit strategies, Gellert Dornay, president and CEO, looked into an ESOP and thought it would fit with the company's innovative and forward-thinking culture. "Studies show that employee-owned companies experience increased employee satisfaction, retention, and productivity gains," Dornay said, adding, "an ESOP rewards employees who contribute to the company's success by allowing them to share in the company's future increase in value."[25]

So what enables one company with an ESOP, such as Axia Home Loans, to be more successful than another, such as Piggly Wiggly? It has a lot to do with the way companies treat employees. You can't just call an employee an owner and expect them to respond positively. You have to do something to make them feel like an owner and then involve them as owners. Piggly Wiggly illustrates that employee ownership is not a magic elixir. "When employees run the company, our decision methodology is different. Everything is in the primary best interest of the shareholders, who are the employees," Dornay said.[26]

Work-Life Benefits

In another growing trend in the workplace, companies are helping their employees to manage the numerous and sometimes competing demands in their lives. Organizations are taking a more active role in helping employees achieve a balance between their work responsibilities and their personal obligations. The desired result is employees who are less stressed, better able to focus on their jobs, and, therefore, more productive. One tool companies are using to help their employees achieve work-life balance is the sabbatical. Sabbaticals can be traced back to the need for an incentive that would attract potential faculty members to Harvard University in the late 1800s. Today, sabbaticals can mean time off of a month or more, paid or unpaid. In today's business environment, companies are juggling cutting costs and increasing profits while simultaneously battling to keep employees motivated and positive about work. Sabbaticals can be an important tool to help managers achieve this balancing act.

Reports vary on whether the use of sabbaticals is rising or declining, but all agree that everyone benefits when employees take them.[27] One benefit is that employees return refreshed and recharged. Morris Financial Concepts, Inc., a small financial planning firm, offers all full-time employees a paid, month-long sabbatical every five years. Kyra Morris, president and owner, says employees were working during vacations, even when discouraged not to. They are required to unplug during sabbaticals. Morris says sabbaticals work for both millennials and older employees and are a great recruiting tool.[28] Zillow, the online real estate giant, offers six-week half-paid sabbaticals to employees at all levels of the organization after six years. Amy Bohutinsky, Zillow Group's chief operating officer, says the company wants to reward long-term employees, encourage them to have a life outside of work, and have them come back recharged.[29] Another benefit is the opportunity to learn new skills, which can be an alternative to layoffs. Buffer, a social media management platform, avoided laying off an employee by creating a 12-week, in-house sabbatical at 50 percent pay for him to learn new skills—skills the company needed—to successfully transition into another department. Learning sabbaticals fit the company's value of self-improvement.[30]

Nurturing Knowledge and Learning Workers

Most organizations have specialized workers, and managing them all effectively is a big challenge. In many companies, knowledge workers may have a supervisor, but they are not "subordinates." They are "associates." Within their area of knowledge, they are supposed to do the telling. Because knowledge is effective only if specialized, knowledge workers are not homogeneous, particularly the fast-growing group of knowledge technologists such as computer systems specialists, lawyers, programmers, and others. And because knowledge work is specialized, it is deeply splintered.

A knowledge-based workforce is qualitatively different from a less-skilled workforce. Increasingly, the success—indeed, the survival—of every business will depend on the performance of its knowledge workforce. The challenging part of managing knowledge workers is finding ways to motivate proud, skilled professionals to share expertise and cooperate in such a way that they advance the frontiers of their knowledge to the benefit of the shareholders and society in general. To achieve that auspicious goal, several companies have created what they call "communities of practice."

Exhibit 9.9   Employers seeking to stem the rising tide of absenteeism are developing innovative, flexible benefits for their employees. SC Johnson offers workers on-site childcare, an in-house doctor, and paternity leave. Prudential allows employees to take time off to care for sick children and elderly parents. Hewlett-Packard boasts a range of flexible work options to fit employees' hectic lives. *Do flexible options and benefits adequately address the root causes of absenteeism?* (Credit: MarylandGovPics/ flickr/ Attribution 2.0 Generic (CC BY 2.0))

Coping with the Rising Costs of Absenteeism

With today's companies trying to do more work with fewer employees, managers must be attentive to two major trends that affect the performance and morale of their employees: absenteeism and turnover. According to the Bureau of Labor Statistics, the absence rate for full-time workers has remained relatively steady in recent years, slightly below 3 percent, for absences due to the employee's own illness, injury, or medical problems; child care problems; other family or personal obligations; civic or military duty; and maternity or paternity leave.[31] Every day almost 3 percent of the full-time workforce does not show up for work, and this costs companies billions per year.[32] However, not all reasons for unscheduled absences are genuine. CareerBuilder, a global end-to-end human capital solutions company, reports that 40 percent of unscheduled absences in 2017 were due to employees calling in sick when not. The top two reasons employees gave were a doctor's appointment and just didn't feel like going to work. Needing to relax, needing to catch up on sleep, running errands, catching up on housework, and plans with family and friends were also listed.[33]

While some employees are taking a day off, employees covering for unscheduled absences are pushed to do more. The result is lower productivity and lower morale, especially if chronic absenteeism is not addressed. In addition to an attendance policy, offering incentives for attendance, wellness programs, employee assistance programs, and other benefits that show care for employees can lower absenteeism rates.[34]

MANAGING CHANGE

Using Communities of Practice to Motivate Knowledge Workers

Communities of practice (CoP) have been so named since the early 1990s as a way to motivate knowledge workers. One company that has experienced tremendous success with CoPs is Schlumberger Limited, an oil-field-services company with nearly $28 billion in annual revenue. As with all CoPs, what Schlumberger calls Eureka groups are comprised of similar professional employees from across the entire organization. Employees participate in one or more of 284 Eureka groups ranging from chemistry to oil-well engineering.

Before the establishment of the communities, Schlumberger's engineers, physicists, and geologists worked well on individual projects, but the company was ignorant of how to help its employees develop the professional sides of their lives. Since the company sells services and expertise, motivating and cultivating its knowledge workers was a critical success factor. Former CEO Euan Baird felt he had tried everything to manage and motivate the company's technical professionals—and failed. That's when he decided to let them manage themselves. He ordered Schulmberger veteran Henry Edmundson to implement communities of practice.

Schlumberger's Eureka communities have been a tremendous success and helped the company leverage its knowledge assets. Today, self-created CVs are posted on the company's internal website, allowing employees across the 85 countries where the company operates to consult the résumé of nearly every company employee to find someone with a particular area of knowledge or expertise. Another reason the Eureka groups are so successful is that they are completely democratic. Participating employees vote on who will lead each community. An employee who is backed by his or her manager and at least one other community member can run for a term of office that lasts one year. The elected leaders of Schlumberger's Eureka communities cost the company about $1 million a year. "Compared with other knowledge initiatives, it's a cheapie," said Edmundson.

John Afilaka, a geological engineer who was a Schlumberger business-development manager in Nigeria, stood for election to the head of the company's rock-characterization community, a group of more than 1,000 people who are experts in determining what might be in an underground reservoir. He beat an opponent and spent 15 to 20 percent of his time organizing the group's annual conference and occasional workshops, overseeing the group's website, coordinating subgroups, and so forth.

Retired CEO Andrew Gould says the self-governing feature is crucial to the Eureka communities' success. Technical professionals are often motivated by peer review and peer esteem, he says, implying that stock options and corner offices aren't sufficient. The election of leaders, he says, "ensures the integrity of peer judgments."

Schlumberger's use of CoPs is known worldwide. The company has been cited a dozen times in the European MAKE (Most Admired Knowledge Enterprises) study and declared the overall winner three times, most recently in 2017.

Critical Thinking Questions

1. How do you think communities of practice help companies like Schlumberger manage in dynamic

business environments?

2. Although communities of practice are commonly thought of in regard to knowledge workers, could they successfully motivate other employees as well? Why do you think as you do?

Sources: Rory L. Chase, "2017 European Most Admired Knowledge Enterprises MAKE Report," *Teleos—The KNOW Network*, http://www.theknowledgebusiness.com, accessed January 24, 2018; "Schlumberger Cited for Knowledge Management," https://www.slb.com, accessed January 24, 2018; "2016 Annual Report," Schlumberger Limited, 2017; "John Afilaka," https://www.zoominfo.com, accessed January 24, 2018; "RezFlo Services Company Limited," http://www.rezflo.com/, accessed January 24, 2018; Olivia Pulsinelli, "Reemerged Energy Co. Hires Halliburton Exec, Names Former Energy CEOs to Board," *Houston Business Journal*, https://www.bizjournals.com, accessed January 24, 2018.

Another trend related to employee morale and absenteeism is turnover. The number of employees who are job-searching is on the rise. A recent Gallup survey found that 51 percent of current employees are looking to leave their current job, but an IBM survey found only 16 percent are actively seeking new employment.[35] Both figures are great cause for concern. A high rate of turnover can be expensive and dampen the morale of other employees who watch their colleagues leave the company. The biggest reasons behind increasing turnover rates: career opportunities elsewhere and to get away from a bad manager.[36]

High rates of turnover (or absenteeism) at the management level can be destabilizing for employees, who need to develop specific strategies to manage a steady flow of new bosses. High rates of turnover (or absenteeism) at the employee level compromises the company's ability to perform at its highest levels. In order to stay competitive, companies need to have programs in place to motivate employees to come to work each day and to stay with the company year after year.

CONCEPT CHECK

1. What benefits can an organization derive from training and educational opportunities and stock ownership programs?
2. Why are sabbaticals growing in popularity as work-life balance tools?
3. How are knowledge workers different from traditional employees?
4. Why are absenteeism and turnover rates increasing, and what is the impact on companies?

🔑 Key Terms

equity theory A theory of motivation that holds that worker satisfaction is influenced by employees' perceptions about how fairly they are treated compared with their coworkers.

expectancy theory A theory of motivation that holds that the probability of an individual acting in a particular way depends on the strength of that individual's belief that the act will have a particular outcome and on whether the individual values that outcome.

goal-setting theory A theory of motivation based on the premise that an individual's intention to work toward a goal is a primary source of motivation.

Hawthorne effect The phenomenon that employees perform better when they feel singled out for attention or feel that management is concerned about their welfare.

hygiene factors Extrinsic elements of the work environment that do not serve as a source of employee satisfaction or motivation.

job enlargement The horizontal expansion of a job by increasing the number and variety of tasks that a person performs.

job enrichment The vertical expansion of a job by increasing the employee's autonomy, responsibility, and decision-making authority.

job rotation The shifting of workers from one job to another; also called cross-training.

job sharing A scheduling option that allows two individuals to split the tasks, responsibilities, and work hours of one 40-hour-per-week job.

Maslow's hierarchy of needs A theory of motivation developed by Abraham Maslow; holds that humans have five levels of needs and act to satisfy their unmet needs. At the base of the hierarchy are fundamental physiological needs, followed in order by safety, social, esteem, and self-actualization needs.

motivating factors Intrinsic job elements that lead to worker satisfaction.

motivation Something that prompts a person to release his or her energy in a certain direction.

need The gap between what is and what is required.

punishment Anything that decreases a specific behavior.

reinforcement theory A theory of motivation that holds that people do things because they know that certain consequences will follow.

reward Anything that increases a specific behavior.

scientific management A system of management developed by Frederick W. Taylor and based on four principles: developing a scientific approach for each element of a job, scientifically selecting and training workers, encouraging cooperation between workers and managers, and dividing work and responsibility between management and workers according to who can better perform a particular task.

Theory X A management style, formulated by Douglas McGregor, that is based on a pessimistic view of human nature and assumes that the average person dislikes work, will avoid it if possible, prefers to be directed, avoids responsibility, and wants security above all.

Theory Y A management style, formulated by Douglas McGregor, that is based on a relatively optimistic view of human nature; assumes that the average person wants to work, accepts responsibility, is willing to help solve problems, and can be self-directed and self-controlled.

Theory Z A theory developed by William Ouchi that combines U.S. and Japanese business practices by emphasizing long-term employment, slow career development, moderate specialization, group decision-making, individual responsibility, relatively informal control over the employee, and concern for workers.

want The gap between what is and what is desired.

🗐 Summary of Learning Outcomes

9.1 Early Theories of Motivation

1. What are the basic principles of Frederick Taylor's concept of scientific management?

Scientific management is based on the belief that employees are motivated by economic incentives and that there is "one best way" to perform any job. The four basic principles of scientific management developed by Taylor are as follows:

1. Develop a scientific approach for each element of a person's job.
2. Scientifically select, train, teach, and develop workers.
3. Encourage cooperation between workers and managers so that each job can be accomplished in a standard, scientifically determined way.
4. Divide work and responsibility between management and workers according to who is better suited to each task.

9.2 The Hawthorne Studies

2. What did Elton Mayo's Hawthorne studies reveal about worker motivation?

The pride that comes from special attention motivates workers to increase their productivity. Supervisors who allow employees to have some control over their situation appeared to further increase the workers' motivation. The Hawthorne effect suggests that employees will perform better when they feel singled out for special attention or feel that management is concerned about employee welfare.

9.3 Maslow's Hierarchy of Needs

3. What is Maslow's hierarchy of needs, and how do these needs relate to employee motivation?

Maslow believed that each individual has a hierarchy of needs, consisting of physiological, safety, social, esteem, and self-actualization needs. Managers who accept Maslow's ideas attempt to increase employee motivation by modifying organizational and managerial practices to increase the likelihood that employees will meet all levels of needs. Maslow's theory has also helped managers understand that it is hard to motivate people by appealing to already-satisfied needs.

9.4 McGregor's Theories X and Y

4. How are McGregor's Theories X and Y and Ouchi's Theory Z used to explain worker motivation?

Douglas McGregor influenced the study of motivation with his formulation of two contrasting sets of assumptions about human nature—designated Theory X and Theory Y. Theory X says people don't like to work and will avoid it if they can. Because people don't like to work, they must be controlled, directed, or threatened to get them to make an effort. Theory Y says that people want to be self-directed and will try to accomplish goals that they believe in. Workers can be motivated with positive incentives. McGregor personally believed that Theory Y assumptions describe most employees and that managers seeking to motivate subordinates should develop management practices based on those assumptions.

William Ouchi's Theory Z combines U.S. and Japanese business practices. Theory Z emphasizes long-term employment, slow career development, and group decision-making. The long-term decline of the Japanese economy has resulted in most U.S. firms moving away from Japanese management practices.

9.5 Herzberg's Motivator-Hygiene Theory

5. What are the basic components of Herzberg's motivator-hygiene theory?

Frederick Herzberg's studies indicated that certain job factors are consistently related to employee job satisfaction whereas others can create job dissatisfaction. According to Herzberg, motivating factors (also called satisfiers) are primarily intrinsic job elements that lead to satisfaction, such as achievement, recognition, the (nature of) work itself, responsibility, advancement, and growth. What Herzberg termed hygiene factors (also called dissatisfiers) are extrinsic elements of the work environment such as company policy, relationships with supervisors, working conditions, relationships with peers and subordinates, salary and benefits, and job security. These are factors that can result in job dissatisfaction if not well managed. One of the most interesting results of Herzberg's studies was the implication that the opposite of satisfaction is not dissatisfaction. Herzberg believed that proper management of hygiene factors could prevent employee dissatisfaction, but that these factors could not serve as a source of satisfaction or motivation.

9.6 Contemporary Views on Motivation

6. What four contemporary theories on employee motivation offer insights into improving employee performance?

According to expectancy theory, the probability of an individual acting in a particular way depends on the strength of that individual's belief that the act will have a particular outcome and on whether the individual values that outcome. Equity theory is based on individuals' perceptions about how fairly they are treated compared with their coworkers. Goal-setting theory states that employees are highly motivated to perform when specific goals are established and feedback on progress is offered. Reinforcement theory states that behavior is a function of consequences; that is, people do things because they know other things will follow.

9.7 From Motivation Theory to Application

7. How can managers redesign existing jobs to increase employee motivation and performance?

The horizontal expansion of a job, which involves increasing the number and variety of tasks that a person performs, is called job enlargement. Increasing task diversity can enhance job satisfaction, particularly when the job is mundane and repetitive in nature. Job enrichment is the vertical expansion of an employee's job to provide the employee with more autonomy, responsibility, and decision-making authority. Other popular motivational tools include work-scheduling options, employee-recognition programs, empowerment, and variable-pay programs.

9.8 Trends in Employee Motivation

8. What initiatives are organizations using today to motivate and retain employees?

Today firms are using several key tactics to motivate and retain workers. First, companies are investing more in employee education and training, which makes employees more productive and confident in their jobs. Second, managers are giving employees the opportunity to participate in the ownership of the company, which can strongly increase employee commitment. Employers are providing more work-life benefits to employees, and a small but growing percentage of companies is offering employees paid sabbaticals in addition to regular vacation and sick time. As the composition of the workforce changes, it is becoming increasingly important for companies to understand how to manage knowledge workers. One method of doing this is establishing communities of practice that enable workers to share expertise across the organization. Finally, managers in today's business environment need to pay special attention to managing absence rates and employee (and management) turnover.

Preparing for Tomorrow's Workplace Skills

1. Are you motivated more by intrinsic rewards (satisfaction, sense of accomplishment, etc.) or by extrinsic

rewards (money, bonuses, etc.)? Interview some friends and classmates to find out what motivates them. Discuss your differences in perspective. (Interpersonal, Information)

2. Think of a task or project you have completed recently that required a great deal of effort. What motivated you to exert so much energy to complete the task or project? Describe your motivation in terms of the theories presented in the chapter. (Systems)

3. Not all jobs are intrinsically motivating. For example, many entry-level jobs often involve repetitive and simple tasks that can become rapidly boring. (You may have worked a job that fits that description.) How can managers motivate frontline employees (such as fast-food cashiers, trash collectors, supermarket cashiers, etc.) to perform at high levels? (Systems, Interpersonal)

4. If you were offered the opportunity to job-share, would you need to have a partner who was motivated by the same things as you are? Why or why not? (Interpersonal)

5. **Team Activity** Assemble a team of three to five students. Imagine that you are the management team for a start-up business with limited resources but a need for a highly motivated, skilled workforce. Brainstorm ways you could motivate your employees other than large bonuses and high salaries. (Resources)

Ethics Activity

You join a large bank that encourages and promotes employee volunteerism, allowing employees one day a month, or up to 12 days a year, to volunteer for a cause of their choosing. Shortly after you start working there as a junior teller, your boss's wife is diagnosed with a particularly aggressive form of breast cancer that carries a very poor prognosis. Realizing it will win you kudos with your boss, you choose the local chapter of the Susan G. Komen for the Cure foundation—a breast cancer charity that sponsors an annual Race for the Cure—for your company-sponsored volunteer work.

In addition to working at the foundation's office one day a month, you spend your own time actively soliciting other staffers at your firm to sign up for the charity walk in a few months' time. Impressed with your qualities of tireless dedication, your boss puts your name forward for promotion to junior bank officer, well before the customary two years of service normally required for being considered for promotion.

Using a web search tool, locate articles about this topic and then write responses to the following questions. Be sure to support your arguments and cite your sources.

Ethical Dilemma: Your company is generous in its approach to employee volunteerism. It gives you paid time off, and you acquire enhanced job skills through your volunteer activities. Have you just been smart in recognizing the value of volunteering for a charity that you know will earn your boss's personal appreciation? Or are you taking unfair advantage of your boss's vulnerability and manipulating the situation?

Working the Net

1. Looking for 1,001 ways to motivate or reward your employees? Bob Nelson can help. Visit his Nelson Motivation site at **http://www.nelson-motivation.com** to get some ideas you can put to use to help you do a better job, either as a manager or as an employee.

2. Some companies offer their employees stock ownership plans. To learn the differences between an ESOP and stock options, visit the National Center for Employee Ownership (NCEO) at **http://www.nceo.org** and the Foundation for Enterprise Development (FED) at **http://www.fed.org**. Which stock plan would you rather have? Why?

3. Open-book management is one of the better-known ways to create a participatory work environment. Over 2,000 companies have adopted this practice, which involves sharing financial information with nonmanagement employees and training them to understand financial information. Does it really motivate employees and improve productivity? The NCEO website, **http://www.nceo.org**, has a number of articles on open-book management. Read several of the articles to get more insight into this practice, and then develop your answers to this question.

4. You've been asked to develop a staff recognition program for your company but don't have a clue where to start. Three sites with articles and other useful information are *Incentive* magazine, **http://www.incentivemag.com**, the National Association for Employee Recognition, **http://www.recognition.org**, and the U.S. Office of Personnel Management, **https://www.opm.gov**. Using the material you'll find there, outline the plan you would recommend for your company.

5. You have two great job opportunities. Both are equally attractive in terms of job content and offer the same salary. However, one offers year-end bonuses, whereas the other includes stock options for employees. How do you compare the offers? Learn how to evaluate stock options at the Money section of How Stuff Works, **https://money.howstuffworks.com**. Prepare a comparison of bonuses versus stock options, and determine which appeals to you more. Explain your reasons.

6. Use a search engine to find companies that offer "work-life benefits." Link to several companies and review their employee programs in this area. How do they compare? Which benefits would be most important to you if you were job hunting, and why?

Critical Thinking Case

Motivating Employees: A Monster of a Problem

As mentioned in earlier, U.S. businesses will face a decrease in the available workforce due in part to a smaller generation of talented workers replacing retiring baby boomers. "Our study reveals that recruiters and hiring managers are not only cognizant of the issue but are concerned about its current and future impact on organizational growth," said Dr. Jesse Harriott, former vice president of research at monster.com (**http://www.monster.com**), one of the leading global online career and recruitment resources. "Businesses of all sizes and across all industries must develop and implement creative programs and strategies to attract and hire top candidates while retaining and motivating current employees. As the talent pool shrinks, it is imperative that immediate action is taken to ensure businesses are properly prepared and staffed for the future."

In a sampling of over 600 human resource managers, Monster's survey showed that over 75 percent believe compensation is one of the top three motivators that prevent employees from leaving their job. The fact that money motivates top-performing employees is supported by almost half the human resources professionals surveyed for a Rewards Program and Incentive Compensation Survey released by the Society of Human Resource Management. The survey also found that neither monetary nor nonmonetary rewards were effective motivators for underperformers.

While compensation is clearly a significant issue, not all companies can offer this advantage. Other strategies that motivate employee loyalty and commitment are necessary. Some of these include making supervisors more accountable for worker retention, promoting work-life balance for employees, fostering a workplace where employee expectations are clearly articulated, creating learning and development programs that groom employees for future management roles, implementing performance-based systems that identify and proactively manage top employees and when possible promote from within, creating mentoring programs that match new employees with seasoned veterans, monitoring sentiment throughout the employee life cycle, and creating an employment brand "experience" that not only motivates and energizes employees but can also be used to attract new talent.

Diana Pohly, president, CEO, and owner of The Pohly Company, keeps vigilant watch over the morale of the office, ensuring that employees are satisfied. "Business owners of growing companies must possess strong leadership and management skills in order to solidify the foundation of their business," said Pohly. "Effective team leadership is imperative to sustain efficient team workflows and contribute to employee morale."

"Employees are the lifeblood of any organization. Building a positive work environment is an important strategy in attracting, retaining and motivating a team," says Michelle Swanda, corporate marketing manager of The Principal. Improving employee morale with creative and effective management tactics ultimately boosts employee productivity, and that goes straight to the bottom line.

Critical Thinking Questions

1. How are social and economic factors influencing companies' approach to hiring, motivating, and retaining employees?
2. What are some of the nonmonetary strategies companies must develop to attract and reward employees and keep them motivated?
3. What "reward factors" would be important to you when working for a company? List at least five in order of importance, and list your reasons for each.

Sources: "Company Overview of Globoforce Group plc," https://www.bloomberg.com, accessed January 24, 2018; "Diana Pohly," The Pohly Company, https://www.pohlyco.com, accessed January 24, 2018; "Michelle Swanson," *Zoom Info*, https://www.zoominfo.com, accessed January 24, 2018; "70 Percent of HR Managers Concerned about Workforce Retention, According to Monster Study," *Business Wire,* Jan 9, 2006, http://www.findarticles.com; "Poll Says Top-Performing Workers Motivated By Money," *Nation's Restaurant News,* April 25, 2005, http://www.findarticles.com; "Team Motivation: Women Business Owners Increase Productivity Through Effective Leadership," *Business Wire,* Oct 27, 2005, http://www.findarticles.com.

Hot Links Address Book

1. What makes a company a good place to work? Find out by reading about the companies on *Fortune* magazine's "100 Best Companies to Work For" at **http://www.fortune.com**.
2. Expand your knowledge about motivation in the workplace at Accel-Team's site, **http://dheise.andrews.edu/Content/leadership/comps/6b/1biblio/accel-team.htm**
3. How do you keep employees satisfied? The Business Research Lab has a series of tips and articles, which you'll find at the Articles & Stories page of **http://busreslab.com**.
4. For many resources to help motivate, reward, and retain employees, visit https://www.thebalance.com/employee-motivation-4073608.
5. Wish you could have flexible hours? For advice on making this wish come true, visit this Career Planning page on flextime, https://www.thebalance.com/flextime-hours-and-benefits-1177979.
6. Association for Training Development is a professional association and leading resource on workplace learning and performance issues. Visit its site, https://www.td.org/, to learn more about it and these topics.

Exhibit 10.1 (Credit: U.S. Geological Survey / flickr/ Attribution 2.0 Generic (CC BY 2.0))

 # Introduction

Learning Outcomes

After reading this chapter, you should be able to answer these questions:

1. Why is production and operations management important in both manufacturing and service firms?
2. What types of production processes do manufacturers and service firms use?
3. How do organizations decide where to put their production facilities? What choices must be made in designing the facility?
4. Why are resource-planning tasks such as inventory management and supplier relations critical to production?
5. How do operations managers schedule and control production?
6. How can quality-management and lean-manufacturing techniques help firms improve production and operations management?
7. What roles do technology and automation play in manufacturing and service-industry operations management?
8. What key trends are affecting the way companies manage production and operations?

EXPLORING BUSINESS CAREERS

Deborah Butler, Caterpillar

Deborah Butler is a certified Master Black Belt, but don't expect to see her working with Jet Li anytime soon. In fact, her job has little to do with martial arts. Employed by Caterpillar, "the world's leading manufacturer of construction and mining equipment, diesel and natural gas engines, and industrial gas turbines," Butler's Master Black Belt status reflects her expertise in Six Sigma, the process Caterpillar employees use to continually manage, improve, and create processes, products, and services. "Sigma" refers to the maximum number of defects tolerated in production or service delivery; Six Sigma is the highest level of quality control, demanding no more than 3.4 defects per million parts. That means if you were to use Six Sigma in your college career, you would miss only *one half of a single question* in over four years of test-taking!

Caterpillar was the first corporation to take Six Sigma global, deploying it corporate-wide in 2001 not only to its almost 300 facilities, but also eventually to every dealer and more than 850 key suppliers throughout the world. The corporation hails the process as a key element of its overall operations management, attributing increased profits, improved customer service, and supply-chain efficiency to Six Sigma.

Caterpillar's more than 300 Master Black Belts lead projects that use Six Sigma and train the company's approximately 3,300 Black Belts in the principles of the process. Butler is currently in charge of updating and implementing *Our Values in Action: Caterpillar's Worldwide Code of Conduct*. Outlining the four core values of integrity, excellence, teamwork, and commitment, the updated code of conduct embodies two important aspects of Caterpillar's philosophy on Six Sigma.

Sigma is a Greek letter that represents a statistical unit of measurement and defines standard deviation. Caterpillar uses this standard deviation for the number of errors in a product, which equates to 3.4 errors per million. Six Sigma is designed to reduce the number of errors in a process by a step-by-step approach. Caterpillar uses the Six Sigma methodology that utilizes the process of gathering information, analyzing the data, and then making decisions based on the facts. This process ensures that Caterpillar is meeting the requirements of the customer.

Caterpillar recognizes that employees are the heart of any operation. Therefore, Caterpillar employees use Six Sigma to improve as people and as workers as much as to improve the products they produce. The core values, reflected in a series of action statements such as "We put Integrity in action when we compete fairly," are the product of a yearlong development process involving Butler's global team. As part of the project research, the team interviewed thousands of Caterpillar employees, from officers of the company to production and hourly workers, for the purpose of, as Butler says, "bringing to the surface the values that have made Caterpillar a successful enterprise, enhancing behavioral expectations, and accurately expressing Caterpillar's corporate culture."

Caterpillar is not content simply to produce *Our Values in Action* and leave it at that, however, and the second aspect of its Six Sigma philosophy is that employees must bring the process to their lives. Butler has worked to inject the code of conduct's values into employees' day-to-day work. If an employee writes about safety-related changes, for example, she would not just list the changes. Instead, she might write first: "According to Our Values In Action, we put Commitment in action when we protect the health and safety of others and ourselves. As such, we are implementing the following changes. . . ." In this way, the code becomes a living part of corporate culture, a critical component of operations management.

Sources: Heather McBroom, "6 Sigma: Foundation for Quality at Caterpillar," *Peoria Magazine*, http://www.peoriamagazines.com, accessed February 20, 2018; John Gillett, Ross Fink, and Nick Bevington, "How Caterpillar Uses 6 Sigma to Execute Strategy," *Strategic Finance Magazine*, http://sfmagazine.com, accessed February 20, 2018; company website, "Christopher Six Sigma Black

Belt," https://www.caterpillar.com, accessed February 20, 2018.

Nearly every type of business organization needs to find the most efficient and effective methods of producing the goods or services it sells to its customers. Technological advances, ongoing competition, and consumer expectations force companies to rethink where, when, and how they will produce products or services.

Manufacturers have discovered that it is no longer enough to simply push products through the factory and onto the market. Consumers demand high quality at reasonable prices. They also expect manufacturers to deliver products in a timely manner. Firms that can't meet these expectations often face strong competition from businesses that can. To compete, many manufacturers are streamlining how they make their products—by automating their factories, developing new production processes, focusing on quality-control techniques, and improving relationships with suppliers.

Service organizations also face challenges. Their customers are demanding better service, shorter waiting periods, and more individualized attention. Like manufacturers, service companies are using new methods to deliver what their customers need and want. Banks, for example, are using technology such as online banking and mobile apps to make their services more accessible to customers. Colleges offer online courses to accommodate the schedules of working students. Tax services file tax returns via the cloud.

This chapter examines how manufacturers and service firms manage and control the creation of products and services. We'll discuss production planning, including the choices firms must make concerning the type of production process they will use; the location where production will occur; the design of the facility; and the management of resources needed in production. Next, we'll explain routing and scheduling, two critical tasks for controlling production and operations efficiency. Then we will look at how firms can improve production and operations by employing quality management and lean-manufacturing techniques. Finally, we will review some of the trends affecting production and operations management.

10.1 Production and Operations Management—An Overview

1. Why is production and operations management important in both manufacturing and service firms?

Production, the creation of products and services, is an essential function in every firm. Production turns inputs, such as natural resources, raw materials, human resources, and capital, into outputs, which are products and services. This process is shown in Exhibit 10.3. Managing this conversion process is the role of **operations management**.

Exhibit 10.2   With new oil reserves now available through "fracking," the United States is challenging Saudi Arabia and is set to become a vast supplier of oil worldwide. Unlike the smooth petroleum that gushes from Arabian wells, however, America's black gold in the Marcellus, Bakken, and other shale regions has to be drilled horizontally through new technology. The process is rigorous: oil and gas companies drill into the ground to extract crude oil and natural gas from the shale rock that lies thousands of feet under the ground. Once the formation is reached, gallons of water, sand, and an extensive list of man-made chemicals are injected into the well under high pressure. This combination inserted in the well will fracture the rock and release crude oil and natural gas. It is estimated that the gas within these rock formations could supply the United States for generations to come as technologies evolve to drill below the earth's surface. *What are key inputs in the fracking process?* (Credit: Mark Dixon/ Flickr/ Attribution 2.0 Generic (CC BY 2.0))

The goal of customer satisfaction is an important part of effective production and operations. In the past, the manufacturing function in most companies was inwardly focused. Manufacturing had little contact with customers and didn't always understand their needs and desires. In the 1980s, many U.S. industries, such as automotive, steel, and electronics, lost customers to foreign competitors because their production systems could not provide the quality customers demanded. As a result, today most American companies, both large and small, consider a focus on quality to be a central component of effective operations management.

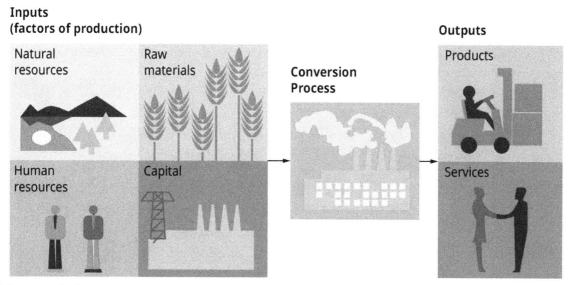

Exhibit 10.3   Production Process for Products and Services (Attribution: Copyright Rice University, OpenStax, under CC BY 4.0 license.)

Stronger links between marketing and manufacturing also encourage production managers to be more outwardly focused and to consider decisions in light of their effect on customer satisfaction. Service companies find that making operating decisions with customer satisfaction in mind can be a competitive advantage.

Operations managers, the people charged with managing and supervising the conversion process, play a vital role in today's firm. They control about three-fourths of a firm's assets, including inventories, wages, and benefits. They also work closely with other major divisions of the firm, such as marketing, finance, accounting, and human resources, to ensure that the firm produces its goods profitably and satisfies its customers. Marketing personnel help them decide which products to make or which services to offer. Accounting and human resources help them face the challenge of combining people and resources to produce high-quality goods on time and at reasonable cost. They are involved in the development and design of goods and determine what production processes will be most effective.

Production and operations management involve three main types of decisions, typically made at three different stages:

1. *Production planning.* The first decisions facing operations managers come at the *planning stage.* At this stage, managers decide where, when, and how production will occur. They determine site locations and obtain the necessary resources.
2. *Production control.* At this stage, the decision-making process focuses on controlling quality and costs, scheduling, and the actual day-to-day operations of running a factory or service facility.
3. *Improving production and operations.* The final stage of operations management focuses on developing more efficient methods of producing the firm's goods or services.

All three decisions are ongoing and may occur simultaneously. In the following sections, we will take a closer look at the decisions and considerations firms face in each stage of production and operations management.

Gearing Up: Production Planning

An important part of operations management is **production planning**. Production planning allows the firm to consider the competitive environment and its own strategic goals to find the best production methods. Good production planning has to balance goals that may conflict, such as providing high-quality service while keeping operating costs low, or keeping profits high while maintaining adequate inventories of finished products. Sometimes accomplishing all these goals is difficult.

Exhibit 10.4   From its storied creation in post-war Italy to its big-screen immortalization in movies such as *Roman Holiday* and *Quadrophenia*, the Vespa scooter has a reputation for romance, rebellion, and style. Manufactured by Italy's Piaggio Group, the Vespa's svelte, stainless-steel chassis and aeronautic-inspired designs are seen everywhere in Europe and more and more in the United States. The Piaggio Group presently operates factories in Italy, Vietnam, India, and China. *What important production-planning decisions does Piaggio need to make as it considers expanding into more overseas markets?* (Credit: Steve Watkins/ Flickr/ Attribution-2.0 Generic (CC BY2.0))

Production planning involves three phases. Long-term planning has a time frame of three to five years. It focuses on which goods to produce, how many to produce, and where they should be produced. Medium-term planning decisions cover about two years. They concern the layout of factory or service facilities, where and how to obtain the resources needed for production, and labor issues. Short-term planning, within a one-year time frame, converts these broader goals into specific production plans and materials management strategies.

Four important decisions must be made in production planning. They involve the type of production process that will be used, site selection, facility layout, and resource planning.

10.2 The Production Process: How Do We Make It?

2. What types of production processes do manufacturers and service firms use?

In production planning, the first decision involves which type of **production process**—the way a good or service is created—best fits with company goals and customer demand. An important consideration is the type of good or service being produced, because different goods may require different production processes. In general, there are three types of production: mass production, mass customization, and customization. In addition to production type, operations managers also classify production processes in two ways: (1) how inputs are converted into outputs and (2) the timing of the process.

One for All: Mass Production

Mass production, manufacturing many identical goods at once, was a product of the Industrial Revolution. Henry Ford's Model-T automobile is a good example of early mass production. Each car turned out by Ford's factory was identical, right down to its color. If you wanted a car in any color except black, you were out of luck. Canned goods, over-the-counter drugs, and household appliances are other examples of goods that are mass-produced. The emphasis in mass production is on keeping manufacturing costs low by producing uniform products using repetitive and standardized processes. As products became more complicated to produce, mass production also became more complex. Automobile manufacturers, for example, must now incorporate more sophisticated electronics into their car designs. As a result, the number of assembly stations in most automobile manufacturing plants has increased.

Just for You: Customizing Goods

In **mass customization**, goods are produced using mass-production techniques, but only up to a point. At that point, the product or service is custom-tailored to the needs or desires of individual customers. For example, American Leather, a Dallas-based furniture manufacturer, uses mass customization to produce couches and chairs to customer specifications within 30 days. The basic frames in the furniture are the same, but automated cutting machinery precuts the color and type of leather ordered by each customer. Using mass-production techniques, they are then added to each frame.

Customization is the opposite of mass production. In customization, the firm produces goods or services one at a time according to the specific needs or wants of individual customers. Unlike mass customization, each product or service produced is unique. For example, a print shop may handle a variety of projects, including newsletters, brochures, stationery, and reports. Each print job varies in quantity, type of printing process, binding, color of ink, and type of paper. A manufacturing firm that produces goods in response to customer orders is called a **job shop**.

Exhibit 10.5   Classification of Production Types (Attribution: Copyright Rice University, OpenStax, under CC BY 4.0 license.)

Mass Production	Mass Customization	Customization
Highly uniform products or services Many products made sequentially	Uniform standardized production to a point, then unique features added to each product	Each product or service produced according to individual customer requirements
Examples: Breakfast cereals, soft drinks, and computer keyboards	**Examples:** Dell Computers, tract homes, and Taylor Made golf clubs	**Examples:** Custom homes, legal services, and haircuts

Some types of service businesses also deliver customized services. Doctors, for instance, must consider the illnesses and circumstances of each individual patient before developing a customized treatment plan. Real estate agents may develop a customized service plan for each customer based on the type of house the person is selling or wants to buy. The differences between mass production, mass customization, and customization are summarized in Exhibit 10.5.

Converting Inputs to Outputs

As previously stated, production involves converting *inputs* (natural resources, raw materials, human resources, capital) into *outputs* (products or services). In a manufacturing company, the inputs, the production process, and the final outputs are usually obvious. Harley-Davidson, for instance, converts steel, rubber, paint, and other inputs into motorcycles. But the production process in a service company involves a less obvious conversion. For example, a hospital converts the knowledge and skills of its medical personnel, along with equipment and supplies from a variety of sources, into health care services for patients. Table 10.1 provides examples of the inputs and outputs used by various other businesses.

There are two basic processes for converting inputs into outputs. In **process manufacturing**, the basic inputs (natural resources, raw materials) are broken down into one or more outputs (products). For instance, bauxite (the input) is processed to extract aluminum (the output). The **assembly process** is just the opposite. The basic inputs, like natural resources, raw materials, or human resources, are either *combined* to create the output or *transformed* into the output. An airplane, for example, is created by assembling thousands of parts, which are its raw material inputs. Steel manufacturers use heat to transform iron and other materials into steel. In services, customers may play a role in the transformation process. For example, a tax preparation service combines the knowledge of the tax preparer with the client's information about personal finances in order to complete the tax return.

Production Timing

A second consideration in choosing a production process is timing. A **continuous process** uses long production runs that may last days, weeks, or months without equipment shutdowns. This is best for high-volume, low-variety products with standardized parts, such as nails, glass, and paper. Some services also use a continuous process. Your local electric company is an example. Per-unit costs are low, and production is easy to schedule.

Converting Inputs to Outputs		
Type of Organization	Input	Output
Airline	Pilots, flight attendants, reservations system, ticketing agents, customers, airplanes, maintenance crews, ground facilities	Movement of customers and freight
Grocery store	Merchandise, building, clerks, supervisors, store fixtures, shopping carts, customers	Groceries for customers
High school	Faculty, curriculum, buildings, classrooms, library, auditorium, gymnasium, students, staff, supplies	Graduates, public service
Manufacturer	Machinery, raw materials, plant, workers, managers	Finished products for consumers and other firms
Restaurant	Food, cooking equipment, servers, chefs, dishwashers, host, patrons, furniture, fixtures	Meals for patrons

Table 10.1

In an **intermittent process**, short production runs are used to make batches of different products. Machines are shut down to change them to make different products at different times. This process is best for low-volume, high-variety products such as those produced by mass customization or customization. Job shops are examples of firms using an intermittent process.

Although some service companies use continuous processes, most service firms rely on intermittent processes. For instance, a restaurant preparing gourmet meals, a physician performing surgical procedures, and an advertising agency developing ad campaigns for business clients all customize their services to suit each customer. They use the intermittent process. Note that their "production runs" may be very short—one grilled salmon or one physical exam at a time.

CONCEPT CHECK

1. Describe the different types of production processes.
2. How are inputs transformed into outputs in a variety of industries?

10.3 Location, Location, Location: Where Do We Make It?

3. How do organizations decide where to put their production facilities? What choices must be made in designing the facility?

A big decision that managers must make early in production and operations planning is where to put the facility, be it a factory or a service office. The facility's location affects operating and shipping costs and, ultimately, the price of the product or service and the company's ability to compete. Mistakes made at this stage can be expensive, because moving a factory or service facility once production begins is difficult and costly. Firms must weigh a number of factors to make the right decision.

Exhibit 10.6   Facing stiff competition from rival automobile companies and sagging demand among German consumers, Germany's BMW (Bavarian Motor Works) opened a factory in Spartanburg, South Carolina. Opened in 1994, the U.S. plant recently produced it four millionth vehicle and now employs 9,000 employees in its six million square foot plant. *What factors determine where auto companies locate their operations?* (Credit: Daniel Chou/ Flickr/ Attribution-NoDerivs 2.0 Generic (CC BY-ND 2.0))

Availability of Production Inputs

As we discussed earlier, organizations need certain resources to produce products and services for sale.

Access to these resources, or inputs, is a huge consideration in site selection. Executives must assess the availability of raw materials, parts, equipment, and available manpower for each site under consideration. The cost of shipping raw materials and finished goods can be as much as 25 percent of a manufacturer's total cost, so locating a factory where these and other costs are as low as possible can make a major contribution to a firm's success.

Companies that use heavy or bulky raw materials, for example, may choose to be located close to their suppliers. Mining companies want to be near ore deposits, oil refiners near oil fields, paper mills near forests, and food processors near farms. Bottlers are discovering that rural western communities in need of an economic boost make rich water sources. In Los Lunas, New Mexico, it made sense for Niagara Purified Drinking Water to produce purified bottled water in a 166,000 square foot building that was vacant. The business helps diversify the town's economy and created 40 new, much-needed jobs.[1]

The availability and cost of labor are also critical to both manufacturing and service businesses, and the unionization of local labor is another point to consider in many industries. Payroll costs can vary widely from one location to another due to differences in the cost of living; the number of jobs available; and the size, skills, and productivity of the local workforce. In the case of the water-bottling company, a ready pool of relatively inexpensive labor was available due to high unemployment in the areas.

Marketing Factors

Businesses must evaluate how their facility location will affect their ability to serve their customers. For some firms it may not be necessary to be located near customers. Instead, the firm will need to assess the difficulty and costs of distributing its goods to customers from its chosen location. Other firms may find that locating near customers can provide marketing advantages. When a factory or service center is close to customers, the firm can often offer better service at a lower cost. Other firms may gain a competitive advantage by locating their facilities so that customers can easily buy their products or services. The location of competitors may also be a consideration. And businesses with more than one facility may need to consider how far to spread their locations in order to maximize market coverage.

Manufacturing Environment

Another factor to consider is the manufacturing environment in a potential location. Some localities have a strong existing manufacturing base. When a large number of manufacturers in a certain industry are already located in an area, that area is likely to offer greater availability of resources, such as manufacturing workers, better accessibility to suppliers and transportation, and other factors that can increase a plant's operating efficiency.

Nestlé is proposing to open a new bottled water plant in the desert city of Phoenix. The plants have provided much-needed employment to replace jobs lost in the recession of 2008. The city of Phoenix faced opposition to the plant because some locals thought that diverting water from tap water to a for-profit entity was not a sound idea. Phoenix officials contend that the source of water is adequate for decades to come.[2]

Local Incentives

Incentives offered by countries, states, or cities may also influence site selection. Tax breaks are a common incentive. A locality may reduce the amount of taxes a firm must pay on income, real estate, utilities, or payroll. Local governments may offer financial assistance and/or exemptions from certain regulations to attract or keep production facilities in their area. For example, many U.S. cities are competing to attract a second Amazon headquarters and, in addition to touting local attractions and a strong workforce, most of them are offering a host of tax incentives.[3]

International Location Considerations

There are often sound financial reasons for considering a foreign location. Labor costs are considerably lower in countries such as Singapore, China, India, and Mexico. Foreign countries may also have fewer regulations governing how factories operate. A foreign location may also move production closer to new markets. Automobile manufacturers such as Toyota, BMW, and Hyundai are among many that build plants in the United States to reduce shipping costs.

Designing the Facility

After the site location decision has been made, the next focus in production planning is the facility's layout. The goal is to determine the most efficient and effective design for the particular production process. A manufacturer might opt for a U-shaped production line, for example, rather than a long, straight one, to allow products and workers to move more quickly from one area to another.

Service organizations must also consider layout, but they are more concerned with how it affects customer behavior. It may be more convenient for a hospital to place its freight elevators in the center of the building, for example, but doing so may block the flow of patients, visitors, and medical personnel between floors and departments.

There are three main types of facility layouts: process, product, and fixed-position. All three layouts are illustrated in **Exhibit 10.7**. Cellular manufacturing is another type of facility layout.

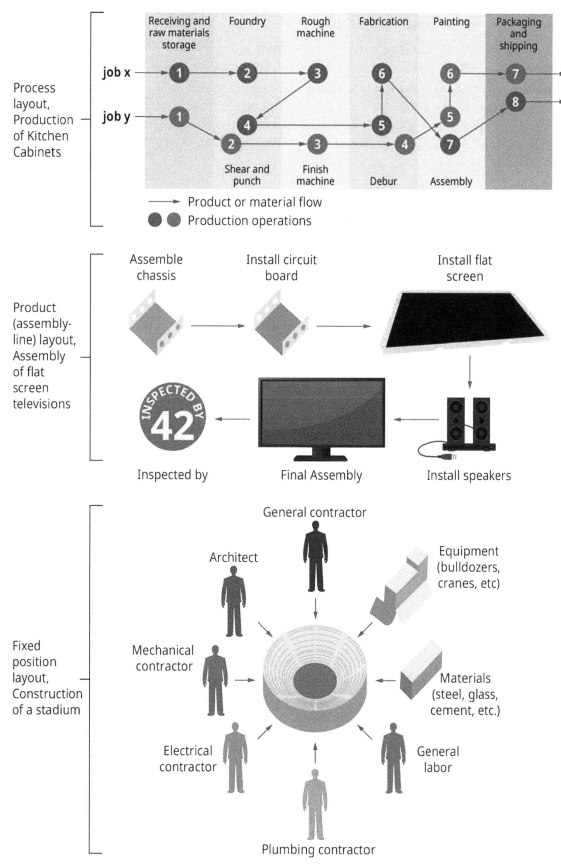

Exhibit 10.7 Types of Facility Layouts Source: Adapted from *Operations Management*, 9th edition, by Gaither/Frazier.

Process Layout: All Welders Stand Here

The **process layout** arranges workflow around the production process. All workers performing similar tasks are grouped together. Products pass from one workstation to another (but not necessarily to every workstation). For example, all grinding would be done in one area, all assembling in another, and all inspection in yet another. The process layout is best for firms that produce small numbers of a wide variety of products, typically using general-purpose machines that can be changed rapidly to new operations for different product designs. For example, a manufacturer of custom machinery would use a process layout.

Product Layout: Moving Down the Line

Products that require a continuous or repetitive production process use the **product** (or **assembly-line**) **layout**. When large quantities of a product must be processed on an ongoing basis, the workstations or departments are arranged in a line with products moving along the line. Automobile and appliance manufacturers, as well as food-processing plants, usually use a product layout. Service companies may also use a product layout for routine processing operations.

Fixed-Position Layout: Staying Put

Some products cannot be put on an assembly line or moved about in a plant. A **fixed-position layout** lets the product stay in one place while workers and machinery move to it as needed. Products that are impossible to move—ships, airplanes, and construction projects—are typically produced using a fixed-position layout. Limited space at the project site often means that parts of the product must be assembled at other sites, transported to the fixed site, and then assembled. The fixed-position layout is also common for on-site services such as housecleaning services, pest control, and landscaping.

Cellular Manufacturing: A Start-to-Finish Focus

Cellular manufacturing combines some aspects of both product and fixed-position layouts. Work cells are small, self-contained production units that include several machines and workers arranged in a compact, sequential order. Each work cell performs all or most of the tasks necessary to complete a manufacturing order. There are usually five to 10 workers in a cell, and they are trained to be able to do any of the steps in the production process. The goal is to create a team environment wherein team members are involved in production from beginning to end.

CONCEPT CHECK

1. What factors does a firm consider when making a site-selection decision?
2. What should be considered when deciding on a production approach?

10.4 | Pulling It Together: Resource Planning

4. Why are resource-planning tasks such as inventory management and supplier relations critical to

production?

As part of the production-planning process, firms must ensure that the resources needed for production—such as raw materials, parts, equipment, and labor—will be available at strategic moments in the production process. This can be a huge challenge. The components used to build just one Boeing airplane, for instance, number in the millions. Cost is also an important factor. In many industries, the cost of materials and supplies used in the production process amounts to as much as half of sales revenues. Resource planning is therefore a big part of any firm's production strategy.

Resource planning begins by specifying which raw materials, parts, and components will be required, and when, to produce finished goods. To determine the amount of each item needed, the expected quantity of finished goods must be forecast. A **bill of material** is then drawn up that lists the items and the number of each required to make the product. **Purchasing**, or *procurement,* is the process of buying production inputs from various sources.

Make or Buy?

The firm must decide whether to make its own production materials or buy them from outside sources. This is the **make-or-buy decision**. The quantity of items needed is one consideration. If a part is used in only one of many products, buying the part may be more cost-effective than making it. Buying standard items, such as screws, bolts, rivets, and nails, is usually cheaper and easier than producing them internally. Purchasing larger components from another manufacturer can be cost-effective as well. When items are purchased from an outside source instead of being made internally, it is called **outsourcing**. Harley-Davidson, for example, purchases its tires, brake systems, and other motorcycle components from manufacturers that make them to Harley's specifications. However, if a product has special design features that need to be kept secret to protect a competitive advantage, a firm may decide to produce all parts internally.

In deciding whether to make or buy, a firm must also consider whether outside sources can provide the high-quality supplies it needs in a reliable manner. Having to shut down production because vital parts aren't delivered on time can be a costly disaster. Just as bad are inferior parts or materials, which can damage a firm's reputation for producing high-quality goods. Therefore, firms that buy some or all of their production materials from outside sources should make building strong relationships with quality suppliers a priority.

Inventory Management: Not Just Parts

A firm's **inventory** is the supply of goods it holds for use in production or for sale to customers. Deciding how much inventory to keep on hand is one of the biggest challenges facing operations managers. On the one hand, with large inventories, the firm can meet most production and customer demands. Buying in large quantities can also allow a company to take advantage of quantity discounts. On the other hand, large inventories can tie up the firm's money, are expensive to store, and can become obsolete.

Inventory management involves deciding how much of each type of inventory to keep on hand and the ordering, receiving, storing, and tracking of it. The goal of inventory management is to keep down the costs of ordering and holding inventories while maintaining enough on hand for production and sales. Good inventory management enhances product quality, makes operations more efficient, and increases profits. Poor inventory management can result in dissatisfied customers, financial difficulties, and even bankruptcy.

One way to determine the best inventory levels is to look at three costs: holding inventory, frequent reordering, and not keeping enough inventory on hand. Managers must measure all three costs and try to minimize them.

To control inventory levels, managers often track the use of certain inventory items. Most companies keep a **perpetual inventory**, a continuously updated list of inventory levels, orders, sales, and receipts, for all major items. Today, companies mostly use computers to track inventory levels, calculate order quantities, and issue purchase orders at the right times.

Computerized Resource Planning

Many manufacturing companies have adopted computerized systems to control the flow of resources and inventory. **Materials requirement planning (MRP)** is one such system. MRP uses a master schedule to ensure that the materials, labor, and equipment needed for production are at the right places in the right amounts at the right times. The schedule is based on forecasts of demand for the company's products. It says exactly what will be manufactured during the next few weeks or months and when the work will take place. Sophisticated computer programs coordinate all the elements of MRP. The computer comes up with materials requirements by comparing production needs to the materials the company already has on hand. Orders are placed so items will be on hand when they are needed for production. MRP helps ensure a smooth flow of finished products.

Manufacturing resource planning II (MRPII) was developed in the late 1980s to expand on MRP. It uses a complex computerized system to integrate data from many departments, including finance, marketing, accounting, engineering, and manufacturing. MRPII can generate a production plan for the firm, as well as management reports, forecasts, and financial statements. The system lets managers make more accurate forecasts and assess the impact of production plans on profitability. If one department's plans change, the effects of these changes on other departments are transmitted throughout the company.

Whereas MRP and MRPII systems are focused internally, **enterprise resource planning (ERP)** systems go a step further and incorporate information about the firm's suppliers and customers into the flow of data. ERP unites all of a firm's major departments into a single software program. For instance, production can call up sales information and know immediately how many units must be produced to meet customer orders. By providing information about the availability of resources, including both the human resources and materials needed for production, the system allows for better cost control and eliminates production delays. The system automatically notes any changes, such as the closure of a plant for maintenance and repairs on a certain date or a supplier's inability to meet a delivery date, so that all functions adjust accordingly. Both large and small organizations use ERP to improve operations.

Keeping the Goods Flowing: Supply-Chain Management

In the past, the relationship between purchasers and suppliers was often competitive and antagonistic. Businesses used many suppliers and switched among them frequently. During contract negotiations, each side would try to get better terms at the expense of the other. Communication between purchasers and suppliers was often limited to purchase orders and billing statements.

Today, however, many firms are moving toward a new concept in supplier relationships. The emphasis is increasingly on developing a strong **supply chain**. The supply chain can be thought of as the entire sequence of securing inputs, producing goods, and delivering goods to customers. If any links in this process are weak, chances are customers—the end point of the supply chain—will end up dissatisfied.

Effective supply-chain strategies reduce costs. For example, integration of the shipper and customer's supply chains allows companies to automate more processes and save time. Technology also improves supply-chain efficiency by tracking goods through the various supply-chain stages and helping with logistics. With better information about production and inventory, companies can order and receive goods at the optimal point to keep inventory holding costs low.

Companies also need contingency plans for supply-chain disruptions. Is there an alternative source of supply if a blizzard closes the airport so that cargo planes can't land or a drought causes crop failures in the Midwest? By thinking ahead, companies can avert major losses. The length and distance involved in a supply line is also a consideration. Importing parts from or outsourcing manufacturing to Asia creates a long supply chain for a manufacturer in Europe or the United States. Perhaps there are closer suppliers or manufacturers who can meet a company's needs at a lower overall cost. Companies should also reevaluate outsourcing decisions periodically.

Strategies for Supply-Chain Management

Ensuring a strong supply chain requires that firms implement supply-chain management strategies. **Supply-chain management** focuses on smoothing transitions along the supply chain, with the ultimate goal of satisfying customers with quality products and services. A critical element of effective supply-chain management is to develop tight bonds with suppliers. This may mean reducing the number of suppliers used and asking them to offer more services or better prices in return for an ongoing relationship.

Exhibit 10.8   Managing an efficient supply chain is critical for businesses, especially when the product being delivered is a bouquet of fresh-cut flowers. To ensure that only the freshest, most colorful floral arrangement arrives for that special someone, online floral delivery acts as a national website that serves customers through reputable local florists that deliver the same day. The site uses a web service that draws in customers through search, combined with coordinated carrier scheduling and a review of local florist quality that allows delivery of flowers fresher than the competition. *What strategies help businesses create and maintain an effective supply chain?* (Credit: Brood_wich/ Flickr/ Attribution-2.0 Generic (CC BY 2.0))

General Motors plans to pare the number of its suppliers to give larger, longer-term contracts to a strategically selected group to be based in a new supplier park near its Texas-based SUV plant. GM is one of several manufacturing firms reconsidering far-flung suppliers in their supply chain. Global parts networks have long been seen as critical to cutting costs, but more companies are concluding they're a risky bet due to political shifts, protectionist measures, and natural disasters. The automaker says its new move was planned before President Donald Trump criticized GM's Mexican imports, and the new supplier park will trim logistics expenses and bring other gains from proximity of parts to the assembly plant.[4]

Instead of being viewed as "outsiders" in the production process, many suppliers play an important role in supporting the operations of their customers. They are expected to meet high quality standards, offer suggestions that can help reduce production costs, and even contribute to the design of new products.

EXPANDING AROUND THE GLOBE

Sophisticated Supply-Chain Strategies Keep Products on the Move

Headquartered in Tokyo but with offices around the world, shipping company MOL (Mitsui O.S.K. Lines, Ltd.) is taking integrating with its customers to new levels. It is joining its customers in a series of joint ventures to build and operate dedicated vessels for as long as 25 years. One such joint venture teamed MOL with a Chinese steel mill to build and sail ships bringing Brazilian iron ore and coal across the Pacific Ocean for processing.

Sophisticated supply-chain systems that control every aspect of production and transportation are the key to making offshore manufacturing work. Supply-chain software that monitors operations and continually makes adjustments ensures that all processes are running at peak efficiency. By tightly mapping an entire sequence—from order to final delivery—and by automating it as much as possible, supply-chain management can deliver products from across the world while at the same time cutting costs. Companies that can carry a small inventory and get paid faster improve their cash flow and profitability.

Acer, a $7 billion Taiwanese computer and electronics maker, brings components from around the world and assembles them into everything from PC notebooks to TVs at factories in Taiwan and mainland China. It then reverses the flow by shipping these products to international buyers. "Acer sold four million portable systems. Without a solid supply-chain infrastructure behind us we couldn't hope to do it," says Sumit Agnihotry, Acer's American director of notebook product marketing.

The synchronizing of trade is essential. If goods don't get into the stores in time, sales might be lost or the company might have to carry larger inventories to avoid sellouts, which would cut into its profits. Companies need to continually monitor demand and react quickly by adjusting production. "This gets increasingly difficult when the supply chain stretches across thousands of miles and a dozen time zones," says David Bovet, managing director of Mercer Management Consulting, a Boston-based firm that advises on business tactics. "There are strategies that smart companies are using to bring costs down to earth. Getting the most of lower labor costs overseas requires an emphasis on transportation, and supply-chain skills are a required core competency," he says. His advice to global manufacturers: cooperate with shippers, and integrate supply chains into one cohesive system.

An important aspect of a solid supply chain is the availability of inventory, as the needs of the customer cannot be met without an in-stock supply of products. Inventory can refer to components such as the goods and materials on hand. In international global supply, some things to consider are the availability of labor, geography, and local regulations.

There needs to be a well-developed strategy in order to have a successful supply chain. Strategies include knowing your customers and their needs and planning what you want to achieve and how you are going to make it happen.

The acknowledged master of supply-chain dynamics is Dell, with its global logistics control room lined with big screens that monitor its shipping lanes at all times. Alongside Dell executives are representatives of its logistics suppliers for guidance and quick action if anything goes wrong.

Risk is the name of the game when it comes to international trade, and companies need to decide whether to play it safe with extra inventory or scramble if a disaster like a port strike occurs. Either way, they need to have contingency plans and be ready to react, and solid supply-chain strategies will ensure they are prepared for any eventuality.

Sources: "About MOL," http://www.mol.co.jp, accessed February 20, 2018; "Supply Chain," http://www.dell.com, accessed February 20, 2018; "Our Supply Chain," https://www.acer-group.com, accessed February 20, 2018; Muddassir Ahmed, "How to Create a Supply Chain Strategic Plan That Will Work for (Nearly) Any Business," http://muddassirism.com, December 4, 2016; Pamela Hyatt, "The 5 Essential Stages in Developing a Successful Supply Chain," *Trade Ready,* http://www.tradeready.ca, February 12, 2016; Crystal Gilliam, "7 Tips for Effective Inventory Management in a Global Supply Chain," *Trade Gecko*, https://www.tradegecko.com, October 19, 2015.

Critical Thinking Questions

1. Why are solid supply-chain strategies so important?
2. What problems is a company likely to experience without such strategies in place?

E-Procurement, Electronic Data Interchange, and Blockchain

Effective supply chain management depends on strong communications with suppliers. Technology, particularly the internet, is providing new ways to do this. **E-procurement**, the process of purchasing supplies and materials online, is booming. Many manufacturing firms use the internet to keep key suppliers informed about their requirements. Intel, for example, has set up a special website for its suppliers and potential suppliers. Would-be suppliers can visit the site to get information about doing business with Intel; once they are approved, they can access a secure area to make bids on Intel's current and future resource needs.

The internet also streamlines purchasing by providing firms with quick access to a huge database of information about the products and services of hundreds of potential suppliers. Many large companies now participate in *reverse auctions* online, which can slash procurement costs. In a reverse auction, the manufacturer posts its specifications for the materials it requires. Potential suppliers then bid against each other to get the job. However, there are risks with reverse auctions. It can be difficult to establish and build ongoing relationships with specific suppliers using reverse auctions because the job ultimately goes to the lowest bidder. Therefore, reverse auctions may not be an effective procurement process for critical production materials. Other types of corporations can use these auctions as well. The U.S. Army utilizes reverse auctions to leverage technology to fight the reality and perception that it is inefficient in its procurement practices. The General Services Administration found that government agencies had 31 suppliers that were charging between $9.76 and $48.77 for the same hammer.[5] In 2005 the U.S. Army began to partner with FedBid, Inc., the largest commercial marketplace for reverse auctions, for a variety of products, from paper to computers to helicopters. Costs dropped by $388 million according to independent government cost estimates over the past decade.[6]

Another communications tool is **electronic data interchange (EDI)**, in which two trading partners exchange information electronically. EDI can be conducted via a linked computer system or over the internet. The advantages of exchanging information with suppliers electronically include speed, accuracy, and lowered communication costs. EDI plays a critical role in Ford Motor Company's efforts to produce and distribute vehicles worldwide. With the emergence of **blockchain technology**, there is the potential to automate these types of processes to cover multiple transactions with a variety of participating organizations.[7]

CONCEPT CHECK

CONCEPT CHECK

1. What are the approaches to inventory that businesses can consider?
2. How is technology being used in resource planning?

10.5 Production and Operations Control

5. How do operations managers schedule and control production?

Every company needs to have systems in place to see that production and operations are carried out as planned and to correct errors when they are not. The coordination of materials, equipment, and human resources to achieve production and operating efficiencies is called *production control*. Two of its key aspects are routing and scheduling.

Routing: Where to Next?

Routing is the first step in production control. It sets out a work flow, the sequence of machines and operations through which a product or service progresses from start to finish. Routing depends on the type of goods being produced and the facility layout. Good routing procedures increase productivity and cut unnecessary costs.

One useful tool for routing is **value-stream mapping**, whereby production managers "map" the flow from suppliers through the factory to customers. Simple icons represent the materials and information needed at various points in the flow. Value-stream mapping can help identify where bottlenecks may occur in the production process and is a valuable tool for visualizing how to improve production routing.

Awning manufacturer Rader Awning & Upholstery used value-stream mapping to automate some of its operations. With the assistance of New Mexico Manufacturing Extension Partnership (MEP), the company evaluated how orders were processed from sales to manufacturing over two days. With the implementation of the processes suggested by MEP, productivity improved by 20 percent per salesperson, production defects decreased by 15 percent, and installation corrections dropped by 25 percent.[8]

Scheduling: When Do We Do It?

Closely related to routing is scheduling. **Scheduling** involves specifying and controlling the time required for each step in the production process. The operations manager prepares timetables showing the most efficient sequence of production and then tries to ensure that the necessary materials and labor are in the right place at the right time.

Scheduling is important to both manufacturing and service firms. The production manager in a factory schedules material deliveries, work shifts, and production processes. Trucking companies schedule drivers, clerks, truck maintenance, and repairs in accordance with customer transportation needs. Scheduling at a college entails deciding when to offer which courses, in which classrooms, with which instructors. A museum must schedule special exhibits, ship works to be displayed, market its offerings, and conduct educational programs and tours. Scheduling can range from simple to complex. Giving numbers to customers waiting to be served in a bakery and making interview appointments with job applicants are examples of simple scheduling. Organizations that must produce large quantities of products or services or service a diverse customer base face more complex scheduling problems.

Three common scheduling tools used for complex situations are Gantt charts, the critical path method, and PERT.

Tracking Progress with Gantt Charts

Named after their originator, Henry Gantt, **Gantt charts** are bar graphs plotted on a time line that show the relationship between scheduled and actual production.

In the example shown in Exhibit 10.9, the left side of the chart lists the activities required to complete the job or project. Both the scheduled time and the actual time required for each activity are shown, so the manager can easily judge progress.

Gantt charts are most helpful when only a few tasks are involved, when task times are relatively long (days or weeks rather than hours), and when job routes are short and simple. One of the biggest shortcomings of Gantt charts is that they are static. They also fail to show how tasks are related. These problems can be solved, however, by using two other scheduling techniques, the critical path method and PERT.

The Big Picture: Critical Path Method and PERT

To control large projects, operations managers need to closely monitor resources, costs, quality, and budgets. They also must be able to see the "big picture"—the interrelationships of the many different tasks necessary to complete the project. Finally, they must be able to revise scheduling and divert resources quickly if any tasks fall behind schedule. The critical path method (CPM) and the program evaluation and review technique (PERT) are related project management tools that were developed in the 1950s to help managers accomplish this.

In the **critical path method (CPM)**, the manager identifies all of the activities required to complete the project, the relationships between these activities, and the order in which they need to be completed. Then, the manager develops a diagram that uses arrows to show how the tasks are dependent on each other. The longest path through these linked activities is called the **critical path**. If the tasks on the critical path are not completed on time, the entire project will fall behind schedule.

To better understand how CPM works, look at Exhibit 10.10, which shows a CPM diagram for constructing a house. All of the tasks required to finish the house and an estimated time for each have been identified. The arrows indicate the links between the various steps and their required sequence. As you can see, most of the jobs to be done can't be started until the house's foundation and frame are completed. It will take five days to finish the foundation and another seven days to erect the house frame. The activities linked by brown arrows form the critical path for this project. It tells us that the fastest possible time the house can be built is 38 days, the total time needed for all of the critical path tasks. The noncritical path jobs, those connected with black arrows, can be delayed a bit or done early. Short delays in installing appliances or roofing won't delay construction of the house because these activities don't lie on the critical path.

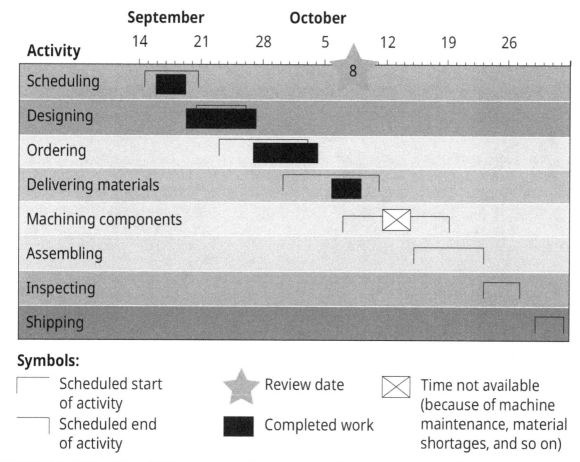

Exhibit 10.9 A Typical Gantt Chart (Attribution: Copyright Rice University, OpenStax, under CC BY 4.0 license.)

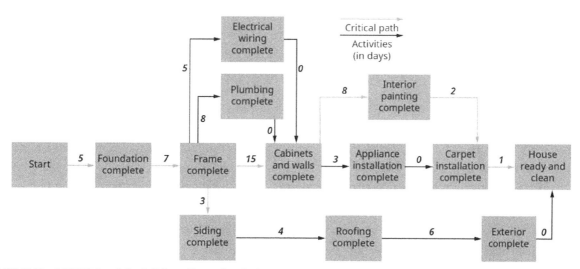

Exhibit 10.10 A CPM Network for Building a House (Attribution: Copyright Rice University, OpenStax, under CC BY 4.0 license.)

Like CPM, the **program evaluation and review technique (PERT)** helps managers identify critical tasks and assess how delays in certain activities will affect operations or production. In both methods, managers use diagrams to see how operations and production will flow. PERT differs from CPM in one important respect. CPM assumes that the amount of time needed to finish a task is known with certainty; therefore, the CPM diagram shows only one number for the time needed to complete each activity. In contrast, PERT assigns three time estimates for each activity: an optimistic time for completion, the most probable time, and a pessimistic time. These estimates allow managers to anticipate delays and potential problems and schedule accordingly.

CONCEPT CHECK

1. What is production control, and what are its key aspects?
2. How can value-stream mapping improve routing efficiency?
3. Identify and describe three commonly used scheduling tools.

10.6 | Looking for a Better Way: Improving Production and Operations

6. How can quality-management and lean-manufacturing techniques help firms improve production and operations management?

Competing in today's business world is challenging. To compete effectively, firms must keep production costs down. At the same time, however, it's becoming increasingly complex to produce and deliver the high-quality goods and services customers demand. Methods to help meet these challenges include quality-management techniques, lean manufacturing, and technology and automation.

Putting Quality First

Successful businesses recognize that quality and productivity must go hand in hand. **Quality** goods and services meet customer expectations by providing reliable performance. Defective products waste materials and time, increasing costs. Worse, poor quality causes customer dissatisfaction, which usually results in lost sales.

A consumer measures quality by how well a product serves its purpose. From the manufacturer's point of view, quality is the degree to which the product conforms to a set of predetermined standards. **Quality control** involves creating quality standards, producing goods that meet them, and measuring finished goods and services against them. It takes more than just inspecting goods at the end of the assembly line to ensure quality control, however. Quality control requires a company-wide dedication to managing and working in a way that builds excellence into every facet of operations.

Dr. W. Edwards Deming, an American management consultant, was the first to say that quality control should be a company-wide goal. His ideas were adopted by the Japanese in the 1950s but largely ignored in the United States until the 1970s. Deming believed that quality control starts with top management, who must foster a company-wide culture dedicated to producing quality.

Deming's concept of **Total Quality Management (TQM)** emphasizes the use of quality principles in all aspects of a company's production and operations. It recognizes that all employees involved with bringing a product or service to customers—marketing, purchasing, accounting, shipping, manufacturing—contribute to its quality. TQM focuses on **continuous improvement**, a commitment to constantly seek better ways of doing things in order to achieve greater efficiency and improve quality. Company-wide teams work together to prevent problems and systematically improve key processes instead of troubleshooting problems only as they arise. Continuous improvement continually measures performance using statistical techniques and looks for ways to apply new technologies and innovative production methods.

Another quality-control method is the **Six Sigma** quality program. Six Sigma is a company-wide process that focuses on measuring the number of defects that occur and systematically eliminating them in order to get as close to "zero defects" as possible. In fact, Six Sigma quality aims to have every process produce no more than 3.4 defects per million. Six Sigma focuses on designing products that not only have fewer defects but that also satisfy customer needs. A key process of Six Sigma is called *DMAIC*. This stands for Define, Measure, Analyze, Improve, and Control. Employees at all levels define what needs to be done to ensure quality, then measure and analyze production results using statistics to see if standards are met. They are also charged with finding ways to improve and control quality.

General Electric was one of the first companies to institute Six Sigma throughout the organization. GE employees are trained in Six Sigma concepts, and many analysts believe this has given GE a competitive manufacturing advantage. Service firms and government entities have applied Six Sigma to their quality initiatives as well.

Malcolm Baldrige National Quality Award

Named for a former secretary of commerce, the **Malcolm Baldrige National Quality Award** was established by the U.S. Congress in 1987 to recognize U.S. companies that offer goods and services of world-class quality. The award promotes awareness of quality and allows the business community to assess which quality control programs are most effective.

Administered by the U.S. Department of Commerce's National Institute of Standards and Technologies (NIST), the award's most important criterion is a firm's effectiveness at meeting customer expectations, as well as demonstrating that it offers quality goods and services. To qualify for the award, a company must also show continuous improvement in internal operations. Company leaders and employees must be active participants in the firm's quality program, and they must respond quickly to data and analysis.

Organizations in a wide variety of industries have won the Baldrige Award since it was first presented in 1987. In 2017, for example, the Baldrige Award winners included Bristol Tennessee Essential Services, an electricity and fiber services utility company, in the small business sector; the city of Fort Collins, Colorado, in the nonprofit sector; and Southcentral Foundation in Anchorage, Alaska, in the health care sector.[9]

Worldwide Excellence: International Quality Standards

The International Organization for Standardization (ISO), located in Geneva, Switzerland, is an industry organization that has developed standards of quality that are used by businesses around the world. **ISO 9000**, introduced in the 1980s, is a set of five technical standards designed to offer a uniform way of determining whether manufacturing plants and service organizations conform to sound quality procedures. To register, a company must go through an audit of its manufacturing and customer service processes, covering everything from how it designs, produces, and installs its products, to how it inspects, packages, and markets them. Over 500,000 organizations worldwide have met ISO 9000 standards.

ISO 14000, launched after ISO 9000, was designed in response to environmental issues such as global warming and water pollution and promotes clean production processes. To meet ISO 14000 standards, a company must commit to continually improving environmental management and reducing pollution resulting from its production processes.

Lean Manufacturing Trims the Fat

Manufacturers are discovering that they can better respond to rapidly changing customer demands, while keeping inventory and production costs down, by adopting lean-manufacturing techniques. **Lean manufacturing** streamlines production by eliminating steps in the production process that do not add benefits customers want. In other words, *non-value-added production processes* are cut so that the company can concentrate its production and operations resources on items essential to satisfying customers. Toyota was a pioneer in developing these techniques, but today manufacturers in many industries have adopted the lean-manufacturing philosophy.

Another Japanese concept, **just-in-time (JIT)**, goes hand in hand with lean manufacturing. JIT is based on the belief that materials should arrive exactly when they are needed for production, rather than being stored on-site. Relying closely on computerized systems such as MRP, MRPII, and ERP, manufacturers determine what parts will be needed and when and then order them from suppliers so they arrive "just in time." Under the JIT system, inventory and products are "pulled" through the production process in response to customer demand. JIT requires close teamwork between vendors and purchasing and production personnel because any delays in deliveries of supplies could bring JIT production to a halt.

Unexpected events like the September 11 terrorist attacks or the shutdown of ports due to Hurricane Harvey and the devastation and flooding caused by Hurricane Maria in Puerto Rico can cause chaos in the supply chains of manufacturers, resulting in problems for firms relying on JIT. But if employed properly, and in spite of these risks, a JIT system can greatly reduce inventory-holding costs and smooth production highs and lows.

CONCEPT CHECK

1. How can managers use techniques to improve efficiency?
2. Define Six Sigma.
3. What was Edward Demming's contribution to operations management?

10.7 Transforming the Factory Floor with Technology

7. What roles do technology and automation play in manufacturing and service-industry operations management?

Technology is helping many firms improve their operating efficiency and ability to compete. Computer systems in particular are enabling manufacturers to automate factories in ways never before possible. Among the technologies helping to automate manufacturing are computer-aided design and manufacturing systems, robotics, flexible manufacturing systems, and computer-integrated manufacturing.

Computer-Aided Design and Manufacturing Systems

Computers have transformed the design and manufacturing processes in many industries. In **computer-aided design (CAD)**, computers are used to design and test new products and modify existing ones. Engineers use these systems to draw products and look at them from different angles. They can analyze the products, make changes, and test prototypes before manufacturing a single item. **Computer-aided manufacturing (CAM)** uses computers to develop and control the production process. These systems analyze the steps required to make the product, then automatically send instructions to the machines that do the work. **CAD/CAM systems** combine the advantages of CAD and CAM by integrating design, testing, and manufacturing control into one linked computer system. The system helps design the product, control the flow of resources needed to produce the product, and operate the production process. Companies can further improve the design and manufacturing processes through the use of additive manufacturing, commonly referred to as 3D printing. Specialized printers can create products or parts for use in early prototypes, and some industries print certain components on site rather than shipping them.

Cardianove Inc., a Montreal-based manufacturer of medical and surgical equipment, used CAD software to develop the world's smallest heart pump. The company says using computer-aided design shaved two years off the normal design time for cardiac devices. The company's CAD program ran complex three-dimensional simulations to confirm that the design would function properly inside the human body. Using CAD software, Cardianove tested over 100 virtual prototypes before the top three designs were produced for real-life testing.

Robotics

Robots are computer-controlled machines that can perform tasks independently. **Robotics** is the technology involved in designing, constructing, and operating robots. The first robot, or "steel-collar worker," was used by General Motors in 1961. Robots can be mobile or fixed in one place. Fixed robots have an arm that moves and does what the computer instructs. Some robots are quite simple, with limited movement for a few tasks such as cutting sheet metal and spot welding. Others are complex, with hands or grippers that can be programmed to perform a series of movements. Some robots are even equipped with sensing devices for sight and touch.

Robots usually operate with little or no human intervention. Replacing human effort with robots is most effective for tasks requiring accuracy, speed, or strength. Although manufacturers such as Harley-Davidson are most likely to use robots, some service firms are also finding them useful. Hospitals, for example, may use robots to sort and process blood samples, freeing medical personnel from a tedious, sometimes hazardous, repetitive task.

Adaptable Factories: Flexible and Computer-Integrated Manufacturing Systems

A **flexible manufacturing system (FMS)** automates a factory by blending computers, robots, machine tools, and materials-and-parts-handling machinery into an integrated system. These systems combine automated workstations with computer-controlled transportation devices. Automatic guided vehicles (AGV) move materials between workstations and into and out of the system.

ETHICS IN PRACTICE

Can Technology Save Your Life?

Using robots to perform surgery once seemed like a futuristic fantasy, but not anymore. An estimated 1.5 million robotic procedures have been performed by the da Vinci Surgical System according to its creator, Intuitive Surgical.

So what accounts for the surge in robotic surgeries? Some preliminary studies suggest improved outcomes for patients. Surgeons who use the da Vinci Surgical System find that patients have less blood loss and pain, lower risks of complications, shorter hospital stays, and quicker recovery times than those who have open surgery—or even, in some cases, laparoscopic procedures that are also performed through multiple small incisions.

In October 2005, Dr. Francis Sutter, chief of cardiology at the Heart Center at Lankenau Hospital near Philadelphia, did the first da Vinci double bypass. His patient, a 65-year-old man, had just a single two-inch incision on the left side of his chest and was walking 30 minutes a day just a week and a half after surgery. Tests show his heart function to be normal again.

So what are the downsides? At a price of $1.3 million each, the cost of the robots can be a barrier. Because insurance companies pay a fixed amount for a procedure regardless of how it is performed, the hospital is left to pick up the tab for the more expensive robotic surgeries. Sutter's center held fundraisers to help pay for the da Vinci Surgical System. And some surgeons are reluctant to commit the time necessary to learn robotic techniques. There is also a concern that once a hospital invests in such an expensive system, surgeons may feel pressured to use it and steer patients toward surgery over other treatment options.

Other types of technology also improve health care. At Aurora St. Luke's Medical Center in Milwaukee, intensive-care nurses check a patient coming out of heart-bypass surgery—from a building several miles away. This is the Aurora eICU, from which a team of doctors and nurses keep constant watch on more than 10 intensive care units in four different hospitals spread across eastern Wisconsin. "The idea is not to make care more remote," says David Rein, the unit's medical director, "but to bring expertise to the patient's bedside faster than we ever could before."

Monitors display vital signs and the patient's electronic chart, with details on medications, lab tests and X-ray results, and notes on the patient's condition. Cameras can zoom in so closely that monitoring staff can see the capillaries in a patient's eyes.

A survey recently found that patient mortality was 7.2 percent lower in hospitals that were "wired," which has a lot of health care researchers excited. Although the survey doesn't prove that technology causes better patient outcomes, it does show there is a strong connection.

Of course, robotic surgery raises some ethical issues. Recent developments suggest ethical issues that may arise when implementing technology into health care practices. Dr. Bertalan Meskó, who wrote the book *The Guide to the Future of Medicine,* identified such issues, including the hacking of medical devices, defending our privacy, scanning ourselves at home (without medical guidance), how society changes if we can prolong life, and possible bioterrorism due to technological advances.

Critical Thinking Questions

1. How is technology being used to streamline hospital operations, improve the quality of patient care, and provide better outcomes for patients?
2. What criteria should hospitals use to evaluate whether these expensive technologies are worthwhile investments?

Sources: Bertalan Meskó, "Ethical Issues of the Future of Medicine: The Top 10," *Medical Futurist,* http://medicalfuturist.com, accessed February 20, 2018; Thomas Macaulay, "Could the 'World's Smallest Surgical Robot' Make Keyhole Surgery Mainstream?" *Tech World,* https://www.techworld.com, December 28, 2017; Greg Adamson, "Ethics and Technology," *IEEE Standards University,* https://www.standardsuniversity.org, March 13, 2017; Nayef Al-Rodhan, "The Many Ethical Implications of Emerging Technologies," *Scientific* American, https://www.scientificamerican.com, March 13, 2015; Nick Glass and Matthew Knight, "Would You Have Surgery at the Hands of a Robot?" *CNN,* http://www.cnn.com, August 5, 2013; Josh Fishman, "Can High Tech Save Your Life?" *U.S. News & World Report,* August 1, 2005, p. 45–52.

Flexible manufacturing systems are expensive. But once in place, a system requires little labor to operate and provides consistent product quality. It can also be adjusted easily and inexpensively. FMS equipment can quickly be reprogrammed to perform a variety of jobs. These systems work well when small batches of a variety of products are required or when each product is made to individual customer specifications.

Computer-integrated manufacturing (CIM) combines computerized manufacturing processes (such as robots and flexible manufacturing systems) with other computerized systems that control design, inventory, production, and purchasing. With CIM, when a part is redesigned in the CAD system, the changes are quickly transmitted both to the machines producing the part and to all other departments that need to know about and plan for the change.

Technology and Automation at Your Service

Manufacturers are not the only businesses benefiting from technology. Nonmanufacturing firms are also using automation to improve customer service and productivity. Banks now offer services to customers through automated teller machines (ATM), via automated telephone systems, and even over the internet. Retail stores of all kinds use point-of-sale (POS) terminals that track inventories, identify items that need to be reordered, and tell which products are selling well. Walmart, the leader in retailing automation, has its own satellite system connecting POS terminals directly to its distribution centers and headquarters.

CONCEPT CHECK

1. Describe total quality management and the role that Six Sigma, ISO 9000, and ISO14000 play in it.
2. How can lean manufacturing and just-in-time inventory management help a firm improve its production and operations?
3. How are both manufacturing and nonmanufacturing firms using technology and automation to improve operations?

10.8 Trends in Production and Operations Management

8. What key trends are affecting the way companies manage production and operations?

What trends will impact U.S. production and operations management both now and in the future? Manufacturing employment has added one million manufacturing factory jobs since the end of the great recession, up to a level of 12.5 million in December 2017. U.S. exports have quadrupled over the past 25 years, and the integration of technology into manufacturing processes has made U.S. manufacturers more competitive. These statistics portray a U.S. economy that is steaming ahead.[10]

Yet rapid changes in technology and intense global competition—particularly from Asia—create anxiety about the future. Is technology replacing too many jobs? Or, with qualified workers predicted to be in short supply, is the increased reliance on technology imperative to the United States' ability to compete in a global marketplace? Will the United States lose its edge in the ongoing war for leadership in innovation? And what should it be doing to ensure that today's students are tomorrow's innovators and scientists?

Recent surveys show finding qualified workers continues to be a major concern facing U.S. industry today. If the United States is to maintain its competitive edge, more investment—both private and federal—is needed for science and research. And what about the crucial role of technology? These are some of the trends facing companies today that we will examine.

U.S. workers no longer compete simply against one another but also against workers in less-developed countries with lower wages and increasing access to modern technology and production techniques. This is particularly true for manufacturers who account for the bulk of U.S. exports and compete directly with most imports. A more integrated global economy with more import competition and more export opportunities offers both new challenges and new opportunities to the United States and its workforce. To maintain its position as the world's leading innovator, it is essential that the United States remain committed to innovation and the concerted development of a more highly educated and skilled workforce.

Looming Workforce Crisis Threatens U.S. Competitiveness

According to the latest National Association of Manufacturers Skills Gap Report, manufacturing executives rank a "high-performing workforce" as the most important factor in their firms' future success. This finding concurs with a recent study by the U.S. Department of Labor, which concluded that 85 percent of future jobs in the United States will require advanced training, an associate degree, or a four-year college degree. Minimum skills will be adequate for only 15 percent of future jobs.

But the National Association of Manufacturers predicts that 3.5 million new jobs will be filled over the next decade, but two million jobs will go unfilled due to a skills gap. When asked to identify the most serious problem for their company, survey respondents ranked "finding qualified employees" above high energy costs and the burdens of taxes, federal regulations, and litigation. Only the cost of health insurance and import competition ranked as more pressing concerns.

As demand for better-educated and more highly skilled workers begins to grow, troubling trends project a severe shortage of such workers. U.S. employers already struggling to find qualified workers will face an increasing shortage of such workers in coming years. To make matters worse, trends in U.S. secondary education suggest that even those future workers who stay in school to study math and science may not receive globally competitive educations.[11]

American Innovation Leadership at Risk

A recently released report shows the United States is in danger of losing its global lead in science and innovation for the first time since World War II. The report was prepared by the Task Force on the Future of American Innovation, a coalition of leaders from industry, science, and higher education. Although the United States is still out front of the world's innovation curve, competing countries are climbing the technology ladder quickly, and the only way the United States can continue to create high-wage, value-added jobs is to climb the innovation ladder faster than the rest of the world.

The task force identified dwindling federal investment in science and research as a root cause of the problem. Federal research as a share of GDP has declined 40 percent over the past 40 years.[12] The U.S. share of worldwide high-tech exports has been in a 10-year decline since 2008, after a dramatic rise from $77 billion in 1990 to $221 billion in 2008. The latest data has the U.S. high-tech exports at $153 billion. Similarly, graduate science and engineering enrollment is declining in the United States while on the rise in China, India, and elsewhere. In addition, retirements from science and engineering jobs here at home could lead to a critical shortage of U.S. talent in these fields in the near future.[13]

So what needs to be done to reverse this alarming trend? More robust investment is part of the solution because federally funded, peer-reviewed, and patented scientific advances are essential to innovation. Such basic research helped bring us lasers, the World Wide Web, magnetic resonance imaging (MRI), and fiber optics. National Association of Manufacturers President Jay Timmons noted that, "Modern manufacturing offers high-paying, long-term careers. It's a high-tech, sleek industry. It's time to close the skills gap and develop the next generation of the manufacturing workforce."[14]

Business Process Management (BPM)—The Next Big Thing?

The twenty-first century is the age of the scattered corporation. With an assortment of partners and an army of suppliers often spread across thousands of miles, many companies find themselves with global design, supply, and logistics chains stretched to the breaking point. Few firms these days can afford to go it alone with their own raw materials, in-house production processes, and exclusive distribution systems.[15]

"**Business Process Management** is the glue to bind it all together," says Eric Austvold, research director at AMR Research. "It provides a unified system for business." This technology has the power to integrate and optimize a company's sprawling functions by automating much of what it does. The results speak for themselves. BPM has saved U.S. firms $117 billion a year on inventory costs alone. Defense contractor Lockheed Martin recently used a BPM system to resolve differences among the hundreds of businesses that it acquired, unifying them into a whole and saving $50 million per year by making better use of existing resources and data.

BPM is the key to the success of such corporate high-flyers as Walmart and Dell, which collect, digest, and utilize all sorts of production, sales, and shipping data to continually hone their operations. So how does BPM actually work? When a Dell system is ordered online, rather than waiting for a person to get the ball rolling, a flurry of electronic traffic flows back and forth between suppliers so that every part arrives within a few hours and the computer's assembly, as well as software loading and testing, are scheduled. Production runs like a well-oiled clock so customers get their computers quickly, and Dell can bill them on shipment. A well-thought-through BPM system can even reschedule production runs, reroute deliveries, or shift work to alternate plants. The key, says Byron Canady of Dell, is "to stay close to customers and the supply chain."[16]

The amount of available data—business intelligence (BI), enterprise resource planning (ERP), customer relationship management (CRM), and other systems—is staggering. "Companies are flooded with information," says Jeanne Baker, chair of the industry support group Business Process Management Initiative (BPMI) and vice president of technology at Sterling Commerce. "The challenge is to make sense of it all. How you leverage the value chain is the true competitive advantage of the 21st century." According to Baker, "BPMI drives growth through the automation of business processes, particularly the processes that integrate organizations. These provide the best opportunities for growth. Studies have shown companies that have good collaborative processes experience 15 percent less inventory; 17 percent stronger order fulfillment; 35 percent shorter cash-to-cash cycles; 10 percent less stock outs; 7 to 8 percent increase in revenues from savings; and overall sales increases."[17]

CONCEPT CHECK

1. Describe the impact of the anticipated worker shortage on U.S. business.
2. How are today's educational trends affecting the future of manufacturing?
3. What is business process management (BPM), and how do businesses use it to improve operations management?

🔑 Key Terms

assembly process A production process in which the basic inputs are either combined to create the output or transformed into the output.

bill of material A list of the items and the number of each required to make a given product.

blockchain technology Refers to a decentralized "public ledger" of all transactions that have ever been executed. It is constantly expanding, as "completed" blocks are added to the ledger with each new transaction.

business process management (BPM) A unified system that has the power to integrate and optimize a company's sprawling functions by automating much of what it does.

CAD/CAM systems Linked computer systems that combine the advantages of computer-aided design and computer-aided manufacturing. The system helps design the product, control the flow of resources needed to produce the product, and operate the production process.

cellular manufacturing Production technique that uses small, self-contained production units, each performing all or most of the tasks necessary to complete a manufacturing order.

computer-aided design (CAD) The use of computers to design and test new products and modify existing ones.

computer-aided manufacturing (CAM) The use of computers to develop and control the production process.

computer-integrated manufacturing (CIM) The combination of computerized manufacturing processes (such as robots and flexible manufacturing systems) with other computerized systems that control design, inventory, production, and purchasing.

continuous improvement A commitment to constantly seek better ways of doing things in order to achieve greater efficiency and improve quality.

continuous process A production process that uses long production runs lasting days, weeks, or months without equipment shutdowns; generally used for high-volume, low-variety products with standardized parts.

critical path In a critical path method network, the longest path through the linked activities.

critical path method (CPM) A scheduling tool that enables a manager to determine the critical path of activities for a project—the activities that will cause the entire project to fall behind schedule if they are not completed on time.

customization The production of goods or services one at a time according to the specific needs or wants of individual customers.

e-procurement The process of purchasing supplies and materials online using the internet.

electronic data interchange (EDI) The electronic exchange of information between two trading partners.

enterprise resource planning (ERP) A computerized resource-planning system that incorporates information about the firm's suppliers and customers with its internally generated data.

fixed-position layout A facility arrangement in which the product stays in one place and workers and machinery move to it as needed.

flexible manufacturing system (FMS) A system that combines automated workstations with computer-controlled transportation devices—automatic guided vehicles (AGV)—that move materials between workstations and into and out of the system.

Gantt charts Bar graphs plotted on a time line that show the relationship between scheduled and actual production.

intermittent process A production process that uses short production runs to make batches of different products; generally used for low-volume, high-variety products.

inventory The supply of goods that a firm holds for use in production or for sale to customers.

inventory management The determination of how much of each type of inventory a firm will keep on hand and the ordering, receiving, storing, and tracking of inventory.

ISO 14000 A set of technical standards designed by the International Organization for Standardization to promote clean production processes to protect the environment.

ISO 9000 A set of five technical standards of quality management created by the International Organization for Standardization to provide a uniform way of determining whether manufacturing plants and service organizations conform to sound quality procedures.

job shop A manufacturing firm that produces goods in response to customer orders.

just-in-time (JIT) A system in which materials arrive exactly when they are needed for production, rather than being stored on-site.

lean manufacturing Streamlining production by eliminating steps in the production process that do not add benefits that customers want.

make-or-buy decision The determination by a firm of whether to make its own production materials or to buy them from outside sources.

Malcolm Baldrige National Quality Award An award given to recognize U.S. companies that offer goods and services of world-class quality; established by Congress in 1987 and named for a former secretary of commerce.

manufacturing resource planning II (MRPII) A complex computerized system that integrates data from many departments to allow managers to more accurately forecast and assess the impact of production plans on profitability.

mass customization A manufacturing process in which goods are mass-produced up to a point and then custom-tailored to the needs or desires of individual customers.

mass production The manufacture of many identical goods at once.

materials requirement planning (MRP) A computerized system of controlling the flow of resources and inventory. A master schedule is used to ensure that the materials, labor, and equipment needed for production are at the right places in the right amounts at the right times.

operations management Management of the production process.

outsourcing The purchase of items from an outside source rather than making them internally.

perpetual inventory A continuously updated list of inventory levels, orders, sales, and receipts.

process layout A facility arrangement in which work flows according to the production process. All workers performing similar tasks are grouped together, and products pass from one workstation to another.

process manufacturing A production process in which the basic input is broken down into one or more outputs (products).

product (or assembly-line) layout A facility arrangement in which workstations or departments are arranged in a line with products moving along the line.

production The creation of products and services by turning inputs, such as natural resources, raw materials, human resources, and capital, into outputs, which are products and services.

production planning The aspect of operations management in which the firm considers the competitive environment and its own strategic goals in an effort to find the best production methods.

production process The way a good or service is created.

program evaluation and review technique (PERT) A scheduling tool that is similar to the CPM method but assigns three time estimates for each activity (optimistic, most probable, and pessimistic); allows managers to anticipate delays and potential problems and schedule accordingly.

purchasing The process of buying production inputs from various sources; also called *procurement*.

quality Goods and services that meet customer expectations by providing reliable performance.

quality control The process of creating quality standards, producing goods that meet them, and measuring finished goods and services against them.

robotics The technology involved in designing, constructing, and operating computer-controlled machines that can perform tasks independently.

routing The aspect of production control that involves setting out the work flow—the sequence of machines and operations through which the product or service progresses from start to finish.

scheduling The aspect of production control that involves specifying and controlling the time required for each step in the production process.

Six Sigma A quality-control process that relies on defining what needs to be done to ensure quality, measuring and analyzing production results statistically, and finding ways to improve and control quality.

supply chain The entire sequence of securing inputs, producing goods, and delivering goods to customers.

supply-chain management The process of smoothing transitions along the supply chain so that the firm can satisfy its customers with quality products and services; focuses on developing tight bonds with suppliers.

Total Quality Management (TQM) The use of quality principles in all aspects of a company's production and operations.

value-stream mapping Routing technique that uses simple icons to visually represent the flow of materials and information from suppliers through the factory to customers.

Summary of Learning Outcomes

10.1 Production and Operations Management—An Overview
1. Why is production and operations management important in both manufacturing and service firms?

In the 1980s, many U.S. manufacturers lost customers to foreign competitors because their production and operations management systems did not support the high-quality, reasonably priced products consumers demanded. Service organizations also rely on effective operations management in order to satisfy consumers. Operations managers, the personnel charged with managing and supervising the conversion of inputs into outputs, work closely with other functions in organizations to help ensure quality, customer satisfaction, and financial success.

10.2 The Production Process: How Do We Make It?
2. What types of production processes do manufacturers and service firms use?

Products are made using one of three types of production processes. In mass production, many identical goods are produced at once, keeping production costs low. Mass production, therefore, relies heavily on standardization, mechanization, and specialization. When mass customization is used, goods are produced using mass-production techniques up to a point, after which the product or service is custom-tailored to individual customers by adding special features. When a firm's production process is built around customization, the firm makes many products one at a time according to the very specific needs or wants of individual customers.

10.3 Location, Location, Location: Where Do We Make It?
3. How do organizations decide where to put their production facilities? What choices must be made in designing the facility?

Site selection affects operating costs, the price of the product or service, and the company's ability to compete. In choosing a production site, firms must weigh the availability of resources—raw materials, manpower, and even capital—needed for production, as well as the ability to serve customers and take advantage of marketing opportunities. Other factors include the availability of local incentives and the manufacturing environment. Once a site is selected, the firm must choose an appropriate design for the facility. The three main production facility designs are process, product, and fixed-position layouts. Cellular manufacturing is another type of facility layout.

10.4 Pulling It Together: Resource Planning

4. Why are resource-planning tasks such as inventory management and supplier relations critical to production?

Production converts input resources, such as raw materials and labor, into outputs, finished products and services. Firms must ensure that the resources needed for production will be available at strategic moments in the production process. If they are not, productivity, customer satisfaction, and quality may suffer. Carefully managing inventory can help cut production costs while maintaining enough supply for production and sales. Through good relationships with suppliers, firms can get better prices, reliable resources, and support services that can improve production efficiency.

10.5 Production and Operations Control

5. How do operations managers schedule and control production?

Routing is the first step in scheduling and controlling production. Routing analyzes the steps needed in production and sets out a workflow, the sequence of machines and operations through which a product or service progresses from start to finish. Good routing increases productivity and can eliminate unnecessary cost. Scheduling involves specifying and controlling the time and resources required for each step in the production process. Operations managers use three methods to schedule production: Gantt charts, the critical path method, and PERT.

10.6 Looking for a Better Way: Improving Production and Operations

6. How can quality-management and lean-manufacturing techniques help firms improve production and operations management?

Quality and productivity go hand in hand. Defective products waste materials and time, increasing costs. Poor quality also leads to dissatisfied customers. By implementing quality-control methods, firms can reduce these problems and streamline production. Lean manufacturing also helps streamline production by eliminating unnecessary steps in the production process. When activities that don't add value for customers are eliminated, manufacturers can respond to changing market conditions with greater flexibility and ease.

10.7 Transforming the Factory Floor with Technology

7. What roles do technology and automation play in manufacturing and service-industry operations management?

Many firms are improving their operational efficiency by using technology to automate parts of production. Computer-aided design and manufacturing systems, for example, help design new products, control the flow of resources needed for production, and even operate much of the production process. By using robotics, human time and effort can be minimized. Factories are being automated by blending computers, robots, and machinery into flexible manufacturing systems that require less labor to operate. Service firms are automating operations too, using technology to cut labor costs and control quality.

10.8 Trends in Production and Operations Management

8. What key trends are affecting the way companies manage production and operations?

Data show the U.S. economy steaming steadily ahead, but dramatic advances in technology, predicted worker shortages, and global competition create challenges for the future. How will companies balance their technology and workforce needs? Will the United States maintain its lead in the ongoing war for leadership in innovation? And what should it be doing to convert today's students into tomorrow's innovators and scientists? Surveys indicate that finding qualified workers continues to be a major concern facing U.S. industry today. If the United States is to maintain its competitive edge, more private and federal investment is needed for science and research. And what of the increasingly crucial role of technology? These are some of the trends facing companies today.

Preparing for Tomorrow's Workplace Skills

1. Tom Lawrence and Sally Zickle are co-owners of L-Z Marketing, an advertising agency. Last week, they landed a major aerospace manufacturer as a client. The company wants the agency to create its annual report. Tom, who develops the art for the agency, needs about a week to develop the preliminary report design, another two weeks to set the type, and three weeks to get the report printed. Sally writes the material for the report and doesn't need as much time: two days to meet with the client to review the company's financial information and about three weeks to write the report copy. Of course, Tom can't set type until Sally has finished writing the report. Sally will also need three days to proofread the report before it goes to the printer. Develop either a Gantt chart or a critical path diagram for Tom and Sally to use in scheduling the project. Explain why you chose the method you did. How long will it take Tom and Sally to finish the project if there are no unforeseen delays? (Resources, Systems)

2. Look for ways that technology and automation are used at your school, in the local supermarket, and at your doctor's office. As a class, discuss how automation affects the service you receive from each of these organizations. Does one organization use any types of automation that might be effectively used by one of the others? Explain. (Interpersonal, Information)

3. Pick a small business in your community. Make a list of the resources critical to the firm's production and operations. What would happen if the business suddenly couldn't acquire any of these resources? Divide the class into small groups and discuss strategies that small businesses can use to manage their supply chain. (Resources, Information, Interpersonal)

4. Broadway Fashions is a manufacturer of women's dresses. The company's factory has 50 employees. Production begins when the fabric is cut according to specified patterns. After being cut, the pieces for each dress style are placed into bundles, which then move through the factory from worker to worker. Each worker opens each bundle and does one assembly task, such as sewing on collars, hemming dresses, or adding decorative items such as appliqués. Then, the worker puts the bundle back together and passes it on to the next person in the production process. Finished dresses are pressed and packaged for shipment. Draw a diagram showing the production process layout in Broadway Fashions' factory. What type of factory layout and process is Broadway using? Discuss the pros and cons of this choice. Could Broadway improve production efficiency by using a different production process or factory layout? How? Draw a diagram to explain how this might look. (Resources, Systems)

5. As discussed in this chapter, many U.S. firms have moved their manufacturing operations to overseas locations in the past decade. Although there can be sound financial benefits to this choice, moving production overseas can also raise new challenges for operations managers. Identify several of these challenges, and offer suggestions for how operations managers can use the concepts in this chapter to minimize or solve them. (Resources, Information)

6. **Team Exercise** Reliance Systems, headquartered in Oklahoma City, is a manufacturer of computer keyboards. The company plans to build a new factory and hopes to find a location with access to low-cost but skilled workers, national and international transportation, and favorable government incentives.

Working in teams, assign tasks, and use the internet and your school library to research possible site locations, both domestic and international. Choose a location you feel would best meet the company's needs. Make a group presentation to the class explaining why you have chosen this location. Include information about the location's labor force, similar manufacturing facilities already located there, availability of resources and materials, possible local incentives, political and economic environment in the location, and any other factors you feel make this an attractive location. After all teams have presented their proposed locations, as a class rank all of the locations and decide the top two Reliance should investigate further. (Interpersonal, Information)

7. Your teacher has just announced a huge assignment, due in three weeks. Develop a Gantt chart to plan and schedule more effectively.
    ◦ Break the assignment down into smaller tasks: pick a topic; conduct research at the library or on the internet; organize your notes; develop an outline; and write, type, and proofread the paper.
    ◦ Estimate how much time each task will take.
    ◦ Across the top of a piece of paper, list all the days until the assignment is due. Along the side of the paper, list all the tasks you've identified in the order they need to be done.
    ◦ Starting with the first task, block out the number of days you estimate each task will take. Include days that you won't be able to work on the project.
    ◦ Track the actual time spent on each task.

After you complete and submit your assignment, compare your time estimates to the actual time each task took. How can these findings help you with future assignments? (Resources, Systems)

Ethics Activity

A recent spate of mine disasters that caused numerous fatalities refocused national attention on the question: is management doing enough to protect employees on the job? Recent serious Occupational Safety and Health Administration (OSHA) violations resulting in the deaths of two workers from falls due to the lack of harnesses or guardrails suggest there is still a long way to go.

Companies are responsible for providing a safe workplace for employees. So why do accidents like these continue to happen? In a word—money. It takes money to purchase harnesses, install guardrails, and otherwise ensure a safe and healthy work environment. And even more is needed to employ the staff necessary to enforce company safety policies. It is often less costly for a company to just pay the fines that are levied for violations.

As a supervisor at a company with frequent violations of OSHA regulations, you worry about your employees' safety. But each time your company needs to implement a new safety feature, end-of-year employee bonuses get smaller. The money has to come from somewhere, management claims.

Using a web search tool, locate articles about this topic, and then write responses to the following questions. Be sure to support your arguments and cite your sources.

Ethical Dilemma: Do you report safety violations to management in the hope they will be corrected before someone gets hurt, or do you stage a total work stoppage to force management's hand, knowing that either way you risk losing popularity at every level, and very possibly your job? Or, of course, you could say nothing and hope for the best. It is not a problem you created, and you're just there to do a job, after all.

Sources: George Avalos, "PG&E Violated Safety Rules, Was Late on Thousands of Wine Country Electricity Inspections and Work Orders," *The Mercury News*, https://www.mercurynews.com, October 25, 2017; Barry

Meier and Danielle Ivory, "Worker Safety Rules Are Among Those Under Fire in Trump Era," *The New York Times*, https://www.nytimes.com, March 13, 2017; Kenneth Cheng, "Senior Managers Could Be Taken to Task for Workplace Safety Violations," *Today Online*, http://www.todayonline.com, March 7, 2017.

Working the Net

1. Use the Google search engine, **http://www.google.com**, to conduct a search for "supplier information," and visit the websites of several firms (for example, Walmart, Northrop Grumman, Verizon, etc.). Compare the requirements companies set for their suppliers. How do they differ? How are they similar?

2. Visit *Site Selection* magazine, **http://www.siteselection.com**. Click on Area Spotlights for information about the manufacturing environment in various U.S. locations. Pick three to four areas to read about. Using this information, what locations would you recommend for firms in the following industries: general services, telecommunications, automotive manufacturing, and electronics manufacturing? Explain.

3. Manufacturers face many federal, state, and local regulations. Visit the National Association of Manufacturers at **http://www.nam.org**. Pick two or three legislative or regulatory issues discussed under their Policy sections, and use a search engine such as Yahoo! (**http://www.yahoo.com**) to find more information.

4. Using a search engine to search for information about technologies such as ERP, CAD/CAM systems, or robotics. Find at least three suppliers for one of these technologies. Visit their websites, and discuss how their clients are using their products to automate production.

5. Research either the Malcolm Baldrige National Quality Award or the ISO 9000 Quality Standards program on the internet. Write an executive summary that explains the basic requirements and costs of participating. What are the benefits of participating? Include a brief example of a company that has participated and their experiences. Include a list of relevant website links for further reading.

Critical Thinking Case

Innovation and E-mail Rules

This chapter provides insights into how manufacturing and service organizations can implement processes and controls to increase efficiency, manage expenditures, and increase profits for the organization. For companies such as General Motors that need to manage suppliers and make sure that all components are procured on time and at the best costs to ensure the final assembly runs efficiently, and for service organizations such as Marriott, which wants to have clean rooms and an efficient check-in process when guests arrive, the main lessons of this chapter are readily apparent.

All companies, however, need to innovate continuously to improve their products and services. Automobile companies such as General Motors have to constantly measure customer tastes and needs and provide products that meet and exceed their expectations. Likewise, Marriott needs to cater to the needs of business and leisure travelers in a variety of locations.

Perhaps no company in recent years has captured the attention of the public more than Tesla and SpaceX, both headed by CEO Elon Musk. Tesla is named after the inventor Nicola Tesla, a contemporary of Thomas Edison, who designed the first electric engine. SpaceX is a company that is known for innovation such as reusing rocket launchers to reduce costs. While Tesla and SpaceX still manage their operations with all the processes covered in this chapter, their constant innovation requires new processes.

Perhaps no aspect of modern business has had a bigger impact than the proliferation of e-mail. No longer confined to the desktop, e-mail messages are delivered via mobile devices, and managers must find ways to manage the proliferation of communication to keep on top of things.

Elon Musk communicated the processes and rules for communicating at Tesla in this e-mail to all employees.

Subject: Communication Within Tesla

> There are two schools of thought about how information should flow within companies. By far the most common way is chain of command, which means that you always flow communication through your manager. The problem with this approach is that, while it serves to enhance the power of the manager, it fails to serve the company.
>
> Instead of a problem getting solved quickly, where a person in one dept talks to a person in another dept and makes the right thing happen, people are forced to talk to their manager who talks to their manager who talks to the manager in the other dept who talks to someone on his team. Then the info has to flow back the other way again. This is incredibly dumb. Any manager who allows this to happen, let alone encourages it, will soon find themselves working at another company. No kidding.
>
> Anyone at Tesla can and should email/talk to anyone else according to what they think is the fastest way to solve a problem for the benefit of the whole company. You can talk to your manager's manager without his permission, you can talk directly to a VP in another dept, you can talk to me, you can talk to anyone without anyone else's permission. Moreover, you should consider yourself obligated to do so until the right thing happens. The point here is not random chitchat, but rather ensuring that we execute ultra-fast and well. We obviously cannot compete with the big car companies in size, so we must do so with intelligence and agility.
>
> One final point is that managers should work hard to ensure that they are not creating silos within the company that create an us vs. them mentality or impede communication in any way. This is unfortunately a natural tendency and needs to be actively fought. How can it possibly help Tesla for depts to erect barriers between themselves or see their success as relative within the company instead of collective? We are all in the same boat. Always view yourself as working for the good of the company and never your dept.
>
> Thanks,
>
> Elon

Critical Thinking Questions

1. Why would an e-mail rules memo like this work better at an innovation-driven company such as Tesla rather than at a manufacturing-driven company such as General Motors?
2. What are the potential problems that could arise out of this approach to e-mail?

Sources: Justin Bariso, "This Email From Elon Musk to Tesla Employees Describes What Great Communication Looks Like," *Inc.*, https://www.inc.com, accessed February 20, 2018; John F. Wasik, "Tesla the Car Is a Household Name. Long Ago, So Was Nikola Tesla," *The New York Times*, https://www.nytimes.com, December 30, 2017; Ken Costlow, "Ground Broken on New General Motors Supplier Park," *Arlington Voice,* https://arlingtonvoice.com, June 19, 2017.

Hot Links Address Book

1. See how American Leather brings it all together to create beautiful customized couches at

https://www.americanleather.com.

2. What characteristics contribute to a city's manufacturing climate? Find out by reading more at *Industry Week*'s website: **http://www.industryweek.com**.

3. How do companies decide whether to make or buy? Find out more at the Outsourcing Institute, a professional association where buyers and sellers network and connect: **http://www.outsourcing.com**.

4. Learn how to build your own Gantt chart at **https://www.mindtools.com/pages/article/ newPPM_03.htm**.

5. What does it take to win the Malcolm Baldrige National Quality Award? Get the details at **https://www.nist.gov/baldrige/baldrige-award**.

6. Want to know more about how robots work? Find out at **https://science.howstuffworks.com/ robot.htm**.

Creating Products and Pricing Strategies to Meet Customers' Needs

Exhibit 11.1 (Credit: Hamza Butt / flickr / Attribution Generic 2.0 (CC BY))

 Introduction

Learning Outcomes

After reading this chapter, you should be able to answer these questions:

1. What is the marketing concept and relationship-building?
2. How do managers create a marketing strategy?
3. What is the marketing mix?
4. How do consumers and organizations make buying decisions?
5. What are the five basic forms of consumer and business market segmentation?
6. What is a product, and how is it classified?
7. How do organizations create new products?
8. What are the stages of the product life cycle?
9. What strategies are used for pricing products, and what are the future trends?
10. What trends are occurring in products and pricing?

EXPLORING BUSINESS CAREERS

Rachel Kuhr: Mark Cuban's Shark Tank Empire

Rachel Kuhr is the product innovation and development specialist for Mark Cuban's investments in the ABC show *Shark Tank*. Two years ago, after watching an episode, Kuhr e-mailed Mark Cuban and attached a resume that highlighted her mechanical engineering and product development expertise. Her approach appealed to Cuban, and she was contacted the next day by Abe Minkara, head of Cuban's business development team. After a Skype interview in which Minkara was impressed with Kuhr's skill set of both creativity and attention to process, she was hired to fill that role and work with several start-ups that Cuban acquired an investment in through the show.

Kuhr now coaches and collaborates with over 60 companies that reside in Cuban's business portfolio. Rather than start out with detailed plans and building sophisticated prototypes, Kuhr favors using things like a whiteboard, Post-it notes, colored pens, and highlighters to sketch out the ideas. Such an approach uses the best practices from brainstorming that allow fatal flaws to steer the direction of product development before spending lots of resources, both human and financial, on a single idea for too long. This approach also allows the product development team to incorporate the user experience, which is sometimes overlooked when the focus is squarely on the product.

One of the companies that Kuhr works with created Chapul Cricket Bars. Chapul Cricket Bars was the first company to use insect-based "flour" in the manufacture of high- energy protein bars. After the deal on Shark Tank, company founder Pat Crowley and Kuhr decided to take the flying insect logo off the product design and renamed the bars with names such as Aztec, Matcha, and Chaco instead of the "Cricket Bar" name.

Another Cuban investment was the Austin, Texas–based BeatBox Beverages. To better understand how typical consumers would relate to boxed flavored cocktails, Kuhr attended several fraternity parties at Southern Methodist University and off-campus bars. She asked questions that addressed how a variety of consumers decide on what to drink on different occasions and in different settings. Since securing a $1 million dollar investment from Cuban, and working with Rachel Kuhr, online and distribution sales through stores has skyrocketed according to Justin Fenchel, BeatBox Beverages' CEO.

Sources: Cheryl Hall, "Why Rachel Kuhr Is the Innovator for Mark Cuban's Shark Tank Startups," *Dallas News*, https://www.dallasnews.com, accessed October 1, 2017; "About Us," https://chapul.com, accessed October 1, 2017; "The Story," https://www.beatboxbeverages.com, accessed October 1, 2017; Teddy Nykiel, "Shark Tank's Biggest Deals and How They Panned Out," *NerdWallet*, https://www.nerdwallet.com, January 9, 2015.

Marketing plays a key role in the success of businesses. It is the task of marketing to generate sales for the firm. Sales revenue, in turn, pays workers' salaries, buys supplies, covers the costs of new buildings and equipment, and hopefully enables the company to earn a profit. This chapter looks at the nature of marketing and the creation of product and pricing strategies to meet customers' needs. In this chapter, you will learn about the marketing concept, marketing strategies, and consumer and business buying decisions. You will also see how the marketing mix is used to create sales opportunities. We discuss how new products are created and how they go through periods of sales growth and then decline. Next you will discover how managers set prices to reach organizational goals.

11.1 The Marketing Concept

1. What is the marketing concept and relationship-building?

Marketing is the process of getting the right goods or services or ideas to the right people at the right place, time, and price, using the right promotion techniques and utilizing the appropriate people to provide the customer service associated with those goods, services, or ideas. This concept is referred to as the *"right" principle* and is the basis of all marketing strategy. We can say that **marketing** is finding out the needs and wants of potential buyers (whether organizations or consumers) and then providing goods and services that meet or exceed the expectations of those buyers. Marketing is about creating exchanges. An **exchange** takes place when two parties give something of value to each other to satisfy their respective needs or wants. In a typical exchange, a consumer trades money for a good or service. In some exchanges, nonmonetary things are exchanged, such as when a person who volunteers for the company charity receives a T-shirt in exchange for time spent. One common misconception is that some people see no difference between marketing and sales. They are two different things that are both part of a company's strategy. Sales incorporates actually selling the company's products or service to its customers, while marketing is the process of communicating the value of a product or service to customers so that the product or service sells.

To encourage exchanges, marketers follow the "right" principle. If a local Avon representative doesn't have the right lipstick for a potential customer when the customer wants it, at the right price, the potential customer will not exchange money for a new lipstick from Avon. Think about the last exchange (purchase) you made: What if the price had been 30 percent higher? What if the store or other source had been less accessible? Would you have bought anything? The "right" principle tells us that marketers control many factors that determine marketing success.

Most successful organizations have adopted the **marketing concept**. The marketing concept is based on the "right" principle. The marketing concept is the use of marketing data to focus on the needs and wants of customers in order to develop marketing strategies that not only satisfy the needs of the customers but also the accomplish the goals of the organization. An organization uses the marketing concept when it identifies the buyer's needs and then produces the goods, services, or ideas that will satisfy them (using the "right" principle). The marketing concept is oriented toward pleasing customers (be those customers organizations or consumers) by offering value. Specifically, the marketing concept involves the following:

- Focusing on the needs and wants of the customers so the organization can distinguish its product(s) from competitors' offerings. Products can be goods, services, or ideas.
- Integrating all of the organization's activities, including production and promotion, to satisfy these wants and needs
- Achieving long-term goals for the organization by satisfying customer wants and needs legally and responsibly

Today, companies of every size in all industries are applying the marketing concept. Enterprise Rent-A-Car found that its customers didn't want to have to drive to its offices. Therefore, Enterprise began delivering vehicles to customers' homes or places of work. Disney found that some of its patrons really disliked waiting in lines. In response, Disney began offering FastPass at a premium price, which allows patrons to avoid standing in long lines waiting for attractions. One important key to understanding the marketing concept is to know that using the marketing concept means the product is created *after* market research is used to identify the needs and wants of the customers. Products are not just created by production departments and then marketing departments are expected to identify ways to sell them based on the research. An organization that truly utilizes the marketing concept uses the data about potential customers from the very inception of the product to create the best good, service, or idea possible, as well as other marketing strategies to support it.

Customer Value

Customer value is the ratio of benefits for the customer (organization or consumer) to the sacrifice necessary to obtain those benefits. The customer determines the value of both the benefits and the sacrifices. Creating customer value is a core business strategy of many successful firms. Customer value is rooted in the belief that price is not the only thing that matters. A business that focuses on the cost of production and price to the customer will be managed as though it were providing a commodity differentiated only by price. In contrast, businesses that provide customer value believe that many customers will pay a premium for superior customer service or accept fewer services for a value price. It is important not to base value on price (instead of service or quality) because customers who only value price will buy from the competition as soon as a competitor can offer a lower price. It is much better to use marketing strategies based on customer relationships and service, which are harder for the competition to replicate. Southwest Airlines doesn't offer assigned seats, meals, or in-flight movies. Instead the budget carrier delivers what it promises: on-time departures. In "service value" surveys, Southwest routinely beats the full-service airlines such as American Airlines, which actually provide passengers with luxuries such as movies and food on selected long-haul flights.

Customer Satisfaction

Customer satisfaction is a theme stressed throughout this text. **Customer satisfaction** is the customer's feeling that a product has met or exceeded expectations. Expectations are often the result of communication, especially promotion. Utilizing marketing research to identify specific expectations and then crafting marketing strategy to meet or exceed those expectations is a major contributor to success for an organization. Lexus consistently wins awards for its outstanding customer satisfaction. JD Powers surveys car owners two years after they make their purchase. Its Customer Satisfaction Survey is made up of four measures that each describe an element of overall ownership satisfaction at two years: vehicle quality/ reliability, vehicle appeal, ownership costs, and service satisfaction from a dealer. Lexus continues to lead the industry and has been America's top-ranked vehicle for five years in a row.[1]

Exhibit 11.2   Geico—the major auto insurer with the scaly mascot—famously boasts a 97 percent customer-satisfaction rating. Although the firm's claim may be exaggerated a bit, consumers get the message that Geico delivers quality insurance coverage at low prices. *In what way does the company's quirky and ubiquitous advertising—in which customers claim to have saved a bunch of money on car insurance by switching to Geico—influence customers' service expectations?* (Credit: Mike Mozart/ Flickr/ Attribution 2.0 Generic (CC BY 2.0))

Building Relationships

Relationship marketing is a strategy that focuses on forging long-term partnerships with customers. Companies build relationships with customers by offering value and providing customer satisfaction. Once relationships are built with customers, customers tend to continue to purchase from the same company, even if the prices of the competitors are less or if the competition offers sales promotions or incentives. Customers (both organizations and consumers) tend to buy products from suppliers whom they trust and feel a kinship with, regardless of offerings of unknown competitors. Companies benefit from repeat sales and referrals that lead to increases in sales, market share, and profits. Costs fall because it is less expensive to serve existing customers than to attract new ones. Focusing on customer retention can be a winning tactic; studies show that increasing customer retention rates by 5 percent increases profits by anywhere from 25 to 95 percent.[2]

Customers also benefit from stable relationships with suppliers. Business buyers have found that partnerships with their suppliers are essential to producing high-quality products while cutting costs. Customers remain loyal to firms that provide them greater value and satisfaction than they expect from competing firms.

Frequent-buyer clubs are an excellent way to build long-term relationships. All major airlines have frequent-flyer programs. After you fly a certain number of miles, you become eligible for a free ticket. Now, cruise lines, hotels, car rental agencies, credit-card companies, and even mortgage companies give away "airline miles" with purchases. Consumers patronize the airline and its partners because they want the free tickets. Thus, the program helps to create a long-term relationship with (and ongoing benefits for) the customer. Southwest Airlines carries its loyalty program a bit further than most. Members get birthday cards, and some even get profiled in the airline's in-flight magazine!

CONCEPT CHECK

1. Explain the marketing concept.
2. Explain the difference between customer value and customer satisfaction.
3. What is meant by relationship marketing?

11.2 Creating a Marketing Strategy

2. How do managers create a marketing strategy?

What Is Marketing Strategy?

Marketers use a number of different "tools" to develop the products or services that meet the needs and wants of their customers, provide excellent value for the customers, and satisfy those customers. Marketing strategy is really five different components of marketing. These components are called "the **Five Ps**" of marketing. They are the methods, tools, and processes used by marketers to develop and market products. These five tools are also called "the marketing mix." These are the 5Ps:

- **Product:** Something offered in exchange and for which marketing actions are taken and marketing decisions made. Products can be goods (physical things such as smartphones) or services (such as the telecommunications that must be used for a smartphone to work) or ideas (such as the thought that being constantly connected through telecommunications is absolutely crucial in today's society). All products have both tangible and intangible aspects.

- **Price:** Something given in exchange for a product. Price may be monetary or nonmonetary (such as waiting in long lines for a restaurant or giving blood at the local blood bank). Price has many names, such as rent, fees, charges, and others.
- **Place:** Some method of getting the product from the creator of the product to the customer. Place includes a myriad of important tasks: transportation, location, supply chain management (managing each entity that deals with the product in its route to the buyer), online presence, inventory, and atmospherics (how the office, store, or even the website looks).
- **Promotion:** Methods for informing and influencing customers to buy the product. Promotion includes several different components – traditional advertising, sales promotion, public relations, personal selling, social media, and e-commerce. Promotion is often mistaken for marketing because it is the most visible part of marketing; however, marketing encompasses much more than just promotion.
- **People:** Methods of utilizing organization employees to support the marketing strategies of the company. All products have both tangible and intangible aspects. People (as a marketing strategy) are crucial to the development of the product's intangible aspects.

Marketers utilize the tools of marketing strategy to develop new products and sell them in the marketplace. But marketers cannot create products in isolation. Marketers must understand and consider all aspects of the external environment in order to create marketing programs (plans) that will be successful in the current market and in future markets. Thus, many organizations assemble a team of specialists to continually collect and evaluate environmental information, a process called **environmental scanning**. The goal in gathering the environmental data is to identify current and future market opportunities and threats.

Computer manufacturers understand the importance of environmental scanning to monitor rapidly changing consumer interests. Since the invention of the personal computer (PC), computer technicians and other enthusiasts have taken two things for granted: processor speeds will grow exponentially, and PCs will become indistinguishable from televisions. The result of this will be "convergence," which means that the digital industry (manufacturers of computers, smartphones, and other mobile devices) will merge together with entertainment (such as television, radio, streaming video, and the internet). This convergence is already creating great opportunities for new products—watches that have both computers and cell phones in them, cell phones used to download videos not available except by independent entertainment producers (who are not affiliated with traditional media) such as Amazon and Google.

One clear winner in this new world so far is Apple, which has leveraged its computer platform to make it easy and fashionable for consumers to become experts in the digital age. Apple has capitalized on this through the development of iTunes, the iPhone and iPads, and the iWatch. Apple sells almost as many iPads per quarter as it does Macintosh computers, and it certainly sells a massive number of iPhones. Microsoft wants in on this business badly, but Hewlett-Packard decided to shift its loyalty to Apple, so Microsoft doesn't have much leverage just now. The other company to watch over the next few years is Samsung, which has doubled its efforts to make its consumer electronics offerings strong competition to Apple products. Finally, the device-free streaming services such as Amazon Music, Pandora, and Spotify have provided competition to Apple while restoring profitability to the music industry.[3]

In general, six categories of environmental data shape most marketing decisions:

- *Cultural/social forces:* Includes such factors as the buying behaviors of specific cultures and subcultures, the values of potential customers, the changing roles of families, and other societal trends such as employees working from home and flexible work hours
- *Demographic forces:* Includes such factors as changes in the ages of potential customers (e.g., baby

boomers, millennials), birth and death rates, and locations of various groups of people
- *Economic forces:* Includes such factors as changing incomes, unemployment levels, inflation, and recession
- *Technological forces:* Includes such factors as advances in telecommunications and computer technology
- *Political and legal forces:* Includes such factors as changes in laws, regulatory agency activities, and political movements
- *Competitive forces:* Includes such factors as new and shifting competition from domestic and foreign-based firms

Defining the Target Market

Marketers develop the information about the environment to get a clear picture of the total market for the product, including environmental factors. Once the marketers understand the various environmental factors, specific target markets must then be chosen from the total market. Marketers focus on providing value for a well-defined target market or target markets. The **target market** is the specific group of customers (which could be organizations or individual consumers) toward which a firm directs its marketing efforts. Quaker Oats targets its grits to blue-collar consumers in the South. Williams Sonoma has several different types of stores, each geared toward a distinct target market: Pottery Barn for upscale home furnishings; its specialty stores, West Elm, Mark and Graham, and Rejuvenation, that specialize in jewelry and other accessories; and home improvement and furnishings that are affordable and sustainable. These target markets are all part of the overall retail market for housewares and lifestyle. Identifying a target market helps a company focus its marketing efforts on those who are most likely to buy its products or services. Concentrating on potential customers lets the firm use its resources efficiently. Examples of the target markets for Marriott Hotel Brands' lodging alternatives are shown in Table 11.1.

Examples of Target Markets for Marriott Hotel Brands		
	Price Range	Target Market
Fairfield Inn	$105–125	Economizing business and leisure travelers
Towne Place Suites	$110–140	Moderate-tier travelers who stay three to four weeks
SpringHill Suites	$120–165	Business and leisure travelers looking for more space and amenities
Courtyard	$120–170	Travelers seeking quality and affordable accommodations designed for the road warrior
Residence Inn	$126–175	Travelers seeking a residential-style hotel
Marriott Hotels, Resorts, and Suites	$135–410	Grounded achievers who desire consistent quality

Table 11.1

Examples of Target Markets for Marriott Hotel Brands		
	Price Range	Target Market
Renaissance Hotels and Resorts	$135–415	Discerning business and leisure travelers who seek creative attention to detail
Ritz-Carlton	$295–1,500	Senior executives and entrepreneurs looking for a unique, luxury, personalized experience

Table 11.1

Creating a Competitive Advantage

A **competitive advantage**, also called a *differential advantage*, is a set of unique features of a company and its products that are perceived by the target market(s) as significant and superior to those of the competition. Competitive advantage is the factor that causes customers to patronize a specific firm and not the competition. There are four types of competitive advantage: cost, product differentiation, service differentiation, and niche.

Cost Competitive Advantage

A firm that has a **cost competitive advantage** can produce a product or service at a lower cost than all its competitors while maintaining satisfactory profit margins. Firms become cost leaders by obtaining inexpensive raw materials, making plant operations more efficient, designing products for ease of manufacture, controlling overhead costs, and avoiding marginal customers.

Over time, the cost competitive advantage may fail. Typically, if one firm is using an innovative technology to reduce its costs, then other firms in the industry will adopt this technology and reduce their costs as well. For example, Bell Labs invented fiber-optic cables that reduced the cost of voice and data transmission by dramatically increasing the number of calls that could be transmitted simultaneously through a two-inch cable. Within five years, however, fiber-optic technology had spread through the industry, and Bell Labs lost its cost competitive advantage. Firms may also lose their cost competitive advantage if competing firms match their low costs by using the same lower-cost suppliers. Therefore, a cost competitive advantage may not offer a long-term competitive advantage.

Product Differentiation Competitive Advantage

Because cost competitive advantages are subject to continual erosion, other types of competitive advantage tend to provide a longer-lasting competitive advantage. The durability of a **differential competitive advantage** can be more successful for the long-term viability of the company. Common differential advantages are brand names (Tide detergent), a strong dealer network (Caterpillar for construction equipment), product reliability (Lexus vehicles), image (Neiman Marcus in retailing), and service (Federal Express). Brand names such as Chanel, BMW, and Cartier stand for quality the world over. Through continual product and marketing innovations and attention to quality and value, marketers at these organizations have created enduring competitive advantages.

Service Differentiation Competitive Advantage

In today's world of instant connection and social media, services are crucial for both tangible and nontangible products. Almost every day, the media report the consequences of poor service that went "viral" on social media because the service interaction was videotaped and uploaded to the internet. Customers now demand a higher level of service for all kinds of products, and if the service level does not meet customer expectations, it is likely that the customer will post negative comments on a review site or upload the interaction to various social media platforms. Some small companies have had to close their doors on the basis of one poor service interaction that went viral. Service levels that delight customers are even more important for intangible products such as engineering and accounting. More than 80 percent of the U.S. GDP is based on services. The ability to create the service product, continually refine the service process, and interact with customers (co-creators of the service) is crucial. Higher-level services require more planning, better execution, and constant evolution through the relationships with the customers. The use of service differentiation as a competitive advantage can be one of the most enduring and viable types of advantage.

Niche Competitive Advantage

A company with a **niche competitive advantage** targets and effectively serves a single segment of the market. For small companies with limited resources that potentially face giant competitors, utilizing a niche competitive advantage may be the only viable option. A market segment that has good growth potential but is not crucial to the success of major competitors is a good candidate for a niche strategy. Once a potential segment has been identified, the firm needs to make certain it can defend against challengers through its superior ability to serve buyers in the segment. For example, Regions Bank–Music Row Private Bank follows a niche strategy with its concentration on country music stars and entertainment industry professionals in Nashville. Its office is in the heart of Nashville's music district. Music Row Private Bank has decided to expand its niche strategy to Miami, the "epicenter" of Latin music, and to Atlanta. The latter is a longtime rhythm-and-blues capital and now is the center of contemporary "urban" music. Both new markets have the kinds of music professionals—entertainers, record executives, producers, agents, and others—that have made Regions Bank–Music Row Private Bank so successful in Nashville.

CONCEPT CHECK

1. What is environmental scanning?
2. What is a target market, and why should a company have one?
3. Explain the four types of competitive advantages and provide examples of each.

11.3   Developing a Marketing Mix

3. What is the marketing mix?

Once a firm has defined its target market and identified its competitive advantage, it can create the **marketing mix**, which is based on the 5Ps discussed earlier, that brings a specific group of consumers a product with superior value. Every target market requires a unique marketing mix to satisfy the needs of the target customers and meet the firm's goals. A strategy must be constructed for each of the 5Ps, and all strategies must be blended with the strategies of the other elements. Thus, the marketing mix is only as good as its weakest part. For example, an excellent product with a poor distribution system could be doomed to failure. An excellent product with an excellent distribution system but an inappropriate price is also doomed to failure. A successful marketing mix requires careful tailoring. For instance, at first glance you might think that McDonald's and Wendy's have roughly the same marketing mix. After all, they are both in the fast-food business. But McDonald's targets parents with young children through Ronald McDonald, heavily promoted children's Happy Meals, and in-store playgrounds. Wendy's is targeted to a more adult crowd. Wendy's has no playgrounds, but it does have flat-screen TVs, digital menu boards, and comfy leather seating by a fireplace in many stores (a more adult atmosphere), and it has expanded its menu to include more items for adult tastes.

Product Strategy

Marketing strategy typically starts with the product. Marketers can't plan a distribution system or set a price if they don't know exactly what product will be offered to the market. Marketers use the term *product* to refer to *goods, services*, or even *ideas*. Examples of goods would include tires, MP3 players, and clothing. Goods can be divided into business goods (commercial or industrial) or consumer goods. Examples of services would be hotels, hair salons, airlines, and engineering and accounting firms. Services can be divided into consumer services, such as lawn care and hair styling, or professional services, such as engineering, accounting, or consultancy. In addition, marketing is often used to "market" ideas that benefit companies or industries, such as the idea to "go green" or to "give blood." Businesses often use marketing to improve the long-term viability of their industries, such as the avocado industry or the milk industry, which run advertising spots and post social media messages to encourage consumers to view their industries favorably. Thus, the heart of the marketing mix is the good, service, or idea. Creating a **product strategy** involves choosing a brand name, packaging, colors, a warranty, accessories, and a service program.

Marketers view products in a much larger context than is often thought. They include not only the item itself but also the brand name and the company image. The names Ralph Lauren and Gucci, for instance, create extra value for everything from cosmetics to bath towels. That is, products with those names sell at higher prices than identical products without the names. Consumers buy things not only for what they do, but also for what they mean.

Exhibit 11.3   With their computerized profile-matching capabilities, online dating services are a high-tech way to make a love connection. Today's date-seeking singles want more than automated personals, however. They want advice from experts. At Match.com, popular shrink Dr. Phil guides subscribers toward healthy relationships. At eHarmony.com, Dr. Neil Clark Warren helps the lovelorn find a soulmate. *How do internet dating services use various elements of the marketing mix to bolster the effectiveness of their product strategies?* (Credit: Bixentro/ Flickr/ Attribution-2.0 Generic (CC BY 2.0))

Pricing Strategy

Pricing strategy is based on demand for the product and the cost of producing that product. However, price can have a major impact on the success of a product if the price is not in balance with the other components of the 5Ps. For some products (especially service products), having a price that is too low may actually hurt sales. In services, a higher price is often equated with higher value. For some types of specialty products, a high price is expected, such as prices for designer clothes or luxury cars. Even costume jewelry is often marked up more than 1000 percent over the cost to produce it because of the image factor of a higher price. Special considerations can also influence the price. Sometimes an introductory price is used to get people to try a new product. Some firms enter the market with low prices and keep them low, such as Carnival Cruise Lines and Suzuki cars. Others enter a market with very high prices and then lower them over time, such as producers of high-definition televisions and personal computers.

Place (Distribution) Strategy

Place (distribution) strategy is creating the means (the channel) by which a product flows from the producer to the consumer. Place includes many parts of the marketing endeavor. It includes the physical location and physical attributes of the business, as well as inventory and control systems, transportation, supply chain management, and even presence on the web. One aspect of distribution strategy is deciding how many stores and which specific wholesalers and retailers will handle the product in a geographic area. Cosmetics, for instance, are distributed in many different ways. Avon has a sales force of several hundred thousand representatives who call directly on consumers. Clinique and Estée Lauder are distributed through selected department stores. Cover Girl and Coty use mostly chain drugstores and other mass merchandisers. Redken products sell through hair salons. Revlon uses several of these distribution channels. For services, place often becomes synonymous with both physical location (and attributes of that location such as atmospherics) and online presence. Place strategy for services also includes such items as supply chain management. An example would be that an engineering firm would develop offices with lush interiors (to denote success) and would also have to manage the supplies for ongoing operations such as the purchase of computers for computer-aided drafting.

Promotion Strategy

Many people feel that promotion is the most exciting part of the marketing mix. **Promotion strategy** covers personal selling, traditional advertising, public relations, sales promotion, social media, and e-commerce. These elements are called the promotional mix. Each element is coordinated with the others to create a promotional blend. An advertisement, for instance, helps a buyer get to know the company and paves the way for a sales call. A good promotional strategy can dramatically increase a firm's sales.

Public relations plays a special role in promotion. It is used to create a good image of the company and its products. Bad publicity costs nothing to send out, but it can cost a firm a great deal in lost business. Public relations uses many tools, such as publicity, crisis management strategy, and in-house communication to employees. Good publicity, such as a television or magazine story about a firm's new product, may be the result of much time, money, and effort spent by a public-relations department. Public-relations activities always cost money—in salaries and supplies. Public-relations efforts are the least "controllable" of all the tools of promotion, and a great deal of effort and relationship-building is required to develop the ongoing goodwill and networking that is needed to enhance the image of a company.

Sales promotion directly stimulates sales. It includes trade shows, catalogs, contests, games, premiums, coupons, and special offers. It is a direct incentive for the customer to purchase the product immediately. It takes many forms and must adhere to strict laws and regulations. For example, some types of contests and giveaways are not allowed in all the states within the United States. McDonald's discount coupons and contests offering money and food prizes are examples of sales promotions.

Social media is a major element of the promotion mix in today's world. Most businesses have a corporate website, as well as pages on different social media sites such as Facebook, Pinterest, and Twitter. Social media is more powerful as a channel for getting the company's message out to the target market (or general public) than traditional advertising, especially for some target markets. Companies (and even individuals) can use social media to create instant branding. E-commerce is the use of the company website to support and expand the marketing strategies of the 5Ps. It can include actual "order online" capabilities, create online communities, and be used to collect data from both existing and potential customers. Some e-commerce websites offer free games and other interactive options for their customers. All of this activity helps to build and strengthen the long-term relationships of customers with the company.

Not-for-Profit Marketing

Profit-oriented companies are not the only ones that analyze the marketing environment, find a competitive advantage, and create a marketing mix. The application of marketing principles and techniques is also vital to not-for-profit organizations. Marketing helps not-for-profit groups identify target markets and develop effective marketing mixes. In some cases, marketing has kept symphonies, museums, and other cultural groups from having to close their doors. In other organizations, such as the American Heart Association, marketing ideas and techniques have helped managers do their jobs better. In the private sector, the profit motive is both an objective for guiding decisions and a criterion for evaluating results. Not-for-profit organizations do not seek to make a profit for redistribution to owners or shareholders. Rather, their focus is often on generating enough funds to cover expenses or generating enough funds to expand their services to assist more people. For example, the Methodist Church does not gauge its success by the amount of money left in offering plates. The Museum of Science and Industry does not base its performance evaluations on the dollar value of tokens put into the turnstile. An organization such as the American Red Cross raises funds to provide basic services, but if enough funds are raised (beyond just the amount to cover expenses), those funds are used to expand services or improve current services.

CONCEPT CHECK

1. What is meant by the marketing mix?
2. What are the components of the marketing mix?
3. How can marketing techniques help not-for-profit organizations?

11.4 | Buyer Behavior

4. How do consumers and organizations make buying decisions?

An organization that wants to be successful must consider buyer behavior when developing the marketing mix. **Buyer behavior** is the actions people take with regard to buying and using products. Marketers must understand buyer behavior, such as how raising or lowering a price will affect the buyer's perception of the product and therefore create a fluctuation in sales, or how a specific review on social media can create an entirely new direction for the marketing mix based on the comments (buyer behavior/input) of the target market.

To understand buyer behavior, marketers must understand how customers make buying decisions. Consumers and businesses have processes for making decisions about purchases. These decision-making processes are affected by cultural, social, individual, and psychological factors. The consumer decision-making process has several steps, which are shown in Exhibit 11.4.

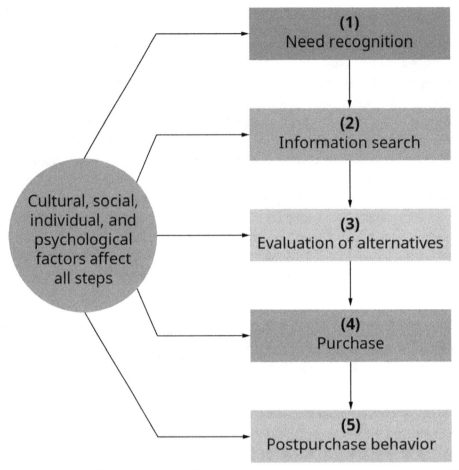

Exhibit 11.4   Consumer Purchase Decision-Making Process (Attribution: Copyright Rice University, OpenStax, under CC BY 4.0 license.)

The process starts with need recognition. Need recognition could be as simple as running out of coffee. Need recognition could also take place over several months, such as when repeated car repairs influence a consumer to make a decision to buy a new car. (Step 1 in **Exhibit 11.4**).

Next, the buyer gathers information. If the consumer is making a decision to purchase a house, he or she might research information about financing, available homes, styles, locations, and so forth (Step 2). Once the consumer has gathered the information, he or she must evaluate alternatives (Step 3). For example, a consumer might eliminate all homes that cost over $150,000 or are more than a 30-minute drive to work. After evaluating the alternatives, the consumer will make a decision based on those alternatives. Then the consumer makes the purchase decision, the decision to buy or not to buy (Step 4). Finally, the consumer assesses the decision itself and his or her satisfaction with the purchase, which would include not only the home, but the buying experience as well (Step 5).

Influences on Consumer Decision-Making

Cultural, social, individual, and psychological factors have an impact on consumer decision-making from the time a person recognizes a need through post-purchase behavior. We will examine each of these factors in more detail. It is important to understand the relevance of these influences on consumer decision-making.

Culture

Purchase roles within the family are influenced by culture. **Culture** is the set of values, ideas, attitudes, and symbols created to shape human behavior. Culture is the part of customs and traditions of a group of people that is transformed into its art, food, costumes/clothing, architecture, and language, as well as other unique manifestations of a specific group of related individuals. Culture is environmentally oriented. For example, the nomads of Finland have developed a culture for Arctic survival. Similarly, the natives of the Brazilian jungle have created a culture suitable for jungle living.

Culture by definition is social in nature. It is human interaction that creates values and prescribes acceptable behavior. Culture gives order to society by creating common expectations. Sometimes these expectations are codified into law; for example, if you come to a red light, you stop the car. In some cultures, a young man undergoes a special rite of passage from youth into adulthood (such as a bar mitzvah in Jewish culture). In other cultures, young women have a rite of passage but young men do not (such as a quinceañera in Hispanic culture). As long as a value or belief meets the needs of society, it will remain part of the culture. If it is no longer functional, the value or belief fades away. For example, the value that very large families are "good" is no longer held by a majority of Americans. This is because most Americans live in an urban rather than a rural environment, and children are no longer needed to perform farm chores.

Social Factors

Most consumers are likely to seek out the opinions of others to reduce their search and evaluation effort or uncertainty, especially as the perceived risk of the decision increases. Consumers may also seek out others' opinions for guidance on new products or services, products with image-related attributes, or products where attribute information is lacking or uninformative. Specifically, consumers interact socially with reference groups, opinion leaders, and family members to obtain product information and decision approval. All the formal and informal groups that influence the buying behavior of an individual are considered that person's **reference groups**. Consumers may use products or brands to identify with or become a member of a group. They learn from observing how members of their reference groups consume, and they use the same criteria to make their own consumer decisions. A reference group might be a fraternity or sorority, a group you work with, or a club to which you belong.

Individual Influences

A person's buying decisions are also influenced by personal characteristics unique to each individual, such as gender and personality. Individual characteristics are generally stable over the course of one's life. For instance, most people do not change their gender, and the act of changing personality requires a complete reorientation of one's life.

Physiological differences between men and women result in different needs, such as health and beauty products. Just as important are the distinct cultural, social, and economic roles played by men and women and the effects that these have on their decision-making processes. Men and women also shop differently. Studies show that men and women share similar motivations in terms of where to shop—that is, seeking reasonable prices, merchandise quality, and a friendly, low-pressure environment—but they don't necessarily feel the same about shopping in general. Most women enjoy shopping; their male counterparts claim to dislike the experience and shop only out of necessity. Furthermore, men desire simple shopping experiences, stores with less variety, and convenience. When it comes to online shopping, gender differences continue. According to recent research, women tend to shop based on their future needs, while men tend to shop when their need is immediate. In addition, women tend to make impulse buys more frequently than men, who tend to think logically when making purchase decisions.[4]

Each consumer has a unique personality. **Personality** is a broad concept that can be thought of as a way of organizing and grouping how an individual typically reacts to situations. Thus, personality combines psychological makeup and environmental forces. It includes people's underlying dispositions, especially their most dominant characteristics. Although personality is one of the least useful concepts in the study of consumer behavior, some marketers believe that personality influences the types and brands of products purchased. For instance, the type of car, clothes, or jewelry a consumer buys may reflect one or more personality traits.

Psychological Influences

An individual's buying decisions are further influenced by psychological factors such as perception, beliefs, and attitudes. These factors are what consumers use to interact with their world. They are the tools consumers use to recognize their feelings, gather and analyze information, formulate thoughts and opinions, and take action. Unlike the other three influences on consumer behavior, psychological influences can be affected by a person's environment because they are applied on specific occasions. For example, individuals will perceive different stimuli and process these stimuli in different ways depending on whether the individual is sitting in class concentrating on an instructor's lecture, sitting outside of class talking to friends, or sitting at home watching television.

B2B Purchase Decision-Making

Business-to-business (B2B) buyer behavior and business markets are different from consumer markets. Business markets include institutions such as hospitals and schools, manufacturers, wholesalers and retailers, and various branches of government. The key difference between a consumer product and a business product is the intended use. For example, if a consumer purchases a certain brand of computer for use at home, it is considered a consumer good. If a purchasing agent for Netflix buys exactly the same computer for Netflix scriptwriter, it is considered a business good. Why? The reason is that Netflix is a business, so the computer will be used in a business environment.

The Decision-Making Process

The purchases that organizations make often involve greater risk than purchases made by individual consumers. For this reason, businesses (and other organizations) tend to base purchase decisions on more data and make purchase decisions based on rational decision-making so purchases will optimize value for the organization and minimize risk. For this reason, the business purchase decision-making process differs from the consumer process. The steps are similar: need recognition, setting specifications, information search (including identification of suppliers), evaluation (including evaluation of suppliers), purchase ("go or no-go"), and post-purchase evaluation. The major difference between the two processes is that businesses decide beforehand what exactly is needed on the purchase (setting specifications) and then seek information regarding products that meet those specifications. In this way, the purchases are more likely to satisfy the needs of the overall organization, thus reducing the risk.

Characteristics of the B2B Market

The main differences between consumer markets and business markets include the following:

1. *Purchase volume:* Business customers buy in much larger quantities than consumers. Mars must purchase many truckloads of sugar to make one day's output of M&Ms. Home Depot buys thousands of batteries each day for resale to consumers. The federal government must use (and purchase) millions of pens each day.

2. *Number of customers:* Business marketers usually have far fewer customers than consumer marketers. As a result, it is much easier to identify prospective buyers and monitor current needs. For example, there are far fewer customers for airplanes or industrial crane companies than there are for consumer goods companies since there are more than 125 million consumer households in the United States.

3. *Location of buyers:* Business customers tend to be much more geographically concentrated than consumers. The computer industry is concentrated in Silicon Valley and a few other areas. Aircraft manufacturing is found in Seattle, Washington; St. Louis, Missouri; and Dallas/Fort Worth, Texas. Suppliers to these manufacturers often locate close to the manufacturers to lower distribution costs and facilitate communication.

4. *Direct distribution:* Business sales tend to be made directly to the buyer because such sales frequently involve large quantities or custom-made items such as heavy machinery. Consumer goods are more likely to be sold through intermediaries such as wholesalers and retailers.

CONCEPT CHECK

1. Explain the consumer purchase decision-making process.
2. Explain the differences between the business purchase decision-making process and the consumer purchase decision-making process.
3. How do business markets differ from consumer markets?

11.5 | Market Segmentation

5. What are the five basic forms of consumer and business market segmentation?

Most organizations cannot target the total market for a specific product. For each separate part of the market that an organization wants to target, a marketing mix (a set of 5Ps) must be created. It would be very expensive to try to create a marketing mix for every part of the target market. Instead, companies cut up those targets into specific "segments" of the market that the organization is more strategically positioned to be successful in targeting. Segmentation also varies based on the target market being a consumer market or a business market.

The study of buyer behavior helps marketing managers better understand why people make purchases. To identify the target markets that may be most profitable for the firm, marketers use **market segmentation**, which is the process of separating, identifying, and evaluating the layers of a market to identify a target market. For instance, a target market might be segmented into two groups: families with children and families without children. Families with young children are likely to buy hot cereals and presweetened cereals. Families with no children are more likely to buy health-oriented cereals. Cereal companies plan their marketing mixes with this difference in mind. A business market may be segmented by large customers and small customers or by geographic area.

The five basic forms of consumer market segmentation are demographic, geographic, psychographic, benefit, and volume. Their characteristics are summarized in **Table 11.2** and discussed in the following sections.

Demographic Segmentation

Demographic segmentation uses categories such as age, education, gender, income, and household size to differentiate among markets. This form of market segmentation is the most common because demographic information is easy to obtain. The U.S. Census Bureau provides a great deal of demographic data, especially about metropolitan areas. For example, marketing researchers can use census data to find areas within cities that contain high concentrations of high-income consumers, singles, blue-collar workers, and so forth. However, even though demographic information is easier to obtain than other types of information, it may not always be the best approach to segmentation because it is limited on what it can reveal about consumers.

Forms of Consumer Market Segmentation	
Form General	Characteristics
Demographic segmentation	Age, education, gender, income, race, social class, household size
Geographic segmentation	Regional location (e.g., New England, Mid-Atlantic, Southeast, Great Lakes, Plains States, Northwest, Central, Southwest, Rocky Mountains, Far West), population density (urban, suburban, rural), city or county size, climate
Psychographic segmentation	Lifestyle, personality, interests, values, attitudes
Benefit segmentation	Benefits provided by the good or service
Volume segmentation	Amount of use (light versus heavy)

Table 11.2

Age Segmentation for Fritos, Doritos, and Tostitos					
	Name Derivation	Year Introduced	Main Ingredients	Demographic	Niche, According to Frito Lay
Fritos	"Little fried bits" (Spanish)	1932	Corn, vegetable oil, salt	33- to 51-year-old males	"Hunger satisfaction"

Table 11.3 Source: Adapted from Frito Lay website, accessed October 1, 2017.

Age Segmentation for Fritos, Doritos, and Tostitos					
	Name Derivation	Year Introduced	Main Ingredients	Demographic	Niche, According to Frito Lay
Doritos	"Little bits of gold"	1964	Corn, vegetable oil, cheddar cheese, salt	Teens, mostly males	"Bold and daring snacking"
Tostitos	"Little toasted bits" (Spanish)	1981	White corn, vegetable oil, salt	Upscale consumers born between 1946 and 1964	"Casual interaction through friends and family . . . a social food that brings people together"

Table 11.3 Source: Adapted from Frito Lay website, accessed October 1, 2017.

Many products are targeted to various age groups. Most music CDs, Pepsi, Coke, many movies, the Honda Fit, and thousands of other products are targeted toward teenagers and persons under 25 years old. In contrast, most cruises, medical products, fine jewelry, vacation homes, Teslas, and denture products are targeted toward people 50 years old and up. An example of how Frito Lay targets various age groups for three of its most popular products is shown in Table 11.3.

Income is another popular way to segment markets. Income level influences consumers' wants and determines their buying power. Housing, clothing, automobiles, and alcoholic beverages are among the many markets segmented by income. Budget Gourmet frozen dinners are targeted to lower-income groups, whereas the Stouffer's line and California Pizza Kitchen frozen pizzas are aimed at higher-income consumers.

Geographic Segmentation

Geographic segmentation means segmenting markets by region of the country, city or county size, market density, or climate. *Market density* is the number of people or businesses within a certain area. Many companies segment their markets geographically to meet regional preferences and buying habits. Pizza Hut, for instance, gives easterners extra cheese, westerners more ingredients, and midwesterners both. Both Ford and Chevrolet sell more pickup trucks and truck parts in the middle of the country than on either coast. The well-defined "pickup truck belt" runs from the upper Midwest south through Texas and the Gulf states. Ford "owns" the northern half of this truck belt and Chevrolet the southern half.

Psychographic Segmentation

Race, income, occupation, and other demographic variables help in developing strategies but often do not paint the entire picture of consumer needs. Demographics provide basic data that can be observed about individuals, but psychographics provide vital information that is often much more useful in crafting the marketing message. Demographics provide the skeleton, but psychographics add meat to the bones.

Psychographic segmentation is market segmentation by personality or lifestyle. People with common activities, interests, and opinions are grouped together and given a "lifestyle name." For example, Harley-Davidson divides its customers into seven lifestyle segments, from "cocky misfits" who are most likely to be arrogant troublemakers, to "laid-back camper types" committed to cycling and nature, to "classy capitalists" who have wealth and privilege. Two different managers could be described by demographics as male, managers, 35 years old, with $80,000 per year income. A marketer who just saw the demographics might create one advertisement to reach both of them. However, if the marketer knew that one of the managers was president of his homeowner's association and captain of a rugby league team and the other manager was a holder of opera season tickets and president of the Friends of the Public Library, the messages might be designed very differently in order to be more successful.

Benefit Segmentation

Benefit segmentation is based on what a product will do rather than on consumer characteristics. For years Crest toothpaste was targeted toward consumers concerned with preventing cavities. Recently, Crest subdivided its market. It now offers regular Crest, Crest Tartar Control for people who want to prevent cavities and tartar buildup, Crest for kids with sparkles that taste like bubble gum, and another Crest that prevents gum disease. Another toothpaste, Topol, targets people who want whiter teeth—teeth without coffee, tea, or tobacco stains. Sensodyne toothpaste is aimed at people with highly sensitive teeth.

Volume Segmentation

The fifth main type of segmentation is **volume segmentation**, which is based on the amount of the product purchased. Just about every product has heavy, moderate, and light users, as well as nonusers. Heavy users often account for a very large portion of a product's sales. Thus, a firm might want to target its marketing mix to the heavy-user segment. For example, in the fast-food industry, the heavy user (a young, single male) accounts for only one in five fast-food patrons. Yet this heavy user makes over 60 percent of all visits to fast-food restaurants.

Retailers are aware that heavy shoppers not only spend more, but also visit each outlet more frequently than other shoppers. Heavy shoppers visit the grocery store 122 times per year, compared with 93 annual visits for the medium shopper. They visit discount stores more than twice as often as medium shoppers, and they visit convenience/gas stores more than five times as often. On each trip, they consistently spend more than their medium-shopping counterparts.

Business Market Segmentation

Business markets are segmented differently than consumer markets. Business markets may segment based on geography, volume, and benefits, just as consumer markets are. However, organizations might also segment based on use of the product (such as a petrochemical company having one market segment for purchasers who use polyethylene for instrumentation panels and one for purchasers who use polyethylene for car seats), characteristics of purchasing function (such as purchasing committees, purchasing managers, or purchasing departments), size of the client (one segment for large customers who have different needs than smaller customers), or industry (such as segmenting food systems into restaurants or government agencies such as schools or military bases), as well as other considerations related to characteristics of business customers.

Using Marketing Research to Serve Existing Customers and Find New Customers

How do successful companies learn what their customers value? Through marketing research, companies can be sure they are listening to the voice of the customer. **Marketing research** is the process of planning, collecting, and analyzing data relevant to a marketing decision. The results of this analysis are then communicated to management. The information collected through marketing research includes the preferences of customers, the perceived benefits of products, and consumer lifestyles. Research helps companies make better use of their marketing budgets. Marketing research has a range of uses, from fine-tuning existing products to discovering whole new marketing concepts.

For example, everything at the Olive Garden restaurant chain, from the décor to the wine list, is based on marketing research. Each new menu item is put through a series of consumer taste tests before being added to the menu. Hallmark Cards uses marketing research to test messages, cover designs, and even the size of the cards. Hallmark's experts know which kinds of cards will sell best in which places. Engagement cards, for instance, sell best in the Northeast, where engagement parties are popular. Birthday cards for "Daddy" sell best in the South because even adult southerners tend to call their fathers Daddy.

Marketing research can use either primary data (where the organization actually gets the data and analyzes it) or secondary data (where the organization uses data that has already been developed and published by another entity and the organization is able to utilize the data for its own purposes). There are three basic research methods used for gathering primary data: survey, observation, and experiment.

With **survey research**, data is gathered from respondents—in person, through the internet, by telephone, or by mail—to obtain facts, opinions, and attitudes. A questionnaire is used to provide an orderly and structured approach to data-gathering. Face-to-face interviews may take place at the respondent's home, in a shopping mall, or at a place of business.

Observation research is research that monitors respondents' actions without direct interaction. In the fastest-growing form of observation research, researchers use cash registers with scanners that read tags with bar codes to identify the item being purchased. Technological advances are rapidly expanding the future of observation research. Arbitron research has developed a portable people meter (PPM) about the size of a cell phone that research participants clip to their belts or any article of clothing. They agree to wear it during all waking hours. Before the study participants go to sleep, they put the PPM in a cradle that automatically sends data back to Arbitron (now Nielsen Audio). The PPM will tell the marketing research company exactly which television programs the person watched and for how long. It also records radio programs listened to, any web streaming, supermarket piped-in music, or any other electronic media that the research participant encountered during the day.[5]

In the third research method, **experiment**, the investigator changes one or more variables—price, package, design, shelf space, advertising theme, or advertising expenditures—while observing the effects of those changes on another variable (usually sales). The objective of experiments is to measure causality. For example, an experiment may reveal the impact that a change in package design has on sales.

CONCEPT CHECK

1. Define market segmentation.
2. List and discuss the five basic forms of consumer market segmentation.
3. What are some additional forms of business segmentation?
4. How does marketing research help companies make better use of their marketing budgets?

11.6 What Is a Product?

6. What is a product, and how is it classified?

The goal of marketing research is to create products that are desired by the target market(s) chosen as strategic markets in line with the organization's goals. In marketing, a **product** (a good, service, or idea), along with its perceived attributes and benefits, creates value for the customer. Attributes can be tangible or intangible. Among the tangible attributes are packaging and warranties as illustrated in Exhibit 11.5. Intangible attributes are symbolic, such as brand image. Intangible attributes can include things like image as well as the depth of the relationship between a service provider and a customer. People make decisions about which products to buy after considering both tangible and intangible attributes of a product. For example, when a consumer buys a pair of jeans, he or she considers price, brand, store image, and style before making the purchase. These factors are all part of the marketing mix.

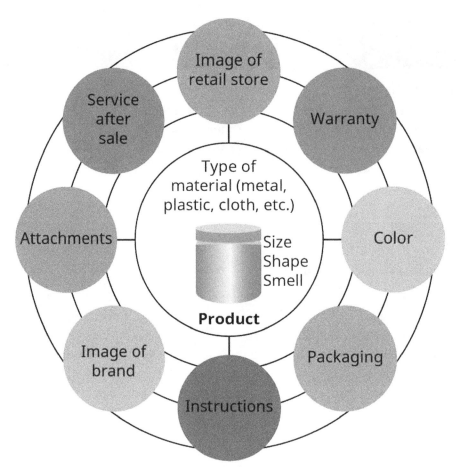

Exhibit 11.5   Tangible and Intangible Attributes of a Product Create Value (Attribution: Copyright Rice University, OpenStax, under CC BY 4.0 license.)

Classifying Consumer Products

Consumers are really buying packages of benefits that deliver value, which always includes some tangible aspects and some intangible aspects. The person who buys a plane ride on United Airlines is looking for a quick way to get from one city to another (the benefit). Providing this benefit requires a tangible part of the product (a plane) and an intangible part of the product (ticketing, maintenance, and piloting services). A person who purchases accounting services buys the benefit of having taxes completed on the correct tax form (tangible part of the service) and having the taxes prepared correctly by a trusted person (intangible part of the service).

Marketers must know how consumers view the types of products their companies sell so that they can design the marketing mix to appeal to the selected target market. To help them define target markets, marketers have devised product categories. Products that are bought by the end user are called *consumer products*. They include electric razors, sandwiches, cars, stereos, magazines, and houses. Consumer products that get used up, such as Nexxus shampoo and Lay's potato chips, are called *consumer nondurables*. Those that last for a long time, such as Whirlpool washing machines and Apple computers, are *consumer durables*.

Another way to classify consumer products is by the amount of effort consumers are willing to make to acquire them. The four major categories of consumer products are unsought products, convenience products, shopping products, and specialty products, as summarized in Table 11.4. **Unsought products** are products unplanned by the potential buyer or known products that the buyer does not actively seek.

Convenience products are relatively inexpensive items that require little shopping effort. Soft drinks, candy bars, milk, bread, and small hardware items are examples. Consumers buy them routinely without much planning. This does not mean that such products are unimportant or obscure. Many, in fact, are well known by their brand names—such as Pepsi-Cola, Pepperidge Farm breads, Domino's pizza, Sure deodorant, and UPS shipping.

In contrast to convenience products, **shopping products** are bought only after a brand-to-brand and store-to-store comparison of price, suitability, and style. Examples are furniture, automobiles, a vacation in Europe, and some items of clothing. Convenience products are bought with little planning, but shopping products may be purchased after months or even years of search and evaluation.

Specialty products are products for which consumers search long and hard and for which they refuse to accept substitutes. Expensive jewelry, designer clothing, state-of-the-art stereo equipment, limited-production automobiles, and gourmet restaurants fall into this category. Because consumers are willing to spend much time and effort to find specialty products, distribution is often limited to one or two sellers in a given region, such as Neiman-Marcus, Gucci, or a Porsche dealer.

Classification of Consumer Products by the Effort Expended to Buy Them		
Consumer	Product Examples	Degree of Effort Expended by Consumer
Unsought products	Life insurance	No effort
	Burial plots	Some to considerable effort
	Time-share condos	Some to considerable effort
Convenience products	Soft drinks	Very little or minimum effort
	Bread	Very little or minimum effort
	Milk	Very little or minimum effort
	Coffee	Very little or minimum effort
Shopping products	Automobiles	Considerable effort
	Homes	Considerable effort
	Vacations	Considerable effort
Specialty products	Expensive jewelry	Maximum effort
	Gourmet restaurants	Maximum effort
	Limited-production automobiles	Maximum effort

Table 11.4

CUSTOMER SATISFACTION AND QUALITY

Ferrari Targets Successful Consumers

Kevin Crowder walked onto the famed Monza, Italy, race track, climbed into a Ferrari F2000 racer, and circled the course with a Grand Prix champion. Mr. Crowder, a Texas businessman who earned millions when he sold a software company he cofounded, isn't himself a professional driver. He's a customer of one of Ferrari's marketing programs: the F-1 Clienti program, under which Ferrari resurrects old race cars that would otherwise be headed for the scrap heap. Instead, it sells them for $1 million or more, along with the chance to drive them with a professional pit crew's help.

Ferrari has long built its business around exclusivity. It limits production to around 4,500 to 5,000 cars a year at around $180,000 and up. Some customers pay additional money to race these street cars against fellow owners at company-sponsored Ferrari Challenge events. The F-1 Clienti program adds a super-premium service by giving people a chance to drive the same Ferraris used in Formula One, a series of auto races that are especially popular among Europeans.

The program gives customers "an experience they can't get elsewhere," says Ferrari CEO Dieter Knechtel. Mr. Knechtel says that the "brand experience is very much related to the ownership experience: It's about driving and the experience of the car while doing it in a community of like-minded people. This is why, we organise track days and tours in Italy with road tours in different countries, we can organise almost any experience with the car—what we offer to our customers is often a 'money can't buy' experience."

Critical Thinking Questions

1. For Mr. Crowder, the Ferrari is a specialty good. What kind of product would it be for you? Why?
2. Do you think that Ferrari has done a good job of building brand loyalty? Could Ford do the same thing?

Sources: "Corse Clienti: Overview," http://races.ferrari.com, accessed October 8, 2017; James Allen, "Ferrari's F1 Clienti Is the World's Ultimate Used Car Buying Program," *Car Buzz*, http://www.carbuzz.com, accessed October 8, 2017; Jonathan Ho, "Ferrari Celebrates 70 Years," *Luxuo*, http://www.luxuo.com, July 13, 2017; Jonathan Welsh, "Checkered-Flag Past Helps Ferrari Unload a Fleet of Used Cars," *The Wall Street Journal*, January 11, 2005, pp. A1, A10.

Classifying Business Products

Products bought by businesses or institutions for use in making other products are called *business products*. These products can be commercial, industrial, or services products. A commercial product would be an 18-wheeler truck used by a major transportation company as part of the business. An industrial product might be a major robotics installation in a state-of-the-art manufacturing facility. A services product (for business) might be telecommunications consulting for a large corporation setting up offices in Singapore. Business products are classified as either capital products or expense items. **Capital products** are usually large, expensive items with a long life span. Examples are buildings, large machines, and airplanes. **Expense items** are typically smaller, less expensive items that usually have a life span of less than a year. Examples are printer cartridges and paper. Industrial products are sometimes further classified in the following categories:

1. *Installations:* These are large, expensive capital items that determine the nature, scope, and efficiency of a company. Capital products such as General Motors' truck assembly plant in Fort Wayne, Indiana, represent a big commitment against future earnings and profitability. Buying an installation requires longer negotiations, more planning, and the judgments of more people than buying any other type of product.

2. *Accessories:* Accessories do not have the same long-run impact on the firm as installations, and they are less expensive and more standardized. But they are still capital products. Minolta photocopy machines, HP laptops, and smaller machines such as Black & Decker table drills and saws are typical accessories. Marketers of accessories often rely on well-known brand names and extensive advertising as well as personal selling.

3. *Component parts and materials:* These are expense items that are built into the end product. Some component parts are custom-made, such as a drive shaft for an automobile, a case for a computer, or a special pigment for painting U.S. Navy harbor buoys; others are standardized for sale to many industrial users. Intel's Pentium chip for PCs and cement for the construction trade are examples of standardized component parts and materials.

4. *Raw materials:* Raw materials are expense items that have undergone little or no processing and are used to create a final product. Examples include lumber, copper, and zinc.

5. *Supplies:* Supplies do not become part of the final product. They are bought routinely and in fairly large quantities. Supply items run the gamut from pencils and paper to paint and machine oil. They have little impact on the firm's long-run profits. Bic pens, Champion copier paper, and Pennzoil machine oil are typical supply items.

6. *Services.* These are expense items used to plan or support company operations—for example, janitorial cleaning and management consulting services.

CONCEPT CHECK

1. What is a product?
2. What are the classes of consumer products?
3. Explain how business products are classified.

11.7 | Creating Products That Deliver Value

7. How do organizations create new products?

New products pump life into company sales, enabling the firm not only to survive but also to grow. Companies like Allegheny Ludlum (steel), Dow (chemicals), Samsung (electronics), Campbell Soup (foods), and Stryker (medical products) get most of their profits from new products. Companies that lead their industries in profitability and sales growth get a large percentage of their revenues from products developed within the last five years. A recent McKinsey survey found that 94 percent of top executives believed that their companies' innovation approach and process needed to be updated, signaling how important new products are as the lifeblood of a company.[6]

Marketers have several different terms for new products, depending on how the product fits into a company's existing product line. When a firm introduces a product that has a new brand name and is in a product category new to the organization, it is classified as a new product.

A new flavor, size, or model using an existing brand name in an existing category is called a **line extension**. Diet Cherry Coke and caffeine-free Coke are line extensions. The strategy of expanding the line by adding new models has enabled companies like Seiko (watches), Kraft (cheeses), Oscar Mayer (lunch meats), and Sony (consumer electronics) to tie up a large amount of shelf space and brand recognition in a product category. Crayola now offers Crayola bubble bath shampoo. Services companies also develop new products—new services based on market research—or make changes in ongoing services. Services companies can often introduce and adapt their products faster than companies that manufacture goods because service delivery can be more flexible and changes can often be made immediately. Due to this, customers often expect and require immediate improvements to services.

How New Products Are Developed

Developing new products is both costly and risky, especially for companies that sell products that are goods. New-product failure rates for household and grocery products can approach 80 percent. Overall, companies report that only 3 percent of their products exceed their initial sales targets in Year 1. Even companies such as Facebook, which launched Facebook Home in 2013 at an initial price of $99 per year, have experienced new product failures.[7] Industrial goods failure rates tend to be lower than those for consumer goods. To increase their chances for success, most firms use the following product development process, which is also summarized in Exhibit 11.6.

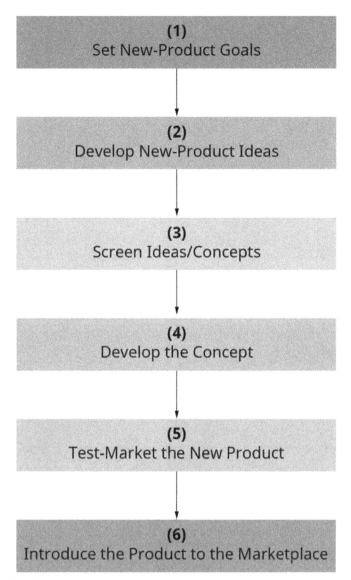

Exhibit 11.6   Steps to Develop New Products That Satisfy Customers (Attribution: Copyright Rice University, OpenStax, under CC BY 4.0 license.)

1. *Set new-product goals:* New-product goals are usually stated as financial objectives. For example, a company may want to recover its investment in three years or less. Or it may want to earn at least a 15 percent return on the investment. Nonfinancial goals may include using existing equipment or facilities.
2. *Develop new-product ideas:* Smaller firms usually depend on employees, customers, investors, and distributors for new ideas. Larger companies use these sources and more-structured marketing research techniques, such as focus groups and brainstorming. A **focus group** consists of eight to 12 participants led by a moderator in an in-depth discussion on one particular topic or concept. The goal of focus group research is to learn and understand what people have to say and why. The emphasis is on getting people to speak at length and in detail about the subject at hand. The intent is to find out how they feel about a product, concept, idea, or organization; how it fits into their lives; and their emotional involvement with it. Focus groups often generate excellent product ideas. A few examples of focus group–influenced products are the interior design of the Toyota RAV4, Stick Ups room deodorizers, Swiffer WetJet, and Wendy's Salad Sensations. In the business market, machine tools, keyboard designs, aircraft interiors, and backhoe

accessories evolved from focus groups.

Brainstorming is also used to generate new-product ideas. With **brainstorming**, the members of a group think of as many ways to vary a product or solve a problem as possible. Criticism is avoided, no matter how ridiculous an idea seems at the time. The emphasis is on sheer numbers of ideas. Evaluation of these ideas is postponed to later steps of development.

3. *Screen ideas and concepts:* As ideas emerge, they are checked against the firm's new-product goals and its long-range strategies. Many product concepts are rejected because they don't fit well with existing products, needed technology is not available, the company doesn't have enough resources, or the sales potential is low.

4. *Develop the concept:* Developing the new-product concept involves creating a prototype of the product, testing the prototype, and building the marketing strategy. Building the marketing strategy means developing a test set of 5Ps. The type and amount of product testing varies, depending on such factors as the company's experience with similar products, how easy it is to make the item, and how easy it will be for consumers to use it. If Kraft wanted to develop a new salad dressing flavor, the company would benefit from the fact that the company already has a lot of experience in this area. The new dressing will go directly into advanced taste tests and perhaps home-use tests. To develop a new line of soft drinks, however, Kraft would most likely do a great deal of testing. It would study many aspects of the new product before actually making it.

   While the product is tested, the marketing strategy is refined. Channels of distribution are selected, pricing policies are developed and tested, the target market is further defined, and demand for the product is estimated. Management also continually updates the profit plan.

   As the marketing strategy and prototype tests mature, a communication strategy is developed. A logo and package wording are created. As part of the communication strategy, promotion themes are developed, and the product is introduced to the sales force.

5. *Test-market the new product:* **Test-marketing** is testing the product among potential users. It allows management to evaluate various strategies and to see how well the parts of the marketing mix fit together. Few new-product concepts reach this stage. For those that pass this stage, the firm must decide whether to introduce the product on a regional or national basis.

   Companies that don't test-market their products run a strong risk of product failure. In essence, test-marketing is the "acid test" of new-product development. The product is put into the marketplace, and then the manufacturer can see how it performs against the competition.

6. *Introduce the product:* A product that passes test-marketing is ready for market introduction, called *rollout,* which requires a lot of logistical coordination. Various divisions of the company must be encouraged to give the new item the attention it deserves. Packaging and labeling in a different language may be required. Sales training sessions must be scheduled, spare parts inventoried, service personnel trained, advertising and promotion campaigns readied, and wholesalers and retailers informed about the new item. If the new product is to be sold internationally, it may have to be altered to meet the requirements of the target countries. For instance, electrical products may have to run on different electrical currents.

For services companies, the new product develop process is similar, but developing the prototype can take less time and resources. It will mean developing the service and training service personnel on the new service in order to test it in the market.

The Role of the Product Manager

When a new product enters the marketplace in large organizations, it is often placed under the control of a product or brand manager. A **product manager** develops and implements a complete strategy and marketing program for a specific product or brand of product. Some companies may have numerous brands of the same type of product, such as many versions of laundry soap, each with different target markets, brand names, and attributes. Product management first appeared at Procter & Gamble in 1929. A new company soap, Camay, was not doing well, so a young Procter & Gamble executive was assigned to devote his exclusive attention to developing and promoting this product. He was successful, and the company soon added other product managers. Since then, many firms, especially consumer products companies, have set up product management organizations.

CONCEPT CHECK

1. How do companies organize for new-product development?
2. What are the steps in the new-product development process?
3. How does new-product development differ for services companies?
4. Explain the role of the product manager.

11.8 | The Product Life Cycle

8. What are the stages of the product life cycle?

Product managers create marketing mixes for their products as they move through the life cycle. The **product life cycle** is a pattern of sales and profits over time for a product (Ivory dishwashing liquid) or a product category (liquid detergents). As the product moves through the stages of the life cycle, the firm must keep revising the marketing mix to stay competitive and meet the needs of target customers.

Stages of the Life Cycle

As illustrated in Exhibit 11.7, the product life cycle consists of the following stages:

1. *Introduction:* When a product enters the life cycle, it faces many obstacles. Although competition may be light, the *introductory stage* usually features frequent product modifications, limited distribution, and heavy promotion. The failure rate is high. Production and marketing costs are also high, and sales volume is low. Hence, profits are usually small or negative.

2. *Growth:* If a product survives the introductory stage, it advances to the *growth stage* of the life cycle. In this stage, sales grow at an increasing rate, profits are healthy, and many competitors enter the market. Large companies may start to acquire small pioneering firms that have reached this stage. Emphasis switches from primary demand promotion to aggressive brand advertising and communicating the differences between brands. For example, the goal changes from convincing people to buy flat-screen TVs to convincing them to buy Sony versus Panasonic or Sharp.

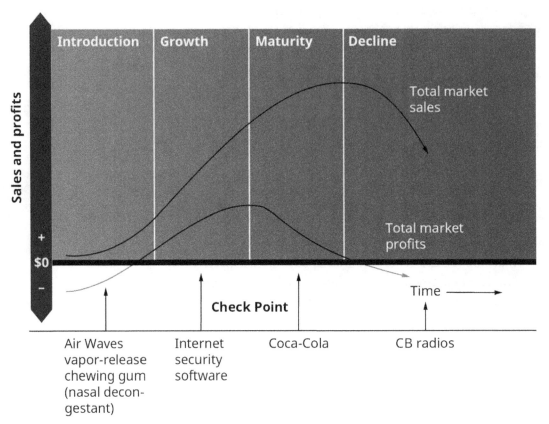

Exhibit 11.7   Sales and Profits during the Product Life Cycle (Attribution: Copyright Rice University, OpenStax, under CC BY 4.0 license.)

Distribution becomes a major key to success during the growth stage, as well as in later stages. Manufacturers scramble to acquire dealers and distributors and to build long-term relationships. Without adequate distribution, it is impossible to establish a strong market position.

Toward the end of the growth phase, prices normally begin falling, and profits peak. Price reductions result from increased competition and from cost reductions from producing larger quantities of items (economies of scale). Also, most firms have recovered their development costs by now, and their priority is in increasing or retaining market share and enhancing profits.

3. *Maturity:* After the growth stage, sales continue to mount—but at a decreasing rate. This is the *maturity stage*. Most products that have been on the market for a long time are in this stage. Thus, most marketing strategies are designed for mature products. One such strategy is to bring out several variations of a basic product (line extension). Kool-Aid, for instance, was originally offered in six flavors. Today there are more than 50, as well as sweetened and unsweetened varieties.

4. *Decline (and death):* When sales and profits fall, the product has reached the *decline stage*. The rate of decline is governed by two factors: the rate of change in consumer tastes and the rate at which new products enter the market. Sony VCRs are an example of a product in the decline stage. The demand for VCRs has now been surpassed by the demand for DVDs and online streaming of content. Sometimes companies can improve a product by implementing changes to the product, such as new ingredients or new services. If the changes are accepted by customers, it can lead to a product moving out of the decline stage and back into the introduction stage.

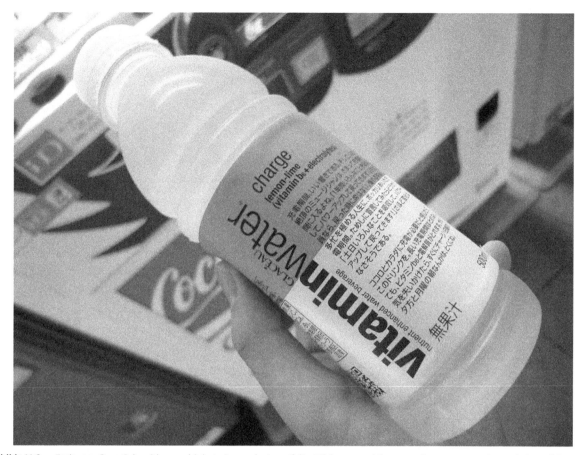

Exhibit 11.8   Each year Coca-Cola adds new drinks to its product portfolio. While some of these new beverages are close relatives of the original Coca-Cola Classic, others, such as Vitaminwater, constitute entirely new categories of soft drink. *What challenges do new products such as Vitaminwater face during the introduction phase of the product life cycle? (Credit: kobakou/ Flickr/ Attribution 2.0 Generic (CC BY 2.0))*

The Product Life Cycle as a Management Tool

The product life cycle may be used in planning. Marketers who understand the cycle concept are better able to forecast future sales and plan new marketing strategies. Table 11.5 is a brief summary of strategic needs at various stages of the product life cycle. Marketers must be sure that a product has moved from one stage to the next before changing its marketing strategy. A temporary sales decline should not be interpreted as a sign that the product is dying. Pulling back marketing support can become a self-fulfilling prophecy that brings about the early death of a healthy product.

Strategies for Success at Each Stage of the Product Life Cycle				
Category	Introduction	Growth	Maturity	Decline
Marketing objectives	Encourage trial, establish distribution	Get triers to repurchase, attract new users	Seek new user or users	Reduce marketing expenses, used to keep loyal users

Table 11.5

Strategies for Success at Each Stage of the Product Life Cycle				
Category	Introduction	Growth	Maturity	Decline
Product	Establish competitive advantage	Maintain product quality	Modify product	Maintain product
Distribution	Establish distribution network	Solidify distribution relationships	Provide additional incentives to ensure support	Eliminate trade allowances
Promotional	Build brand awareness	Provide information	Reposition product	Eliminate most advertising and sales promotions
Pricing	Set introductory price (skimming or penetration pricing)	Maintain prices	Reduce prices to meet competition	Maintain prices

Table 11.5

CONCEPT CHECK

1. What is the product life cycle?
2. Describe each stage of the product life cycle.
3. What are the marketing strategies for each stage of the product life cycle?

11.9 Pricing Strategies and Future Trends

9. What strategies are used for pricing products, and what are the future trends?

An important part of the marketing planning process is setting the right price. Price is the perceived value that is exchanged for something else. Value in our society is most commonly expressed in dollars and cents. Thus, price is typically the amount of money exchanged for a product. Note that *perceived value* refers to the perception of the product's value at the time of the transaction. After a consumer has used a product, the consumer may decide that its actual value was less than its perceived value at the time it was purchased. The price paid for a product is based on the *expected satisfaction* that the customer will receive and not necessarily the *actual satisfaction of the customer*.

Although price is usually a dollar amount, it can be anything with perceived value. When products are exchanged for each other, the trade is called *barter*. If a student exchanges this book for a math book at the end of the term, that student has engaged in barter.

Pricing Objectives

Price is important in determining how much a firm earns. The prices charged customers times the number of units sold equals the *gross revenue* for the firm. Revenue is what pays for every activity of the company (production, finance, sales, distribution, and so forth). The money that is left over (if any) is profit. Managers strive to charge a price that will allow the firm to earn a fair return on its investment and will maximize return on investment to the highest extent while still maintaining a fair return.

The chosen price must be neither too high nor too low, and the price must equal the perceived value to target consumers. If consumers think the price is too high, sales opportunities will be lost. Lost sales mean lost revenue. If the price is too low, consumers may view the product as a great value, but the company may not meet its profit goals. Sometimes, as in the case of services, a price that is too low will cause the product to viewed as less than credible and lose sales for the company.

Product Pricing

Managers use various pricing strategies when determining the price of a product, as this section explains. Price skimming and penetration pricing are strategies used in pricing new products; other strategies such as leader pricing and bundling may be used for established products as well.

Price Skimming

The practice of introducing a new product on the market with a high price and then lowering the price over time is called **price skimming**. As the product moves through its life cycle, the price usually is lowered because competitors are entering the market. As the price falls, more and more consumers can buy the product. Recent example are DVD players and flat-screen televisions. When they first came out, DVD players were priced at around $500 while flat-screen televisions were priced at over $1,000. Over time, the price of DVD players has sunk to under $100, while 4-inch Insignia brand flat-screen TVs can be purchased for under $220.

Price skimming has four important advantages. First, a high initial price can be a way to find out what buyers are willing to pay. Second, if consumers find the introductory price too high, it can be lowered. Third, a high introductory price can create an image of quality and prestige. Fourth, when the price is lowered later, consumers may think they are getting a bargain. The disadvantage is that high prices attract competition.

Price skimming can be used to price virtually any new products, such as high-definition televisions, new cancer drugs, and color computer printers. For example, the Republic of Tea recently launched Emperor's White Tea, which it says is among the rarest of teas. Because it is minimally processed, white tea is said to retain the highest level of antioxidants and has a lower caffeine content than black and green teas. The company says the tea is picked only a few days each year, right before the leaf opens, yielding a small harvest. The product retails for $16 per tin of 50 bags. Products don't have to cost hundreds of dollars to use a skimming strategy.

Penetration Pricing

A company that doesn't use price skimming will probably use **penetration pricing**. With this strategy, the company offers new products at low prices in the hope of achieving a large sales volume. Procter & Gamble did this with its SpinBrush toothbrush. Penetration pricing requires more extensive planning than skimming does because the company must gear up for mass production and marketing. When Texas Instruments entered the digital-watch market, its facilities in Lubbock, Texas, could produce 6 million watches a year, enough to meet the entire world demand for low-priced watches. If the company had been wrong about demand, its losses would have been huge.

Penetration pricing has two advantages. First, the low initial price may induce consumers to switch brands or companies. Using penetration pricing on its jug wines, Gallo has lured customers away from Taylor California Cellars and Inglenook. Second, penetration pricing may discourage competitors from entering the market. Their costs would tend to be higher, so they would need to sell more at the same price to break even.

Leader Pricing

Pricing products below the normal markup or even below cost to attract customers to a store where they wouldn't otherwise shop is **leader pricing**. A product priced below cost is referred to as a **loss leader**. Retailers hope that this type of pricing will increase their overall sales volume and thus their profit.

Items that are leader priced are usually well known and priced low enough to appeal to many customers. They also are items that consumers will buy at a lower price, even if they have to switch brands. Supermarkets often feature coffee and bacon in their leader pricing. Department stores and specialty stores also rely heavily on leader pricing.

Pricing of Services

Pricing of services tends to be more complex than pricing of products that are goods. Services may be priced as standard services, such as the price a hair stylist might charge for a haircut, or pricing may be based on tailored services designed for a specific buyer, such as the prices charged for the design of a new building by an architect.

ETHICS IN PRACTICE

Pricing Before, During, and After Hurricanes

The late summer of 2017 brought several devastating hurricanes that impacted large areas of Texas, Florida, Puerto Rico, and the Virgin Islands. As often happens during events like these, there were several reports of stores, hotels, and service stations engaging in price gouging. Many states have laws against price gouging during natural disasters, but a Twitter photo of a Best Buy store charging $42 for a case of 24 bottles of water was widely circulated. Usually a case of water can be purchased for about $5 to $8, so the $42 price was thought to be an instance of price gouging. Best Buy quickly addressed the exorbitant price and issued an apology, stating they normally do not sell cases of water, and that an employee wanting to provide a service in advance of the hurricane simply multiplied the price of a single bottle they normally sell by 24 to arrive at the price-per-case total. Best Buy's response was clearly aimed at deflecting any negative public reaction to the pricing "error."

Another example of how companies might be accused of price gouging occurs with companies that use **"dynamic pricing,"** which uses computer algorithms to analyze demand and automatically raises prices as demand increases. Amazon, the large online retailer, uses dynamic pricing, and consumers saw an increase in the price of things like generators and water in the days prior to hurricanes Harvey, Irma, and Juan in 2017.

There are some economists and business thought leaders who believe that price increases during events like hurricanes is a good thing. Economists from the Chicago School of Economics state that regulating lower prices during natural disasters actually discourages consumers from purchasing essential supplies such as water and gasoline until the disaster occurs because they can anticipate regulated prices. In addition, let's say that a hotel usually rents a room for $50 a night and decides to raise the price during a hurricane to $100. A family might decide to stay in one room rather than rent two rooms, thus saving some money while at the same time increasing the supply of hotel rooms for people who need them the most.

Critical Thinking Questions
1. What risks do companies such as Best Buy and Amazon face when selling a product that they normally don't sell and then are accused of price gouging, or when they using dynamic pricing?
2. Why is the use of dynamic pricing deemed acceptable for selling tickets to sporting events but not during a natural disaster?
3. Do you agree with the arguments in support of higher prices put forth by free-market economists?

Sources: Andrew Ross Sorkin, "Hurricane Price Gouging Is Despicable Right? Not to Some Economists," *The New York Times*, https://www.nytimes.com, September 11, 2017; Tom Popomaronis, "Amid Preparations for Hurricane Irma, Amazon Draws Scrutiny for Price Increases," *Forbes*, https://www.forbes.com, September 6, 2017; Dennis Green, "Best Buy Explains Why It Charges $42 for a Case of Water in Texas During the Hurricane in 'a Big Mistake,'" *Business Insider*, http://www.businessinsider.com, August 29, 2017; Matt Zwolinski, "The Ethics of Price Gouging," *Business Ethics Quarterly,* 18(3): 347–378, 2008, http://facpub.stjohns.edu.

Bundling

Bundling means grouping two or more related products together and pricing them as a single product. Marriott's special weekend rates often include the room, breakfast, and free Wi-Fi. Department stores may offer a washer and dryer together for a price lower than if the units were bought separately.

The idea behind bundling is to reach a segment of the market that the products sold separately would not reach as effectively. Some buyers are more than willing to buy one product but have much less use for the second. Bundling the second product to the first at a slightly reduced price thus creates some sales that otherwise would not be made. For example, Aussie 3-Minute Miracle Shampoo is typically bundled with its conditioner because many people use shampoo more than conditioner, so they don't need a new bottle of conditioner.

Odd-Even Pricing

Psychology often plays a big role in how consumers view prices and what prices they will pay. **Odd-even pricing** (or **psychological pricing**) is the strategy of setting a price at an odd number to connote a bargain and at an even number to imply quality. For years, many retailers have priced their products in odd numbers—for example, $99.95 or $49.95—to make consumers feel that they are paying a lower price for the product.

Prestige Pricing

The strategy of raising the price of a product so consumers will perceive it as being of higher quality, status, or value is called **prestige pricing**. This type of pricing is common where high prices indicate high status. In the specialty shops on Rodeo Drive in Beverly Hills, which cater to the super-rich of Hollywood, shirts that would sell for $65 elsewhere sell for at least $150. If the price were lower, customers would perceive them as being of low quality. Prestige pricing is also very prevalent in services because services providers with reputations for excellent service are more in demand, often with a waiting list. This is due to the fact that services are tied directly to the people who provide them and those people have only so much time in a week in which to provide services. Once the calendar fills up, the demand goes up, and the prices become prestige prices.

CONCEPT CHECK

1. What is the difference between penetration pricing and price skimming?
2. Explain the concept of price bundling.
3. Describe odd-even pricing and prestige pricing.
4. Why is prestige pricing prevalent in services?

| 11.10 | # Trends in Developing Products and Pricing |

10. What trends are occurring in products and pricing?

As customer expectations increase and competition becomes fiercer, perceptive managers will find innovative strategies to satisfy demanding consumers and establish unique products in the market. Satisfying customers requires the right prices. The internet has delivered pricing power to both buyers and sellers. Another significant trend is the use of one-to-one marketing to create a customized marketing mix for each consumer.

Impact of the Internet on Pricing

The internet, corporate networks, and wireless setups are linking people, machines, and companies around the globe—and connecting sellers and buyers as never before. This link is enabling buyers to quickly and easily compare products and prices, putting them in a better bargaining position. At the same time, the technology enables sellers to collect detailed data about customers' buying habits, preferences, and even spending limits so that they can tailor their products and prices. Amazon, as well as online businesses from traditional retailers such as Walmart, have drastically changed the retail landscape. Amazon's Prime membership, which offers free shipping and other amenities for an annual fee, has also taken market share from traditional low-cost warehouse clubs such as Costco and Sam's Club.[8]

Online price-comparison engines, known as shopbots, are continuing to add new features. ShopSmarter.com now includes coupons and additional retailer discounts in its price results. In the past, consumers had to click deep into a retailer's site to find out about these additional savings. Vendio eCommerce introduced a toolbar that people can download. If a person is on the web page of a particular product—whether it's an iPhone or a Canon digital camera—the toolbar flashes a blinking alert when it finds a lower price for that same item somewhere else. The person can then open a window on the side of the site to learn details of the cheaper price—or simply ignore the alert. BuySAFE introduced a website that lets consumers search among about 1.5 million products that are backed by antifraud guarantees. If a buyer purchases one of the items and the seller fails to deliver, the buyer can get reimbursed for the full cost up to $25,000. Merchants on the site include those that sell on eBay and Overstock.com.

Use of these sites has boomed in the past few years as people have become more reliant on the web both as a research tool and as a place to shop. According to a recent survey, more than 90 percent of consumers have used a smartphone when comparison-shopping in stores.[9] Much of the growth has come from the more-established sites such as Shopify, Bizrate, and NexTag, as well as the shopping sections of Amazon, Microsoft's MSN, and Google. The big attraction with shopping comparison services, of course, is the hunt for a better bargain. Merchants like the sites because they help drive consumer spending. Consumers who use comparison-shopping sites for product information or in-store discount coupons spend more than those who don't.[10]

One-to-One Marketing

One-to-one marketing is creating a unique marketing mix for every consumer. The key to creating one-to-one marketing is a good marketing database. The information contained in a marketing database helps managers know and understand customers, and potential customers, on an individual basis. A **marketing database** is a computerized file of customers' and potential customers' profiles and purchase patterns.

In the 1960s, network television enabled advertisers to "get the same message to everyone simultaneously." Database marketing can get a customized, individual message to everyone simultaneously through direct mail or through the internet. This is why database marketing is sometimes called *micromarketing.* Database marketing can create a computerized form of the old-fashioned relationship that people used to have with the corner grocer, butcher, or baker. "A database is sort of a collective memory," says Richard G. Barlow, president of Frequency Marketing, Inc., a Cincinnati-based consulting firm. "It deals with you in the same personalized way as a mom-and-pop grocery store, where they knew customers by name and stocked what they wanted."

You have also probably heard the term **big data**. Companies such as Facebook and Google can process information and then tailor information to provide marketers with higher-probability targets. For instance, imagine that you and some friends are discussing a spring break vacation and you are searching for possible locations on the Florida gulf coast. That data, along with the social group considering the vacation, can be sold to companies that provide travel services, airline flights, hotel rentals, and the like. Suddenly, you and your friends see travel offers and alternate destinations on your Facebook page. Likewise, imagine you are looking for a mystery novel to read on a long flight. Let's say that you are also searching for ways to remove a rust stain on a favorite sweater. When you go to your Amazon page, you see several new mystery novels as well as cleaning solutions highlighted on your page. All of this was done through the use of big data and analytics to provide consumers solutions they are looking for as well as products that they don't even know that they want. **Exhibit 11.9** contrasts the differences in approaches in traditional advertising versus targeted marketing using big data.

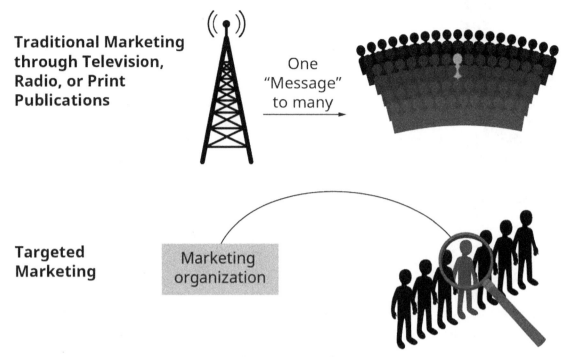

Exhibit 11.9 Traditional Advertising and Targeted Marketing Using Big Data (Attribution: Copyright Rice University, OpenStax, under CC BY 4.0 license.)

The size of some databases is impressive: Ford Motor Company's is about 50 million names; Kraft General Foods, 30 million; Citicorp, 30 million; and Kimberly Clark, maker of Huggies diapers, 10 million new parents. American Express can pull from its database all cardholders who made purchases at golf pro shops in the past six months, who attended symphony concerts, or who traveled to Europe more than once in the past year, as well as the very few people who did all three.

Companies are using their marketing databases to implement one-to-one marketing. For example, Novartis Seeds, Inc., a Minneapolis-based agriculture business, produces individually customized, full-color brochures for 7,000 farmers. Each piece features products selected by Novartis dealers specifically for the farmer based on information collected about the farm operation and the types of crops grown. Instead of the 30-page catalog Novartis traditionally sent, these customers get a one-page brochure with only the five or six products they need, plus other complementary products dealers feel they should consider.

CONCEPT CHECK

1. How have online price-comparison engines helped consumers shop for the best price?
2. Describe one-to-one marketing and the role of marketing databases.

🔑 Key Terms

benefit segmentation The differentiation of markets based on what a product will do rather than on customer characteristics.

big data Large data sets and systems and solutions developed to manage large accumulations of data.

brainstorming A method of generating ideas in which group members suggest as many possibilities as they can without criticizing or evaluating any of the suggestions.

bundling The strategy of grouping two or more related products together and pricing them as a single product.

buyer behavior The actions people take in buying and using goods and services.

capital products Large, expensive items with a long life span that are purchased by businesses for use in making other products or providing a service.

competitive advantage A set of unique features of a company and its products that are perceived by the target market as significant and superior to those of the competition; also called differential advantage.

convenience products Relatively inexpensive items that require little shopping effort and are purchased routinely without planning.

cost competitive advantage A firm's ability to produce a product or service at a lower cost than all other competitors in an industry while maintaining satisfactory profit margins.

culture The set of values, ideas, attitudes, and other symbols created to shape human behavior.

customer satisfaction The customer's feeling that a product has met or exceeded expectations.

customer value The ratio of benefits to the sacrifice necessary to obtain those benefits, as determined by the customer; reflects the willingness of customers to actually buy a product.

demographic segmentation The differentiation of markets through the use of categories such as age, education, gender, income, and household size.

differential competitive advantage A firm's ability to provide a unique product or service with a set of features that the target market perceives as important and better than the competitor's.

distribution strategy Creating the means by which products flow from the producer to the consumer.

dynamic pricing Computer algorithms that allow for prices to change based on demand.

environmental scanning The process in which a firm continually collects and evaluates information about its external environment.

exchange The process in which two parties give something of value to each other to satisfy their respective needs.

expense items Items (purchased by businesses) that are smaller and less expensive than capital products and usually have a life span of less than one year.

experiment A marketing research method in which the investigator changes one or more variables—price, packaging, design, shelf space, advertising theme, or advertising expenditures—while observing the effects of these changes on another variable (usually sales).

five Ps Product, price, promotion, place (distribution), and people, which together make up the marketing mix.

focus group A group of eight to 12 participants led by a moderator in an in-depth discussion on one particular topic or concept.

geographic segmentation The differentiation of markets by region of the country, city or county size, market density, or climate.

leader pricing The strategy of pricing products below the normal markup or even below cost to attract customers to a store where they would not otherwise shop.

line extension A new flavor, size, or model using an existing brand name in an existing category.

loss leader A product priced below cost as part of a leader-pricing strategy.

market segmentation The process of separating, identifying, and evaluating the layers of a market in order to identify a target market.

marketing The process of discovering the needs and wants of potential buyers and customers and then providing goods and services that meet or exceed their expectations.

marketing concept Identifying consumer needs and then producing the goods or services that will satisfy them while making a profit for the organization.

marketing database Computerized file of customers' and potential customers' profiles and purchase patterns.

marketing mix The blend of product offering, pricing, promotional methods, distribution system, and strategies for utilizing people that creates an offering that brings a specific group of consumers superior value.

marketing research The process of planning, collecting, and analyzing data relevant to a marketing decision.

niche competitive advantage A firm's ability to target and effectively serve a single segment of the market, often within a limited geographic area.

observation research A marketing research method in which the investigator monitors respondents' actions without interacting directly with the respondents; for example, by using cash registers with scanners.

odd-even (psychological) pricing The strategy of setting a price at an odd number to connote a bargain and at an even number to suggest quality.

one-to-one marketing Creating a unique marketing mix for every customer.

penetration pricing The strategy of selling new products at low prices in the hope of achieving a large sales volume.

personality A way of organizing and grouping how an individual reacts to situations.

prestige pricing The strategy of increasing the price of a product so that consumers will perceive it as being of higher quality, status, or value.

price skimming The strategy of introducing a product with a high initial price and lowering the price over time as the product moves through its life cycle.

pricing strategy Setting a price based upon the demand for and cost of a good or service.

product In marketing, a good, service or idea, along with its perceived attributes and benefits, that creates value for the customer.

product life cycle The pattern of sales and profits over time for a product or product category; consists of an introductory stage, growth stage, maturity, and decline (and death).

product manager The person who develops and implements a complete strategy and marketing program for a specific product or brand.

product strategy Taking the good or service and selecting a brand name, packaging, colors, a warranty, accessories, and a service program.

promotion strategy The unique combination of personal selling, traditional advertising, publicity, sales promotion, social media, and e-commerce to stimulate the target market to buy a product. Sometimes referred to as the promotion mix.

psychographic segmentation The differentiation of markets by personality or lifestyle.

reference groups Formal and informal groups that influence buyer behavior.

relationship marketing A strategy that focuses on forging long-term partnerships with customers by offering value and providing customer satisfaction.

shopping products Items that are bought after considerable planning, including brand-to-brand and store-to-store comparisons of price, suitability, and style.

specialty products Items for which consumers search long and hard and for which they refuse to accept substitutes.

survey research A marketing research method in which data is gathered from respondents, either in person, by telephone, by mail, at a mall, or through the internet to obtain facts, opinions, and attitudes.

target market The specific group of consumers toward which a firm could direct its marketing efforts. It is often divided into segments so that marketing strategies can be directed to a more specific target.

test marketing The process of testing a new product among potential users.

unsought products Products that either are not planned as a purchase by a potential buyer or are known but the buyer does not actively seek them, such as funeral services.

volume segmentation The differentiation of markets based on the amount of the product purchased.

Summary of Learning Outcomes

11.1 The Marketing Concept

1. What is the marketing concept and relationship-building?

Marketing includes those business activities that are designed to satisfy consumer needs and wants through the exchange process. Marketing managers use the "right" principle—getting the right goods or services to the right people at the right place, time, and price, using the right promotional techniques. Today, many firms have adopted the marketing concept. The marketing concept involves identifying consumer needs and wants and then producing products (which can be goods, services, or ideas) that will satisfy them while making a profit. Relationship marketing entails forging long-term relationships with customers, which can lead to repeat sales, reduced costs, and stable relationships.

11.2 Creating a Marketing Strategy

2. How do managers create a marketing strategy?

A firm creates a marketing strategy by understanding the external environment, defining the target market, determining a competitive advantage, and developing a marketing mix. Environmental scanning enables companies to understand the external environment. The target market is the specific group of consumers toward which a firm directs its marketing efforts. A competitive advantage is a set of unique features of a company and its products that are perceived by the target market as significant and superior to those of the competition.

11.3 Developing a Marketing Mix

3. What is the marketing mix?

To carry out the marketing strategy, firms create a marketing mix—a blend of products, distribution (place) systems, prices, promotion, and people. Marketing managers use this mix to satisfy target consumers. The mix can be applied to nonbusiness as well as business situations.

11.4 Buyer Behavior

4. How do consumers and organizations make buying decisions?

Buyer behavior is what consumers and businesses do in order to buy and use products. The consumer purchase decision-making process consists of the following steps: recognizing a need, seeking information, evaluating alternatives, purchasing the product, judging the purchase outcome, and engaging in post-purchase behavior. A number of factors influence the process. Cultural, social, individual, and psychological factors have an impact on consumer decision-making. The business purchase decision-making model includes the following steps: need recognition, setting specifications, information search, evaluation of alternatives against specifications, purchase, and post-purchase behavior. The main differences between consumer and business markets are purchase volume, number of customers, location of buyers, direct distribution, and rational purchase decisions. Companies learn more about their target markets by conducting marketing research—the process of planning, collecting, and analyzing data relevant to a marketing decision.

11.5 Market Segmentation

5. What are the five basic forms of consumer and business market segmentation?

Success in marketing depends on understanding the target market. One technique used to identify a target market is market segmentation. The five basic forms of segmentation are demographic (population statistics), geographic (location), psychographic (personality or lifestyle), benefit (product features), and volume (amount purchased).

Business markets may segment based on geography, volume, and benefits, just as consumer markets are. However, organizations might also segment based on use of the product, characteristics of purchasing function, and size of the client or industry, as well as other considerations related to characteristics of business customers.

11.6 What Is a Product?

6. What is a product, and how is it classified?

A product can be a good, service, or idea, along with its perceived attributes and benefits, that creates customer value. Tangible attributes include the good itself, packaging, and warranties. Intangible attributes can include the brand's image or relational attributes such as the credibility of its service providers. Products are categorized as either consumer products or business-to-business products, which can be commercial, industrial, or services products. Consumer products are bought and used by the end user, sometimes called "the ultimate consumer." They can be classified as unsought products, convenience products, shopping products, or specialty products, depending on how much effort consumers are willing to exert to get them.

Business-to-business products are those bought by organizations for use in making other products or in rendering services to other organizations and include capital products and expense items.

11.7 Creating Products That Deliver Value

7. How do organizations create new products?

To succeed, most firms must continue to design new products to satisfy changing customer demands. But new-product development can be risky. Many new products fail. The steps in new-product development are setting new-product goals, exploring ideas, screening ideas, developing the concept (creating a prototype and building the marketing strategy), test-marketing, and introducing the product. When the product enters the marketplace, it is often managed by a product manager.

11.8 The Product Life Cycle

8. What are the stages of the product life cycle?

After a product reaches the marketplace, it enters the product life cycle. This cycle typically has four stages: introduction, growth, maturity, and decline (and possibly death). Profit margins are usually small in the introductory phase, reach a peak at the end of the growth phase, and then decline.

Price indicates value, helps position a product in the marketplace, and is the means for earning a fair return on investment. If a price is too high, the product won't sell well and the firm will lose money. If the price is too low, the firm may lose money even if the product sells well. Prices are set according to pricing objectives.

11.9 Pricing Strategies and Future Trends

9. What strategies are used for pricing products, and what are the future trends?

The two main strategies for pricing a new product are price skimming and penetration pricing. Price skimming involves charging a high introductory price and then, usually, lowering the price as the product moves through its life cycle. Penetration pricing involves selling a new product at a low price in the hope of achieving a large sales volume.

Pricing tactics are used to fine-tune the base prices of products. Sellers that use leader pricing set the prices of some of their products below the normal markup or even below cost to attract customers who might otherwise not shop at those stores. Bundling is grouping two or more products together and pricing them as one. Psychology often plays a role in how consumers view products and in determining what they will pay. Setting a price at an odd number tends to create a perception that the item is cheaper than the actual price. Prices in even numbers denote quality or status. Raising the price so an item will be perceived as having high quality and status is called prestige pricing. Pricing for services is more complicated and is often tailored to specific services for a specific customer.

11.10 Trends in Developing Products and Pricing

10. What trends are occurring in products and pricing?

The internet has given pricing power to both buyers and sellers. A second trend is that many firms are using databases to create one-to-one marketing. Also, the large amount of information that is available to marketers is being mined and analyzed to target specific customers with personalized messages rather than creating one message that is aimed at a broad audience.

Preparing for Tomorrow's Workplace Skills

1. Can the marketing concept be applied effectively by a sole proprietorship, or is it more appropriate for larger businesses with more managers? Explain. (Information)
2. Before starting your own business, you should develop a marketing strategy to guide your efforts. Choose one of the business ideas listed below, and develop a marketing strategy for the business. Include the type of market research you will perform and how you will define your target market. (Information, Systems)
    ◦ Crafts store to capitalize on the renewed interest in knitting and other crafts
    ◦ Online corporate-training company
    ◦ Ethnic restaurant near your campus
    ◦ Another business opportunity that interests you
3. "Market segmentation is the most important concept in marketing." Why do you think some marketing professionals make this statement? Give an example of each form of segmentation. (Systems)
4. Pick a specific product that you use frequently, such as a cosmetic or toiletry item, snack food, article of clothing, book, computer program, or video game. What is the target market for this product, and does the company's marketing strategy reflect this? Now consider the broader category of your product. How can this product be changed and/or the marketing strategy adjusted to appeal to other market segments? (Systems)
5. Under what circumstances would a jeans maker market the product as a convenience product? A shopping product? A specialty product? (Information)
6. Go to the library, and look through magazines and newspapers to find examples of price skimming,

penetration pricing, and value pricing. Make copies and show them to the class. (Information)

7. Explain how something as obvious as a retail price can have a psychological dimension. (Information)

8. **Team Activity** Divide the class into teams. Create a single market list of products. Each team should go to a different supermarket chain store or an independent supermarket and write down the prices of the goods selected. Report your findings to the class. (Interpersonal)

9. How does the stage of a product's life cycle affect price? Give some examples. (Informational)

Ethics Activity

As cosmetics companies roll out line after line of products to satisfy consumers' quest for youth, the shelves are getting crowded. How can a company stand out? Products such as the Cosmedicine and Rodan+Fields lines promote their affiliation with research institutions and medical doctors to distinguish them from their competition.

Shortly after Johns Hopkins University began consulting with the then-owner of the company that produced Cosmedicine products, medical ethicists criticized Johns Hopkins for this arrangement. Hopkins initially defended its position, claiming that its consulting work does not imply any endorsement of Cosmedicine. "We have been pretty clear about our role," said Hopkins CEO Edward Miller. "We are reporting on the scientific validity of studies that were done by outside testing agencies." Cosmedicine packaging includes a disclaimer that discloses the nature of the research and financial relationship between Hopkins and the cosmetics company. Similarly, Rodan+Fields was established as a cosmetics company by two medical doctors. They began their company by starting out as a multi-level marketing company. The practice of multi-level marketing by companies like Herbalife, Rodan+Fields, Beachbody, and Plexus also is controversial to some. Basically, multi-level marketing enlists a new salesperson by making the individual purchase training and inventory of the company product at a discount and begin selling the product at retail prices, while also recruiting new salespeople as their "downline" salespeople. The idea is that eventually you will make most of your income via the results of your downline salespeople—the people you brought into the business.

There are numerous critiques of multi-level marketing, the most notable being investor Bill Ackman's accusation that weight loss company Herbalife was engaging in a pyramid scheme. A pyramid scheme is an arrangement whose entire whole purpose is the enrichment of the top of the pyramid at the expense of new recruits. Herbalife was able to refute Ackman's accusations in a lawsuit brought against them by showing that their results were based on product sales rather than recruitment and that they offered money-back guarantees if the recruits were unable to sell the product.

Ethical Dilemma: Is it ethical for research institutions like Johns Hopkins and medical doctors to endorse products such as skin care? Is the practice of multi-level marketing ethical? Does the money-back guarantee provided by Herbalife provide evidence that they are not engaged in a pyramid scheme?

Sources: "Multi-Level Marketing," *Investopedia,* http://www.investopedia.com, accessed October 1, 2017; Alissa Fleck, "How Women Making Men Rich Has Been Misbranded as Feminism," *Huffington Post,* http://www.huffingtonpost.com, August 28, 2017; Kristen Calderaro, "Why Are Doctors Becoming Rodan+Fields Consultants?" *LinkedIn,* https://www.linkedin.com, October 29, 2015; Rhonda L. Rundle, "A New Name in Skin Care: Johns Hopkins," *The Wall Street Journal,* April 11, 2006, p. B1.

 # Working the Net

1. You want to start a job at a company like Herbalife or Rodan+Fields and work at home. Do a search of the U.S. Census database at **http://www.census.gov** to get information about the work-at-home market. Then visit **http://www.jbsba.com** to expand your research. Then visit the Rodan+Fields (**http://www.rodanandfields.com**) or Herbalife (**http://www.herbalife.com**) website and explore the career opportunities. Summarize your findings.

2. Visit the Strategic Business Insights website at **http://www.strategicbusinessinsights**.com, and click on the VALS™ link. First, read about the VALS survey and how marketers can use it. Describe its value. Then take the survey to find out which psychographic segment you're in. Do you agree or disagree with the results? Why or why not?

3. How good was the marketing strategy you developed in Question 2 of Preparing for Tomorrow's Workplace? Using advice from the marketing section of *Entrepreneur* (**http://www.entrepreneur.com**) or other resources, revisit your marketing strategy for the business you selected, and revise the plan accordingly. (*Entrepreneur*'s article "Write a Simple Marketing Plan" is a good place to start.) What did you overlook? (If you didn't do this exercise, pick one of the businesses and draft a marketing strategy using online resources to guide you.)

4. Visit an online retailer such as Amazon.com (**http://www.amazon.com**), PCConnection.com (**http://www.pcconnection.com**), or cvs.com (). At the site, try to identify examples of leader pricing, bundling, odd-even pricing, and other pricing strategies. Do online retailers have different pricing considerations than "real-world" retailers? Explain.

5. Do a search on Yahoo! (**http://www.yahoo.com**) for online auctions for a product you are interested in buying. Visit several auctions, and get an idea of how the product is priced. How do these prices compare with the price you might find in a local store? What pricing advantages or disadvantages do companies face in selling their products through online auctions? How do online auctions affect the pricing strategies of other companies? Why?

6. Pick a new consumer electronic product such as a digital camera, HDTV, or laptop computer. Then go to shopping bot **http://www.dealio.com.** Compare prices, information, and ease-of-use of the site. Report your findings to the class.

 ## Critical Thinking Case

The Brandfather Strikes Gold

Coca-Cola is promoting its new Full Throttle energy drink, PepsiCo Inc. is marketing energy drinks under its SoBe and Mountain Dew brands, and smaller companies are challenging the soft drink giants with products such as Powerade, Rockstar, and FUZE Mega Energy. With concerns about the amount of sugar in soft drinks and the negative health effects that can cause, brands such as Vitaminwater and Bai have garnered significant market share and have been acquired by soft drink giants such as Coca-Cola and Dr Pepper.

The person behind the success of Powerade, Vitaminwater, and Bai is Rohan Oza. After graduating from the University of Michigan's business school, Oza began working at Coca Cola, where he worked on brands such as Sprite and Powerade. After Oza left Coca Cola for more entrepreneurial challenges, he scored a coup with Smartwater, where he was able to approach Jennifer Aniston to become the endorser of the product. He also was able to attract rapper 50 Cent as an endorser of Vitaminwater. On the arrangement with 50 Cent, he took no fees for the endorsement, instead opting for equity in the company. It looks like this was a sound strategy, since Vitaminwater parent Glaceau sold to Oza's former employer, Coca Cola, for $4.2 billion in 2007.

Oza did not stop after the Vitaminwater success. He started Bai and partnered with Justin Timberlake to establish that brand. Just as he did with Jennifer Aniston and Smartwater, and with 50 Cent and Vitaminwater, Oza works on making sure that he has the correct strategy to match the features and benefits of the brand with just the right celebrity endorser. With Bai, a sparkling drink that features antioxidants as a product benefit, Oza was able to convince Timberlake, an entrepreneur in his own right, to invest in Bai. So Timberlake was not only an endorser but a part owner, and he has been intimately involved in the brand strategy. This partnership worked as well, because Bai was sold to the Dr Pepper Snapple Group for $1.7 billion in 2016.

Critical Thinking Questions
- Oza has established several successful products in the competitive beverage industry. Why has he been able to achieve this success when large organizations with more resources, such as Coca Cola and Pepsi, are forced to buy these new successful brands?
- What types of unique marketing support helped to sustain Vitaminwater and Bai's tremendous growth?
- Suggest a celebrity endorsement with a beverage brand, and tell why that pairing would lead to success. What are the brand attributes and the reputation of the endorser that would resonate with specific consumer segments?

Sources: John Lynch, "Hollywood's 'Brandfather' Talks About His New Role on 'Shark Tank,' Working with 50 Cent and Justin Timberlake," *Business Insider*, http://www.businessinsider.com, October 1, 2017; Heidi Parker, "She Has Great Ideas and Is Savvy," *The Daily Mail,* http://www.dailymail.co.uk, September 17, 2017; Katie Benner, "He's Like to Buy the World Something Other Than a Coke," *The New York Times*, https://www.nytimes.com, January 6, 2017.

Hot Links Address Book

1. What's the latest in customer loyalty programs? For the answer, do a search for "loyalty programs" at SearchCRM.com, **http://searchcrm.techtarget.com**.
2. Considering a career in marketing? Read articles about different marketing topics of interest and visit the Marketing Jobs and Career Services and Student Resources areas at the American Marketing Association site, **http://www.marketingpower.com**.
3. What's different about business-to-business marketing? Find out at the Business Marketing Association site, **http://www.marketing.org**.
4. How satisfied are American consumers today? The American Customer Satisfaction Index (ACSI) is an economic indicator based on modeling of customer evaluations. Find the latest survey results at **http://www.theacsi.org**.
5. So what's so important about branding? Learn more about branding products at **http://www.allaboutbrands.com**.
6. See how one consulting firm helps clients pick the right name by pointing your web browser to **http://www.namebase.com**.
7. At Brandchannel.com, an online exchange, you'll find branding success stories, failures, debates, and more: **http://www.brandchannel.com**.
8. Companies are turning to smart-pricing software to improve margins on products. Find out how one company's software works at Zilliant's website, **http://www.zilliant.com**.
9. If you have ever wondered how manufacturers make certain types of products, this is the site for you! At How Products Are Made, you can find the details on everything from accordions and action figures to zippers, and everything in between: **http://www.madehow.com**.

Exhibit 12.1 (Credit: OIST / flickr/ Attribution 2.0 Generic (CC BY 2.0))

 Introduction

Learning Outcomes

After reading this chapter, you should be able to answer these questions:

1. What is the nature and function of distribution (place)?
2. What is wholesaling, and what are the types of wholesalers?
3. What are the different kinds of retail operations?
4. How can supply-chain management increase efficiency and customer satisfaction?
5. What is promotion, and what are the key elements of a promotional mix?
6. How are advertising media selected?
7. What is personal selling?
8. What are the goals of a sales promotion, and what are several types of sales promotion?
9. How does public relations fit into the promotional mix?
10. What is social media, and how has it changed promotion?
11. What is e-commerce, and how does it affect promotion?

EXPLORING BUSINESS CAREERS

Steve Piehl, Harley-Davidson

A road not taken is the next adventure waiting. Live to ride; ride to live. These are just a few of the creeds that Harley riders live by. Whether it's the vision of the open road, the shine of chrome, or the smell of dust mixed with exhaust, people are drawn to Harley-Davidson motorcycles. How often do you see someone with "Honda" tattooed on their chest? Harleys are the stuff that dreams and identities are made of.

Steve Piehl, who was the director of communications at Harley-Davidson before retiring in 2015, helped shape people's dreams for more than 25 years. He used traditional marketing channels such as print, radio, and television advertising; however, Harley also, understandably, approaches marketing nontraditionally.

The focus of Harley marketing is not selling a product, but selling an experience. Piehl explains, "The difference of that experience is what has given us success. We don't categorize what that experience is. We leave it up to people to make it their own." For some, a Harley is a ticket to freedom; for others, it is a knockout ride to work. Harley's promotion of accessories supports this idea. As Piehl says, "No two Harleys on the street are the same." A part of the purchasing process is a meeting with a "chrome consultant" who can help with customizing and accessorizing your bike. In this way, the bike becomes part of one's identity.

Part of Harley's focus on experience is its support of motorcycle riding as a sport. On its website and at the dealerships, it provides tips and classes for rider improvement. Through the Harley Owners Group (HOG), a membership group of Harley owners, Harley promotes events and rallies where owners can get together and ride. They form what Piehl calls "brothers and sisters of the road."

It is with this focus on the "sport" that Harley creates its most powerful marketing tool: the motorcycle mentor. Through the nature of the Harley community, previous owners coach new owners on buying a more advanced bike, taking an overnight trip, or packing for long-distance rides. Piehl says, "We would be doing a disservice if we said we reach everyone with our product announcements. But when we put it out, it works its way through the customer base. Our owners sell our products. They encourage people to get more involved in the sport." And tools such as chat rooms on the Harley website or magazines such as *HOGtales* and *Motorcycle Enthusiast* facilitate that sharing.

So how does Harley-Davidson measure its marketing success? It participates in Customer Satisfaction Index studies to measure satisfaction for people who purchase new motorcycles. But it is the statistic that over 90 percent of Harley owners will repurchase a Harley that carries the weight. "When we get a customer, we can pretty much keep them. Our marketing is to get new customers and to keep existing [customers] happy," Piehl says.

It is just another part of Harley's creed: We believe life is what you make it, and we make it one heck of a ride.

Sources: Interview with Steve Piehl, "Sturgis Motorcycle Rally Is Tamer, Still not a family Affair," *Hagerty*, https://www.hagerty.com, August 29, 2016; "What Is Harley Davidson's Marketing Strategy?" http://marketrealist.com, March 31, 2016; "Steve Piehl Is Retiring from Harley Davidson," Cyrilhuzblog.com, July 23, 2015, http://cyrilhuzeblog.com/2015/06/23/steve-piehl-is-retiring-from-harley-davidson.

This chapter continues to reveal the role of marketing, starting with a discussion of the distribution system and concluding with a look at traditional and nontraditional marketing channels. It explores how organizations use a distribution system to enhance the value of a product and examines the methods used to move products to locations where consumers wish to buy them. Distribution is also known as "place" in terms of the **5Ps**, key components of the marketing mix. It is important to have an understanding of the members of a distribution system and to explore the role of wholesalers and retailers in delivering products to customers. In addition to understanding how the supply chain works to increase efficiency and customer satisfaction, marketers must also develop tactics for promotion, the last element of the marketing mix. Promotion is comprised of six parts, which include traditional advertising, sales promotion, personal selling, public relations, social media, and e-commerce.

12.1 The Nature and Functions of Distribution (Place)

1. What is the nature and function of distribution (place)?

Distribution is efficiently managing the acquisition of raw materials by the factory and the movement of products from the producer or **manufacturer** to business-to-business (B2B) users and consumers. It includes many facets, such as location, hours, website presence, logistics, atmospherics, inventory management, supply-chain management, and others. Logistics activities are usually the responsibility of the marketing department and are part of the large series of activities included in the supply chain. A supply chain is the system through which an organization acquires raw material, produces products, and delivers the products and services to its customers. Exhibit 12.2 illustrates a typical supply chain. Supply chain management helps increase the efficiency of logistics service by minimizing inventory and moving goods efficiently from producers to the ultimate users.

On their way from producers to end users and consumers, products pass through a series of marketing entities known as a **distribution channel**. We will look first at the entities that make up a distribution channel and then examine the functions that channels serve.

Marketing Intermediaries in the Distribution Channel

A distribution channel is made up of **marketing intermediaries**, or organizations that assist in moving goods and services from producers to end users and consumers. Marketing intermediaries are in the middle of the distribution process, between the producer and the end user. The following marketing intermediaries most often appear in the distribution channel:

- *Agents and brokers:* **Agents** are sales representatives of manufacturers and wholesalers, and **brokers** are entities that bring buyers and sellers together. Both agents and brokers are usually hired on commission basis by either a buyer or a seller. Agents and brokers are go-betweens whose job is to make deals. They do not own or take possession of goods.
- *Industrial distributors:* **Industrial distributors** are independent wholesalers that buy related product lines from many manufacturers and sell them to industrial users. They often have a sales force to call on purchasing agents, make deliveries, extend credit, and provide information. Industrial distributors are used in such industries as aircraft manufacturing, mining, and petroleum.
- *Wholesalers:* **Wholesalers** are firms that sell finished goods to retailers, manufacturers, and institutions (such as schools and hospitals). Historically, their function has been to buy from manufacturers and sell to retailers.
- *Retailers:* **Retailers** are firms that sell goods to consumers and to industrial users for their own consumption.

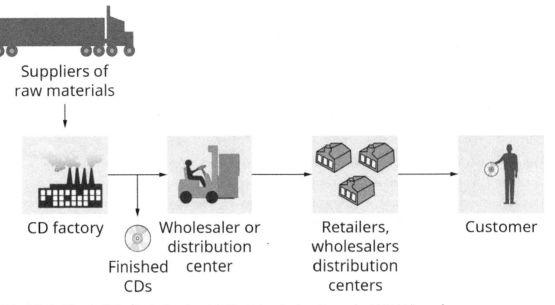

Exhibit 12.2   A Typical Supply Chain (Attribution: Copyright Rice University, OpenStax, under CC BY 4.0 license.)

At the end of the distribution channel are final consumers and industrial users. Industrial users are firms that buy products for internal use or for producing other products or services. They include manufacturers, utilities, airlines, railroads, and service institutions such as hotels, hospitals, and schools.

Exhibit 12.3 shows various ways marketing intermediaries can be linked. For instance, a manufacturer may sell to a wholesaler that sells to a retailer that in turn sells to a customer. In any of these distribution systems, goods and services are physically transferred from one organization to the next. As each takes possession of the products, it may take legal ownership of them. As the exhibit indicates, distribution channels can handle either consumer products or industrial products.

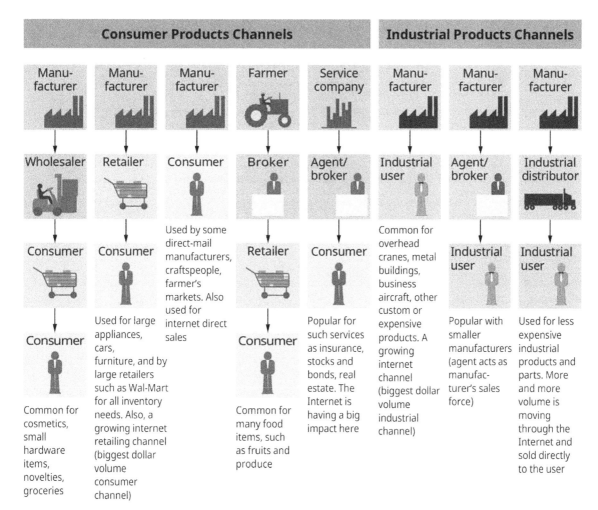

Exhibit 12.3 Channels of Distribution for B2B and Consumer Products (Attribution: Copyright Rice University, OpenStax, under CC BY 4.0 license.)

Nontraditional Channels

Often nontraditional channel arrangements help differentiate a firm's product from the competition. For example, manufacturers may decide to use nontraditional channels such as the internet, mail-order channels, or infomercials to sell products instead of going through traditional retailer channels. Although nontraditional channels may limit a brand's coverage, they can give a producer serving a niche market a way to gain market access and customer attention without having to establish channel intermediaries. Nontraditional channels can also provide another avenue of sales for larger firms. For example, a London publisher sells short stories through vending machines in the London Underground. Instead of the traditional book format, the stories are printed like folded maps, making them an easy-to-read alternative for commuters.

Kiosks, long a popular method for ordering and registering for wedding gifts, dispersing cash through ATMs, and facilitating airline check-in, are finding new uses. Ethan Allen furniture stores use kiosks as a product locator tool for consumers and salespeople. Kiosks on the campuses of Cheney University allow students to register for classes, see their class schedule and grades, check account balances, and even print transcripts. The general public, when it has access to the kiosks, can use them to gather information about the university.

Small and medium-sized New Orleans food and beverage companies and restaurants banded together to

promote their goods and establishments over the internet on a specific website at
http://www.nolacuisine.com. They also have found that they can successfully sell their offerings through the websites of the profiled restaurants and food outlets, such as Cochon Butcher (**https://cochonbutcher.com**). With technology rapidly evolving, downloading first-run movies to mobile devices may not be far off. The changing world of technology opens many doors for new, nontraditional distribution channels.

The Functions of Distribution Channels

Why do distribution channels exist? Why can't every firm sell its products directly to the end user or consumer? Why are go-betweens needed? Channels serve a number of functions.

Channels Reduce the Number of Transactions

Channels make distribution simpler by reducing the number of transactions required to get a product from the manufacturer to the consumer. For example, if there are four students in a course and a professor requires five textbooks (each from a different publisher), a total of 20 transactions would be necessary to accomplish the sale of the books. If the bookstore serves as a go-between, the number of transactions is reduced to nine. Each publisher sells to one bookstore rather than to four students. Each student buys from one bookstore instead of from five publishers (see **Exhibit 12.4**).

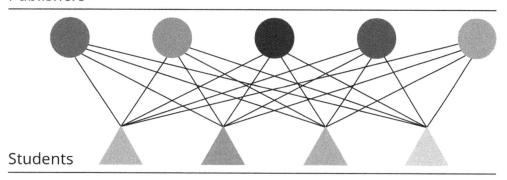

Without a Marketing Intermediary:
5 publishers × 4 students = 20 transactions

Publishers

Students

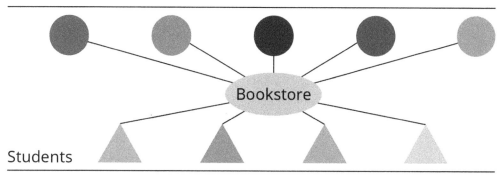

With a Marketing Intermediary:
5 publishers + 4 students = 9 transactions

Publishers

Bookstore

Students

Exhibit 12.4   How Distribution Channels Reduce the Number of Transactions (Attribution: Copyright Rice University, OpenStax, under CC BY 4.0 license.)

Dealing with channel intermediaries frees producers from many of the details of distribution activity. Producers are traditionally not as efficient or as enthusiastic about selling products directly to end users as channel members are. First, producers may wish to focus on production. They may feel that they cannot both produce and distribute in a competitive way. On the other hand, manufacturers are eager to deal directly with giant retailers, such as Walmart, which offer huge sales opportunities to producers.

Channels Ease the Flow of Goods

Channels make distribution easier in several ways. The first is by *sorting,* which consists of the following:

- *Sorting out:* Breaking many different items into separate stocks that are similar. Eggs, for instance, are sorted by grade and size. Another example would be different lines of women's dresses—designer, moderate, and economy lines.
- *Accumulating:* Bringing similar stocks together into a larger quantity. Twelve large Grade A eggs could be placed in some cartons and 12 medium Grade B eggs in other cartons. Another example would be to merge several lines of women's dresses from different designers together.
- *Allocating:* Breaking similar products into smaller and smaller lots. (Allocating at the wholesale level is called **breaking bulk**.) For instance, a tank-car load of milk could be broken down into gallon jugs. The

process of allocating generally is done when the goods are dispersed by region and as ownership of the goods changes.

Without the sorting, accumulating, and allocating processes, modern society would not exist. Instead, there would be home-based industries providing custom or semicustom products to local markets. In short, society would return to a much lower level of consumption.

A second way channels ease the flow of goods is by locating buyers for merchandise. A wholesaler must find the right retailers to sell a profitable volume of merchandise. A sporting-goods wholesaler, for instance, must find the retailers who are most likely to reach sporting-goods consumers. Retailers have to understand the buying habits of consumers and put stores where consumers want and expect to find the merchandise. Every member of a distribution channel must locate buyers for the products it is trying to sell.

Channel members also store merchandise so that goods are available when consumers want to buy them. The high cost of retail space often means many goods are stored by the wholesaler or manufacturer.

CONCEPT CHECK

1. List and define the marketing intermediaries that make up a distribution channel.
2. Provide an example of a strategic channel alliance.
3. How do channels reduce the number of transactions?

12.2 Wholesaling

2. What is wholesaling, and what are the types of wholesalers?

Wholesalers are channel members that buy finished products from manufacturers and sell them to retailers. Retailers in turn sell the products to consumers.

Wholesalers also sell products to institutions, such as manufacturers, schools, and hospitals, for use in performing their own missions. A manufacturer, for instance, might buy computer paper from Nationwide Papers, a wholesaler. A hospital might buy its cleaning supplies from Lagasse Brothers, one of the nation's largest wholesalers of janitorial supplies.

Sometimes wholesalers sell products to manufacturers for use in the manufacturing process. A builder of custom boats, for instance, might buy batteries from a battery wholesaler and switches from an electrical wholesaler. Some wholesalers even sell to other wholesalers, creating yet another stage in the distribution channel.

Types of Wholesaler Intermediaries

The two main types of wholesalers are merchant wholesalers and agents and brokers. Merchant wholesalers take title to the product (ownership rights); agents and brokers simply facilitate the sale of a product from producer to end user.

Merchant Wholesalers

Merchant wholesalers make up 80 percent of all wholesaling establishments and conduct slightly less than 60 percent of all wholesale sales. A **merchant wholesaler** is an institution that buys goods from manufacturers and resells them to businesses, government agencies, other wholesalers, or retailers. All merchant wholesalers take title to the goods they sell.

Agents and Brokers

As mentioned earlier, agents represent manufacturers and wholesalers. **Manufacturers' representatives** (also called **manufacturers' agents**) represent noncompeting manufacturers. These salespeople function as independent agents rather than as salaried employees of manufacturers. They do not take title to or possession of merchandise. They get commissions if they make sales—and nothing if they don't. They are found in a variety of industries, including electronics, clothing, hardware, furniture, and toys.

Exhibit 12.5   If diamonds are a girl's best friend, then women can find plenty of friends at Sam's and Costco. The two leading membership warehouse chains recently entered the luxury market, offering expensive diamond rings at steeply discounted prices. At Sam's, a 3.74-carat pink diamond pendant was reportedly priced 25 percent below its $750,000 valuation. At Costco, a 5.6-carat yellow-diamond ring valued at $280,000 listed for $99,999. *Why do cash-and-carry wholesalers offer jewelry for considerably lower prices than those offered by high-end retailers such as Tiffany and Neiman Marcus?* (Credit: Phillip Pressard/ Flickr/ Attribution 2.0 Generic (CC BY 2.0))

Brokers bring buyers and sellers together. Like agents, brokers do not take title to merchandise, they receive commissions on sales, and they have little say over company sales policies. They are found in markets where the information that would join buyers and sellers is scarce. These markets include real estate, agriculture, insurance, and commodities.

CONCEPT CHECK

1. Define wholesaling, and describe what wholesalers do.
2. Describe merchant wholesalers.
3. Explain the difference between agents and brokers.

12.3 The Competitive World of Retailing

3. What are the different kinds of retail operations?

Some 15 million Americans are engaged in retailing. Of this number, almost half work in service businesses such as barbershops, lawyers' offices, and amusement parks. Although most retailers are involved in small businesses, most sales are made by the giant retail organizations, such as Walmart, Target, and Macy's. Half of all retail sales come from fewer than 10 percent of all retail businesses. This small group employs about 40 percent of all retail workers. Retailers feel the impact of changes in the economy more than many other types of businesses. Survival depends on keeping up with changing lifestyles and customer shopping patterns. In recent years, online retailing trends have significantly impacted retailing organizations, providing more opportunity for smaller retailers and more competition for larger retailers.

Types of Retail Operations

There is a great deal of variety in retail operations. The major types of retailers are described in **Table 12.1**, which divides them into two main categories: in-store and nonstore retailing. Examples of *in-store retailing* include Walmart, Target, Macy's, and Neiman Marcus. These retailers get most of their revenue from people who come to the store to buy what they want. Many in-store retailers also do some catalog and telephone sales.

Retailing Takes Many Forms		
Types of In-Store Retailing	Description	Examples
Department store	Houses many departments under one roof with each treated as a separate buying center to achieve economies of buying, promotion, and control	Macy's, Nordstrom, Bloomingdale's, Kohl's

Table 12.1

Retailing Takes Many Forms		
Types of In-Store Retailing	Description	Examples
Specialty store	Specializes in a category of merchandise and carries a complete assortment	Toys "R" Us, Zales Jewelers
Convenience store	Offers convenience goods with long store hours and quick checkout	7-Eleven, Circle K
Supermarket	Specializes in a wide assortment of food, with self-service	Safeway, Kroger, Winn-Dixie
Discount store	Competes on the basis of low prices and high turnover; offers few services	Walmart, Target
Off-price retailer	Sells at prices 25 percent or more below traditional department store prices in a spartan environment	TJ Maxx, HomeGoods
Factory outlet	Owned by manufacturer; sells closeouts, factory seconds, and canceled orders	Levi Strauss, Dansk
Catalog store	Sends catalogs to customers and displays merchandise in showrooms where customers can order from attached warehouse	Ikea
Types of Nonstore Retailing	Description	Examples
Vending machine	Sells merchandise by machine	Canteen
Direct selling	Sells face-to-face, usually in the person's home	Avon, Amway
Direct-response marketing	Attempts to get immediate consumer sale through media advertising, catalogs, pop-up ads, or direct mail	K-Tel Music, Ronco
Home shopping networks	Selling via cable television	Home Shopping Network, QVC

Table 12.1

Retailing Takes Many Forms		
Types of In-Store Retailing	Description	Examples
Internet retailing (e-retailing)	Selling over the internet	Bluefly.com, landsend.com, gap.com, Amazon.com, Wayfair.com, Dell.com

Table 12.1

Nonstore retailing includes vending, direct selling, direct-response marketing, home shopping networks, and internet retailing. Vending uses machines to sell food and other items, usually as a convenience in institutions such as schools and hospitals.

Atmosphere and Retail Image

In considering retailing as a distribution strategy (place in the 5Ps), it is important to understand that place includes more than channel members or logistics. It also includes atmospherics—the image of the actual retailing store (or, in the case of nonstore retailing, the platform from which the product is offered, such as a website or vending machine). An important task in retailing is to create this image. Marketers combine the store's merchandise mix, service level, and atmosphere to make up a retail image. *Atmosphere* refers to the physical layout and décor of the store. They can create a relaxed or busy feeling, a sense of luxury, a friendly or cold attitude, and a sense of organization or clutter.

These are the most influential factors in creating a store's atmosphere:

- *Employee type and density:* Employee type refers to an employee's general characteristics—for instance, neat, friendly, knowledgeable, or service-oriented. Density is the number of employees per 1,000 square feet of selling space. A discount retailer such as Target has a low employee density that creates a "do-it-yourself" casual atmosphere.
- *Merchandise type and density:* The type of merchandise carried and how it is displayed add to the atmosphere the retailer is trying to create. A prestigious retailer such as Saks or Nordstrom carries the best brand names and displays them in a neat, uncluttered arrangement. Other retailers such as Dollar Tree may display goods in a more cluttered, crowded, disheveled way because their target market (lower-income individuals) equates clutter with open markets (and with lower prices and "deals").

Exhibit 12.6   Whether peering through department store windows, buying holiday gifts, or going on a spending spree, people love to shop. Shopping makes people feel good, and a growing body of research suggests that shopping activates key areas of the brain, boosting one's mood—at least until the bill arrives. Feelings of pleasure and satisfaction derived from a buying binge may be linked to brain chemicals that produce a "shopping high." *How might retailers use atmosphere to stimulate consumers' natural impulse to shop?* (Montgomery County Planning Commission/ Flickr/ Attribution 2.0 Generic (CC BY 2.0))

- *Fixture type and density:* Fixtures can be elegant (rich woods) or trendy (chrome and smoked glass), or they can be old, beat-up tables, as in an antique store. The fixtures should be consistent with the general atmosphere the store is trying to create. By displaying its merchandise on tables and shelves rather than on traditional pipe racks, the Gap creates a relaxed and uncluttered atmosphere that enables customers to see and touch the merchandise more easily. In addition to traditional display racks, Cabela's retail stores feature two 5,000-gallon aquariums stocked with carp, trout, and other fish and a diorama featuring elephants, lions, zebras, hyenas, and other animals. A typical Cabela's has several million customers a year. It is not unusual for someone to drive many miles to get to a Cabela's, where you can often see license plates from many states and Canadian provinces.[1]

- *Sound:* Sound can be pleasant or unpleasant for a customer. Classical music at a nice Italian restaurant helps create ambiance, just as country and western music does at a truck stop. Music can also entice customers to stay in the store longer and buy more, or it can encourage them to eat quickly and leave a table for others.

- *Odors:* Smell can either stimulate or detract from sales. The wonderful smell of pastries and breads entices bakery customers, as does the smell of freshly brewed coffee in a shopping mall. Conversely, customers can be repulsed by bad odors, such as cigarette smoke, musty smells, antiseptic odors, and overly powerful room deodorizers.

EXPANDING AROUND THE GLOBE

Creative Retailing at Selfridges

To steer traffic to its flagship store in London, Selfridges sought divine intervention—that is, a 50-foot statue of Jesus. The small-scale replica of Rio de Janeiro's famous monument gazed down on shoppers during a month-long Brazilian-themed promotion.

Combined with a radical redesign of the retail space that makes each of Selfridges' four outlets feel more like a collection of quirky boutiques than one gargantuan marketplace, stunts like the Brazil 40° celebration have transformed the once-staid 95-year-old British retail chain into a premier arbiter of hip. Selfridges' success has spurred retailers worldwide to take a closer look. "A department store chief who has not made his way to Selfridges to study its operation," says Arnold Aronson, former CEO of Saks Fifth Avenue, "is an executive not doing his job."

Typically, department stores develop their own merchandising strategies, resulting in a retail space crowded with Tommy Hilfiger, Ralph Lauren, and other predictable names arranged in displays that rarely vary from one chain to the next. Selfridges, however, operates on the theory that no one understands a product better than the designer or vendor that created it. So individual designers are allotted space in Selfridges and asked to create in-store displays that highlight their work. Traditional "departments" such as shoes, cosmetics, and men's business wear have been organized by lifestyle—youth, sports, or women's contemporary. This helps expose customers to merchandise they might not otherwise see.

Recently, Selfridges asked a tattoo and body-piercing parlor called Metal Morphosis to set up shop next to some women's fashion vendors. Metal Morphosis was such a huge hit with shoppers en route to the clothing racks that it will soon expand to other Selfridges outlets.

Selfridges is also known for its "happenings." They recently opened a low-cost interfaith charity shop within the confines of their luxury brand Oxford street store in London. Performance artist Miranda July was involved in the creation of this shop-within-a-shop, which partners with Islamic, Jewish, and other faith groups to promote the charity store. Ironically, shoppers can find bargain-priced donated blouses just feet away from some priced at over $3,000.

Critical Thinking Questions

1. Selfridges opened a new store described as a "silver blob" or "spaceship." The building has no straight lines and is covered with 15,000 anodized aluminum disks. The atrium is an array of high-gloss white elevators and balconies that are all slanted to avoid "the atrium look." Do you think Selfridges is becoming too cool or hip? What impact will this have on sales?
2. Would Selfridges be successful in the United States? Why or why not?

Sources: "The Secrets Behind Our House," http://www.selfridges.com/US/en, accessed September 27, 2017; Barry Toberman, "Norwood Delight as Interfaith Shop at Selfridges Brings in the Punters," *The Jewish Chronicle,* https://www.thejc.com, September 1, 2017; Hannah Ellis-Petersen, "Miranda July Curates Interfaith Charity Shop Opening up in Selfridges," *The Guardian,* https://www.theguardian.com, August 30, 2017.

CONCEPT CHECK

1. Describe at least five types of in-store retailing and four forms of nonstore retailing.
2. What factors most influence a retail store's atmosphere?

12.4 | Using Supply Chain Management to Increase Efficiency and Customer Satisfaction

4. How can supply-chain management increase efficiency and customer satisfaction?

Distribution (place) is an important part of the marketing mix. Retailers don't sell products they can't deliver, and salespeople don't (or shouldn't) promise deliveries they can't make. Late deliveries and broken promises may mean the loss of a customer. Accurate order filling and billing, timely delivery, and arrival in good condition are important to the success of the product.

The goal of supply-chain management is to create a satisfied customer by coordinating all of the activities of the supply-chain members into a seamless process. Therefore, an important element of supply-chain management is that it is completely customer driven. In the mass-production era, manufacturers produced standardized products that were "pushed" through the supply channel to the consumer. In contrast, in today's marketplace, products are being driven by customers, who expect to receive product configurations and services matched to their unique needs. For example, Dell builds computers according to its customers' precise specifications, such as the amount of memory, type of monitor, and amount of hard-drive space. The process begins with Dell purchasing partly built laptops from contract manufacturers. The final assembly is done in Dell factories in Ireland, Malaysia, or China, where microprocessors, software, and other key components are added. Those finished products are then shipped to Dell-operated distribution centers in the United States, where they are packaged with other items and shipped to the customer.

Through the channel partnership of suppliers, manufacturers, wholesalers, and retailers along the entire supply chain who work together toward the common goal of creating customer value, supply-chain management allows companies to respond with the unique product configuration demanded by the customer. Today, supply-chain management plays a dual role: first, as a *communicator* of customer demand that extends from the point of sale all the way back to the supplier, and second, as a *physical flow process* that engineers the timely and cost-effective movement of goods through the entire supply pipeline.

Accordingly, supply-chain managers are responsible for making channel strategy decisions, coordinating the sourcing and procurement of raw materials, scheduling production, processing orders, managing inventory, transporting and storing supplies and finished goods, and coordinating customer-service activities. Supply-chain managers are also responsible for the management of information that flows through the supply chain. Coordinating the relationships between the company and its external partners, such as vendors, carriers, and third-party companies, is also a critical function of supply-chain management. Because supply-chain managers play such a major role in both cost control and customer satisfaction, they are more valuable than ever.

For products that are services, the distribution channel is based primarily on location of the services, such as where the company has its headquarters; the layout of the area in which the service is provided (for example, the interior of a dry cleaners' store); alternative locations for the presentation of services, such as an architect visiting a client's site location; and elements of atmosphere, such as dark wooden bookcases for bound legal volumes in an attorney's office, which provide credibility. Services companies also utilize the traditional entities of distribution for any actual goods they sell or supplies they must purchase.

CONCEPT CHECK

1. What is the goal of supply-chain management?
2. What does it mean for a supply chain to be customer driven?
3. How does distribution (place) differ for services products?

12.5 Promotion Strategy

5. What is promotion, and what are the key elements of a promotional mix?

Promotion is an attempt by marketers to inform, persuade, or remind consumers and B2B users to influence their opinion or elicit a response. Most firms use some form of promotion. Because company goals vary widely, so do promotional strategies. The goal is to stimulate action from the people or organizations of a target market. In a profit-oriented firm, the desired action is for the consumer to buy the promoted item. Mrs. Smith's, for instance, wants people to buy more frozen pies. Not-for-profit organizations seek a variety of actions with their promotions. They tell us not to litter, to buckle up, to join the military, or to attend the ballet. (These are examples of products that are ideas marketed to specific target markets.)

Promotional goals include creating awareness, getting people to try products, providing information, retaining loyal customers, increasing the use of products, and identifying potential customers, as well as teaching potential service clients what is needed to "co-create" the services provided. Any promotional campaign may seek to achieve one or more of these goals:

1. *Creating awareness:* All too often, firms go out of business because people don't know they exist or what they do. Small restaurants often have this problem. Simply putting up a sign and opening the door is rarely enough. Promotion through ads on social media platforms and local radio or television, coupons in local papers, flyers, and so forth can create awareness of a new business or product.
   Large companies often use catchy slogans to build brand awareness. For example, Dodge's wildly successful ads where a guy in a truck yells over to another truck at a stoplight, "Hey, that thing got a Hemi?" has created a huge number of new customers for Dodge trucks. Hemi has become a brand within a brand. Now, Chrysler is extending the Hemi engine to the Jeep brand, hoping for the same success.
2. *Getting consumers to try products:* Promotion is almost always used to get people to try a new product or to get nonusers to try an existing product. Sometimes free samples are given away. Lever, for instance, mailed over two million free samples of its Lever 2000 soap to targeted households. Coupons and trial-size containers of products are also common tactics used to tempt people to try a product. Celebrities are also used to get people to try products. Oprah Winfrey, for example, recently partnered with Kraft Heinz to launch a new line of refrigerated soups and side dishes made with no artificial flavors or dyes. Kate Murphy, director of strategic partnerships at the social marketing platform Crowdtap, weighed in on the strategy. "Celebrity endorsements can provide immense value to a product/brand when done right," Murphy said. "If a celebrity aligns with a product, they bring a level of trust and familiarity to the table."[2]
3. *Providing information:* Informative promotion is more common in the early stages of the product life cycle. An informative promotion may explain what ingredients (for example, fiber) will do for a consumer's health, describe why the product is better (for example, high-definition television versus regular

television), inform the customer of a new low price, or explain where the item may be purchased. People typically will not buy a product or support a not-for-profit organization until they know what it will do and how it may benefit them. Thus, an informative ad may stimulate interest in a product. Consumer watchdogs and social critics applaud the informative function of promotion because it helps consumers make more intelligent purchase decisions. StarKist, for instance, lets customers know that its tuna is caught in dolphin-safe nets.

4. *Keeping loyal customers:* Promotion is also used to keep people from switching brands. Slogans such as Campbell's soups are "M'm! M'm! Good!" and "Intel Inside" remind consumers about the brand. Marketers also remind users that the brand is better than the competition. For years, Pepsi has claimed it has the taste that consumers prefer. Southwest Airlines brags that customers' bags fly free. Such **advertising** reminds customers about the quality of the product or service.

   Firms can also help keep customers loyal by telling them when a product or service is improved. Domino's recently aired candid advertisements about the quality of their product and completely revamped their delivery operations to improve their service. This included advertisements highlighting a Domino's pizza being delivered by reindeer in Japan and by drone in New Zealand. According to University of Maryland marketing professor Roland Rust, "delivery" stands out in how Domino's has broadly improved its quality, and "the customized delivery vehicles are a competitive advantage."[3]

5. *Increasing the amount and frequency of use:* Promotion is often used to get people to use more of a product and to use it more often. The National Cattlemen's Beef Association reminds Americans to "Eat More Beef." The most popular promotion to increase the use of a product may be frequent-flyer or -user programs. The Marriott Rewards program awards points for each dollar spent at a Marriott property. At the Platinum level, members receive a guaranteed room, an upgrade to the property's finest available accommodations, access to the concierge lounge, a free breakfast, free local phone calls, and a variety of other goodies.[4]

6. *Identifying target customers:* Promotion helps find customers. One way to do this is to list a website as part of the promotion. For instance, promotions in *The Wall Street Journal* and *Bloomberg Businessweek* regularly include web addresses for more information on computer systems, corporate jets, color copiers, and other types of business equipment to help target those who are truly interested. Fidelity Investments ads trumpet, "Solid investment opportunities are out there," and then direct consumers to go to **http://www.fidelity.com.** A full-page ad in *The Wall Street Journal* for Sprint unlimited wireless service invites potential customers to visit **http://www.sprint.com.** These websites typically will ask for your e-mail address when you seek additional information.

7. *Teaching the customer:* For service products, it is often imperative to actually teach the potential client the reasons for certain parts of a service. In services, the service providers work with customers to perform the service. This is called "co-creation." For example, an engineer will need to spend extensive time with team members from a client company and actually teach the team members what the design process will be, how the interaction of getting information for the design will work, and at what points each part of the service will be delivered so that ongoing changes can be made to the design. For services products, this is more involved than just providing information—it is actually teaching the client.

The Promotional Mix

The combination of traditional advertising, personal selling, sales promotion, public relations, social media, and e-commerce used to promote a product is called the **promotional mix**. Each firm creates a unique promotional mix for each product. But the goal is always to deliver the firm's message efficiently and effectively to the target audience. These are the elements of the promotional mix:

- *Traditional advertising:* Any paid form of nonpersonal promotion by an identified sponsor that is delivered through traditional media channels.
- *Personal selling:* A face-to-face presentation to a prospective buyer.
- *Sales promotion:* Marketing activities (other than personal selling, traditional advertising, public relations, social media, and e-commerce) that stimulate consumer buying, including coupons and samples, displays, shows and exhibitions, demonstrations, and other types of selling efforts.
- *Public relations:* The linking of organizational goals with key aspects of the public interest and the development of programs designed to earn public understanding and acceptance. Public relations can include lobbying, publicity, special events, internal publications, and media such as a company's internal television channel.
- *Social media:* The use of social media platforms such as Facebook, Twitter, Pinterest, Instagram, and various blogs to generate "buzz" about a product or company. The skills and knowledge needed to generate information as well as to defend the company against problems (such as incriminating videos "going viral") are separate skills from those related to traditional advertising. Even promotional strategies such as paying celebrities to wear a specific line of clothing and posting these images on Twitter or Instagram (a form of advertising) requires different types of planning and expertise than traditional advertising.
- *E-commerce:* The use of a company's website to generate sales through online ordering, information, interactive components such as games, and other elements of the website. Website development is mandatory is today's business world. Understanding how to develop and utilize a website to generate sales is imperative for any marketer.

Ideally, marketing communications from each promotional-mix element (personal selling, traditional advertising, sales promotion, public relations, social media, and e-commerce) should be integrated. That is, the message reaching the consumer should be the same regardless of whether it comes from an advertisement, a salesperson in the field, a magazine article, a blog, a Facebook posting, or a coupon in a newspaper insert.

Integrated Marketing Communications

This disjointed approach to promotion has propelled many companies to adopt the concept of **integrated marketing communications (IMC)**. IMC involves carefully coordinating all promotional activities—traditional advertising (including direct marketing), sales promotion, personal selling, public relations, social media and e-commerce, packaging, and other forms of promotion—to produce a consistent, unified message that is customer focused. Following the concept of IMC, marketing managers carefully work out the roles the various promotional elements will play in the marketing mix. Timing of promotional activities is coordinated, and the results of each campaign are carefully monitored to improve future use of the promotional mix tools. Typically, a company appoints a marketing communications director who has overall responsibility for integrating the company's marketing communications.

Exhibit 12.7   When Weight Watchers signed up DJ Khaled to be one of its celebrity endorsers, many were surprised by the choice. Khaled will broadcast his quest to slim down across Facebook, Instagram, Twitter, and Snapchat in a bid to attract more men to sign up for the program. Khaled is not the usual choice for a Weight Watchers spokesperson, but once you scratch below the surface, he's actually a great brand fit. Authenticity and relevance are words bandied about like the gospel in influencer marketing, but they are the most important ingredients when it comes to working with any level of influencer. *What challenges and payoffs are associated with integrated marketing communications?* (Credit: megran.roberts/ Flickr/ Attribution 2.0 Generic (CC BY 2.0))

Southwest Airlines relied on IMC to launch its "Transfarency" campaign. The campaign integrated and promoted the concept on its website, as well as through advertising and airport signage. The campaign has resonated with consumers because most competitors add extra fees for baggage and premium seats. One of the taglines Southwest uses is "Reward seats only on days ending with the letter 'y.'" The integrated marketing campaign was created in collaboration with Southwest's advertising agency, GSD&M, based in Dallas, Texas.[5]

The sections that follow examine the elements of the promotional mix in more detail.

CONCEPT CHECK

1. What is the objective of a promotional campaign?
2. What is the promotional mix?
3. What are the features of an integrated marketing communications campaign?

12.6 | The Huge Impact of Advertising

6. How are advertising media selected?

Most Americans are bombarded daily with advertisements to buy things. **Traditional advertising** is any paid form of nonpersonal presentation by an identified sponsor. It may appear on television or radio; in newspapers, magazines, books, or direct mail; or on billboards or transit cards. In the United States, children between the ages of two and 11 are exposed to more than 25,600 exposures to advertising through TVs and online exposures a year. Adults are exposed to three times as many—more than two million commercials in a lifetime.[6]

The money that big corporations spend on advertising is mind-boggling. Total advertising expenses in this country were estimated at more than $206 billion in 2017.[7] Global advertising expenditures are approximately $546 billion annually.[8] General Motors is America's largest advertiser, spending over $3.1 billion annually. This is slightly over $350,000 per hour, seven days a week, 24 hours per day. America's biggest global spender on advertising is Procter & Gamble at $4.6 billion.[9]

Nissan was a sponsor of the 2016 Rio Olympic Games and provided 5,000 vehicles for the events. Ads for the 2018 Super Bowl cost between $5 million and $5.5 million for a 30-second commercial. A 30-second spot on NBC's *Sunday Night Football* costs about $650,000.

The Impact of Technology and the Internet on Traditional Advertising

Many new media are not hardwired or regulated, and digital technology is delivering content anytime, anywhere. Cable, satellite, and the internet have highly fragmented audiences, making them tougher than ever to reach. In the late 1950s, *Gunsmoke* on CBS captured a 65 percent share of the TV audience nearly every Saturday night. Only one event, the Super Bowl, has a chance to do that now.

Traditional forms of entertainment are being rapidly digitized. Magazines, books, movies, shows, and games can be accessed through a laptop or a cell phone. In 2017, 93 million U.S. homes have broadband connections—nearly as many as the 119.6 million that now have cable and satellite hookups.[10]

Technology is driving many of the changes, but so is consumer behavior. Advertiser questions abound. How do you market a product to young people when millions of them are glued to video game screens instead of TVs? How do you reach TV audiences when viewers can TiVo their way past your ads? How do you utilize social media to get the word out about your product, and once you do, how do you control the message if something goes viral? What role do influencers play in promoting products and services via various electronic platforms? What should you make of blogs? How do you plan a website that fosters sales and continually provides information and other forms of value for your customers? Product placements in films and streaming content? Podcasts? We will touch on each of these later in the chapter.

Choosing Advertising Media

The channels through which advertising is carried to prospective customers are the **advertising media**. Both product and institutional ads appear in all the major advertising media. Each company must decide which media are best for its products. Two of the main factors in making that choice are the cost of the medium and the audience reached by it.

Advertising Costs and Market Penetration

Cost per contact is the cost of reaching one member of the target market. Naturally, as the size of the audience increases, so does the total cost. Cost per contact enables an advertiser to compare media vehicles, such as television versus radio or magazine versus newspaper, or, more specifically, *Forbes* versus The Wall Street Journal. An advertiser debating whether to spend local advertising dollars for TV spots or radio spots could consider the cost per contact of each. The advertiser might then pick the vehicle with the lowest cost per contact to maximize advertising punch for the money spent. Often costs are expressed on a **cost per thousand (CPM)** contacts basis.

Reach is the number of different target consumers who are exposed to a commercial at least once during a specific period, usually four weeks. Media plans for product introductions and attempts at increasing brand awareness usually emphasize reach. For example, an advertiser might try to reach 70 percent of the target audience during the first three months of the campaign. Because the typical ad is short-lived and often only a small portion of an ad may be perceived at one time, advertisers repeat their ads so consumers will remember the message. **Frequency** is the number of times an individual is exposed to a message. Average frequency is used by advertisers to measure the intensity of a specific medium's coverage.

Exhibit 12.8   In addition to listing hundreds of scrumptious menu choices and cheesecakes, the Cheesecake Factory's magazine-sized menus feature a number of full-page glossy ads for Bebe, Macy's, Mercedes-Benz, and more. An increasingly popular media option, menu advertising offers many promotional benefits: huge readership by a captive audience, outstanding demographic selectivity, and great value—less than a penny per exposure. *How do advertisers decide whether or not menu advertising is right for their promotional mixes?* (Credit: Mighell xp/ Flickr/ Attribution 2.0 Generic (CC BY 2.0)

Media selection is also a matter of matching the advertising medium with the product's target market. If marketers are trying to reach teenage females, they might select *Seventeen* magazine. If they are trying to reach consumers over 50 years old, they may choose *AARP: The Magazine.* A medium's ability to reach a precisely defined market is its **audience selectivity**. Some media vehicles, such as general newspapers and network television, appeal to a wide cross section of the population. Others—such as *Brides, Popular Mechanics, Architectural Digest,* MTV, ESPN, and Christian radio stations—appeal to very specific groups. Marketers must also consider utilizing various social media platforms and which platforms are most likely to reach the targeted market.

CONCEPT CHECK

1. How is technology impacting the way advertisers reach their markets?
2. What are the two main factors that should be considered when selecting advertising media?

12.7 The Importance of Personal Selling

7. What is personal selling?

Advertising acquaints potential customers with a product and thereby makes personal selling easier. **Personal selling** is a face-to-face sales presentation to a prospective customer. Sales jobs range from salesclerks at clothing stores to engineers with MBAs who design large, complex systems for manufacturers. About 6.5 million people are engaged in personal selling in the United States. Slightly over 45 percent of them are women. The number of people who earn a living from sales is huge compared, for instance, with the nearly 300,000 workers employed in the traditional advertising sector. Personal selling offers several advantages over other forms of promotion:

- Personal selling provides a detailed explanation or demonstration of the product. This capability is especially desirable for complex or new goods and services.
- The sales message can be varied according to the motivations and interests of each prospective customer. Moreover, when the prospect has questions or raises objections, the salesperson is there to provide explanations. In contrast, advertising and sales promotion can respond only to the objections the copywriter thinks are important to customers.
- Personal selling can be directed only to qualified prospects. Other forms of promotion include some unavoidable waste because many people in the audience are not prospective customers.
- Personal selling costs can be controlled by adjusting the size of the sales force (and resulting expenses) in one-person increments. In contrast, advertising and sales promotion must often be purchased in fairly large amounts.
- Perhaps the most important advantage is that personal selling is considerably more effective than other forms of promotion in obtaining a sale and gaining a satisfied customer.

The Selling Process

Selling is a process that can be learned. Experts have spelled out the steps of the selling process, shown in

Exhibit 12.9, and professional salespeople use them all the time. These steps are as follows:

1. *Prospecting and qualifying:* To start the process, the salesperson looks for **sales prospects**, those companies and people who are most likely to buy the seller's offerings. This activity is called **prospecting**. Because there are no surefire ways to find prospects, most salespeople try many methods.

   For many companies, the inquiries generated by advertising and promotion are the most likely source of prospects. Inquiries are also known as sales leads. Leads usually come in the form of letters, cards, e-mail addresses, telephone calls, or through social media sites. Some companies supply salespeople with prospect lists compiled from external sources, such as Chamber of Commerce directories, newspapers, public records, club membership lists, internet inquiries, and professional or trade publication subscription lists. Meetings, such as professional conventions and trade shows, are another good source of leads. Sales representatives attend such meetings to display and demonstrate their company's products and to answer the questions of those attending. The firm's files and records can be another source of prospects. Correspondence with buyers can be helpful. Records in the service department can identify people who already own equipment and might be prospects for new models. Finally, friends and acquaintances of salespeople can often supply leads.

   One guideline is that not all prospects are "true" opportunities for a sale. Just because someone has been referred or has made an inquiry does not mean that the person is a genuine prospect. Salespeople can avoid wasting time and increase their productivity by qualifying all prospects. **Qualifying questions** are used to separate prospects from those who do not have the potential to buy. The following three questions help determine who is a real prospect and who is not:

   ◦ Does the prospect have a need for our product?
   ◦ Can the prospect make the buying decision?
   ◦ Can the prospect afford our product?

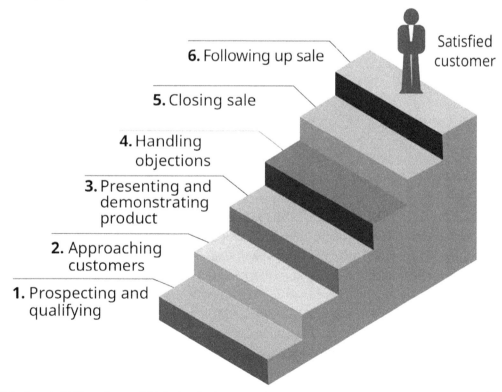

Exhibit 12.9 Steps in Making a Successful Sale (Attribution: Copyright Rice University, OpenStax, under CC BY 4.0 license.)

2. *Approaching customers:* After identifying a prospect, the salesperson explains the reason for wanting an

appointment and sets a specific date and time. At the same time, the salesperson tries to build interest in the coming meeting. One good way to do this is to impart an interesting or important piece of information—for instance, "I think my product can cut your shipping and delivery time by two days."

3. *Presenting and demonstrating the product:* The presentation and demonstration can be fully automated, completely unstructured, or somewhere in between. In a fully automated presentation, the salesperson shows a movie or slides or makes a PowerPoint presentation and then answers questions and takes any orders. In today's business world, in which relationships are most important for long-term sales, canned or structured presentations are not well received, nor do they support the idea of building a great bond with the customer. A completely unstructured presentation that has no set format is a much more successful approach. It may be a casual conversation, with the salesperson presenting product benefits and assisting the customer in solving his or her problems (like a partner on the client company's team) in a way that might interest the potential buyer.

4. *Handling objections:* Almost every sales presentation, structured or unstructured, meets with some objection. Rarely does a customer say, "I'll buy it," without asking questions or voicing concerns. The professional salesperson tries to anticipate objections so they can be countered quickly and with assurance. The best way to counter objections is to have a thorough knowledge of the product offering so that a solution can be found that overcomes the objection.

   Often employed in business, the "higher authority" objection is frequently used when one of the parties says, "This agreement looks good, but I'll have to run it by my committee" (or wife or any other "higher authority"). The result is that that sales presentation turns out to be just a preliminary, nonbinding round. After the higher authority responds, often disapproving the agreement, the sale goes into round two or starts all over again.

   For example, when a customer wants to buy a house, car, or anything expensive, the salesperson will say, "If we find the house (or car) that you really like, is there any reason you could not make the purchase today?" Once they get the green light, the salesperson will spend whatever time it takes to find the right product for the customer. However, if the client says his uncle has to give the final approval because he will be loaning the money, the salesperson will try and set up an appointment when the uncle can be present.

5. *Closing the sale:* After all the objections have been dealt with, it's time to close the sale. Even experienced salespeople sometimes find this part of the sales process awkward. Perhaps the easiest way to close a sale is to ask for it: "Ms. Jones, may I write up your order?" One of the best techniques is to act as though the deal has been concluded: "Mr. Bateson, we'll have this equipment in and working for you in two weeks." If Mr. Bateson doesn't object, the salesperson can assume that the sale has been made.

6. *Following up on the sale:* The salesperson's job isn't over when the sale is made. In fact, the sale is just the start. The salesperson must write up the order properly and turn it in promptly. This part of the job may be easy for many consumer products, but for B2B products or services, it may be more complex. An order for a complex piece of industrial equipment may include a hundred pages of detail. Each detail must be carefully checked to ensure that the equipment is exactly what was ordered.

   After the product is delivered to the customer, the salesperson must make a routine visit to see that the customer is satisfied. This follow-up call may also be a chance to make another sale. But even if it isn't, it will build goodwill for the salesperson's company and may bring future business. Repeat sales over many years are the goal of professional salespeople.

CONCEPT CHECK

1. What are the advantages of personal selling?
2. Explain the selling process.

12.8 Sales Promotion

8. What are the goals of sales promotion, and what are several types of sales promotion?

Sales promotion helps make personal selling and advertising more effective. **Sales promotions** are marketing events or sales efforts—not including traditional advertising, personal selling, and public relations—that stimulate buying. Sales promotion can be developed as part of the social media or e-commerce effort just as advertising can, but the methods and tactics are much different. Sales promotion is a $300 billion—and growing— industry. Sales promotion is usually targeted toward either of two distinctly different markets. Consumer sales promotion is targeted to the ultimate consumer market. Trade sales promotion is directed to members of the marketing channel, such as wholesalers and retailers.

The goal of many promotion tactics is immediate purchase. Therefore, it makes sense when planning a sales-promotion campaign to target customers according to their general behavior. For instance, is the consumer loyal to the marketer's product or to the competitor's? Does the consumer switch brands readily in favor of the best deal? Does the consumer buy only the least expensive product, no matter what? Does the consumer buy any products in your category at all?

Procter & Gamble believes shoppers make up their mind about a product in about the time it takes to read this paragraph.

This "first moment of truth," as P&G calls it, is the three to seven seconds when someone notices an item on a store shelf. Despite spending billions on traditional advertising, the consumer-products giant thinks this instant is one of its most important marketing opportunities. It recently created a position entitled Director of First Moment of Truth, or Director of FMOT (pronounced "EFF-mott"), to produce sharper, flashier in-store displays. There is a 15-person FMOT department at P&G headquarters in Cincinnati as well as 50 FMOT leaders stationed around the world.[11]

Exhibit 12.10   Pet lovers want the best for their animals, and choosing a proper diet is an essential part of raising happy, healthy pets. That's why many dog food providers such as Purina and Blue Buffalo are creating specific size- and age-appropriate diets for dogs. They often use sales promotion to encourage animal lovers to transition their pets to premium-brand food, encourage pet owners to track their pets' performance during the trial, and evaluate the "before and after" health of their pets. *What promotional objectives underlie these practices?* (Credit: Ted Van Pelt/ Flickr/ Attribution 2.0 Generic (CC BY 2.0))

One of P&G's most prominent in-store promotions has been for a new line of Pampers. In the United States, P&G came up with what it calls a "shopper concept"—a single promotional theme that allows it to pitch products in a novel way. The theme for Pampers was "Babies First." In stores, the company handed out information on childhood immunizations, car-seat safety, and healthy diets while promoting its diapers and wipes in other parts of the store. To market Pampers diapers in the United Kingdom, P&G persuaded retailers earlier this year to put fake doorknobs high up on restroom doors, to remind parents how much babies need to stretch.

The objectives of a promotion depend on the general behavior of target consumers, as described in Table 12.2. For example, marketers who are targeting loyal users of their product don't want to change behavior. Instead, they want to reinforce existing behavior or increase product usage. Frequent-buyer programs that reward consumers for repeat purchases can be effective in strengthening brand loyalty. Other types of promotions are more effective with customers prone to brand switching or with those who are loyal to a competitor's product. Cents-off coupons, free samples, or an eye-catching display in a store will often entice shoppers to try a different brand.

The use of sales promotion for services products depends on the type of services. Consumer services, such as hairstyling, rely heavily on sales promotions (such as providing half off the price of a haircut for senior citizens on Mondays). Professional services, however, use very little sales promotion. Doctors, for example, do not often use coupons for performing an appendectomy, for example. In fact, service product companies must be careful not to utilize too many sales-promotion tactics because they can lower the credibility of the firm. Attorneys do not have a sale on providing services for divorce proceedings, for example.

Types of Consumers and Sales Promotion Goals		
Type of Behavior	**Desired Results**	**Sales Promotion Examples**
Loyal customers: People who buy your product most or all of the time	Reinforce behavior, increase consumption, change purchase timing	Loyalty marketing programs, such as frequent-buyer cards and frequent-shopper clubs Bonus packs that give loyal consumers an incentive to stock up or premiums offered in return for proof of purchase
Competitor's customers: People who buy a competitor's product most or all of the time	Break loyalty, persuade to switch to your brand	Sweepstakes, contests, or premiums that create interest in the product
Brand switchers: People who buy a variety of products in the category	Persuade to buy your brand more often	Sampling to introduce your product's superior qualities compared to their brand
Price buyers: People who consistently buy the least expensive brand	Appeal with low prices or supply added value that makes price less important	Trade deals that help make the product more readily available than competing products Coupons, cents-off packages, refunds, or trade deals that reduce the price of the brand to match that of the brand that would have been purchased

Table 12.2

Two growing areas of sales promotion are couponing and product placement. American consumers receive over $321 billion worth of coupons each year and redeem about $3 billion.[12] Almost 85 percent of all Americans redeem coupons. Sunday newspaper supplements remain the number one source, but there has been explosive growth of online or consumer-printed coupons. General Mills, Kimberly-Clark, and General Electric like online coupons because they have a higher redemption rate. Coupons are used most often for grocery shopping. Do they save you money? One study found that people using coupons at the grocery store spent eight percent more than those who didn't.[13]

Product placement is paid inclusion of brands in mass media programming. This includes movies, TV, books, music videos, and video games. So when you see Ford vehicles in the latest James Bond movie or Tom Hanks putting on a pair on Nikes on-screen, that is product placement. Product placement has become a huge business. For example, companies paid more than $6 billion in a recent year to have their products placed prominently in a film or television program; that figure is expected to reach more than $11 billion by 2019.[14] It is easy to go overboard with this trend and be portrayed as a parody, however. The 2017 *Emoji Movie* is an example of failed product placements. The theme of the movie centered on various emojis caught in a smartphone as they are forced to play Candy Crush and say glowing things about such apps as Dropbox and Instagram as they make their way through the phone.[15] Also, some have suggested that product placement might doom the products and companies. For example, Atari products appeared in the classic 1982 film *Blade Runner*, but the original company went out of business shortly after the movie was released, while another product, the Cuisinart food processor, had to settle a price-fixing scandal after making an appearance in the film. This has not stopped companies such as Sony, Peugeot, and Coca-Cola from tempting fate by appearing in the recently released *Blade Runner 2049*.[16] Many large companies are cutting their advertising budgets to spend more on product placements. One area of product placement that continues to raise ethical issues is so-called "experts" being paid to mention brands on the air.

Exhibit 12.11   Whether making a cameo appearance or starring in a major role, brands are top talent in the entertainment world. NASCAR drivers, racing cars, and tracks are speckled with corporate brands, and Coca-Cola sits at the judges' table on *American Idol*. Drive through the video game *Need for Speed* and you will see Best Buy stores along the way, as well as billboards for Burger King and other products. And Reese's Pieces are forever immortalized in the movie *E.T. the Extra-Terrestrial*. *Does product placement blur the lines between advertising and content, and should viewers be concerned?* (Credit: roger blake/ Flickr/ Attribution 2.0 Generic (CC BY 2.0))

ETHICS IN PRACTICE

Influencer Marketing and Product Placement: Are They Always Ethical?

Traditional marketing vehicles such as advertising have been regulated to include limitations on promotions for such products as tobacco and alcohol. One area that has not had the same type of regulatory oversight has been the practice of product placement and companies working with "influencers" to market their products.

In a classic scene from *Forrest Gump,* actor Tom Hanks, who plays Gump, meets President Kennedy and says, "The best thing about visiting the president is the food! Now, since it was all free, and I wasn't hungry but thirsty, I must have drank me 15 Dr Peppers." Since Forrest Gump was a family film seen by many children, this scene could influence them to think that consuming large quantities of the beverage was appropriate and might even give them the stamina to undertake cross-country marathons (one of Gump's other activities in the film). Unlike traditional television and print advertising, product placement in films, television shows, and even video games has not been heavily regulated, but that's about to change. For instance, in Australia, the Alcohol Beverages Advertising Code (ABAC) is instituting expanded regulation of advertising and product placement for new, nontraditional media that have not been regulated previously.

Companies are also enlisting influencers to help them reach customers. Influencers might be people who have achieved recognition as an expert in a certain area, or someone who has amassed a large number of followers on platforms such as Facebook, Twitter, or Instagram. The use of influencers has raised concern about the ethics of companies such as Amazon, Apple, and Google when they enlist teachers such as Kayla Delzer, who has her own brand, Top Dog Teacher (**http://www.topdogteaching.com**), that touts her teaching approaches through workshops. Since Delzer incorporates technology into her classroom, she has attracted the attention of both small start-ups such as Seesaw and large companies such as Apple, which provide her with products and services in the hope that disseminating her experiences through blogs, tweets, and workshops will encourage her followers to adopt their technologies. Because there is little research-based evidence that these technologies actually improve student outcomes, this situation presents an ethical dilemma for school administrators.

Another ethical dilemma is that some influencers use fake followers to increase the appearance of extended media reach, thus being able to command larger sums of money from various companies for their services. One of the most blatant examples of signing up fake followers was the appearance of a vending machine in Moscow where patrons could use a credit card to purchase likes, favorites, and followers for their social media sites.

Critical Thinking Questions
1. What is the role of industry trade groups, government agencies, and marketers to self-regulate ethical practices?
2. Do you think it's unethical to pay people to use products and services that influence consumer purchases? Explain your reasoning.

Sources: Natasha Singer, "Silicon Valley Courts Name-Brand Teachers Raising Ethical Issues," *The New York Times*, https://www.nytimes.com, September 2, 2017; Natalie Koltun, "Insta-Fakers: When Fraud Hits Influencer Marketing," *Mobile Marketer*, http://www.mobilemarketer.com, August 14, 2017; Rosie Baker, "New Rules on Placement of Alcohol Ads Loom Large," *AdNews*, http://www.adnews.com, August 9, 2017.

1. How does sales promotion differ from advertising?
2. Describe several types of sales promotion.

12.9 Public Relations Helps Build Goodwill

9. How does public relations fit into the promotional mix?

Like sales promotion, public relations can be a vital part of the promotional mix. **Public relations** is any communication or activity designed to win goodwill or prestige for a company or person. This could include **publicity**, information about a company or product that appears in the news media and is not directly paid for by the company. Publicity can be good or bad. Reports of children overeating fast food, which can lead to obesity, is an example of negative publicity. Public relations includes many other activities, such as lobbying, event planning, acting as a press agent, managing internal communication, and coordinating crisis management for communications.

Naturally, firms' public relations departments try to create as much good publicity as possible. They furnish company speakers for business and civic clubs, write speeches for corporate officers, and encourage employees to take active roles in such civic groups as the United Way and the Chamber of Commerce. One of the tools of the public relations department is the *press release,* a formal announcement of some newsworthy event connected with the company, such as the start of a new program, the introduction of a new product, or the opening of a new plant. Public relations departments may perform any or all of the functions described in Table 12.3.

The Functions of a Public Relations Department	
Public Relations	**Function Description**
Press relations	Placing positive, newsworthy information in the news media to attract attention to a product, a service, or a person associated with the firm or institution
Product publicity	Publicizing specific products or services
Corporate communications	Creating internal and external messages to promote a positive image of the firm or institution
Public affairs	Building and maintaining national or local community relations
Lobbying	Influencing legislators and government officials to promote or defeat legislation and regulation

Table 12.3

The Functions of a Public Relations Department	
Public Relations	**Function Description**
Employee and investor relations	Maintaining positive relationships with employees, shareholders, and others in the financial community
Crisis management	Responding to unfavorable publicity or a negative event

Table 12.3

Much of sales promotion and publicity is about creating buzz. Buzz marketing (or viral marketing) is intense word-of-mouth marketing. Word-of-mouth is essentially a linear process with information passing from one individual to another, then to another. A marketer has successfully created a buzz when the interactions are so intense that the information moves in a matrix pattern rather than a linear one and everyone is talking about the topic. Leading-edge firms now feel that they get more bang for their buck using buzz marketing than other forms of promotion.

CONCEPT CHECK

1. How does public relations differ from advertising?
2. Describe several types of publicity.

12.10 Trends in Social Media

10. What is social media, and how has it changed promotion?

Advances in technology continue to change the marketing landscape. As you will see in the following sections, marketers are harnessing new technology to hone their marketing message and reach more customers.

The business world now relies on the internet for much of its communications, marketing or otherwise. Almost all companies have Facebook accounts, and individual leaders of companies have separate individual accounts on Linked In, Twitter, Instagram, and other social media sites. New social media sites are popping up almost every week. The phenomenon of social media has created a business climate in which thousands of impressions can be made with one social media post. That impression could be positive or negative. Within social media, there are "stars" of social media—individuals who have developed audiences in the millions who follow their posts every day. **Social media** is a hugely powerful tool for marketers. It has it challenges, though, because the platforms are constantly changing and evolving. Also, the audiences being reached often read (or view) and believe the messages seen on various social media platforms without understanding the context of the message. A social media post that goes viral can close down a business, even if the post is not true. That's what makes social media the newest challenge/opportunity for marketers. Companies that want to retain market share and build their image must develop tactics for the use of social media and for defending against problems created by the use of this powerful marketing tool.

Promotion through Blogs

Blogs provide marketers with a real-time dialogue with customers and an avenue to promote their products or services. A *blog* is an online journal with regularly updated content. This content is pushed to subscribers by RSS (really simple syndication) or e-mail and allows for response and discussion from site visitors. RSS enables users to automatically gather updates from various websites, especially news sites and blogs, and display headlines and a brief summary of those updates in a single location. Blogs can be considered to be offerings of social media unless the site is actually part of the company's main web page.

Well-run marketing blogs usually focus tightly on one niche area, product line, or vertical market segment. The aim is to provide the blog's readers with a constantly renewing source of news and insight about that topic. About 366 million blogs are registered on Tumblr, and more than 23 million blog entries are posted daily.[17]

Many companies have set up their own blogs, including General Motors, Apple, the American Cancer Society, and Microsoft, to name a few. These companies blog because they: (1) get real-time input from customers and prospects; (2) create and maintain relationships; (3) can have a continuing dialogue with loyal customers and prospective clients; and (4) can zero in on specific marketing goals. For example, Disney uses a blog called Disney Baby to cater to the needs of new mothers. Each of their bloggers has a personal bio that helps provide a connection for the new mother to the blogger and provides a deeper connection to the Disney brand.[18]

Firms can also use emerging search tools such as BlogPulse, Feedster, PubSub, and Technorati to monitor conversations about their company and brands. A public relations department might then decide to feed new-product information to bloggers who are evangelists for their brand.

Advertisers Jump on Podcasts and Videos

Podcasts are basically blogs with a multimedia file. The trend developed when a new version of iTunes software made it easy for people to create their own podcasts and post them on a website. There are more than 8,000 podcasters in the United States. Besides individuals, companies are beginning to do their own podcasts as well as posting videos from the company on YouTube as another marketing channel. For listeners, the advantage of a podcast is convenience. Companies now have the ability to use streaming video, which potential customers can download to their mobile devices; for example, ABC News offering a digital version of its programming. The customers' favorite programs download automatically from the internet, usually free of charge, and they can listen to the programs any time they wish. They can also listen wherever they wish, if they have a mobile device to receive the downloads.

Gimlet Media is one of the nation's largest podcasters, offering material from nearly 40 different stations as podcasts. At first ad-free, Gimlet's podcasts are done for direct-to-consumer companies like Blue Apron, as well as for traditional advertisers like Pepsi and Ford. Gimlet now includes a short advertisement before the programming—short enough that people won't fast-forward through it. Gimlet also received a $5 million investment from advertising giant WPP, a clear sign that the business community sees a bright future in podcasts.[19]

Pet owners can go to **http://www.purina.com** and opt in to receive Purina's podcasts. The products will offer advice ranging from animal training to pet insurance to nutrition for older pets. Weekly tips will also be sent on things such as how to help your dog lose weight. Owners spend close to $25 billion a year on pet food. The aim of the podcasts is to build brand loyalty with a soft sell.[20]

Videos have become another important promotions channel. Literally hundreds of thousands of videos can be viewed on YouTube, the top video-hosting site on the internet. Many people now log in to YouTube to watch videos on a particular product and how the product can be used. Entrepreneurs and other small-business owners have made extensive use of YouTube to provide value to their customers by creating and uploading informational videos that highlight their products.

CONCEPT CHECK

1. How are companies embracing social media as a way to connect with customers?
2. What has been the effect of social media on traditional advertising?

12.11 Trends in E-Commerce

11. What is e-commerce, and how has it affected the retail sector?

E-commerce is related to social media and other new online platforms because it utilizes the internet for marketing communication. **E-commerce** refers to the development and maintenance of a company's website and the facilitation of commerce on the website, such as the ability for customers to order products online, to get questions answered about products, and for the company to introduce new products and ideas. E-commerce can include special components designed specifically for separate target market segments, such as information boxes or games. Anything associated with an actual company website related to marketing can be considered e-commerce.

Estimates by various researchers say that more than half of all retail sales involve an online component; direct internet purchases in 2016 were more than 13 percent of *all* retail sales, and that percentage will continue to grow.[21] Why? One reason is the economics of shopping. Think about time spent engaged in making a purchase in a brick-and-mortar location: the cost of fuel, finding a parking spot, locating your intended store, deciding on a purchase, and then driving home. Now think about the time spent reviewing products on a website, deciding what to purchase, and clicking a mouse or swiping a mobile device screen—it takes no time at all!

Countless small businesses have taken the plunge to serve the growing army of online shoppers. Many e-commerce businesses, including e-jeweler Blue Nile, luggage site eBags, and shoe and accessory retailer Zappos, are experiencing sales of $100 million a year or more. The increasing sophistication of search technology and comparison-shopping sites have allowed online businesses to market their products to millions of potential customers cheaply and effectively. Often, these innovations are bringing less-well-known brands and merchants to consumers' attention.

Online merchants can offer a far broader array of merchandise than specialty brick-and-mortar retailers because they don't have to keep the products on store shelves. In response to this challenge, traditional retailers are turning to technology to gain an advantage, outfitting their sales associates with voice headgear so they can look up prices and product information to assist customers.[22]

After a slow start, the world's largest retailer, Walmart, has begun moving into e-retailing in a big way. It is now in almost every major category of web-related consumer commerce. It is estimated that Walmart has approximately 200 million items across all of its outlets, compared to 300 million items available through Amazon. The company has taken some innovative steps to leverage the web to drive people to its stores. In

2016, CEO Doug McMillon purchased Jet.com for $3.3 billion and put Jet.com's CEO Mark Lore in charge of running Walmart's online business. A case in point is the company's online tire service, which allows you to order automobile tires to be picked up and mounted at a Walmart tire center. Customers can order prescription refills for delivery by mail or for pickup at a Walmart pharmacy department. Walmart's online photo service, in addition to providing a way to store pictures on the web, allows customers to send digital pictures to be printed in a Walmart store of their choice, with a one-hour turnaround.[23]

CONCEPT CHECK

1. How can brick-and-mortar stores use technology to compete with online giants such as Amazon?
2. What factors contribute to the internet's soaring growth in retailing?

🔐 Key Terms

5Ps The traditional 4Ps of marketing: product, price, promotion, and place (distribution), now with packaging added as a key marketing component.

advertising Any paid form of nonpersonal presentation by an identified sponsor.

advertising media The channels through which advertising is carried to prospective customers; includes newspapers, magazines, radio, television, outdoor advertising, direct mail, social media, and the internet.

agents Sales representatives of manufacturers and wholesalers.

audience selectivity An advertising medium's ability to reach a precisely defined market.

breaking bulk The process of breaking large shipments of similar products into smaller, more usable lots.

brokers Go-betweens that bring buyers and sellers together.

cost per thousand (CPM) Cost per thousand contacts is a term used in expressing advertising costs; refers to the cost of reaching 1,000 members of the target market.

distribution (logistics) Efficiently managing the acquisition of raw materials by the factory and the movement of products from the producer to industrial users and consumers.

distribution channel The series of marketing entities through which goods and services pass on their way from producers to end users.

e-commerce E-commerce refers to the development and maintenance of a company's website and the facilitation of commerce on the website, such as the ability for customers to order products online and other activities.

frequency The number of times an individual is exposed to an advertising message.

industrial distributors Independent wholesalers that buy related product lines from many manufacturers and sell them to industrial users.

integrated marketing communications (IMC) The careful coordination of all promotional activities—media advertising, sales promotion, personal selling, and public relations, as well as direct marketing, packaging, and other forms of promotion—to produce a consistent, unified message that is customer focused.

manufacturer A producer; an organization that converts raw materials to finished products.

manufacturers' representatives Salespeople who represent noncompeting manufacturers; function as independent agents rather than as salaried employees of the manufacturers.

marketing intermediaries Organizations that assist in moving goods and services from producers to end users.

merchant wholesaler An institution that buys goods from manufacturers (takes ownership) and resells them to businesses, government agencies, other wholesalers, or retailers.

personal selling A face-to-face sales presentation to a prospective customer.

promotion The attempt by marketers to inform, persuade, or remind consumers and industrial users to engage in the exchange process.

promotional mix The combination of advertising, personal selling, sales promotion, and public relations used to promote a product.

prospecting The process of looking for sales prospects.

public relations Any communication or activity designed to win goodwill or prestige for a company or person.

publicity Information about a company or product that appears in the news media and is not directly paid for by the company.

qualifying questions Inquiries used by salespeople to separate prospects from those who do not have the potential to buy.

reach The number of different target consumers who are exposed to a commercial at least once during a specific period, usually four weeks.

retailers Firms that sell goods to consumers and to industrial users for their own consumption.

sales promotion Marketing events or sales efforts—not including advertising, personal selling, and public relations—that stimulate buying.

sales prospects The companies and people who are most likely to buy a seller's offerings.

social media A relatively new marketing channel that includes platforms such as Facebook, Twitter, LinkedIn, Pinterest, and Instagram.

wholesalers Firms that sell finished goods to retailers, manufacturers, and institutions.

Summary of Learning Outcomes

12.1 The Nature and Functions of Distribution (Place)
1. What is the nature and function of distribution (place)?

Distribution (place) includes the efficient managing of the acquisition of raw materials by the factory and the movement of products from the producer or manufacturer to business-to-business users and consumers. Place includes such activities as location selection, store layout, atmosphere and image-building for the location, inventory, transportation, and logistics. Logistics activities are usually the responsibility of the marketing department and are part of the large series of activities included in the supply chain.

Distribution channels are the series of marketing entities through which goods and services pass on their way from producers to end users. Distribution systems focus on the physical transfer of goods and services and on their legal ownership at each stage of the distribution process. Channels reduce the number of transactions and ease the flow of goods.

12.2 Wholesaling
2. What is wholesaling, and what are the types of wholesalers?

Wholesalers typically sell finished products to retailers and to other institutions, such as manufacturers, schools, and hospitals. The two main types of wholesalers are merchant wholesalers and agents and brokers. Merchant wholesalers buy from manufacturers and sell to other businesses. Agents and brokers are essentially independents who provide buying and selling services. They receive commissions according to their sales and don't take title (ownership) of the merchandise.

12.3 The Competitive World of Retailing
3. What are the different kinds of retail operations?

Some 15 million Americans are engaged in retailing. Retailing can be either in-store or nonstore. In-store retail operations include department stores, specialty stores, discount stores, off-price retailers, factory outlets, and catalog showrooms. Nonstore retailing includes vending machines, direct sales, direct-response marketing, home shopping networks, and internet retailing. The most important factors in creating a store's atmosphere are employee type and density, merchandise type and density, fixture type and density, sound, and odors.

12.4 Using Supply Chain Management to Increase Efficiency and Customer Satisfaction
4. How can supply-chain management increase efficiency and customer satisfaction?

The goal of supply-chain management is to coordinate all of the activities of the supply-chain members into a seamless process, thereby increasing customer satisfaction. Supply-chain managers have responsibility for main channel strategy decisions, coordinating the sourcing and procurement of raw materials, scheduling production, processing orders, managing inventory, transporting and storing supplies and finished goods, and coordinating customer-service activities.

12.5 Promotion Strategy

5. What is promotion, and what are the key elements of a promotional mix?

Promotion aims to stimulate demand for a company's goods or services. Promotional strategy is designed to inform, persuade, or remind target audiences about those products. The goals of promotion are to create awareness, get people to try products, provide information, keep loyal customers, increase use of a product, identify potential customers, and even teach clients about potential services.

The unique combination of advertising, personal selling, sales promotion, public relations, social media, and e-commerce used to promote a product is called the promotional mix. Advertising is any paid form of nonpersonal promotion by an identified sponsor. Personal selling consists of a face-to-face presentation in a conversation with a prospective purchaser. Sales promotion consists of marketing activities—other than personal selling, advertising, and public relations—that stimulate consumers to buy. These activities include coupons and samples, displays, shows and exhibitions, demonstrations, and other selling efforts. Public relations is the marketing function that links the policies of the organization with the public interest and develops programs designed to earn public understanding and acceptance. IMC is being used by more and more organizations. It is the careful coordination of all of the elements of the promotional mix to produce a consistent, unified message that is customer focused.

12.6 The Huge Impact of Advertising

6. How are traditional advertising media selected?

Cost per contact is the cost of reaching one member of the target market. Often costs are expressed on a cost per thousand basis. Reach is the number of different target customers who are exposed to a commercial at least once during a specific period, usually four weeks. Frequency is the number of times an individual is exposed to a message. Media selection is a matter of matching the advertising medium with the target audience. Technology continues to drive many of the recent changes to traditional advertising strategies.

12.7 The Importance of Personal Selling

7. What is personal selling?

About 6.5 million people in the United States are directly engaged in personal selling. Personal selling enables a salesperson to demonstrate a product and tailor the message to the prospect; it is effective in closing a sale. Professional salespeople are knowledgeable and creative. They also are familiar with the selling process, which consists of prospecting and qualifying, approaching customers, presenting and demonstrating the product, handling objections, closing the sale, and following up on the sale.

12.8 Sales Promotion

8. What are the goals of sales promotion, and what are several types of sales promotion?

Immediate purchase is the goal of most sales promotion, whether it is aimed at consumers or the trade (wholesalers and retailers). The most popular sales promotions are coupons, samples, product placement, premiums, contests, and sweepstakes. Trade shows, conventions, and point-of-purchase displays are other types of sales promotion.

12.9 Public Relations Helps Build Goodwill

9. How does public relations fit into the promotional mix?

Public relations is mostly concerned with getting good publicity for companies and other organizations. Publicity is any information about a company or product that appears in the news media and is not directly paid for by the company. Public relations departments furnish company speakers for business and civic clubs, write speeches for corporate officers, and encourage employees to take active roles in civic groups. These activities help build a positive image for an organization and create buzz, which is a good backdrop for selling its products.

12.10 Trends in Social Media

10. What is social media, and how does it affect promotion?

Social media is a relatively new marketing channel that includes platforms such as Facebook, Twitter, LinkedIn, Pinterest, and Instagram. The phenomenon of social media has created a business climate in which thousands of impressions (marketing messages) can be achieved with one creative social media post. Social media is a hugely powerful tool for marketers. It has it challenges, though, because a social media post that goes viral can close down a business, even if it is not true. That's what makes social media the newest challenge/ opportunity for marketers. The internet and new technology are having a major impact on promotion and promotion expenditures. Traditional media are losing advertising funds to the internet. Many companies are now creating blogs to get closer to customers and potential customers. Podcasts offer advertisers a new medium to reach consumers. Streaming video and videos uploaded to YouTube are also important social media channels.

12.11 Trends in E-Commerce

11. What is e-commerce, and how does it affect promotion?

E-commerce refers to the development and maintenance of a company's website and the facilitation of commerce on the website, such as the ability for customers to order products on line, to get questions answered about products, and for the company to introduce new products and ideas. E-commerce can include special components designed specifically for separate target market segments, such as information boxes or games.

The ease of use and ability to comparison-shop is driving millions of people to the internet to purchase goods and services. Major retailers such as Walmart are quickly increasing their web presence in an effort to stay relevant in this ever-changing business environment and to attract even more loyal customers who have made the switch to doing most of their shopping on line.

Preparing for Tomorrow's Workplace Skills

1. **Team Activity** Divide the class into two groups with one taking the "pro" position and the other the "con" position on the following issue: "The only thing marketing intermediaries really do is increase prices for consumers. It is always best to buy direct from the producer." (Interpersonal)

2. Trace the distribution channel for some familiar product. Compose an e-mail that explains why the channel has evolved as it has and how it is likely to change in the future. (Systems)

3. You work for a small chain of department stores (six stores total) located within a single state. Write a memo to the president explaining how e-retailing may affect the chain's business. (Technology)

4. How does supply-chain management increase customer value? (Systems)

5. Think of a product that you use regularly. Find several examples of how the manufacturer markets this product, such as ads in different media, sales promotions, and publicity. Assess each example for effectiveness in meeting one or more of the six promotional goals described in the chapter. Then analyze them for effectiveness in reaching you as a target consumer. Consider such factors as the media used, the style of the ad, and ad content. Present your findings to the class. (Information)

6. Go to the blogging search sites listed in the text and find personal blogs, both positive and negative, for a brand. Also report on a consumer good manufacturer's blogging site. Was it appealing? Why or why not? (Technology)

7. *The internet and technology has changed the world of promotion forever.* Explain the meaning of this sentence. (Technology)

8. What advantages does personal selling offer over types of promotion? (Information)

9. Choose a current advertising campaign for a beverage product. Describe how the campaign uses different media to promote the product. Which media is used the most, and why? What other promotional strategies does the company use for the product? Evaluate the effectiveness of the campaign. Present your results to the class. (Information)

10. The Promotional Products Association International is a trade association of the promotional-products industry. Its website, **http://www.ppai.org**, provides an introduction to promotional products and how they are used in marketing. Read its FAQ page and the Industry Sales Volume statistics (both reached through the Education link). Then go to the Resources and Technology section, then case studies, and link to the most recent Golden Pyramid Competition. Choose three to four winners from different categories. Now prepare a short report on the role of promotional products in the promotional mix. Include the examples you selected, and explain how the products helped the company reach its objective. (Technology)

🖼 Ethics Activity

After working really hard to distinguish yourself, you've finally been promoted to senior account executive at a major advertising agency and placed in charge of the agency's newest account, a nationally known cereal company. Their product is one you know contains excessive amounts of sugar as well as artificial colorings and lacks any nutritional value whatsoever. In fact, you have never allowed your own children to eat it.

Your boss has indicated that the cereal company would like to use the slogan "It's good for you" in their new television and print advertising campaign. You know that a $2 billion lawsuit has been filed against the Kellogg and Viacom corporations for marketing junk food to young children. The suit cited "alluring product packaging, toy giveaways, contests, collectibles, kid-oriented websites, magazine ads, and branded toys and clothes." In addition, two consumer groups have brought suit against children's television network Nickelodeon for "unfair and deceptive junk-food marketing."

Your new role at the agency will be tested with this campaign. Doing a good job on it will cement your position and put you in line for a promotion to vice president. But as a responsible parent, you have strong feelings about misleading advertising targeted at susceptible children.

Using a web search tool, locate articles about this topic and then write responses to the following questions. Be sure to support your arguments and cite your sources.

Ethical Dilemma: Do you follow your principles and ask to be transferred to another account? Or do you help promote a cereal you know may be harmful to children in order to secure your career?

Sources: James Schroeder, "To the Heart of the Matter: We Are What We Eat," *Evansville Courier & Press*, http://www.courierpress.com, September 11, 2017; Lizzie Parry, "Popular Cereals Contain Up to a Third of Your Kids' Sugar Intake," *The Sun*, https://www.thesun.co.uk, February 8, 2017; Stephanie Thompson, "Kellogg Co. Might as Well Have Painted a Bull's-eye on Itself," *Advertising Age*, January 23, 2006; and Abbey Klaassen, "Viacom Gets Nicked," *Advertising Age*, January 23, 2006.

⊕ Working the Net

1. Visit *Industry Week*'s website at **http://www.industryweek.com**. Under Archives, do a search using the search term "supply-chain management." Choose an article from the results that describes how a company has used supply-chain management to improve customer satisfaction, performance, or profitability. Give a brief presentation to your class on your findings.

2. What are some of the logistics problems facing firms that operate internationally? Visit the *Logistics Management* magazine website at **http://www.logisticsmgmt.com**, and see if you can find information about how firms manage global logistics. Summarize the results.

3. Go to **http://www.woot.com**. Why do you think that this e-retailer is successful? How can it expand its market? Why do you think that the site has such a cult following?

4. A competitive advantage of the internet is the ability to comparison-shop like never before. To compare brands, features, and prices of products, go to two of these sites: **http://www.pricegrabber.com** or **http://mysimon.com**, or, for the best bargains, **http://www.overstock.com**, **http://www.smartbargains.com**, **http://www.bluefly.com**, **http://www.nextag.com**, or **http://www.shopzilla.com**. Which is the easiest site to use? The most difficult? Which site provides the most information?

5. The Zenith Media site at **http://www.zenithmedia.com** is a good place to find links to internet resources on advertising. Research the leading brands listed on the site. Pick three of the company sites listed, and review them using the concepts in this chapter.

6. Go to the *Sales and Marketing* magazine site at **http://www.salesandmarketing.com**. Read several of the free recent articles from the magazine as well as online exclusives, and prepare a brief report on current trends in one of the following topics: sales strategies, marketing strategies, customer relationships, or training. Also check out their new blog, "Closers." What is your opinion of this blog?

7. Entrepreneurs and small businesses don't always have big sales promotion budgets. The Guerrilla Marketing page at **http://www.gmarketing.com** has many practical ideas for those with big ideas but small budgets. After exploring the site, explain the concept of guerrilla marketing. Then list five ideas or tips that appeal to you, and summarize why they are good marketing strategies.

8. Press releases are a way to get free publicity for your company and products. Visit the following site to learn how to write a press release: **http://www.press-release-examples.com**. Was this helpful, and why? Develop a short "how-to" guide on press releases for your classmates. Then write a press release that announces the opening of your new health food restaurant, Zen Foods, located just two blocks from campus.

⌁ Critical Thinking Case

Advertisers Score with the Super Bowl

What sporting event is televised in 170 countries and has created a quasi–national holiday in the United States? The Super Bowl is considered by football fans as the ultimate game and known as the largest advertising opportunity for media companies that broadcast the game and companies that want to reach a large audience. The history of impactful advertising shown as part of Super Bowl viewing includes the famous 1984 Apple advertisement that "breaks" the PC wall. The ad was only shown once, but it is recognized as one of the most iconic moments in the history of advertising.

In recent years companies have used football's popularity and the Super Bowl as a global program to get their message out to a worldwide audience. While the high cost of advertising during the Super Bowl may deter some advertisers, the impact of an ad like Clint Eastwood's 2012 "Halftime in America" for Chrysler or the 2017 Heinz "Dachhund" ad has been hailed as dramatic and created buzz that ads running in traditional spots do not generate.

One additional thing that advertisers have to consider is the infusion of politics into more aspects of life and how players or outside groups might create a diversion that could impact advertisers, and the amount that the networks pay the NFL for the right to air the Super Bowl. NFL games, and the Super Bowl in particular, provide a large audience for players to voice their concerns with issues such as race, or a newsworthy protest of kneeling for the National Anthem prior to the game. Likewise, controversy can occur during a halftime show or by protesters unfurling a banner, as occurred at a Minnesota Vikings game in 2017. Just as advertisers would rather not show their ads during natural disasters or live coverage of a plane crash or terrorist attack, a large-scale live event always provides the possibility of something happening that could not be anticipated. Companies with creative and adept social media departments can, however, make a positive impact by reacting to events as they occur. For example, during the 2013 Super Bowl in New Orleans, a faulty transformer caused a power outage just before halftime, which caused a 30-minute delay. A clever worker in the Oreo's social media department sent out a Tweet saying, "Power out? No problem. You can still dunk in the dark," with a picture of an Oreo cookie on a dark background.

Critical Thinking Questions
1. Name some of the challenges marketers encounter when developing advertising and promotional campaigns. How does the type of product affect the promotional strategies?
2. You work for an ad agency that has a Super Bowl sponsor as a client. What approach would you recommend for your agency as it develops a campaign—universal, customized for each geographical region, or something else, and why?
3. What types of companies could benefit from placing ads on the NFL website, and how can they use the internet effectively to promote their products?

Sources: Benjamin Hoffman, Victor Mather, and Jacey Fortin, "After Trump Blasts N.F.L., Players Kneel and Lock Arms in Solidarity," *The New York Times*, http://www.nytimes.com, September 25, 2017; Jason Notte, "How NFL Sponsors Get Ambushed at the Super Bowl," *The Street*, https://www.thestreet.com, January 24, 2017; Rochelle Olsen and Andrew Krammer, **"**Two Pipeline Protesters Arrested after Hanging Banner in U.S. Bank Stadium during Vikings Game," *Star Tribune*, http://www.startribune.com, January 2, 2017; Rick Porter, "The 100 Most-Watched TV Programs of 2016: Super Bowl 50 Leads by a Mile," *TV by the Numbers,* http://tvbythenumbers.zap2it.com, December 27, 2016; Angele Watercutter, "How Oreo Won the Marketing Super Bowl with a Timely Blackout Ad on Twitter," *Wired*, https://www.wired.com, February 4, 2013; "Super Bowl XLVI: Most Watched TV Show Ever!" http://www.justjared.com, February 6, 2012.

Hot Links Address Book

1. Consumers can now comparison-shop like never before. To compare brands, features, and prices of products, go to one of these sites: **http://www.pricegrabber.com**, **http://www.mysimon.com**, or **http://www.compare.net.http://www.bottomdollar.com**
2. At the National Retail Federation's website, you'll find current retail statistics, links to retailing resources, and information about retailing careers: **http://www.nrf.com**.
3. The American Wholesale Marketers Association is an international trade organization for distributors of

convenience products in the United States. Visit its website to browse the latest issue of *Distribution Channels* magazine and learn more about this field: **http://www.awmanet.org**.

4. *Stores* magazine offers hundreds of ideas for putting together a successful retail strategy: **http://www.stores.org**.

5. Freightworld offers detailed information on various modes of transportation and links to transportation companies: **http://www.freightworld.com**.

6. For articles on supply-chain management along with information on the latest technology in the field, check out *Supply Chain Management Review: http://scmr.com*.

7. A good site for the latest on interactive and internet marketing is ClickZ network, where you'll find news, advice from experts, statistics, feature articles, and more: **http://www.clickz.com**.

8. How can you find the right magazine in which to advertise? The Media Finder website has a searchable database of thousands of magazines: **http://www.mediafinder.com**.

9. What should a media kit for the press include? 101 Public Relations provides the answer, along with other good information about getting publicity for your company: **http://www.101publicrelations.com**.

10. *Advertising Age* magazine has a wealth of information about the latest in advertising, including videos and ratings of new ads: **http://www.adage.com**.

13

Using Technology to Manage Information

Exhibit 13.1 (Credit: OIST / flickr / Attribution 2.0 Generic (CC BY 2.0))

 Introduction

Learning Outcomes

After reading this chapter, you should be able to answer these questions:

1. How has information technology transformed business and managerial decision-making?
2. Why are computer networks an important part of today's information technology systems?
3. What types of systems make up a typical company's management information system?
4. How can technology management and planning help companies optimize their information technology systems?
5. What are the best ways to protect computers and the information they contain?
6. What are the leading trends in information technology?

EXPLORING BUSINESS CAREERS

John Daly, Daly Investment Management, LLC

When meeting with a Daly Investment (**https://www.dalyinvestment.com**) financial consultant, most likely you are thinking about money, *your* money. Whether you seek a short-term investment or a retirement nest egg, money will be your focus. You probably will not be thinking about the technological infrastructure required to transmit information throughout a multibillion dollar, nationwide institution such as TD Ameritrade—information that often is private and financial in nature. Luckily for you, however, the company is led by financial advisor John Daly, who works with TD Ameritrade to support his company's technology needs.

After successful careers at Charles Schwab and Morgan Stanley, Daly knew when he started his own firm he would need IT support so that he could ensure the security of the funds he managed for his customers while focusing on the financial aspects of managing their finances. In addition to providing a financial trading platform for individual investors, TD Ameritrade has a robust set of software as a service cloud-based tools that allow Daly to focus on his core competencies rather than having to hire, train, and maintain a complex set of IT resources that his clients can trust.

Given the size of the assets it manages, TD Ameritrade's management information system (MIS) is necessarily large. TD Ameritrade's open architecture environment enables financial advisors like John Daly to select the technology they want to use. The lesson is that Daly could act as an entrepreneur and start his own firm while providing information technology with the scale that customers expect and providing the personal service that is often missing when dealing with larger organizations.

Sources: "Innovative Technologies," *TD Ameritrade Institutional*, http://www.tdainstitutional.com, accessed February 21, 2018; Daly Investment Management website, https://www.dalyinvestment.com, accessed February 21, 2018; Daly Investment Management Facebook page, https://www.facebook.com/ dalyinvestment, accessed February 21, 2018.

This chapter focuses on the role of information technology (IT) in business, examining the details of MIS organization, as well as the challenges companies encounter in an increasingly technological world. As John Daly learned, harnessing the power of information technology gives a company a significant competitive advantage.

13.1 | Transforming Businesses through Information

1. How has information technology transformed business and managerial decision-making?

Information technology (IT) includes the equipment and techniques used to manage and process information. Information is at the heart of all organizations. Without information about the processes of and participants in an organization—including orders, products, inventory, scheduling, shipping, customers, suppliers, and employees—a business cannot operate.

In less than 70 years, we have shifted from an industrial society to a knowledge-based economy driven by information. Businesses depend on information technology for everything from running daily operations to making strategic decisions. Computers are the tools of this information age, performing extremely complex operations as well as everyday jobs such as word processing and creating spreadsheets. The pace of change has been rapid since the personal computer became a fixture on most office desks. Individual units became part of small networks, followed by more sophisticated enterprise-wide networks. Table 13.1 and Table 13.2 summarize the types of computer equipment and software, respectively, most commonly used in business management information systems today.

Business Computing Equipment		
Computer Type	Description	Comments
Tablets	Self-contained computers in which applications (apps) can reside. These devices can also be linked into a network over which other programs can be accessed.	Increasing power, speed, and memory accessed via the cloud make these tablets the dominant computer for many business processes.
Desktop personal computers (PC)	Self-contained computers on which software can reside. These PCs can also be linked into a network over which other programs can be accessed.	Increasing power, speed, memory, and storage make these commonly used for many business processes. Can handle text, audio, video, and complex graphics.
Laptop computers	Portable computers similar in power to desktop computers.	Smaller size and weight make mobile computing easier for workers.
Minicomputers	Medium-sized computers with multiple processors, able to support from four to about 200 users at once.	The distinction between the larger minicomputers and smaller mainframes is blurring.
Mainframe computers	Large machines about the size of a refrigerator; can simultaneously run many different programs and support hundreds or thousands of users.	Extremely reliable and stable, these are used by companies and governments to process large amounts of data. They are more secure than PCs.
Servers	Greatest storage capacity and processing speeds.	These are not subject to crashes and can be upgraded and repaired while operating.
Supercomputers	Most powerful computers, now capable of operating at speeds of 280 trillion calculations per second.	Companies can rent time to run projects from special supercomputer centers.

Table 13.1

Application Type	Description
Word processing software	Used to write, edit, and format documents such as letters and reports. Spelling and grammar checkers, mail merge, tables, and other tools simplify document preparation.

Table 13.2

Application Type	Description
Spreadsheet software	Used for preparation and analysis of financial statements, sales forecasts, budgets, and similar numerical and statistical data. Once the mathematical formulas are keyed into the spreadsheet, the data can be changed and the solution will be recalculated instantaneously.
Database management programs	Serve as electronic filing cabinets for records such as customer lists, employee data, and inventory information. Can sort data based on various criteria to create different reports.
Graphics and presentation programs	Create tables, graphs, and slides for customer presentations and reports. Can add images, video, animation, and sound effects.
Desktop publishing software	Combines word processing, graphics, and page layout software to create documents. Allows companies to design and produce sales brochures, catalogs, advertisements, and newsletters in-house.
Communications programs	Translate data into a form for transmission and transfer it across a network to other computers. Used to send and retrieve data and files.
Integrated software suites	Combine several popular types of programs, such as word processing, spreadsheet, database, graphics presentation, and communications programs. Component programs are designed to work together.
Groupware	Facilitates collaborative efforts of workgroups so that several people in different locations can work on one project. Supports online meetings and project management (scheduling, resource allocation, document and e-mail distribution, etc.).
Financial software	Used to compile accounting and financial data and create financial statements and reports.

Table 13.2

Although most workers spend their days at powerful desktop computers, other groups tackle massive computational problems at specialized supercomputer centers. Tasks that would take years on a PC can be completed in just hours on a supercomputer. With their ability to perform complex calculations quickly, supercomputers play a critical role in national security research, such as analysis of defense intelligence; scientific research, from biomedical experiments and drug development to simulations of earthquakes and star formations; demographic studies such as analyzing and predicting voting patterns; and weather and environmental studies. Businesses, too, put supercomputers to work by analyzing big data to gain insights into customer behavior, improving inventory and production management and for product design.[1] The speed of these special machines has been rising steadily to meet increasing demands for greater computational capabilities, and the next goal is quadrillions of computations per second, or *petaflops*. Achieving these incredible speeds is critical to future scientific, medical, and business discoveries. Many countries, among them the United States, China, France, and Japan, have made petascale computing a priority.[2]

In addition to a business's own computers and internal networks, the internet makes it effortless to connect quickly to almost anyplace in the world. As Thomas Friedman points out in his book The World Is Flat, "We are now connecting all of the knowledge centers on the planet together into a single global network, which . . . could usher in an amazing era of prosperity and innovation."[3] The opportunities for collaboration on a global scale increase daily. A manager can share information with hundreds of thousands of people worldwide as easily as with a colleague on another floor of the same office building. The internet and the web have become indispensable business tools that facilitate communication within companies as well as with customers.

The rise of electronic trading hubs is just one example of how technology is facilitating the global economy. Electronic trading hubs are not reserved for large companies of developed economies, however. Alibaba is piloting an e-hub called eWTP in Malaysia that will provide access to small businesses. As Jack Ma, Alibaba co-founder, said at eWTP's launch, "There are a lot of free-trade zones for efficient trade facilitation, but only for big companies. There is no free-trade zone designed for small companies. I have been shouting everywhere, screaming, that every government should do it."[4]

Many companies entrust an executive called the **chief information officer (CIO)** with the responsibility of managing all information resources. The importance of this responsibility is immense. In addition to the massive expansion of information gathered by today's businesses, most of us are **knowledge workers** who develop or use knowledge. Knowledge workers contribute to and benefit from information they use to perform planning, acquiring, searching, analyzing, organizing, storing, programming, producing, distributing, marketing, or selling functions. We must know how to gather and use information from the many resources available to us.

Exhibit 13.2   In today's high-tech world, CIOs must possess not only the technical smarts to implement global IT infrastructures, integrate communications systems with partners, and protect customer data from insidious hackers, but they must also have strong business acumen. Google's acclaimed tech chief Ben Fried manages the technology necessary to deliver more than 9 billion searches daily, with an eye towards greater business efficiency, growth, and profits. *Why is it important for CIOs to possess both technological and business expertise?* (Credit: Enterprise 2.0 Conference/ flickr/ Attribution 2.0 Generic (CC BY 2.0)

EXPANDING AROUND THE GLOBE

E-Hubs Integrate Global Commerce

Thanks to the wonders of technological advancement, global electronic trading now goes far beyond the internet retailing and trading that we are all familiar with. Special websites known as trading hubs, or eMarketplaces, facilitate electronic commerce between businesses in specific industries such as automotive manufacturing, retailing, telecom provisioning, aerospace, financial products and services, and more. Virtually all Forex (Foreign Exchange) is done via trading hubs that provide an open market for trading of a variety of currencies. Because there are a large number of trades involving currencies, the price is discoverable and there is transparency in the market. By contrast, Bitcoin is mainly traded in smaller quantities, and there are often large discrepancies between prices for the cryptocurrency in different exchanges.

The trading hub functions as a means of integrating the electronic collaboration of business services. Each hub provides standard formats for the electronic trading of documents used in a particular industry, as well as an array of services to sustain e-commerce between businesses in that industry. Services include demand forecasting, inventory management, partner directories, and transaction settlement services. And the payoff is significant—lowered costs, decreased inventory levels, and shorter time to market—resulting in bigger profits and enhanced competitiveness. For example, large-scale manufacturing procurement can amount to billions of dollars. Changing to "just-in-time purchasing" on the e-hub can save a considerable percentage of these costs.

Electronic trading across a hub can range from the collaborative integration of individual business processes to auctions and exchanges of goods (electronic barter). Global content management is an essential factor in promoting electronic trading agreements on the hub. A globally consistent view of the "content" of the hub must be available to all. Each participating company handles its own content, and applications such as *content managers* keep a continuously updated master catalog of the inventories of all members of the hub. The *transaction manager* application automates trading arrangements between companies, allowing the hub to provide aggregation and settlement services.

Ultimately, trading hubs for numerous industries could be linked together in a global e-commerce web—an inclusive *"hub of all hubs."* One creative thinker puts it this way: "The traditional linear, one step at a time, supply chain is dead. It will be replaced by parallel, asynchronous, real-time marketplace decision-making. Take manufacturing capacity as an example. Enterprises can bid their excess production capacity on the world e-commerce hub. Offers to buy capacity trigger requests from the seller for parts bids to suppliers who in turn put out requests to other suppliers, and this whole process will all converge in a matter of minutes."

Sources: "Asian Companies Count Losses—Hatch Ways to Cope with Weak Dollar," *Reuters*, https://www.reuters.com, January 24, 2018; Rob Verger, "This Is What Determines the Price of Bitcoin," *Popular Science*, https://www.popsci.com, January 22, 2018; Bhavan Jaipragas, "Alibaba's Electronic Trading Hub to Help Small and Medium-sized Enterprises Goes Live in Malaysia," *This Week in Asia*, http://www.scmp.com, November 3, 2017.

Critical Thinking Questions
1. How do companies benefit from participating in an electronic trading hub?
2. What impact does electronic trading have on the global economy?

Because most jobs today depend on information—obtaining, using, creating, managing, and sharing it—this chapter begins with the role of information in decision-making and goes on to discuss computer networks and management information systems. The management of information technology—planning and protection—follows. Finally, we'll look at the latest trends in information technology. Throughout the chapter, examples show how managers and their companies are using computers to make better decisions in a highly competitive world.

Data and Information Systems

Information systems and the computers that support them are so much a part of our lives that we almost take them for granted. These **management information systems** methods and equipment that provide information about all aspects of a firm's operations provide managers with the information they need to make decisions. They help managers properly categorize and identify ideas that result in substantial operational and cost benefits.

Businesses collect a great deal of *data*—raw, unorganized facts that can be moved and stored—in their daily operations. Only through well-designed IT systems and the power of computers can managers process these data into meaningful and useful *information* and use it for specific purposes, such as making business decisions. One such form of business information is the **database**, an electronic filing system that collects and organizes data and information. Using software called a *database management system (DBMS)*, you can quickly and easily enter, store, organize, select, and retrieve data in a database. These data are then turned into information to run the business and to perform business analysis.

Databases are at the core of business information systems. For example, a customer database containing name, address, payment method, products ordered, price, order history, and similar data provides information to many departments. Marketing can track new orders and determine what products are selling best; sales can identify high-volume customers or contact customers about new or related products; operations managers use order information to obtain inventory and schedule production of the ordered products; and finance uses sales data to prepare financial statements. Later in the chapter, we will see how companies use very large databases called data warehouses and data marts.

Companies are discovering that they can't operate well with a series of separate information systems geared to solving specific departmental problems. It takes a team effort to integrate the systems described and involves employees throughout the firm. Company-wide *enterprise resource planning (ERP)* systems that bring together human resources, operations, and technology are becoming an integral part of business strategy. So is managing the collective knowledge contained in an organization, using data warehouses and other technology tools. Technology experts are learning more about the way the business operates, and business managers are learning to use information systems technology effectively to create new opportunities and reach their goals.

CONCEPT CHECK

1. What are management information systems, and what challenges face the CIO in developing the company's MIS?
2. Distinguish between data and information. How are they related? Why are data considered a valuable asset for a firm?
3. How does systems integration benefit a company?

13.2 | Linking Up: Computer Networks

2. Why are computer networks an important part of today's information technology systems?

Today most businesses use networks to deliver information to employees, suppliers, and customers. A **computer network** is a group of two or more computer systems linked together by communications channels to share data and information. Today's networks often link thousands of users and can transmit audio and video as well as data.

Networks include clients and servers. The *client* is the application that runs on a personal computer or workstation. It relies on a *server* that manages network resources or performs special tasks such as storing files, managing one or more printers, or processing database queries. Any user on the network can access the server's capabilities.

By making it easy and fast to share information, networks have created new ways to work and increase productivity. They provide more efficient use of resources, permitting communication and collaboration across distance and time. With file-sharing, all employees, regardless of location, have access to the same information. Shared databases also eliminate duplication of effort. Employees at different sites can "screen-share" computer files, working on data as if they were in the same room. Their computers are connected by phone or cable lines, they all see the same thing on their display, and anyone can make changes that are seen by the other participants. The employees can also use the networks for videoconferencing.

Networks make it possible for companies to run enterprise software, large programs with integrated modules that manage all of the corporation's internal operations. Enterprise resource planning systems run on networks. Typical subsystems include finance, human resources, engineering, sales and order distribution, and order management and procurement. These modules work independently and then automatically exchange information, creating a company-wide system that includes current delivery dates, inventory status, quality control, and other critical information. Let's now look at the basic types of networks companies use to transmit data—local area networks and wide area networks—and popular networking applications such as intranets and virtual private networks.

Connecting Near and Far with Networks

Two basic types of networks are distinguished by the area they cover. A **local area network (LAN)** lets people at one site exchange data and share the use of hardware and software from a variety of computer manufacturers. LANs offer companies a more cost-effective way to link computers than linking terminals to a mainframe computer. The most common uses of LANs at small businesses, for example, are office automation, accounting, and information management. LANs can help companies reduce staff, streamline operations, and cut processing costs. LANs can be set up with wired or wireless connections.

A **wide area network (WAN)** connects computers at different sites via telecommunications media such as phone lines, satellites, and microwaves. A modem connects the computer or a terminal to the telephone line and transmits data almost instantly, in less than a second. The internet is essentially a worldwide WAN. Communications companies, such as AT&T, Verizon, and Sprint, operate very large WANs. Companies also connect LANs at various locations into WANs. WANs make it possible for companies to work on critical projects around the clock by using teams in different time zones.

Several forms of WANs—intranets, virtual private networks (VPN), and extranets—use internet technology. Here we'll look at intranets, internal corporate networks that are widely available in the corporate world, and VPNs. Although wireless networks have been around for more than a decade, they are increasing in use because of falling costs, faster and more reliable technology, and improved standards. They are similar to their wired LAN and WAN cousins, except they use radio frequency signals to transmit data. You use a wireless WAN (WWAN) regularly when you use your cellular phone. WANs' coverage can span several countries.

Telecommunications carriers operate using wireless WANs.

Wireless LANs (WLAN) that transmit data at one site offer an alternative to traditional wired systems. WLANs' reach is a radius of 500 feet indoors and 1,000 feet outdoors and can be extended with antennas, transmitters, and other devices. The wireless devices communicate with a wired access point into the wired network. WLANs are convenient for specialized applications where wires are in the way or when employees are in different locations in a building. Hotels, airports, restaurants, hospitals, retail establishments, universities, and warehouses are among the largest users of WLANs, also known as Wi-Fi. For example, the Veterans Administration Hospital in West Haven, Connecticut, recently added Wi-Fi access in all patient rooms to upgrade its existing WLAN to improve patient access, quality, and reliability. The new WLAN supports many different functions, from better on-site communication among doctors and nurses through both data transmission and voice-over-internet phone systems to data-centric applications such as its Meditech clinical information system and pharmacy management.[5]

CATCHING THE ENTREPRENEURIAL SPIRIT

Documenting the Future

Potential customers of Captiva Software didn't share company cofounder and chief executive Reynolds Bish's belief that paper wasn't going away. They held to the idea that personal computers and the internet would make paper disappear, and they weren't going to invest in software to organize their documents. That almost caused Captiva to go under. "We really were afraid we weren't going to make it," said Jim Berglund, an early investor in Captiva and a former board member.

But Bish asked investors for another $4 million commitment—on a bet that paper was here to stay. Bish recalls a board member telling him, "Five years from now people are going to either think you're a genius or a complete idiot."

That conversation took place 20 years ago. Captiva Software was named one of the fastest-growing technology companies in San Diego in the early 2000s for its 172 percent increase in revenues. The company was then acquired by EMC Corp.—the sixth-largest software company in the world and top maker of corporate data-storage equipment, with projected annual revenues of more than $9 billion—for $275 million in cash, rewarding embattled early Captiva investors with 10 times their money back. (In 2016, Dell acquired EMC for more than $67 billion.)

Captiva began its journey to the big time in 1989 in Park City, Utah, as TextWare Corp., a small data-entry company. Cofounder Steven Burton's technical expertise, Bish's business background, and a credit card helped them get the business going. "It was pure bootstrapping," Bish said. "We did everything from going without a salary for a year or more to using up our credit cards."

Bish and Burton quickly saw the need for employees to enter data more directly and accurately. The software they developed still required clerks to type information from a paper document, but it could check for inaccuracies, matching zip codes to cities, for instance. In 1996, TextWare produced software that could "read" typewritten words on a scanned piece of paper, which significantly reduced the number of data-entry clerks needed. It found popularity with credit-card processors, insurance companies, shipping companies, and other corporations that handled thousands of forms every day.

TextWare acquired or merged with five firms, went public, changed its name twice, and in 1998 set up its headquarters in San Diego, California, after buying Wheb Systems, which is based there. In 2002, the company merged with publicly held ActionPoint, a San Jose, California, document-processing company, and changed its name to Captiva.

An estimated 80 percent of all information is still paper-based, according to market research firm Forrester Research. Captiva's flagship products, InputAccel and FormWare, process over 85 million pieces of paper worldwide every day, leaving no doubt that Bish's vision was on target. Paper is indeed here to stay.

Sources: "Why Captiva?" https://www.emc.com, accessed February 21, 2018; EMC corporate website, "About Us," https://dellemc.com, accessed February 21, 2018; "Lucera Uses Connectivity Routes of Chicago, New York, London and Tokyo as a Trading Hub in Trading Increases," *BSO*, https://www.bsonetwork.com, October 19, 2017; Ron Miller, "$67 Billion Dell–EMC Deal Closes Today," *Tech Crunch,* https://techcrunch.com, September 7, 2016; Brian Sherman, "Input Management and Opportunities for the Reseller Channel: An Interview with Wayne Ford, VP of Partner Alliances at Captiva," *ECM Connection*, http://www.ecmconnection.com, December 27, 2005; Kathryn Balint, "Captiva's Paper Chase Paying Off," *San Diego Union-Tribune,* December 9, 2005, pp. C1, C5.

Critical Thinking Questions
1. What role did co-founders Reynolds Bish and Steven Burton play in the evolution of tiny TextWare into hugely successful Captiva?
2. What other unique factors were responsible for the company's remarkable growth?

An Inside Job: Intranets

Like LANs, **intranets** are private corporate networks. Many companies use both types of internal networks. However, because they use internet technology to connect computers, intranets are WANs that link employees in many locations and with different types of computers. Essentially mini-internets that serve only the company's employees, intranets operate behind a *firewall* that prevents unauthorized access. Employees navigate using a standard web browser, which makes the intranet easy to use. They are also considerably less expensive to install and maintain than other network types and take advantage of the internet's interactive features such as chat rooms and team workspaces. Many software providers now offer off-the-shelf intranet packages so that companies of all sizes can benefit from the increased access to and distribution of information.

Companies now recognize the power of intranets to connect employers and employees in many ways, promoting teamwork and knowledge-sharing. Intranets have many applications, from human resource (HR) administration to logistics. For instance, a benefits administration intranet can become a favorite with employees. Instead of having to contact an HR representative to make any changes in personnel records or retirement plan contributions or to submit time sheets, staff members simply log on to the intranet and update the information themselves. Managers can also process staffing updates, performance reviews, and incentive payments without filing paperwork with human resources. Employees can regularly check an online job board for new positions. Shifting routine administrative tasks to the intranet can bring additional benefits such as reducing the size of the HR department by 30 percent and allowing HR staff members to turn their attention to more substantive projects.[6]

Enterprise Portals Open the Door to Productivity

Intranets that take a broader view serve as sophisticated knowledge management tools.

One such intranet is the **enterprise portal**, an internal website that provides proprietary corporate information to a defined user group. Portals can take one of three forms: business to employee (B2E), business to business (B2B), and business to consumer (B2C). Unlike a standard intranet, enterprise portals allow individuals or user groups to customize the portal home page to gather just the information they need for their particular job situations and deliver it through a single web page. Because of their complexity, enterprise portals are typically the result of a collaborative project that brings together designs developed and perfected through the effort of HR, corporate communications, and information technology departments.

More companies use portal technology to provide:

- A consistent, simple user interface across the company
- Integration of disparate systems and multiple sets of data and information
- A single source for accurate and timely information that integrates internal and external information
- A shorter time to perform tasks and processes
- Cost savings through the elimination of information intermediaries
- Improved communications within the company and with customers, suppliers, dealers, and distributors

No More Tangles: Wireless Technologies

Wireless technology has become commonplace today. We routinely use devices such as cellular phones, mobile devices, garage door openers, and television remote controls—without thinking of them as examples of wireless technology. Businesses use wireless technologies to improve communications with customers, suppliers, and employees.

Companies in the package delivery industry, such as UPS and FedEx, were among the first users of wireless technology. Delivery personnel use handheld computers to send immediate confirmation of package receipt. You may also have seen meter readers and repair personnel from utility and energy companies send data from remote locations back to central computers.

Bluetooth short-range wireless technology is a global standard that improves personal connectivity for users of mobile phones, portable computers, and stereo headsets, and Bluetooth wirelessly connects keyboards and mice to computers and headsets to phones and music players. A Bluetooth-enabled mobile phone, for example, provides safer hands-free phone use while driving. The technology is finding many applications in the auto industry as well. Bluetooth wireless technology is now standard in many vehicles today. Many car, technology, and cell phone companies—among them Amazon, Apple, Audi, BMW, DaimlerChrysler, Google, Honda, Saab, Toyota, and Volkswagen—already offer Bluetooth hands-free solutions. Other uses include simplifying the connection of portable digital music players to the car's audio system and transferring downloaded music to the system.[7]

Exhibit 13.3   Although designing a true mobile replacement for the desktop PC has proved elusive for computer manufacturers, ultramobile PCs offer wireless functions many professionals want—web browsing, e-mail, Microsoft Office, and telephony. The Apple iPad Pro runs iOS 10, and with its 10.5-inch LCD touch screen and stylus, the mini-tablet provides the power of a desktop PC and freedom from pen and paper. *What impact might ultramobile computing have on business?* (Credit: Tinh t? Photo/ flickr/ Public Domain)

Private Lines: Virtual Private Networks

Many companies use **virtual private networks** to connect two or more private networks (such as LANs) over a public network, such as the internet. VPNs include strong security measures to allow only authorized users to access the network and its sensitive corporate information. Companies with widespread offices may find that a VPN is a more cost-effective option than creating a network using purchased networking equipment and leasing expensive private lines. This type of private network is more limited than a VPN, because it doesn't allow authorized users to connect to the corporate network when they are at home or traveling.

As Exhibit 13.4 shows, the VPN uses existing internet infrastructure and equipment to connect remote users and offices almost anywhere in the world—without long-distance charges. In addition to saving on telecommunications costs, companies using VPNs don't have to buy or maintain special networking equipment and can outsource management of remote access equipment. VPNs are useful for salespeople and telecommuters, who can access the company's network as if they were on-site at the company's office. On the downside, the VPN's availability and performance, especially when it uses the internet, depends on factors largely outside of an organization's control.

VPNs are popular with many different types of organizations. Why? Security is one of the main reasons to always use a VPN to access the internet. Because all your data is encrypted once tunneled, if a hacker were trying to intercept your browsing activity, say, while you were entering your credit card number to make an online purchase, the encryption would stymie their efforts. That's why it's a particularly good idea to use VPNs in public settings such as coffee shops and airports.[8]

Software on Demand: Application Service Providers

As software developers release new types of application programs and updated versions of existing ones every year or two, companies have to analyze whether they can justify buying or upgrading to the new software—in terms of both cost and implementation time. **Application service providers (ASP)** offer a different approach to this problem. Companies subscribe, usually on a monthly basis, to an ASP and use the applications much like you'd use telephone voice mail, the technology for which resides at the phone company. Other names for ASPs include on-demand software, hosted applications, and software-as-a-service. Exhibit 13.5 shows how the ASP interfaces with software and hardware vendors and developers, the IT department, and users.

Exhibit 13.4   Virtual Private Networks (VPNs) (Attribution: Copyright Rice University, OpenStax, under CC BY 4.0 license.)

The simplest ASP applications are automated—for example, a user might use one to build a simple e-commerce site. ASPs provide three major categories of applications to users:

- Enterprise applications, including customer relationship management (CRM), enterprise resource planning, e-commerce, and data warehousing
- Collaborative applications for internal communications, e-mail, groupware, document creation, and management messaging
- Applications for personal use—for example, games, entertainment software, and home-office applications

According to recent surveys, more companies are currently using an ASP, and even moving their legacy systems to the cloud. Estimates suggest revenues from subscriptions to on-demand cloud services were about $180 billion in 2017. This sector is growing much more rapidly—three times faster—than traditional hardware and software.[9] As this market grows, more companies are adding on-demand offerings to their traditional software packages. Amazon (Amazon Web Services), IBM, Microsoft, and Salesforce.com are among the leading cloud service providers.[10]

Until recently, many companies were reluctant to outsource critical enterprise applications to third-party providers. As ASPs improved their technologies and proved to be reliable and cost-effective, attitudes have changed. Companies, both large and small, seek cost advantages such as the convenience ASPs provide. The basic idea behind subscribing to an ASP is compelling. Users can access any of their applications and data from any computer, and IT can avoid purchasing, installing, supporting, and upgrading expensive software applications. ASPs buy and maintain the software on their servers and distribute it through high-speed networks. Subscribers rent the applications they want for a set period of time and price. The savings in licensing fees, infrastructure, time, and staff are significant.

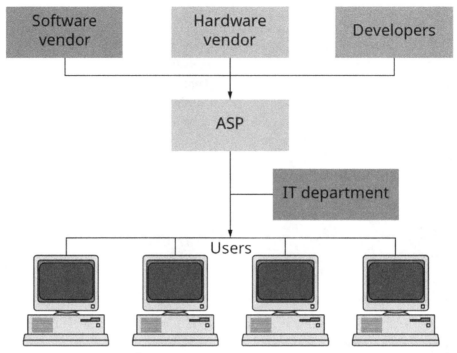

Exhibit 13.5   Structure of an ASP Relationship   (Attribution: Copyright Rice University, OpenStax, under CC BY 4.0 license.)

Managed service providers (MSP) represent the next generation of ASPs, offering greater customization and expanded capabilities that include business processes and complete management of the network servers. The global market for managed IT services reached $149.1 billion in 2016. This market is estimated to reach $256.5 billion in 2021, from $166.7 billion in 2017, at a compound annual growth rate of 11.5 percent for the period 2018 through 2021.[11]

CONCEPT CHECK

1.   What is a computer network? What benefits do companies gain by using networks?
2.   How do a LAN and a WAN differ? Why would a company use a wireless network?
3.   What advantages do VPNs offer a company? What about the cloud, ASPs, and MSPs?

13.3   Management Information Systems

3.   What types of systems make up a typical company's management information system?

Whereas individuals use business productivity software such as word processing, spreadsheet, and graphics programs to accomplish a variety of tasks, the job of managing a company's information needs falls to *management information systems:* users, hardware, and software that support decision-making. Information systems collect and store the company's key data and produce the information managers need for analysis, control, and decision-making.

Factories use computer-based information systems to automate production processes and order and monitor inventory. Most companies use them to process customer orders and handle billing and vendor payments.

Banks use a variety of information systems to process transactions such as deposits, ATM withdrawals, and loan payments. Most consumer transactions also involve information systems. When you check out at the supermarket, book a hotel room online, or download music over the internet, information systems record and track the transaction and transmit the data to the necessary places.

Companies typically have several types of information systems, starting with systems to process transactions. Management support systems are dynamic systems that allow users to analyze data to make forecasts, identify business trends, and model business strategies. Office automation systems improve the flow of communication throughout the organization. Each type of information system serves a particular level of decision-making: operational, tactical, and strategic. Exhibit 13.6 shows the relationship between transaction processing and management support systems as well as the management levels they serve. Let's take a more detailed look at how companies and managers use transaction processing and management support systems to manage information.

Transaction Processing Systems

A firm's integrated information system starts with its **transaction processing system (TPS)**. The TPS receives raw data from internal and external sources and prepares these data for storage in a database similar to a microcomputer database but vastly larger. In fact, all the company's key data are stored in a single huge database that becomes the company's central information resource. As noted earlier, the *database management system* tracks the data and allows users to query the database for the information they need.

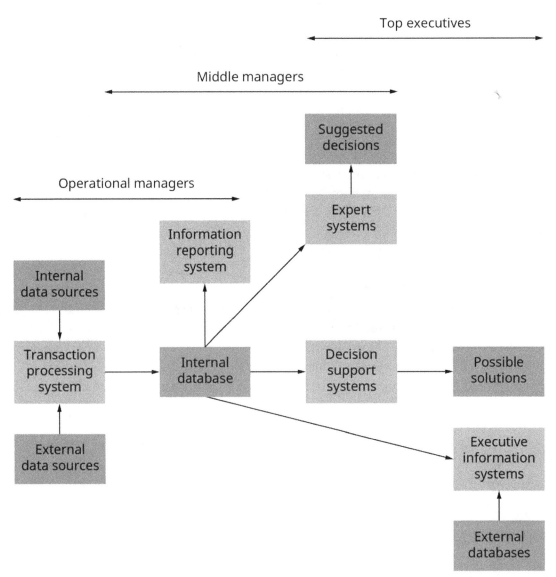

Exhibit 13.6   A Company's Integrated Information System   (Attribution: Copyright Rice University, OpenStax, under CC BY 4.0 license.)

The database can be updated in two ways: **batch processing**, where data are collected over some time period and processed together, and **online**, or **real-time**, **processing**, which processes data as they become available. Batch processing uses computer resources very efficiently and is well-suited to applications such as payroll processing that require periodic rather than continuous processing. Online processing keeps the company's data current. When you make an airline reservation, the information is entered into the airline's information system, and you quickly receive confirmation, typically through an e-mail. Online processing is more expensive than batch processing, so companies must weigh the cost versus the benefit. For example, a factory that operates around the clock may use real-time processing for inventory and other time-sensitive requirements but process accounting data in batches overnight.

Decisions, Decisions: Management Support Systems

Transaction processing systems automate routine and tedious back-office processes such as accounting, order processing, and financial reporting. They reduce clerical expenses and provide basic operational information quickly. **Management support systems (MSS)** use the internal master database to perform high-level analyses that help managers make better decisions.

Information technologies such as data warehousing are part of more advanced MSSs. A **data warehouse** combines many databases across the whole company into one central database that supports management decision-making. With a data warehouse, managers can easily access and share data across the enterprise to get a broad overview rather than just isolated segments of information. Data warehouses include software to extract data from operational databases, maintain the data in the warehouse, and provide data to users. They can analyze data much faster than transaction-processing systems. Data warehouses may contain many **data marts**, special subsets of a data warehouse that each deal with a single area of data. Data marts are organized for quick analysis.

Companies use data warehouses to gather, secure, and analyze data for many purposes, including customer relationship management systems, fraud detection, product-line analysis, and corporate asset management. Retailers might wish to identify customer demographic characteristics and shopping patterns to improve direct-mailing responses. Banks can more easily spot credit-card fraud, as well as analyze customer usage patterns.

According to Forrester Research, about 60 percent of companies with $1 billion or more in revenues use data warehouses as a management tool. Union Pacific (UP), a $19 billion railroad, turned to data warehouse technology to streamline its business operations. By consolidating multiple separate systems, UP achieved a unified supply-chain system that also enhanced its customer service. "Before our data warehouse came into being we had stovepipe systems," says Roger Bresnahan, principal engineer. "None of them talked to each other. . . . We couldn't get a whole picture of the railroad."

UP's data warehouse system took many years and the involvement of 26 departments to create. The results were well worth the effort: UP can now make more accurate forecasts, identify the best traffic routes, and determine the most profitable market segments. The ability to predict seasonal patterns and manage fuel costs more closely has saved UP millions of dollars by optimizing locomotive and other asset utilization and through more efficient crew management. In just three years, Bresnahan reports, the data warehouse system had paid for itself.[12]

At the first level of an MSS is an *information-reporting system,* which uses summary data collected by the TPS to produce both regularly scheduled and special reports. The level of detail would depend on the user. A company's payroll personnel might get a weekly payroll report showing how each employee's paycheck was determined. Higher-level mangers might receive a payroll summary report that shows total labor cost and overtime by department and a comparison of current labor costs with those in the prior year. Exception reports show cases that fail to meet some standard. An accounts receivable exception report that lists all customers with overdue accounts would help collection personnel focus their work. Special reports are generated only when a manager requests them; for example, a report showing sales by region and type of customer can highlight reasons for a sales decline.

Decision Support Systems

A **decision support system (DSS)** helps managers make decisions using interactive computer models that describe real-world processes. The DSS also uses data from the internal database but looks for specific data that relate to the problems at hand. It is a tool for answering "what if" questions about what would happen if the manager made certain changes. In simple cases, a manager can create a spreadsheet and try changing some of the numbers. For instance, a manager could create a spreadsheet to show the amount of overtime required if the number of workers increases or decreases. With models, the manager enters into the computer the values that describe a particular situation, and the program computes the results. Marketing executives at a furniture company could run DSS models that use sales data and demographic assumptions to develop forecasts of the types of furniture that would appeal to the fastest-growing population groups.

Companies can use a predictive analytics program to improve their inventory management system and use big data to target customer segments for new products and line extensions.

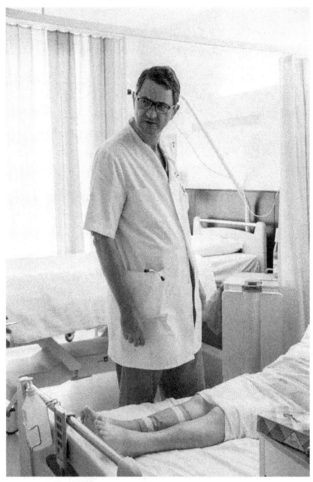

Exhibit 13.7   Decision support systems help businesses by providing quantitative data and predictive models that aid problem-solving and decision-making. Now the health-care industry wants this technology in hospitals to improve the practice of medicine. Spearheading the effort for a clinical decision-support system is the American Medical Informatics Association, which believes a national DSS could help physicians with diagnosing and treating illnesses. *What are the pros and cons to having medical professionals rely on a DSS for help in treating patients?* (Credit: Axelle Geelen/ flickr/ Attribution 2.0 Generic (CC BY 2.0))

Executive Information Systems

Although similar to a DSS, an **executive information system (EIS)** is customized for an individual executive. These systems provide specific information for strategic decisions. For example, a CEO's EIS may include special spreadsheets that present financial data comparing the company to its principal competitors and graphs showing current economic and industry trends.

Expert Systems

An **expert system** gives managers advice similar to what they would get from a human consultant. Artificial intelligence enables computers to reason and learn to solve problems in much the same way humans do, using what-if reasoning. Although they are expensive and difficult to create, expert systems are finding their way into more companies as more applications are found. Lower-end expert systems can even run on mobile devices. Top-of-the-line systems help airlines appropriately deploy aircraft and crews, critical to the carriers' efficient operations. The cost of hiring enough people to do these ongoing analytical tasks would be prohibitively expensive. Expert systems have also been used to help explore for oil, schedule employee work shifts, and diagnose illnesses. Some expert systems take the place of human experts, whereas others assist them.

CONCEPT CHECK

1. What are the main types of management information systems, and what does each do?
2. Differentiate between the types of management support systems, and give examples of how companies use each.

13.4 Technology Management and Planning

4. How can technology management and planning help companies optimize their information technology systems?

With the help of computers, people have produced more data in the last 30 years than in the previous 5,000 years combined. Companies today make sizable investments in information technology to help them manage this overwhelming amount of data, convert the data into knowledge, and deliver it to the people who need it. In many cases, however, the companies do not reap the desired benefits from these expenditures. Among the typical complaints from senior executives are that the company is spending too much and not getting adequate performance and payoff from IT investments, these investments do not relate to business strategy, the firm seems to be buying the latest technology for technology's sake, and communications between IT specialists and IT users are poor.

Optimize IT!

Managing a company's enterprise-wide IT operations, especially when those often stretch across multiple locations, software applications, and systems, is no easy task. IT managers must deal not only with on-site systems; they must also oversee the networks and other technology, such as mobile devices that handle e-mail messaging, that connect staff working at locations ranging from the next town to another continent. At the same time, IT managers face time constraints and budget restrictions, making their jobs even more challenging.

Growing companies may find themselves with a decentralized IT structure that includes many separate systems and duplication of efforts. A company that wants to enter or expand into e-commerce needs systems flexible enough to adapt to this changing marketplace. Security for equipment and data is another critical area, which we will cover later in the chapter.

The goal is to develop an integrated, company-wide technology plan that balances business judgment, technology expertise, and technology investment. IT planning requires a coordinated effort among a firm's top executives, IT managers, and business-unit managers to develop a comprehensive plan. Such plans must take into account the company's strategic objectives and how the right technology will help managers reach those goals.

Technology management and planning go beyond buying new technology. Today companies are cutting IT budgets so that managers are being asked to do more with less. They are implementing projects that leverage their investment in the technology they already have, finding ways to maximize efficiency and optimize utilization.

Managing Knowledge Resources

As a result of the proliferation of information, we are also seeing a major shift from information management to a broader view that focuses on finding opportunities in and unlocking the value of intellectual rather than physical assets. Whereas *information management* involves collecting, processing, and condensing information, the more difficult task of **knowledge management (KM)** focuses on researching, gathering, organizing, and sharing an organization's collective knowledge to improve productivity, foster innovation, and gain competitive advantage. Some companies are even creating a new position, *chief knowledge officer,* to head up this effort.[13]

Companies use their IT systems to facilitate the physical sharing of knowledge. But better hardware and software are not the answer to KM. KM is not technology-based, but rather a business practice that uses technology. Technology alone does not constitute KM, nor is it the solution to KM. Rather, it facilitates KM. Executives with successful KM initiatives understand that KM is not a matter of buying a major software application that serves as a data depository and coordinates all of a company's intellectual capital. According to Melinda Bickerstaff, vice president of knowledge management at Bristol-Myers Squibb (BMS), any such "leading with technology" approach is a sure path to failure. "Knowledge management has to be perceived as a business problem solver, not as an abstract concept," Bickerstaff explains.

Effective KM calls for an interdisciplinary approach that coordinates all aspects of an organization's knowledge. It requires a major change in behavior as well as technology to leverage the power of information systems, especially the internet, and a company's human capital resources. The first step is creating an information culture through organizational structure and rewards that promotes a more flexible, collaborative way of working and communicating. Moving an organization toward KM is no easy task, but it is well worth the effort in terms of creating a more collaborative environment, reducing duplication of effort, and increasing shared knowledge. The benefits can be significant in terms of growth, time, and money.

At Bristol-Meyers Squibb, a major pharmaceutical company, Bickerstaff began the KM implementation by looking for specific information-related problems to solve so that the company would save time and/or money. For example, she learned that company scientists were spending about 18 percent of their time searching multiple databases to find patents and other information. Simply integrating the relevant databases gave researchers the ability to perform faster searches. A more complex project involved compiling the best practices of drug-development teams with the best FDA approval rates so that other groups could benefit. Rather than send forms that could be easily set aside, Bickenstaff arranged to conduct interviews and lessons-learned sessions. The information was then developed into interesting articles rather than dry corporate reports.[14]

Technology Planning

A good technology plan provides employees with the tools they need to perform their jobs at the highest levels of efficiency. The first step is a general needs assessment, followed by ranking of projects and the specific choices of hardware and software. Table 13.3 poses some basic questions departmental managers and IT specialists should ask when planning technology purchases.

Questions for IT Project Planning
• What are the company's overall objectives?
• What problems does the company want to solve?
• How can technology help meet those goals and solve the problems?
• What are the company's IT priorities, both short- and long-term?
• What type of technology infrastructure (centralized or decentralized) best serves the company's needs?
• Which technologies meet the company's requirements?
• Are additional hardware and software required? If so, will they integrate with the company's existing systems?
• Does the system design and implementation include the people and process changes, in addition to the technological ones?
• Do you have the in-house capabilities to develop and implement the proposed applications, or should you bring in an outside specialist?

Table 13.3

Once managers identify the projects that make business sense, they can choose the best products for the company's needs. The final step is to evaluate the potential benefits of the technology in terms of efficiency and effectiveness. For a successful project, you must evaluate and restructure business processes, choose technology, develop and implement the system, and manage the change processes to best serve your organizational needs. Installing a new IT system on top of inefficient business processes is a waste of time and money!

CONCEPT CHECK

1. What are some ways a company can manage its technology assets to its advantage?
2. Differentiate between information management and knowledge management. What steps can companies take to manage knowledge?
3. List the key questions managers need to ask when planning technology purchases.

13.5 Protecting Computers and Information

5. What are the best ways to protect computers and the information they contain?

Have you ever lost a term paper you worked on for weeks because your hard drive crashed or you deleted the wrong file? You were upset, angry, and frustrated. Multiply that paper and your feelings hundreds of times over, and you can understand why companies must protect computers, networks, and the information they store and transmit from a variety of potential threats. For example, security breaches of corporate information systems—from human hackers or electronic versions such as viruses and worms—are increasing at an alarming rate. The ever-increasing dependence on computers requires plans that cover human error, power outages, equipment failure, hacking, and terrorist attacks. To withstand natural disasters such as major fires, earthquakes, and floods, many companies install specialized fault-tolerant computer systems.

Disasters are not the only threat to data. A great deal of data, much of it confidential, can easily be tapped or destroyed by anyone who knows about computers. Keeping your networks secure from unauthorized access—from internal as well as external sources—requires formal security policies and enforcement procedures. The increasing popularity of mobile devices—laptops, tablets, and cell phones—and wireless networks requires new types of security provisions.

In response to mounting security concerns, companies have increased spending on technology to protect their IT infrastructure and data. Along with specialized hardware and software, companies need to develop specific security strategies that take a proactive approach to prevent security and technical problems before they start. However, a recent CIO article lamented the lack of basic security policies that companies only implement after a hack or data crisis.[15]

Data Security Issues

Unauthorized access into a company's computer systems can be expensive, and not just in monetary terms. Juniper Networks estimates that cybercrime will cost businesses more than $2 trillion in 2019, compared to just $450 million in 2001. The most costly categories of threats include worms, viruses, and Trojan horses (defined later in this section); computer theft; financial fraud; and unauthorized network access. The report also states that almost all U.S. businesses report at least one security issue, and almost 20 percent have experienced multiple security incidents.[16]

Computer crooks are becoming more sophisticated all the time, finding new ways to get into ultra-secure sites. "As companies and consumers continue to move towards a networked and information economy, more opportunity exists for cybercriminals to take advantage of vulnerabilities on networks and computers," says Chris Christiansen, program vice president at technology research firm IDC.[17] Whereas early cybercrooks were typically amateur hackers working alone, the new ones are more professional and often work in gangs to commit large-scale internet crimes for large financial rewards. The internet, where criminals can hide behind anonymous screen names, has increased the stakes and expanded the realm of opportunities to commit identity theft and similar crimes. Catching such cybercriminals is difficult, and fewer than 5 percent are caught.[18]

Exhibit 13.8   Data security is under constant attack. In 2017, cybercriminals penetrated Equifax, one of the largest credit bureaus in the nation, and stole the personal data of more than 145 million people. To date, it is considered one of the worst data breaches of all time because of the amount of sensitive data stolen, including consumers' Social Security numbers. *What impact do identity theft and other data-security issues have on global networking and e-commerce?* (Credit: Blogtrepreneur/ flickr/ Attribution 2.0 Generic (CC BY 2.0))

Firms are taking steps to prevent these costly computer crimes and problems, which fall into several major categories:

- *Unauthorized access and security breaches.* Whether from internal or external sources, unauthorized access and security breaches are a top concern of IT managers. These can create havoc with a company's systems and damage customer relationships. Unauthorized access also includes employees, who can copy confidential new-product information and provide it to competitors or use company systems for personal business that may interfere with systems operation. Networking links also make it easier for someone outside the organization to gain access to a company's computers.

  One of the latest forms of cybercrime involves secretly installing keylogging software via software downloads, e-mail attachments, or shared files. This software then copies and transmits a user's keystrokes—passwords, PINs, and other personal information—from selected sites, such as banking and credit card sites, to thieves.

- *Computer viruses, worms, and Trojan horses.* Computer viruses and related security problems such as worms and Trojan horses are among the top threats to business and personal computer security. A computer program that copies itself into other software and can spread to other computer systems, a **computer virus** can destroy the contents of a computer's hard drive or damage files. Another form is called a *worm* because it spreads itself automatically from computer to computer. Unlike a virus, a worm doesn't require e-mail to replicate and transmit itself into other systems. It can enter through valid access points.

  Trojan horses are programs that appear to be harmless and from legitimate sources but trick the user into installing them. When run, they damage the user's computer. For example, a Trojan horse may claim to get rid of viruses but instead infects the computer. Other forms of Trojan horses provide a "trapdoor" that allows undocumented access to a computer, unbeknownst to the user. Trojan horses do not, however, infect other files or self-replicate.[19]

Viruses can hide for weeks, months, or even years before starting to damage information. A virus that "infects" one computer or network can be spread to another computer by sharing disks or by downloading infected files over the internet. To protect data from virus damage, virus protection software automatically monitors computers to detect and remove viruses. Program developers make regular updates available to guard against newly created viruses. In addition, experts are becoming more proficient at tracking down virus authors, who are subject to criminal charges.

- *Deliberate damage to equipment or information.* For example, an unhappy employee in the purchasing department could get into the company's computer system and delete information on past orders and future inventory needs. The sabotage could severely disrupt production and the accounts payable system. Willful acts to destroy or change the data in computers are hard to prevent. To lessen the damage, companies should back up critical information.
- *Spam.* Although you might think that *spam,* or unsolicited and unwanted e-mail, is just a nuisance, it also poses a security threat to companies. Viruses spread through e-mail attachments that can accompany spam e-mails. Spam is now clogging blogs, instant messages, and cell phone text messages as well as e-mail inboxes. Spam presents other threats to a corporation: lost productivity and expenses from dealing with spam, such as opening the messages and searching for legitimate messages that special spam filters keep out.
- *Software and media piracy.* The copying of copyrighted software programs, games, and movies by people who haven't paid for them is another form of unauthorized use. Piracy, defined as using software without a license, takes revenue away from the company that developed the program—usually at great cost. It includes making counterfeit CDs to sell as well as personal copying of software to share with friends.

Preventing Problems

Creating formal written information security policies to set standards and provide the basis for enforcement is the first step in a company's security strategy. Unfortunately, a recent survey of IT executives worldwide revealed that over two-thirds expect a cyberattack in the near future. Stephanie Ewing, a data security expert, states, "Having a documented, tested process brings order to chaotic situations and keeps everyone focused on solving the most pressing issues." Without information security strategies in place, companies spend too much time in a reactive mode—responding to crises—and don't focus enough on prevention.[20]

Security plans should have the support of top management, and then follow with procedures to implement the security policies. Because IT is a dynamic field with ongoing changes to equipment and processes, it's important to review security policies often. Some security policies can be handled automatically, by technical measures, whereas others involve administrative policies that rely on humans to perform them. Examples of administrative policies are "Users must change their passwords every 90 days" and "End users will update their virus signatures at least once a week." Table 13.4 shows the types of security measures companies use to protect data.

Five Areas of Concern Regarding the Protection of Data	
Percentage	Concern for Protecting Data
52	Aren't sure how to secure connected devices and apps
40	Don't immediately change default passwords
33	Don't think they can control how companies collect personal information
33	Parents admit they don't know the risks well enough to explain to children
37	Use credit-monitoring services

Table 13.4 Source: Adapted from Tony Bradley, "Top 5 Concerns to Focus on for Privacy Day," *Forbes*, https://forbes.com, January 27, 2017.

Preventing costly problems can be as simple as regularly backing up applications and data. Companies should have systems in place that automatically back up the company's data every day and store copies of the backups off-site. In addition, employees should back up their own work regularly. Another good policy is to maintain a complete and current database of all IT hardware, software, and user details to make it easier to manage software licenses and updates and diagnose problems. In many cases, IT staff can use remote access technology to automatically monitor and fix problems, as well as update applications and services.

Companies should never overlook the human factor in the security equation. One of the most common ways that outsiders get into company systems is by posing as an employee, first getting the staffer's full name and username from an e-mail message and then calling the help desk to ask for a forgotten password. Crooks can also get passwords by viewing them on notes attached to a desk or computer monitor, using machines that employees leave logged on when they leave their desks, and leaving laptop computers with sensitive information unsecured in public places.

Portable devices, from handheld computers to tiny plug-and-play flash drives and other storage devices (including mobile phones), pose security risks as well. They are often used to store sensitive data such as passwords, bank details, and calendars. Mobile devices can spread viruses when users download virus-infected documents to their company computers.

Imagine the problems that could arise if an employee saw a calendar entry on a mobile device like "meeting re: layoffs," an outsider saw "meeting about merger with ABC Company," or an employee lost a flash drive containing files about marketing plans for a new product. Manufacturers are responding to IT managers' concerns about security by adding password protection and encryption to flash drives. Companies can also use flash drive monitoring software that prevents unauthorized access on PCs and laptops.

Companies have many ways to avoid an IT meltdown, as Table 13.5 describes.

Procedures to Protect IT Assets
• Develop a comprehensive plan and policies that include portable as well as fixed equipment.
• Protect the equipment itself with stringent physical security measures to the premises.
• Protect data using special *encryption* technology to encode confidential information so only the recipient can decipher it.
• Stop unwanted access from inside or outside with special authorization systems. These can be as simple as a password or as sophisticated as fingerprint or voice identification.
• Install *firewalls*, hardware or software designed to prevent unauthorized access to or from a private network.
• Monitor network activity with intrusion-detection systems that signal possible unauthorized access, and document suspicious events.
• Conduct periodic IT audits to catalog all attached storage devices as well as computers.
• Use technology that monitors ports for unauthorized attached devices and turn off those that are not approved for business use.
• Train employees to troubleshoot problems in advance, rather than just react to them.
• Hold frequent staff-training sessions to teach correct security procedures, such as logging out of networks when they go to lunch and changing passwords often.
• Make sure employees choose sensible passwords, at least six and ideally eight characters long, containing numbers, letters, and punctuation marks. Avoid dictionary words and personal information.
• Establish a database of useful information and FAQ (frequently asked questions) for employees so they can solve problems themselves.
• Develop a healthy communications atmosphere.

Table 13.5

Keep IT Confidential: Privacy Concerns

The very existence of huge electronic file cabinets full of personal information presents a threat to our personal privacy. Until recently, our financial, medical, tax, and other records were stored in separate computer systems. Computer networks make it easy to pool these data into data warehouses. Companies also sell the information they collect about you from sources like warranty registration cards, credit-card records, registration at websites, personal data forms required to purchase online, and grocery store discount club cards. Telemarketers can combine data from different sources to create fairly detailed profiles of consumers.

The September 11, 2001, tragedy and other massive security breaches have raised additional privacy concerns. As a result, the government began looking for ways to improve domestic-intelligence collection and analyze terrorist threats within the United States. Sophisticated database applications that look for hidden patterns in a group of data, a process called **data mining**, increase the potential for tracking and predicting people's daily activities. Legislators and privacy activists worry that such programs as this and ones that eavesdrop electronically could lead to excessive government surveillance that encroaches on personal privacy. The stakes are much higher as well: errors in data mining by companies in business may result in a consumer being targeted with inappropriate advertising, whereas a governmental mistake in tracking suspected terrorists could do untold damage to an unjustly targeted person.

Increasingly, consumers are fighting to regain control of personal data and how that information is used. Privacy advocates are working to block sales of information collected by governments and corporations. For example, they want to prevent state governments from selling driver's license information and supermarkets from collecting and selling information gathered when shoppers use barcoded plastic discount cards. With information about their buying habits, advertisers can target consumers for specific marketing programs.

The challenge to companies is to find a balance between collecting the information they need while at the same time protecting individual consumer rights. Most registration and warranty forms that ask questions about income and interests have a box for consumers to check to prevent the company from selling their names. Many companies now state in their privacy policies that they will not abuse the information they collect. Regulators are taking action against companies that fail to respect consumer privacy.

CONCEPT CHECK

1. Describe the different threats to data security.
2. How can companies protect information from destruction and unauthorized use?
3. Why are privacy rights advocates alarmed over the use of techniques such as data warehouses and data mining?

13.6 | Trends in Information Technology

6. What are the leading trends in information technology?

Information technology is a continually evolving field. The fast pace and amount of change, coupled with IT's broad reach, make it especially challenging to isolate industry trends. From the time we write this chapter to the time you read it—as little as six months—new trends will appear, and those that seemed important may fade. However, some trends that are reshaping today's IT landscape are digital forensics, the shift to a distributed workforce, and the increasing use of grid computing.

Cyber Sleuthing: A New Style of Crime Busting

What helped investigators bring suit against Enron, Merck's Vioxx medication, and the BTK serial killer? Digital evidence taken from an individual's computer or corporate network—web pages, pictures, documents, and e-mails are part of a relatively new science called *digital forensics*. Digital-forensics software safeguards electronic evidence used in investigations by creating a duplicate of a hard drive that an investigator can search by keyword, file type, or access date. Digital forensics is also evolving into areas such as cloud computing and blockchain technology. For instance, it is estimated that as much as 3.9 million of the original 21 million bitcoins are "lost" on hard drives confined to landfills and flash drives located in the back of old office desks.[21]

But nowadays digital sleuthing is not limited to law enforcement. Companies such as Walmart, Target, and American Express have their own secret in-house digital forensics teams. And what if you're in New York and need to seize a hard drive in Hong Kong? No problem. Over 75 members of the Fortune 500 now use technology that allows them to search hard drives remotely over their corporate networks. Digital forensics makes it possible to track down those who steal corporate data and intellectual property. Broadcom, a semiconductor chip designer, used computer forensics to investigate and apprehend former employees who were attempting to steal trade secrets. In the process, Broadcom gathered incriminating e-mails, including deleted documents, that gave it solid evidence to use the 2013 Federal Computer Fraud and Abuse Act to stop the former employees from starting up a rival firm.[22]

However, there is a downside to having these advanced capabilities. If this kind of software falls into the wrong hands, sophisticated hackers could access corporate networks and individual computers as easily as taking candy from a baby—and the victims would not even know it was happening. In an age of corporate wrongdoing, sexual predators, and computer porn, your hard drive will tell investigators everything they need to know about your behavior and interests, good and bad. Cybersleuthing means we are all potential targets of digital forensics. As evidenced by the huge increase in identity theft, personal privacy—once an unassailable right—is no longer as sacred as it once was.

ETHICS IN PRACTICE

Unearthing Your Secrets

Cybercrimes in our technologically driven world are on the increase—identity theft, pornography, and sexual predator victim access, to name a few. The FBI's computer analysis response team confirms their caseload includes 800 cases reported *per day* in 2017. To keep up with the changing world we live in, law enforcement, corporations, and government agencies have turned to new crime-fighting tools, one of the most effective being digital forensics.

The leader in this technology is Guidance Software, founded in 1997 to develop solutions that search, identify, recover, and deliver digital information in a forensically sound and cost-effective manner. Headquartered in Pasadena, California, the company employs 391 people at offices and training facilities in Chicago, Illinois; Washington, DC; San Francisco, California; Houston, Texas; New York City; and Brazil, England, and Singapore. The company's more than 20,000 high-profile clients include leading police agencies, government investigation and law enforcement agencies, and Fortune 1000 corporations in the financial service, insurance, high-tech and consulting, health care, and utility industries.

Guidance Software's suite of EnCase® solutions is the first computer forensics tool able to provide world-class electronic investigative capabilities for large-scale complex investigations. Law enforcement officers, government/corporate investigators, and consultants around the world can now benefit from computer forensics that exceed anything previously available. The software offers an investigative infrastructure that provides network-enabled investigations, enterprise-wide integration with other security technologies, and powerful search and collection tools. With EnCase, clients can conduct digital investigations, handle large-scale data collection needs, and respond to external attacks.

Notably, the company's software was used by law enforcement in the Casey Anthony murder case and the Sony PlayStation security breach, and was used to examine data retrieved by the U.S. special forces in the Osama bin Laden raid.

Guidance Software also helps reduce corporate and personal liability when investigating computer-related fraud, intellectual property theft, and employee misconduct. It protects against network threats such as hackers, worms, and viruses and hidden threats such as malicious code.

In response to increases in the number and scope of discovery requests, Guidance Software developed its eDiscovery Suite. The software package dramatically improves the practice of large-scale discovery—the identification, collection, cataloging, and saving of evidence—required in almost every major legal case these days. eDiscovery integrates with other litigation-support software to significantly decrease the time for corporations to accomplish these tasks. At the same time, it improves regulatory compliance and reduces disruption. The result is many millions of dollars in cost savings. In late 2017, Guidance Software was acquired by OpenText, an enterprise information management company that employs more than 10,000 people worldwide.

Sources: FBI website, https://www.fbi.gov, accessed January 15, 2018; Guidance Software website, https://www.guidancesoftware.com, accessed January 15, 2018; OpenText website, https://www.opentext.com, accessed January 15, 2018; "Casey Anthony: The Computer Forensics," *The State v Casey Anthony website*, https://statevcasey.wordpress.com, July 18, 2011; Declan McCullagh, "Finding Treasures in Bin Laden Computers," *CBS News*, https://www.cbsnews.com, May 6, 2011; Evan Narcisse, " Who's Cleaning Up the PSN Debacle for Sony?" *Time,* http://techland.time.com, May 4, 2011.

Critical Thinking Questions
1. How is Guidance Software responding to and helping to manage changes in our technology-driven world?
2. What other types of forensics software do you foresee a need for in the future? Do you think there are ethical issues in using forensics software, and why?
3. What are the benefits and risks of Guidance Software being acquired by a larger company?

The Distributed Workforce

Insurance company Aetna shuttered 2.7 million square feet of office space, saving the company $78 million, while American Express estimates it saved between $10 to $15 million dollars per year by expanding its distributed workforce. Was this a sign that these company were in trouble? Far from it. Instead of maintaining expensive offices in multiple locations, they sent employees home to work and adopted a new model for employees: the distributed workforce. Employees have no permanent office space and work from home or on the road. The shift to virtual workers has been a huge success, and not only do companies save on their personnel and related costs, but they also have happier, more productive employees.

Aetna and American Express are not alone in recognizing the benefits of distributed workers, especially in companies that depend on knowledge workers. Work Design Collaborative LLC in Prescott, Arizona, estimates that about 12 percent of all workers in the United States fall into this category, and in urban areas the number could be as high as 15 percent. There are estimates that this trend could eventually reach 40 percent over the next decade, as long commutes, high gas costs, and better connecting tools and technologies make this an attractive option for many workers who like the flexibility of not working in an office.[23] Already, employees use the internet to conduct video-conferenced meetings and collaborate on teams that span the globe. On the downside, working from home can also mean being available 24/7—although most workers consider the trade-off well worth it.

According to recent statistics, close to four million U.S. workers work from home at least half of the time.

Remote workers continue to be recruited by companies of all sizes, including Amazon, Dell, Salesforce, and others.[24] Intel has a successful virtual-work program that has been popular with working parents. "Technology allows working remotely to be completely invisible," says Laura Dionne, the company's director of supply-chain transformation. At Boeing, thousands of employees participate in the virtual-work program, and it has been a critical factor in attracting and retaining younger workers. Almost half of Sun Microsystems' employees are "location-independent," reducing real estate costs by $300 million. Additional benefits for Sun are higher productivity from these workers and the ability to hire the best talent. "Our people working these remote schedules are the happiest employees we have, and they have the lowest attrition rates," says Bill MacGowan, senior vice president for human resources at Sun. "Would I rather settle on someone mediocre in the Bay Area, or get the best person in the country who is willing to work remotely?"[25]

Grid and Cloud Computing Offer Powerful Solutions

How can smaller companies that occasionally need to perform difficult and large-scale computational tasks find a way to accomplish their projects? They can turn to *grid* or **cloud computing**, also called *utility computing* or *peer-to-peer computing*. Cloud and grid technology provides a way to divide the job into many smaller tasks and distribute them to a virtual supercomputer consisting of many small computers linked into a common network. Combining multiple desktop machines results in computing power that exceeds supercomputer speeds. A hardware and software infrastructure clusters and integrates computers and applications from multiple sources, harnessing unused power in existing PCs and networks. This structure distributes computational resources but maintains central control of the process. A central server acts as a team leader and traffic monitor. The controlling cluster server divides a task into subtasks, assigns the work to computers on the grid with surplus processing power, combines the results, and moves on to the next task until the job is finished. **Exhibit 13.9** shows how typical grid and cloud setups work, and the differences between the two.

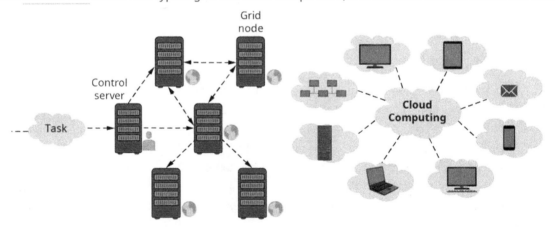

Exhibit 13.9   How Grid and Cloud Computing Work (Attribution: Copyright Rice University, OpenStax, under CC BY 4.0 license.)

With utility computing, any company—large or small—can access the software and computer capacity on an as-needed basis. One of the big advantages of cloud computing is that companies can update their inventory in real time across their entire organization. For example, suppose you are an appliance retailer and have several outlets throughout the Midwest. If you have one model of a Whirlpool washing machine in your Des Moines, Iowa, store, and a salesperson in your Chicago location can sell that model in Chicago, the sale can be accomplished pretty easily. They can finalize the sale, create the shipping instructions, and update the inventory record automatically—and the Chicago consumer's needs will be met.[26]

Amazon, Google, IBM, Salesforce.com, Oracle, and Hewlett-Packard Enterprise are among the companies providing as-needed cloud and grid services. Although cloud and grid computing appears similar to outsourcing or on-demand software from ASPs, it has two key differences:

- Pricing is set per-use, whereas outsourcing involves fixed-price contracts.
- Cloud and grid computing goes beyond hosted software and includes computer and networking equipment as well as services.

The cloud and grids provide a very cost-effective way to provide computing power for complex projects in areas such as weather research and financial and biomedical modeling. Because the computing infrastructure already exists—they tap into computer capacity that is otherwise unused—the cost is quite low. The increased interest in cloud and grid technology will continue to contribute to high growth.

CONCEPT CHECK

1. How are companies and other organizations using digital forensics to obtain critical information?
2. Why do companies find that productivity rises when they offer employees the option of joining the virtual workforce?
3. What advantages do grid and cloud computing offer a company? What are some of the downsides to using this method?

Key Terms

application service providers (ASP) A service company that buys and maintains software on its servers and distributes it through high-speed networks to subscribers for a set period and price.

batch processing A method of updating a database in which data are collected over some time period and processed together.

chief information officer (CIO) An executive with responsibility for managing all information resources in an organization.

cloud computing A general term for the delivery of hosted services over the internet.

computer network A group of two or more computer systems linked together by communications channels to share data and information.

computer virus A computer program that copies itself into other software and can spread to other computer systems.

data mart Special subset of a data warehouse that deals with a single area of data and is organized for quick analysis.

data mining Sophisticated database applications that look for hidden patterns in a group of data to help track and predict future behavior.

data warehouse An information technology that combines many databases across a whole company into one central database that supports management decision-making.

database An electronic filing system that collects and organizes data and information.

decision support system (DSS) A management support system that helps managers make decisions using interactive computer models that describe real-world processes.

enterprise portal A customizable internal website that provides proprietary corporate information to a defined user group, such as employees, supply-chain partners, or customers.

executive information system (EIS) A management support system that is customized for an individual executive; provides specific information for strategic decisions.

expert system A management support system that gives managers advice similar to what they would get from a human consultant; it uses artificial intelligence to enable computers to reason and learn to solve problems in much the same way humans do.

information technology (IT) The equipment and techniques used to manage and process information.

intranet An internal corporate-wide area network that uses internet technology to connect computers and link employees in many locations and with different types of computers.

knowledge management (KM) The process of researching, gathering, organizing, and sharing an organization's collective knowledge to improve productivity, foster innovation, and gain competitive advantage.

knowledge worker A worker who develops or uses knowledge, contributing to and benefiting from information used to perform planning, acquiring, searching, analyzing, organizing, storing, programming, producing, distributing, marketing, or selling functions.

local area network (LAN) A network that connects computers at one site, enabling the computer users to exchange data and share the use of hardware and software from a variety of computer manufacturers.

managed service providers (MSP) Next generation of ASPs, offering customization and expanded capabilities such as business processes and complete management of the network servers.

management information system (MIS) The methods and equipment that provide information about all aspects of a firm's operations.

management support system (MSS) An information system that uses the internal master database to perform high-level analyses that help managers make better decisions.

online (real-time) processing A method of updating a database in which data are processed as they become available.

transaction processing system (TPS) An information system that handles the daily business operations of a firm. The system receives and organizes raw data from internal and external sources for storage in a database using either batch or online processing.

virtual private networks (VPN) Private corporate networks connected over a public network, such as the internet. VPNs include strong security measures to allow only authorized users to access the network.

wide area network (WAN) A network that connects computers at different sites via telecommunications media such as phone lines, satellites, and microwaves.

Summary of Learning Outcomes

13.1 Transforming Businesses through Information
1. How has information technology transformed business and managerial decision-making?

Businesses depend on information technology for everything from running daily operations to making strategic decisions. Companies must have management information systems that gather, analyze, and distribute information to the appropriate parties, including employees, suppliers, and customers. These systems are comprised of different types of computers that collect data and process it into usable information for decision-making. Managers tap into databases to access the information they need, whether for placing inventory orders, scheduling production, or preparing long-range forecasts. They can compare information about the company's current status to its goals and standards. Company-wide enterprise resource planning systems that bring together human resources, operations, and technology are becoming an integral part of business strategy.

13.2 Linking Up: Computer Networks
2. Why are computer networks an important part of today's information technology systems?

Today companies use networks of linked computers that share data and expensive hardware to improve operating efficiency. Types of networks include local area networks, wide area networks, and wireless local area networks. Intranets are private WANs that allow a company's employees to communicate quickly with one other and work on joint projects, regardless of their location. Companies are finding new uses for wireless technologies such as tablets, cell phones, and other mobile devices. Virtual private networks give companies a cost-effective secure connection between remote locations by using public networks such as the internet.

13.3 Management Information Systems
3. What types of systems make up a typical company's management information system?

A management information system consists of a transaction processing system, management support systems, and an office automation system. The transaction processing system collects and organizes operational data on the firm's activities. Management support systems help managers make better decisions. They include an information-reporting system that provides information based on the data collected by the TPS to the managers who need it; decision support systems that use models to assist in answering "what if" types of questions; and expert systems that give managers advice similar to what they would get from a human consultant. Executive information systems are customized to the needs of top management.

13.4 Technology Management and Planning
4. How can technology management and planning help companies optimize their information technology

systems?

To get the most value from IT, companies must go beyond simply collecting and summarizing information. Technology planning involves evaluating the company's goals and objectives and using the right technology to reach them. IT managers must also evaluate the existing infrastructure to get the best return on the company's investment in IT assets. Knowledge management focuses on sharing an organization's collective knowledge to improve productivity and foster innovation. Some companies establish the position of chief knowledge officer to head up KM activities.

13.5 Protecting Computers and Information

5.   What are the best ways to protect computers and the information they contain?

Because companies are more dependent on computers than ever before, they need to protect data and equipment from natural disasters and computer crime. Types of computer crime include unauthorized use and access, software piracy, malicious damage, and computer viruses. To protect IT assets, companies should prepare written security policies. They can use technology such as virus protection, firewalls, and employee training in proper security procedures. They must also take steps to protect customers' personal privacy rights.

13.6 Trends in Information Technology

6.   What are the leading trends in information technology?

IT is a dynamic industry, and companies must stay current on the latest trends to identify ones that help them maintain their competitive edge, such as digital forensics, the distributed workforce, and grid computing. With digital forensics techniques, corporations, government agencies, attorneys, and lawmakers can obtain evidence from computers and corporate networks—web pages, pictures, documents, and e-mails. Many knowledge workers now work remotely rather than from an office. Companies adopting the distributed workforce model gain many benefits, such as cost savings, more satisfied and productive employees, and increased employee retention. Cloud computing harnesses the power of computers, online software, and data storage to create a virtual computing environment that is invisible to the user. A company can access the cloud on an as-needed basis instead of investing in its own supercomputer equipment. Outsourcing a portion of the company's computing needs provides additional flexibility and cost advantages. Companies can also set up internal grids.

📖 Preparing for Tomorrow's Workplace Skills

1.   How has information technology changed your life? Describe at least three areas (both personal and school- or work-related) where having access to better information has improved your decisions. Are there any negative effects? What steps can you take to manage information better? (Information, Technology)

2.   Visit or conduct a phone interview with a local small-business owner about the different ways her or his firm uses information technology. Prepare a brief report on your findings that includes the hardware and software used, how it was selected, benefits of technology for the company, and any problems in implementing or using it. (Interpersonal, Information)

3.   Your school wants to automate the class-registration process. Prepare a memo to the dean of information systems describing an integrated information system that would help a student choose and register for courses. Make a list of the different groups that should be involved and questions to ask during the planning process. Include a graphic representation of the system that shows how the data become useful

information. Indicate the information a student needs to choose courses and its sources. Explain how several types of management support systems could help students make better course decisions. Include ways the school could use the information it collects from this system. Have several students present their plans to the class, which will take the role of university management in evaluating them. (Resources, Systems, Technology)

4. You recently joined the IT staff of a midsized consumer products firm. After a malicious virus destroys some critical files, you realize that the company lacks a security strategy and policies. Outline the steps you'd take to develop a program to protect data and the types of policies you'd recommend. How would you present the plan to management and employees to encourage acceptance? (Resources, Technology)

5. **Team Activity** Should companies outsource IT? Some executives believe that IT is too important to outsource and that application service providers don't have a future. Yet spending for ASP subscriptions, MSPs, and other forms of IT outsourcing such as cloud computing continue to grow. What's your position? Divide the class into groups designated "for" or "against" outsourcing and/or ASPs. Have them research the current status of ASPs using publications such as *CIO* and *Computerworld* and websites such as Enterprise Apps Today, http://www.enterpriseappstoday.com. (Interpersonal, Information)

Ethics Activity

As the owner of a small but growing business, you are concerned about employees misusing company computers for personal matters. Not only does this cost the company in terms of employee productivity, but it also ties up bandwidth that may be required for company operations and exposes the firm's networks to increased risks of attacks from viruses, spyware, and other malicious programs. Installing e-mail monitoring and web security and filtering software programs would allow you to track e-mail and internet use, develop use policies, block access to inappropriate sites, and limit the time employees can conduct personal online business. At the same time, the software will protect your IT networks from many types of security concerns, from viruses to internet fraud. You are concerned, however, that employees will take offense and consider such software an invasion of privacy.

Using a web search tool, locate articles about this topic and then write responses to the following questions. Be sure to support your arguments and cite your sources.

Ethical Dilemma: Should you purchase employee-monitoring software for your company, and on what do you base your decision? If you install the software, do you have an obligation to tell employees about it? Explain your answers and suggest ways to help employees understand your rationale.

Sources: KC Agu, "6 Software Tools for Monitoring Employee Productivity," *Huffington Post*, https://www.huffingtonpost.com, December 6, 2017; Marissa Lang, "Electronic Tracking Spurs Workplace Privacy Debate," *Government Technology*, http://www.govtech.com, October 18, 2017; Mike Rogoway, "Jive's Buyer Responds to Employee Anxiety over Workplace Monitoring Tool," *The Oregonian*, http://www.oregonlive.com.

Working the Net

1. Enterprise resource planning is a major category of business software. Visit the site of one of the following companies: SAP (**http://www.sap.com**), or Oracle (**http://www.oracle.com**). Prepare a short presentation for the class about the company's ERP product offerings and capabilities. Include examples

of how companies use the ERP software. What are the latest trends in ERP?

2. What can intranets and enterprise portals accomplish for a company? Find out by using such resources as Brint.com's Intranet Portal, **http://www.brint.com/Intranets.htm**. Look for case studies that show how companies apply this technology. Summarize the different features an intranet or enterprise portal provides.

3. Learn more about the CERT Coordination Center (CERT/CC), which serves as a center of internet security expertise. Explore its website, **https://www.cert.org/index.cfm**. What are the latest statistics on incidents reported, vulnerabilities, security alerts, security notes, mail messages, and hotline calls? What other useful information does the site provide to help a company protect IT assets?

4. Research the latest developments in computer security at *Computerworld*'s site, **http://computerworld.com/**. What types of information can you find here? Pick one of the categories in this area (Cybercrime, Encryption, Disaster Recovery, Firewalls, Hacking, Privacy, Security Holes, Vhttp://computerworld.com/securitytopics/securityiruses and Worms, and VPN), and summarize your findings.

5. How can someone steal your identity? Using information at the Federal Trade Commission's central website for information about identity theft, https://www.consumer.ftc.gov/features/feature-0014-identity-theft, compile a list of the ways thieves can access key information to use your identity. What steps should you take if you've been a victim of identity theft? Summarize key provisions of federal laws dealing with this crime and the laws in your state.

 # Critical Thinking Case

Novartis's Prescription for Invoice Processing

What do you do when you have more than 600 business units operating through 360 independent affiliates in 140 countries around the world—processing complex invoices in various languages and currencies? You seek out the best technology solution to make the job easier.

At global pharmaceutical giant Novartis, the IT department is a strategic resource, a community of 2,000 people serving 63,000 customers in 200 locations and 25 data centers. Because most of the company's invoices come from international suppliers, they have differences in design, language, taxes, and currency. Consequently, many ended up as "query items" requiring manual resolution by Novartis accounting staff—which delayed payments and made those invoices extremely costly to process. In fact, finance personnel spent so much of their time resolving queried invoices that other work suffered. A solution was badly needed.

To maximize its investment, Novartis needed a flexible solution that would meet its current and future needs and function in other business departments in a variety of geographic locations. It should provide fast, accurate document capture and multi-language support, and should extend to other types of information—such as faxes and electronic data—in addition to paper documents. Finally, in order to obtain financing for the project, return on investment (ROI) was required within nine months of project implementation.

Input*Accel* for Invoices from EMC/Captiva was the answer. The software extracts data from paper documents, applies intelligent document recognition (IDR) technology to convert them to digital images, and sends relevant data to enterprise resource planning, accounts payable (A/P), and other back-end management systems. The specialized Input*Accel* server manages output by recognizing and avoiding holdups in the workflow process. It also ensures if a server goes offline, others will carry on functioning, thus avoiding downtime.

Now Novartis scans incoming invoices at a centrally located site, and the images are transmitted to the Input*Accel* for Invoices server for image improvement. Invoice data is then extracted and validated against supplier information. Most invoices are transferred directly for payment, with relatively few invoices requiring transfer to one of three accounts payable clerks who deal with queries manually. Novartis is a global leader in research and development of products that improve health issues. Input*Accel* was selected by Novartis to be part of its accounting system.

Thanks to IT, overall efficiency has increased, processing errors are reduced, and accounting personnel can use their time and expert knowledge for more meaningful tasks than resolving invoice errors. For Novartis, it is "mission accomplished."

Critical Thinking Questions
1. What factors contributed to Novartis's invoice processing being so complex?
2. How did IT help the company solve that problem?
3. What other uses and functions does Input*Accel* serve, and how will this be useful to Novartis over the long term? (You may want to visit the EMC/Captiva website, **https://www.emc.com**, for more information on Input*Accel*'s capabilities.)

Sources: "OpenText Acquires EMC Enterprise Division," *MetaSource*, http://www.metasource.com, September 20, 2016; Novartis corporate website, http://www.novartis.com, March 20, 2006; "Processing Invoices From Around the World," *ECM Connection,* https://www.ecmconnection, February 2, 2006; Kathryn Balint, "Captiva's Paper Chase Paying Off," *San Diego Union-Tribune,* December 9, 2005, pp. C1, C5.

Hot Links Address Book

1. If you want to know the definition of a computer term or more about a particular topic, Webopedia has the answer: **http://www.webopedia.com**.
2. Can't tell a LAN from a WAN? Learn more about networking at Lifewire's Internet & Networking pages, **https://www.lifewire.com**.
3. To find out if that e-mail alerting you to another virus threat is real or a hoax, check out the latest information at **http://www.snopes.com**.
4. How can you "inoculate" your computer against viruses? Symantec's Security Center has the latest details on virus threats and security issues: **http://www.symantec.com**.
5. The CIO digital magazine offers helpful articles that provide a good introduction to key IT topics: **http://www.cio.com**.
6. Curious about how companies are using on-demand grid computing? Read the Grid FAQ at the Grid Computing Technology Centre, **http://www.gridcomputing.com**, and then check out some of the many links to other resources.

14

Using Financial Information and Accounting

Exhibit 14.1 (Credit: Matt Madd /flickr / Attribution 2.0 Generic (CC BY 2.0))

 Introduction

Learning Outcomes

After reading this chapter, you should be able to answer these questions:

1. Why are financial reports and accounting information important, and who uses them?
2. What are the differences between public and private accountants, and how has federal legislation affected their work?
3. What are the six steps in the accounting cycle?
4. In what terms does the balance sheet describe the financial condition of an organization?
5. How does the income statement report a firm's profitability?
6. Why is the statement of cash flows an important source of information?
7. How can ratio analysis be used to identify a firm's financial strengths and weaknesses?
8. What major trends affect the accounting industry today?

EXPLORING BUSINESS CAREERS

Theresa Lee

Future Glory

Theresa Lee always knew she would start her own business; it was just a matter of time. In 2013, after working as a designer in the Bay Area for more than a decade, Lee cofounded Future Glory, which specializes in handmade leather bags and accessories, now made in a small studio in the Dogpatch neighborhood of San Francisco.

Lee would be the first to tell you that she is a creative person and not so great with numbers and other business details. But the business details, including financial statements and cash flow, are key to any company. That's where accounting software like QuickBooks Online comes in handy. QuickBooks is a global online accounting program that has helped tech-savvy entrepreneurs take the worry out of crunching the numbers that can make or break their business ventures.

Intuit, the global leader in accounting software, has revolutionized the approach taken by small businesses with its products, including QuickBooks and TurboTax, programs that can be used by new businesses, independent contractors, product sellers, accountants, and other types of businesses. The company estimates more than two million global customers are currently using the online version of QuickBooks. Intuit provides online support that includes expert help, a resource blog, accounting advice, and other features utilized by QuickBooks users and those wanting more information about how to track typical business accounting functions.

As Lee points out, using a cloud-based accounting program has helped her gain control over company finances and provided insight into key business components such as profit and loss, cost of goods sold, and labor. In addition, QuickBooks' ability to work with other apps has helped her manage e-commerce sales efficiently. Lee uses Shopify as an e-commerce platform and PayPal as a payment system. By using a version of these apps designed to work with QuickBooks, Lee can import sales data (line items, fees, and taxes) as well as customer information into the accounting program. In addition, Shopify e-commerce data automatically syncs with QuickBooks, allowing her to keep bookkeeping activities to a minimum and giving her more time to focus on designing and creating new products and fulfilling the social goals of her business.

According to Lee, a significant part of her operation is dedicated to providing training and jobs to members of the local community. In addition, Future Glory supports various social causes, donating a portion of revenue to various organizations that assistant women and children in need.

Keeping a close eye on financial and accounting information is an important part of any business, whether it's a startup or a global conglomerate. The continuing revolution in technology has enabled bookkeeping and accounting activities to be done more efficiently while giving business owners, particularly small businesses like Future Glory, the time to spend expanding their business and giving back to their local communities.

Sources: "Corporate Profile," https://www.intuit.com, accessed August 11, 2017; "QuickBooks Online," https://quickbooks.intuit.com, accessed August 11, 2017; "Our Story," https://futureglory.co, accessed August 10, 2017; "It's in the Bag—Future Glory Blends Apps with QuickBooks to Craft Fine Leather Goods," https://quickbooks.intuit.com, accessed August 10, 2017; Jordan Kushins, "Guide to Dogpatch's Flourishing Design Shops," *San Francisco Chronicle,* http://www.sfchronicle.com, March 1, 2017; David Leøng Photography blog, "November—Theresa Lee," http://www.davidleongphoto.com, November 30, 2016.

Financial information is central to every organization. To operate effectively, businesses must have a way to track income, expenses, assets, and liabilities in an organized manner. Financial information is also essential for decision-making. Managers prepare financial reports using accounting, a set of procedures and guidelines for companies to follow when preparing financial reports. Unless you understand basic accounting concepts, you will not be able to "speak" the standard financial language of businesses. This module examines the role of accounting in business, how accounting contributes to a company's overall success, the three primary financial statements, and careers in accounting.

14.1 Accounting: More than Numbers

1. Why are financial reports and accounting information important, and who uses them?

Prior to 2001, accounting topics rarely made the news. That changed when Enron Corp.'s manipulation of accounting rules to improve its financial statements hit the front pages of newspapers. The company filed bankruptcy in 2001, and its former top executives were charged with multiple counts of conspiracy and fraud. Arthur Andersen, Enron's accounting firm, was indicted and convicted of obstruction of justice, and in 2002, the once-respected firm went out of business. Soon financial abuses at other companies—among them Tyco, Adelphia, WorldCom, and more recently Madoff Investment Securities—surfaced. Top executives at these and other companies were accused of knowingly flouting accepted accounting standards to inflate current profits and increase their compensation. Many were subsequently convicted:

- Investment securities broker Bernard Madoff and his accountant bilked investors out of more than $65 billion; Madoff is currently serving a 150-year prison term.
- Andrew Fastow, Enron's former chief financial officer, and Ben Glisan Jr., its former treasurer, pleaded guilty and received prison terms of 10 and five years, respectively. The company's former chairman, Ken Lay, and CEO, Jeffrey Skilling, were convicted of multiple charges.
- Bernard Ebbers, WorldCom's CEO, was sentenced to 25 years in prison for conspiracy, securities fraud, and filing false reports with regulatory agencies—crimes that totaled $11 billion in accounting fraud.
- Tyco's CEO L. Dennis Kozlowski was fined $70 million and sentenced to 8 to 25 years.[1]

These and other cases raised critical concerns about the independence of those who audit a company's financial statements, questions of integrity and public trust, and issues with current financial reporting standards. Investors suffered as a result because the crisis in confidence sent stock prices tumbling, and companies lost billions in value.

So it's no surprise that more people are paying attention to accounting topics. We now recognize that accounting is the backbone of any business, providing a framework to understand the firm's financial condition. Reading about accounting irregularities, fraud, audit (financial statement review) shortcomings, out-of-control business executives, and bankruptcies, we have become very aware of the importance of accurate financial information and sound financial procedures.

All of us—whether we are self-employed, work for a local small business or a multinational Fortune 100 firm, or are not currently in the workforce—benefit from knowing the basics of accounting and financial statements. We can use this information to educate ourselves about companies before interviewing for a job or buying a company's stock or bonds. Employees at all levels of an organization use accounting information to monitor operations. They also must decide which financial information is important for their company or business unit, what those numbers mean, and how to use them to make decisions.

Exhibit 14.2   This advertisement by the U.S. Marshals Service underscores the greed and financial abuse caused by Bernard Madoff, as his personal belongings were seized by the government and auctioned off to help pay for the $65 billion lost by individuals who invested in his financial securities firm. Madoff is serving a jail term of 150 years for his fraudulent actions. *What should be the lessons learned by executives and accounting professionals about Madoff's behavior?* (Credit: P K /Flickr/ Attribution 2.0 Generic (CC BY 2.0))

This chapter starts by discussing why accounting is important for businesses and for users of financial information. Then it provides a brief overview of the accounting profession and the post-Enron regulatory environment. Next it presents an overview of basic accounting procedures, followed by a description of the three main financial statements—the balance sheet, the income statement, and the statement of cash flows. Using these statements, we then demonstrate how ratio analysis of financial statements can provide valuable information about a company's financial condition. Finally, the chapter explores current trends affecting the accounting profession.

Accounting Basics

Accounting is the process of collecting, recording, classifying, summarizing, reporting, and analyzing financial activities. It results in reports that describe the financial condition of an organization. All types of organizations—businesses, hospitals, schools, government agencies, and civic groups—use accounting procedures. Accounting provides a framework for looking at past performance, current financial health, and possible future performance. It also provides a framework for comparing the financial positions and financial performances of different firms. Understanding how to prepare and interpret financial reports will enable you to evaluate two companies and choose the one that is more likely to be a good investment.

The accounting system shown in Exhibit 14.3 converts the details of financial transactions (sales, payments, purchases, and so on) into a form that people can use to evaluate the firm and make decisions. Data become information, which in turn becomes reports. These reports describe a firm's financial position at one point in time and its financial performance during a specified period. Financial reports include *financial statements,* such as balance sheets and income statements, and special reports, such as sales and expense breakdowns by product line.

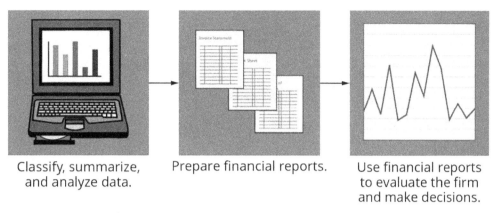

Classify, summarize, and analyze data.   Prepare financial reports.   Use financial reports to evaluate the firm and make decisions.

Exhibit 14.3   The Accounting System (Attribution: Copyright Rice University, OpenStax, under CC BY 4.0 license.)

Who Uses Financial Reports?

The accounting system generates two types of financial reports, as shown in Exhibit 14.4: internal and external. Internal reports are used within the organization. As the term implies, **managerial accounting** provides financial information that managers inside the organization can use to evaluate and make decisions about current and future operations. For instance, the sales reports prepared by managerial accountants show how well marketing strategies are working, as well as the number of units sold in a specific period of time. This information can be used by a variety of managers within the company in operations as well as in production or manufacturing to plan future work based on current financial data. Production cost reports can help departments track and control costs, as well as zero in on the amount of labor needed to produce goods or services. In addition, managers may prepare very detailed financial reports for their own use and provide summary reports to top management, providing key executives with a "snapshot" of business operations in a specific timeframe.

Financial accounting focuses on preparing external financial reports that are used by outsiders; that is, people who have an interest in the business but are not part of the company's management. Although they provide useful information for managers, these reports are used primarily by lenders, suppliers, investors, government agencies, and others to assess the financial strength of a business.

To ensure accuracy and consistency in the way financial information is reported, accountants in the United States follow **generally accepted accounting principles (GAAP)** when preparing financial statements. The **Financial Accounting Standards Board (FASB)** is a private organization that is responsible for establishing financial accounting standards used in the United States.

Currently there are no international accounting standards. Because accounting practices vary from country to country, a multinational company must make sure that its financial statements conform to both its own country's accounting standards and those of the parent company's country. Often another country's standards are quite different from U.S. GAAP. In the past, the U.S. Financial Accounting Standards Board and the International Accounting Standards Board (IASB) worked together to develop global accounting standards that would make it easier to compare financial statements of foreign-based companies. However, as of this writing, the two organizations have not agreed on a global set of accounting standards.

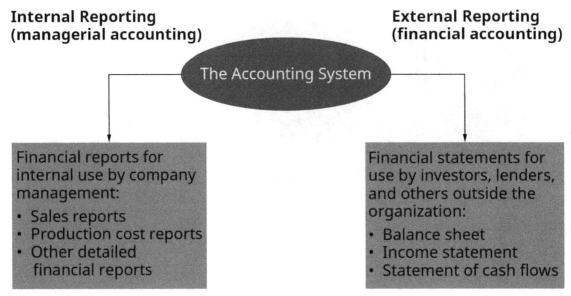

Exhibit 14.4   Reports Provided by the Accounting System (Attribution: Copyright Rice University, OpenStax, under CC BY 4.0 license.)

EXPANDING AROUND THE GLOBE

Global Accounting Standards Unlikely to Happen

Imagine being a CFO of a major multinational company with significant operations in 10 other countries. Because the accounting rules in those countries don't conform to GAAP, your staff has to prepare nine sets of financial reports that comply with the host country's rules—and also translate the figures to GAAP for consolidation into the parent company's statements in the United States. It's a massive undertaking for anyone.

The U.S. FASB and the IASB have tried to make this task easier, but progress has been slow. These groups hoped to develop international accounting standards that remove disparities between national and international standards, improve the quality of financial information worldwide, and simplify comparisons of financial statements across borders for both corporations and investors. Unfortunately, it looks like this goal of convergence is slipping away.

More than a decade ago, the FASB and the IASB jointly published a memorandum of understanding (MOU) reaffirming the two organizations' desire to create uniform global accounting standards. "This document underscores our strong commitment to continue to work together with the IASB to bring about a common set of accounting standards that will enhance the quality, comparability, and consistency of global financial reporting, enabling the world's capital markets to operate more effectively," said Robert Herz, FASB's former chairman. Sir David Tweedie, then chairman of the IASB, agreed: "The pragmatic approach described in the MOU enables us to provide much-needed stability for companies using IFRS [the IASB's International Financial Reporting Standards] in the near term," he commented. (About 150 countries worldwide currently use IFRS.)

As they worked toward convergence, the board members decided to develop a new set of common standards rather than try to reconcile the two standards. These new standards had to be better than existing ones, not simply eliminate differences. Unfortunately, merging GAAP and IFRS into a consistent set of international accounting standards has proven to be very difficult because of different approaches used in the two sets. For example, because of frequent litigation surrounding financial information in the United States, preparers of financial statements demand very detailed rules in all areas of accounting, in contrast to the IASB's approach of setting accounting principles and leaving preparers to apply them to individual situations they encounter. In addition, many companies doing business in the United States fear that moving toward global accounting standards would be very costly and time-consuming in terms of changing accounting software, employee and vendor training, and other business-related practices.

For now, the two organizations agree to disagree on when and if they can "converge" GAAP and IFRS into a global set of standards. However, they continue to keep each other informed about upcoming changes in standards that may impact accounting practices worldwide.

Critical Thinking Questions
1. Is it important to have a single set of international accounting standards for at least publicly owned companies? Defend your answer.
2. Do you think the two organizations will ever come close to uniform global accounting standards? Use a search engine and the archives of *CFO* magazine, **http://www.cfo.com**, to research this topic, and summarize your findings.

Sources: "Who Uses IFRS Standards?" http://www.ifrs.org, accessed August 10, 2017; "FASB and IASB Reaffirm Commitment to Enhance Consistency, Comparability and Efficiency in Global Capital Markets," (press release), http://www.fasb.org, accessed August 10, 2017; Ken Tysiac, "Will Brexit, Trump Affect Global Accounting Standards?" http://www.journalofaccountancy.com, December 6, 2016; Bruce Cowie, "Insights: IFRS/US GAAP Convergence and Global Accounting Standards—Where Are We Now?" https://kaplan.co.uk, September 26, 2016; Michael Cohn, "IASB and FASB Look Beyond Convergence," https://www.accountingtoday.com, December 9, 2014; David M. Katz, "The Split over Convergence," *CFO*, http://ww2.cfo.com, October 17, 2014.

Financial statements are the chief element of the **annual report**, a yearly document that describes a firm's financial status. Annual reports usually discuss the firm's activities during the past year and its prospects for the future. Three primary financial statements included in the annual report are discussed and shown later in this chapter:

- The balance sheet
- The income statement
- The statement of cash flows

CONCEPT CHECK

1. Explain who uses financial information.
2. Differentiate between financial accounting and managerial accounting.
3. How do GAAP, the FASB, and the IASB influence the accounting industry?

14.2 | The Accounting Profession

2. What are the differences between public and private accountants, and how has federal legislation affected their work?

When you think of accountants, do you picture someone who works in a back room, hunched over a desk, wearing a green eye shade and scrutinizing pages and pages of numbers? Although today's accountants still must love working with numbers, they now work closely with their clients to not only prepare financial reports but also help them develop good financial practices. Advances in technology have taken the tedium out of the number-crunching and data-gathering parts of the job and now offer powerful analytical tools as well. Therefore, accountants must keep up with information technology trends. The accounting profession has grown due to the increased complexity, size, and number of businesses and the frequent changes in the tax laws. Accounting is now a $95 billion-plus industry. The more than 1.4 million accountants in the United States are classified as either public accountants or private (corporate) accountants. They work in public accounting firms, private industry, education, and government, and about 10 percent are self-employed. The job outlook for accountants over the next decade is positive; the Bureau of Labor Statistics projects that accounting and auditing jobs will increase 11 percent faster than many other industries in the U.S. economy.[2]

Public Accountants

Independent accountants who serve organizations and individuals on a fee basis are called **public accountants**. Public accountants offer a wide range of services, including preparation of financial statements and tax returns, independent auditing of financial records and accounting methods, and management consulting. **Auditing**, the process of reviewing the records used to prepare financial statements, is an important responsibility of public accountants. They issue a formal *auditor's opinion* indicating whether the statements have been prepared in accordance with accepted accounting rules. This written opinion is an important part of a company's annual report.

The largest public accounting firms, called the Big Four, operate worldwide and offer a variety of business consulting services in addition to accounting services. In order of size, they are Deloitte, PwC (PricewaterhouseCoopers), EY (Ernst & Young), and KPMG International.[3] A former member of this group, Arthur Andersen, disbanded in 2002 as a result of the Enron scandal.

To become a **certified public accountant (CPA)**, an accountant must complete an approved bachelor's degree program and pass a test prepared by the American Institute of CPAs (AICPA). Each state also has requirements for CPAs, such as several years' on-the-job experience and continuing education. Only CPAs can issue the auditor's opinion on a firm's financial statements. Most CPAs first work for public accounting firms and later may become private accountants or financial managers. Of the more than 418,000 accountants who belong to the AICPA, 47 percent work in public accounting firms and 39 percent in business and industry.[4]

Private Accountants

Accountants employed to serve one particular organization are **private accountants**. Their activities include preparing financial statements, auditing company records to be sure employees follow accounting policies and procedures, developing accounting systems, preparing tax returns, and providing financial information for management decision-making. Whereas some private accountants hold the CPA designation, managerial accountants also have a professional certification program. Requirements to become a **certified**

management accountant (CMA) include passing an examination.

Reshaping the Accounting Environment

Although our attention was focused on big-name accounting scandals in the late 1990s and early 2000s, an epidemic of accounting irregularities was also taking place in the wider corporate arena. The number of companies restating annual financial statements grew at an alarming rate, tripling from 1997 to 2002. In the wake of the numerous corporate financial scandals, Congress and the accounting profession took major steps to prevent future accounting irregularities. These measures targeted the basic ways, cited by a report from the AICPA, that companies massaged financial reports through creative, aggressive, or inappropriate accounting techniques, including:

- Committing fraudulent financial reporting
- Stretching accounting rules to significantly enhance financial results
- Following appropriate accounting rules but using loopholes to manage financial results

Why did companies willfully push accounting to the edge—and over it—to artificially pump up revenues and profits? Looking at the companies involved in the scandals, some basic similarities have emerged:

- A company culture of arrogance and above-average tolerance for risk
- Interpretation of accounting policies to their advantage and manipulation of the rules to get to a predetermined result and conceal negative financial information
- Compensation packages tied to financial or operating targets, making executives and managers greedy and pressuring them to find sometimes-questionable ways to meet what may have been overly optimistic goals
- Ineffective checks and balances, such as audit committees, boards of directors, and financial control procedures, that were not independent from management
- Centralized financial reporting that was tightly controlled by top management, increasing the opportunity for fraud
- Financial performance benchmarks that were often out of line with the companies' industry
- Complicated business structures that clouded how the company made its profits
- Cash flow from operations that seemed out of line with reported earnings (You'll learn about this important difference between cash and reported earnings in the sections on the income statement and statement of cash flows.)
- Acquisitions made quickly, often to show growth rather than for sound business reasons; management focused more on buying new companies than making the existing operations more profitable[5]

Companies focused on making themselves look good in the short term, doing whatever was necessary to top past performance and to meet the expectations of investment analysts, who project earnings, and investors, who panic when a company misses the analysts' forecasts. Executives who benefited when stock prices rose had no incentive to question the earnings increases that led to the price gains.

These number games raised serious concerns about the quality of earnings and questions about the validity of financial reports. Investors discovered to their dismay that they could neither assume that auditors were adequately monitoring their clients' accounting methods nor depend on the integrity of published financial information.

Better Numbers Ahead

Over the past 15 years, a number of accounting reforms have been put in place to set better standards for accounting, auditing, and financial reporting. Investors, now aware of the possibility of various accounting shenanigans, are avoiding companies that use complicated financial structures and off-the-books financing.

In 2002, the **Sarbanes-Oxley Act** (commonly referred to as SOX) went into effect. This law, one of the most extensive pieces of business legislation passed by Congress, was designed to address the investing public's lack of trust in corporate America. It redefines the public corporation–auditor relationship and restricts the types of services auditors can provide to clients. The Act clarifies auditor-independence issues, places increased accountability on a company's senior executives and management, strengthens disclosure of insider transactions (an employee selling stock based on information not known by the public), and prohibits loans to executives.

An independent five-member Public Company Accounting Oversight Board (PCAOB) was given the authority to set and amend auditing, quality control, ethics, independence, and other standards for audit reports. The Act specifies that all PCAOB members be financially literate. Two members must have their CPA designation, and the other three cannot be or have been CPAs. Appointed and overseen by the Securities and Exchange Commission (SEC), the PCAOB can also inspect accounting firms; investigate breaches of securities law, standards, competency, and conduct; and take disciplinary action. The corporate Board registers public accounting firms, as the Act now requires. Altering or destroying key audit documents now carries felony charges and increased penalties.

Other key provisions of the Act cover the following areas:

- *Auditing standards:* The Board must include in its standards several requirements, such as maintaining audit work papers and other documentation for audit reports for seven years, the review and approval of audit reports by a second partner, and audit standards for quality control and review of internal control procedures.
- *Financial disclosure:* Companies must clearly disclose all transactions that may have a material current or future effect on their financial condition, including those that are off the books or with unconsolidated entities (related companies whose results the company is not required to combine with its own financial statements under current accounting rules). Management and major stockholders must disclose transactions such as sales of company stock within two days of the transaction. The company must disclose its code of ethics for senior financial executives. Any significant changes in a company's operations or financial condition must be disclosed "on a rapid and current basis."
- *Financial statement certification:* Chief executive officers and chief financial officers must certify company financial statements, with severe criminal and civil penalties for false certification. If securities fraud results in restatement of financial reports, these executives will lose any stock-related profits and bonuses they received prior to the restatement.
- *Internal controls:* Each company must have appropriate internal control procedures in place for financial reporting, and its annual report must include a report on implementation of those controls to assure the integrity of financial reports.
- *Consulting work:* The Act restricts the non-auditing work auditors may perform for a client. In the past, the large accounting firms had expanded their role to include a wide range of advisory services that went beyond their traditional task of validating a company's financial information. Conflicts of interest arose when the same firm earned lucrative fees for both audit and consulting work for the same client.[6]

Other regulatory organizations also took steps to prevent future abuses. In September 2002, the AICPA Auditing Standards Board (ASB) issued expanded guidelines to help auditors uncover fraud while conducting audits. The New York Stock Exchange stiffened its listing requirements so that the majority of directors at listed companies must be independent and not employees of the corporation. Nor can auditors serve on clients' boards for five years. Companies listed in the Nasdaq marketplace cannot hire former auditors at any level for three years.

In response to the passage of Sarbanes-Oxley and other regulations, companies implemented new control measures and improved existing ones. The burdens in both cost and time have been considerable. Many companies had to redesign and restructure financial systems to improve efficiency. Some finance executives believe that their investment in increased controls has improved shareholder perceptions of their company's ethics. Others, however, reported that costs depressed earnings and negatively affected stock prices. Despite the changes and costs associated with SOX compliance, 15 years after the law's implementation, many business executives believe that the process has helped them fine-tune financial activities and reporting while addressing dynamic changes in the market and other economic challenges.[7]

CONCEPT CHECK

1. Compare the responsibilities of public and private accountants. How are they certified?
2. Summarize the major changes affecting accounting and corporate reporting and the reasons for them.

14.3   Basic Accounting Procedures

3. What are the six steps in the accounting cycle?

Using generally accepted accounting principles, accountants record and report financial data in similar ways for all firms. They report their findings in financial statements that summarize a company's business transactions over a specified time period. As mentioned earlier, the three major financial statements are the balance sheet, income statement, and statement of cash flows.

People sometimes confuse accounting with bookkeeping. Accounting is a much broader concept. *Bookkeeping,* the system used to record a firm's financial transactions, is a routine, clerical process. Accountants take bookkeepers' transactions, classify and summarize the financial information, and then prepare and analyze financial reports. Accountants also develop and manage financial systems and help plan the firm's financial strategy.

The Accounting Equation

The accounting procedures used today are based on those developed in the late 15th century by an Italian monk, Brother Luca Pacioli. He defined the three main accounting elements as assets, liabilities, and owners' equity. **Assets** are things of value owned by a firm. They may be *tangible,* such as cash, equipment, and buildings, or *intangible,* such as a patent or trademarked name. **Liabilities**—also called *debts*—are what a firm owes to its creditors. **Owners' equity** is the total amount of investment in the firm minus any liabilities. Another term for owners' equity is *net worth.*

The relationship among these three elements is expressed in the accounting equation:

$$\text{Assets} - \text{Liabilities} = \text{Owners' equity}$$

The accounting equation must always be in balance (that is, the total of the elements on one side of the equals sign must equal the total on the other side).

Suppose you start a coffee shop and put $10,000 in cash into the business. At that point, the business has assets of $10,000 and no liabilities. This would be the accounting equation:

$$
\begin{array}{ccccc}
\text{Assets} & = & \text{Liabilities} & + & \text{Owners' equity} \\
\$10,000 & = & \$0 & + & \$10,000
\end{array}
$$

The liabilities are zero and owners' equity (the amount of your investment in the business) is $10,000. The equation balances.

To keep the accounting equation in balance, every transaction must be recorded as two entries. As each transaction is recorded, there is an equal and opposite event so that two accounts or records are changed. This method is called **double-entry bookkeeping**.

Suppose that after starting your business with $10,000 cash, you borrow another $10,000 from the bank. The accounting equation will change as follows:

$$
\begin{array}{cccccl}
\text{Assets} & = & \text{Liabilities} & + & \text{Owners' equity} & \\
\$10,000 & = & \$0 & + & \$10,000 & \text{Initial equation} \\
\$10,000 & = & \$10,000 & + & \$0 & \text{Borrowing transaction} \\
\$20,000 & = & \$10,000 & + & \$10,000 & \text{Equation after borrowing}
\end{array}
$$

Now you have $20,000 in assets—your $10,000 in cash and the $10,000 loan proceeds from the bank. The bank loan is also recorded as a liability of $10,000 because it's a debt you must repay. Making two entries keeps the equation in balance.

The Accounting Cycle

The *accounting cycle* refers to the process of generating financial statements, beginning with a business transaction and ending with the preparation of the report. Exhibit 14.5 shows the six steps in the accounting cycle. The first step in the cycle is to analyze the data collected from many sources. All transactions that have a financial impact on the firm—sales, payments to employees and suppliers, interest and tax payments, purchases of inventory, and the like—must be documented. The accountant must review the documents to make sure they're complete.

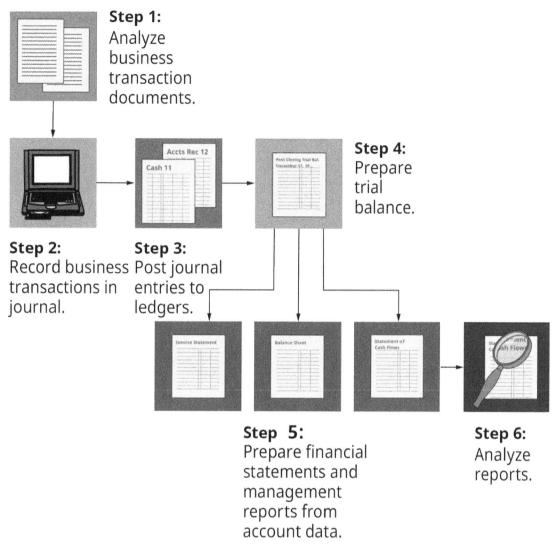

Exhibit 14.5   The Accounting Cycle (Attribution: Copyright Rice University, OpenStax, under CC BY 4.0 license.)

Next, each transaction is recorded in a *journal,* a listing of financial transactions in chronological order. The journal entries are then recorded in *ledgers,* which show increases and decreases in specific asset, liability, and owners' equity accounts. The ledger totals for each account are summarized in a *trial balance,* which is used to confirm the accuracy of the figures. These values are used to prepare financial statements and management reports. Finally, individuals analyze these reports and make decisions based on the information in them.

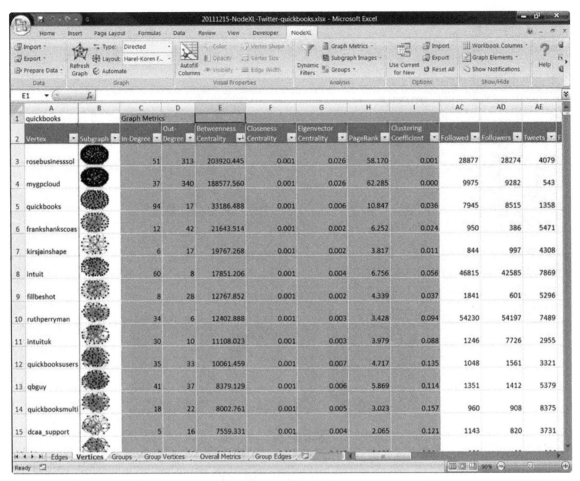

Exhibit 14.6   QuickBooks is a well-known software developer that provides business-management solutions to businesses of different sizes. The company's accounting software tools benefit professionals by automating a broad range of accounting and other business tasks. QuickBooks has become standard in the accounting and business fields, assisting in managerial decision-making and streamlining bookkeeping and accounting processes. *What accounting functions are typically incorporated into basic accounting software programs?* (Credit: Marc Smith/ Flickr/ Attribution 2.0 Generic (CC BY 2.0))

Technological Advances

Over the past decade, technology has had a significant impact on the accounting industry. Computerized and online accounting programs now do many different things to make business operations and financial reporting more efficient. For example, most accounting packages offer basic modules that handle general ledger, sales order, accounts receivable, purchase order, accounts payable, and inventory control functions. Tax programs use accounting data to prepare tax returns and tax plans. Point-of-sale terminals used by many retail firms automatically record sales and do some of the bookkeeping. The Big Four and many other large public accounting firms develop accounting software for themselves and for clients.

Accounting and financial applications typically represent one of the largest portions of a company's software budget. Accounting software ranges from off-the-shelf programs for small businesses to full-scale customized enterprise resource planning systems for major corporations. Although these technological advances in accounting applications have made the financial aspects of running a small business much easier, entrepreneurs and other small-business owners should take to time to understand underlying accounting principles, which play an important role in evaluating just how financially sound a business enterprise really is.

MANAGING CHANGE

Data Analytics Become Effective CPA Tool

Knowledge is power, and understanding what your customers want and how your company can provide it often differentiates you from the competition. As the accounting field continues to take advantage of technological advances, it is important that data analytics become a key element of any accounting professional's toolbox.

Historically described as "paper pushers" who track financial information, today's accountants need to learn about big data and data analytics as part of their continuing education. Not long ago, an accountant's work finished when business financial statements were finalized and tax forms were ready to be filed with federal, state, and local governing bodies. Not anymore. With the revolution of computer technology, automation, and data collection from a myriad of sources, accountants can use data analytics to provide a clearer picture of the overall business environment for their companies and clients on an ongoing basis.

Data analytics can be defined as the process of examining numerous data sets (sometimes called big data) to draw conclusions about the information they contain, with the assistance of specialized systems and software. Using data analytics effectively can help businesses increase revenue, expand operations, maximize customer service, and more. Accountants can use data analytics to make more accurate and detailed forecasts; help companies link diverse financial and nonfinancial data sets, which provides a more comprehensive reporting of their overall performance to shareholders and others; assess and manage risk across the entire organization; and identify possible fraud.

Data analytics can also improve and enhance the auditing process because more information will now be collected, which allows for analysis of *full* data sets in situations where only samples were audited previously. In addition, continuous monitoring will be easier to accomplish using data sets that are comprehensive.

Accounting professionals who can adapt to quickly changing technology such as data analytics will not only expand the scope of their expertise but also provide financial guidance that will give their companies and clients a strong strategic advantage over competitors.

Critical Thinking Questions

1. How can accountants use data analytics to enhance the services they provide to their clients?
2. Is the seismic shift in technology a good thing for professional accountants? Explain your reasoning.

Sources: "Data Analytics," http://searchdatamanagement.techtarget.com, accessed August 11, 2017; Jiali Tang and Khondkar E. Karim, "Big Data in Business Analytics: Implications for the Audit Profession," *The CPA Journal,* http://www.cpajournal.com, June 2017 issue; Clarence Goh, "Are You Ready? Data Analytics Is Reshaping the Work of Accountants," https://www.cfoinnovation.com, February 28, 2017; Norbert Tschakert, Julia Kokina, Stephen Kozlowski, and Miklos Vasarhelyi, "The Next Frontier in Data Analytics," *Journal of Accountancy,* http://www.journalofaccountancy.com, August 1, 2016.

CONCEPT CHECK

1. Explain the accounting equation.
2. Describe the six-step accounting cycle.
3. What role do computers and other technology play in accounting?

14.4 The Balance Sheet

4. In what terms does the balance sheet describe the financial condition of an organization?

The **balance sheet**, one of three financial statements generated from the accounting system, summarizes a firm's financial position at a specific point in time. It reports the resources of a company (assets), the company's obligations (liabilities), and the difference between what is owned (assets) and what is owed (liabilities), or owners' equity.

The assets are listed in order of their **liquidity**, the speed with which they can be converted to cash. The most liquid assets come first, and the least liquid are last. Because cash is the most liquid asset, it is listed first. Buildings, on the other hand, have to be sold to be converted to cash, so they are listed after cash. Liabilities are arranged similarly: liabilities due in the short term are listed before those due in the long term.

The balance sheet as of December 31, 2018, for Delicious Desserts, Inc., a fictitious bakery, is illustrated in Table 14.1. The basic accounting equation is reflected in the three totals highlighted on the balance sheet: assets of $148,900 equal the sum of liabilities and owners' equity ($70,150 + $78,750). The three main categories of accounts on the balance sheet are explained below.

Balance Sheet for Delicious Desserts		
Delicious Desserts, Inc.		
Balance Sheet as of December 31, 2018		
Assets		
Current assets:		$15,000
Cash		4,500
Marketable securities		
Accounts receivable	$45,000	
Less: Allowance for doubtful accounts	1,300	43,700
Notes receivable		5,000
Inventory		15,000
Total current assets		83,200

Table 14.1

Balance Sheet for Delicious Desserts		
Delicious Desserts, Inc.		
Balance Sheet as of December 31, 2018		

Fixed assets:			
Bakery equipment	$56,000		
Less: Accumulated depreciation	16,000	$40,000	
Furniture and fixtures	$18,450		
Less: Accumulated depreciation	4,250	14,200	
Total fixed assets			54,200
Intangible assets:			
Trademark			
Goodwill		$ 4,500	
		7,000	
Total intangible assets			11,500
Total assets			$148,900

Liabilities and owners' equity

Current liabilities:			
Accounts payable	$30,650		
Notes payable	15,000		
Accrued expenses	4,500		
Income taxes payable	5,000		
Current portion of long-term debt	5,000		
Total current liabilities		$60,150	
Long-term liabilities:			
Bank loan for bakery equipment	$10,000		
Total long-term liabilities		10,000	
Total liabilities			$ 70,150
Owners' equity:			
Common stock		$30,000	
(10,000 shares outstanding)			
Retained earnings		48,750	
Total owners' equity			78,750
Total liabilities and owners' equity			$148,900

Table 14.1

Assets

Assets can be divided into three broad categories: current assets, fixed assets, and intangible assets. **Current assets** are assets that can or will be converted to cash within the next 12 months. They are important because they provide the funds used to pay the firm's current bills. They also represent the amount of money the firm can quickly raise. Current assets include:

- *Cash:* Funds on hand or in a bank
- *Marketable securities:* Temporary investments of excess cash that can readily be converted to cash
- *Accounts receivable:* Amounts owed to the firm by customers who bought goods or services on credit
- *Notes receivable:* Amounts owed to the firm by customers or others to whom it lent money
- *Inventory:* Stock of goods being held for production or for sale to customers

Fixed assets are long-term assets used by the firm for more than a year. They tend to be used in production and include land, buildings, machinery, equipment, furniture, and fixtures. Except for land, fixed assets wear out and become outdated over time. Thus, they decrease in value every year. This declining value is accounted for through depreciation. **Depreciation** is the allocation of the asset's original cost to the years in which it is expected to produce revenues. A portion of the cost of a depreciable asset—a building or piece of equipment, for instance—is charged to each of the years in which it is expected to provide benefits. This practice helps match the asset's cost against the revenues it provides. Because it is impossible to know exactly how long an asset will last, estimates are used. They are based on past experience with similar items or IRS guidelines for assets of that type. Notice that, through 2018, Delicious Desserts has taken a total of $16,000 in depreciation on its bakery equipment.

Intangible assets are long-term assets with no physical existence. Common examples are patents, copyrights, trademarks, and goodwill. *Patents* and *copyrights* shield the firm from direct competition, so their benefits are more protective than productive. For instance, no one can use more than a small amount of copyrighted material without permission from the copyright holder. *Trademarks* are registered names that can be sold or licensed to others. One of Delicious Desserts' intangible assets is a trademark valued at $4,500. *Goodwill* occurs when a company pays more for an acquired firm than the value of its tangible assets. Delicious Desserts' other tangible asset is goodwill of $7,000.

Liabilities

Liabilities are the amounts a firm owes to creditors. Those liabilities coming due sooner—current liabilities—are listed first on the balance sheet, followed by long-term liabilities.

Current liabilities are those due within a year of the date of the balance sheet. These short-term claims may strain the firm's current assets because they must be paid in the near future. Current liabilities include:

- *Accounts payable:* Amounts the firm owes for credit purchases due within a year. This account is the liability counterpart of accounts receivable.
- *Notes payable:* Short-term loans from banks, suppliers, or others that must be repaid within a year. For example, Delicious Desserts has a six-month, $15,000 loan from its bank that is a note payable.
- *Accrued expenses:* Expenses, typically for wages and taxes, that have accumulated and must be paid at a specified future date within the year although the firm has not received a bill
- *Income taxes payable:* Taxes owed for the current operating period but not yet paid. Taxes are often shown separately when they are a large amount.
- *Current portion of long-term debt:* Any repayment on long-term debt due within the year. Delicious Desserts is scheduled to repay $5,000 on its equipment loan in the coming year.

Long-term liabilities come due more than one year after the date of the balance sheet. They include bank loans (such as Delicious Desserts' $10,000 loan for bakery equipment), mortgages on buildings, and the company's bonds sold to others.

Owners' Equity

Owners' equity is the owners' total investment in the business after all liabilities have been paid. For sole proprietorships and partnerships, amounts put in by the owners are recorded as capital. In a corporation, the owners provide capital by buying the firm's common stock. For Delicious Desserts, the total common stock investment is $30,000. **Retained earnings** are the amounts left over from profitable operations since the firm's beginning. They are total profits minus all dividends (distributions of profits) paid to stockholders. Delicious Desserts has $48,750 in retained earnings.

CONCEPT CHECK

1. What is a balance sheet?
2. What are the three main categories of accounts on the balance sheet, and how do they relate to the accounting equation?
3. How do retained earnings relate to owners' equity?

14.5 The Income Statement

5. How does the income statement report a firm's profitability?

The balance sheet shows the firm's financial position at a certain point in time. The **income statement** summarizes the firm's revenues and expenses and shows its total profit or loss over a period of time. Most companies prepare monthly income statements for management and quarterly and annual statements for use by investors, creditors, and other outsiders. The primary elements of the income statement are revenues, expenses, and net income (or net loss). The income statement for Delicious Desserts for the year ended December 31, 2018, is shown in **Table 14.2**.

Income Statement for Delicious Desserts	
Delicious Desserts, Inc.	
Income Statement for the Year Ending December 31, 2018	
Revenues	
Gross sales	$275,000
Less: Sales discounts	2,500
Less: Returns and allowances	2,000
Net sales	$270,500
Cost of Goods Sold	

Table 14.2

Income Statement for Delicious Desserts			
Delicious Desserts, Inc.			
Income Statement for the Year Ending December 31, 2018			
Beginning inventory, January 1		$ 18,000	
Cost of goods manufactured		109,500	
Total cost of goods available for sale		$127,500	
Less: Ending inventory December 31		15,000	
Cost of goods sold			112,500
Gross profit			**$158,000**
Operating Expenses			
Selling expenses			
Sales salaries	$31,000		
Advertising	16,000		
Other selling expenses	18,000		
Total selling expenses		$ 65,000	
General and administrative expenses			
Professional and office salaries	$20,500		
Utilities	5,000		
Office supplies	1,500		
Interest	3,600		
Insurance	2,500		
Rent	17,000		
Total general and administrative expenses		50,100	
Total operating expenses			115,100
Net profit before taxes			**$ 42,900**
Less: Income taxes			10,725
Net profit			**$ 32,175**

Table 14.2

Revenues

Revenues are the dollar amount of sales plus any other income received from sources such as interest, dividends, and rents. The revenues of Delicious Desserts arise from sales of its bakery products. Revenues are determined starting with **gross sales**, the total dollar amount of a company's sales. Delicious Desserts had two deductions from gross sales. *Sales discounts* are price reductions given to customers that pay their bills early. For example, Delicious Desserts gives sales discounts to restaurants that buy in bulk and pay at delivery. *Returns and allowances* is the dollar amount of merchandise returned by customers because they didn't like a product or because it was damaged or defective. **Net sales** is the amount left after deducting sales discounts and returns and allowances from gross sales. Delicious Desserts' gross sales were reduced by $4,500, leaving net sales of $270,500.

Expenses

Expenses are the costs of generating revenues. Two types are recorded on the income statement: cost of goods sold and operating expenses.

The **cost of goods sold** is the total expense of buying or producing the firm's goods or services. For manufacturers, cost of goods sold includes all costs directly related to production: purchases of raw materials and parts, labor, and factory overhead (utilities, factory maintenance, machinery repair). For wholesalers and retailers, it is the cost of goods bought for resale. For all sellers, cost of goods sold includes all the expenses of preparing the goods for sale, such as shipping and packaging.

Delicious Desserts' cost of goods sold is based on the value of inventory on hand at the beginning of the accounting period, $18,000. During the year, the company spent $109,500 to produce its baked goods. This figure includes the cost of raw materials, labor costs for bakery workers, and the cost of operating the bakery area. Adding the cost of goods manufactured to the value of beginning inventory, we get the total cost of goods available for sale, $127,500. To determine the cost of goods sold for the year, we subtract the cost of inventory at the end of the period:

$$\$127,500 - \$15,000 = \$112,500$$

The amount a company earns after paying to produce or buy its products but before deducting operating expenses is the **gross profit**. It is the difference between net sales and cost of goods sold. Because service firms do not produce goods, their gross profit equals net sales. Gross profit is a critical number for a company because it is the source of funds to cover all the firm's other expenses.

The other major expense category is **operating expenses**. These are the expenses of running the business that are not related directly to producing or buying its products. The two main types of operating expenses are selling expenses and general and administrative expenses. *Selling expenses* are those related to marketing and distributing the company's products. They include salaries and commissions paid to salespeople and the costs of advertising, sales supplies, delivery, and other items that can be linked to sales activity, such as insurance, telephone and other utilities, and postage. *General and administrative expenses* are the business expenses that cannot be linked to either cost of goods sold or sales. Examples of general and administrative expenses are salaries of top managers and office support staff; utilities; office supplies; interest expense; fees for accounting, consulting, and legal services; insurance; and rent. Delicious Desserts' operating expenses totaled $115,100.

Net Profit or Loss

The final figure—or bottom line—on an income statement is the **net profit** (or **net income**) or **net loss**. It is calculated by subtracting all expenses from revenues. If revenues are more than expenses, the result is a net profit. If expenses exceed revenues, a net loss results.

Several steps are involved in finding net profit or loss. (These are shown in the right-hand column of Table 14.2.) First, cost of goods sold is deducted from net sales to get the gross profit. Then total operating expenses are subtracted from gross profit to get the net profit before taxes. Finally, income taxes are deducted to get the net profit. As shown in Table 14.2, Delicious Desserts earned a net profit of $32,175 in 2018.

It is very important to recognize that profit does not represent cash. The income statement is a summary of the firm's operating results during some time period. It does not present the firm's actual cash flows during the period. Those are summarized in the statement of cash flows, which is discussed briefly in the next section.

CONCEPT CHECK

1. What is an income statement? How does it differ from the balance sheet?
2. Describe the key parts of the income statement. Distinguish between gross sales and net sales.
3. How is net profit or loss calculated?

14.6 The Statement of Cash Flows

6. Why is the statement of cash flows an important source of information?

Net profit or loss is one measure of a company's financial performance. However, creditors and investors are also keenly interested in how much cash a business generates and how it is used. The **statement of cash flows**, a summary of the money flowing into and out of a firm, is the financial statement used to assess the sources and uses of cash during a certain period, typically one year. All publicly traded firms must include a statement of cash flows in their financial reports to shareholders. The statement of cash flows tracks the firm's cash receipts and cash payments. It gives financial managers and analysts a way to identify cash flow problems and assess the firm's financial viability.

Exhibit 14.7 Coinstar is a cash cow—literally. The company established a niche counting loose change at the exits of supermarkets and other retailers everywhere. For a small fee, Coinstar's coin-counting machines turn penny jars and piggy banks into cash vouchers, a no-fee eGift card, or a charity donation. Recently Coinstar's parent company, Outerwall, was acquired by a private equity firm in a $1.6 billion deal to take the holding company private. *What does the statement of cash flows indicate about a company's financial status?* (Credit: Mike Mozart/ Flickr/ Attribution 2.0 Generic (CC BY 2.0))

Using income statement and balance sheet data, the statement of cash flows divides the firm's cash flows into three groups:

- *Cash flow from operating activities:* Those related to the production of the firm's goods or services
- *Cash flow from investment activities:* Those related to the purchase and sale of fixed assets
- *Cash flow from financing activities:* Those related to debt and equity financing

Delicious Desserts' statement of cash flows for 2018 is presented in Table 14.3. It shows that the company's cash and marketable securities have increased over the last year. And during the year the company generated enough cash flow to increase inventory and fixed assets and to reduce accounts payable, accruals, notes payable, and long-term debt.

Statement of Cash Flows for Delicious Desserts		
Delicious Desserts, Inc. Statement of Cash Flows for 2018		
Cash Flow from Operating Activities		
Net profit after taxes	$27,175	
Depreciation	1,500	
Decrease in accounts receivable	3,140	
Increase in inventory	(4,500)	
Decrease in accounts payable	(2,065)	
Decrease in accruals	(1,035)	
Cash provided by operating activities		$24,215
Cash Flow from Investment Activities		
Increase in gross fixed assets	($ 5,000)	
Cash used in investment activities		($5,000)
Cash Flow from Financing Activities		
Decrease in notes payable	($ 3,000)	
Decrease in long-term debt	(1,000)	
Cash used by financing activities		($4,000)
Net increase in cash and marketable securities		**$15,215**

Table 14.3

CONCEPT CHECK

1. What is the purpose of the statement of cash flows?
2. Why has cash flow become such an important measure of a firm's financial condition?
3. What situations can you cite from the chapter that support your answer?

14.7 Analyzing Financial Statements

7. How can ratio analysis be used to identify a firm's financial strengths and weaknesses?

Individually, the balance sheet, income statement, and statement of cash flows provide insight into the firm's operations, profitability, and overall financial condition. By studying the relationships among the financial statements, however, one can gain even more insight into a firm's financial condition and performance. A good way to think about analyzing financial statements is to compare it a fitness trainer putting clients through various well-established assessments and metrics to determine whether a specialized fitness program is paying dividends for the person in terms of better strength, endurance, and overall health. Financial statements at any given time can provide a snapshot of a company's overall health. Company management must use certain standards and measurements to determine whether they need to implement additional strategies to keep the company fit and making a profit.

Ratio analysis involves calculating and interpreting financial ratios using data taken from the firm's financial statements in order to assess its condition and performance. A financial ratio states the relationship between financial data on a percentage basis. For instance, current assets might be viewed relative to current liabilities or sales relative to assets. The ratios can then be compared over time, typically three to five years. A firm's ratios can also be compared to industry averages or to those of another company in the same industry. Period-to-period and industry ratios provide a meaningful basis for comparison, so that we can answer questions such as, "Is this particular ratio good or bad?"

It's important to remember that ratio analysis is based on historical data and may not indicate future financial performance. Ratio analysis merely highlights potential problems; it does not prove that they exist. However, ratios can help managers monitor the firm's performance from period to period to understand operations better and identify trouble spots.

Ratios are also important to a firm's present and prospective creditors (lenders), who want to see if the firm can repay what it borrows and assess the firm's financial health. Often loan agreements require firms to maintain minimum levels of specific ratios. Both present and prospective shareholders use ratio analysis to look at the company's historical performance and trends over time.

Ratios can be classified by what they measure: liquidity, profitability, activity, and debt. Using Delicious Desserts' 2018 balance sheet and income statement (Table 14.1 and Table 14.2), we can calculate and interpret the key ratios in each group. Table 14.4 summarizes the calculations of these ratios for Delicious Desserts. We'll now discuss how to calculate the ratios and, more important, how to interpret the ratio value.

Liquidity Ratios

Liquidity ratios measure the firm's ability to pay its short-term debts as they come due. These ratios are of special interest to the firm's creditors. The three main measures of liquidity are the current ratio, the acid-test (quick) ratio, and net working capital.

The **current ratio** is the ratio of total current assets to total current liabilities. Traditionally, a current ratio of 2 ($2 of current assets for every $1 of current liabilities) has been considered good. Whether it is sufficient depends on the industry in which the firm operates. Public utilities, which have a very steady cash flow, operate quite well with a current ratio well below 2. A current ratio of 2 might not be adequate for manufacturers and merchandisers that carry high inventories and have lots of receivables. The current ratio for Delicious Desserts for 2018, as shown in Table 14.4, is 1.4. This means little without a basis for comparison. If the analyst found that the industry average for small bakeries was 2.4, Delicious Desserts would appear to have low liquidity.

The **acid-test (quick) ratio** is like the current ratio except that it excludes inventory, which is the least-liquid current asset. The acid-test ratio is used to measure the firm's ability to pay its current liabilities without selling inventory. The name *acid-test* implies that this ratio is a crucial test of the firm's liquidity. An acid-test ratio of at least 1 is preferred. But again, what is an acceptable value varies by industry. The acid-test ratio is a good measure of liquidity when inventory cannot easily be converted to cash (for instance, if it consists of very specialized goods with a limited market). If inventory is liquid, the current ratio is better. Delicious Desserts' acid-test ratio for 2018 is 1.1. Because the bakery's products are perishable, it does not carry large inventories. Thus, the values of its acid-test and current ratios are fairly close. At a manufacturing company, however, inventory typically makes up a large portion of current assets, so the acid-test ratio will be lower than the current ratio.

Ratio Analysis for Delicious Desserts at Year-End 2018			
Ratio	Formula	Calculation	Result
Liquidity Ratios			
Current ratio	$\dfrac{\text{Total current assets}}{\text{Total current liabilities}}$	$\dfrac{\$83{,}200}{\$60{,}150}$	1.4
Acid-test (quick) ratio	$\dfrac{\text{Total current assets–inventory}}{\text{Total current liabilities}}$	$\dfrac{\$83{,}200 - \$15{,}000}{\$60{,}150}$	1.1
Net working capital	Total current assets $-$ Total current liabilities	$\$83{,}200 - \$60{,}150$	$23,050
Profitability Ratios			
Net profit margin	$\dfrac{\text{Net profi}}{\text{Net sales}}$	$\dfrac{\$32{,}175}{\$270{,}500}$	11.9%
Return on equity	$\dfrac{\text{Net profi}}{\text{Total owners' equity}}$	$\dfrac{\$32{,}175}{\$78{,}750}$	40.9%
Earnings per share	$\dfrac{\text{Net profi}}{\text{Number of shares of common stock outstanding}}$	$\dfrac{\$32{,}175}{10{,}000}$	$3.22
Activity Ratio			
Inventory turnover	$\dfrac{\text{Cost of goods sold}}{\text{Average inventory}}$		
	$\dfrac{\text{Cost of goods sold}}{(\text{Beginning inventory} + \text{Ending inventory})/\ 2}$	$\dfrac{\$112{,}500}{(\$18{,}000 + \$15{,}000)/\ 2}$	
		$\dfrac{\$112{,}500}{\$16{,}500}$	6.8 times

Table 14.4

Ratio Analysis for Delicious Desserts at Year-End 2018			
Ratio	Formula	Calculation	Result
Debt Ratio			
Debt-to-equity ratio	$\dfrac{\text{Total liabilities}}{\text{Owners' equity}}$	$\dfrac{\$70,150}{\$78,750}$	89.1%

Table 14.4

Net working capital, though not really a ratio, is often used to measure a firm's overall liquidity. It is calculated by subtracting total current liabilities from total current assets. Delicious Desserts' net working capital for 2018 is $23,050. Comparisons of net working capital over time often help in assessing a firm's liquidity.

Profitability Ratios

To measure profitability, a firm's profits can be related to its sales, equity, or stock value. **Profitability ratios** measure how well the firm is using its resources to generate profit and how efficiently it is being managed. The main profitability ratios are net profit margin, return on equity, and earnings per share.

The ratio of net profit to net sales is the **net profit margin**, also called *return on sales.* It measures the percentage of each sales dollar remaining after all expenses, including taxes, have been deducted. Higher net profit margins are better than lower ones. The net profit margin is often used to measure the firm's earning power. "Good" net profit margins differ quite a bit from industry to industry. A grocery store usually has a very low net profit margin, perhaps below 1 percent, whereas a jewelry store's net profit margin would probably exceed 10 percent. Delicious Desserts' net profit margin for 2018 is 11.9 percent. In other words, Delicious Desserts is earning 11.9 cents on each dollar of sales.

Exhibit 14.8   For giant retailers such as Macy's, the high expense of operating a brick-and-mortar store counters the elevated markup on merchandise, resulting in slim profit margins. Because competition forces marketers to keep prices low, it is often a retailer's cost-cutting strategy, not initial markup or sales volume, that determines whether a business will be profitable. *What expenses other than payroll and the cost of merchandise affect a retailer's net profit margin?* (Credit: Mike Mozart/ Flickr/ Attribution 2.0 Generic (CC BY 2.0))

The ratio of net profit to total owners' equity is called **return on equity (ROE)**. It measures the return that owners receive on their investment in the firm, a major reason for investing in a company's stock. Delicious Desserts has a 40.9 percent ROE for 2018. On the surface, a 40.9 percent ROE seems quite good. But the level of risk in the business and the ROE of other firms in the same industry must also be considered. The higher the risk, the greater the ROE investors look for. A firm's ROE can also be compared to past values to see how the company is performing over time.

Earnings per share (EPS) is the ratio of net profit to the number of shares of common stock outstanding. It measures the number of dollars earned by each share of stock. EPS values are closely watched by investors and are considered an important sign of success. EPS also indicates a firm's ability to pay dividends. Note that EPS is the dollar amount earned by each share, not the actual amount given to stockholders in the form of dividends. Some earnings may be put back into the firm. Delicious Desserts' EPS for 2018 is $3.22.

Activity Ratios

Activity ratios measure how well a firm uses its assets. They reflect the speed with which resources are converted to cash or sales. A frequently used activity ratio is inventory turnover. The **inventory turnover ratio** measures the speed with which inventory moves through the firm and is turned into sales. It is calculated by dividing cost of goods sold by the average inventory. (Average inventory is estimated by adding the beginning and ending inventories for the year and dividing by 2.) Based on its 2018 financial data, Delicious Desserts' inventory, on average, is turned into sales 6.8 times each year, or about once every 54 days (365 days ÷ 6.8). The acceptable turnover ratio depends on the line of business. A grocery store would have a high turnover ratio, maybe 20 times a year, whereas the turnover for a heavy equipment manufacturer might be only three times a year.

Debt Ratios

Debt ratios measure the degree and effect of the firm's use of borrowed funds (debt) to finance its operations. These ratios are especially important to lenders and investors. They want to make sure the firm has a healthy mix of debt and equity. If the firm relies too much on debt, it may have trouble meeting interest payments and repaying loans. The most important debt ratio is the debt-to-equity ratio.

The **debt-to-equity ratio** measures the relationship between the amount of debt financing (borrowing) and the amount of equity financing (owners' funds). It is calculated by dividing total liabilities by owners' equity. In general, the lower the ratio, the better. But it is important to assess the debt-to-equity ratio against both past values and industry averages. Delicious Desserts' ratio for 2018 is 89.1 percent. The ratio indicates that the company has 89 cents of debt for every dollar the owners have provided. A ratio above 100 percent means the firm has more debt than equity. In such a case, the lenders are providing more financing than the owners.

CONCEPT CHECK

1. How can ratio analysis be used to interpret financial statements?
2. Name the main liquidity and profitability ratios, and explain what they indicate.
3. What kinds of information do activity ratios give? Why are debt ratios of concern to lenders and investors?

14.8 | Trends in Accounting

8. What major trends affect the accounting industry today?

The post-SOX business environment has brought many changes to the accounting profession. When the public accounting industry could no longer regulate itself back in the late 1990s and early 2000s, it became subject to formal regulation for the first time. This regulatory environment set higher standards for audit procedures, which actually helped public companies fine-tune their financial reporting procedures, despite the added costs and labor hours needed to comply with SOX. Once again the core auditing business, rather than financial advisory and management consulting services, became the primary focus of public accounting firms. The relationship between accountants and their clients has also changed, and the role of chief audit executive has taken on more visibility in many large organizations. In addition, the FASB has made slow but steady progress in making changes related to GAAP, including a separate decision-making framework for users and preparers of private company financial statements.[8] There are several other important trends that may affect the accounting industry over the next several years, including cloud computing services, automation, and staffing challenges.

Cloud-Based Services

The internet and cloud technology continue to disrupt many industries, including accounting, and clients expect their accountants to be up to speed on how financial data and other accounting information can be entered, accessed, and discussed in a very short period of time. For the most part, gone are the days when accountants and their support staff spend hours manually inputting data that gets "re-hydrated" into standardized accounting and financial statements, and reams of paper generate a company's weekly, monthly, or yearly reports.

According to recent research, cloud-based accounting firms add five times more clients than traditional accounting firms because businesses expect their accountants to be able to use technology to create the company's financial picture in real time, while assisting them in decision-making about where to go next in terms of profitability, sales, expansion, etc. In addition, it is estimated that more than 90 percent of small and medium-sized companies use cloud-based accounting software, which helps them synthesize the information they collect for their many important financial statements. This use of computerized accounting programs offers many opportunities to accountants to shift their focus when it comes to attracting and retaining business clients.[9]

Automation

In addition to cloud-based services, automation will continue to play an important role in the accounting industry, particularly in auditing services, where the manual gathering and inputting of information can be an inefficient and sometimes inaccurate process. Being able to automate this process will help generate complete sets of data that will improve the overall details of the auditing process. In addition, accountants who can use a client's data files from their business operations and import this information into a tax or accounting software package will streamline the overall accounting process and lessen the tedious work of data entry.[10]

Staffing Challenges

As these and other disruptive technologies change the focus of accounting work, the challenge of hiring the right staff to use these new tools intensifies. With accounting processes becoming automated and less time-intensive, some accounting firms are becoming more connected to their clients and increasing their advisory services when it comes to daily business operations. This change in approach will likely have an impact on the type of experienced employees accountants hire in the future. In addition, because most services are now cloud-based and financial data is available rather quickly, businesses are apt to change accounting firms faster than in the past if they are unsatisfied with the services they receive. Accountants have a great opportunity to expand their business portfolios and increase their client list by leveraging technology as part of their overall corporate strategies.[11]

MANAGING CHANGE

Attracting and Retaining Millennial CPAs

Much has been written about millennials, the population segment born between 1980 and 2000. As the older baby boomer generation continues to retire, millennials now make up the largest group in the U.S. labor force. This group will continue to shape the workplace over the next few decades.

Businesses and other organizations cannot ignore this group and their expectations about employment. To be successful, today's accounting firms—whether Big 4 firms or small and mid-sized businesses—need to understand what makes millennials tick, what is important to them, what makes them look for new opportunities both within and outside the organization—and how to retain them.

Global accounting services company PwC recently partnered with several other institutions to conduct a two-year generational study about the attitudes of millennial employees. Key findings suggest that millennials want flexibility in their work lives that leads to an enjoyable work-life balance, appreciation for the work they accomplish, challenges that will help them grow in their careers, and continued support from employers. As a result of this study, PwC made several changes to its own work environment to attract and retain millennial workers, including flexible schedules, relaxed dress codes, greater communication at all levels of the company, and a renewed commitment to transparency within the organization.

PwC is not alone in shifting its organizational culture to address some of the issues millennials say are important factors for them within the work environment. For example, Baker Tilly, another top accounting firm, recognizes that more than half its workforce consists of millennials who have helped shape the company's approach to work. The themes of flexibility and trust permeate the company's culture, which reinforces employees' motivation to be engaged in work that is meaningful, satisfying, and helps them develop as individuals.

Here are some other strategies accounting firms might employ to keep their 30-something employees from jumping ship:

- *Initiate onboarding activities quickly:* Although training accounting professionals takes time, companies should engage and train new employees quickly to immerse them in organizational culture and assign them work they view as meaningful.
- *Assign mentors from the start:* Millennials want to know their work makes a difference, so what better way to get them involved right from the start than to make sure they are connected to mentors who can guide their work and career path.
- *Support a flexible approach to work:* Some millennials are in the prime of their career, and many may also be juggling a family life that requires a lot of their time. Companies need to remember that millennials like being productive, although they may not think a long workday equates to a productive one. The use of cloud-based technology encourages employees to do their work in a productive atmosphere that may not take place in the office.

Recognizing generational traits of millennials not only demonstrates commitment on the part of the company, but also helps keep these employees engaged and involved in their work.

Critical Thinking Questions

1. Do you think a shift in thinking when it comes to managing millennials is a smart strategy? Why or

why not?

2. Will accounting firms be required to rethink their billing strategies to address millennials' insistence on a more flexible approach to work? Explain your reasoning.

Sources: "Workforce of the Future: The Competing Forces Shaping 2030," https://www.pwc.com, accessed August 11, 2017; Hitendra Patil, "The 7 Experiences Millennials Want from Your Firm," http://www.cpatrendlines.com, accessed August 11, 2017; "Millennial Accountants Don't Want a Corner Office with a View," https://www.rogercpareview.com, April 24, 2017; David Isaacs, "Voices: Confessions of a Millennial CPA: The Most Productive Generation," https://www.accountingtoday.com, April 20, 2017; Teri Saylor, "How CPA Firms Are Evolving to Meet Millennials' Desires," http://www.journalofaccountancy.com, March 6, 2017.

CONCEPT CHECK

1. How has the relationship between public accounting firms and their clients changed since SOX became law?
2. Describe how cloud computing and automation are changing the accounting industry.
3. What are some of the challenges encountered by accounting firms when introducing new technologies into their workflow process?

🔑 Key Terms

accounting The process of collecting, recording, classifying, summarizing, reporting, and analyzing financial activities.

acid-test (quick) ratio The ratio of total current assets excluding inventory to total current liabilities; used to measure a firm's liquidity.

activity ratios Ratios that measure how well a firm uses its assets.

annual report A yearly document that describes a firm's financial status and usually discusses the firm's activities during the past year and its prospects for the future.

assets Things of value owned by a firm.

auditing The process of reviewing the records used to prepare financial statements and issuing a formal auditor's opinion indicating whether the statements have been prepared in accordance with accepted accounting rules.

balance sheet A financial statement that summarizes a firm's financial position at a specific point in time.

certified management accountant (CMA) A managerial accountant who has completed a professional certification program, including passing an examination.

certified public accountant (CPA) An accountant who has completed an approved bachelor's degree program, passed a test prepared by the American Institute of CPAs, and met state requirements. Only a CPA can issue an auditor's opinion on a firm's financial statements.

cost of goods sold The total expense of buying or producing a firm's goods or services.

current assets Assets that can or will be converted to cash within the next 12 months.

current liabilities Short-term claims that are due within a year of the date of the balance sheet.

current ratio The ratio of total current assets to total current liabilities; used to measure a firm's liquidity.

debt ratios Ratios that measure the degree and effect of a firm's use of borrowed funds (debt) to finance its operations.

debt-to-equity ratio The ratio of total liabilities to owners' equity; measures the relationship between the amount of debt financing (borrowing) and the amount of equity financing (owner's funds).

depreciation The allocation of an asset's original cost to the years in which it is expected to produce revenues.

double-entry bookkeeping A method of accounting in which each transaction is recorded as two entries so that two accounts or records are changed.

earnings per share (EPS) The ratio of net profit to the number of shares of common stock outstanding; measures the number of dollars earned by each share of stock.

expenses The costs of generating revenues.

financial accounting Accounting that focuses on preparing external financial reports that are used by outsiders such as lenders, suppliers, investors, and government agencies to assess the financial strength of a business.

Financial Accounting Standards Board (FASB) The private organization that is responsible for establishing financial accounting standards in the United States.

fixed assets Long-term assets used by a firm for more than a year such as land, buildings, and machinery.

generally accepted accounting principles (GAAP) The financial accounting standards followed by accountants in the United States when preparing financial statements.

gross profit The amount a company earns after paying to produce or buy its products but before deducting operating expenses.

gross sales The total dollar amount of a company's sales.

income statement A financial statement that summarizes a firm's revenues and expenses and shows its total profit or loss over a period of time.

intangible assets Long-term assets with no physical existence, such as patents, copyrights, trademarks, and goodwill.

inventory turnover ratio The ratio of cost of goods sold to average inventory; measures the speed with which inventory moves through a firm and is turned into sales.

liabilities What a firm owes to its creditors; also called debts.

liquidity The speed with which an asset can be converted to cash.

liquidity ratios Ratios that measure a firm's ability to pay its short-term debts as they come due.

long-term liabilities Claims that come due more than one year after the date of the balance sheet.

managerial accounting Accounting that provides financial information that managers inside the organization can use to evaluate and make decisions about current and future operations.

net loss The amount obtained by subtracting all of a firm's expenses from its revenues, when the expenses are more than the revenues.

net profit (net income) The amount obtained by subtracting all of a firm's expenses from its revenues, when the revenues are more than the expenses.

net profit margin The ratio of net profit to net sales; also called return on sales. It measures the percentage of each sales dollar remaining after all expenses, including taxes, have been deducted.

net sales The amount left after deducting sales discounts and returns and allowances from gross sales.

net working capital The amount obtained by subtracting total current liabilities from total current assets; used to measure a firm's liquidity.

operating expenses The expenses of running a business that are not directly related to producing or buying its products.

owners' equity The total amount of investment in the firm minus any liabilities; also called net worth.

private accountants Accountants who are employed to serve one particular organization.

profitability ratios Ratios that measure how well a firm is using its resources to generate profit and how efficiently it is being managed.

public accountants Independent accountants who serve organizations and individuals on a fee basis.

ratio analysis The calculation and interpretation of financial ratios using data taken from the firm's financial statements in order to assess its condition and performance.

retained earnings The amounts left over from profitable operations since the firm's beginning; equal to total profits minus all dividends paid to stockholders.

return on equity (ROE) The ratio of net profit to total owners' equity; measures the return that owners receive on their investment in the firm.

revenues The dollar amount of a firm's sales plus any other income it received from sources such as interest, dividends, and rents.

Sarbanes-Oxley Act Legislation passed in 2002 that sets new standards for auditor independence, financial disclosure and reporting, and internal controls; establishes an independent oversight board; and restricts the types of non-audit services auditors can provide audit clients.

statement of cash flows A financial statement that provides a summary of the money flowing into and out of a firm during a certain period, typically one year.

🗐 Summary of Learning Outcomes

14.1 Accounting: More than Numbers

1. Why are financial reports and accounting information important, and who uses them?

Accounting involves collecting, recording, classifying, summarizing, reporting, and analyzing a firm's financial activities according to a standard set of procedures. The financial reports resulting from the accounting process give managers, employees, investors, customers, suppliers, creditors, and government agencies a way to analyze a company's past, current, and future performance. Financial accounting is concerned with the preparation of financial reports using generally accepted accounting principles. Managerial accounting provides financial information that management can use to make decisions about the firm's operations.

14.2 The Accounting Profession

2. What are the differences between public and private accountants, and how has federal legislation affected their work?

Public accountants work for independent firms that provide accounting services—such as financial report preparation and auditing, tax return preparation, and management consulting—to other organizations on a fee basis. Private accountants are employed to serve one particular organization and may prepare financial statements, tax returns, and management reports.

The bankruptcies of companies such as Enron and WorldCom, plus widespread abuses of accounting practices, raised critical issues of auditor independence and the integrity and reliability of financial reports. To set better standards for accounting, auditing, and financial reporting and prevent future accounting irregularities, Congress passed the Sarbanes-Oxley Act in 2002. This Act created an independent board to oversee the accounting profession, set stricter auditing and financial disclosure standards, and placed increased accountability on a company's senior executives and management. In addition, the law restricts auditors from providing certain types of consulting services to clients. Other organizations such as the SEC, the New York Stock Exchange, and accounting industry professional associations issued new regulations and guidelines related to compliance with the Act.

14.3 Basic Accounting Procedures

3. What are the six steps in the accounting cycle?

The accounting cycle refers to the process of generating financial statements. It begins with analyzing business transactions, recording them in journals, and posting them to ledgers. Ledger totals are then summarized in a trial balance that confirms the accuracy of the figures. Next the accountant prepares the financial statements and reports. The final step involves analyzing these reports and making decisions. Computers have simplified many of these labor-intensive tasks.

14.4 The Balance Sheet

4. In what terms does the balance sheet describe the financial condition of an organization?

The balance sheet represents the financial condition of a firm at one moment in time, in terms of assets, liabilities, and owners' equity. The key categories of assets are current assets, fixed assets, and intangible assets. Liabilities are divided into current and long-term liabilities. Owners' equity, the amount of the owners' investment in the firm after all liabilities have been paid, is the third major category.

14.5 The Income Statement

5. How does the income statement report a firm's profitability?

The income statement is a summary of the firm's operations over a stated period of time. The main parts of the statement are revenues (gross and net sales), cost of goods sold, operating expenses (selling and general and administrative expenses), taxes, and net profit or loss.

14.6 The Statement of Cash Flows

6. Why is the statement of cash flows an important source of information?

The statement of cash flows summarizes the firm's sources and uses of cash during a financial-reporting period. It breaks the firm's cash flows into those from operating, investment, and financing activities. It shows the net change during the period in the firm's cash and marketable securities.

14.7 Analyzing Financial Statements

7. How can ratio analysis be used to identify a firm's financial strengths and weaknesses?

Ratio analysis is a way to use financial statements to gain insight into a firm's operations, profitability, and overall financial condition. The four main types of ratios are liquidity ratios, profitability ratios, activity ratios, and debt ratios. Comparing a firm's ratios over several years and comparing them to ratios of other firms in the same industry or to industry averages can indicate trends and highlight financial strengths and weaknesses.

14.8 Trends in Accounting

8. What major trends affect the accounting industry today?

The post-SOX business environment has brought many changes to the accounting profession, including higher standards for audit procedures. In addition, the FASB has made slow but steady progress in making changes related to GAAP; however, the implementation of global accounting standards may not occur anytime soon. Several important trends will continue to impact the accounting industry going forward, including cloud-based services, automation, and staffing challenges, as accountants shift the focus of their practice to one incorporating technological advances and a more comprehensive approach to their companies' and clients' overall business environment.

Preparing for Tomorrow's Workplace Skills

1. Your firm has been hired to help several small businesses with their year-end financial statements.
    a. Based on the following account balances, prepare the Marbella Design Enterprises balance sheet as of December 31, 2018:

Cash	$30,250
Accounts payable	28,500
Fixtures and furnishings	85,000
Notes payable	15,000
Retained earnings	64,450
Accounts receivable	24,050
Inventory	15,600
Equipment	42,750
Accumulated depreciation on fixtures and furnishings	12,500
Common shares (50,000 shares at $1)	50,000

Long-term debt	25,000
Accumulated depreciation on equipment	7,800
Marketable securities	13,000
Income taxes payable	7,500

b. The following are the account balances for the revenues and expenses of the Windsor Gift Shop for the year ending December 31, 2018. Prepare the income statement for the shop. (Resources, Information)

Rent	$ 15,000
Salaries	23,500
Cost of goods sold	98,000
Utilities	8,000
Supplies	3,500
Sales	195,000
Advertising	3,600
Interest	3,000
Taxes	12,120

2. During the year ended December 31, 2018, Lawrence Industries sold $2 million worth of merchandise on credit. A total of $1.4 million was collected during the year. The cost of this merchandise was $1.3 million. Of this amount, $1 million has been paid, and $300,000 is not yet due. Operating expenses and income taxes totaling $500,000 were paid in cash during the year. Assume that all accounts had a zero balance at the beginning of the year (January 1, 2018). Write a brief report for the company controller that includes calculation of the firm's (a) net profit and (b) cash flow during the year. Explain why there is a difference between net profit and cash flow. (Information, Systems)

3. A friend has been offered a sales position at Draper Media, Inc., a small publisher of computer-related publications, but wants to know more about the company. Because of your expertise in financial analysis, you offer to help analyze Draper's financial health. Draper has provided the following selected financial information:

Account balances on December 31, 2018:

Inventory	$ 72,000

Net sales	450,000
Current assets	150,000
Cost of goods sold	290,000
Total liabilities	180,000
Net profit	35,400
Total assets	385,000
Current liabilities	75,000
Other information	
Number of common shares outstanding	25,000
Inventory at January 1, 2018	48,000

Calculate the following ratios for 2018: acid-test (quick) ratio, inventory turnover ratio, net profit margin, return on equity, debt-to-equity ratio, and earnings per share. Summarize your assessment of the company's financial performance, based on these ratios, in a report for your friend. What other information would you like to have to complete your evaluation? (Information, Systems)

4. Use the internet and business publications to research how companies and accounting firms are implementing the provisions of the Sarbanes-Oxley Act. What are the major concerns they face? What rules have other organizations issued that relate to Act compliance? Summarize your findings. (Information)

5. **Team Activity** Two years ago, Rebecca Mardon started a computer consulting business, Mardon Consulting Associates. Until now, she has been the only employee, but business has grown enough to support hiring an administrative assistant and another consultant this year. Before she adds staff, however, she wants to hire an accountant and computerize her financial recordkeeping. Divide the class into small groups, assigning one person to be Rebecca and the others to represent members of a medium-sized accounting firm. Rebecca should think about the type of financial information systems her firm requires and develop a list of questions for the firm. The accountants will prepare a presentation making recommendations to her as well as explaining why their firm should win the account. (Resources, Interpersonal)

6. One of the best ways to learn about financial statements is to prepare them. Put together your personal balance sheet and income statement, using Table 14.1 and Table 14.2 as samples. You will have to adjust the account categories to fit your needs. Here are some suggestions:
   ◦ Current assets—cash on hand, balances in savings and checking accounts
   ◦ Investments—stocks and bonds, retirement funds
   ◦ Fixed assets—real estate, personal property (cars, furniture, jewelry, etc.)
   ◦ Current liabilities—charge-card balances, loan payments due in one year
   ◦ Long-term liabilities—auto loan balance, mortgage on real estate, other loan balances that will not come due until after one year
   ◦ Income—employment income, investment income (interest, dividends)
   ◦ Expenses—housing, utilities, food, transportation, medical, clothing, insurance, loan payments, taxes,

personal care, recreation and entertainment, and miscellaneous expenses

After you complete your personal financial statements, use them to see how well you are managing your finances. Consider the following questions:

a. Should you be concerned about your debt ratio?

b. Would a potential creditor conclude that it is safe or risky to lend you money?

c. If you were a company, would people want to invest in you? Why or why not? What could you do to improve your financial condition? (Information)

Ethics Activity

As the controller of a medium-sized financial services company, you take pride in the accounting and internal control systems you have developed for the company. You and your staff have kept up with changes in the accounting industry and been diligent in updating the systems to meet new accounting standards. Your outside auditor, which has been reviewing the company's books for 15 years, routinely complimented you on your thorough procedures.

The passage of the Sarbanes-Oxley Act, with its emphasis on testing internal control systems, initiated several changes. You have studied the law and made adjustments to ensure you comply with the regulations, even though it has created additional work. Your auditors, however, have chosen to interpret SOX very aggressively—too much so, in your opinion. The auditors have recommended that you make costly improvements to your systems and also enlarged the scope of the audit process, raising their fees. When you question the partner in charge, he explains that the complexity of the law means that it is open to interpretation and it is better to err on the side of caution than risk noncompliance. You are not pleased with this answer, as you believe that your company is in compliance with SOX, and consider changing auditors.

Using a web search tool, locate articles about this topic and then write responses to the following questions. Be sure to support your arguments and cite your sources.

Ethical Dilemma: Should you change auditors because your current one is too stringent in applying the Sarbanes-Oxley Act? What other steps could you take to resolve this situation?

Sources: Loren Kasuske, "The 4 Biggest Pros and Cons of the Sarbanes-Oxley Act," https://ktconnections.com, June 8, 2017; Terry Sheridan, "Financial Services Spend More than $1M Annually on SOX," https://www.accountingweb.com, August 2, 2016; "Sarbanes-Oxley Is Paying Off for Companies Despite Increased Costs and Hours, Protiviti Survey Finds," http://www.prnewswire.com, June 2, 2016; Daniel Kim, "Top 3 Ways to Reduce SOX Compliance Costs," https://www.soxhub.com, December 14, 2015.

Working the Net

1. Visit the website of one of the following major U.S. public accounting firms: Deloitte (**http://www.deloitte.com**), Ernst & Young (**http://www.ey.com**), KPMG (**http://www.kpmg.com**), PricewaterhouseCoopers (**http://www.pwc.com**), Grant Thornton (**http://www.grantthornton.com**), or BDO (**http://www.bdo.com**). Explore the site to learn the services the firm offers. What other types of resources does the firm have on its website? How well does the firm communicate via the website with existing and prospective clients? Summarize your findings in a brief report.

2. Do annual reports confuse you? Many websites can take the mystery out of this important document. See IBM's Guide to Understanding Financials at **https://www.ibm.com/investor/help/guide/**

Moneychimp's "How to Read an Annual Report" features an interactive diagram that provides a big-picture view of what the report's financial information tells you: **http://www.moneychimp.com**. Which site was more helpful to you, and why?

3. Corporate reports filed with the SEC are now available on the web at the EDGAR (Electronic Data Gathering, Analysis, and Retrieval system) website, **https://www.sec.gov/edgar**. First, read about the EDGAR system; then go to the search page. To see the type of information that companies must file with the SEC, use the search feature to locate a recent filing by Microsoft. What types of reports did you find, and what was the purpose of each report?

 ## Critical Thinking Case

Accountingfly Changes How CPAs Get Hired

Filling accounting positions, especially at the CPA level, can be a challenge. Until a few years ago, businesses other than the Big 4 firms basically had two options: post openings on general job platforms such as Monster and Indeed, or go through a staffing agency that charged a hefty fee for finding just the right accounting professional.

Jeff Phillips, a professional recruiter who previously worked for Monster.com, saw the opportunity to create a job site that caters strictly to accounting and bookkeeping jobs and started Accountingfly.com with brothers John and James Hosman. After studying various industries, the founders decided to focus on accounting because of the "massive imbalance" when it came to recruiting for private and public accountants. In their research, the trio found that most of the talent was snapped up by Big 4 accounting firms, leaving other accounting businesses struggling to find the right experienced people to fill key positions.

Despite the record number of students currently majoring in accounting, Phillips discovered the number of graduates taking the CPA exam was declining rapidly, signaling to him that people were losing interest in public accounting jobs. He sees Accountingfly as a way to alert job seekers (and companies) about the good jobs available for new and experienced CPAs outside of the four major players in the accounting field.

As the accounting talent pool evolves, millennials are looking to make their mark in the industry and tend to look for new jobs with organizations that pay competitive salaries, encourage job flexibility, and offer multiple career opportunities for the long haul. Accountingfly attracts both experienced CPAs and college students to its website by providing job boards, webinars, and virtual career fairs. There are more than one million job seekers and 200,000 user profiles on the website. Recently Accountingfly acquired Going Concern, a leading accounting news website that features original content and an insider's perspective on the people, firms, and culture that shape the accounting profession in this country. According to Phillips, Going Concern has a large, well-informed, highly engaged audience of early-career accountants who could benefit from connecting with accounting firms seeking exceptional talent.

Critical Thinking Questions

1. How does the company's focus on recruiting accountants and related services give Accountingfly a competitive advantage?
2. Do you think Accountingfly's approach can compete with the Big 4's expensive and comprehensive recruiting efforts for new accountants? Explain your reasoning.
3. How can Accountingfly use its recent acquisition of Going Concern as a recruiting tool for experienced CPAs who desire a different career track? Provide some examples to support your answer.

Sources: "Who We Are," https://accountingfly.com, accessed August 11, 2017; Ian Welham, "How

Accountingfly Is Revolutionizing the Way CPAs Are Hired," http://cpatrendlines.com, August 5, 2017; "Millennial Businesses to Accounting Firms: Diversify Services, Go Digital and Embrace the Cloud," https://www.bill.com, May 30, 2017; Carlos Gieseken, "Accountingfly Gains Influence in Industry," http://www.pnj.com, October 5, 2015; Sherman G. Mohr, Jr., "Meet Jeff Phillips, CEO of Accountingfly. Tech Is Thriving in the Florida Panhandle," *LinkedIn,* https://www.linkedin.com, August 24, 2015; "Accountingfly Acquires Going Concern, a Leading Accounting News Publication," http://www.prweb.com, August 20, 2015.

▣ Hot Links Address Book

1. What issues is the FASB working on now? Check it out at **http://www.fasb.org**.
2. Two good sites to learn about the latest news in the accounting industry are Accounting Today, **http://www.accountingtoday.com**, and AccountingWEB, **http://www.accountingweb.com**.
3. To become more familiar with annual reports and key financial statements, head for IBM's Guide to Financial Statements. The material offers a good overview of financial reporting and shows you what to look for when you read these documents: **https://www.ibm.com/investor/help/guide**.
4. To find free information about business statistics and financial ratios, go to the BizStats website at **http://www.bizstats.com**. There you will find industry financial ratios for corporations in more than 200 different industries.
5. To find out more about the accounting profession and becoming a CPA, visit the American Institute of CPAs' website at **http://www.aicpa.org**, and click on the Career tab to explore various career paths in the accounting industry.
6. Forensic accountants combine their accounting knowledge with investigative skills in various legal and investigative settings, looking for fraud in various accounting transactions. To learn more about this accounting specialty, go to the website of the Association of Certified Fraud Examiners at **http://www.acfe.com**.
7. A comprehensive site with information about careers in accounting, certification programs, internships, and links to many related websites can be found at **http://accountingmajors.com**.
8. At their websites, you can learn about the types of services the Big Four accounting firms are now offering their clients: **http://www.deloitte.com**, **http://www.kpmg.com**, **http://www.ey.com**, and **https://www.pwc.com/us/en.html**.

15 Understanding Money and Financial Institutions

Exhibit 15.1 (Credit: The Fed/US Government Works)

 Introduction

Learning Outcomes

After reading this chapter, you should be able to answer these questions:

1. What is money, what are its characteristics and functions, and what are the three parts of the U.S. money supply?
2. How does the Federal Reserve manage the money supply?
3. What are the key financial institutions, and what role do they play in the process of financial intermediation?
4. How does the Federal Deposit Insurance Corporation (FDIC) protect depositors' funds?
5. What roles do U.S. banks play in the international marketplace?
6. What trends are reshaping financial institutions?

Michelle Moore

Bank of America

Technology continues to change every facet of daily life, including how consumers interact with banks and other financial institutions. Whether large or small, banks have to stay one step ahead of the competition when it comes to providing top-notch service to their customers, including digital and mobile channels. Michelle Moore, head of digital banking at Bank of America, has worked in various parts of the company for more than 14 years. Regardless of her role within the organization, Moore has consistently demonstrated her obsession with exceptional service and how best to make sure the bank is providing customers with products and features that will make their lives easier, keep them loyal to the organization, and ultimately increase sales.

Exhibit 15.2   Michelle Moore is the head of digital banking at Bank of America. (Credit: Mike Mozart/ Flickr/ Attribution 2.0 Generic (CC BY 2.0))

While overseeing the bank's call center operations, Moore was asked to take on the bank's mobile initiatives, a request that befuddled her. Moore is the first to tell you she is no techy—she admits she kept her beloved flip phone too long before opting for a smartphone. Yet, her people skills and her drive to provide the best customer service made her the perfect person to take on the bank's digital and mobile efforts.

Like other major financial institutions, Bank of America did not have a stellar reputation when it came to digital or mobile banking. Although customers used the bank's digital offerings, the services were basic, even as the smartphone revolution changed many of life's daily activities. Once Moore and her digital team got the bank's mobile app up to speed, they began to figure out how to make it better. The team started to add features to the app, making sure that nearly everything customers can do at a bank branch they can do on the new and improved app. In addition, Moore and her group created a digital assistant feature that uses artificial intelligence and predictive analytics to provide customers with the same level of advice and expertise that previously would have been reserved for customers with high-end wealth-management accounts.

A play on the word "America," the app called Erica recently debuted to the public, and customer reaction has been positive. But Moore is never satisfied with the status quo. She encourages her team to constantly ask how customers will use the app and what will it take to make and keep them happy with the digital assistant's features. For example, after Moore read an article on the success of Apple's Siri and Amazon's Alexa, she wondered, "Why can't our banking app talk to clients?" She pushed her team to add a voice feature to Erica, which gives the digital assistant a competitive edge over other banking mobile apps for now.

Moore knows that customer sentiment is critical to the bank's success, especially in mobile banking. She continues to be obsessed by customer reviews and how the bank can increase customer satisfaction quickly and efficiently, and she knows that agility is critical in an ever-changing bank environment. Her efforts are paying off. Several years ago, Bank of America had 6 million mobile banking users; today, that number has jumped to more than 22 million. In a recent three-month period, mobile banking customers logged in to their accounts more than 967 million times—more than double the number of desktop logins. And when customers need to visit a local bank branch, more and more of them are booking appointments via the mobile app each week. Although she knows there is more work to do, Moore's common-sense approach to listening to customers while leveraging technology will help Bank of America increase sales and stay ahead of the competition.

Sources: Robert Barba, "Digital Banker of the Year: B of A's Michelle Moore," *American Banker,* https://www.americanbanker.com, May 31, 2017; Robert Barba, "Mom, Marathoner, App Maker: B of A's Michelle Moore," *American Banker,* https://www.americanbanker.com, May 31, 2017; Ayoub Aouad and Jaime Toplin, "Bank of America Boosts Digital Banking Segment," *Business Insider,* http://www.businessinsider.com, April 19, 2017; Michelle Moore, "Leading the Way in Digital Banking," *The Financial Brand,* https://the financial brand.com, February 20, 2017; Hilary Burns, "Michelle Moore on the Latest for BofA's Digital Operations," *Charlotte Business Journal,* https://www.bizjournals.com, December 21, 2016.

Advanced technology, globalization of markets, and the relaxation of regulatory restrictions continue to accelerate the pace of change in the financial services industry. These changes are giving businesses and consumers new options for conducting their financial transactions. The competitive landscape for financial institutions is also changing, creating new ways for these firms to increase their market share and boost profits.

This chapter focuses on the role of financial institutions in U.S. and international economies. It discusses different types of financial institutions, how they are set up and how they function internally, and government oversight of their operations. Because financial institutions connect people with money, this chapter begins with a discussion of money, its characteristics and functions, and the components of the U.S. money supply. Next, it explains the role of the Federal Reserve System in managing the money supply. Then it describes different types of financial institutions and their services and the organizations that insure customer deposits. The chapter ends with a discussion of international banking and trends in financial institutions.

15.1 Show Me the Money

1. What is money, what are its characteristics and functions, and what are the three parts of the U.S. money supply?

Money is anything that is acceptable as payment for goods and services. It affects our lives in many ways. We earn it, spend it, save it, invest it—and often wish we had more of it. Businesses and government use money in similar ways. Both require money to finance their operations. By controlling the amount of money in circulation, the federal government can promote economic growth and stability. For this reason, money has been called the lubricant of the machinery that drives our economic system. Our banking system was developed to ease the handling of money.

Characteristics of Money

For money to be a suitable means of exchange, it should have these key characteristics:

- *Scarcity:* Money should be scarce enough to have some value but not so scarce as to be unavailable. Pebbles, which meet some of the other criteria, would not work well as money because they are widely available. Too much money in circulation increases prices and inflation. Governments control the scarcity of money by limiting the quantity of money in circulation.
- *Durability:* Any item used as money must be durable. A perishable item such as a banana becomes useless as money when it spoils. Even early societies used durable forms of money, such as metal coins and paper money, which lasted for a long time.
- *Portability:* Money must be easily moved around. Large or bulky items, such as boulders or heavy gold bars, cannot be transported easily from place to place.
- *Divisibility:* Money must be capable of being divided into smaller parts. Divisible forms of money help make transactions of all sizes and amounts possible.

Table 15.1 provides some interesting facts about our money.

Functions of Money

Using a variety of items as money would be confusing. Thus, societies develop a uniform money system to measure the value of goods and services. For money to be acceptable, it must function as a medium of exchange, as a standard of value, and as a store of value.

As a *medium of exchange,* money makes transactions easier. Having a common form of payment is much less complicated than having a barter system, wherein goods and services are exchanged for other goods and services. Money allows the exchange of products to be a simple process.

Money also serves as a *standard of value.* With a form of money whose value is accepted by all, goods and services can be priced in standard units. This makes it easy to measure the value of products and allows transactions to be recorded in consistent terms.

As a *store of value,* money is used to hold wealth. It retains its value over time, although it may lose some of its purchasing power due to inflation. Individuals may choose to keep their money for future use rather than exchange it today for other types of products or assets.

Fun Facts about U.S. Currency

Did you know . . .

- Currency paper is composed of 25% linen and 75% cotton.
- About 4,000 double folds (first forward and then backwards) are required before a note will tear.
- As of mid-July 2017, there was more than $1.56 trillion in U.S. currency in circulation, with $40 billion in coins.
- 95% of the notes printed each year are used to replace notes already in circulation.
- The largest note ever printed by the Bureau of Engraving and Printing was the $100,000 Gold Certificate, Series 1934.
- During fiscal year 2017, it cost approximately 5.4 cents per note to produce nearly 40 billion U.S. paper currency notes.
- A stack of currency one mile high would contain over 14 million notes.
- If you had 10 billion $1 notes and spent one every second of every day, it would require 317 years for you to go broke.

Table 15.1 Source: Bureau of Engraving and Printing, "Resources," https://www.moneyfactory.gov, accessed September 7, 2017.

The U.S. Money Supply

The U.S. money supply is composed of currency, demand deposits, and time deposits. **Currency** is cash held in the form of coins and paper money. Other forms of currency include travelers' checks, cashier's checks, and money orders. The amount of currency in circulation depends on public demand. Domestic demand is influenced primarily by prices for goods and services, income levels, and the availability of alternative payment methods such as credit cards. Until the mid-1980s, nearly all U.S. currency circulated only domestically. Today domestic circulation totals only a small fraction of the total amount of U.S. currency in circulation.

Over the past decade, the amount of U.S. currency has doubled to more than $1.56 trillion and is held both inside and outside the country.[1] Foreign demand is influenced by the political and economic uncertainties associated with some foreign currencies, and recent estimates suggest that between one-half and two-thirds of the value of currency in circulation is held abroad. Some residents of foreign countries hold dollars as a store of value, whereas others use it as a medium of exchange.

Federal Reserve notes make up more than 99 percent of all U.S. currency in circulation. Each year the Federal Reserve Board determines new currency demand and submits a print order to the Treasury's Bureau of Engraving and Printing (BEP). The order represents the Federal Reserve System's estimate of the amount of currency the public will need in the upcoming year and reflects estimated changes in currency usage and destruction rates of unfit currency. Table 15.2 shows how long we can expect our money to last on average.

How Long Will Your Money Last?	
Have you ever wondered how quickly money wears out from being handled or damaged? Not surprisingly, smaller denominations have a shorter life span.	
$1 bill	5.8 years
$5 bill	5.5 years
$10 bill	4.5 years
$20 bill	7.9 years
$50 bill	8.5 years
$100 bill	15.0 years

Table 15.2 Source: "How Long Is the Lifespan of U.S. Paper Money?" https://www.federalreserve.gov, accessed September 7, 2017.

Demand deposits consist of money kept in checking accounts that can be withdrawn by depositors on demand. Demand deposits include regular checking accounts as well as interest-bearing and other special types of checking accounts. **Time deposits** are deposits at a bank or other financial institution that pay interest but cannot be withdrawn on demand. Examples are certain savings accounts, money market deposit accounts, and certificates of deposit. Economists use two terms to report on and discuss trends in the U.S. monetary system: M1 and M2. **M1** (the *M* stands for money) is used to describe the total amount of readily available money in the system and includes currency and demand deposits. As of August 2017, the M1 monetary supply was $3.5 trillion. **M2** includes all M1 monies plus time deposits and other money that is not immediately accessible. In August 2017, the M2 monetary supply was $13.6 trillion.[2] Credit cards, sometimes referred to as "plastic money," are routinely used as a substitute for cash and checks. Credit cards are not money; they are a form of borrowing. When a bank issues a credit card to a consumer, it gives a short-term loan to the consumer by directly paying the seller for the consumer's purchases. The consumer pays the credit card company after receiving the monthly statement. Credit cards do not replace money; they simply defer payment.

CONCEPT CHECK

1. What is money, and what are its characteristics?
2. What are the main functions of money?
3. What are the three main components of the U.S. money supply? How do they relate to M1 and M2?

15.2 | The Federal Reserve System

2. How does the Federal Reserve manage the money supply?

Before the twentieth century, there was very little government regulation of the U.S. financial or monetary systems. In 1907, however, several large banks failed, creating a public panic that led worried depositors to withdraw their money from other banks. Soon many other banks had failed, and the U.S. banking system was near collapse. The panic of 1907 was so severe that Congress created the Federal Reserve System in 1913 to provide the nation with a more stable monetary and banking system.

The **Federal Reserve System** (commonly called the **Fed**) is the central bank of the United States. The Fed's primary mission is to oversee the nation's monetary and credit system and to support the ongoing operation of America's private-banking system. The Fed's actions affect the interest rates banks charge businesses and consumers, help keep inflation under control, and ultimately stabilize the U.S. financial system. The Fed operates as an independent government entity. It derives its authority from Congress but its decisions do not have to be approved by the president, Congress, or any other government branch. However, Congress does periodically review the Fed's activities, and the Fed must work within the economic framework established by the government.

The Fed consists of 12 district banks, each covering a specific geographic area. Exhibit 15.3 shows the 12 districts of the Federal Reserve. Each district has its own bank president who oversees operations within that district.

Originally, the Federal Reserve System was created to control the money supply, act as a borrowing source for banks, hold the deposits of member banks, and supervise banking practices. Its activities have since broadened, making it the most powerful financial institution in the United States. Today, four of the Federal Reserve System's most important responsibilities are carrying out monetary policy, setting rules on credit, distributing currency, and making check clearing easier.

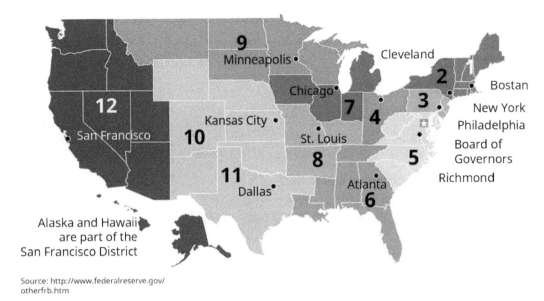

Source: http://www.federalreserve.gov/
otherfrb.htm

Exhibit 15.3   Federal Reserve Districts and Banks Source: "Federal Reserve Banks," https://www.richmondfed.org, accessed September 7, 2017.

Carrying Out Monetary Policy

The most important function of the Federal Reserve System is carrying out monetary policy. The Federal Open Market Committee (FOMC) is the Fed policy-making body that meets eight times a year to make monetary policy decisions. It uses its power to change the money supply in order to control inflation and interest rates, increase employment, and influence economic activity. Three tools used by the Federal Reserve System in managing the money supply are open market operations, reserve requirements, and the discount rate. Table 15.3 summarizes the short-term effects of these tools on the economy.

Open market operations—the tool most frequently used by the Federal Reserve—involve the purchase or sale of U.S. government bonds. The U.S. Treasury issues bonds to obtain the extra money needed to run the government (if taxes and other revenues aren't enough). In effect, Treasury bonds are long-term loans (five years or longer) made by businesses and individuals to the government. The Federal Reserve buys and sells these bonds for the Treasury. When the Federal Reserve buys bonds, it puts money into the economy. Banks have more money to lend, so they reduce interest rates, which generally stimulates economic activity. The opposite occurs when the Federal Reserve sells government bonds.

The Federal Reserve System's Monetary Tools and Their Effects				
Tool	Action	Effect on Money Supply	Effect on Interest Rates	Effect on Economic Activity
Open market operations	Buy government bonds	Increases	Lowers	Stimulates
	Sell government bonds	Decreases	Raises	Slows Down

Table 15.3

The Federal Reserve System's Monetary Tools and Their Effects				
Tool	Action	Effect on Money Supply	Effect on Interest Rates	Effect on Economic Activity
Reserve requirements	Raise reserve requirements	Decreases	Raises	Slows Down
	Lower reserve requirements	Increases	Lowers	Stimulates
Discount rate	Raise discount rate	Decreases	Raises	Slows Down
	Lower discount rate	Increases	Lowers	Stimulates

Table 15.3

Banks that are members of the Federal Reserve System must hold some of their deposits in cash in their vaults or in an account at a district bank. This **reserve requirement** ranges from 3 to 10 percent on different types of deposits. When the Federal Reserve raises the reserve requirement, banks must hold larger reserves and thus have less money to lend. As a result, interest rates rise, and economic activity slows down. Lowering the reserve requirement increases loanable funds, causes banks to lower interest rates, and stimulates the economy; however, the Federal Reserve seldom changes reserve requirements.

The Federal Reserve is called "the banker's bank" because it lends money to banks that need it. The interest rate that the Federal Reserve charges its member banks is called the **discount rate**. When the discount rate is less than the cost of other sources of funds (such as certificates of deposit), commercial banks borrow from the Federal Reserve and then lend the funds at a higher rate to customers. The banks profit from the *spread,* or difference, between the rate they charge their customers and the rate paid to the Federal Reserve. Changes in the discount rate usually produce changes in the interest rate that banks charge their customers. The Federal Reserve raises the discount rate to slow down economic growth and lowers it to stimulate growth.

Setting Rules on Credit

Another activity of the Federal Reserve System is setting rules on credit. It controls the credit terms on some loans made by banks and other lending institutions. This power, called **selective credit controls**, includes consumer credit rules and margin requirements. *Consumer credit rules* establish the minimum down payments and maximum repayment periods for consumer loans. The Federal Reserve uses credit rules to slow or stimulate consumer credit purchases. *Margin requirements* specify the minimum amount of cash an investor must put up to buy securities or investment certificates issued by corporations or governments. The balance of the purchase cost can be financed through borrowing from a bank or brokerage firm. By lowering the margin requirement, the Federal Reserve stimulates securities trading. Raising the margin requirement slows trading.

Distributing Currency: Keeping the Cash Flowing

The Federal Reserve distributes the coins minted and the paper money printed by the U.S. Treasury to banks. Most paper money is in the form of Federal Reserve notes. Look at a dollar bill and you'll see "Federal Reserve

Note" at the top. The large letter seal on the left indicates which Federal Reserve Bank issued it. For example, bills bearing a *D* seal are issued by the Federal Reserve Bank of Cleveland, and those with an *L* seal are issued by the San Francisco district bank.

Making Check Clearing Easier

Another important activity of the Federal Reserve is processing and clearing checks between financial institutions. When a check is cashed at a financial institution other than the one holding the account on which the check is drawn, the Federal Reserve's system lets that financial institution—even if distant from the institution holding the account on which the check is drawn—quickly convert the check into cash. Checks drawn on banks within the same Federal Reserve district are handled through the local Federal Reserve Bank using a series of bookkeeping entries to transfer funds between the financial institutions. The process is more complex for checks processed between different Federal Reserve districts.

The time between when the check is written and when the funds are deducted from the check writer's account provides float. *Float* benefits the check writer by allowing it to retain the funds until the check clears—that is, when the funds are actually withdrawn from its accounts. Businesses open accounts at banks around the country that are known to have long check-clearing times. By "playing the float," firms can keep their funds invested for several extra days, thus earning more money. To reduce this practice, in 1988 the Fed established maximum check-clearing times. However, as credit cards and other types of electronic payments have become more popular, the use of checks continues to decline. Responding to this decline, the Federal Reserve scaled back its check-processing facilities over the past decade. Current estimates suggest that the number of check payments has declined by two billion annually over the last couple of years and will continue to do so as more people use online banking and other electronic payment systems.[3]

Managing the 2007–2009 Financial Crisis

Much has been written over the past decade about the global financial crisis that occurred between 2007 and 2009. Some suggest that without the Fed's intervention, the U.S. economy would have slipped deeper into a financial depression that could have lasted years. Several missteps by banks, mortgage lenders, and other financial institutions, which included approving consumers for home mortgages they could not afford and then packaging those mortgages into high-risk financial products sold to investors, put the U.S. economy into serious financial trouble.[4]

In the early 2000s, the housing industry was booming. Mortgage lenders were signing up consumers for mortgages that "on paper" they could afford. In many instances, lenders told consumers that based on their credit rating and other financial data, they could easily take the next step and buy a bigger house or maybe a vacation home because of the availability of mortgage money and low interest rates. When the U.S. housing bubble burst in late 2007, the value of real estate plummeted, and many consumers struggled to pay mortgages on houses no longer worth the value they borrowed to buy the properties, leaving their real estate investments "underwater." Millions of consumers simply walked away from their houses, letting them go into foreclosure while filing personal bankruptcy. At the same time, the overall economy was going into a recession, and millions of people lost their jobs as companies tightened their belts to try to survive the financial upheaval affecting the United States as well as other countries across the globe.[5]

In addition, several leading financial investment firms, particularly those that managed and sold the high-risk, mortgage-backed financial products, failed quickly because they had not set aside enough money to cover the billions of dollars they lost on mortgages now going into default. For example, the venerable financial company Bear Stearns, which had been a successful business for more than 85 years, was eventually sold to JP Morgan for less than $10 a share, even after the Federal Reserve made more than $50 billion dollars available to help prop up financial institutions in trouble.[6]

After the collapse of Bear Stearns and other firms such as Lehman Brothers and insurance giant AIG, the Fed set up a special loan program to stabilize the banking system and to keep the U.S. bond markets trading at a normal pace. It is estimated that the Federal Reserve made more than $9 trillion in loans to major banks and other financial firms during the two-year crisis—not to mention bailing out the auto industry and buying several other firms to keep the financial system afloat.[7]

As a result of this financial meltdown, Congress passed legislation in 2010 to implement major regulations in the financial industry to prevent the future collapse of financial institutions, as well to put a check on abusive lending practices by banks and other firms. Among its provisions, the Dodd-Frank Wall Street Reform and Consumer Protection Act (known as Dodd-Frank) created an oversight council to monitor risks that affect the financial industry; requires banks to increase their cash reserves if the council feels the bank has too much risk in its current operations; prohibits banks from owning, investing, or sponsoring hedge funds, private equity funds, or other proprietary trading operations for profit; and set up a whistle-blower program to reward people who come forward to report security and other financial violations.[8]

Another provision of Dodd-Frank legislation requires major U.S. banks to submit to annual stress tests conducted by the Federal Reserve. These annual checkups determine whether banks have enough capital to survive economic turbulence in the financial system and whether the institutions can identify and measure risk as part of their capital plan to pay dividends or buy back shares. In 2017, seven years after Dodd-Frank became law, all of the country's major banks passed the annual examination.[9]

Exhibit 15.4   The Federal Reserve kept short-term interest rates close to 0 percent for more than seven years, from 2009 to December 2015, as a result of the global financial crisis. Now that the economy seems to be recovering at a slow but steady pace, the Fed began to raise the interest rate to 1.00–1.25 percent in mid-2017. *What effect do higher interest rates have on the U.S. economy?* (Credit: ./ Pexels/ CC0 License/✓ Free for personal and commercial use/✓ No attribution required)

CONCEPT CHECK

1. What are the four key functions of the Federal Reserve System?
2. What three tools does the Federal Reserve System use to manage the money supply, and how does each affect economic activity?
3. What was the Fed's role in keeping the U.S. financial markets solvent during the 2007–2009 financial crisis?

15.3 | U.S. Financial Institutions

3. What are the key financial institutions, and what role do they play in the process of financial intermediation?

The well-developed financial system in the United States supports our high standard of living. The system allows those who wish to borrow money to do so with relative ease. It also gives savers a variety of ways to earn interest on their savings. For example, a computer company that wants to build a new headquarters in

Atlanta might be financed partly with the savings of families in California. The Californians deposit their money in a local financial institution. That institution looks for a profitable and safe way to use the money and decides to make a real estate loan to the computer company. The transfer of funds from savers to investors enables businesses to expand and the economy to grow.

Households are important participants in the U.S. financial system. Although many households borrow money to finance purchases, they supply funds to the financial system through their purchases and savings. Overall, businesses and governments are users of funds. They borrow more money than they save.

Sometimes those who have funds deal directly with those who want them. A wealthy realtor, for example, may lend money to a client to buy a house. Most often, financial institutions act as intermediaries—or go-betweens—between the suppliers and demanders of funds. The institutions accept savers' deposits and invest them in financial products (such as loans) that are expected to produce a return. This process, called **financial intermediation,** is shown in Exhibit 15.5. Households are shown as suppliers of funds, and businesses and governments are shown as demanders. However, a single household, business, or government can be either a supplier or a demander, depending on the circumstances.

Financial institutions are the heart of the financial system. They are convenient vehicles for financial intermediation. They can be divided into two broad groups: depository institutions (those that accept deposits) and nondepository institutions (those that do not accept deposits).

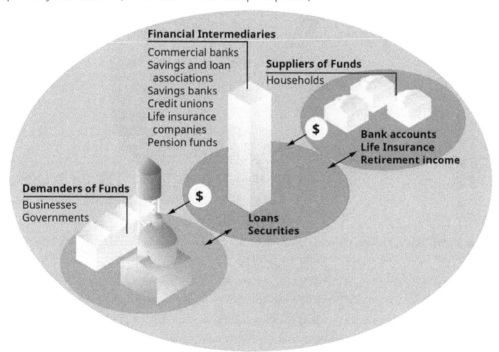

Exhibit 15.5   The Financial Intermediation Process* Only the dominant suppliers and demanders are shown here. Clearly, a single household, business, or government can be either a supplier or demander, depending on circumstances. (Attribution: Copyright Rice University, OpenStax, under CC BY 4.0 license.)

Depository Financial Institutions

Not all depository financial institutions are alike. Most people call the place where they save their money a "bank." Some of those places are indeed banks, but other depository institutions include thrift institutions and credit unions.

Commercial Banks

A **commercial bank** is a profit-oriented financial institution that accepts deposits, makes business and consumer loans, invests in government and corporate securities, and provides other financial services. Commercial banks vary greatly in size, from the "money center" banks located in the nation's financial centers to smaller regional and local community banks. As a result of consolidations, small banks are decreasing in number. A large share of the nation's banking business is now held by a relatively small number of big banks. There are approximately 5,011 commercial banks in the United States, accounting for nearly $16 trillion in assets and $9 trillion in total liabilities.[10] Banks hold a variety of assets, as shown in the diagram in Exhibit 15.6.

Table 15.4 lists the top 10 insured U.S.-chartered commercial banks, based on their consolidated assets.

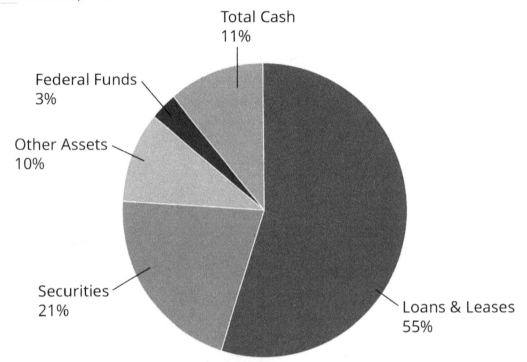

Exhibit 15.6   Assets of FDIC-Insured Commercial Banks, 2017 Source: "FDIC: Statistics on Depository Institutions Report for Commercial Banks as of 6/30/17," https://www5.fdic.gov, accessed September 7, 2017.

Customers' deposits are a commercial bank's major source of funds, the main use for which is loans. The difference between the interest the bank earns on loans and the interest it pays on deposits, plus fees it earns from other financial services, pays the bank's costs and provides a profit.

Commercial banks are corporations owned and operated by individuals or other corporations. They can be either national or state banks, and to do business, they must get a **bank charter**—an operating license—from a state or federal government. *National banks* are chartered by the Comptroller of the Currency, who is part of the U.S. Treasury Department. These banks must belong to the Federal Reserve System and must carry insurance on their deposits from the Federal Deposit Insurance Corporation. *State banks* are chartered by the state in which they are based. Generally, state banks are smaller than national banks, are less closely regulated than national banks, and are not required to belong to the Federal Reserve System.

Thrift Institutions

A **thrift institution** is a depository institution formed specifically to encourage household saving and to make home mortgage loans. Thrift institutions include *savings and loan associations (S&Ls)* and *savings banks.* S&Ls keep large percentages of their assets in home mortgages. Compared with S&Ls, savings banks focus less on mortgage loans and more on stock and bond investments. Thrifts are declining in number. At their peak in the late 1960s, there were more than 4,800. But a combination of factors, including sharp increases in interest rates in the late 1970s and increased loan defaults during the recession of the early 1980s, has reduced their ranks significantly. By year-end 2016, due mostly to acquisitions by or conversions to commercial banks or other savings banks, the number of thrifts had fallen to fewer than 800.[11]

Top Ten Insured U.S.-Chartered Commercial Banks, Based on Consolidated Assets, 2016	
Bank	Consolidated Assets
1. JP Morgan Chase & Co.	2,082,803,000
2. Wells Fargo & Co.	1,727,235,000
3. Bank of America Corp.	1,677,490,000
4. Citigroup	1,349,581,000
5. U.S. Bancorp	441,010,000
6. PNC Financial Services Group	356,000,000
7. Capital One Financial Corp.	286,080,000
8. TD Bank North America	269,031,000
9. Bank of New York Mellon Corp.	257,576,000
10. State Street Bank and Trust Corp.	239,203,000

Table 15.4 Source: "Insured U.S.-Chartered Commercial Banks That Have Consolidated Assets of $300 Million or More as of 12/31/16," https://www.federalreserve.gov, accessed September 7, 2017.

CUSTOMER SATISFACTION AND QUALITY

Rating Banks: Mobile and Branch Banking a Must

Which banks provide the best customer satisfaction? J.D. Power (JDP), based in Costa Mesa, California, ranked 136 major banks in 11 U.S. regions based on responses from more than 78,000 retail banking customers. In the research company's 2017 U.S. Retail Banking Satisfaction Study, top performers received high ratings in account information, channel activities (such as branch, mobile, website, and ATM), fees, problem resolution, and product offerings.

While specific banks took the top spots in various areas of the country, the overall customer sentiment in the JDP survey was clear: consumers wants banks that offer both digital experience and personal interaction in local branches—and the ones that can make these two channels work together effortlessly will be the most successful, especially among millennials. Findings also suggest banks that provide a user-friendly digital experience will attract and retain customers, and this digital experience must work seamlessly with a local branch system as younger customers avail themselves of other banking services such as mortgages and wealth management in the future. Other key survey findings include:

- Regardless of age group, more customers than ever are using mobile banking.
- More than 70 percent of all customers visited a local branch an average of 14 times over the past year, and their overall satisfaction was 27 index points higher than those who did not visit a bank branch.
- Close to 65 percent of bank customers have mobile payment services linked to their accounts.
- Successful problem resolution is a key driver of customer satisfaction, and younger customers prefer to resolve issues online or via social media.

Assessing customer satisfaction is also the goal of the American Customer Satisfaction Index (ACSI), which granted Citibank the top spot in the national bank category in its most recent survey, with a 12 percent jump in its overall score. Other top super regional banks in the ACSI study include BB&T, Fifth Third Bank, Capital One, and Citizens Bank. Overall, national banks improved their overall customer experience the most, up more than 6 percent from ACSI's previous survey.

Sources: "Digital, Branch, Drive-Through or ATM? Yes, Please! Say Bank Customers in J.D. Power Study," http://www.jdpower.com, accessed September 11, 2017; ACSI: Customer Satisfaction with Banks, Insurance Rebounds, http://www.theacsi.org, accessed September 11, 2017; American Bankers Association, "Millennials and Banking," https://www.aba.com, accessed September 11, 2017; Tanya Gazdik, "Citibank Leads National Banks in Study," https://www.mediapost.com, November 15, 2016.

Critical Thinking Questions
1. What can banks and financial institutions do to retain their customers and make them feel valued?
2. Is there a cost involved in not making customer service a priority? Explain your answer.

Credit Unions

A **credit union** is a not-for-profit, member-owned financial cooperative. Credit union members typically have something in common: they may, for example, work for the same employer, belong to the same union or professional group, or attend the same church or school. The credit union pools their assets, or savings, in order to make loans and offer other services to members. The not-for-profit status of credit unions makes them tax-exempt, so they can pay good interest rates on deposits and offer loans at favorable interest rates. Like banks, credit unions can have either a state or federal charter.

The approximately 5,700 credit unions in the United States have more than 108 million members and over $1.34 trillion in assets. The five largest credit unions in the United States are shown in Table 15.5. Although the U.S. credit union system remained strong during the 2007–2009 financial crisis, consumer-owned credit unions in several regions weakened as a result of home foreclosures, business failures, and unemployment rates. Today, the credit union system continues to demonstrate its resilience as the economy continues to rebound.[12]

Services Offered

Commercial banks, thrift institutions, and credit unions offer a wide range of financial services for businesses and consumers. Typical services offered by depository financial institutions are listed in Table 15.6. Some financial institutions specialize in providing financial services to a particular type of customer, such as consumer banking services or business banking services.

MANAGING CHANGE

Banks Take on P2P Payments

Person-to-person (P2P) payment systems are big business, and U.S. banks are now working together to compete in this billion-dollar industry. P2P transfers made through mobile apps such as Venmo, PayPal, Square Cash, and others accounted for more than $147 billion in digital payments in 2016, according to recent research by the Aite Group.

The simplicity of P2P apps has made them a part of everyday life for millions, especially millennials and young adults who use their smartphones for many daily activities. Venmo, for example, requires merely a phone number and email in order for someone to transfer money to a friend (and the friend creates a Venmo account to receive payment). Social media sites also encourage their members to transfer money via mobile apps, such as Google Wallet and Facebook Messenger.

Banks have been successful allowing their own customers to transfer money via apps; however, P2P transfers have been limited to other customers of the same bank—until now. A consortium of more than 30 banks recently introduced a mobile app called Zelle, which can be used by anyone to transfer funds to customers across these banking institutions.

A downside of using Venmo is that it may take a day or two for money to arrive in a recipient's account because the money flows through an intermediary. With Zelle, the transfer of money between two accounts will occur instantaneously, making payments happen quickly. For now, most banks using Zelle are making the service free of charge—knowing that it is in their best interest to migrate people to a cashless and checkless environment, which will eventually lower their costs in terms of services, labor, overhead, etc.

Is a cashless society imminent now that major banks have gotten on board with P2P payments? Probably not, but the banking industry's commitment to challenging Venmo and other digital payment systems eventually may result in a stronger revenue stream and underscores their business strategy of staying connected to customers of all ages.

Critical Thinking Questions
1. Does working together on a P2P system help banks stay competitive? Explain your reasoning.
2. Do you think P2P payment systems will eventually eliminate the use of cash in our society? Why or why not?

Sources: "Use Venmo with Anyone," https://venmo.co, accessed September 12, 2017; Sarah Perez, "Zelle, the U.S. Banks' Venmo Rival, Will Launch Its Mobile App Next Week," *Tech Crunch,* https://techcrunch.com, September 8, 2017; Kevin Wack, "Zelle Says 4M Users Have Enrolled Since June Launch," *American Banker,* https://www.americanbanker.com, September 8, 2017; Jennifer Surane,

"Venmo Killer? Banks Roll Out Faster P2P Payments with Zelle," *Bloomberg Technology,* https://www.bloomberg.com, June 12, 2017; James Rufus Koren, "As Millennials 'Venmo' Each Other Money, Banks Fight Back with Their Own Mobile Apps," *Los Angeles Times,* http://www.latimes.com, March 27, 2017.

Five Largest U.S. Credit Unions
1. Navy Federal Credit Union, Vienna, Virginia
2. State Employees Credit Union, Raleigh, North Carolina
3. Pentagon Federal Credit Union, Alexandria, Virginia
4. Boeing Employees Credit Union, Tukwila, Washington
5. Schoolfirst Federal Credit Union, Santa Ana, California

Table 15.5 Source: "Top 100 Credit Unions," http://www.usacreditunions.com, accessed September 7, 2017.

Nondepository Financial Institutions

Some financial institutions provide certain banking services but do not accept deposits. These nondepository financial institutions include insurance companies, pension funds, brokerage firms, and finance companies. They serve both individuals and businesses.

Insurance Companies

Insurance companies are major suppliers of funds. Policyholders make payments (called *premiums*) to buy financial protection from the insurance company. Insurance companies invest the premiums in stocks, bonds, real estate, business loans, and real estate loans for large projects.

599

Exhibit 15.7 Insurance companies, hurt by billions of dollars in unforeseen payouts during natural disasters such as Hurricane Irma in 2017, are rethinking their reliance on catastrophe-risk modelers, whose risk estimates failed to anticipate cataclysmic storms such as Hurricanes Katrina, Irma, and Harvey. Cat-risk businesses forecast potential weather-related expenses for insurers through sophisticated computer modeling that analyzes historical meteorological data. *How do frequent natural disasters affect insurance companies and their policyholders?* (Credit: Cayobo/ Flickr/ Attribution 2.0 Generic (CC BY 2.0))

Services Offered by Depository Financial Institutions	
Service	Description
Savings accounts	Pay interest on deposits
Checking accounts	Allow depositors to withdraw any amount of funds at any time up to the amount on deposit
Money market deposit accounts	Savings accounts on which the interest rate is set at market rates
Certificates of deposit (CD)	Pay a higher interest rate than regular savings accounts, provided that the deposit remains for a specified period

Table 15.6

Services Offered by Depository Financial Institutions	
Service	Description
Consumer loans	Loans to individuals to finance the purchase of a home, car, or other expensive items
Business loans	Loans to businesses and other organizations to finance their operations
Electronic funds transfer	Use of computers and mobile devices to conduct financial transactions
Automated teller machine (ATM)	Allows bank customers to make deposits, withdrawals, and transfers from their accounts 24 hours a day
Debit cards	Allow customers to transfer money from their bank account directly to a merchant's account to pay for purchases
Online banking	Allows customers to conduct financial transactions via the internet or through a dial-in line that operates with a bank's software
Mobile apps	Technology that allows consumers to download programs to mobile devices that enable them to take care of banking, financial, and other transactions
Direct deposit of paychecks	Enabled through employers and payroll service vendors; allows financial institutions to accept direct deposits of payroll checks to consumers' checking and/or savings accounts on a regular basis

Table 15.6

Pension Funds

Corporations, unions, and governments set aside large pools of money for later use in paying retirement benefits to their employees or members. These **pension funds** are managed by the employers or unions themselves or by outside managers, such as life insurance firms, commercial banks, and private investment firms. Pension plan members receive a specified monthly payment when they reach a given age. After setting aside enough money to pay near-term benefits, pension funds invest the rest in business loans, stocks, bonds, or real estate. They often invest large sums in the stock of the employer. U.S. pension fund assets total nearly $3.4 trillion.[13]

Brokerage Firms

A *brokerage firm* buys and sells securities (stocks and bonds) for its clients and gives them related advice.

Many brokerage firms offer some banking services. They may offer clients a combined checking and savings account with a high interest rate and also make loans, backed by securities, to them.

Finance Companies

A *finance company* makes short-term loans for which the borrower puts up tangible assets (such as an automobile, inventory, machinery, or property) as security. Finance companies often make loans to individuals or businesses that cannot get credit elsewhere. Promising new businesses with no track record and firms that can't get more credit from a bank often obtain loans from *commercial finance companies. Consumer finance companies* make loans to individuals, often to cover the lease or purchase of large consumer goods such as automobiles or major household appliances. To compensate for the extra risk, finance companies usually charge higher interest rates than banks.

CONCEPT CHECK

1. What is the financial intermediation process?
2. Differentiate between the three types of depository financial institutions and the services they offer.
3. What are the four main types of nondepository financial institutions?

15.4 | Insuring Bank Deposits

4. How does the Federal Deposit Insurance Corporation (FDIC) protect depositors' funds?

The U.S. banking system worked fairly well from when the Federal Reserve System was established in 1913 until the stock market crash of 1929 and the Great Depression that followed. Business failures caused by these events resulted in major cash shortages as people rushed to withdraw their money from banks. Many cash-starved banks failed because the Federal Reserve did not, as expected, lend money to them. The government's efforts to prevent bank failures were ineffective. Over the next two years, 5,000 banks—about 20 percent of the total number—failed.

President Franklin D. Roosevelt made strengthening the banking system his first priority. After taking office in 1933, Roosevelt declared a bank holiday, closing all banks for a week so he could take corrective action. Congress passed the Banking Act of 1933, which empowered the Federal Reserve System to regulate banks and reform the banking system. The act's most important provision was the creation of the **Federal Deposit Insurance Corporation (FDIC)** to insure deposits in commercial banks. The 1933 act also gave the Federal Reserve authority to set reserve requirements, ban interest on demand deposits, regulate the interest rates on time deposits, and prohibit banks from investing in specified types of securities. In 1934 the Federal Savings and Loan Insurance Corporation (FSLIC) was formed to insure deposits at S&Ls. When the FSLIC went bankrupt in the 1980s, the FDIC took over responsibility for administering the fund that insures deposits at thrift institutions.

Today, the major deposit insurance funds include the following:

- *The Deposit Insurance Fund (DIF):* Administered by the FDIC, this fund provides deposit insurance to commercial banks and thrift institutions.
- *The National Credit Union Share Insurance Fund:* Administered by the National Credit Union Administration,

this fund provides deposit insurance to credit unions.

Role of the FDIC

The FDIC is an independent, quasi-public corporation backed by the full faith and credit of the U.S. government. It examines and supervises about 4,000 banks and savings banks, more than half the institutions in the banking system. It insures trillions of dollars of deposits in U.S. banks and thrift institutions against loss if the financial institution fails.[14] The FDIC insures all member banks in the Federal Reserve System. The ceiling on insured deposits is $250,000 per account. Each insured bank pays the insurance premiums, which are a fixed percentage of the bank's domestic deposits. In 1993, the FDIC switched from a flat rate for deposit insurance to a risk-based premium system because of the large number of bank and thrift failures during the 1980s and early 1990s. Some experts argue that certain banks take too much risk because they view deposit insurance as a safety net for their depositors—a view many believe contributed to earlier bank failures.

Enforcement by the FDIC

To ensure that banks operate fairly and profitably, the FDIC sets guidelines for banks and then reviews the financial records and management practices of member banks at least once a year. Bank examiners perform these reviews during unannounced visits, rating banks on their compliance with banking regulations—for example, the Equal Credit Opportunity Act, which states that a bank cannot refuse to lend money to people because of their color, religion, or national origin. Examiners also rate a bank's overall financial condition, focusing on loan quality, management practices, earnings, liquidity, and whether the bank has enough capital (equity) to safely support its activities.

When bank examiners conclude that a bank has serious financial problems, the FDIC can take several actions. It can lend money to the bank, recommend that the bank merge with a stronger bank, require the bank to use new management practices or replace its managers, buy loans from the bank, or provide extra equity capital to the bank. The FDIC may even cover all deposits at a troubled bank, including those over $250,000, to restore the public's confidence in the financial system.

With the fallout from the financial crisis of 2007–2009 still having an effect on banking and financial markets in this country and abroad, the FDIC works closely with the Federal Reserve to make sure that banks continue to maintain healthy balance sheets by "testing" their solvency on a regular basis. Although the future of Dodd-Frank regulations is open to speculation in 2017, the consequences of thinking that banks and other financial institutions were "too big to fail" has had a positive impact on banking and financial transactions with the hope that such a financial crisis can be avoided in the future.

CONCEPT CHECK

1. What is the FDIC, and what are its responsibilities?
2. What are the major deposit insurance funds?
3. What can the FDIC do to help financially troubled banks?

15.5   International Banking

5.   What roles do U.S. banks play in the international marketplace?

The financial marketplace spans the globe, with money routinely flowing across international borders. U.S. banks play an important role in global business by providing loans to foreign governments and businesses. Multinational corporations need many special banking services, such as foreign-currency exchange and funding for overseas investments. U.S. banks also offer trade-related services, such as global cash management, that help firms manage their cash flows, improve their payment efficiency, and reduce their exposure to operational risks. Sometimes consumers in other nations have a need for banking services that banks in their own countries don't provide. Therefore, large banks often look beyond their national borders for profitable banking opportunities.

Many U.S. banks have expanded into overseas markets by opening offices in Europe, Latin America, and Asia. They often provide better customer service than local banks and have access to more sources of funding. Citibank, for example, was the first bank to offer banking by phone and 24-hour-a-day ATM service in Japan.

For U.S. banks, expanding internationally can be difficult. Banks in other nations are often subject to fewer regulations than U.S. banks, making it easier for them to undercut American banks on the pricing of loans and services. Some governments also protect their banks against foreign competition. For example, the Chinese government imposes high fees and limits the amount of deposits that foreign banks can accept from customers. It also controls foreign-bank deposit and loan interest rates, limiting the ability of foreign banks to compete with government-owned Chinese banks. Despite the banking restrictions for foreign banks in China, many of the large U.S. banking institutions continue to do business there. [15]

International banks operating within the United States also have a substantial impact on the economy through job creation—they employ thousands of people in the United States, and most workers are U.S. citizens—operating and capital expenditures, taxes, and other contributions. According to March 2017 Federal Reserve data, the combined banking and nonbanking assets of the U.S. operations of foreign banks total more than $24 trillion. [16]

The World's Biggest Banks, 2017
Industrial and Commercial Bank of China
China Construction Bank
JPMorgan Chase & Co. (USA)
Wells Fargo & Co. (USA)
Agricultural Bank of China
Bank of America Corp. (USA)
Bank of China Ltd.
Citigroup (USA)

Table 15.7 Source: "The World's Biggest Banks in 2017: The American Bull Market Strengthens," *Forbes,* http://www.forbes.com, May 24, 2017.

The World's Biggest Banks, 2017
BNP Paribas (France)
Mitsubishi UFJ Financial Group (Japan)

Table 15.7 Source: "The World's Biggest Banks in 2017: The American Bull Market Strengthens," *Forbes,* http://www.forbes.com, May 24, 2017.

The United States has four banks listed in the top 10 world's biggest banks, as shown in **Table 15.7**.

Political and economic uncertainty in other countries can make international banking a high-risk venture. European and Asian banks were not immune to the financial crisis of 2007–2009. In fact, several countries, including Greece, Portugal, Spain, and Ireland, continue to rebound slowly from the near-collapse of their economic and financial systems they experienced a decade ago. Financial bailouts spearheaded by the European Union and the International Monetary Fund have helped stabilize the European and global economy. It is unclear at this writing, however, whether the impending "Brexit" move by the United Kingdom (leaving the European Union) will impact international banking, as many of the world's top financial institutions seek to move their global operations out of London and shift them to other financial capitals within the eurozone.[17]

CONCEPT CHECK

1. What is the role of U.S. banks in international banking?
2. What challenges do U.S. banks face in foreign markets?

15.6 | Trends in Financial Institutions

6. What trends are reshaping financial institutions?

What factors will influence financial institutions in the coming years? The latest reports suggest there will be a continued focus on regulatory and compliance issues (especially after the recent financial crisis), as well as on operational efficiency and technological advances.

Banks will continue to tackle customer engagement and technology initiatives over the next few years. According to a report by Aite Group, a Boston-based firm that forecasts U.S. banking trends, technology continues to empower consumers to control their banking and commerce experiences. Financial institutions have become better at using data and data analytics to help them better understand their customers' needs and behaviors, which may provide them the competitive advantage they seek in the retail banking industry.[18]

Financial technology (or "fintech" services) will continue to disrupt the banking industry and provide opportunities for banks and other institutions to work closely with fintech companies that can help them innovate and streamline their business practices. According to recent research by Goldman Sachs, fintech startups have the potential to take away billions of dollars in business from traditional investment and lending institutions. Some of the services offered by fintech firms include payment transaction processing, mobile and web payment services for e-commerce firms, peer-to-peer lending, and integrated financial software programs.[19]

Mobile financial apps will continue to be a strategic advantage that separates traditional banking approaches from innovative companies that can offer their clients a connected, digital experience when it comes to their money and investments. Consumers will expect personalization of bank products and services as part of their routine interaction with financial institutions. Otherwise, they will look elsewhere for a competitive platform to meet all of their financial and banking needs.[20]

Although most banks continue to offer local branch offices, the next few years will see branch banking become less prevalent as online and mobile services become more popular. Most banking institutions already offer apps that allow customers to move money between accounts or deposit a check via their smartphones, which happens almost instantaneously, rather than get in a car, drive to the bank, and deposit the check in person. In addition, online payment platforms such as PayPal, Apple Pay, Google Wallet, Shopify, Stripe, and others continue to make personal and business transactions seamless. In this 24/7 world, consumers expect their banking and financial transactions to happen quickly and efficiently.[21]

Exhibit 15.8   Online payment platforms such as Google Wallet, Apple Pay, and others continue to make personal and business transactions seamless and efficient. *How can companies continue to leverage technology to make financial transactions as easy as a swipe or tap on a mobile device?* (Credit: Sergio Uceda/ flickr/ Attribution 2.0 Generic (CC BY 2.0))

MANAGING CHANGE

Chatbots Help Banks Connect with Customers

Computer software using artificial intelligence (AI) to simulate conversation with humans, chatbots have become an integral part of the banking industry's push to connect with customers while keeping operations and costs in line. They can be an effective tool in what banks call "conversational commerce"—interacting with customers via messaging and digital platforms.

Typically banks engage their customers through various channels, including human channels (in-person transactions or service calls with a live agent) and digital channels (websites, mobile apps, e-mail, and online ads). Although customers may have a favorite way to interact with their bank, these channels can cost banks a substantial amount of money, and financial institutions are constantly looking for ways to reduce costs while maintaining quality customer service.

It is not surprising that in-person transactions are the most expensive service provided by banks; however, not every transaction with a customer requires human intervention. As technology continues to evolve, more banks have figured out they can leverage their services to fit the everyday activities of their tech-savvy customers by using chatbots as the next step in customer service.

For example, as mentioned in the opening feature in this module, Bank of America recently introduced Erica, a voice- and text-enabled chatbot that helps customers make smarter banking decisions. Erica sends customers notifications, points out areas where they can save money, updates credit ratings, and can help facilitate bill payments within the bank's mobile app.

Capital One, another player in the U.S. banking industry, launched Eno, a text-enabled chatbot that helps customers manage their money via smartphone. Customers can ask Eno questions about account balances, credit history, recent transactions, payment history, etc. via text messaging. Eno is the second virtual assistant created by Capital One; it already launched its own Amazon Alexa feature, which allows customers to ask about checking account balances and when upcoming bills are due and pay credit card bills in conversations with Alexa.

AI chatbots provide benefits to both banks and customers. Banks are using them to streamline operations, automate customer support, and provide a convenient and positive customer experience. Customers rely on this type of digital assistant to make their lives easier and keep them current on personal and business transactions without having to wait on hold for a person to respond to questions that can easily be answered by chatbots. A recent report by Gartner, an IT research firm, estimates that by the year 2020, consumers will manage 85 percent of their banking relationships via chatbots, saving customers time and banks millions of dollars. With more than 1.2 billion users of mobile banking worldwide, chatbots can be an effective tool to help banks become more efficient, more proactive in anticipating customer needs, and more sensitive to their bottom line.

Critical Thinking Questions
1. Do you think chatbots will eventually replace customer service representatives at U.S. banks? Explain your reasoning.
2. What are some advantages and disadvantages of using a digital assistant as part of your banking routine?

Sources: Yue Cathy Chang and Cindi Thompson, "Chatbots in Banking," *Silicon Valley Data Science*, https://svds.com, accessed September 11, 2017; Maruti Techlabs, "Banking Chatbots," https://chatbotmagazine.com, accessed September 11, 2017; "Number of Mobile Payment Users from 2009 to 2016, by Region (in Millions)," *Statista,* https://www.statista.com, accessed September 11, 2017; Blake Morgan, "5 Ways Chatbots Can Improve Customer Experience in Banking," *Forbes,* http://www.forbes.com, August 6, 2017; Elizabeth Mills, "How 10 Big Banks Are Using Chatbots to Boost Their Business," https://www.abe.ai, March 13, 2017.

CONCEPT CHECK

1. How will fintech services enhance the overall banking experience?
2. What challenges do banks face when it comes to offering local branch services to customers?

🔑 Key Terms

bank charter An operating license issued to a bank by the federal government or a state government; required for a commercial bank to do business.

commercial banks Profit-oriented financial institutions that accept deposits, make business and consumer loans, invest in government and corporate securities, and provide other financial services.

credit unions Not-for-profit, member-owned financial cooperatives.

currency Cash held in the form of coins and paper money.

demand deposits Money kept in checking accounts that can be withdrawn by depositors on demand.

discount rate The interest rate that the Federal Reserve charges its member banks.

Federal Deposit Insurance Corporation (FDIC) An independent, quasi-public corporation backed by the full faith and credit of the U.S. government that insures deposits in commercial banks and thrift institutions for up to a ceiling of $250,000 per account.

Federal Reserve System (Fed) The central bank of the United States; consists of 12 district banks, each located in a major U.S. city.

financial intermediation The process in which financial institutions act as intermediaries between the suppliers and demanders of funds.

M1 The total amount of readily available money in the system; includes currency and demand deposits.

M2 A term used by economists to describe the U.S. monetary supply. Includes all M1 monies plus time deposits and other money that is not immediately accessible.

money Anything that is acceptable as payment for goods and services.

open market operations The purchase or sale of U.S. government bonds by the Federal Reserve to stimulate or slow down the economy.

pension funds Large pools of money set aside by corporations, unions, and governments for later use in paying retirement benefits to their employees or members.

reserve requirement Requires banks that are members of the Federal Reserve System to hold some of their deposits in cash in their vaults or in an account at a district bank.

selective credit controls The power of the Federal Reserve to control consumer credit rules and margin requirements.

thrift institutions Depository institutions formed specifically to encourage household saving and to make home mortgage loans.

time deposits Deposits at a bank or other financial institution that pay interest but cannot be withdrawn on demand.

📋 Summary of Learning Outcomes

15.1 Show Me the Money

1. What is money, what are its characteristics and functions, and what are the three parts of the U.S. money supply?

Money is anything accepted as payment for goods and services. For money to be a suitable means of exchange, it should be scarce, durable, portable, and divisible. Money functions as a medium of exchange, a standard of value, and a store of value. The U.S. money supply consists of currency (coins and paper money), demand deposits (checking accounts), and time deposits (interest-bearing deposits that cannot be withdrawn on demand).

15.2 The Federal Reserve System

2. How does the Federal Reserve manage the money supply?

The Federal Reserve System (the Fed) is an independent government agency that performs four main functions: carrying out monetary policy, setting rules on credit, distributing currency, and making check clearing easier. The three tools it uses in managing the money supply are open market operations, reserve requirements, and the discount rate. The Fed played a major role in keeping the U.S. financial system solvent during the financial crisis of 2007–2009 by making more than $9 trillion available in loans to major banks and other financial firms, in addition to bailing out the auto industry and other companies and supporting congressional passage of Dodd-Frank federal legislation.

15.3 U.S. Financial Institutions

3. What are the key financial institutions, and what role do they play in the process of financial intermediation?

Financial institutions can be divided into two main groups: depository institutions and nondepository institutions. Depository institutions include commercial banks, thrift institutions, and credit unions. Nondepository institutions include insurance companies, pension funds, brokerage firms, and finance companies. Financial institutions ease the transfer of funds between suppliers and demanders of funds.

15.4 Insuring Bank Deposits

4. How does the Federal Deposit Insurance Corporation (FDIC) protect depositors' funds?

The Federal Deposit Insurance Corporation insures deposits in commercial banks through the Bank Insurance Fund and deposits in thrift institutions through the Savings Association Insurance Fund. Deposits in credit unions are insured by the National Credit Union Share Insurance Fund, which is administered by the National Credit Union Administration. The FDIC sets banking policies and practices and reviews banks annually to ensure that they operate fairly and profitably.

15.5 International Banking

5. What role do U.S. banks play in the international marketplace?

U.S. banks provide loans and trade-related services to foreign governments and businesses. They also offer specialized services such as cash management and foreign-currency exchange.

15.6 Trends in Financial Institutions

6. What trends are reshaping financial institutions?

There will be a continued focus on regulatory and compliance issues, especially after the recent financial crisis, as well as on operational efficiency and technological advances. Banks will continue to tackle customer engagement and technology initiatives, as consumers will control more than 85 percent of their ongoing relationships with banks and other financial institutions. Fintech services will continue to disrupt the banking industry and will enable some banks to increase innovation and streamline operational efficiencies. Mobile financial apps will continue to provide banks with a strategic advantage, as well as enable them to collect and utilize customer data as part of their overall business strategy. Finally, online payment platforms will play an integral role in the banking and financial sector, as consumers' expectations continue to drive innovation in the banking industry.

Preparing for Tomorrow's Workplace Skills

1. How much does a checking account cost? Call or visit websites of several local banks and weigh prices and services. Take into consideration how you use your checking account, how many checks a month you write, and the average balances you keep. On the internet, BankRate.com (**http://www.bankrate.com**) lets you digitally compare bank products, including those banking institutions that are strictly internet-based. Could you pay lower fees elsewhere? Could you earn interest on your checking account at a credit union? Would you be better off paying a monthly fee with unlimited check-writing privileges? Crunch the numbers to find the best deal. (Resources, Information)

2. You are starting a small business selling collectible books over the internet and need to establish a business banking account that will provide the following services: business checking, credit-card processing, a business savings account, and perhaps a line of credit. Call or visit at least three banks, including an internet-based one, to gather information about their business banking services, including data about fees, service options, and other features of interest to entrepreneurs. Write a short summary of each bank's offerings and benefits and make a recommendation about which bank you would choose for your new business. (Interpersonal, Information)

3. If you watch the news, you've undoubtedly heard mention that the Fed is going to raise or lower interest rates. What exactly does this mean? Explain how the Fed's decision to raise and lower its discount rate might affect (a) a large manufacturer of household appliances, (b) a mid-sized software firm, (c) a small restaurant, (d) a family hoping to purchase their first home, and (e) a college student. (Information)

4. Research the banking system of another country, and write a report on your findings by answering these questions: Is there a central banking system similar to the U.S. Federal Reserve System in place? Which government agency or department controls it, and how does it operate? How stable is the country's central banking system? How does it compare in structure and operation to the Federal Reserve System? How much control does the government have over banks operating in the country? Are there any barriers to entry specifically facing foreign banks? What would this mean to a foreign business attempting to do business in this country? (Information)

5. Banks use databases to identify profitable and unprofitable customers. Bankers say they lose money on customers who typically keep less than $1,000 in their checking and savings accounts and frequently call or visit the bank. Profitable customers keep several thousand dollars in their accounts and seldom visit a teller or call the bank. To turn unprofitable customers into profitable ones, banks have assessed fees on many of their services, including using a bank teller, although many of the fees are waived for customers who maintain high account balances. Bankers justify the fees by saying they're in business to earn a profit. Discuss whether banks are justified in treating profitable and unprofitable customers differently. Defend your answers. (Information, Systems)

6. **Team Activity** During its regular meetings, the Federal Open Market Committee, the Federal Reserve's monetary policy-making body, considers a number of economic indicators and reports before making decisions. The decisions made by the Fed include whether to sell or purchase Federal treasury bonds, whether to raise or lower bank reserve requirements, and whether to raise or lower the Federal Reserve discount rate. Divide your class into groups (if possible, try to use seven members, the size of the FOMC), and assign each group one of these decisions. As a group, identify the types of information used by the Fed in making their assigned decision and how that information is used. Find the most recent information (sources may include newspapers, business publications, online databases, etc.) and analyze it. Based on this information and your group's analysis, what should the Fed do now? Present your findings and recommendations to the class. (Interpersonal, Information)

Ethics Activity

You are a loan officer with a financial company that specializes in auto loans. The senior vice president in charge of your area sets new loan quotas for your group and suggests that courting more subprime borrowers would make the new quotas easier to meet. He reminds you that the company can justifiably charge higher interest rates, loan fees, and servicing costs for these higher-risk loans. He also points out that the loans will earn you and your team larger commissions as well. "Everyone wins," he tells you. "We help people who might otherwise not be able to get the financing they need, the company makes money, and so do you."

But you are uneasy about the company's focus on subprime borrowers, low-income applicants with poor or limited credit histories, many of whom are also minorities. You suspect the company's tactics could be considered "predatory lending" or "reverse redlining." You are also convinced that the cost of the company's subprime loans aren't tied to the increased risk factor at all, but to how much profit the company can squeeze from a group of unsophisticated borrowers with few other options.

Using a web search tool, locate articles about the topic of subprime auto loans, and then write responses to the following questions. Be sure to support your arguments and cite your sources.

Ethical Dilemma: Should you seek out subprime loans, knowing that you will have to charge borrowers the high fees your company demands, while believing they may not be totally justified?

Sources: Adam Tempkin, "'Deep' Subprime Car Loans Hit Crisis-Era Milestone," *Bloomberg Markets,* https://www.bloomberg.com, August 15, 2017; Shannara Johnson, "Subprime Auto Loans Up, Car Sales Down: Why This Could Be Good for Gold," *Forbes,* https://www.forbes.com, July 13, 2017; Mark Huffman, "Santander Settles Subprime Auto Loan Suit with Massachusetts," *Consumer Affairs,* https://www.consumeraffairs.com, March 31, 2017; Michael Corkery and Jessica Silver-Greenberg, "Prosecutors Scrutinize Minority Borrowers' Auto Loans," *The New York Times,* https://www.nytimes.com, March 30, 2015.

Working the Net

1. Banking on a great career? Go to **http://www.careerbank.com** to explore what positions are available in banking, finance, and accounting. Make a presentation on the type of job you might choose and its location.

2. Visit the International Money Laundering Network Services Association (**http://www.imolin.org**) for the latest information on what organizations are doing to ensure international monetary transfers remain out of terrorists' hands. Summarize your findings.

3. Find out everything you want to know about financial institutions and banking careers from the latest edition of the Bureau of Labor Statistics' *Occupational Outlook Handbook.* Visit the OOH's website at **https://www.bls.gov/ooh**, and click on the A–Z Index to explore banking and other financial occupations, including the forecast for these careers in the coming decade. Explain why this information should be important to you.

4. Using an internet search engine, research information on digital banking branches used around the country by companies such as Citibank. Make a presentation describing the merits of this trend to your class.

5. The recent Wells Fargo scandal in which bank employees created more than three million fake customer accounts as a result of pressure from their managers to meet sales quotas still has the banking

community and consumers up in arms regarding the ethics of fraudulent banking practices, ongoing credit issues, and customer privacy. Using an internet search engine, research what happened at Wells Fargo, what fallout it caused for consumers as well as bank employees, and what the Fed did to intervene. Summarize your findings, and provide recommendations on what banking executives and employees could have done differently.

6. What are your rights to privacy when dealing with financial institutions? Use the internet to research the specific privacy provisions related to banking and financial services, and write a paper on how you can use this information to protect your privacy and financial identity.

Critical Thinking Case

Stripe Revolutionizes Digital Payments

Raised in Ireland, Patrick and John Collison were precocious, inquisitive youngsters who taught themselves computer coding at an early age. By the time they were teenagers, the brothers were developing iPhone apps and eventually became college dropouts after a few semesters at MIT (Patrick) and Harvard (John). During this time they started a company called Auctomatic Inc., which created an online marketplace management system for companies such as eBay, and then sold the company for $5 million in 2008.

After selling the business, they continued to work on simplifying the payment process for startup businesses that use the internet to sell goods and services. As the internet entered its second decade and more and more entrepreneurs were using the web to do business, the Collisons recognized that the payment transaction process for online purchases needed an overhaul. In 2011, they opened their new company, Stripe, after testing their service and building relationships with banks, credit card companies, and regulators, so clients could focus their energies on building their businesses—and not building a payment infrastructure from scratch.

Using Stripe, businesses only need to add seven lines of coding to their websites to handle payments—a process that previously could have taken weeks to perfect. Word spread quickly among developers that the Collison brothers' simple coding architecture could indeed disrupt the payment processing industry. As more and more marketplace companies and other online services needed to divvy up payments between vendors and consumers, Stripe became the go-to company to figure out how to move money online quickly and to get people (and companies) paid. The company's engineers determined how to separate payments for some of the internet's startups such as Lyft, which needed consumers to pay for rides and drivers to be compensated quickly. Stripe engineers worked their magic to bypass typical banking protocol and linked payments to Lyft drivers via their debit cards, which allowed them to be paid promptly.

After seven years in business, Stripe is now the financial "back office" for more than 100,000 businesses that take mobile payments—some of them startups and some of them big businesses such as Amazon, Salesforce, and Target. The company charges a 2.9 percent fee on credit card payments in exchange for its services. Although Stripe's sales data is confidential, analysts estimate Stripe handles more than $50 billion in commerce annually, which translates to nearly $1.5 billion in revenue.

With more than 750 employees, Stripe continues to expand its product offerings in an effort to give customers and potential clients new tools they can use to help grow their business. For example, Radar, Stripe's fraud detection service, uses artificial intelligence to analyze payments on its extensive network to identify suspicious activity. By looking at such a large data set on its own network, Stripe can spot patterns better than a single company reviewing its own transactions. The company recently rolled out another tool called Atlas, which can help a local or overseas startup incorporate, get a taxpayer ID number and U.S. bank account, and receive legal and tax advice on forming a company—for a fee of $500 and a few simple clicks. Typically this process would take months, many visits to the United States (if a foreign business), and large legal fees.

Stripe continues to disrupt the payment processing industry, and its Irish cofounders believe they have what it takes to continue building a simple internet infrastructure that will allow startups across the globe to do business and handle mobile payments efficiently—giving entrepreneurs more time to focus on growing successful businesses.

Critical Thinking Questions

1. Do you think Stripe's strategy of keeping things simple is a sound business plan? Explain your reasoning.
2. What impact do you think the company's Atlas product offering will have on Stripe's global expansion?
3. Do you think Stripe's agility in working with so many different businesses provides the company with a competitive advantage over big banks and credit card companies? Justify your answer.

Sources: "About Us," https://stripe.com, accessed September 12, 2017; Matt Weinberger, "$9 Billion Stripe Has a Master Plan to Take Over the World—or at Least, Open It Up for Business," *Business Insider,* http://www.businessinsider.com, August 10, 2017; Ashlee Vance, "How Two Brothers Turned Seven Lines of Code into a $9.2 Billion Startup," *Bloomberg Businessweek,* https://www.businessweek.com, August 1, 2017; "Stripe CEO Patrick Collison on Recode Decode (Podcast transcript)," *Recode,* https://www.recode.net, June 13, 2017; Marguerite Ward, "Meet the 20-Something Stripe Founders Who Are Now Worth More Than $1 Billion Each," *CNBC,* https://www.cnbc.com, March 20, 2017; Rolfe Winkler and Telis Demos, "Stripe's Valuation Nearly Doubles to $9.2 Billion," *The Wall Street Journal,* https://www.wsj.com, November 25, 2016.

Hot Links Address Book

1. Tour the American Currency Exhibit to learn the history of our nation's money at **http://www.frbsf.org/ currency**.
2. The website of the Federal Reserve Bank of St. Louis offers an easy-to-understand explanation of how the Federal Reserve System works, called "In Plain English": **https://www.stlouisfed.org/in-plain-english/ landing/home**.
3. The FDIC gets so many requests about banks' insurance status that it added an option to determine "Is my account fully insured?" on its website. Visit **http://www.fdic.gov**.
4. What goes on at a Federal Open Market Committee meeting? Find out by reading the minutes of the Committee's latest meeting at **http://www.federalreserve.gov/fomc**.
5. Find out what other services the Federal Reserve provides to financial institutions at **http://www.frbservices.org**.
6. How did Abraham Lincoln do his banking? Take a cybertour of American banking history by clicking on the About the OCC tab at **https://www.occ.treas.gov**.
7. To find out if you're eligible to join a credit union, visit the National Credit Union Administration's credit union locator at **https://www.ncua.gov**.

16

Understanding Financial Management and Securities Markets

Exhibit 16.1 (Credit: skys the limit2 / flickr / Attribution 2.0 Generic (CC BY 2.0))

 Introduction

Learning Outcomes

After reading this chapter, you should be able to answer these questions:

1. How do finance and the financial manager affect a firm's overall strategy?
2. What types of short-term and long-term expenditures does a firm make?
3. What are the main sources and costs of unsecured and secured short-term financing?
4. What are the key differences between debt and equity, and what are the major types and features of long-term debt?
5. When and how do firms issue equity, and what are the costs?
6. How do securities markets help firms raise funding, and what securities trade in the capital markets?
7. Where can investors buy and sell securities, and how are securities markets regulated?
8. What are the current developments in financial management and the securities markets?

EXPLORING BUSINESS CAREERS

Vicki Saunders, Venture Capitalist & Entrepreneur

Many women dream of starting their own business. But this involves a large investment of time, dedication, creativity—and money. Even the best ideas fall flat without strong financial backing and fiscal management. Most start-ups don't have a chief financial officer, let alone an unlimited amount of cash to fund their owners' dreams.

According to a recent report, there are more than 11 million woman-owned businesses in the United

States that employ close to 9 million people and generate more than $1.6 trillion in revenues. And revenues have increased for these businesses more than 35% over the last decade compared to 27% among all U.S. companies. Despite these impressive statistics, less than 4 percent of venture capital funding goes to this group of entrepreneurs. That's where Vicki Saunders and SheEO, her venture capital start-up, come into the picture.

Saunders, who describes herself as a serial entrepreneur, previously cofounded and ran four different business ventures. She believes that the funding universe for women entrepreneurs needs to be fixed and offers her plan via SheEO, a platform to enlist women "activators" to invest money to create a pool of capital distributed to select woman-owned businesses in the form of 0% interest loans that are paid back within five years. The activators are more than just investors, however. Saunders envisions these women as being a crucial part of the businesses in which they invest, by providing operational support, resources for suppliers and other vendors, and a solid networking opportunity for everything from legal support to cultivating new customers. In a recent campaign called Radical Generosity, $1,000 was raised from each of 500 women, and that pool of $500,000 was split among five woman-led businesses.

In year three of the funding venture in 2017, SheEO funded 15 companies and invested $1.5 million. SheEO has funded entrepreneurs working on a variety of businesses, including artificial intelligence, hardware for people with disabilities, food, and education. While SheEO currently operates in four regions, Canada, Los Angeles, San Francisco, and Colorado, Saunders's goals for funding woman-led businesses are lofty. By 2020, Saunders hopes to have a million investors and a billion dollars to fund 10,000 entrepreneurs. But her ultimate goal is to change the culture around how investors support businesses—all businesses. According to Saunders, activating women on behalf of other women will change the world.

Sources: Company website, "About Us," https://sheeo.world, accessed November 5, 2017; Emma Hinchliffe, "SheEO Has a Plan to Build a $1 Billion Fund for Female Founders," *Mashable,* http://mashable.com, October 24, 2017; Catherine McIntyre, "How Vicki Saunders Plans to Get a Million Women Involved in Venture Capital," *Canadian Business,* http://www.canadianbusiness.com, accessed October 24, 2017; Kimberly Weisul, "Venture Capital Is Broken. These Women Are Trying to Fix It," *Inc.,* https://www.inc.com, accessed October 24, 2017; Geri Stengel, "Women Become Financiers to Disrupt the Funding Landscape for Entrepreneurs," *Forbes,* https://www.forbes.com, October 18, 2017; Kathleen Chaykowski, "Meet the Top Women Investors in VC in 2017," *Forbes,* https://www.forbes.com, April 18, 2017; Jill Richmond, "Everything May Be Broken But This CEO's Glasses Are a Rose Hue," *Forbes,* https://www.forbes.com, December 16, 2016.

In today's fast-paced global economy, managing a firm's finances is more complex than ever. For financial managers, a thorough command of traditional finance activities—financial planning, investing money, and raising funds—is only part of the job. Financial managers are more than number crunchers. As part of the top management team, chief financial officers (CFOs) need a broad understanding of their firm's business and industry, as well as leadership ability and creativity. They must never lose sight of the primary goal of the financial manager: to maximize the value of the firm to its owners.

Financial management—spending and raising a firm's money—is both a science and an art. The science part is analyzing numbers and flows of cash through the firm. The art is answering questions such as these: Is the firm using its financial resources in the best way? Aside from costs, why choose a particular form of financing? How risky is each option? Another important concern for both business managers and investors is understanding the basics of securities markets and the securities traded on them, which affect both corporate plans and investor pocketbooks. About 52 percent of adult Americans now own stocks, compared to just 25 percent in 1981.[1]

This chapter focuses on the financial management of a firm and the securities markets in which firms raise funds. We'll start with an overview of the role of finance and of the financial manager in the firm's overall business strategy. Discussions of short- and long-term uses of funds and investment decisions follow. Next, we'll examine key sources of short- and long-term financing. Then we'll review the function, operation, and regulation of securities markets. Finally, we'll look at key trends affecting financial management and securities markets.

16.1 | The Role of Finance and the Financial Manager

1. How do finance and the financial manager affect the firm's overall strategy?

Any company, whether it's a small-town bakery or General Motors, needs money to operate. To make money, it must first spend money—on inventory and supplies, equipment and facilities, and employee wages and salaries. Therefore, finance is critical to the success of all companies. It may not be as visible as marketing or production, but management of a firm's finances is just as much a key to the firm's success.

Financial management—the art and science of managing a firm's money so that it can meet its goals—is not just the responsibility of the finance department. All business decisions have financial consequences. Managers in all departments must work closely with financial personnel. If you are a sales representative, for example, the company's credit and collection policies will affect your ability to make sales. The head of the IT department will need to justify any requests for new computer systems or employee laptops.

Revenues from sales of the firm's products should be the chief source of funding. But money from sales doesn't always come in when it's needed to pay the bills. Financial managers must track how money is flowing into and out of the firm (see **Exhibit 16.2**). They work with the firm's other department managers to determine how available funds will be used and how much money is needed. Then they choose the best sources to obtain the required funding.

For example, a financial manager will track day-to-day operational data such as cash collections and disbursements to ensure that the company has enough cash to meet its obligations. Over a longer time horizon, the manager will thoroughly study whether and when the company should open a new manufacturing facility. The manager will also suggest the most appropriate way to finance the project, raise the funds, and then monitor the project's implementation and operation.

Financial management is closely related to accounting. In most firms, both areas are the responsibility of the vice president of finance or CFO. But the accountant's main function is to collect and present financial data. Financial managers use financial statements and other information prepared by accountants to make financial decisions. Financial managers focus on **cash flows**, the inflows and outflows of cash. They plan and monitor the firm's cash flows to ensure that cash is available when needed.

The Financial Manager's Responsibilities and Activities

Financial managers have a complex and challenging job. They analyze financial data prepared by accountants, monitor the firm's financial status, and prepare and implement financial plans. One day they may be developing a better way to automate cash collections, and the next they may be analyzing a proposed acquisition. The key activities of the financial manager are:

- *Financial planning:* Preparing the financial plan, which projects revenues, expenditures, and financing needs over a given period.
- *Investment (spending money):* Investing the firm's funds in projects and securities that provide high returns in relation to their risks.
- *Financing (raising money):* Obtaining funding for the firm's operations and investments and seeking the best balance between debt (borrowed funds) and equity (funds raised through the sale of ownership in the business).

The Goal of the Financial Manager

How can financial managers make wise planning, investment, and financing decisions? The main goal of the financial manager is to maximize the value of the firm to its owners. The value of a publicly owned corporation is measured by the share price of its stock. A private company's value is the price at which it could be sold.

To maximize the firm's value, the financial manager has to consider both short- and long-term consequences of the firm's actions. Maximizing profits is one approach, but it should not be the only one. Such an approach favors making short-term gains over achieving long-term goals. What if a firm in a highly technical and competitive industry did no research and development? In the short run, profits would be high because research and development is very expensive. But in the long run, the firm might lose its ability to compete because of its lack of new products.

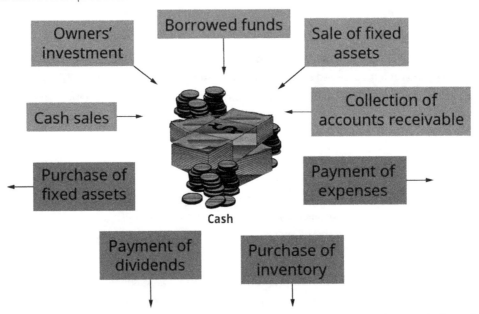

Exhibit 16.2   How Cash Flows through a Business (Attribution: Copyright Rice University, OpenStax, under CC BY 4.0 license.)

This is true regardless of a company's size or point in its life cycle. At Corning, a company founded more than 160 years ago, management believes in taking the long-term view and not managing for quarterly earnings to satisfy Wall Street's expectations. The company, once known to consumers mostly for kitchen products such as Corelle dinnerware and Pyrex heat-resistant glass cookware, is today a technology company that manufactures specialized glass and ceramic products. It is a leading supplier of Gorilla Glass, a special type of glass used for the screens of mobile devices, including the iPhone, the iPad, and devices powered by Google's Android operating system. The company was also the inventor of optical fiber and cable for the telecommunications industry. These product lines require large investments during their long research and development (R&D) cycles and for plant and equipment once they go into production.[2]

This can be risky in the short term, but staying the course can pay off. In fact, Corning recently announced plans to develop a separate company division for Gorilla Glass, which now has more than 20 percent of the phone market—with over 200 million devices sold. In addition, its fiber-optic cable business is back in vogue and thriving as cable service providers such as Verizon have doubled down on upgrading the fiber-optic network across the United States. As of 2017, Corning's commitment to repurposing some of its technologies and developing new products has helped the company's bottom line, increasing revenues in a recent quarter by more than 16 percent.[3]

As the Corning situation demonstrates, financial managers constantly strive for a balance between the opportunity for profit and the potential for loss. In finance, the opportunity for profit is termed **return**; the potential for loss, or the chance that an investment will not achieve the expected level of return, is **risk**. A basic principle in finance is that the higher the risk, the greater the return that is required. This widely accepted concept is called the **risk-return trade-off**. Financial managers consider many risk and return factors when making investment and financing decisions. Among them are changing patterns of market demand, interest rates, general economic conditions, market conditions, and social issues (such as environmental effects and equal employment opportunity policies).

CONCEPT CHECK

1. What is the role of financial management in a firm?
2. How do the three key activities of the financial manager relate?
3. What is the main goal of the financial manager? How does the risk-return trade-off relate to the financial manager's main goal?

16.2 How Organizations Use Funds

2. What types of short-term and long-term expenditures does a firm make?

To grow and prosper, a firm must keep investing money in its operations. The financial manager decides how best to use the firm's money. Short-term expenses support the firm's day-to-day activities. For instance, athletic-apparel maker Nike regularly spends money to buy such raw materials as leather and fabric and to pay employee salaries. Long-term expenses are typically for fixed assets. For Nike, these would include outlays to build a new factory, buy automated manufacturing equipment, or acquire a small manufacturer of sports apparel.

Short-Term Expenses

Short-term expenses, often called operating expenses, are outlays used to support current production and selling activities. They typically result in current assets, which include cash and any other assets (accounts receivable and inventory) that can be converted to cash within a year. The financial manager's goal is to manage current assets so the firm has enough cash to pay its bills and to support its accounts receivable and inventory.

Cash Management: Assuring Liquidity

Cash is the lifeblood of business. Without it, a firm could not operate. An important duty of the financial manager is **cash management**, or making sure that enough cash is on hand to pay bills as they come due and to meet unexpected expenses.

Businesses estimate their cash requirements for a specific period. Many companies keep a minimum cash balance to cover unexpected expenses or changes in projected cash flows. The financial manager arranges loans to cover any shortfalls. If the size and timing of cash inflows closely match the size and timing of cash outflows, the company needs to keep only a small amount of cash on hand. A company whose sales and receipts are fairly predictable and regular throughout the year needs less cash than a company with a seasonal pattern of sales and receipts. A toy company, for instance, whose sales are concentrated in the fall, spends a great deal of cash during the spring and summer to build inventory. It has excess cash during the winter and early spring, when it collects on sales from its peak selling season.

Because cash held in checking accounts earns little, if any, interest, the financial manager tries to keep cash balances low and to invest the surplus cash. Surpluses are invested temporarily in **marketable securities**, short-term investments that are easily converted into cash. The financial manager looks for low-risk investments that offer high returns. Three of the most popular marketable securities are Treasury bills, certificates of deposit, and commercial paper. (**Commercial paper** is unsecured short-term debt—an IOU—issued by a financially strong corporation.) Today's financial managers have new tools to help them find the best short-term investments, such as online trading platforms that save time and provide access to more types of investments. These have been especially useful for smaller companies who don't have large finance staffs.

Companies with overseas operations face even greater cash management challenges. Developing the systems for international cash management may sound simple in theory, but in practice it's extremely complex. In addition to dealing with multiple foreign currencies, treasurers must understand and follow banking practices and regulatory and tax requirements in each country. Regulations may impede their ability to move funds freely across borders. Also, issuing a standard set of procedures for every office may not work because local business practices differ from country to country. In addition, local managers may resist the shift to a centralized structure because they don't want to give up control of cash generated by their units. Corporate financial managers must be sensitive to and aware of local customs and adapt the centralization strategy accordingly.

In addition to seeking the right balance between cash and marketable securities, the financial manager tries to shorten the time between the purchase of inventory or services (cash outflows) and the collection of cash from sales (cash inflows). The three key strategies are to collect money owed to the firm (accounts receivable) as quickly as possible, to pay money owed to others (accounts payable) as late as possible without damaging the firm's credit reputation, and to minimize the funds tied up in inventory.

Managing Accounts Receivable

Accounts receivable represent sales for which the firm has not yet been paid. Because the product has been sold but cash has not yet been received, an account receivable amounts to a use of funds. For the average manufacturing firm, accounts receivable represent about 15 to 20 percent of total assets.

The financial manager's goal is to collect money owed to the firm as quickly as possible, while offering customers credit terms attractive enough to increase sales. Accounts receivable management involves setting credit policies, guidelines on offering credit, credit terms, and specific repayment conditions, including how long customers have to pay their bills and whether a cash discount is given for quicker payment. Another aspect of accounts receivable management is deciding on collection policies, the procedures for collecting overdue accounts.

Setting up credit and collection policies is a balancing act for financial managers. On the one hand, easier credit policies or generous credit terms (a longer repayment period or larger cash discount) result in increased sales. On the other hand, the firm has to finance more accounts receivable. The risk of uncollectible accounts receivable also rises. Businesses consider the impact on sales, timing of cash flow, experience with bad debt, customer profiles, and industry standards when developing their credit and collection policies.

Companies that want to speed up collections actively manage their accounts receivable, rather than passively letting customers pay when they want to. According to recent statistics, more than 90 percent of businesses experience late payments from customers, and some companies write off a percentage of their bad debt, which can be expensive.[4]

Technology plays a big role in helping companies improve their credit and collections performance. For example, many companies use some type of automated decision-making, whether that comes in the form of an ERP system or a combination of software programs and supplemental modules that help companies make informed decisions when it comes to credit and collection processes.[5]

Other companies choose to outsource financial and accounting business processes to specialists rather than develop their own systems. The availability of cutting-edge technology and specialized electronic platforms that would be difficult and expensive to develop in-house is winning over firms of all sizes. Giving up control of finance to a third party has not been easy for CFOs. The risks are high when financial and other sensitive corporate data are transferred to an outside computer system: data could be compromised or lost, or rivals could steal corporate data. It's also harder to monitor an outside provider than your own employees. One outsourcing area that has attracted many clients is international trade, which has regulations that differ from country to country and requires huge amounts of documentation. With specialized IT systems, providers can track not only the physical location of goods, but also all the paperwork associated with shipments. Processing costs for goods purchased overseas are about twice those of domestic goods, so more efficient systems pay off.[6]

Inventory

Another use of funds is to buy inventory needed by the firm. In a typical manufacturing firm, inventory is nearly 20 percent of total assets. The cost of inventory includes not only its purchase price, but also ordering, handling, storage, interest, and insurance costs.

Production, marketing, and finance managers usually have differing views about inventory. Production managers want lots of raw materials on hand to avoid production delays. Marketing managers want lots of finished goods on hand so customer orders can be filled quickly. But financial managers want the least inventory possible without harming production efficiency or sales. Financial managers must work closely with production and marketing to balance these conflicting goals. Techniques for reducing the investment in inventory are inventory management, the just-in-time system, and materials requirement planning.

For retail firms, inventory management is a critical area for financial managers, who closely monitor inventory turnover ratios. This ratio shows how quickly inventory moves through the firm and is turned into sales. If the inventory number is too high, it will typically affect the amount of working capital a company has on hand, forcing the company to borrow money to cover the excess inventory. If the turnover ratio number is too high, it means the company does not have enough inventory of products on hand to satisfy customer needs, which means they could take their business elsewhere.[7]

Long-Term Expenditures

A firm also invests funds in physical assets such as land, buildings, machinery, equipment, and information systems. These are called **capital expenditures**. Unlike operating expenses, which produce benefits within a year, the benefits from capital expenditures extend beyond one year. For instance, a printer's purchase of a new printing press with a usable life of seven years is a capital expenditure and appears as a fixed asset on the firm's balance sheet. Paper, ink, and other supplies, however, are expenses. Mergers and acquisitions are also considered capital expenditures.

Firms make capital expenditures for many reasons. The most common are to expand, to replace or renew fixed assets, and to develop new products. Most manufacturing firms have a big investment in long-term assets. Boeing Company, for instance, puts billions of dollars a year into airplane-manufacturing facilities. Because capital expenditures tend to be costly and have a major effect on the firm's future, the financial manager uses a process called **capital budgeting** to analyze long-term projects and select those that offer the best returns while maximizing the firm's value. Decisions involving new products or the acquisition of another business are especially important. Managers look at project costs and forecast the future benefits the project will bring to calculate the firm's estimated return on the investment.

CONCEPT CHECK

1. Distinguish between short- and long-term expenses.
2. What is the financial manager's goal in cash management? List the three key cash management strategies.
3. Describe a firm's main motives in making capital expenditures.

16.3 | Obtaining Short-Term Financing

3. What are the main sources and costs of unsecured and secured short-term financing?

How do firms raise the funding they need? They borrow money (debt), sell ownership shares (equity), and retain earnings (profits). The financial manager must assess all these sources and choose the one most likely to help maximize the firm's value.

Like expenses, borrowed funds can be divided into short- and long-term loans. A short-term loan comes due within one year; a long-term loan has a maturity greater than one year. Short-term financing is shown as a current liability on the balance sheet and is used to finance current assets and support operations. Short-term loans can be unsecured or secured.

Unsecured Short-Term Loans

Unsecured loans are made on the basis of the firm's creditworthiness and the lender's previous experience with the firm. An unsecured borrower does not have to pledge specific assets as security. The three main types of unsecured short-term loans are trade credit, bank loans, and commercial paper.

Trade Credit: Accounts Payable

When Goodyear sells tires to General Motors, GM does not have to pay cash on delivery. Instead, Goodyear regularly bills GM for its tire purchases, and GM pays at a later date. This is an example of **trade credit**: the seller extends credit to the buyer between the time the buyer receives the goods or services and when it pays for them. Trade credit is a major source of short-term business financing. The buyer enters the credit on its books as an **account payable**. In effect, the credit is a short-term loan from the seller to the buyer of the goods and services. Until GM pays Goodyear, Goodyear has an account receivable from GM, and GM has an account payable to Goodyear.

Bank Loans

Unsecured bank loans are another source of short-term business financing. Companies often use these loans to finance seasonal (cyclical) businesses. Unsecured bank loans include lines of credit and revolving credit agreements. A **line of credit** specifies the maximum amount of unsecured short-term borrowing the bank will allow the firm over a given period, typically one year. The firm either pays a fee or keeps a certain percentage of the loan amount (generally 10 to 20 percent) in a checking account at the bank. Another bank loan, the **revolving credit agreement**, is basically a guaranteed line of credit that carries an extra fee in addition to interest. Revolving credit agreements are often arranged for a period of two to five years.

Commercial Paper

As noted earlier, commercial paper is an unsecured short-term debt—an IOU—issued by a financially strong corporation. Thus, it is both a short-term investment and a financing option for major corporations. Corporations issue commercial paper in multiples of $100,000 for periods ranging from 3 to 270 days. Many big companies use commercial paper instead of short-term bank loans because the interest rate on commercial paper is usually 1 to 3 percent below bank rates.

Secured Short-Term Loans

Secured loans require the borrower to pledge specific assets as collateral, or security. The secured lender can legally take the collateral if the borrower doesn't repay the loan. Commercial banks and commercial finance companies are the main sources of secured short-term loans to business. Borrowers whose credit is not strong enough to qualify for unsecured loans use these loans. Typically, the collateral for secured short-term loans is accounts receivable or inventory. Because accounts receivable are normally quite liquid (easily converted to cash), they are an attractive form of collateral. The appeal of inventory—raw materials or finished goods—as collateral depends on how easily it can be sold at a fair price.

Another form of short-term financing using accounts receivable is **factoring**. A firm sells its accounts receivable outright to a factor, a financial institution (often a commercial bank or commercial finance company) that buys accounts receivable at a discount. Factoring is widely used in the clothing, furniture, and appliance industries. Factoring is more expensive than a bank loan, however, because the factor buys the receivables at a discount from their actual value.

Exhibit 16.3 For businesses with steady orders but a lack of cash to make payroll or other immediate payments, factoring is a popular way to obtain financing. In factoring, a company sells its invoices to a third-party funding source for cash. The factor purchasing the invoices then collects on the due payments over time. Trucking companies with voluminous accounts receivable in the form of freight bills are good candidates for the use of short-term financing such as factoring. *Why might firms choose factoring instead of loans?* (Credit: Mike's Photos/ flickr/ Creative Commons Zero (CC0) license)

CONCEPT CHECK

1. Distinguish between unsecured and secured short-term loans.
2. Briefly describe the three main types of unsecured short-term loans.
3. Discuss the two ways that accounts receivable can be used to obtain short-term financing.

16.4 | Raising Long-Term Financing

4. What are the key differences between debt and equity, and what are the major types and features of long-term debt?

A basic principle of finance is to match the term of the financing to the period over which benefits are expected to be received from the associated outlay. Short-term items should be financed with short-term funds, and long-term items should be financed with long-term funds. Long-term financing sources include both debt (borrowing) and equity (ownership). Equity financing comes either from selling new ownership interests or from retaining earnings. Financial managers try to select the mix of long-term debt and equity that results in the best balance between cost and risk.

Debt versus Equity Financing

Say that the Boeing Company plans to spend $2 billion over the next four years to build and equip new factories to make jet aircraft. Boeing's top management will assess the pros and cons of both debt and equity and then consider several possible sources of the desired form of long-term financing.

The major advantage of debt financing is the deductibility of interest expense for income tax purposes, which lowers its overall cost. In addition, there is no loss of ownership. The major drawback is **financial risk**: the chance that the firm will be unable to make scheduled interest and principal payments. The lender can force a borrower that fails to make scheduled debt payments into bankruptcy. Most loan agreements have restrictions to ensure that the borrower operates efficiently.

Equity, on the other hand, is a form of permanent financing that places few restrictions on the firm. The firm is not required to pay dividends or repay the investment. However, equity financing gives common stockholders voting rights that provide them with a voice in management. Equity is more costly than debt. Unlike the interest on debt, dividends to owners are not tax-deductible expenses. Table 16.1 summarizes the major differences between debt and equity financing.

Debt Financing

Long-term debt is used to finance long-term (capital) expenditures. The initial maturities of long-term debt typically range between 5 and 20 years. Three important forms of long-term debt are term loans, bonds, and mortgage loans.

Major Differences between Debt and Equity Financing		
	Debt Financing	Equity Financing
Have a say in management	Creditors typically have none, unless the borrower defaults on payments. Creditors may be able to place restraints on management in event of default.	Common stockholders have voting rights.
Have a right to income and assets	Debt holders rank ahead of equity holders. Payment of interest and principal is a contractual obligation of the firm.	Equity owners have a residual claim on income (dividends are paid only after paying interest and any scheduled principal) and no obligation to pay dividends.
Maturity (date when debt needs to be paid back)	Debt has a stated maturity and requires repayment of principal by a specified date.	The company is not required to repay equity, which has no maturity date.

Table 16.1

Major Differences between Debt and Equity Financing		
	Debt Financing	Equity Financing
Tax treatment	Interest is a tax-deductible expense.	Dividends are not tax-deductible and are paid from after-tax income.

Table 16.1

A **term loan** is a business loan with a maturity of more than one year. Term loans generally have maturities of 5 to 12 years and can be unsecured or secured. They are available from commercial banks, insurance companies, pension funds, commercial finance companies, and manufacturers' financing subsidiaries. A contract between the borrower and the lender spells out the amount and maturity of the loan, the interest rate, payment dates, the purpose of the loan, and other provisions such as operating and financial restrictions on the borrower to control the risk of default. The payments include both interest and principal, so the loan balance declines over time. Borrowers try to arrange a repayment schedule that matches the forecast cash flow from the project being financed.

Bonds are long-term debt obligations (liabilities) of corporations and governments. A bond certificate is issued as proof of the obligation. The issuer of a bond must pay the buyer a fixed amount of money—called **interest**, stated as the *coupon rate*—on a regular schedule, typically every six months. The issuer must also pay the bondholder the amount borrowed—called the **principal**, or *par value*—at the bond's maturity date (due date). Bonds are usually issued in units of $1,000—for instance, $1,000, $5,000, or $10,000—and have initial maturities of 10 to 30 years. They may be secured or unsecured, include special provisions for early retirement, or be convertible to common stock.

A **mortgage loan** is a long-term loan made against real estate as collateral. The lender takes a mortgage on the property, which lets the lender seize the property, sell it, and use the proceeds to pay off the loan if the borrower fails to make the scheduled payments. Long-term mortgage loans are often used to finance office buildings, factories, and warehouses. Life insurance companies are an important source of these loans. They make billions of dollars' worth of mortgage loans to businesses each year.

CONCEPT CHECK

1. Distinguish between debt and equity.
2. Identify the major types and features of long term debt.

16.5 Equity Financing

5. When and how do firms issue equity, and what are the costs?

Equity refers to the owners' investment in the business. In corporations, the preferred and common stockholders are the owners. A firm obtains equity financing by selling new ownership shares (external financing), by retaining earnings (internal financing), or for small and growing, typically high-tech, companies, through venture capital (external financing).

Selling New Issues of Common Stock

Common stock is a security that represents an ownership interest in a corporation. A company's first sale of stock to the public is called an *initial public offering (IPO)*. An IPO often enables existing stockholders, usually employees, family, and friends who bought the stock privately, to earn big profits on their investment. (Companies that are already public can issue and sell additional shares of common stock to raise equity funds.)

But going public has some drawbacks. For one thing, there is no guarantee an IPO will sell. It is also expensive. Big fees must be paid to investment bankers, brokers, attorneys, accountants, and printers. Once the company is public, it is closely watched by regulators, stockholders, and securities analysts. The firm must reveal such information as operating and financial data, product details, financing plans, and operating strategies. Providing this information is often costly.

Going public is the dream of many small company founders and early investors, who hope to recoup their investments and become instant millionaires. Google, which went public in 2004 at $85 a share and soared to $475 in early 2006 before settling back to trade in the high-300 range in August 2006. More than a decade later, in October 2017, Google continues to be a successful IPO, trading at more than $990 per share.

In recent years, the number of IPOs has dropped sharply, as start-ups think long and hard about going public, despite the promise of millions of dollars for investors and entrepreneurs. For example, in 2017, Blue Apron, a meal-kit delivery service, went public with an opening stock price of $10 per share. Several months later, the share price dropped more than 40 percent. Some analysts believe that Amazon's possible entry into the meal-kit delivery sector has hurt Blue Apron's value, as well as the company's high marketing costs to attract and retain monthly subscribers.[8]

Some companies choose to remain private. Cargill, SC Johnson, Mars, Publix Super Markets, and Bloomberg are among the largest U.S. private companies.

Exhibit 16.4   Snap Inc., the parent company of Snapchat, went public in 2017 under the ticker symbol "SNAP." The much-anticipated IPO was popular at an opening price of $17 per share and rose that same day by more than 40 percent, which initially put the company's market capitalization at about $30 billion. *What are the pros and cons of going public?* (Credit: Tim Savage/ pexels/ Creative Commons Zero (CC0) license)

Dividends and Retained Earnings

Dividends are payments to stockholders from a corporation's profits. Dividends can be paid in cash or in stock. **Stock dividends** are payments in the form of more stock. Stock dividends may replace or supplement cash dividends. After a stock dividend has been paid, more shares have a claim on the same company, so the value of each share often declines. A company does not have to pay dividends to stockholders. But if investors buy the stock expecting to get dividends and the firm does not pay them, the investors may sell their stocks.

At their quarterly meetings, the company's board of directors (typically with the advice of its CFO) decides how much of the profits to distribute as dividends and how much to reinvest. A firm's basic approach to paying dividends can greatly affect its share price. A stable history of dividend payments indicates good financial health. For example, cable giant Comcast has increased its dividend more than 20 percent over the past five years, giving shareholders a healthy return on their investment.[9]

If a firm that has been making regular dividend payments cuts or skips a dividend, investors start thinking it has serious financial problems. The increased uncertainty often results in lower stock prices. Thus, most firms set dividends at a level they can keep paying. They start with a relatively low dividend payout ratio so that they can maintain a steady or slightly increasing dividend over time.

Retained earnings, profits that have been reinvested in the firm, have a big advantage over other sources of equity capital: They do not incur underwriting costs. Financial managers strive to balance dividends and retained earnings to maximize the value of the firm. Often the balance reflects the nature of the firm and its industry. Well-established and stable firms and those that expect only modest growth, such as public utilities, financial services companies, and large industrial corporations, typically pay out much of their earnings in dividends. For example, in the 2016 fiscal year, ExxonMobil paid dividends of $3.08 per share, Altria Group paid $2.64 per share, Apple paid $2.23 per share, and Costco paid $2.00 per share.

Most high-growth companies, such as those in technology-related fields, finance much of their growth through retained earnings and pay little or no dividends to stockholders. As they mature, many decide to begin paying dividends, as Apple decided to do in 2012, after 17 years of paying no annual dividends to shareholders.[10]

Preferred Stock

Another form of equity is **preferred stock**. Unlike common stock, preferred stock usually has a dividend amount that is set at the time the stock is issued. These dividends must be paid before the company can pay any dividends to common stockholders. Also, if the firm goes bankrupt and sells its assets, preferred stockholders get their money back before common stockholders do.

Like debt, preferred stock increases the firm's financial risk because it obligates the firm to make a fixed payment. But preferred stock is more flexible. The firm can miss a dividend payment without suffering the serious results of failing to pay back a debt.

Preferred stock is more expensive than debt financing, however, because preferred dividends are not tax-deductible. Also, because the claims of preferred stockholders on income and assets are second to those of debtholders, preferred stockholders require higher returns to compensate for the greater risk.

Venture Capital

Venture capital is another source of equity capital. It is most often used by small and growing firms that aren't big enough to sell securities to the public. This type of financing is especially popular among high-tech companies that need large sums of money.

Venture capitalists invest in new businesses in return for part of the ownership, sometimes as much as 60 percent. They look for new businesses with high growth potential, and they expect a high investment return within 5 to 10 years. By getting in on the ground floor, venture capitalists buy stock at a very low price. They earn profits by selling the stock at a much higher price when the company goes public. Venture capitalists generally get a voice in management through seats on the board of directors. Getting venture capital is difficult, even though there are hundreds of private venture-capital firms in this country. Most venture capitalists finance only about 1 to 5 percent of the companies that apply. Venture-capital investors, many of whom experienced losses during recent years from their investments in failed dot-coms, are currently less willing to take risks on very early-stage companies with unproven technology. As a result, other sources of venture capital, including private foundations, states, and wealthy individuals (called *angel investors*), are helping start-up firms find equity capital. These private investors are motivated by the potential to earn a high return on their investment.

CONCEPT CHECK

1. Compare the advantages and disadvantages of debt and equity financing.

2. Discuss the costs involved in issuing common stock.
3. Briefly describe these sources of equity: retained earnings, preferred stock, venture capital.

16.6 Securities Markets

6. How do securities markets help firms raise funding, and what securities trade in the capital markets?

Stocks, bonds, and other securities trade in securities markets. These markets streamline the purchase and sales activities of investors by allowing transactions to be made quickly and at a fair price. **Securities** are investment certificates that represent either *equity* (ownership in the issuing organization) or *debt* (a loan to the issuer). Corporations and governments raise capital to finance operations and expansion by selling securities to investors, who in turn take on a certain amount of risk with the hope of receiving a profit from their investment.

Securities markets are busy places. On an average day, individual and institutional investors trade billions of shares of stock in more than 10,000 companies through securities markets. *Individual investors* invest their own money to achieve their personal financial goals. **Institutional investors** are investment professionals who are paid to manage other people's money. Most of these professional money managers work for financial institutions, such as banks, mutual funds, insurance companies, and pension funds. Institutional investors control very large sums of money, often buying stock in 10,000-share blocks. They aim to meet the investment goals of their clients. Institutional investors are a major force in the securities markets, accounting for about half of the dollar volume of equities traded.

Types of Markets

Securities markets can be divided into primary and secondary markets. The **primary market** is where *new* securities are sold to the public, usually with the help of investment bankers. In the primary market, the issuer of the security gets the proceeds from the transaction. A security is sold in the primary market just once—when the corporation or government first issues it. The Blue Apron IPO is an example of a primary market offering.

Later transactions take place in the **secondary market**, where *old* (already issued) securities are bought and sold, or traded, among investors. The issuers generally are not involved in these transactions. The vast majority of securities transactions take place in secondary markets, which include broker markets, dealer markets, the over-the-counter market, and the commodities exchanges. You'll see *tombstones,* announcements of both primary and secondary stock and bond offerings, in the *Wall Street Journal* and other newspapers.

The Role of Investment Bankers and Stockbrokers

Two types of investment specialists play key roles in the functioning of the securities markets. **Investment bankers** help companies raise long-term financing. These firms act as intermediaries, buying securities from corporations and governments and reselling them to the public. This process, called **underwriting**, is the main activity of the investment banker, which acquires the security for an agreed-upon price and hopes to be able to resell it at a higher price to make a profit. Investment bankers advise clients on the pricing and structure of new securities offerings, as well as on mergers, acquisitions, and other types of financing. Well-known investment banking firms include Goldman Sachs, Morgan Stanley, JP Morgan, Bank of America Merrill Lynch, and Citigroup.

A **stockbroker** is a person who is licensed to buy and sell securities on behalf of clients. Also called *account executives,* these investment professionals work for brokerage firms and execute the orders customers place for stocks, bonds, mutual funds, and other securities. Investors are wise to seek a broker who understands their investment goals and can help them pursue their objectives.

Brokerage firms are paid commissions for executing clients' transactions. Although brokers can charge whatever they want, most firms have fixed commission schedules for small transactions. These commissions usually depend on the value of the transaction and the number of shares involved.

Online Investing

Improvements in internet technology have made it possible for investors to research, analyze, and trade securities online. Today almost all brokerage firms offer online trading capabilities. Online brokerages are popular with "do-it-yourself" investors who choose their own stocks and don't want to pay a full-service broker for these services. Lower transaction costs are a major benefit. Fees at online brokerages range from about $4.95 to $8.00, depending on the number of trades a client makes and the size of a client's account. Although there are many online brokerage firms, the four largest—Charles Schwab, Fidelity, TD Ameritrade, and E*Trade—account for more than 80 percent of all trading volume and trillions in assets in customer accounts.[11] The internet also offers investors access to a wealth of investment information.

MANAGING CHANGE

Competition Causes Online Fees to Drop

With the U.S. stock market reaching an all-time high in 2017, private investors continue to look for ways to get in or stay in the market without paying exorbitant fees to execute their own trades. Historically, fees associated with buying and selling stocks have been high and considered one reason why investors sought alternatives via online trading platforms offered by firms such as Fidelity, Charles Schwab, TD Ameritrade, and E*Trade. With advances in technology, including the use of artificial intelligence, the costs associated with handling stock trades has dropped dramatically over the last decade, and investors are looking for the best possible deal.

With competition from companies such as Robinhood, a start-up app that offers $0 fees for stock trades, online trading firms have rushed to reduce their fees to attract more overall business, and a price war has ensued. Fidelity and Charles Schwab lowered their fees for online stock and exchange-traded funds to $4.95; Ameritrade and E*Trade reduced their fees from $9.99 to $6.95.

So how will these firms continue to make money? They believe that lowering the price of entry for trading stocks will allow them to "sweep up" customer assets—meaning firms have an opportunity to attract new customers who not only will take advantage of low trading fees but will be interested in other financial products offered by these investment companies. Some of the other services being touted by online trading firms include loaning money to investors to buy stock and cross-selling customers on wealth management services and other investment products.

According to some industry analysts, one downside to matching competitors' low fees could be a strategy of consolidation within the online trading industry. Unless firms can increase their overall business by reaching out to current customers and potential ones, some may be forced to join up with competitors.

Critical Thinking Questions
1. From a business standpoint, do you think the "almost-free" trading fees make sense? Explain.
2. What can online trading firms do to increase their overall business, particularly when it comes to attracting new investors?

Sources: Simone Foxman, "The Future Price of Investing: Zilch," *Bloomberg Businessweek,* http://www.bloomberg.com, October 31, 2017; Evelyn Chang, "Robinhood, Trading App for Millennials, Still Betting on Stocks over Bitcoin," *CNBC,* https://www.cnbc.com, October 10, 2017; Taylor Tepper, "You Probably Have the Wrong Idea When It Comes to Investments. Let's Fix That," http://www.bankrate.com, July 19, 2017; Trevor Hunnicutt and Tim McLaughlin, "Brokerages' Race to Zero Fees Points to a Bigger War to Come," *Reuters,* https://www.reuters.com, February 27, 2017.

Investing in Bonds

When many people think of financial markets, they picture the equity markets. However, the bond markets are huge—the Securities Industry and Financial Markets Association (SIFMA) estimates that the global bond market is nearly $88 trillion. In the United States, companies and government entities sold about $2 billion in new bond issues in 2016. Average daily trading volume exceeded $760 billion, with U.S. Treasury securities accounting for more than 60 percent of the total.[12]

Bonds can be bought and sold in the securities markets. However, the price of a bond changes over its life as market interest rates fluctuate. When the market interest rate drops below the fixed interest rate on a bond, it becomes more valuable, and the price rises. If interest rates rise, the bond's price will fall. *Corporate bonds,* as the name implies, are issued by corporations. They usually have a par value of $1,000. They may be secured or unsecured (called *debentures*), include special provisions for early retirement, or be convertible to common stock. Corporations can also issue *mortgage bonds*, bonds secured by property such as land, buildings, or equipment. Approximately $1.5 trillion in new corporate bonds were issued in 2016.[13]

In addition to regular corporate debt issues, investors can buy *high-yield*, or *junk, bonds*—high-risk, high-return bonds often used by companies whose credit characteristics would not otherwise allow them access to the debt markets. They generally earn 3 percent or more above the returns on high-quality corporate bonds. Corporate bonds may also be issued with an option for the bondholder to convert them into common stock. These *convertible bonds* generally allow the bondholder to exchange each bond for a specified number of shares of common stock.

Exhibit 16.5   Elon Musk and his electric car company, Tesla, issued high-yield junk bonds in August 2017 and raised nearly $1.8 billion to help finance the production and launch of Tesla's new Model 3. Tesla has spent billions of dollars in its efforts to develop electric cars in the past few years. *What are the risks and rewards of buying junk bonds?* (Credit: Steve Jurvetson/ flickr/ Attribution 2.0 Generic (CC BY 2.0))

U.S. Government Securities and Municipal Bonds

Both the federal government and local government agencies also issue bonds. The U.S. Treasury sells three major types of federal debt securities: Treasury bills, Treasury notes, and Treasury bonds. All three are viewed as default-risk-free because they are backed by the U.S. government. Treasury bills mature in less than a year and are issued with a minimum par value of $1,000. Treasury notes have maturities of 10 years or less, and Treasury bonds have maturities as long as 25 years or more. Both notes and bonds are sold in denominations of $1,000 and $5,000. The interest earned on government securities is subject to federal income tax but is free from state and local income taxes. According to SIFMA, a total of $1.7 trillion U.S. treasuries were issued in 2016, down 20 percent from 2015.[14]

Municipal bonds are issued by states, cities, counties, and other state and local government agencies. Almost $445.8 billion in municipal bonds were issued in 2016.[15] These bonds typically have a par value of $5,000 and are either general obligation or revenue bonds. *General obligation bonds* are backed by the full faith and credit (and taxing power) of the issuing government. *Revenue bonds*, on the other hand, are repaid only from income generated by the specific project being financed. Examples of revenue bond projects include toll highways and bridges, power plants, and parking structures. Because the issuer of revenue bonds has no legal obligation to back the bonds if the project's revenues are inadequate, they are considered more risky and therefore have higher interest rates than general obligation bonds.

Municipal bonds are attractive to investors because interest earned on them is exempt from federal income tax. For the same reason, the coupon interest rate for a municipal bond is lower than for a similar-quality corporate bond. In addition, interest earned on municipal bonds issued by governments within the taxpayer's home state is exempt from state income tax as well. In contrast, all interest earned on corporate bonds is fully taxable.

Bond Ratings

Bonds vary in quality, depending on the financial strength of the issuer. Because the claims of bondholders come before those of stockholders, bonds are generally considered less risky than stocks. However, some bonds are in fact quite risky. Companies can default—fail to make scheduled interest or principal payments—on their bonds. Investors can use **bond ratings**, letter grades assigned to bond issues to indicate their quality or level of risk. Ratings for corporate bonds are easy to find. The two largest and best-known rating agencies are Moody's and Standard & Poor's (S&P), whose publications are in most libraries and in stock brokerages. Table 16.2 lists the letter grades assigned by Moody's and S&P. A bond's rating may change if a company's financial condition changes.

Other Popular Securities

In addition to stocks and bonds, investors can buy mutual funds, a very popular investment category, or exchange-traded funds (ETFs). Futures contracts and options are more complex investments for experienced investors.

Mutual Funds

Suppose that you have $1,000 to invest but don't know which stocks or bonds to buy, when to buy them, or when to sell them. By investing in a mutual fund, you can buy shares in a large, professionally managed portfolio, or group, of stocks and bonds. A **mutual fund** is a financial-service company that pools its investors' funds to buy a selection of securities—marketable securities, stocks, bonds, or a combination of securities—that meet its stated investment goals. Each mutual fund focuses on one of a wide variety of possible investment goals, such as growth or income. Many large financial-service companies, such as Fidelity and Vanguard, sell a wide variety of mutual funds, each with a different investment goal. Investors can pick and choose funds that match their particular interests. Some specialized funds invest in a particular type of company or asset: in one industry such as health care or technology, in a geographical region such as Asia, or in an asset such as precious metals.

Mutual funds are one of the most popular investments for individuals today: they can choose from about 9,500 different funds. Investments in mutual funds are more than $40 trillion worldwide, of which U.S. mutual funds hold more than $19 trillion. About 94 million individuals, representing 55 percent of all U.S. households, own mutual funds.[16] Mutual funds appeal to investors for three main reasons:

Moody's and Standard & Poor's Bond Ratings		
Moody's Ratings	S & P Ratings	Description
Aaa	AAA	**Prime-quality investment bonds:** Highest rating assigned; indicates extremely strong capacity to pay.
Aa, A	AA, A	**High-grade investment bonds:** Also considered very safe bonds, although not quite as safe as Aaa/AAA issues; Aa/AA bonds are safer (have less risk of default) than single As.
Baa	BBB	**Medium-grade investment bonds:** Lowest of investment-grade issues; seen as lacking protection against adverse economic conditions.
Ba B	BB B	**Junk bonds:** Provide little protection against default; viewed as highly speculative.
Caa Ca C	CCC CC C D	**Poor-quality bonds:** Either in default or very close to it.

Table 16.2

- They are a good way to hold a diversified, and thus less risky, portfolio. Investors with only $500 or $1,000 to invest cannot diversify much on their own. Buying shares in a mutual fund lets them own part of a portfolio that may contain 100 or more securities.
- Mutual funds are professionally managed.
- Mutual funds may offer higher returns than individual investors could achieve on their own.

Exchange-Traded Funds

Another type of investment, the **exchange-traded fund (ETF)**, has become very popular with investors. ETFs are similar to mutual funds because they hold a broad basket of stocks with a common theme, giving investors instant diversification. ETFs trade on stock exchanges (most trade on the American Stock Exchange, AMEX), so their prices change throughout the day, whereas mutual fund share prices, called net asset values (NAVs), are calculated once a day, at the end of trading. Worldwide, ETF assets in 2016 were more than $3.5 trillion, with the U.S. ETF market accounting for 73 percent of the global market.[17]

Investors can choose from more than 1,700 ETFs that track almost any market sector, from a broad market index such as the S&P 500 (described later in this chapter), industry sectors such as health care or energy, and geographical areas such as a particular country (Japan) or region (Latin America). ETFs have very low expense ratios. However, because they trade as stocks, investors pay commissions to buy and sell these shares.

Futures Contracts and Options

Futures contracts are legally binding obligations to buy or sell specified quantities of commodities (agricultural or mining products) or financial instruments (securities or currencies) at an agreed-on price at a future date. An investor can buy commodity futures contracts in cattle, pork bellies (large slabs of bacon), eggs, coffee, flour, gasoline, fuel oil, lumber, wheat, gold, and silver. Financial futures include Treasury securities and foreign currencies, such as the British pound or Japanese yen. Futures contracts do not pay interest or dividends. The return depends solely on favorable price changes. These are very risky investments because the prices can vary a great deal.

Options are contracts that entitle holders to buy or sell specified quantities of common stocks or other financial instruments at a set price during a specified time. As with futures contracts, investors must correctly guess future price movements in the underlying financial instrument to earn a positive return. Unlike futures contracts, options do not legally obligate the holder to buy or sell, and the price paid for an option is the maximum amount that can be lost. However, options have very short maturities, so it is easy to quickly lose a lot of money with them.

CONCEPT CHECK

1. Distinguish between primary and secondary securities markets. How does an investment banker work with companies to issue securities?
2. Describe the types of bonds available to investors and the advantages and disadvantages they offer.
3. Why do mutual funds and exchange-traded funds appeal to investors? Discuss why futures contracts and options are risky investments.

16.7 Buying and Selling at Securities Exchanges

7. Where can investors buy and sell securities, and how are securities markets regulated?

When we think of stock markets, we are typically referring to secondary markets, which handle most of the securities trading activity. The two segments of the secondary markets are broker markets and dealer markets, as **Exhibit 16.6** shows. The primary difference between broker and dealer markets is the way each executes securities trades. Securities trades can also take place in alternative market systems and on non-U.S. securities exchanges.

The securities markets both in the United States and around the world are in flux and undergoing tremendous changes. We present the basics of securities exchanges in this section and discuss the latest trends in the global securities markets later in the chapter.

Broker Markets

The **broker market** consists of national and regional securities exchanges that bring buyers and sellers together through brokers on a centralized trading floor. In the broker market, the buyer purchases the securities directly from the seller through the broker. Broker markets account for about 60 percent of the total dollar volume of all shares traded in the U.S. securities markets.

Exhibit 16.6   The Secondary Markets: Broker and Dealer Markets (Attribution: Copyright Rice University, OpenStax, under CC BY 4.0 license.)

New York Stock Exchange

The oldest and most prestigious broker market is the *New York Stock Exchange (NYSE),* which has existed since 1792. Often called the Big Board, it is located on Wall Street in downtown New York City. The NYSE, which lists the shares of some 2,400 corporations, had a total market capitalization (domestic and foreign companies) of $25.8 trillion at year-end 2016. On a typical day, more than 3 billion shares of stock are traded on the NYSE.[18] It represents 90 percent of the trading volume in the U.S. broker marketplace. Major companies such as IBM, Coca-Cola, AT&T, Procter & Gamble, Ford Motor Co., and Chevron list their shares on the NYSE. Companies that list on the NYSE must meet stringent listing requirements and annual maintenance requirements, which give them creditability.

The NYSE is also popular with non-U.S. companies. More than 490 foreign companies with a global market capitalization of almost $63 trillion now list their securities on the NYSE. [19]

Until recently, all NYSE transactions occurred on the vast NYSE trading floor. Each of the companies traded at the NYSE is assigned to a trading post on the floor. When an exchange member receives an order to buy or sell a particular stock, the order is transmitted to a floor broker at the company's trading post. The floor brokers then compete with other brokers on the trading floor to get the best price for their customers.

In response to competitive pressures from electronic exchanges, the NYSE created a hybrid market that combines features of the floor auction market and automated trading. Its customers now have a choice of how they execute trades. In the trends section, we'll discuss other changes the NYSE is making to maintain a leadership position among securities exchanges.

Another national stock exchange, the American Stock Exchange (AMEX), lists the securities of more than 700 corporations but handles only 4 percent of the annual share volume of shares traded on U.S. securities exchanges. Because the AMEX's rules are less strict than those of the NYSE, most AMEX firms are smaller and less well known than NYSE-listed corporations. Some firms move up to the NYSE once they qualify for listing there. Other companies choose to remain on the AMEX. Companies cannot be listed on both exchanges at the same time. The AMEX has become a major market, however, for exchange-traded funds and in options trading.

Exhibit 16.7   The New York Stock Exchange (NYSE) is the largest securities market in the world. Its market capitalization dwarfs both foreign and domestic markets. Unlike other financial markets, the NYSE trades mostly through specialists, financial professionals who match up buyers and sellers of securities, while pocketing the spread between the bid and ask price on market orders. *How does the NYSE's hybrid trading system differ from fully automated, electronic trading?* (Credit: Kevin Hutchison/ flickr/ Attribution 2.0 Generic (CC BY 2.0))

Regional Exchanges

The remaining 6 percent of annual share volume takes place on several regional exchanges in the United States. These exchanges list about 100 to 500 securities of firms located in their area. Regional exchange membership rules are much less strict than for the NYSE. The top regional exchanges are the Boston, Chicago, Philadelphia, and National (formerly the Cincinnati) exchanges. An electronic network linking the NYSE and many of the regional exchanges allows brokers to make securities transactions at the best prices.

The regional exchanges, which have struggled to compete, benefited from the passage of the Securities and Exchange Commission's (SEC's) Regulation NMS (National Market System), which became fully effective in 2007. Regulation NMS makes price the most important factor in making securities trades, and all orders must go to the trading venue with the best price.[20]

Dealer Markets

Unlike broker markets, **dealer markets** do not operate on centralized trading floors but instead use sophisticated telecommunications networks that link dealers throughout the United States. Buyers and sellers do not trade securities directly, as they do in broker markets. They work through securities dealers called *market makers*, who make markets in one or more securities and offer to buy or sell securities at stated prices. A security transaction in the dealer market has two parts: the selling investor sells his or her securities to one dealer, and the buyer purchases the securities from another dealer (or in some cases, the same dealer).

Exhibit 16.8   The New York Stock Exchange (NYSE) named Stacy Cunningham the first female head of the exchange in its 226-year history. Outside the exchange, the statue "Fearless Girl" by Kristen Virbal stared down the "bull" statue and represented the need for more female representation on the world's most important exchange. *How does the naming of Stacy Cunningham as head of the NYSE demonstrate that the glass ceiling has been shattered?* (Anthony Quintano/ Flickr/ Attribution 2.0 Generic (CC BY 2.0))

NASDAQ

The largest dealer market is the **National Association of Securities Dealers Automated Quotation system**, commonly referred to as NASDAQ. The first electronic-based stock market, the NASDAQ is a sophisticated telecommunications network that links dealers throughout the United States. Founded in 1971 with origins in the over-the-counter (OTC) market, today NASDAQ is a separate securities exchange that is no longer part of the OTC market. The NASDAQ lists more companies than the NYSE, but the NYSE still leads in total market capitalization. An average of 1.6 billion shares were exchanged daily in 2016 through NASDAQ, which is now the largest electronic stock market.[21] It provides up-to-date bid and ask prices on about 3,700 of the most active OTC securities. Its sophisticated electronic communication system provides faster transaction speeds than traditional floor markets and is the main reason for the popularity and growth of the OTC market.

In January 2006, the SEC approved NASDAQ's application to operate as a national securities exchange. As a result, the NASDAQ Stock Market LLC began operating independently in August 2006.[22] The securities of many well-known companies, some of which could be listed on the organized exchanges, trade on the NASDAQ. Examples include Amazon, Apple, Costco, Comcast, JetBlue, Microsoft, Qualcomm, and Starbucks. The stocks of most commercial banks and insurance companies also trade in this market, as do most government and corporate bonds. More than 400 foreign companies also trade on the NASDAQ.

More than a decade ago, the NASDAQ changed its structure to a three-tier market:

- The NASDAQ Global Select Market, a new tier with "financial and liquidity requirements that are higher than those of any other market," according to NASDAQ. More than 1,000 NASDAQ companies qualify for this group.
- The NASDAQ Global Market (formerly the NASDAQ National Market), which will list about 1,650 companies.
- The NASDAQ Capital Market will replace the NASDAQ Small Cap Market and list about 550 companies.

All three market tiers adhere to NASDAQ's rigorous listing and corporate governance standards.[23]

The Over-the-Counter Market

The **over-the-counter (OTC) markets** refer to those other than the organized exchanges described above. There are two OTC markets: the *Over-the-Counter Bulletin Board (OTCBB)* and the *Pink Sheets*. These markets generally list small companies and have no listing or maintenance standards, making them attractive to young companies looking for funding. OTC companies do not have to file with the SEC or follow the costly provisions of Sarbanes-Oxley. Investing in OTC companies is therefore highly risky and should be for experienced investors only.

Alternative Trading Systems

In addition to broker and dealer markets, alternative trading systems such as **electronic communications networks (ECNs)** make securities transactions. ECNs are private trading networks that allow institutional traders and some individuals to make direct transactions in what is called the *fourth market*. ECNs bypass brokers and dealers to automatically match electronic buy and sell orders. They are most effective for high-volume, actively traded stocks. Money managers and institutions such as pension funds and mutual funds with large amounts of money to invest like ECNs because they cost far less than other trading venues.

Global Trading and Foreign Exchanges

Improved communications and the elimination of many legal barriers are helping the securities markets go global. The number of securities listed on exchanges in more than one country is growing. Foreign securities are now traded in the United States. Likewise, foreign investors can easily buy U.S. securities.

Stock markets also exist in foreign countries: more than 60 countries operate their own securities exchanges. NASDAQ ranks second to the NYSE, followed by the London Stock Exchange (LSE) and the Tokyo Stock Exchange. Other important foreign stock exchanges include Euronext (which merged with the NYSE but operates separately) and those in Toronto, Frankfurt, Hong Kong, Zurich, Australia, Paris, and Taiwan.[24] The number of big U.S. corporations with listings on foreign exchanges is growing steadily, especially in Europe. For example, significant activity in NYSE-listed stocks also occurs on the LSE. The LSE also is getting a growing share of the world's IPOs. Emerging markets such as India, whose economy has been growing 6 percent or more a year, continue to attract investor attention. The Sensex, the benchmark index of the Bombay Stock Exchange, increased close to 40 percent between 2013 and 2017 as foreign investors continue to pump billions into Indian stocks.[25]

Why should U.S. investors pay attention to international stock markets? Because the world's economies are increasingly interdependent, businesses must look beyond their own national borders to find materials to make their goods and markets for foreign goods and services. The same is true for investors, who may find that they can earn higher returns in international markets.

Regulation of Securities Markets

Both state and federal governments regulate the securities markets. The states were the first to pass laws aimed at preventing securities fraud. But most securities transactions occur across state lines, so federal securities laws are more effective. In addition to legislation, the industry has self-regulatory groups and measures.

Securities Legislation

Congress passed the Securities Act of 1933 in response to the 1929 stock market crash and subsequent problems during the Great Depression. It protects investors by requiring full disclosure of information about new securities issues. The issuer must file a *registration statement* with the SEC, which must be approved by the SEC before the security can be sold.

The *Securities Exchange Act of 1934* formally gave the SEC power to regulate securities exchanges. The act was amended in 1964 to give the SEC authority over the dealer markets as well. The amendment included rules for operating the stock exchanges and granted the SEC control over all participants (exchange members, brokers, dealers) and the securities traded in these markets.

The 1934 act also banned **insider trading**, the use of information that is not available to the general public to make profits on securities transactions. Because of lax enforcement, however, several big insider trading scandals occurred during the late 1980s. The *Insider Trading and Fraud Act of 1988* greatly increased the penalties for illegal insider trading and gave the SEC more power to investigate and prosecute claims of illegal actions. The meaning of *insider* was expanded beyond a company's directors, employees, and their relatives to include anyone who gets private information about a company.

Other important legislation includes the *Investment Company Act of 1940,* which gives the SEC the right to regulate the practices of investment companies (such as mutual funds managed by financial institutions), and the *Investment Advisers Act of 1940,* which requires investment advisers to disclose information about their background. The *Securities Investor Protection Corporation (SIPC)* was established in 1970 to protect customers if a brokerage firm fails, by insuring each customer's account for up to $500,000.

In response to corporate scandals that hurt thousands of investors, the SEC passed new regulations designed to restore public trust in the securities industry. It issued *Regulation FD* (for "fair disclosure") in October 2000. Regulation FD requires public companies to share information with all investors at the same time, leveling the information playing field. The *Sarbanes-Oxley Act of 2002* has given the SEC more power when it comes to regulating how securities are offered, sold, and marketed.

Self-Regulation

The investment community also regulates itself, developing and enforcing ethical standards to reduce the potential for abuses in the financial marketplace. The Financial Industry Regulatory Authority (FINRA) oversees the nation's more than 3,700 brokerage firms and more 600,000 registered brokers. It develops rules and regulations, provides a dispute resolution forum, and conducts regulatory reviews of member activities for the protection and benefit of investors.

In response to "Black Monday"—October 19, 1987, when the Dow Jones Industrial Average plunged 508 points and the trading activity severely overloaded the exchange's computers—the securities markets instituted corrective measures to prevent a repeat of the crisis. Now, under certain conditions, **circuit breakers** stop trading for a 15-minute cooling-off period to limit the amount the market can drop in one day. Under revised rules approved in 2012 by the SEC, market-wide circuit breakers kick in when the S&P 500 Index drops 7 percent (level 1), 13 percent (level 2), and 20 percent (level 3) from the prior day's closing numbers.[26]

ETHICS IN PRACTICE

Blowing the Whistle on Financial Fraud

As part of the 2010 Dodd-Frank legislation passed by Congress in response to the 2008 financial crisis, the Securities and Exchange Commission (SEC) established a whistleblower-rewards program to provide employees and other individuals with the opportunity to report financial securities misconduct. More than seven years after starting the Office of the Whistleblower, the SEC reports that the rewards program has recovered almost $1 billion in financial penalties from companies that have done things to damage their own reputation as well as those of employees and other stakeholders.

According to a recent SEC report, 2016 was a banner year for individuals reporting financial wrongdoings and whistleblowers being rewarded for what they discovered. In 2016 alone, more than $57 million was awarded to whistleblowers—an amount greater than the total amount of rewards issued since the program's inception in 2011.

The whistleblower program is based on three key components: monetary awards, prohibition of employer retaliation, and protection of the whistleblower's identity. The program requires the SEC to pay out monetary awards to eligible individuals who voluntarily provide original information about a violation of federal securities laws that has occurred, is ongoing, or is about to take place. The information supplied must lead to a successful enforcement action or monetary sanctions exceeding $1 million. No awards are paid out until the sanctions are collected from the offending firm.

A whistleblower must be an individual (not a company), and that individual does not need to be employed by a company to submit information about that specific organization. A typical award to a whistleblower is between 10 and 30 percent of the monetary sanctions the SEC and others (for example, the U.S. attorney general) are able to collect from the company in question.

Through September 2016, the whistleblower program received more than 18,000 tips, with more than 4,200 tips reported in 2016 alone. The program is not limited to U.S. citizens or residents; foreign persons living abroad may submit tips and are eligible to receive a monetary award. In fact, the SEC gave the largest monetary award to date of $30 million to a foreign national living abroad for original information relating to an ongoing fraud.

Despite criticisms from some financial institutions, the whistleblower-rewards program continues to be a success—reinforcing the point that financial fraud will not go unnoticed by the SEC, employees, and others individuals.

Critical Thinking Questions
1. Despite assurances that companies involved in financial fraud are not allowed to retaliate against

their accusers, would you blow the whistle on your employer? Why or why not?

2. What can companies do to make sure their employees are aware of the consequences of financial securities fraud? Provide several examples.

Sources: "Office of the Whistleblower," https://www.sec.gov, accessed November 1, 2017; Erika A. Kelton, "Four Important Dodd-Frank Whistleblower Program Developments to Watch for in 2017," https://wp.nyu.edu, accessed November 1, 2017; Jason Zuckerman and Matt Stock, "One Billion Reasons Why the SEC Whistleblower-Reward Program Is Effective," *Forbes,* http://www.forbes.com, July 18, 2017; John Maxfield, "The Dodd-Frank Act Explained," *USA Today,* https://www.usatoday.com, February 3, 2017; Eduardo Singerman and Paul Hugel, "The Tremendous Impact of the Dodd-Frank Whistleblower Program in 2016," *Accounting Today,* https://www.accountingtoday.com, December 28, 2016; Samuel Rubenfeld, "Dodd-Frank Rollback to Spare SEC Whistleblower Program, Experts Say," *The Wall Street Journal,* https://www.blogs.wsj.com, November 15, 2016.

CONCEPT CHECK

1. How do the broker markets differ from dealer markets, and what organizations compose each of these two markets?
2. Why is the globalization of the securities markets important to U.S. investors? What are some of the other exchanges where U.S companies can list their securities?
3. Briefly describe the key provisions of the main federal laws designed to protect securities investors. What is insider trading, and how can it be harmful? How does the securities industry regulate itself?

16.8   Trends in Financial Management and Securities Markets

8. What are the current developments in financial management and the securities markets?

Many of the key trends shaping the practice of financial management echo those in other disciplines. For example, technology is improving the efficiency with which financial managers run their operations. In the wake of a slowing economy and corporate scandals, the SEC assumed a stronger role and implemented additional regulations to protect investors from fraud and misinformation. A wave of merger mania hit the global securities markets as the securities exchanges themselves have begun to consolidate to capture larger shares of the world's trading volume in multiple types of securities. Online brokerage firms are seeking new ways to capture and keep their customers by broadening the services they offer and keeping the fees they charge highly competitive. Let's now look at two key trends in greater detail. In the era of the Sarbanes-Oxley Act, CFOs find themselves balancing a strategic focus with overseeing corporate compliance with the act. The NYSE and NASDAQ are battling for supremacy as the regional exchanges look for niche markets to exploit.

Finance Looks Outward

No longer does finance operate in its own little world of spreadsheets and banking relationships. Most CFOs want the finance function to be viewed by their company's business units as a strategic partner who can contribute to their success. Finance professionals therefore need a broad view of company operations to communicate effectively with business unit managers, board members, creditors, and investors. The goal is productive cooperation and teamwork between finance and the business units to meet corporate objectives. CFOs are more highly visible and active in company management than ever before. They serve as both business partner to the chief executive and a fiduciary to the board.

In the aftermath of recent accounting scandals and the global recession of 2008–2009, CFOs consider accuracy of financial reporting their top priority, and they also must now provide more detailed explanations of what's behind the numbers to board members and other stakeholders. Rather than showering the board with financial reports and statistics, CFOs are crafting more focused presentations that deal with the company's overall financial health and future prospects.[27] They must also educate board members about the implications of Sarbanes-Oxley and other legislation, such as Dodd-Frank, and what the company is doing to comply with federal regulations.

Vying for the Crown

The NYSE and NASDAQ continue to wage a heated battle for supremacy in the global securities markets. The NYSE fell behind its more nimble rival, which already had an electronic platform. Its answer was to make sweeping changes in its organizational structure by going public and merging with Archipelago, a major ECN, to enter the electronic marketplace. NASDAQ responded immediately by acquiring another ECN, Instinet's INET. The NYSE then made history by signing an agreement to merge with Euronext and create the first exchange to span the Atlantic. Not to be outdone, the NASDAQ increased its ownership of shares in the London Stock Exchange to 25 percent. These transactions reduced the fragmentation in the marketplace and also eliminated many of the differences between the two exchanges.

But the competition between the two companies continued in 2017, as the London Stock Exchange looks for a buyer after the European Commission refused to allow a merger between LSE and Germany's Deutsche Borse.[28] It remains to be seen whether either U.S. exchange is ready to purchase an international exchange; however, their recent strategic moves have made them stronger and more competitive.

CONCEPT CHECK

1. How has the role of CFO changed since the passage of the Sarbanes-Oxley Act?
2. Describe the major changes taking place in the U.S. securities markets. What trends are driving these changes?

Key Terms

accounts payable Purchases for which a buyer has not yet paid the seller.

accounts receivable Sales for which a firm has not yet been paid.

bond ratings Letter grades assigned to bond issues to indicate their quality or level of risk; assigned by rating agencies such as Moody's and Standard & Poor's (S&P).

bonds Long-term debt obligations (liabilities) issued by corporations and governments.

broker markets National and regional securities exchanges that bring buyers and sellers together through brokers on a centralized trading floor.

capital budgeting The process of analyzing long-term projects and selecting those that offer the best returns while maximizing the firm's value.

capital expenditures Investments in long-lived assets, such as land, buildings, machinery, equipment, and information services, that are expected to provide benefits over a period longer than one year.

cash flows The inflow and outflow of cash for a firm.

cash management The process of making sure that a firm has enough cash on hand to pay bills as they come due and to meet unexpected expenses.

circuit breakers Corrective measures that, under certain conditions, stop trading in the securities markets for a short cooling-off period to limit the amount the market can drop in one day.

commercial paper Unsecured short-term debt—an IOU—issued by a financially strong corporation.

common stock A security that represents an ownership interest in a corporation.

dealer markets Securities markets where buy and sell orders are executed through dealers, or "market makers," linked by telecommunications networks.

dividends Payments to stockholders from a corporation's profits.

electronic communications networks (ECNs) Private trading networks that allow institutional traders and some individuals to make direct transactions in the fourth market.

exchange traded fund (ETF) A security similar to a mutual fund; holds a broad basket of stocks with a common theme but trades on a stock exchange so that its price changes throughout the day.

factoring A form of short-term financing in which a firm sells its accounts receivable outright at a discount to a factor.

financial management The art and science of managing a firm's money so that it can meet its goals.

financial risk The chance that a firm will be unable to make scheduled interest and principal payments on its debt.

futures contracts Legally binding obligations to buy or sell specified quantities of commodities or financial instruments at an agreed-on price at a future date.

insider trading The use of information that is not available to the general public to make profits on securities transactions.

institutional investors Investment professionals who are paid to manage other people's money.

interest A fixed amount of money paid by the issuer of a bond to the bondholder on a regular schedule, typically every six months; stated as the coupon rate.

investment bankers Firms that act as intermediaries, buying securities from corporations and governments and reselling them to the public.

line of credit An agreement between a bank and a business that specifies the maximum amount of unsecured short-term borrowing the bank will allow the firm over a given period, typically one year.

marketable securities Short-term investments that are easily converted into cash.

mortgage loan A long-term loan made against real estate as collateral.

municipal bonds Bonds issued by states, cities, counties, and other state and local government agencies.

mutual fund A financial-service company that pools investors' funds to buy a selection of securities that meet its stated investment goals.

National Association of Securities Dealers Automated Quotation (NASDAQ) system The first and largest electronic stock market, which is a sophisticated telecommunications network that links dealers throughout the United States.

options Contracts that entitle holders to buy or sell specified quantities of common stocks or other financial instruments at a set price during a specified time.

over-the-counter (OTC) market Markets, other than the exchanges, on which small companies trade; includes the Over-the-Counter Bulletin Board (OTCBB) and the Pink Sheets.

preferred stock An equity security for which the dividend amount is set at the time the stock is issued and the dividend must be paid before the company can pay dividends to common stockholders.

primary market The securities market where new securities are sold to the public.

principal The amount borrowed by the issuer of a bond; also called par value.

retained earnings Profits that have been reinvested in a firm.

return The opportunity for profit.

revolving credit agreement A guaranteed line of credit whereby a bank agrees that a certain amount of funds will be available for a business to borrow over a given period, typically two to five years.

risk The potential for loss or the chance that an investment will not achieve the expected level of return.

risk-return trade-off A basic principle in finance that holds that the higher the risk, the greater the return that is required.

secondary market The securities market where old (already issued) securities are bought and sold, or traded, among investors; includes broker markets, dealer markets, the over-the-counter market, and the commodities exchanges.

secured loans Loans for which the borrower is required to pledge specific assets as collateral, or security.

securities Investment certificates issued by corporations or governments that represent either equity or debt.

stock dividends Payments to stockholders in the form of more stock; may replace or supplement cash dividends.

stockbroker A person who is licensed to buy and sell securities on behalf of clients.

term loan A business loan with a maturity of more than one year; can be unsecured or secured.

trade credit The extension of credit by the seller to the buyer between the time the buyer receives the goods or services and when it pays for them.

underwriting The process of buying securities from corporations and governments and reselling them to the public; the main activity of investment bankers.

unsecured loans Loans for which the borrower does not have to pledge specific assets as security.

▣ Summary of Learning Outcomes

16.1 The Role of Finance and the Financial Manager

1. How do finance and the financial manager affect the firm's overall strategy?

Finance involves managing the firm's money. The financial manager must decide how much money is needed and when, how best to use the available funds, and how to get the required financing. The financial manager's responsibilities include financial planning, investing (spending money), and financing (raising money). Maximizing the value of the firm is the main goal of the financial manager, whose decisions often have long-term effects.

16.2 How Organizations Use Funds
2. What types of short-term and long-term expenditures does a firm make?

A firm incurs short-term expenses—supplies, inventory, and wages—to support current production, marketing, and sales activities. The financial manager manages the firm's investment in current assets so that the company has enough cash to pay its bills and support accounts receivable and inventory. Long-term expenditures (capital expenditures) are made for fixed assets such as land, buildings, equipment and information systems. Because of the large outlays required for capital expenditures, financial managers carefully analyze proposed projects to determine which offer the best returns.

16.3 Obtaining Short-Term Financing
3. What are the main sources and costs of unsecured and secured short-term financing?

Short-term financing comes due within one year. The main sources of unsecured short-term financing are trade credit, bank loans, and commercial paper. Secured loans require a pledge of certain assets, such as accounts receivable or inventory, as security for the loan. Factoring, or selling accounts receivable outright at a discount, is another form of short-term financing.

16.4 Raising Long-Term Financing
4. What are the key differences between debt and equity, and what are the major types and features of long-term debt?

Financial managers must choose the best mix of debt and equity for their firm. The main advantage of debt financing is the tax-deductibility of interest. But debt involves financial risk because it requires the payment of interest and principal on specified dates. Equity—common and preferred stock—is considered a permanent form of financing on which the firm may or may not pay dividends. Dividends are not tax-deductible.

The main types of long-term debt are term loans, bonds, and mortgage loans. Term loans can be unsecured or secured and generally have maturities of 5 to 12 years. Bonds usually have initial maturities of 10 to 30 years. Mortgage loans are secured by real estate. Long-term debt usually costs more than short-term financing because of the greater uncertainty that the borrower will be able to make the scheduled loan payments.

16.5 Equity Financing
5. When and how do firms issue equity, and what are the costs?

The chief sources of equity financing are common stock, retained earnings, and preferred stock. The cost of selling stock includes issuing costs and potential dividend payments. Retained earnings are profits reinvested in the firm. For the issuing firm, preferred stock is more expensive than debt because its dividends are not tax-deductible and its claims are secondary to those of debtholders but less expensive than common stock. Venture capital is often a source of equity financing for young companies.

16.6 Securities Markets
6. How do securities markets help firms raise funding, and what securities trade in the capital markets?

Securities markets allow stocks, bonds, and other securities to be bought and sold quickly and at a fair price. New issues are sold in the primary market. After that, securities are traded in the secondary market. Investment bankers specialize in issuing and selling new security issues. Stockbrokers are licensed professionals who buy and sell securities on behalf of their clients.

In addition to corporate securities, investors can trade U.S. government Treasury securities and municipal bonds, mutual funds, futures, and options. Mutual funds are managed by financial-service companies that pool the funds of many investors to buy a diversified portfolio of securities. Investors choose mutual funds because they offer a convenient way to diversify and are professionally managed. Exchange-traded funds (ETFs) are similar to mutual funds but trade on stock exchanges similar to common stock. Futures contracts are legally binding obligations to buy or sell specified quantities of commodities or financial instruments at an agreed-on price at a future date. They are very risky investments because the price of the commodity or financial instrument may change drastically. Options are contracts that entitle the holder the right to buy or sell specified quantities of common stock or other financial instruments at a set price during a specified time. They, too, are high-risk investments.

16.7 Buying and Selling at Securities Exchanges

7.   Where can investors buy and sell securities, and how are securities markets regulated?

Securities are resold in secondary markets, which include both broker markets and dealer markets. The broker market consists of national and regional securities exchanges, such as the New York Stock Exchange, that bring buyers and sellers together through brokers on a centralized trading floor. Dealer markets use sophisticated telecommunications networks that link dealers throughout the United States. The NASDAQ and over-the-counter markets are examples of dealer markets. In addition to broker and dealer markets, electronic communications networks (ECNs) can be used to make securities transactions. In addition to the U.S. markets, more than 60 countries have securities exchanges. The largest non-U.S. exchanges are the London, Tokyo, Toronto, Frankfurt, Hong Kong, and Taiwan exchanges.

The Securities Act of 1933 requires disclosure of important information regarding new securities issues. The Securities Exchange Act of 1934 and its 1964 amendment formally empowered the Securities and Exchange Commission and granted it broad powers to regulate the securities exchanges and the dealer markets. The Investment Company Act of 1940 places investment companies such as companies that issue mutual funds under SEC control. The securities markets also have self-regulatory groups such as the Financial Industry Regulatory Authority (FINRA) and measures such as "circuit breakers" to halt trading if the S&P 500 Index drops rapidly.

16.8 Trends in Financial Management and Securities Markets

8.   What are the current developments in financial management and the securities markets?

The role of the CFO has continued to expand since the passage of the Sarbanes-Oxley Act, with CFOs taking the central role in overseeing corporate compliance with the act and reestablishing public trust. CFOs must look outward and be business focused. Most CFOs are promoting strategic finance and encouraging finance staff to be team players who work closely with business units to achieve corporate goals.

Competition among the world's major securities exchanges has changed the composition of the financial marketplace. The NYSE and NASDAQ went head to head in the United States. The NYSE became a for-profit company, acquired Archipelago, an electronic exchange, and merged with Euronext to form the first transatlantic exchange. NASDAQ also expanded by acquiring its own ECN and buying a 25 percent stake in the London Stock Exchange, which continues to look for a potential buyer.

⬚ Preparing for Tomorrow's Workplace Skills

1.   The head of your school's finance department has asked you to address a group of incoming business students about the importance of finance to their overall business education. Develop an outline with the key points you would cover in your speech. (Information)

2.   You are the chief financial officer of Discovery Labs, a privately held biotechnology company that needs to raise $3 million to fund the development of a new drug. Prepare a report for the board of directors that

discusses the types of long-term financing available to the firm, their pros and cons, and the key factors to consider in choosing a financing strategy. (Information)

3. **Team Activity** Does paying dividends enhance the value of a company? Some financial experts caution companies to look long and hard before beginning to pay dividends. They believe that committing yourself to a regular dividend curtails financial flexibility and reduces debt capacity. Dividends might also signal that the company doesn't have good growth opportunities in which to invest its excess cash. Others counter that dividends can help a company's stock by making it less volatile. Standard & Poor's data supports this; typically, dividend-paying stocks in the S&P 500 outperform nonpayers. Divide the class into two teams to debate whether dividends add value to a company's stock. (Interpersonal, Information)

4. Research the trends in the IPO marketplace from 2009 to 2017. Then select two IPO success stories and two failures. Prepare a report for the class on their performance. What lessons about the securities markets can you learn from their stories? (Information)

5. While having dinner at a Manhattan restaurant, you overhear two investment bankers at the next table. They are discussing the takeover of Bellamco Industries by Gildmart Corp., a deal that has not yet been announced. You have been thinking about buying Bellamco stock for a while, so the next day you buy 500 shares for $30 each. Two weeks later, Gildmart announces its acquisition of Bellamco at a price of $45 per share. Have you fairly earned a profit, or are you guilty of insider trading? What's wrong with insider trading? (Information)

6. **Team Activity** Is joining an investment club a good way to learn about investing in the stock market? Divide the class into groups of five to eight students to develop a strategy to form their own investment club. Use the National Association of Investors Corporation (NAIC) website at **http://www.betterinvesting.org** to learn how investment clubs operate and the investment strategy the organization teaches. Each group should then set up guidelines for their investment club and present their plan to the class. After the presentations, the class members should discuss whether they would prefer to start investing through an investment club or on their own. (Resources, Interpersonal, Information)

Ethics Activity

In late July 2017, senior management at Equifax, a U.S. credit-reporting company, discovered that hackers had stolen the personal data of more than 145 million U.S. customers, including names, birthdates, Social Cecurity numbers, and driver's license information. In addition, the hackers stole credit card information for more than 200,000 Equifax customers.

If that weren't bad enough, reports soon surfaced that three top executives, including Equifax's chief financial officer, sold close to $2 million in shares of company stock days after learning about the breach and more than a month before the company announced the data hack publicly. In a company statement, Equifax says the executives "had no knowledge that an intrusion had occurred at the time they sold their shares." The day after the company's announcement about the breach, Equifax's stock dropped by double digits, and the Department of Justice opened a criminal investigation.

Less than three weeks after the public announcement, Equifax announced its CEO, Richard Smith, would retire, taking a multimillion-dollar payout with him—even after shareholders lost more than $5 *billion* in stock value after the data breach was acknowledged.

Ethical Dilemma: Is it legal for company executives to sell stock shares for financial gain when they know impending bad news will cause the stock price to plummet? Does this constitute insider trading?

Sources: Verne Kopytoff, "Equifax Board Reviews Executive Stock Sales after Data Breach," *Fortune,* http://fortune.com, September 29, 2017; Jen Wieczner, "Equifax CEO Richard Smith Who Oversaw Breach to Collect $90 Million," *Fortune,* http://www.fortune.com, September 26, 2017; Tom Schoenberg, Anders Melin, and Matt Robinson, "Equifax Stock Sales Are the Focus of U.S. Criminal Probe," *Bloomberg Markets,* https://www.bloomberg.com, September 18, 2017; Liz Moyer, "Suspect Trading in Equifax Options before Breach Might Have Generated Millions in Profit," *CNBC,* https://www.cnbc.com, September 8, 2017; Alina Selyukh, "3 Equifax Executives Sold Stock Days after Hack That Wasn't Disclosed for a Month," *NPR,* http://www.npr.org, September 8, 2017; Anders Melin, "Three Equifax Managers Sold Stock Before Cyber Hack Revealed," *Bloomberg News,* https://www.bloomberg.com, September 7, 2017.

Working the Net

1. If factoring accounts receivable is still a mystery to you, visit the 21st Financial Solutions site, **http://www.21stfinancialsolutions.com**. Follow the links on the home page to answer these questions: What are factoring's advantages? What are the additional benefits, and what types of companies can use factoring to their advantage? Then summarize the factoring process.

2. Go to the AdvisoryHQ website at **https://www.advisoryhq.com**, and link to three different venture capital firms listed in the website's "best" list. Compare the firms' investment strategies (industry specialization, age of companies in which they invest, etc.). Also do a web search to check out two angel investor firms. How do their requirements differ from the venture firms?

3. Compare the listing requirements of the NYSE and NASDAQ, using the information at their websites: **http://www.nyse.com** and **http://www.nasdaq.com**. Search the sites for listing requirements. What types of companies qualify for listing on each exchange? Why does NASDAQ offer alternative listing standards?

4. Choose a company currently traded on the NYSE (**http://www.nyse.com**). Find the company's website using a search engine such as Google. At the website, find the firm's investor relations information. Review the information, including, if available, the most recent online annual report. Follow up by researching if any SEC actions have been taken against the firm at the SEC website, **http://www.sec.gov**. Summarize your findings in a brief report that discusses whether you would recommend this company's stock as an investment.

5. Using the information and links available at the Securities Industry and Financial Markets Association's (SIFMA) website, **https://www.sifma.org,** write a brief paper explaining the pros and cons of investing in corporate bonds. In your paper, provide at least three examples of currently available corporate bonds from a site such as **http://www.investinginbonds.com**, and explain why they would be good investments.

6. Research the job responsibilities of a corporate investor relations officer (IRO). If possible, try to interview an IRO, by either phone or email. The National Investor Relations Institute (**http://www.niri.org**), a trade association for IROs, is an alternate source of information. What types of experience and education does an IRO need in order to perform effectively? How are their roles changing? Write a paper summarizing your findings. (Interpersonal, Information)

Critical Thinking Case

Blue Apron IPO Leaves a Bad Taste

Founded in 2012, Blue Apron is one of the top meal-kit delivery services doing business in the United States. Started by three cofounders—Matt Salzberg, Matt Wadiak, and Ilia Pappas—Blue Apron provides preportioned ingredients (and recipes) for a meal, delivered to consumers' front doors.

According to recent research, the U.S. meal-kit delivery industry is an $800 million business with the potential to scale up quickly, as more and more consumers struggle to find time to go grocery shopping, make meals, and spend time with family and friends in their hectic daily lives.

As word spread among foodies about the quality and innovative meals put together by Blue Apron, the company's popularity took off, supported by millions in start-up funding. Costs to scale the business have not been cheap—estimates suggest that Blue Apron's marketing costs have been high.

Despite the challenges, by early 2017 the company was selling more than 8 million meal kits a month and decided to go public in an effort to raise more money and scale its operations, including a new fulfillment facility in New Jersey. According to IPO paperwork filed with the SEC, the company had net revenues of $84 million in 2014, which increased to $795 million in 2016. However, those ambitious numbers were not without warnings: company losses increased in the same time period from $33 million to $55 million.

Even with those larges losses on its balance sheet, Blue Apron decided to go ahead with the IPO and hired Goldman Sachs and Morgan Stanley, two top stock underwriters, to figure out the right price for the initial offering. While Blue Apron and its underwriters were finalizing stock prices, Amazon announced plans to acquire Whole Foods—a move that could negatively affect Blue Apron's business going forward.

Even after Amazon's announcement, Blue Apron and its financial advisors priced the initial offering at $15 to $17 a share and met with investors across the country to inform them about the IPO, which would value the company on paper at more than $3 billion. As part of the IPO strategy, Blue Apron executives needed to communicate a strong financial picture while providing potential investors with an honest assessment of investor demand, especially for institutional investors, who typically are repeat buyers when it comes to IPOs.

According to sources close to the IPO experience, Blue Apron's bankers told investors late in the IPO pricing process that they were "closing their order books early," which meant there was a heightened demand for the stock—a signal that the stock would be priced in the original $15–$17 range.

A day later, however, Blue Apron amended its prospectus with a price range between $10 and $11 a share, which shocked potential investors—a move greeted with criticism that Blue Apron's messaging now lacked credibility in the eyes of the investment community if the company priced the IPO $5 lower per share than originally estimated. With that sudden change in the IPO offering, investors walked away, and the $10 initial offering for Blue Apron stock actually declined on its first day of trading. As of this writing, the stock has lost close to 40 percent from the original $10-per-share price.

With continued consolidation in the meal-kit delivery sector inevitable, Blue Apron is at a crossroads when it comes to generating revenue and stabilizing costs while trying to sign up more subscribers. One of its competitors, Plated, was recently acquired by the Alberstons grocery chain, and Amazon has already trademarked the phrase, "We do the prep. You be the chef," as it relates to prepared food kits.

Sources: Wolf Richter, "Blue Apron's Cash Burn Is a Threat Just 3 Months after Its IPO," *Business Insider,* http://www.businessinsider.com, October 19, 2017; Graham Rapier, "Blue Apron CEO: Amazon and Whole Foods Aren't the Competition," *Business Insider,* http://markets.businessinsider.com, September 13, 2017; Matthew Lynley, "Where Does Blue Apron Go after Amazon Wraps Up Its Whole Foods Deal?" *Tech Crunch,* https://techcrunch.com, August 27, 2017; Leslie Picker, "Inside Blue Apron's IPO: Communication Lapse Chased Away Investors," *CNBC,* https://www.cnbc.com, August 23, 2017; Imani Moise, "Blue Apron Co-Founder to Step Aside as Operating Chief," *The Wall Street Journal,* https://www.wsj.com, July 25, 2017; Phil Lempert, "Understanding Blue Apron's IPO and the Future of Meal Kits," *Forbes,* http://www.forbes.com, June 2, 2017; John Kell, "Meals in the Mail: How Blue Apron Got Started and Where It's Heading," *Fortune,* http://fortune.com, September 11, 2016.

Critical Thinking Questions

1. What issues should executives of a company such as Blue Apron consider before deciding to go public? In your opinion, was the company ready for an IPO? Why or why not?
2. How else could Blue Apron have raised funds to continue to grow? Compare the risks of raising private funding to going public.
3. Use a search engine and a site such as Yahoo! Finance to learn about Blue Apron's current situation. Prepare a brief summary, including the company's current financial situation. Is it still a public company, and how has its stock fared? Would you invest in it? Explain your reasoning.

Sources: Wolf Richter, "Blue Apron's Cash Burn Is a Threat Just 3 Months after Its IPO," *Business Insider,* http://www.businessinsider.com, October 19, 2017; Graham Rapier, "Blue Apron CEO: Amazon and Whole Foods Aren't the Competition," *Business Insider,* http://markets.businessinsider.com, September 13, 2017; Matthew Lynley, "Where Does Blue Apron Go after Amazon Wraps Up Its Whole Foods Deal?" *Tech Crunch,* https://techcrunch.com, August 27, 2017; Leslie Picker, "Inside Blue Apron's IPO: Communication Lapse Chased Away Investors," *CNBC,* https://www.cnbc.com, August 23, 2017; Imani Moise, "Blue Apron Co-Founder to Step Aside as Operating Chief," *The Wall Street Journal,* https://www.wsj.com, July 25, 2017; Phil Lempert, "Understanding Blue Apron's IPO and the Future of Meal Kits," *Forbes,* http://www.forbes.com, June 2, 2017; John Kell, "Meals in the Mail: How Blue Apron Got Started and Where It's Heading," *Fortune,* http://fortune.com, September 11, 2016.

Hot Links Address Book

1. What challenges do today's financial managers face? To find out, browse through recent issues of *CFO* magazine at **http://www.cfo.com**
2. Find an introduction to the types of cash management services banks offer their customers at the Royal Bank of Canada website, **https://rbcbank.com**
3. Start your online exploring at Yahoo! Finance, **http://finance.yahoo.com,** which offers everything from breaking business and world news to stock research, portfolio tracking tools, and educational articles.
4. For small businesses just starting out or entrepreneurs who have invented the next great product but need some financial assistance, several crowdfunding platforms can help. Both Kiva (**https://www.kiva.org**) and IndieGoGo (**https://www.indiegogo.com**) offer loans or financial backing to help people start up new businesses or match potential investors with entrepreneurs looking for some financial backing.
5. The Motley Fool, **http://www.fool.com,** is a favorite site for both novice and experienced investors. In addition to the latest stock picks, the website offers detailed information on a variety of topics, such as how to invest, retirement, and personal finance.
6. You'll find a minicourse on municipal bonds when you click on "Learn More" at the top of the page at **http://www.investingbonds.com**.
7. Moneychimp (**http://www.moneychimp.com**) strives to educate investors by offering clear, practical articles on a complete range of finance and investing topics, including investment basics, understanding annual reports, stock valuation, and more.

8. Thinking of investing in a particular company? Go to the SEC's website to access the EDGAR database of the financial reports filed by all public companies with the SEC: **http://www.sec.gov**.

17

Your Career in Business

Exhibit 17.1 (Credit: public Information Office / flickr / Attribution 2.0 Generic (CC BY 2.0))

 # Introduction

Learning Outcomes

After reading this chapter, you should be able to answer these questions:

1. How can you enhance your interpersonal skills?
2. Why is learning to plan so important in school and in the real world?
3. What skills should you develop in school that can transfer easily to your professional life and make it a success?
4. What are some strategies that will help you find, keep, and advance in your dream job?
5. What key attributes do employers look for when interviewing job candidates?

You Are a Winner Because You Elected to Go to College!

Never Quit Until You Have Your Degree in Hand!

What makes someone a winner in life? A winner is someone who goes through the various stages of life satisfied in knowing that they have done their best: their best at work, home, and in all pursuits of life. A big part of having a happy life is pursuing a career that offers job satisfaction and financial rewards. If you are going to "be all that you can be," you need a good education.

A college degree unlocks doors to economic opportunity.

Why get a degree?

- **Get and keep a better job.** Because the world is changing rapidly and many jobs rely on new technology, more jobs require education beyond high school. With a college education, you will have more jobs from which to choose.
- **Earn more money.** People who go to college usually earn more than those who do not. Currently, a bachelor's degree is worth a minimum of $20,000 a year more than a high school diploma. If your career spans 45 years, you could earn close to $1 million more than a high school graduate.

- **Get a good start in life.** A business college education helps you acquire a wide range of knowledge in many subjects as well as an advanced understanding of your specialized area of business. College also trains you to express your thoughts clearly in speech and in writing and to make informed decisions.

Simply stated, a degree in business gives you the chance to achieve the quality of life you deserve. The lifestyle, the new friends, the purchasing power of a degree won't guarantee happiness but will put you well on the road to finding it.

17.1 | Learn the Basics of Business

You might want to pursue a career as a physician, florist, game warden, systems analyst, or any of a thousand other opportunities. One thing that all careers have in common is that you need to have a basic understanding of business. We hope that you will consider a career in business, but if not, your success in whatever you choose will partially depend on your basic business skills. And that is why this text is so important.

Exhibit 17.2   Finding one's dream job requires combing through job descriptions, researching salary information, taking career-assessment tests, and shadowing others in the workplace. But sometimes people need some career advice or mentorship to "pivot" to a new career or to fine-tune their current job skills. That's where Pivot Planet comes in—the company connects people around the world for a reasonable fee with advisors who offer one-on-one video and phone sessions to answers questions and provide insights about their particular profession. *How can this type of advice and mentorship help individuals longing to change their career paths?* (Credit: U.S. Fish and Wildlife Service Southeast Region/ flickr/ Attribution 2.0 Generic (CC BY 2.0))

Choose a Career

Because this introductory business course gives you a detailed overview of all of the areas of commerce, it will guide you in selecting a major should you elect to get a degree in business. Choosing a major in college is one of life's true milestones. Your major essentially determines how you will spend the next four decades of your life. A marketing major will find a career in sales, marketing research, advertising, or other marketing-related fields. An accounting major will become (you guessed it) an accountant. *Never* take selecting a major lightly. If you work 40 hours a week for the next 45 years (less vacations), you will put in about 90,000 hours on the job. Don't you think you should choose something that you will enjoy?

17.2 Developing Interpersonal Skills Is Key to Your Success

A degree in business is going to offer you many great career opportunities. Once you take your first job, how rapidly you move up the ladder is up to you. People with great interpersonal skills will always do better on and off the job than those who lack them. It has been estimated that up to 90 percent of our workplace success depends on an understanding of other people.[1] Here's how to enhance your interpersonal skills:

1. **Build your people skills.** Learn to build alliances in a group and establish harmony. Make a concerted effort to know what is happening in the lives of those on your team at school and work. About once a month, get together with your group, and pass out a list of issues, concerns, fears, and potential problems. Then invite everyone to give input to solve little problems before the problems become big. If something goes wrong, try to find out where things are not running smoothly and improve them. Be sure to compliment someone in your group who is doing an exceptional job.

   Become a good listener. When you listen well, you are in effect telling the other person that he or she is worth listening to. Listening well includes listening to both what is said and what is not said. Learn to read unspoken gestures and expressions. When giving feedback, plan what you will say in advance. Be positive and specific. Ask the person receiving the feedback if they would like to discuss your comments further.

2. **Understand how to persuade others.** Remember: we all must sell ourselves and our ideas to get ahead in life and in business. Influencing others means overcoming objections, igniting passions, or changing minds. The first step is to build *esprit de corps,* a shared enthusiasm and devotion to the group. Make your vision their vision so that everyone is working toward a common goal. Praise the team as a whole, but recognize the unique contributions different team members have made. The trick is to praise everyone but for different reasons. When you and your team successfully solve a problem, change will result. Persuasion rests on trust. You can build trust by being honest, fulfilling your commitments, being concerned about others, and minimizing problems and pain for others whenever possible. In short, if you have integrity, building trust becomes a simple task.

   When people raise objections to your plans or ideas, try to fully understand their comments and the motivation for making them. When you feel that you understand the true objection, answer the objection in the form of a benefit: "Yes, you will need to work next Saturday, but then you can have compensatory time off anytime you wish next month." Determine your persuasion skills by taking the quiz in **Table 17.1.**

3. **Learn to think on your feet.** Top executives say that thinking and speaking well on your feet while under pressure is the best thing that you can do for your career. If you cannot quickly express yourself with confidence, others will lose confidence in you.[2]

Fun Self-Test—Can You Persuade Others?				
Rate your level of agreement with the statements below using the following scale:				
Strongly Agree	Agree	Neither Agree nor Disagree	Disagree	Strongly Disagree

1. I prefer to work in a team rather than individually.
2. I enjoy motivating others to help accomplish objectives.
3. I avoid working with difficult people or trying to resolve group differences.
4. I can learn more working in a team rather than working by myself.
5. I would prefer to work with individuals I have known previously.
6. I give up if my team members do not agree with me.
7. I may not always convince my team members to agree with my opinions, but I will go ahead and do what I feel is correct.
8. I think people who can persuade others always possess sound judgment.
9. I will do the work myself if others do not agree to do it.
10. To get the work done, I will listen to a person to understand how he/she wants it to be done.
11. I can get people to voluntarily make commitments and get the work done.[3]

See the scoring guidelines at the end of this chapter to obtain your score.

Table 17.1

It will not happen overnight, but you can become an outstanding thinker and speaker. A simple technique is to set a timer for two minutes and ask a friend to begin speaking. When the timer goes off, your friend stops speaking, and you begin talking. The challenge is to use the final thought that your friend spoke as the first word of your two-minute talk. Another technique is to have someone supply you with a series of quotes. Then, without hesitation, give your interpretation.

4. **Empower yourself.** No matter who you are, what position you will hold, or where you will work, you probably will have to report to somebody. If you are fortunate enough to work in a culture of empowerment, you are allowed control over your job (not complete control, but enough control to make you feel your opinion matters). When you are not given an opportunity to provide input, you will eventually lose interest in your job. When empowered, you have the confidence to do something to alter your circumstances. On the job, empowerment means that you can make decisions to benefit the organization and its customers.

    If you want to gain empowerment in your life and work, here are a few tips: be assertive, ask for credit for yourself when it is due, propose ideas to your group and your supervisor, initiate projects without being asked, tie your personal goals to those of the organization, develop your leadership skills, plan to learn on a continuous basis, be informed, don't let others intimidate you, and don't complain about a bad situation—instead, take action to improve it.

5. **Become politically savvy.** Politics is an inevitable part of every organization in the United States, including your school. Politics has always been a part of the workplace and always will be. The trick is to learn to play the political game to your own advantage *and* to the advantage of others without causing harm to anyone else. Being political means getting along with others in order to move them toward accomplishing a specific goal. It does not mean maneuvering for selfish purposes, manipulating in order to deceive, or scheming so others lose while you win.

    Here are some tips and techniques to be an effective player in the political game:

    ◦ *Think about what you say.* Understand the effect your words will have on others before you say or write them.

- *Empathize.* Try to think of a situation from the other person's perspective.
- *Suggest a trial period if you meet opposition to an idea you're proposing.* If you are as successful as you are confident, you can then ask to have the trial period extended.
- *Learn about the political climate in which you are working.* This means knowing, among other things, what actions have led to failure for others, knowing who is "in" and why, determining who is "out" and why, and learning what behaviors lead to promotion.
- *Volunteer to do the jobs no one else wants to do.* Occasionally pitching in shows your willingness to get the job done. However, do not make this your trademark; you do not want others to think they can take advantage of you.
- *Work hard to meet the needs of those in authority.* Make certain you fully understand management's requirements; then go out of your way to meet them. If in time you do not think you are getting the recognition or respect you deserve, make your own needs known.
- *Give credit to others.* You never know who may be in a position to hurt or harm you. Consequently, the best policy is to treat everyone with respect and dignity. Show your appreciation to everyone who has helped you. Do not steal credit that belongs to someone else.
- *Learn your supervisor's preferences.* The more you are in sync with your supervisor's style, wishes, and preferences, the better you can do your job. However, do not be a rubber stamp. Rather, work the way your manager works. When necessary, suggest better ways of doing things.
- *Keep secrets—your own and others'.* Resist the temptation to tell all. Not only do you run the risk of being labeled a gossip, but if you share too much about yourself, your words may come back to haunt you. If you are revealing information told to you in confidence, you are bound to lose the trust and respect of those who originally confided in you.

Find out how well you play the political game by taking the quiz in Table 17.2.

6. **Become a team builder.** Throughout your college and business career, you will participate on teams. Most U.S. business organizations employ some sort of teamwork. An effective team is one that meets its goals on time and, if a budget is involved, within budget. The first step in creating an effective team is to have goals that are clear, realistic, and supported by each team member and that parallel the larger organization goals. Table 17.3 lists the questions that teams should answer to ensure their success.

Fun Self-Test—Can You Play the Political Game?				
Rate your level of agreement with the statements below using the following scale:				
Strongly Agree	Agree	Neither Agree nor Disagree	Disagree	Strongly Disagree

1. To be successful, you should have a strong relationship with your boss and subordinates.
2. Office politics is not very challenging.
3. Tough people give you a tough time but also teach you tough lessons.
4. Networking and observation play a major role in being good at office politics.
5. There is no ethics or morals in office politics.
6. Corporate politics is not about the individuals; it is about the survival of the corporation.
7. Office politics is the only way; you gain real access to your boss's ear.
8. Those who avoid being political at work may not move forward in their careers, may find themselves resentful and frustrated, and run the risk of being isolated.
9. If you do all of the work on a project, you won't tell the boss because you don't want your coworkers to get in trouble.
10. When faced with gossip and rumors, you prefer to be silent but aware.
11. To master office politics, you should seek a win-lose situation.
12. If a person in authority is out to get rid of you, a good tactic would be to establish allies and position yourself for another job in the company.
13. If you have made any significant contribution to a project, you always make sure that others know about it, which, in turn, adds to your reputation.[4]

See the scoring guidelines at the end of this chapter to obtain your score.

Table 17.2

Key Questions That Teams Should Answer before Starting a Project

1. What are the goals?
2. Who provides the mission statement?
3. What are our limits?
4. Where will support come from? Who will be our sponsor?
5. Who will be team leader? How is that person selected?
6. What are the deadlines we face?
7. What resources are available?
8. What data will we need to collect?
9. For how long will our team exist?
10. Who are the customers for our team results? What do they expect of us?
11. Will our team responsibilities conflict with our regular jobs?
12. What is the reward for success?
13. How will decisions be made?
14. How will our efforts be measured?
15. Will our intended success be replicated? If so, how and by whom?[5]

Table 17.3

See the scoring guidelines at the end of this chapter to obtain your score.

Table 17.3

7. **Handle conflict well.** The world is not a perfect place, and there are no perfect people living in it. The best we can hope for is people's willingness to improve life's circumstances. If we are truly committed to the idea of reducing school and workplace conflict, there is much we can do to inspire such willingness in others. Bringing conflict into the open has its advantages. Talking about conflict often helps to clear the air, and thinking about the possibility of conflict often helps to avoid it.

When conflicts occur, try the K-I-N-D technique. The letters stand for:

K = Kind

I = Informed

N = New

D = Definite

The technique involves your requesting a meeting with the difficult person, whether he or she is having a conflict with you or with others. Start off with kind words, words that encourage cooperation, words that show your determination to make the conflict situation better. Next, demonstrate that you have taken the time to learn more about the person, what is important to him or her, what he or she prefers in terms of work. Show by your words that you have taken the time to become informed about the individual.

The third step requires you to do something novel, something you have not tried before. Put your creativity to work, and discover a plan to which you can both subscribe (for example, keeping a journal regarding the problem and possible solutions).

Finally, do not permit the exchange to conclude until you have made a definite overture to ensure future success. What can you promise the other person you will do differently? What are you asking him or her to do differently? Set a time to meet again and review your individual attempts to achieve collective improvement.

17.3 | Make Your Future Happen: Learn to Plan

There is a natural conflict between planning and being impulsive, between pursuing a long-range goal and doing what you feel like doing right now. If you have ever had to study while the rest of the family was watching television, you know what that conflict feels like. If you have ever been invited to go eat pizza and hang out with friends but stayed home to work on a class assignment, you know that sticking to a plan is not easy.[6]

Of course, planning and being impulsive are both good. They both have a place in your life. You need to balance them. Having a plan does not mean that you can't act on the spur of the moment and do something that was not planned. Spontaneous events produce some of the happiest, most meaningful times of your life. Problems arise when you consistently substitute impulsive actions for goal-oriented planning. Success in life requires a balance between the two.

If you do not engage in long-range planning and lack the discipline for it, you may limit your opportunities to be impulsive. You are not going to take a weekend fun trip just because you need a break if you have not saved the money to do it. In the short run, planning involves sacrifice, but in the long run, it gives you more options.

Exhibit 17.3   Life requires planning, and the more important one's goals, the more important planning is to achieve these goals. Whether the objective is to graduate from college, develop a professional career, or build a brighter future for one's family and community, personal success depends on a good plan. *How can the six steps of the planning process help individuals achieve their educational, personal, and career dreams?* (Credit: Rodney Martin/ Flickr/ Attribution 2.0 Generic (CC BY 2.0))

What Is a Plan?

A **plan** is a method or process worked out in advance that leads to the achievement of some goal. A plan is systematic, which means it relies on using a step-by-step procedure. A plan also needs to be flexible so that it may be adapted to gradual changes in your goal.

The Planning Process

Whether choosing a college or finding financial aid, you should understand how the planning process helps you accomplish your goals. The following steps outline the planning process.

Step 1: Set a Goal. Identify something you want to achieve or obtain, your **goal**. The goal, which is usually longer term in nature, will require planning, patience, and discipline to achieve. Just living in the present moment is not a goal.

Step 2: Acquire Knowledge. Gain an understanding of your goal and what will be required to achieve it. Gather information about your goal through research, conversation, and thought.

Step 3: Compare Alternatives. Weigh your options, which are the different paths you might take to achieve your goal. Analyze the pluses and minuses of each—the costs, the demands, the likelihood of success.

Step 4: Choose a Strategy. Select one option as the best plan of action. The choice is based on sound information, the experience of others, and your own interests and abilities.

Step 5: Make a Commitment. Resolve to proceed step-by-step toward achieving your goal. Keep your eyes on the prize.

Step 6: Stay Flexible. Evaluate your progress, and when necessary, revise your plan to deal with changing circumstances and new opportunities.

An Example of Planning

The following example illustrates the process of buying a new pair of wireless headphones using this planning process.

Step 1: Set a Goal. Purchase a pair of wireless headphones.

Step 2: Acquire Knowledge. Ask friends if you can try out their headphones. Study standards and specifications. Check on retailers, brands, models, and prices. Consult *Consumer Reports.*

Step 3: Compare Alternatives.

> **Alternative 1:** Purchase a pair of headphones from an online auction website such as eBay.
> *Pro:* Affordable high-end equipment. Can buy right now.
> *Con:* Uncertain condition of equipment. Limited warranty.

> **Alternative 2:** Buy wireless headphones for $110.
> *Pro:* Can afford now; new equipment with warranty.
> *Con:* Not the best sound quality.

> **Alternative 3:** Buy a high-quality pair of headphones for $500.
> *Pro:* Excellent sound; new equipment with warranty.
> *Con:* Costs more than prepared to pay now.

Step 4: Choose a Strategy. Decide to buy the high-quality headphones, but rather than using a credit card and paying interest, will delay the purchase for six months in order to save for them.

Step 5: Make a Commitment. Give up going to the movies or buying coffee drinks from Starbucks for the six-month period, carry a lunch and stop eating out, and place the savings in a designated headphones fund.

Step 6: Stay Flexible. Four months into the plan, a model change sale provides an opportunity to buy comparable equipment for $300. Make the purchase, paying cash.

Planning for Your Life

Using the planning process to make a buying decision is a simple exercise. Making a decision about major parts of your life is far more complex. You will see that no part of life is exempt from the need for planning. It is important to apply thought, creativity, and discipline to all the interrelated phases of our lives. These phases include the following:

- **Career:** Choosing a field of work and developing the knowledge and skills needed to enter and move ahead in that field. We will offer you some tips to get started on a great career later in this chapter.
- **Self:** Deciding who you are and what kind of person you want to be, working to develop your strengths

and overcome your weaknesses, refining your values.

- **Lifestyle:** Expressing yourself in the nature and quality of your everyday life, your recreation and hobbies, how you use your time and money.
- **Relationships:** Developing friendships and learning to get along with people in a variety of contexts. Building family and community ties.
- **Finances:** Building the financial resources and the economic security needed to pursue all the other dimensions of your life.

Dreams and Plans

People are natural dreamers. Dreams give us pleasure. They are also part of making a future. If you do not have dreams or think that you are not worthy of dreaming, something very important may be missing from your life. You have a right to your dreams, and you need them—even if there is little possibility that they will ever come true.

Planning is not the same as dreaming, but it uses dreams as raw materials. It translates them into specific goals. It tests them. It lays out a course of action that moves you toward realizing these goals and sets up milestones you need to achieve. Planning brings dreams down to earth and turns them into something real and attainable. For example, assume you have a dream to visit Spain as an exchange student. To translate this dream into a specific goal, you will need to follow the planning process—gather information about the exchange process, discuss the program with parents and teachers, and improve your Spanish-language skills.

Directions for Your Life

One of the best things about pursuing our dreams is that, even when you fall short, the effort leads to growth and opens a path to other opportunities. The person who practices the piano every day may not achieve the dream of becoming a concert pianist but may eventually put appreciation of music to work as the director of an arts organization. A basketball player may not make it to a professional team but may enjoy a satisfying career as a coach or a sports writer. Without a plan, dreams simply dissolve. With a plan, they give shape and direction to our lives.

Planning involves a lot of thinking and finding answers to lots of questions. The answers and even the plan will change over time as you gain more knowledge and life experience. Planning is a skill that is useful in every area of your life. It is something you have to pursue consciously and thoughtfully. When you plan, you translate your goals and dreams into step-by-step strategies, specific things you can do to test your goals and bring them to reality. You often have to revise your plans, but even when your plans are not fulfilled, planning will have a positive effect on the course of your life.

17.4 | Going to College Is an Opportunity of a Lifetime—Never Drop Out

You have already had one of your dreams come true—you are in college. It is indeed a rare privilege because far less than 1 percent of traditional college-age people around the world get to attend college. You're lucky! So make the best of it by finishing your degree and learning the following college skills.[7]

Learn to Concentrate

Concentration is the art of being focused, the ability to pay attention. Without concentration, you have no memory of what you hear, see, and read. Concentration is a frame of mind that enables you to stay centered on the activity or work you are doing. You know when you're concentrating because time seems to go by quickly, distractions that normally take you off task don't bother you, and you have a lot of mental or physical energy for the task.

You are ultimately in charge of how well you concentrate. Here are some ways to make it happen:

- *Choose a workplace.* Avoid the bed—you associate it with relaxing or sleeping. Try a desk or table for studying; you will concentrate better and accomplish more in less time. You will also have a convenient writing space and plenty of space to spread out. Be sure to have good lighting.
- *Feed your body right.* What you eat plays an important role in how well or how poorly you concentrate. Protein foods (such as cheese, meat, fish, and vegetables) keep the mind alert, while carbohydrates (such as pasta, bread, and processed sugars) make you sleepy. Caffeine (commonly found in coffee, tea, soft drinks, and chocolate) acts as a stimulant in low doses.
- *Avoid food.* Food and serious learning don't mix well. Think about it. When you try to eat and study at the same time, which gets more of your concentration? The food, of course. You will be more effective if you eat first and then study.
- *Listen to your own thoughts.* Listening to anything but your own thoughts interferes with good concentration. Eliminating distractions such as music, television, cell phones, email and text beeps, and other people can greatly increase the amount of studying you can accomplish. Hold all calls, and let email and texts wait.
- *Make a to-do list.* If you are trying to study but get distracted by all of the things you need to do, take time to make a to-do list. Keeping track of your thoughts on paper and referring to the paper from time to time can be very effective for clearing your mind and focusing on your task.
- *Take short, frequent breaks.* Since people concentrate for about 20 minutes or less at a time, it would make sense to capitalize on your natural body rhythms and take a short break every 20 to 30 minutes. If you feel you are fully concentrating and involved in a task, then work until a natural break occurs.

Learn to Manage Your Time

There are two ways to make sure you have more time in a day. *The first and most important way to gain more time is to plan it.* It's like getting in a car and going somewhere. You need to know where you are going and have a plan to get there. Without a plan, you will waste your time and take longer to get to your destination—if you get there at all!

A **weekly project planner** will allow you to keep track of your assignments in more detail. It contains a to-do list specific to one day. It looks like a calendar but is divided into five one-day periods with plenty of space to write. Using a weekly project planner is an effective way to keep track of assignments and plan study time according to the school calendar. Free calendars are available at **https://calendar.google.com**.

A second way to gain more time in a day is to do more in less time. This can be as simple as doubling up on activities. For example, if you have three errands, you might try to combine them instead of doing one at a time, making one round-trip instead of three. If you commute on a bus, on a train, or in a carpool, you can study during your ride. At lunch, you can review notes. Use your imagination as to how you can get more done in less time.

Exhibit 17.4   Personal digital assistants (PDAs) have morphed into sophisticated mobile devices that now include phone, internet, email, messaging, and other wireless functions. Putting even more computing power at consumers' fingertips, mobile devices now provide users with personal information managers, to-do lists, calendars, and other functions to help us organize and manage our time. *How might mobile devices help college students to accomplish more and make better use of their time when it comes to everyday activities and learning job skills?* (Credit: Riaz Kanani/ Flickr/ Attribution 2.0 Generic (CC BY 2.0))

Here are some ideas to help you master your time:

- *Prepare for the morning the night before.* Put out your clothes; make lunches; pack your books.
- *Get up 15 minutes earlier in the morning.* Use the time to plan your day, review your assignments, or catch up on the news.
- *Schedule a realistic day.* Avoid planning for every minute. Leave extra time in your day for getting to appointments and studying.
- *Leave room in your day for the unexpected.* This will allow you to do what you need to do, regardless of what happens. If the unexpected never happens, you will have more time for yourself.
- *Do one thing at a time.* If you try to do two things at once, you become inefficient. Concentrate on the here and now.
- *Learn to say "No."* Say no to social activities or invitations when you don't have the time or energy.

How well do you manage your time? Take the quiz in **Table 17.4** to find out.

Use Your Money Wisely

You can get college money from several different sources, including the following.

- **Grants and Scholarships.** This refers to aid you do not have to repay. Grants are usually based on need while scholarships are frequently based on academic merit or other qualifying factors.
- **Educational Loans.** These are usually subsidized by federal and state governments, private lenders, or

the colleges themselves. Generally, the loans carry lower interest rates than commercial loans, and you do not have to pay them off until after graduation.

- **Work Aid.** This is financial aid you have to work for, frequently 10 or 15 hours a week on campus.

There are many ways to cut the cost of going to college. Consider these:

- Going to a community college for the first two years and then transferring to a four-year institution
- Attending a nearby college and living at home
- Enrolling in one of thousands of college and universities with cooperative educational programs that alternate between full-time studies and full-time employment
- Taking a full-time job at a company that offers free educational opportunities as an employee benefit

Fun Self-Test—How Well Do You Manage Your Time?
Rate your level of agreement with the following statements using the scale below:
Strongly Agree   Agree   Neither Agree nor Disagree   Disagree   Strongly Disagree

1. I rarely feel driven by the urgencies that come my way.
2. I keep a log of each activity to be performed in a day. I prioritize them accordingly.
3. I prioritize not by the importance of the work but by its nature.
4. I can manage my schedule without preparing a weekly plan that includes specific activities.
5. I always want to do all the work myself, thinking I can do it better than anyone else.
6. I plan my weekends with my family and friends.
7. I can delegate work to people so that the work gets done on time and the people feel they are a part of the team.
8. I allow time for the unexpected things I cannot control.
9. If something doesn't happen as per my schedule, it doesn't get done.
10. To accomplish a set of objectives doesn't mean to avoid other unexpected problems.
11. I seldom work after office hours.
12. I would never work by hand if a machine could do it faster.
13. I feel it is easier and time-saving to try new ways of doing things.
14. I always find time to do what I want to do and what I should do.[8]

See the scoring guidelines at the end of this chapter to obtain your score.

Table 17.4

To learn about college costs and financial aid, one of the first sources to consult is the website of The College Board, a not-for-profit organization that connects students to college success and opportunity. Some of the important topics covered at **www.collegeboard.org** include explaining financial aid, facilitating the application process, and finding colleges that fit. There are other websites that also offer information on financial aid:

- **http://www.fastweb.com:** Fastweb has a database of more than 1.5 million private-sector scholarships, grants, and loans.
- **http://www.ed.gov:** This is the U.S. Department of Education information site for federal aid programs, including student loans and grants.

Gain some insight into your money management skills by taking the quiz in Table 17.5.

Study Well

The first key to doing well in a subject is to complete your assignments on time. Most instructors base their assignments on what they will be discussing in class on a given day. So, if you read the pages you are assigned for the day they are due, you will better understand the day's lecture. If you don't complete an assignment when it is due, not only will you be at a disadvantage in the class, but you will also have twice as much work to do for the following class.

Second, know what material to study. This may sound simple, but all too often students do not ask what material they should study and find out too late that they studied the wrong information. The easiest and most accurate way to learn what will be covered on a test is to ask your instructor or read the syllabus.

Tests measure your working memory and knowledge base. To help yourself remember, you can use several memory devices to recall the information you need to study. Here are a few memory devices that have been proven to work:

Fun Self-Test—Are You Good at Managing Money?				
Rate your level of agreement with the following statements, using the scale below:				
Strongly Agree	Agree	Neither Agree nor Disagree	Disagree	Strongly Disagree

1. I eagerly wait for the day I get my paycheck, because my bank balance is generally below the minimum.
2. I have set my savings and spending priorities and have a budget.
3. When I go shopping, I don't buy anything unless it is on sale or is required.
4. I can easily spend money when I am in school.
5. I can differentiate between what I want and what I truly need.
6. I always max out my credit cards.
7. I don't need to plan for my child's education because there will be plenty of government programs.
8. I don't plan to open or have a savings account.
9. I was raised in a family where I always felt that money was quite tight.
10. Credit cards have been useful to me during times of emergency.
11. It is easy for me to resist buying on credit.[9]

See the scoring guidelines at the end of this chapter to obtain your score.

Table 17.5

- *Recite information using your own words.* You will learn more when you reinforce your learning in as many ways as possible. You can reinforce your learning through hearing, writing, reading, reviewing, and reciting.
- *Develop acronyms.* Acronyms are words or names formed from the first letters or groups of letters in a phrase. Acronyms help you remember because they organize information according to the way you need or want to learn it. For example, COD means "cash on delivery," and GDP refers to "gross domestic product." When you study for a test, be creative and make up your own acronyms.
- *Try mnemonic sentences, rhymes, or jingles.* Mnemonic sentences are similar to acronyms; they help you organize your ideas. But instead of creating a word, you make up a sentence. Creating a rhyme, song, or

jingle can make the information even easier to remember. The more creative and silly the sentence, the easier it is to remember. Take, for example, the nine planets listed in order according to their distance from the sun:

Mercury Venus Earth Mars Jupiter Saturn Uranus Neptune

The first letters of these words are: M V E M J S U N .

An acronym using these letters would be difficult to remember. But if you create a sentence using the letters in order, you will remember the sequence better. For example: My Very Educated Mother Just Served Us Nine Pizzas.

- *Visualize.* Visualization refers to creating or recalling mental pictures related to what you are learning. Have you ever tried to remember something while taking a test and visualized the page the information was on? This is your visual memory at work. Approximately 90 percent of your memory is stored visually in pictures, so trying to visualize what you want to remember is a powerful study tool.

Table 17.6 helps you evaluate your study skills.

Become a Master at Taking Tests

Taking a formal test is like playing a game. The object is to get as many points as possible in the time you are allowed. Tests are evaluations of what you know and what you can do with what you know. Here are the rules of the test-taking game:

Rule 1: Act As If You Will Succeed. Thought is powerful. When you think negative thoughts, your stress level rises. Your confidence level may drop, which often leads to feelings of failure. When this happens, think about success. Smile and take deep, slow breaths. Close your eyes, and imagine getting the test back with a good grade written at the top.

Fun Self-Test—Do You Have Good Study Habits?

Answer "yes" or "no" to the following questions:

1. Do you usually spend too much time studying for the amount you are learning?
2. Do you spend hours cramming the night before an exam?
3. Do you find it easy to balance your social life with your study schedule?
4. Do you prefer to study with sound (TV or music) around you?
5. Can you sit for long periods and study for several hours without getting distracted?
6. Do you always borrow notes/materials from your friends before the exam?
7. Do you review your class notes periodically throughout the semester while preparing for tests?
8. Is it easy for you to recall what you studied at the beginning of the semester?
9. Do you need to change your reading/learning style in response to the difficulty level of the course?
10. Do you normally write your papers or prepare for your presentations the night before they are due?
11. Do you feel comfortable contacting the instructor and asking questions or for help whenever you need it?
12. Do you prefer to study lying on a bed or couch rather than sitting at a desk or table?[10]

See the scoring guidelines at the end of this chapter to obtain your score.

Table 17.6

Rule 2: Arrive Ahead of Time. Being on time or early for a test sets your mind at ease. You will have a better chance of getting your favorite seat, relaxing, and preparing yourself mentally for the game ahead.

Rule 3: Bring the Essential Testing Tools. Don't forget to bring the necessary testing tools along with you, including extra pens, sharpened pencils, erasers, a calculator, laptop, dictionary, and other items you may need.

Rule 4: Ignore Panic Pushers. Some people become nervous before a test and hit the panic button, afraid they don't know the material. **Panic pushers** are people who ask you questions about the material they are about to be tested on. If you know the answers, you will feel confident; however, if you don't, you may panic and lose your confidence. Instead of talking with a panic pusher before a test, spend your time concentrating on what you know, not on what you don't know.

Rule 5: Preview the Playing Field. Here's how to do a preview:

- Listen to instructions, and read directions carefully.
- Determine the point spread. Look at the total number of questions and the point value of each. Decide how much time you can spend on each question and still finish the test on time.
- Budget your time. If you budget your time and stick to your time limits, you will always complete the test in the amount of time given.
- Use the test as an information tool. Be on the lookout for clues that answer other questions. Frequently, instructors will test you on a single topic in more than one way.

Rule 6: Write in the Margin. Before you begin the test, write key terms, formulas, names, dates, and other information in the margin so you won't forget them.

Rule 7: Complete the Easy Questions First. Answering easy questions first helps build your confidence.

If you come across a tough question, mark it so you can come back to it later. Avoid spending so much time on a challenging question that you might run out of time to answer the questions you do know.

Rule 8: Know If There Is a Guessing Penalty. Chances are your tests will carry no penalty for guessing. If your time is about to run out and there is no penalty, take a wild guess. On the other hand, if your test carries a penalty for guessing, choose your answers wisely, and leave blank the answers you do not know.

Rule 9: Avoid Changing Your Answers. Have you ever chosen an answer, changed it, and learned later that your first choice was correct? Research indicates that three out of four times, your first choice is correct; therefore, you should avoid changing an answer unless you are *absolutely sure* the answer is wrong.

Rule 10: Write Clearly and Neatly. If you are handwriting your test (versus using a computer), imagine your instructor reading your writing. Is it easy to read or difficult? The easier your test is for the instructor to read, the better your chances of getting a higher grade.

Here are some websites to help you learn more about taking tests:

Essay tests and a checklist for essay tests
> **http://www.calpoly.edu/~sas/asc/ael/tests.essay.html**

Checklist for essay tests
> **http://www.mtsu.edu/~studskl/essay.html**

General test taking
> **http://www.calpoly.edu/~sas/asc/ael/tests.general.html**

Post-test analysis
> **http://www.calpoly.edu/~sas/asc/ael/tests.post.test.analysis.html**

17.5 Get Your Career Off on the Right Track

Mark this section of the text with a permanent bookmark because you are going to want to refer back to it many times during the remainder of your college career. Yes, we are going to give you a road map to find, keep, and advance in that job that is perfect for you.

Think Positively

To be successful in life and in a career, you need to be positive. *Positive thinking* is making a conscious effort to think with an optimistic attitude and to anticipate positive outcomes. *Positive behavior* means purposely acting with energy and enthusiasm. When you think and behave positively, you guide your mind toward your goals and generate matching mental and physical energy.

Positive thinking and behavior are often deciding factors in landing top jobs: your first job, a promotion, a change of jobs—whatever career step you are targeting. That's because the subconscious is literal; it accepts what you regard as fact. Follow these steps to form the habit of positive thinking and to boost your success:

1. **Deliberately motivate yourself every day.** Think of yourself as successful, and expect positive outcomes for everything you attempt.
2. **Project energy and enthusiasm.** Employers hire people who project positive energy and enthusiasm. Develop the habit of speaking, moving, and acting with these qualities.
3. **Practice this positive-expectation mindset until it becomes a habit.** Applicants who project enthusiasm and positive behavior generate a positive chemistry that rubs off. Hiring decisions are

influenced largely by this positive energy. The habit will help you reach your peak potential.

4. **Dwell on past successes.** Focusing on past successes to remind yourself of your abilities helps in attaining goals. For example, no one is ever born knowing how to ride a bicycle or how to use a computer software program. Through training, practice, and trial and error, you master new abilities. During the trial-and-error phases of development, remind yourself of past successes; look at mistakes as part of the natural learning curve. Continue until you achieve the result you want, and remind yourself that you have succeeded in the past and can do so again. You fail only when you quit trying![11]

Exhibit 17.5   Aligning one's lifestyle interests with one's career trajectory is essential to long-term career satisfaction. If the idea of working in a big city captivates the imagination, it can become a guide to the types of jobs to pursue. If one is motivated to work with people or animals, then charity organizations or zoos might be a good place to look. *What jobs do you visualize yourself doing, and how can that vision guide your career search?* (Credit: Rich Bowen/ Flickr/ Attribution 2.0 Generic (CC BY 2.0))

Take a Good Look at Yourself

Once you've developed a positive, "can do" attitude, the next step is to better understand yourself. Ask yourself two basic questions: "Who am I?" and "What can I do?"

Who Am I? This question is the start of *self-assessment*, examining your likes and dislikes and basic values. You may want to ask yourself the following questions:

- Do I want to help society?
- Do I want to help make the world a better place?
- Do I want to help other people directly?
- Is it important for me to be seen as part of a big corporation? Or do I prefer to be part of a smaller organization?
- Do I prefer working indoors or outdoors?
- Do I like to meet new people, or do I want to work alone?

Are you assertive? Assess your assertiveness by taking the quiz in **Table 17.7**.

What Can I Do? After determining what your values are, take the second step in career planning by asking, "What can I do?" This question is the start of *skill assessment*, evaluating your key abilities and characteristics for dealing successfully with problems, tasks, and interactions with other people. Many skills—for instance, the ability to speak clearly and strongly—are valuable in many occupations.

Be sure to consider the work experience you already have, including part-time jobs while going to school, summer jobs, volunteer jobs, and internships. These jobs teach you skills and make you more attractive to potential employers. It's never too early or too late to take a part-time job in your chosen field. For instance, someone with an interest in accounting would do well to try a part-time job with a CPA (certified public accountant) firm.

Fun Self-Test—How Assertive Are You?				
Rate your level of agreement with the following statements using the scale below:				
Strongly Agree	Agree	Neither Agree nor Disagree	Disagree	Strongly Disagree

1. I don't easily agree to work for others.
2. There are some people who make jokes about the way I communicate and put me down repeatedly.
3. I speak up without fear of what others will think of me.
4. I rarely have to repeat my thoughts to make people understand.
5. I sound like I am asking a question when I am making a statement.
6. I'm more reluctant to speak up on the job than in other situations.
7. I can always think of something to say when faced with rude remarks.
8. I tend to suffer in silence when unfairly criticized or insulted.
9. I tend to respond aggressively when criticized unfairly.
10. People don't listen when I am speaking.
11. If I say "no," I feel guilty.
12. When I have a conflict with someone, the results seem to always go their way.
13. When I speak, people listen.[12]

See the scoring guidelines at the end of this chapter to obtain your score.

Table 17.7

In addition to examining your job-related skills, you should also look at your leisure activities. Some possible questions: Am I good at golf? Do I enjoy sailing? Tennis? Racquetball? In some businesses, transactions are made during leisure hours. In that case, being able to play a skillful, or at least adequate, game of golf or tennis may be an asset.

It's hard to like your job if you don't like the field that you're in. Most career counselors agree that finding work you're passionate about is one of the critical factors behind career success. That's why so many career counselors love all those diagnostic tools that measure your personality traits, skill levels, professional interests, and job potential.

The internet is virtually exploding with tests and assessments that you can take. Try, for example, **http://www.self-directed-search.com**. This test is based on the theory that people and work environments can be classified into six basic types: realistic, investigative, artistic, social, enterprising, and conventional. The test determines which three types best describe you, and it suggests occupations that could be a good match. The **Keirsey Character Sorter (http://www.keirsey.com)** is a first cousin of Myers-Briggs. It sorts people into four temperaments: idealists, rationals, artisans, and guardians. Like Myers-Briggs, it not only places you in an overall category, but it also offers a more detailed evaluation of your personality traits. To find a bunch of tests in one place, use a search engine and search "online personality tests."

Understand What Employers Want

Employers want to hire people who will make their businesses more successful. The most desirable employees have the specific skills, transferable career competencies, work values, and personal qualities necessary to be successful in the employers' organizations. The more clearly you convey your skills as they relate to your job target, the greater your chance of landing your ideal job.[13]

Job-Specific Skills. Employers seek job-specific skills (skills and technical abilities that relate specifically to a particular job). Two examples of job-specific skills are using specialized tools and equipment and using a custom-designed software program.

Transferable Skills and Attitudes. Change is a constant in today's business world. Strong transferable career skills are the keys to success in managing your career through change. The most influential skills and attitudes are the abilities to:

- Work well with people.
- Plan and manage multiple tasks.
- Maintain a positive attitude.
- Show enthusiasm.

Employers need workers who have transferable career competencies—basic skills and attitudes that are important for all types of work. These skills make you highly marketable because they're needed for a wide variety of jobs and can be transferred from one task, job, or workplace to another. Examples include these:

- Planning skills
- Research skills
- Communication skills
- Human relations and interpersonal skills
- Critical thinking skills
- Management skills
- Project management skills

Take, for example, a construction supervisor and an accountant. Both must work well with others, manage time and specific tasks, solve problems, read, and communicate effectively—all transferable competencies. They both must be competent in these areas even though framing a house and balancing a set of financial information (the job-specific skill for each field, respectively) are not related. In every occupation, transferable competencies are as important as technical expertise and job-specific skills.

Find Your First Professional Job

The next step is landing the job that fits your skills and desires. You need to consider not only a general type of work but also your lifestyle and leisure goals. If you like to be outdoors most of the time, you might be very unhappy spending eight hours a day in an office. Someone who likes living in small towns may dislike working at the headquarters of a big corporation in Los Angeles, New York City, or Chicago. But make sure that your geographic preferences are realistic. Some parts of the country will experience much greater growth in jobs than others in the coming years.

According to recent research by Glassdoor, the online job listings and career site, the top 10 best cities for jobs in 2017 are:

1. Pittsburgh, PA
2. Indianapolis, IN
3. Kansas City, MO
4. Raleigh-Durham, NC
5. St. Louis, MO
6. Memphis, TN
7. Columbus, OH
8. Cincinnati, OH
9. Cleveland, OH
10. Louisville, KY[14]

You might start answering the question "What will I do?" by studying the *Occupational Outlook Handbook*, published every two years by the U.S. Department of Labor **(https://www.bls.gov/ooh)**. The most recent *Handbook* edition projects job opportunities by industry through the year 2026. The *Handbook* is divided into 25 occupational clusters describing 325 job profiles (with a section on military careers). Among the clusters are education, sales and marketing, transportation, health, and social services. Each job description tells about the nature of the work, working conditions, required training, other qualifications, chances for advancement, employment outlook, earnings, related occupations, and sources of more information. Another good source of job information is the website for the National Association of Colleges and Employers **(http://www.naceweb.org)**. If you are a member of a minority group, you might want to check out **https://www.blackcareernetwork.com** or **http://www.saludos.com**.

Use the Internet to Find a Job

Today, most job searches are done online. Rarely do job seekers use "snail mail" to send a résumé to a potential employer. Therefore, you need to do your homework when it comes to creating a résumé and posting it to various websites, as well as sending it electronically to a specific company's careers web page.

Let's start with the résumé. There are thousands of job-related sites and millions of résumés on the internet. To break through the clutter, you must start with a great résumé—a written description of your education, work experience, personal data, and interests. There are plenty of online resources that can provide you with tips and actual templates to use when creating your résumé. For example, CollegeGrad **(https://collegegrad.com)** provides more than 100 preformatted templates for over 30 college majors on its website that you can use to tailor your résumé and highlight your specific skills and talents.[15] Of course, there are many other sources for creating a résumé, including the actual websites of most online job-listing services.

Once you have created an electronic résumé, you have several options when it comes to your job search. First, you can target specific companies where you would like to work. Then go to their corporate websites and look for a careers page on the website. For example, Google has an extensive careers section on its website that provides detailed information on how to apply to become a "Googler," along with a section on what the company's interview process entails and how Google makes hiring decisions.[16]

You can also try posting your résumé on the top 10 most popular job websites. They are so large that they are worth checking out first. They tend to have more jobs listed, represent more companies, and have larger résumé databases, which attract even more companies.[17]

- Indeed (**https://www.indeed.com**)
- Monster (**https://www.monster.com**)
- Glassdoor (**https://www.glassdoor.com**)
- CareerBuilder (**https://www.careerbuilder.com**)
- SimplyHired (**https://www.simplyhired.com**)
- JobDiagnosis (**https://www.jobdiagnosis.com**)
- Nexxt (**https://www.nexxt.com**)
- ZipRecruiter (**https://www.ziprecruiter.com**)
- USAJobs (**https://www.usajobs.gov**)

The Multimedia Résumé

If you are going to become a computer programmer, web developer, graphics designer, artist, sculptor, singer, dancer, actor, model, animator, cartoonist, or anyone who would benefit by the photographs, graphics, animation, sound, color, or movement inherent in a multimedia résumé, then this résumé is for you. For most people, however, a multimedia résumé and personal home page on the internet aren't necessary. Most internet service providers and commercial online services provide some space on their sites for subscriber home pages.[18]

Getting Your Electronic Résumé into the Short Pile

Applicant tracking systems (ATSs) screen for keywords, which either reject your résumé or move it on to the short list. Your task is to use keywords that will produce as many "hits" as possible. Keywords tend to be more of the noun or noun phrase type (Total Quality Management, Walmart, Sales Manager) as opposed to power action verbs often found in traditional résumés (developed, coordinated, organized). Every occupation and career field has its own jargon, acronyms, and buzzwords. There are also general keywords that apply to transferable skills important in many jobs, such as teamwork, writing, and planning.

Use these tips for adding effective keywords to your résumé:

- The best source of keywords is the actual job listing, which is likely to contain many, if not all, of the keywords that an employer will use to search the résumé database.
- Include plenty of keyword nouns and noun phrases throughout your résumé. If you have a "Summary of Qualifications" section at the beginning of your résumé, try not to repeat verbatim the contents of this section.
- If you are applying for technical positions, you can list your skills, separating each noun or phrase by a comma.
- In some fields, a simple list of skills does not sufficiently describe the job seeker's background. Where appropriate, include accomplishments, as well, but be sure to include enough keywords to satisfy the ATS searches.[19]

There are several ways to determine what keywords are appropriate for your industry and job.

- Look through recent job postings online. Certain words will reappear consistently. Those are your "key" words.
- Make sure your résumé contains the keywords and concepts used in the *particular job listing* you are

applying to.

- Talk to people in the career field you are targeting, and ask them what keywords are appropriate to the positions you are applying to.
- Research specific company websites that appeal to you in terms of getting a job with that specific organization, and review the "About Us" section. Try to use some of the key words the company uses to describe its corporate environment as part of your résumé descriptions.[20]
- Visit professional association websites, and read the content carefully. Many of these are loaded with industry-related jargon that may be appropriate for your résumé.

If you are *still in college*, try to get at least one internship in the career field you're targeting. Even if your internship lasts only a few weeks, you will significantly increase your keyword count to build a resume, not to mention gain valuable experience that will get the attention of hiring professionals.[21]

I've Landed a Job Interview

If some of the companies you contacted want to speak with you, your résumé achieved its goal of getting you a job interview. Look at the interview as a chance to describe your knowledge and skills and interpret them in terms of the employer's specific needs. To make this kind of presentation, you need to do some research on the company. A great place to start is the company's own corporate website.

As you do your information search, you should build your knowledge in these three areas:

1. **General Information about the Occupational Field.** Learn about the current and predicted industry trends, general educational requirements, job descriptions, growth outlook, and salary ranges in the industry.
2. **Information about Prospective Employers.** Learn whether the organization is publicly or privately owned. Verify company names, addresses, products, or services (current and predicted, as well as trends); history; culture; reputation; performance; divisions and subsidiaries; locations (U.S. and global); predicted growth indicators; number of employees; company philosophies and procedures; predicted job openings; salary ranges; and listings of managers of your targeted department within the organization. Also learn about the competitors and customers.
3. **Information about Specific Jobs.** Obtain job descriptions; identify the required education and experience; and determine prevalent working conditions, salary, and fringe benefits.

Interview Like a Pro

An interview tends to have three parts: icebreaking (about five minutes), in which the interviewer tries to put the applicant at ease; questioning (directly or indirectly) by the interviewer; and questioning by the applicant. Almost every recruiter you meet will be trying to rate you in 5 to 10 areas. The questions will be designed to assess your skills and personality.

Many firms start with a *screening interview*, a rather short interview (about 30 minutes) to decide whether to invite you back for a second interview. Sometimes screening interviews can take place online via Skype, FaceTime, or some other form of videoconferencing. Only about 20 percent of job applicants are invited back. The second interview is usually a half day or a day of meetings set up by the human resource department with managers in different departments. After the meetings, someone from the human resource department will discuss other application materials with you and tell you when a letter of acceptance or rejection is likely to be sent. (The wait may be weeks or even months.) Many applicants send follow-up letters in the meantime to show they are still interested in the firm.

For the interview, you should dress conservatively. Plan to arrive about 10 to 15 minutes ahead of time. Try to relax. Smile and make eye contact with (but do not stare at) the interviewer. Body language is an important communicator. The placement of your hands and feet and your overall posture say a good deal about you. Here are some other tips for interviewing like a pro:

1. **Concentrate on being likable.** As simplistic as it seems, research proves that one of the most essential goals in successful interviewing is to be liked by the interviewer. Interviewers want to hire pleasant people others will like working with on a daily basis. Pay attention to the following areas to project that you are highly likable:
    - Be friendly, courteous, and enthusiastic.
    - Speak positively.
    - Smile.
    - Use positive body language.
    - Make certain your appearance is appropriate.
    - Make eye contact when you speak.

2. **Project an air of confidence and pride.** Act as though you want and deserve the job, not as though you are desperate.

3. **Demonstrate enthusiasm.** The applicant's level of enthusiasm often influences employers as much as any other interviewing factor. The applicant who demonstrates little enthusiasm for a job will never be selected for the position.

4. **Demonstrate knowledge of and interest in the employer.** "I really want this job" is not convincing enough. Explain why you want the position and how the position fits your career plans. You can cite opportunities that may be unique to a firm or emphasize your skills and education that are highly relevant to the position.

5. **State your name and the position you're seeking.** When you enter the interviewer's office, begin with a friendly greeting and state the position you're interviewing for: "Hello, Ms. Levine, I'm Bella Reyna. I'm here to interview for the accounting position." If someone has already introduced you to the interviewer, simply say, "Good morning, Ms. Levine." Identifying the position is important because interviewers often interview for many different positions.

6. **Focus on how you fit the job.** Near the beginning of your interview, as soon as it seems appropriate, ask a question similar to this: "Could you describe the scope of the job and tell me what capabilities are most important in filling the position?" The interviewer's response will help you focus on emphasizing your qualifications that best match the needs of the employer.

7. **Speak correctly.** Grammatical errors can cost applicants the job. Use correct grammar, word choice, and a businesslike vocabulary, not an informal, chatty one. Avoid slang. When under stress, people often use pet phrases (such as *you know*) too often. This is highly annoying and projects immaturity and insecurity. Don't use *just* or *only*. "I just worked as a waiter." Don't say "I guess." Avoid the word *probably* because it suggests unnecessary doubt. Ask a friend or family member to help you identify any speech weaknesses you have. Begin eliminating these speech habits now.

Also, you should avoid the following "disqualifiers" at all costs. Any one of these blunders could cost you your dream job:

1. Don't sit down until the interviewer invites you to; waiting is courteous.
2. Don't bring anyone else to the interview; it makes you look immature and insecure.
3. Don't smoke or bring a beverage with you.
4. Don't put anything on or read anything on the interviewer's desk; it's considered an invasion of personal space.

5. Don't chew gum or have anything else in your mouth; this projects immaturity.

6. If you are invited to a business meal, don't order alcohol. When ordering, choose food that's easy to eat while carrying on a conversation.

7. Don't offer a limp handshake; it projects weakness. Use a firm handshake.[22]

Select the Right Job for You

Hard work and a little luck may pay off with multiple job offers. Your happy dilemma is deciding which one is best for you. Start by considering the "FACTS":

*   *Fit:* Do the job and the employer fit your skills, interests, and lifestyle?
*   *Advancement and growth*: Will you have the chance to develop your talents and move up within the organization?
*   *Compensation*: Is the employer offering a competitive salary and benefits package?
*   *Training:* Will the employer provide you with the tools needed to be successful on the job?
*   *Site:* Is the job location a good match for your lifestyle and your budget?

A great way to evaluate a new location is through Homefair **(http://www.homefair.com)**. This site offers tools to help you calculate the cost of moving, the cost of living, and the quality of life in various places. The Moving Calculator helps you figure out how much it will cost to ship your worldly possessions to a particular city. The Relocation Crime Lab compares crime rates in various locations. The City Snapshots feature compares demographic, economic, and climate information for two cities of your choosing. The Salary Calculator computes cost-of-living differences between hundreds of U.S. and international cities and tells you how much you'd need to make in your new city to maintain your current standard of living.

Start Your New Job

No time is more crucial, and possibly nerve-racking, than the first few months at a new job. During this breaking-in period, the employer decides whether a new employee is valuable enough to keep and, if so, in what capacity. Sometimes the employee's whole future with the company rides on the efforts of the first few weeks or months. Most firms offer some sort of formal orientation. But generally speaking, they expect employees to learn quickly—and often on their own. You will be expected to become familiar with the firm's goals; its organization, including your place in the company; and basic personnel policies, such as coffee breaks, overtime, and parking.

Here are a few tips on making your first job rewarding and productive:

*   *Listen and learn:* When you first walk into your new job, let your eyes and ears take everything in. Do people refer to one another by first names, or is the company more formal? How do people dress? Do the people you work with drop into one another's open offices for informal chats about business matters? Or have you entered a "memo mill," where anything of substance is put on email and talks with other employees are scheduled through their administrative assistants? Size up where the power lies. Who seems to most often assume a leadership role? Who is the person others turn to for advice? Why has that person achieved that position? What traits have made this person a "political leader"? Don't be misled by what others say, but also don't dismiss their evaluations. Make your own judgments based on what you see and hear. Effective listening skills help you learn your new job responsibilities quickly. Take the quiz in Table 17.8 to see if you are a good listener.
*   *Do unto others:* Be nice. Nice people are usually the last to be fired and among the first to be promoted. Don't be pleasant only with those who can help you in the company. Be nice to everyone. You never know

who can help you or give you information that will turn out to be useful. Genuinely nice people make routine job assignments, and especially pressure-filled ones, more pleasant. And people who are dealt with pleasantly usually respond in kind.

- *Don't start out as a maverick:* If every new employee tried to change tried-and-true methods to suit his or her whims, the firm would quickly be in chaos. Individual needs must take a back seat to established procedures. Devote yourself to getting things done within the system. Every manager realizes that it takes time for a new person to adjust. But the faster you start accomplishing things, the faster the boss will decide that you were the right person to hire.
- *Find a great mentor:* The leading cause of career unhappiness is working for a bad boss. Good jobs can easily be ruined by supervisors who hold you back. In contrast, your career will soar (and you will smile every day) when you have a great mentor helping you along the way. If you find a job with a super mentor, jump at the chance to take it.

Fun Self-Test—Are You a Good Listener?
Rate your level of agreement with the statements below using the following scale:
Strongly Agree   Agree   Neither Agree nor Disagree   Disagree   Strongly Disagree

1. A person who takes time to ask for clarification about something that might be unclear is not a good listener.
2. While listening, I am distracted by the sounds around me.
3. I try to not only understand what is being said but also analyze the strength of any ideas that are being presented.
4. I ask questions, make observations, or give opinion when necessary for clarifications.
5. While I am listening, I avoid eye contact but am polite.
6. I am tempted to judge a person whether or not he or she is a good speaker.
7. I feel more comfortable when someone talks to me about a topic that I find interesting.
8. I always jot down key phrases/points that strike me as important points of concern that require a response.
9. My listening style varies from the speaker's style of communication.
10. A good listener requires a good speaker.[23]

See the scoring guidelines at the end of this chapter to obtain your score.

Table 17.8

Moving Up

Once you have been on the job for a while, you will want to get ahead and be promoted. Table 17.9 offers several suggestions for improving your chances of promotion. The first item might seem a bit strange, yet it's there for a practical reason. If you don't really like what you do, you won't be committed enough to compete with those who do. The passionate people are the ones who go the extra mile, do the extra work, and come up with fresh out-of-the-box ideas.

So there you have it. Remember: it's never too early to begin planning your career—the future is now.

How to Move Up

- Love what you do, which entails first figuring out who you are.
- Never stop learning about new technologies and new skills that will help you build a successful career.
- Try to get international experience even if it is only a short stint overseas.
- Create new business opportunities—they could lead to a promotion.
- Be really terrific at what you're doing now, this week, this month.

Table 17.9

17.6 Self-Test Scoring Guidelines

After you answer the questions in each of the fun self-tests that appear in this chapter, determine your score and evaluate your skills using the following scoring guidelines.

Table 1 Fun Self-Test: Can You Persuade Others?

For questions 1, 2, 4, 8, 10, and 11, use the following to calculate your score:

Strongly Agree	Agree	Neither Agree nor Disagree	Disagree	Strongly Disagree
2 points	1 point	0 points	0 points	0 points

For questions 3, 5, 6, 7, and 9 use the following to calculate your score:

Strongly Agree	Agree	Neither Agree nor Disagree	Disagree	Strongly Disagree
0 points	0 points	0 points	4 points	5 points

If your score is between 40 and 55, you have an excellent ability to persuade others. A score between 30 and 39 means you have reasonably good persuasion skills. However, you may need to improve your listening and communicating skills. A score below 30 means that you should consider reading a book or taking a short course on how to persuade others.

Table 2 Fun Self-Test: Are You Good at Office Politics?

For questions 1, 3, 4, 7, 8, 10, 12, and 13, give yourself 1 point if you said "true." For questions 2, 5, 6, 9, and 11, give yourself 1 point if you said "false." If your score is 9 or below, you may be good at managing your work, but you need to improve your political skills. Being political means getting along with others in order to move them toward accomplishing a specific goal. If your score is low, consider reviewing the tips offered in the chapter on how to be an effective political player.

Table 4 Fun Self-Test: How Well Do You Manage Your Time?

For questions 2, 6, 8, 9, 11, 13, 14, and 15, use the following to calculate your score:

Strongly Disagree	Disagree	Neither Agree nor Disagree	Agree	Strongly Agree
0 points	0 points	0 points	4 points	5 points

For questions 1, 3, 4, 5, 7, 10, and 12, use the following to calculate your score:

Strongly Disagree	Disagree	Neither Agree nor Disagree	Agree	Strongly Agree
5 points	4 points	0 points	0 points	0 points

If your score is 60 or higher, you have excellent time management skills. Congratulations—you use your time well! If your score is below 60, consider reading a book on time management, taking a course on time management, or investing in time-management tools such as a weekly project planner. The chapter has additional tips that may be useful in improving your time-management skills.

Table 5 Fun Self-Test: Are You Good at Managing Money?

For questions 2, 3, 5, 6, 10, and 11, use the following to calculate your score:

Strongly Disagree	Disagree	Neither Agree nor Disagree	Agree	Strongly Agree
0 points	0 points	0 points	4 points	5 points

For questions 1, 4, 7, 8, and 9, use the following to calculate your score:

Strongly Disagree	Disagree	Neither Agree nor Disagree	Agree	Strongly Agree
5 points	4 points	0 points	0 points	0 points

If your score is 44 or higher, you are able to manage money while balancing your expenses and income. You will be ready to handle financial emergencies without turning to friends or relatives. If your score is between 36 and 43, your savings habits may be inconsistent. To achieve better savings, control your expenses and avoid unnecessary purchases. If your score is 35 or below, you spend too much! Remember: it's a lot more painful to earn money than to spend it. You need to gain control of your finances by limiting your spending, paying off credit cards, or investing in a good personal finance book or course. You may also need to meet with a financial advisor to seek direction on your spending and saving habits.

Table 6 Fun Self-Test: Do You Have Good Study Habits?

If you answered "yes" to questions 3, 5, 7, 8, and 11, give yourself 1 point for each answer.

If you answered "no" to questions 1, 2, 4, 6, 9, 10, and 12, give yourself 1 point for each answer.

If your score is 10 or above, congratulations! You have good study habits. If your score is below 10, read the tips offered in the chapter on improving your study skills. You may also meet with someone at your school to help maximize your study time.

Table 7 Fun Self-Test: How Assertive Are You?

For questions 1, 3, 4, 7, 9, and 13, use the following to calculate your score:

Strongly Agree	Agree	Neither Agree nor Disagree	Disagree	Strongly Disagree
5 points	4 points	0 points	0 points	0 points

For questions 2, 5, 6, 8, 10, 11, and 12, use the following to calculate your score:

Strongly Agree	Agree	Neither Agree nor Disagree	Disagree	Strongly Disagree
0 points	0 points	0 points	4 points	5 points

If your score is 44 or higher, you stand up for your rights while showing respect for others. You quickly respond to unfair criticism. You should be able to fare well in office politics. If your score is 43 or lower, you may want to consider ways to become more comfortable communicating your ideas and opinions and managing your relationships with others.

Table 8 Fun Self-Test: Are You a Good Listener?

For questions 3, 4, 8, and 9, use the following to calculate your score:

Strongly Agree	Agree	Neither Agree nor Disagree	Disagree	Strongly Disagree
5 points	4 points	0 points	0 points	0 points

For questions 1, 2, 5, 6, 7, and 10, use the following to calculate your score:

Strongly Agree	Agree	Neither Agree nor Disagree	Disagree	Strongly Disagree
0 points	0 points	0 points	4 points	5 points

Listening is an important communication skill that will help you succeed in your career. By becoming an effective listener, you gain respect from your colleagues, pick up insights and ideas on improving your job performance, and develop a skill that is important in managing others. If you have a score of 32 or above, then you are a good listener. If your score falls below 32, you need to improve your listening skills. Search the internet for articles and ideas on becoming a better listener, and begin practicing your new skills with your friends and coworkers.

A   Understanding the Legal and Tax Environment

Learning Outcomes

After reading this appendix, you should be able to answer these questions:

1. How does the legal system govern business transactions and settle disputes?
2. What are the required elements of a valid contract, and what are the key types of business law?
3. What are the most common taxes paid by businesses?

Understanding the Legal Environment

1. How does the legal system govern business transactions and settle disputes?

Our legal system affects everyone who lives and does business in the United States. The smooth functioning of society depends on the law, which protects the rights of people and businesses. The purpose of law is to keep the system stable while allowing orderly change. The law defines which actions are allowed or banned and regulates some practices. It also helps settle disputes. The legal system both shapes and is shaped by political, economic, and social systems. As Judge Learned Hand wrote in *The Spirit of Liberty,* "Without [the law] we cannot live; only with it can we insure the future which by right is ours."

In any society, **laws** are the rules of conduct created and enforced by a controlling authority, usually the government. They develop over time in response to the changing needs of people, property, and business. The legal system of the United States is thus the result of a long and continuing process. In each generation, new social problems occur, and new laws are created to solve them. For instance, in the late 1800s corporations in certain industries, such as steel and oil, merged and became dominant. The Sherman Antitrust Act was passed in 1890 to control these powerful firms. Eighty years later, in 1970, Congress passed the National Environmental Policy Act. This law dealt with pollution problems, which no one had thought about in 1890. Today new areas of law are developing to deal with the internet and the recent financial scandals.

The Main Sources of Law

Common law is the body of unwritten law that has evolved out of judicial (court) decisions rather than being enacted by legislatures. It is also called case law. It developed in England and came to America with the colonists. All states except Louisiana, which follows the Napoleonic Code inherited from French settlers, follow the English system. Common law is based on community customs that were recognized and enforced by the courts.

Statutory law is written law enacted by legislatures at all levels, from city and state governments to the federal government. Examples of statutory law are the federal and state constitutions, bills passed by Congress, and ordinances, which are laws enacted by local governments. Statutory law is the chief source of new laws in the United States. Among the business activities governed by statutory law are securities regulation, incorporation, sales, bankruptcy, and antitrust.

Related to statutory law is **administrative law**, or the rules, regulations, and orders passed by boards, commissions, and agencies of federal, state, and local governments. The scope and influence of administrative law have expanded as the number of these government bodies has grown. Federal agencies issue more rulings and settle more disputes than all the courts and legislatures combined. Some federal agencies that issue rules are the Civil Aeronautics Board, the Internal Revenue Service, the Securities and Exchange Commission, the Federal Trade Commission, and the National Labor Relations Board.

Business law is the body of law that governs commercial dealings. These laws provide a protective environment within which businesses can operate. They serve as guidelines for business decisions. Every businessperson should be familiar with the laws governing his or her field. Some laws, such as the Internal Revenue Code, apply to all businesses. Other types of business laws may apply to a specific industry, such as Federal Communications Commission laws that regulate radio and TV stations.

In 1952 the United States grouped many business laws into a model that could be used by all the states. The **Uniform Commercial Code (UCC)** sets forth the rules that apply to commercial transactions between businesses and between individuals and businesses. It has been adopted by 49 states; Louisiana uses only part of it. By standardizing laws, the UCC simplifies the process of doing business across state lines. It covers the sale of goods, bank deposits and collections, letters of credit, documents of title, and investment securities.

The Court System

The United States has a highly developed court system. This branch of government, the **judiciary**, is responsible for settling disputes by applying and interpreting points of law. Although court decisions are the basis for common law, the courts also answer questions left unanswered by statutes and administrative rulings. They have the power to assure that these laws do not violate the federal or state constitutions.

Trial Courts

Most court cases start in the **trial courts**, also called courts of general jurisdiction. The main federal trial courts are the U.S. district courts. There is at least one federal district court in each state. These courts hear cases involving serious federal crimes, immigration, postal regulations, disputes between citizens of different states, patents, copyrights, and bankruptcy. Specialized federal courts handle tax matters, international trade, and claims against the United States.

Appellate Courts

The losing party in a civil (noncriminal) case and a losing defendant in a criminal case may appeal the trial court's decision to the next level in the judicial system, the **appellate courts (courts of appeals)**. There are 12 U.S. circuit courts of appeals. Cases that begin in a federal district court are appealed to the court of appeals for that district. These courts may also review orders from administrative agencies. Likewise, the states have appellate courts and supreme courts for cases tried in state district or superior courts.

No cases start in appellate courts. Their purpose is to review decisions of the lower courts and affirm, reverse, or modify the rulings.

The Supreme Court

The U.S. Supreme Court is the highest court in the nation. It is the only court specifically established by the U.S. Constitution. Any cases involving a state or in which an ambassador, public minister, or consul is a party are heard directly by the Supreme Court. Its main function is to review decisions by the U.S. circuit courts of appeals. Parties not satisfied with a decision of a state supreme court can appeal to the U.S. Supreme Court. But the Supreme Court accepts only those cases that it believes will have the greatest effect on the country, only about 200 of the thousands of appeals it gets each year.

Administrative Agencies

Administrative agencies have limited judicial powers to regulate their special areas. These agencies exist at the federal, state, and local levels. For example, in 2017, the Federal Trade Commission (FTC) ordered satellite TV provider Dish Network to pay a fine of $280 million for violating the Do Not Call Registry, a clearinghouse for consumers who do not want to be contacted by telemarketers. A federal judge ruled that Dish Network was liable for more than 66 million calls that violated the FTC's Telemarketing Sales Rule. A list of selected federal agencies is shown in Table A1.

Federal Regulatory Agencies	
Agency	**Function**
Federal Trade Commission (FTC)	Enforces laws and guidelines regarding unfair business practices and acts to stop false and deceptive advertising and labeling.
Food and Drug Administration (FDA)	Enforces laws and regulations to prevent distribution of adulterated or misbranded foods, drugs, medical devices, cosmetics, veterinary products, and hazardous consumer products.
Consumer Products Safety Commission	Ensures compliance with the Consumer Product Safety Act and seeks to protect the public from unreasonable risk of injury from any consumer product not covered by other regulatory agencies.
Federal Communications Commission (FCC)	Regulates wire, radio, and TV communication in interstate and foreign commerce.
Environmental Protection Agency (EPA)	Develops and enforces environmental protection standards and researches the effects of pollution.
Federal Energy Regulatory Commission (FERC)	Regulates rates and sales of natural gas products, thereby affecting the supply and price of gas available to consumers; also regulates wholesale rates for electricity and gas, pipeline construction, and U.S. imports and exports of natural gas and electricity.
Federal Aviation Administration (FAA)	Oversees the policies and regulations of the airline industry.
Federal Highway Administration (FHA)	Regulates vehicle safety requirements.

Table A1

Nonjudicial Methods of Settling Disputes

Settling disputes by going to court is both expensive and time-consuming. Even if the case is settled prior to the actual trial, sizable legal expenses can be incurred in preparing for trial. Therefore, many companies now use private arbitration and mediation firms as alternatives to litigation. Private firms offer these services, which are a high growth area within the legal profession.

With **arbitration**, the parties agree to present their case to an impartial third party and are required to accept the arbitrator's decision. **Mediation** is similar, but the parties are not bound by the mediator's decision. The mediator suggests alternative solutions and helps the parties negotiate a settlement. Mediation is more flexible than arbitration and allows for compromise. If the parties cannot reach a settlement, they can then go to court, an option not available in most arbitration cases.

In addition to saving time and money, corporations like the confidentiality of testimony and settlement terms in these proceedings. Arbitration and mediation also allow businesses and medical professionals to avoid jury trials, which can result in large settlements in certain types of lawsuits, such as personal injury, discrimination, medical malpractice, and product liability.

Contract Law

2. What are the required elements of a valid contract, and what are the key types of business law?

Linda Price, a 22-year-old college student, is looking at a car with a sticker price of $18,000. After some negotiating, she and the salesperson agree on a price of $17,000, and the salesperson writes up a contract, which they both sign. Has Linda legally bought the car for $17,000? The answer is yes, because the transaction meets all the requirements for a valid contract.

A **contract** is an agreement that sets forth the relationship between parties regarding the performance of a specified action. The contract creates a legal obligation and is enforceable in a court of law. Contracts are an important part of business law. Contract law is also incorporated into other fields of business law, such as property and agency law. Some of the business transactions that involve contracts are buying materials and property, selling goods, leasing equipment, and hiring consultants.

A contract can be an *express contract,* which specifies the terms of the agreement in either written or spoken words, or an *implied contract*, which depends on the acts and conduct of the parties to show agreement. An example of an express contract is the written sales contract for Linda Price's new car. An implied contract exists when you order and receive a sandwich at Jason's Grill. You and the restaurant have an implied contract that you will pay the price shown on the restaurant's menu in exchange for an edible sandwich.

Contract Requirements

Businesses deal with contracts all the time, so it's important to know the requirements of a valid contract. For a contract to be legally enforceable, all of the following elements must be present:

- *Mutual assent.* Voluntary agreement by both parties to the terms of the contract. Each party to the contract must have entered into it freely, without duress. Using physical or economic harm to force the signing of the contract—threatening injury or refusing to place another large order, for instance—invalidates a contract. Likewise, fraud—misrepresenting the facts of a transaction—makes a contract unenforceable. Telling a prospective used-car buyer that the brakes are new when in fact they have not been replaced makes the contract of sale invalid.
- *Capacity.* Legal ability of a party to enter into contracts. Under the law, minors (those under 18), mental incompetents, drug and alcohol addicts, and convicts cannot enter into contracts.
- *Consideration.* Exchange of some legal value or benefit between the parties. Consideration can be in the form of money, goods, or a legal right given up. Suppose that an electronics manufacturer agrees to rent an industrial building for a year at a monthly rent of $1,500. Its consideration is the rent payment of $1,500, and the building owner's consideration is permission to occupy the space. But if you offer to type a term paper for a friend for free and your offer is accepted, there is no contract. Your friend has not given up anything, so you are not legally bound to honor the deal.
- *Legal purpose.* Absence of illegality. The purpose of the contract must be legal for it to be valid. A contract cannot require performance of an illegal act. A contract to smuggle drugs into a state for a specified

amount of money would not be legally enforceable.

- *Legal form.* Oral or written form, as required. Many contracts can be oral. For instance, an oral contract exists when Bridge Corp. orders office supplies by phone from Ace Stationery Store and Ace delivers the requested goods. Written contracts include leases, sales contracts, and property deeds. Some types of contracts must be in writing to be legally binding. In most states, written contracts are required for the sale of goods costing more than $500, for the sale of land, for contract performance that cannot be carried out within a year, and for guarantees to pay the debts of someone else.

As you can see, Linda Price's car purchase meets all the requirements for a valid contract. Both parties have freely agreed to the terms of the contract. Linda is not a minor and presumably does not fit any of the other categories of incapacity. Both parties are giving consideration, Linda by paying the money and the salesperson by turning over the car to her. The purchase of the car is a legal activity. And the written contract is the correct form because the cost of the car is over $500.

Breach of Contract

A **breach of contract** occurs when one party to a contract fails (without legal excuse) to fulfill the terms of the agreement. The other party then has the right to seek a remedy in the courts. There are three legal remedies for breach of contract:

- *Payment of damages.* Money awarded to the party who was harmed by the breach of contract, to cover losses incurred because the contract wasn't fulfilled. Suppose that Ajax Roofing contracts with Fred Wellman to fix the large hole in the roof of his factory within three days. But the roofing crew doesn't show up as promised. When a thunderstorm four days later causes $45,000 in damage to Wellman's machinery, Wellman can sue for damages to cover the costs of the water damage because Ajax breached the contract.
- *Specific performance of the contract.* A court order requiring the breaching party to perform the duties under the terms of the contract. Specific performance is the most common method of settling a breach of contract. Wellman might ask the court to direct Ajax to fix the roof at the price and conditions in the contract.
- *Restitution.* Canceling the contract and returning to the situation that existed before the contract. If one party fails to perform under the contract, neither party has any further obligation to the other. Because Ajax failed to fix Wellman's roof under the terms of the contract, Wellman does not owe Ajax any money. Ajax must return the 50 percent deposit it received when Wellman signed the contract.

Warranties

Express warranties are specific statements of fact or promises about a product by the seller. This form of warranty is considered part of the sales transaction that influences the buyer. Express warranties appear in the form of statements that can be interpreted as fact. The statement "This machine will process 1,000 gallons of paint per hour" is an express warranty, as is the printed warranty that comes with a computer or a telephone answering machine.

Implied warranties are neither written nor oral. These guarantees are imposed on sales transactions by statute or court decision. They promise that the product will perform up to expected standards. For instance, a man bought a used car from a dealer, and the next day the transmission fell out as he was driving on the highway. The dealer fixed the car, but a week later the brakes failed. The man sued the car dealer. The court ruled in favor of the car owner because any car without a working transmission or brakes is not fit for the ordinary purpose of driving. Similarly, if a customer asks to buy a copier to handle 5,000 copies per month, she relies on the salesperson to sell her a copier that meets those needs. The salesperson implicitly warrants that the copier purchased is appropriate for that volume.

Patents, Copyrights, and Trademarks

The U.S. Constitution protects authors, inventors, and creators of other intellectual property by giving them the rights to their creative works. Patents, copyrights, and registration of trademarks and servicemarks are legal protection for key business assets.

A **patent** gives an inventor the exclusive right to manufacture, use, and sell an invention for 20 years. The U.S. Patent Office, a government agency, grants patents for ideas that meet its requirements of being new, unique, and useful. The physical process, machine, or formula is what is patented. Patent rights—pharmaceutical companies' rights to produce drugs they discover, for example—are considered intangible personal property.

The government also grants copyrights. A **copyright** is an exclusive right, shown by the symbol ©, given to a writer, artist, composer, or playwright to use, produce, and sell her or his creation. Works protected by copyright include printed materials (books, magazine articles, lectures), works of art, photographs, and movies. Under current copyright law, the copyright is issued for the life of the creator plus 70 years after the creator's death. Patents and copyrights, which are considered intellectual property, are the subject of many lawsuits today.

A **trademark** is a design, name, or other distinctive mark that a manufacturer uses to identify its goods in the marketplace. Apple's "bitten apple" logo (symbol) is an example of a trademark. A **servicemark** is a symbol, name, or design that identifies a service rather than a tangible object. The Travelers Insurance umbrella logo is an example of a servicemark.

Most companies identify their trademark with the ® symbol in company ads. This symbol shows that the trademark is registered with the Register of Copyrights, Copyright Office, Library of Congress. The trademark is followed by a generic description: Fritos corn chips, Xerox copiers, Scotch brand tape, Kleenex tissues.

Trademarks are valuable because they create uniqueness in the minds of customers. At the same time, companies don't want a trademark to become so well known that it is used to describe all similar types of products. For instance, Coke is often used to refer to any cola soft drink, not just those produced by The Coca-Cola Company. Companies spend millions of dollars each year to keep their trademarks from becoming *generic words,* terms used to identify a product class rather than the specific product. The Coca-Cola Company employs many investigators and files many lawsuits each year to prevent its trademarks from becoming generic words.

Once a trademark becomes generic (which a court decides), it is public property and can be used by any person or company. Names that were once trademarked but are now generic include *aspirin, thermos, linoleum,* and *toll house cookies.*

Tort Law

A **tort** is a civil, or private, act that harms other people or their property. The harm may involve physical injury, emotional distress, invasion of privacy, or *defamation* (injuring a person's character by publication of false statements). The injured party may sue the wrongdoer to recover damages for the harm or loss. A tort is not the result of a breach of contract, which would be settled under contract law. Torts are part of common law. Examples of tort cases are medical malpractice, *slander* (an untrue oral statement that damages a person's reputation), *libel* (an untrue written statement that damages a person's reputation), product liability (discussed in the next section), and fraud.

A tort is generally not a crime, although some acts can be both torts and crimes. (Assault and battery, for instance, is a criminal act that would be prosecuted by the state and also a tort because of the injury to the person.) Torts are private wrongs and are settled in civil courts. *Crimes* are violations of public law punishable by the state or county in the criminal courts. The purpose of criminal law is to punish the person who committed the crime. The purpose of tort law is to provide remedies to the injured party.

For a tort to exist and damages to be recovered, the harm must be done through either negligence or deliberate intent. *Negligence* occurs when reasonable care is not taken for the safety of others. For instance, a woman attending a New York Mets baseball game was struck on the head by a foul ball that came through a hole in the screen behind home plate. The court ruled that a sports team charging admission has an obligation to provide structures free from defects and seating that protects spectators from danger. The Mets were found negligent. Negligence does not apply when an injury is caused by an unavoidable accident, an event that was not intended and could not have been prevented even if the person used reasonable care. This area of tort law is quite controversial, because the definition of negligence leaves much room for interpretation.

Product-Liability Law

Product liability refers to manufacturers' and sellers' responsibility for defects in the products they make and sell. It has become a specialized area of law combining aspects of contracts, warranties, torts, and statutory law (at both the state and federal levels). A product-liability suit may be based on negligence or strict liability (both of which are torts) or misrepresentation or breach of warranty (part of contract law).

An important concept in product-liability law is **strict liability**. A manufacturer or seller is liable for any personal injury or property damage caused by defective products or packaging—even if all possible care was used to prevent such defects. The definition of defective is quite broad. It includes manufacturing and design defects and inadequate instructions on product use or warnings of danger.

Product-liability suits are very costly. More than 100,000 product-liability suits were filed against hundreds of companies that made or used asbestos, a substance that causes lung disease and cancer but was once used widely in insulation, brake linings, textiles, and other products. Scores of companies were forced into bankruptcy as a result of asbestos-related lawsuits, and the total cost of asbestos cases to defendants and their insurers exceeds $70 billion (most of which was paid not to the victims but to lawyers and experts).

Bankruptcy Law

Congress has given financially distressed firms and individuals a way to make a fresh start. **Bankruptcy** is the legal procedure by which individuals or businesses that cannot meet their financial obligations are relieved of their debts. A bankruptcy court distributes any assets to the creditors.

Bankruptcy can be either voluntary or involuntary. In a *voluntary bankruptcy,* the debtor files a petition with the court, stating that debts exceed assets and asking the court to declare the debtor bankrupt. In an *involuntary bankruptcy,* the creditors file the bankruptcy petition.

The *Bankruptcy Reform Act* of 1978, amended in 1984 and 1986, provides for the resolution of bankruptcy cases. Under this act, two types of bankruptcy proceedings are available to businesses: *Chapter 7* (liquidation) and *Chapter 11* (reorganization). Most bankruptcies, an estimated 70 percent, use Chapter 7. After the sale of any assets, the cash proceeds are given first to secured creditors and then to unsecured creditors. A firm that opts to reorganize under Chapter 11 works with its creditors to develop a plan for paying part of its debts and writing off the rest.

The Bankruptcy Abuse Prevention and Consumer Protection Act went into effect October 17, 2005. Under this law, Americans with heavy debt will find it difficult to avoid meeting their financial obligations. Many debtors will have to work out repayment plans instead of having their obligations erased in bankruptcy court.[1]

---

1   "Changes in Bankruptcy Laws—Credit Counseling, Means Test," http://www.creditinfocenter.com, May 10, 2016.

The law requires people with incomes above a certain level to pay some or all of their credit-card charges, medical bills, and other obligations under a court-ordered bankruptcy plan. Supporters of the 2005 law argue that bankruptcy frequently is the last refuge of gamblers, impulsive shoppers, the divorced or separated, and fathers avoiding child support. Now there is an objective, needs-based bankruptcy test to determine whether filers should be allowed to cancel their debts or be required to enter a repayment plan. Generally, people with incomes above the state median income would be required to use a plan to repay their debts. People with special circumstances, such as serious medical conditions, would be allowed to cancel debts despite this income level.

Also, companies will need a lot more cash to enter into a bankruptcy than in the past. Before the 2005 law, utilities could not discontinue service as a result of a bankruptcy filing. But under the new act, the filing company must post a cash deposit or equivalent in order to continue their service. Sellers also have priority over other claims with regard to merchandise distributed to the debtor within 20 days prior to the bankruptcy filing.

The act limits the debtor's exclusivity period, which was a real boon of filing for bankruptcy. Past law allowed for indefinite extensions, which served to drag out the time before bondholders and other creditors get any money. But now that period is capped at 18 months, with no room for extension. For large corporations with complicated bankruptcies, such a quick turnaround may not be possible, and if a plan is not filed at the end of 18 months, the company must put itself at the mercy of creditors.

Laws to Promote Fair Competition

Many measures have been taken to try to keep the marketplace free from influences that would restrict competition. These efforts include **antitrust regulation**, laws that prevent companies from entering into agreements to control trade through a monopoly. The first act regulating competition was the *Sherman Antitrust Act*, passed in 1890 to prevent large companies from dominating an industry and making it hard for smaller firms to compete. This broad act banned monopolies and contracts, mergers, or conspiracies in restraint of trade. In 1914 the *Clayton Act* added to the more general provisions of the Sherman Antitrust Act. It outlawed the following:

- *Price discrimination.* Offering a customer discounts that are not offered to all other purchasers buying on similar terms
- *Exclusive dealing.* Refusing to let the buyer purchase a competitor's products for resale
- *Tying contracts.* Requiring buyers to purchase merchandise they may not want in order to get the products they do want
- *Purchase of stock in competing corporations so as to lessen competition.* Buying competitors' stock in such quantity that competition is reduced

The 1950 *Celler-Kefauver Act* amended the Clayton Act. It bans the purchase of one firm by another if the resulting merger decreases competition within the industry. As a result, all corporate acquisitions are subject to regulatory approval before they can be finalized. Most antitrust actions are taken by the U.S. Department of Justice, based on federal law. Violations of the antitrust acts are punishable by fines, imprisonment, or civil damage payments that can be as high as three times the actual damage amount. These outcomes give defendants an incentive to resolve cases.

The *Federal Trade Commission Act,* also passed in 1914, bans unfair trade practices. This act created the Federal Trade Commission (FTC), an independent five-member board with the power to define and monitor unfair trade practices, such as those prohibited by the Sherman and Clayton Acts. The FTC investigates complaints and can issue rulings called *cease-and-desist orders* to force companies to stop unfair business practices. Its powers have grown over the years. Today the FTC is one of the most important agencies regulating the competitive practices of business.

Regulation of Advertising and Pricing

A number of federal laws directly affect the promotion and pricing of products. The *Wheeler-Lea Act* of 1938 amended the Federal Trade Commission Act and gave the FTC authority to regulate advertising. The FTC monitors companies' advertisements for false or misleading claims.

The most important law in the area of pricing is the *Robinson-Patman Act,* a federal law passed in 1936 that tightened the Clayton Act's prohibitions against price discrimination. An exception is made for circumstances like discounts for quantity purchases, as long as the discounts do not lessen competition. But a manufacturer cannot sell at a lower price to one company just because that company buys all its merchandise from the manufacturer. Also, if one firm is offered quantity discounts, all firms buying that quantity of goods must get the discounts. The FTC and the antitrust division of the Justice Department monitor pricing.

Consumer Protection Laws

Consumerism reflects the struggle for power between buyers and sellers. Specifically, it is a social movement seeking to increase the rights and powers of buyers vis-à-vis sellers. Sellers' rights and powers include the following:

- To introduce into the marketplace any product, in any size and style, that is not hazardous to personal health or safety, or if it is hazardous, to introduce it with the proper warnings and controls
- To price the product at any level they wish, provided they do not discriminate among similar classes of buyers
- To spend any amount of money they wish to promote the product, so long as the promotion does not constitute unfair competition
- To formulate any message they wish about the product, provided that it is not misleading or dishonest in content or execution
- To introduce any buying incentives they wish

Meanwhile, buyers have the following rights and powers:

- To refuse to buy any product that is offered to them
- To expect products to be safe
- To expect a product to be essentially as the seller represents it
- To receive adequate information about the product

Many laws have been passed to protect consumer rights. Table A2 lists the major consumer protection laws.

Key Consumer Protection Laws	
Mail Fraud Act (1872)	Makes it a federal crime to defraud consumers through use of the mail.
Pure Food and Drug Act (1906)	Created the Food and Drug Administration (FDA); protects consumers against the interstate sale of unsafe and adulterated foods and drugs.

Table A2

Key Consumer Protection Laws	
Food, Drug, and Cosmetic Act (1938)	Expanded the power of the FDA to cover cosmetics and therapeutic devices and to establish standards for food products.
Flammable Fabrics Act (1953)	Prohibits sale or manufacture of clothing made of dangerously flammable fabric.
Child Protection Act (1966)	Prohibits sale of harmful toys and gives the FDA the right to remove dangerous products from the marketplace.
Cigarette Labeling Act (1965)	Requires cigarette manufacturers to put labels warning consumers about health hazards on cigarette packages.
Fair Packaging and Labeling Act (1966)	Regulates labeling and packaging of consumer products.
Consumer Credit Protection Act (Truth-in-Lending Act) (1968)	Requires lenders to fully disclose to borrowers the loan terms and the costs of borrowing (interest rate, application fees, etc.).
Fair Credit Reporting Act (1971)	Requires consumers denied credit on the basis of reports from credit agencies to be given access to their reports and to be allowed to correct inaccurate information.
Consumer Product Safety Act (1972)	Created the Consumer Product Safety Commission, an independent federal agency, to establish and enforce consumer product safety standards.
Equal Credit Opportunity Act (1975)	Prohibits denial of credit on the basis of gender, marital status, race, religion, age, or national origin.
Magnuson-Moss Warranty Act (1975)	Requires that warranties be written in clear language and that terms be fully disclosed.

Table A2

Key Consumer Protection Laws	
Fair Debt Collection Practice Act (1978)	Makes it illegal to harass or abuse any person, to make false statements, or to use unfair methods when collecting a debt.
Alcohol Labeling Legislation (1988)	Provides for warning labels on liquor saying that women shouldn't drink when pregnant and that alcohol impairs our abilities.
Nutrition Labeling and Education Act (1990)	Requires truthful and uniform nutritional labeling on every food the FDA regulates.
Children's Television Act (1990)	Limits the amount of advertising to be shown during children's television programs to not more than 10.5 minutes per hour on weekends and not more than 12.0 minutes per hour on weekdays.
Americans with Disabilities Act (ADA) (1990)	Protects the rights of people with disabilities; makes discrimination against the disabled illegal in public accommodations, transportation, and telecommunications.
Brady Law (1998)	Imposes a 5-day waiting period and a background check before a gun purchaser can take possession of the gun.
Children's Online Privacy Protection Act (2002)	Regulates the collection of personally identifiable information (name, address, e-mail address, phone number, hobbies, interests, or other information collected through cookies) online from children under age 13.
Can-Spam Anti-Spam Law (2004)	Requires marketers to remove customers from their lists when requested, and provide automated opt-out methods as well as complete contact information (address and phone) with alternate means of removal. It also bans common practices such as false headers and e-mail harvesting (the use of software that spies on Web sites to collect e-mail addresses). Subject lines must be truthful and contain a notice that the message is an ad.

Table A2

Key Consumer Protection Laws	
Credit Card Accountability and Disclosure Act (2009)	Amends the Truth in Lending Act to prescribe open-end credit lending procedures and enhanced disclosures to consumers, limit related fees and charges to consumers, increase related penalties, and establish constraints and protections for issuance of credit cards to minors and students.
Dodd Frank Wall Street Reform and Consumer Protection Act (2010)	The act established after the financial crisis of 2008 created a number of new government agencies tasked with overseeing various components of the act and by extension various aspects of the banking system. President Donald Trump has pledged to repeal Dodd-Frank, and on May 22, 2018, the House of Representatives voted to roll back significant pieces of Dodd-Frank.

Table A2

Deregulation of Industries

During the 1980s and 1990s, the U.S. government actively promoted **deregulation**, the removal of rules and regulations governing business competition. Deregulation drastically changed some once-regulated industries (especially the transportation, telecommunications, and financial services industries) and created many new competitors. The result has been entries into and exits from some industries. One of the latest industries to deregulate is the electric power industry. With almost 200 investor-owned electric utilities, it is the largest industry to be deregulated so far.

Consumers typically benefit from deregulation. Increased competition often means lower prices. Businesses also benefit because they have more freedom to operate and can avoid the costs associated with government regulations. But more competition can also make it hard for small or weak firms to survive.

Regulation of the Internet

Use of the internet has exploded over the past decade. Recent estimates suggest that more than half of the world's population use the web to purchase goods and services, book travel plans, conduct banking and pay bills, stream original content, read the latest news and sports information, look up facts and figures, and keep up with friends, family, and business associates via Skype, FaceTime, Twitter, Facebook, and other platforms.[2]

Internet access and regulation continue to be a concern for many interest groups, including privacy advocates, internet providers, private citizens, technology companies, and the government, to name a few. In 2017, President Trump signed legislation overturning the internet privacy protections originally put in place by the Obama administration. Under the new legislation, internet providers will now be able to collect, store, share, and sell certain types of customer information without their consent. Under previous legislation, sharing this type of data would have required consumers' permission. With this new law, companies such as Verizon and Comcast will be able to mine user data and use that information to compete in the $83 billion digital advertising market with companies such as Google and Facebook.[3] The internet environment is extremely dynamic, so consumers and other interest groups should monitor how regulations and other policies will continue to change the ground rules for internet use.

---

2   "Digital in 2017: Global Overview," *The Next Web*, https://thenextweb.com, accessed June 23, 2017.
3   Brian Fung, "Trump Has Signed Repeal of FCC's Internet Privacy Rule. Here's What Happens Next," *Los Angeles Times*, http://www.latimes.com, April 4, 2017.

Understanding the Tax Environment of Business

3. What are the most common taxes paid by businesses?

Taxes are sometimes seen as the price we pay to live in this country. Taxes are assessed by all levels of government on both business and individuals, and they are used to pay for the services provided by government. The federal government is the largest collector of taxes, accounting for 52 percent of all tax dollars. States are next, followed closely by local government taxes. The average American family pays about 37 percent of its income for taxes, 28 percent to the federal government and 9 percent to state and local governments.

Income Taxes

Income taxes are based on the income received by businesses and individuals. The income taxes paid to the federal government are set by Congress, regulated by the Internal Revenue Code, and collected by the Internal Revenue Service. These taxes are *progressive*, meaning that rates increase as income increases. Most of the states and some large cities also collect income taxes from individuals and businesses. The state and local governments establish their own rules and tax rates.

Other Types of Taxes

Besides income taxes, individuals and businesses pay a number of other taxes. The four main types are property taxes, payroll taxes, sales taxes, and excise taxes.

Property taxes are assessed on real and personal property, based on the assessed value of the property. They raise quite a bit of revenue for state and local governments. Most states tax land and buildings. Property taxes may be based on fair market value (what a buyer would pay), a percentage of fair market value, or replacement value (what it would cost today to rebuild or buy something like the original). The value on which the taxes are based is the assessed value.

Any business that has employees and meets a payroll must pay **payroll taxes**, the employer's share of Social Security taxes and federal and state unemployment taxes. These taxes must be paid on wages, salaries, and commissions. State unemployment taxes are based on the number of employees in a firm who have become eligible for unemployment benefits. A firm that has never had an employee become eligible for unemployment will pay a low rate of state unemployment taxes. The firm's experience with employment benefits does not affect federal unemployment tax rates.

Sales taxes are levied on goods when they are sold and are a percentage of the sales price. These taxes are imposed by states, counties, and cities. They vary in amount and in what is considered taxable. Some states have no sales tax. Others tax some categories (such as appliances) but not others (such as clothes). Still others tax all retail products except food, magazines, and prescription drugs. Sales taxes increase the cost of goods to the consumer. Businesses bear the burden of collecting sales taxes and sending them to the government.

Excise taxes are placed on specific items, such as gasoline, alcoholic beverages, cigarettes, airline tickets, cars, and guns. They can be assessed by federal, state, and local governments. In many cases, these taxes help pay for services related to the item taxed. For instance, gasoline excise taxes are often used to build and repair highways. Other excise taxes—such as those on alcoholic beverages, cigarettes, and guns—are used to control practices that may cause harm.

References

The Nature of Business
1. "Mercer 2017 Quality of Life Rankings," http://mercer.com/qol, May 15, 2017. **2.** Rob Fahey, "Sony's Entire Future Now Rests on PlayStation," http://www.gamesindustry.biz, July 1, 2016. **3.** "Quick Facts about Nonprofits," National Center for Charitable Statistics, http://nccs.urban.org, accessed May 15, 2017; Brice S. McKeever, "The Nonprofit Sector in Brief 2015," *Urban Institute*, http://www.urban.org, accessed May 15, 2017. **4.** Julia Halperin, "As a Generation of Directors Reaches Retirement, Fresh Faces Prepare to Take Over US Museums," *The Art Newspaper*, http://www.russellreynolds.com, June 2, 2015; "Museum Succession in America: Onwards and Upwards," *The Economist*, www.economist.com, May 9, 2015. **5.** Kerry A. Dolan, "Forbes 2017 Billionaires List: Meet the Richest People on the Planet," *Forbes*, https://www.forbes.com, March 20, 2017. **6.** Caroline Beaton, "Why Knowledge Workers Are Bad at Making Decisions," *Forbes*, http://www.forbes.com, January 23, 2017; Josh Zumbrun, "The Rise of Knowledge Workers Is Accelerating Despite the Threat of Automation," *The Wall Street Journal*, http://www.wsj.com, May 4, 2016.

Understanding the Business Environment
7. Environmental Defense Fund, "Seven Years Later: What's Ahead for the Gulf," http://www.edf.org, accessed May 15, 2017; "Oil Spills Fast Facts," *CNN*, http://www.cnn.com, February 9, 2017; Steven Mufson, "BP's Big Bill for the World's Largest Oil Spill Reaches $61.6 Billion," *Washington Post*, https://www.washingtonpost.com, July 14, 2016; Debbie Elliott, "5 Years after BP Oil Spill, Effects Linger and Recovery Is Slow," *NPR*, http://www.npr.org, April 20, 2015. **8.** Melissa Healy, "Speed Up Drug Approvals at FDA? It's Already Faster Than Europe's Drug Agency," *Los Angeles Times*, http://www.latimes.com, April 6, 2017. **9.** Hamza Shaban, "Google for the First Time Outspent Every Other Company to Influence Washington in 2017," *Washington Post*, https://www.washingtonpost.com, January 23, 2018; Saleha Mohsin, "Silicon Valley Cozies Up to Washington, Outspending Wall Street 2–1," *Bloomberg*, http://www.bloomberg.com, October 18, 2016. **10.** "CIO Journal: 2017 Telecommunications Outlook," *The Wall Street Journal*, http://deloitte.wsj.com, March 1, 2017. **11.** Richard Fry, "Millennials Overtake Baby Boomers as America's Largest Generation," *Pew Research Center*, http://www.pewresearch.org, April 25, 2016. **12.** Ashley Lutz, "Everything You Know about Millennial Spending Is about to Change," *Business Insider*, http://www.businessinsider.com, October 1, 2016. **13.** Geoff Gross, "5 Ways to Effectively Market to Baby Boomers," *Entrepreneur*, http://www.entrepreneur.com, June 1, 2016. **14.** U.S. Census Bureau, "Projections of the Size and Composition of the U.S. Population: 2014 to 2060," http://www.census.gov, accessed May 15, 2017. **15.** "Why Move to the Cloud? 10 Benefits of Cloud Computing," http://www.salesforce.com, accessed May 15, 2017; Jim Rock, "How Robots Will Reshape the U.S. Economy," *Tech Crunch*, http://techcrunch.com, March 21, 2016.

How Business and Economics Work
16. "What the Future Holds for U.S.–Cuba Relations," *Knowledge@Wharton*, http://knowledge.wharton.upenn.edu, April 11, 2017. **17.** France Accountants, "French Tax Summary 2017," http://www.franceaccountants.com, accessed May 15, 2017; "2017 Tax Brackets," http://www.bankrate.com, accessed May 15, 2017. **18.** Simon Kennedy, "Brexit Timeline: From the Referendum to Article 50," *Bloomberg*, http://www.bloomberg.com, March 20, 2017.

Macroeconomics: The Big Picture
19. Maggie McGrath, "Unemployment Rate Holds Steady at 4.1% as U.S. Adds 148,000 Jobs in December," *Forbes*, https://www.forbes.com, January 5, 2018; Bureau of Labor Statistics, "Spotlight on Statistics: The Recession of 2007–2009," http://www.bls.gov/spotlight, accessed May 15, 2017. **20.** Marcus Bensasson, "Youth Unemployment Shows Euro-Area Recovery Not Working for All," *Bloomberg Markets*, http://www.bloomberg.com, April 3, 2017; Dorota Bartyzel and Konrad Krasuski, "Brexit Flight to Shift 30,000

Jobs to Poland, Minister Says," *Bloomberg Politics,* http://www.bloomberg.com, January 23, 2017. **21.** Bureau of Labor Statistics, "Employees in Motor Vehicle and Parts Industry," https://data.bls.gov, data extracted on May 19, 2017; Christina Rogers, "Ford Aims to Cut Global Workforce by Roughly 10%," *The Wall Street Journal,* http://www.wsj.com, May 15, 2017. **22.** "Historical Inflation Rates: 1914–2017," http://www.usinflationcalculator.com, accessed May 19, 2017. **23.** Trading Economics, "Inflation Rate by Country," http://www.tradingeconomics.com, accessed May 19, 2017.

Achieving Macroeconomic Goals
24. Binyamin Appelbaum, "Fed Raises Interest Rates for Third Time Since Financial Crisis," *The New York Times,* http://www.nytimes.com, March 15, 2017; Lauren Lyons Cole, "How the Fed's Interest-Rate Hike Affects Consumers," *Consumer Reports,* http://www.consumerreports.org, March 15, 2017. **25.** Mike Patton, "U.S. Government Deficit Is Rising Again," *Forbes,* http://www.forbes.com, April 28, 2016. **26.** "Quantifying the National Debt," http://www.justfacts.com, accessed May 23, 2017; "U.S. National Debt Clock: U.S. Total Interest Paid," http://usdebtclock.org, accessed May 23, 2017.

Microeconomics: Zeroing in on Businesses and Consumers
27. Kimberly Amadeo, "Hurricane Katrina Facts: Damage and Costs," *The Balance,* http://www.thebalance.com, February 9, 2017. **28.** "18-Month Average Retail Price Chart (2015–2017)," http://www.gasbuddy.com, accessed May 23, 2017; JPMorgan Chase Institute, "How Falling Gas Prices Fuel the Consumer," https://www.jpmorganchase, accessed May 23, 2017.

Trends in the Business Environment and Competition
29. "The Retirement Problem: What Will You Do with All That Time?" *Knowledge@Wharton,* http://knowledge.wharton.upenn.edu, January 14, 2016. **30.** Michael Zimmerman, "Millennials in the Workforce: What They Want, and How to Manage Them," http://www.smartceo.com, January 11, 2017; Kathy Gurchiek, "What Motivates Your Workers? It Depends on Their Generation," *Society for Human Resource Management,* http://www.shrm.org, May 9, 2016. **31.** Tom Anderson, "Employers Offer Older Workers Flexible Retirement," *CNBC,* http://www.cnbc.com, August 21, 2016. **32.** Blaze Stutes, "The State of US Workforce Diversity in 14 Statistics," http://archpointgroup.com, December 1, 2016; Vivian Hunt, Dennis Layton, and Sara Prince, "Why Diversity Matters," *McKinsey & Company,* http://www.mckinsey.com, January 2015. **33.** Global Energy Statistical Yearbook 2016, "Oil Products Domestic Consumption," https://yearbook.enerdata.net, accessed May 23, 2017; Joe Carroll, "Big Oil Heads for Back-to-Back Profit Triumphs as Fortunes Turn," *Bloomberg Markets,* http://www.bloomberg.com, April 28, 2017. **34.** U.S. Energy Information Administration, "Frequently Asked Questions about Petroleum Imports and Exports," https://www.eia.gov, accessed May 23, 2017; European Commission, "Energy: Supplier Countries," https://ec.europa.eu, accessed May 23, 2017. **35.** Kenneth Rapoza, "Russia's Gazprom Doubling Down on 'Anti-Ukraine' Baltic Pipeline," *Forbes,* http://www.forbes.com, March 14, 2017; Nataliya Vasilyeva, "Ukraine Stops Buying Russian Gas, Closes Airspace," *USA Today,* http://www.usatoday.com, November 25, 2015. **36.** "U.S. Shale Is Turning Up the Heat on OPEC," http://oilprice.com, May 20, 2017; Matt Egan, "Oil Milestone: Fracking Fuels Half of U.S. Output," *CNN Money,* http://money.cnn.com, March 24, 2016; Ed Crooks, "The US Shale Revolution," *Financial Times,* http://www.ft.com, April 24, 2015. **37.** Kavita Kumar, "Target Sharpens Edge Through Partnerships with Harry's and Bevel Razor Companies," *Minneapolis Star Tribune,* http://www.startribune.com, April 15, 2017; Daphne Howland, "Target to Sell Harry's Men's Grooming Products," *Retail Dive,* http://www.retaildive.com, August 4, 2016.

Understanding Business Ethics
1. Renae Merle, "'Pharma Bro' Martin Shkreli Goes on Trial, Where He Finds Another Kind of Limelight," *Washington Post,* https://www.washingtonpost.com, June 27, 2017. **2.** Arthur Schwartz, "The 5 Most Common Unethical Behaviors in the Workplace," *Philadelphia Business Journal,* http://www.bizjournals.com, January 26,

2015; Marianne Moody Jennings, *Case Studies in Business Ethics,* 2nd edition (St. Paul: West Publishing Company, 1996), pp. xx–xxii.

How Organizations Influence Ethical Conduct

3. "Top 10 Crooked CEOs," *TIME,* http://content.time.com, accessed June 23, 2017; Jena McGregor, "More CEOs Are Getting Forced Out for Ethics Violations," *Washington Post,* https://www.washingtonpost.com, May 15, 2017; Adam Hartung, "Wells Fargo CEO Stumpf Is Gone: Is This the Beginning of Wholesale Leadership Change?" *Forbes,* http://www.forbes.com, October 13, 2016. **4.** Dori Meinert, "Creating an Ethical Workplace," Society for Human Resource Management, https://www.shrm.org, accessed June 23, 2017; Jeff Kauflin, "The World's Most Ethical Companies 2017," *Forbes,* http://www.forbes.com, March 14, 2017. **5.** "The 2017 100 Best Corporate Citizens," *Corporate Responsibility,* http://www.thecro.com, accessed June 23, 2017; Karsten Strauss, "America's 100 Best Corporate Citizens in 2017," *Forbes,* http://www.forbes.com, May 11, 2017.

Managing a Socially Responsible Business

6. "Starbucks 2016 Global Social Impact Report," https://globalassets.starbucks.com, accessed June 23, 2017; "Celebrating Volunteerism at Deloitte and in Our Communities," https://www2.deloitte.com, accessed June 23, 2017; Linda Novick O'Keefe, "CSR Grows in 2016 as Companies Embrace Employees' Values," *The Huffington Post,* http://www.huffingtonpost.com, December 15, 2016; Kia Kokalitcheva, "These 8 Employers Will Pay You to Volunteer," *Forbes,* http://www.forbes.com, March 21, 2016. **7.** John Ewoldt, "Better Business Bureau Revokes MyPillow Accreditation over Ad Dispute," *Minneapolis Star Tribune,* http://www.startribune.com, January 4, 2017; Herb Weisbaum, "Full of Fluff? MyPillow Ordered to Pay $1M for Bogus Ads," *NBC News,* http://www.nbcnews.com, November 3, 2016. **8.** "REI Co-op Gives Back Nearly 70 Percent of Profits to the Outdoor Community after Year of Record Revenues in 2016," http://newsroom.rei.com, March 15, 2017.

Responsibilities to Stakeholders

9. "The 100 Best Companies to Work For 2017," *Fortune,* http://fortune.com, accessed June 23, 2017; "Genentech Perks and Programs," http://reviews.greatplacetowork.com, accessed June 23, 2017. **10.** Sarah Landrum, "Millennials Driving Brands to Practice Socially Responsible Marketing," *Forbes,* http://www.forbes.com, March 17, 2017. **11.** "Why B Corps Matter," https://www.bcorporation.net, accessed June 27, 2017; Suntae Kim, Matthew J. Karlesky, Christopher G. Meyers, and Todd Schifeling, "Why Companies Are Becoming B Corporations," *Harvard Business Review,* https://hbr.org, June 17, 2016. **12.** Becky May, "Creating One Toyota," *American Builders Quarterly,* http://americanbuildersquarterly.com, accessed June 23, 2017; Jessica Lyons Hardcastle, "Toyota Headquarters Will Use 100% Renewable Energy," *Environmental Leader,* https://www.environmentalleader.com, June 10, 2016. **13.** "Charitable Giving Statistics," *National Philanthropic Trust,* https://www.nptrust.org, accessed June 23, 2017. **14.** "American Express Company Corporate Social Responsibility: Philanthropy 2016," http://about.americanexpress.com, accessed June 23, 2017. **15.** Ryan Scott, "How Hurricane Katrina Changed Corporate Social Responsibility Forever," *The Huffington Post,* http://www.huffingtonpost.com, accessed June 23, 2017; Del Jones, "Corporate Giving for Katrina Reaches $547 Million," *USA Today,* http://www.usatoday.com, September 12, 2005. **16.** Nellie S. Huang, "7 Great Socially Responsible Mutual Funds," *Kiplinger's Personal Finance,* http://www.kiplinger.com, accessed June 23, 2017. **17.** Per-Ola Karlsson, DeAnne Aquirre, and Kristin Rivera, "Are CEOs Less Ethical Than in the Past?" *Strategy + Business,* https://www.strategy-business.com, accessed June 27, 2017; Emily C. Bianchi and Aharon Mohliver, "CEOs Who Began Their Careers During Booms Tend to Be Less Ethical," *Harvard Business Review,* https://hbr.org, May 12, 2017.

Trends in Ethics and Corporate Social Responsibility

18. "The 50 Best Workplaces for Giving Back," *Fortune,* http://fortune.com, February 9, 2017. **19.** Andie Burjek, Lauren Dixon, Geri Anne Fennessy, and Sarah Fister Gale, "The New Employer-Employee Contract," *Talent Economy,* http://www.talenteconomy.io, May 8, 2017. **20.** "Global Sustainability: Improving Factory Working

Conditions," http://www.gapincsustainability.com, accessed June 23, 2017; "Gap Inc. Joins Global Brands That Publish Factory List," *Human Rights Watch,* https://www.hrw.org, accessed June 23, 2017.

Global Trade in the United States

1. International Trade Administration: US Department of Commerce Website, accessed August 1, 2017. http://tse.export.gov/tse/MapDisplay.aspx. **2.** "In the Stock Market, International Is Actually First," *New York Times,* May 21, 2017, Page BU6. **3.** "Starbucks Coffee International," https://www.starbucks.com, accessed June 20, 2017; Trefis Team, "How Starbucks Plans to Grow Its International Operations," *Forbes,* https://www.forbes.com, January 18, 2016. **4.** "Market Share by Manufacturer, October 2016 Data," https://www.edmunds.com, accessed June 25, 2016. **5.** "Trade (% of GDP)," http://data.worldbank.org, accessed June 26, 2017. **6.** "The Impact of Trade on U.S. and State Level Employment," http://businessroundtable.org, accessed June, 26, 2017. **7.** "Small Business Key Players in International Trade," https://www.sba.gov/sites/default/files/advocacy/Issue-Brief-11-Small-Biz-Key-Players-International-Trade.pdf, June 26, 2017. **8.** "Globalization took hits in 2016; will 2017 lead to more?" http://www.denverpost.com/2017/01/01/globalization-2016-and-2017/, January 1, 2017. **9.** "How Venezuela Ruined Its Oil Industry", https://www.forbes.com/sites/rrapier/2017/05/07/how-venezuela-ruined-its-oil-industry/#4a066087399d, May 7, 2017. **10.** Daniel Workman, "Top 10 Major Export Companies," http://www.worldtopexports.com, accessed July 4, 2017. **11.** "U.S. Exports and Imports," https://www.thebalance.com, accessed June 26, 2017. **12.** "What We Investigate: International Property Theft/ Piracy," https://www.fbi.gov, accessed June 26, 2017. **13.** "International Economic Accounts," https://www.bea.gov/International/index.htm, accessed July 17, 2017. **14.** "Fact Sheet: Commerce Finds Dumping and Countervailable Subsidies of Imports of Stainless Steel Sheet and Strip from the People's Republic of China," http://enforcement.trade.gov, accessed June 26, 2017.

Why Nations Trade

15. Danielle Paquette, "Trump Said He Would Save Jobs at Carrier. The Layoffs Start July 20," *The Washington Post,* https://www.washingtonpost.com, May 24, 2017. **16.** "Jobs Overseas Statistics," http://www.statisticbrain.com, accessed June 26, 2017. **17.** Mike Collins, "The Pros and Cons of Globalization," *Forbes,* https://www.forbes.com, May 6, 2015.

Barriers to Trade

18. Wendy Wu, "China Upset at High U.S. Tariffs on Steel Imports," *South China Morning Post,* http://www.scmp.com, February 4, 2017. **19.** "Commodities Subject to Import Quotas," https://www.cbp.gov, accessed June 25, 2017.

Fostering Global Trade

20. "Members and Observers," https://www.wto.org, accessed June 25, 2017. **21.** https://www.wto.org/ english/tratop_e/dda_e/dda_e.htm, accessed June 25, 2017. **22.** "WTO Technical Notes," https://www.wto.org/ english/res_e/booksp_e/anrep_e/wtr10_tech_notes_e.pdf, accessed July 17, 2017. **23.** "EC and Certain Member States—Large Civil Aircraft," https://www.wto.org, accessed June 25, 2017.

International Economic Communities

24. "Facts about NAFTA: Statistics and Accomplishments," https://www.thebalance.com/facts-about-nafta-statistics-and-accomplishments-3306280, July 7, 2017. **25.** "Mexico Nominal Hourly Wages in Manufacturing," https://tradingeconomics.com, accessed June 25, 2017; Julie Hirschfeld Davis, "Trump Sends NAFTA Renegotiation Notice to Congress," *The New York Times,* http://www.nytimes.com, May 18, 2017; Kate Linthicum, "What Happened When Factory Jobs Moved from Warren, Ohio, to Juarez, Mexico," *Los Angeles Times,* http://www.latimes.com, February 17, 2017. **26.** https://ec.europa.eu/info/policies/eu-enlargement_en#bootstrap-fieldgroup-nav-item--details--2, June 25, 2017. **27.** "Brexit: All You Need to Know About the UK Leaving the EU," *BBC,* (June 26, 2017), http://www.bbc.com/news/uk-politics-32810887, June 26,

2017. **28.** "Is Europe Outperforming the US?" *World Economic Forum,* https://www.weforum.org/agenda/2015/ 10/is-europe-outperforming-the-us/, October 30, 2015. **29.** Mark Scott, "Google Fined $2.7 Billion in E.U. Antitrust Case," *The New York Times,* http://www.nytimes.com, June 26, 2017. **30.** "EU Makes Coke Throw Open Fridges," *BBC,* http://news.bbc.co.uk, June 22, 2005.

Participating in the Global Marketplace
31. https://www.cia.gov/library/publications/the-world-factbook/rankorder/2078rank.html, accessed June 25, 2017. **32.** "McDonald's Sells Control of China Business to Citic, Carlyle," *Bloomberg News,* https://www.bloomberg.com/news/articles/2017-01-09/mcdonald-s-sells-control-of-china-business-to-citic-carlyle, January 9, 2017. **33.** "Famous Failures in China," http://www.1421.consulting, February 2, 2016. **34.** General Motors website, http://www.gmcamiassembly.ca/Facilities/public/ca/en/CAMI/about_us.html, accessed July 17, 2017. **35.** Wuling Sunshine, http://media.gm.com/media/cn/en/wuling/vehicles/sunshine/ 2010.html, accessed June 27, 2017. **36.** "Walmart 2017 Annual Report," http://stock.walmart.com, accessed June 27, 2017.

Threats and Opportunities in the Global Marketplace
37. Ellen Proper, "Dutch See Red Over Foreign Bid For Paint Giant," *Bloomberg News,* https://www.bloomberg.com, March 10, 2017.

The Impact of Multinational Corporations
38. Source: "The World's Largest Corporations," *Fortune,* http://fortune.com/global500/, accessed June 30, 2017.

Trends in Global Competition
39. Vijay Govindarajan and Gunjan Bagla, "Understanding the Rise of Manufacturing in India," *Harvard Business Review,* September 18, 2015. **40.** "As IMF Says, India Should Be One Of World's Largest Economies, Only Bad Policy Has Prevented It," *Forbes,* https://www.forbes.com/sites/timworstall/2017/04/28/as-imf-says-india-should-be-one-of-worlds-largest-economies-only-bad-policy-has-prevented-it/#160c27b05a6b, April 28, 2017.

Going It Alone: Sole Proprietorships
1. Tara Siegel Bernard, "Building a Luxury Retail Business on the Web," *The Wall Street Journal-Small Business,* July 12, 2005, p. B4; Pearl Paradise corporate website, http://www.pearlparadise.com (August 17, 2017); Jeremy Shepherd, "My Journey From Flight Attendant To CEO Of A $20 Million Company," The Blog, Huffington Post, November 1, 2010 (accessed August 17, 2017); Syl Tang , "Rarest of pearls face a less than golden future," *Financial Times,* https://www.ft.com, accessed August 17, 2017.

Corporations: Limiting Your Liability
2. "LLC vs. S Corp.: What's the Best Setup for Your Startup?" Young Upstarts, http://www.youngupstarts.com, August 28, 2017; "Be Careful! Structuring Your Business as an LLC Is Not a Guarantee of Liability Protection," allBusiness, https://www.allbusiness.com, accessed September 30, 2017; Linda Ravden, based on personal interview on May 25, 2006. **3.** "Fortune 500 Companies 2017," *Fortune,* http://www.fortune.com, accessed March 31, 2018; "America's Top Public Companies in 2017: A Buffett Buy List", *Forbes,* https://www.forbes.com, accessed March 31, 2018; Alex Gray, "These Are the World's 10 Biggest Corporate Giants," World Economic Forum, https://www.weforum.org, January 16, 2017.

Specialized Forms of Business Organization
4. "Measuring the Size and Scope of the Cooperative Economy: Results of the 2014 Global Census on Co-operatives," prepared by Dave Grace and Associates for the United Nation's Secretariat Department of Economic and Social Affairs Division for Social Policy and Development, April 2014. **5.** "Ace Hardware Reports Second Quarter 2017 Results," http://www.acehardware.com, accessed August 17, 2017. **6.** "7 Cooperative

Principles," *San Luis Valley REC,* https://www.slvrec.com; "Co-operative Principles," *International Co-operative Alliance,* ica.coop; and "The Principles of Cooperation," *Daman Prakash,* www.uwcc.wisc.edu. **7.** Joyce Lee, "Hyundai Motor to Begin Production at Fifth China Factory in August," Thomson Reuters, July 18, 2017; Jin, Hyunjoo, and Samuel Shen, "Hyundai Motor to Build Two New Plants in China Instead of One: Sources," Thomson Reuters, accessed August 17, 2017; Seon-Jin Cha, "Hyundai Forms China Joint Venture," *The Wall Street Journal,* June 22, 2005, p. B4.

Franchising: A Popular Trend
8. "About Us," http://www.geeksoncall.com, accessed August 17, 2017; Megan Barnett, "Size up a Ready-Made Business," *U.S. News & World Report,* August 2, 2004, p. 69. **9.** "The Economic Impact of Franchised Businesses in the United States," *International Franchise Association*, http://www.franchise.org; "FAQs about Franchising." FAQs about Franchising | International Franchise Association, (August 17, 2017). **10.** "2017 New Franchises," *Entrepreneur,* https://www.entreneur.com, accessed August 17, 2017; "2017 Fastest Growing Franchises," *Franchise Gator,* https://www.franchisegator.com, August 17, 2017; Mosquito Joe, "About MoJo," https://mosquitojoe.com, accessed August 17, 2017.

Mergers and Acquisitions
11. Thomas Content, "With acquisition of Tyco, Johnson Controls will become global 'one-stop shop' for building controls," Journal Sentinel, January 25, 2016, http://archive.jsonline.com, (accessed August 17, 2017); Johnson Control Media Center, http://www.johnsoncontrols.com (accessed August 17, 2017); Brian Steinberg, "AT&T Opens New Advertising Unit in Advance of Time Warner Merger," *Variety,* August 4, 2017, (August 6, 2017). **12.** Christina Mercer, "We List the Most Notable Tech Acquisitions of 2017, So Far," *ComputerworldUK,* https://www.computeruk.com, December 12, 2017. **13.** Gemma Acton, "Number of Global M&A Deals Tumbles in Q1 2017 While Overall Value Rises," *CNBC,* https://www.cnbc.com, accessed August 6, 2017. **14.** Harry R. Webber, "UPS to Buy Trucking Company Overnight for $1.25 Billion to Expand Its Freight Business," *USA Today*, May 17, 2005, p. 6B. **15.** Kevin J. Delaney, "Google to Buy Urchin Software, Provider of Data for Advertisers,"*Wall Street Journal,* March 29, 2005, p. B4. **16.** Koh Gui Qing and Greg Roumeliotis, "Apollo Global Braves LBO Rout with $7 Billion ADT Deal," *Reuters,* https://www.reuters.com, accessed August 6, 2017. **17.** Laurie J. Flynn, "Oracle Acquiring Another Big Rival," *San Diego Union–Tribune,* September 13, 2005, p. C1. **18.** Joe McDonald, "Yahoo Buys Stake in China's No. 1 Web Shopping Firm," *Associated Press, San Diego Union- Tribune,* August 12, 2005, p. C1. **19.** Greg Petro, "Amazon's Acquisition of Whole Foods Is About Two Things: Data and Product," *Forbes,* http://www.forbes.com, accessed March 31, 2018; Kate Taylor, "Here Are All the Changes Amazon Is Making to Whole Foods," *Business Insider,* www.businessinsider.com, March 2, 2018. **20.** Tom Hals and Jessica DiNapoli, "Brookfield Business Partners to Buy Westinghouse for $4.6 Billion," *Reuters,* https://www.reuters.com, January 4, 2018. **21.** Brad Gevurtz, "'Fasten Your Seat Belt': There's Going to Be a Dealmaking Bonanza in 2017," *Business Insider,* www.businessinsider.com, accessed August 6, 2017.

Trends in Business Ownership
22. "Personal-Care Businesses Franchises," *Entrepreneur*, www.entrepreneur.com, accessed August 6, 2017; "IHRSA—Consumer Research," *IHRSA – Home*, 2017, accessed August 6, 2017; Jeanette Borzo, "Follow the Money: More Businesses Are Starting to Cater to an Affluent—and Discriminating—'Mature Market'," *Wall Street Journal*, September 26, 2005. p. R9; and Sara Wilson, "All the 'Rage,' " *Entrepreneur*, January 2005, http://www.entrepreneur.com. **23.** Home Instead corporate website, http://www.homeinstead.com, accessed August 17, 2017; "Cost Analysis," Care Advantage, 2017 (August 17, 2017) **24.** "Cost Comparisons," http://sarahcare.com, accessed August 17, 2017; "Sarah Adult Day Services," *Franchise Zone,* http://www.entrepreneur.com/franzone/ (May 31, 2006). **25.** Judy Kneiszel, "Millennials' Next Frontier: Franchising," *QSR,* http://www.qsr.com, accessed March 31, 2018); Danny Rivera, "The Impact of Millennials on the Franchise Industry," International Franchise Association, https://www.franchise.org, accessed March 31,

2018. **26.** Stephanie Clifford, "What You Need To Know Now," *Inc. Magazine,* September 2005, p. 27. **27.** Laura Shin, "Why the New Retirement Involves Working Past 65," Forbes, https://www.forbes.com, accessed August 17, 2017. **28.** "M&A Statistics," Institute for Mergers, Acquisitions, and Alliances, https://imaa-institute.org, accessed August 17, 2017. **29.** "Expenditures by Foreign Direct Investors for New Investment in the United States, 2014–2016," Bureau of Economic Analysis, July 12, 2017. **30.** James K. Jackson, "U.S. Direct Investment Abroad: Trends and Current Issues," Congressional Research Services Report, https://fas.org, accessed August 17, 2017.

Entrepreneurship Today

1. Shannon McMahon, "Stepping into a Fortune," *San Diego Union-Tribune,* April 5, 2005, p. C4. **2.** Dashel Pierson, "10 Things You Should Know about Surfing in the Olympics," *Surfline,* http://www.surfline.com, August 5, 2016. **3.** Steve Chapple, "Reef Brand's Co-founder Eyes the Horizon," *San Diego Union Tribune,* https://www.sandiegouniontribune.com, December 13, 2013. **4.** Andrew Morse, "An Entrepreneur Finds Tokyo Shares Her Passion for Bagels," *The Wall Street Journal,* October 18, 2005, p. B1. **5.** Barbara Farfan, "Amazon.com's Mission Statement", *The Balance.* April 15, 2018, https://www.thebalance.com/amazon-mission-statement-4068548. **6.** "About StartupNation," https://startupnation.com, accessed February 1, 2018; Jim Morrison, "Entrepreneurs," *American Way Magazine,* October 15, 2005, p. 94.

Characteristics of Successful Entrepreneurs

7. Martha Irvine, "More 20-Somethings Are Blazing Own Paths in Business," *San Diego Union-Tribune,* November 22, 2004, p. C6. **8.** Keith McFarland, "What Makes Them Tick," *Inc. 500,* October 19, 2005, http://www.inc.com. **9.** Ibid.

Small Business: Driving America's Growth

10. U.S. Small Business Administration, "Make Sure You Meet SBA Size Standards," https://www.sba.gov, accessed February 1, 2018. **11.** "Who We Are," http://www.kauffman.org, accessed February 1, 2018; "Ewing Marion Kauffman Foundation," http://en.wikipedia.org, accessed February 1, 2018. **12.** "Annual Survey of Entrepreneurs," https://www.census.gov, accessed February 1, 2018. **13.** "The Kauffman Index," http://www.kauffman.org, accessed February 2, 2018.

Ready, Set, Start Your Own Business

14. Adapted from "They've Founded Million Dollar Companies and They're not Even 30,"https://www.inc.com/30-under-30. **15.** McFarland, "What Makes Them Tick." **16.** "The Kauffman Index," http://www.kauffman.org, accessed February 2, 2018. **17.** Andrew Blackman, "Know When to Give Up," *The Wall Street Journal,* May 9, 2005, p. R9.

Managing a Small Business

18. Michelle Prather, "Talk of the Town," *Entrepreneur Magazine,* February 2003, http://www.entrepreneur.com.

Small Business, Large Impact

19. Forbes, "Ten Best Cities for Entrepreneurs" https://www.forbes.com/pictures/feki45igde/10-best-cities-for-young-entrepreneurs/#5bc189726058. **20.** Don Debelak, "Rookie Rules," *Business Start-Ups Magazine,* http://www.entrepreneur.com, March 2, 2006. **21.** McFarland, "What Makes Them Tick."

The Small Business Administration

22. Much of the statistical information for the SBA section is from the Small Business Administration website at http://www.sba.gov. **23.** "SBA Lending Activity in FY 2017 Shows Consistent Growth," https://www.sba.gov, October 13, 2017.

Trends in Entrepreneurship and Small-Business Ownership

24. "Small Business Profile: 2016," https://www.sba.gov, accessed February 2, 2018. **25.** "The State of Women-

Owned Businesses: 2017," http://about.americanexpress.com, accessed February 2, 2018. **26.** Ibid. **27.** Steve Strauss, "Boomers' Role in Entrepreneurship Is, Well, Booming," *USA Today,* https://www.usatoday.com, August 25, 2017. **28.** Scott Hanson, "Baby Boomers Are Rewriting Retirement History," *Kiplinger,* https://www.kiplinger.com, January 3, 2018. **29.** "SBA Lending Activity in FY 2017 Shows Consistent Growth." **30.** SBA Office of Advocacy, "Annual Report of the Office of Economic Research: 2016," https://www.sba.gov, accessed February 2, 2018. **31.** Lora Kolodny, "This Start-up Fled the High Cost of Silicon Valley to Help Non-Tech Workers Get an Education," *CNBC,* https://www.cnbc.com, September 6, 2017. **32.** Tamara Chuang, "4 Silicon Valley Venture Firms Invest $21 Million in Denver's Guild Education," *The Denver Post,* https://www.denverpost.com, September 6, 2017. **33.** PwC/CB Insights, "MoneyTree Report Q3 2017," https://www.pwc.com, accessed February 2, 2018. **34.** Ibid.

The Role of Management

1. Source: US DOT Form 41 via BTS, Schedules P12 and T2. **2.** Matthew C. Klein, "Traders Appreciate United Airlines Commitment to 'Cost Efficiency Targets'," *Financial Times*, https://ftalphaville.ft.com, April 10, 2017; Robert Silk, "UPDATED: JetBlue Founder Neeleman Working on New Company," *Travel Weekly,* http://www.travelweekly.com, July 31, 2017; Karsten Strauss, "When CEOs Get Demoted (By Companies They Founded)," *Forbes,* https://www.forbes.com, March 28, 2013. **3.** I-Chun Chen, "Sketchers Hires Former Disney and Mattel Exec as CFO," *L. A. Biz,* https://www.bizjournals.com, November 15, 2017.

Planning

4. Christina Cheddar, "Famed Retailer Mickey Drexler Leaving CEO Job at J. Crew," *CNBC,* https://www.cnbc.com, June 5, 2017; John Kell, "J. Crew CEO Mickey Drexler Steps Down," *Fortune,* http://fortune.com, June 5, 2017; Vanessa Friedman and Julie Creswell, "Mickey Drexler Steps Down as Chief of J. Crew, Ending an Era," *The New York Times*, https://www.nytimes.com, June 5, 2017; Steven Solomon, "J. Crew Struggles with Its 'Great Man' Dilemma," *The New York Times*, https://www.nytimes.com, June 10, 2015; Julia Boorstin. "Mickey Drexler's Second Coming," *Fortune,* May 2, 2005, p. 101. **5.** Boorstin, "Mickey Drexler's Second Coming." **6.** Hallie Busta, "Q&A: Former Autodesk CEO Carol Bartz on the Past, Present and Future of Construction Tech," http://www.constructiondive.com, March 29, 2017; David Bank, "Autodesk Stages Revival," *Wall Street Journal,* August 19, 2005, p. B3. **7.** Richard Levick, "Crisis Contingency Planning, Risk Assessment Vitally Important in Today's Climate," *Forbes,* https://www.forbes.com, November 16, 2017. **8.** Trip Advisor website, https://www.tripadvisor.com/ShowUserReviews-g147320-d149920-r526998919-San_Juan_Marriott_Resort_Stellaris_Casino-San_Juan_Puerto_Rico.html, accessed November 15, 2017. **9.** San Juan Marriott website, http://www.marriott.com/hotels/travel/sjupr-san-juan-marriott-resort-and-stellaris-casino/, accessed November 15, 2017.

Organizing

10. Jeffery Garten, "Jack Welch: A Role Model for Today's CEO," *Business Week* (September 10, 2001).

Leading, Guiding, and Motivating Others

11. Ghazal Hashemipour, "A.G. Lafley: A Look Back at the Career of the Most Successful CEO in P&G History," *Chief Executive,* https://chiefexecutive.net, June 13, 2016; Jennifer Reingold, "P&G Chairman A.G. Lafley Steps Down—For Good, This Time?" *Fortune,* http://fortune.com, June 1, 2016; Nancy Brumback, "6. A.G. Lafley, Chairman and CEO, Procter & Gamble Company," *Supermarket News*, July 25, 2005. **12.** Linda Hill, Greg Brandeau, Emily Truelove, and Kent Linebeck, *Collective Genius* (Boston: *Harvard Business Review Press,* 2015). **13.** Carol Hymowitz, "Middle Managers Are Unsung Heroes on Corporate Stage," *Wall Street Journal*, September 19, 2005, p. B1. **14.** Andrew S. Grove 1936-2016, Intelcom, https://newsroom.intel.com/news-releases/andrew-s-grove-1936-2016/, accessed September 16, 2017.) **15.** "How the Best Are Measured," *Great Place to Work,* https://www.greatplacetowork.com, accessed October 30, 2017. **16.** Oscar Raymundo, "5 Reasons Googlers Think It's the Best Place to Work," *Inc.,* https://www.inc.com, accessed November 11,

2017. **17.** "Fortune 100 Best Companies to Work For 2017," Fortune.com, http://fortune.com/best-companies/google/, accessed October 30, 2017.

Managerial Roles

18. Megan Bruneau, "Overcome 'Analysis Paralysis' and Execute on Your Idea: 5 Tips from Ollie Cofounder Gabby Slome," *Forbes*, https: www.forbes.com, November 19, 2017.

Trends in Management and Leadership

19. Elliot Mest, "6 Ways That Hotels Can Prevent, Prepare for Crisis Situations," *Hotel Management*, https://www.hotelmanagement.net, November 15, 2017. **20.** Rajiv Joseph, "More Than the Usual Opening Night Jitters," *The New York Times*, https://www.nytime.com, November 26, 2017. **21.** Ibid. **22.** This section is adapted from Vivian Giang, "The 7 Types of Power That Shape the Workplace," *Business Insider,* http://www.businessinsider.com, July 31, 2013. **23.** Andrew White, "Put Data and Analytics at the Heart of Your Digital Business," *Gartner Blog Network,* https://blogs.gartner.com, November 20, 2017, **24.** David J. Parnell, "Robert Romanoff of Levenfeld Pearlstein: Real Change Requires Leadership, Not Consensus," *Forbes,* http://www.forbes.com, November 6, 2017; "Matthew W. Schuyler," HiltonWorldwide.com, accessed September 16, 2017. **25.** Richard Lewis, "How Different Cultures Understand Time," *Business Insider,* http://www.businessinsider.com, June 1, 2014.

Building Organizational Structures

1. "2016 Annual Report," http://www.ethanallen.com, accessed July 18, 2017. **2.** "ITT 2016 Fact Sheet V2," https://www.itt.com, accessed July 18, 2017. **3.** "Our Business," http://www.gazprom-neft.com, accessed July 18, 2017. **4.** "Pixar Animation Studios," *The Disney Wiki,* http://disney.wiki.com, accessed July 18, 2017; Bob Gower, "Want a Creative Culture? Pixar Says Do These 3 Things," *Inc.,* https://www.inc.com, August 9, 2016. **5.** "Corporate Overview," https://www.pnc.com, accessed July 18, 2017. **6.** "Corporate Structure," http://us.pg.com, accessed July 18, 2017.

Contemporary Structures

7. Herman Vantrappen and Frederic Wirtz, "Making Matrix Organizations Actually Work," *Harvard Business Review,* https://hbr.org, March 1, 2016. **8.** "Executive Committee and Organizational Structure," https://www.novartis.com, accessed July 19, 2017.

Using Teams to Enhance Motivation and Performance

9. Ethan Chazin, "Self-Managed Teams: The Future of Employee Engagement," *LinkedIn,* https://www.linkedin.com, July 19, 2017. **10.** Jennifer Reingold, "How a Radical Shift Left Zappos Reeling," *Fortune,* http://fortune.com, March 4, 2016. **11.** Christian Wissmuller, "String Theory: Prominent Suppliers Discuss the Electric Guitar and Bass String Market," *Musical Merchandise Review,* http://mmrmagazine.com, June 14, 2017; Alan Deutschman, "The Fabric of Creativity," *Fast Company,* https://www.fastcompany.com, December 1, 2004.

Authority—Establishing Organizational Relationships

12. "Morning Star's Success Story: No Bosses, No Titles, No Structural Hierarchy," *Corporate Rebels,* http://corporate-rebels.com, November 14, 2016. **13.** Justin Young, "Unilever's Organizational Structure for Product Innovation," *Panmore Institute,* http://panmore.com, February 21, 2017; "Unilever UK Gets Its House in Order," *Grocer,* February 12, 2005; "From Rivalry to Mergers: Anglo-Dutch Companies," *The Economist,* February 12, 2005, p. 61.

Organizational Design Considerations

14. Steve Lohr, "Microsoft to Cut Up to 4,000 Sales and Marketing Jobs," *The New York Times,* http://www.nytimes.com, July 6, 2017. **15.** "Fortune 2017 100 Best Companies to Work For: #52 W.L. Gore & Associates," *Fortune,* http://fortune.com, accessed July 19, 2017.

The Informal Organization

16. "I Heard It Through the Grapevine," *American Management Association,* http://www.amanet.org, accessed July 19, 2017.

Trends in Organizational Structure

17. "Key Outsourcing Trends from Deloitte's 2016 Global Outsourcing Survey," https://www2.deloitte.com, accessed July 19, 2017. **18.** Patrick Gillespie, "Intuit: Gig Economy Is 34% of US Workforce," *CNN Money,* http://money.cnn.com, May 24, 2017. **19.** Missy Chaiet, "6 Steps to Creating Better Strategic Outsourcing Partnerships," https://www.cgsinc.com, July 1, 2016. **20.** Allan Steinmetz, "Seven Steps for Cultural Integration During a Merger or Acquisition," http://www.inwardconsulting.com, accessed July 21, 2017.

Achieving High Performance through Human Resources Management

1. Maria M. Perotin, "New Alcon Soft Lens Solutions Approved," *Fort Worth Star-Telegram*, October 13, 2005, p. 2c. **2.** Kate Taylor and Dennis Green, "Best Buy's CEO Led the Retailer in an Incredible Turnaround," *Business Insider*, www.businessinsider.com/best-buy-ceo-hubert-joly-interview-2018-3, March 25, 2018. **3.** *Ibid*.

Employee Recruitment

4. "About Carbone Smolan Agency," https://www.carbonesmolan.com, accessed February 8, 2018.

Employee Selection

5. "The Wonderlic Personnel Tests," https://www.wonderlic.com, accessed February 8, 2018. **6.** "Yankee Candle Improves Performance by 40% with the Predictive Index®," https://olivergroup.com, accessed February 8 2018; Eric Krell, "Personality Counts," *HR Magazine*, vol. 50 (November 2005), pp. 46–52. **7.** Carolyn Murray LinkedIn Profile, accessed February 15, 2018, https://www.linkedin.com/in/jcarolynmurray/; "Gore-Tex," *Fast Company*, January, 1999, p. 160.

Employee Training and Development

8. "Work, Environment & Culture," https://www.dow.com, accessed February 8, 2018; Stephanie Oferman, "Mentors without Borders," *HR Magazine*, vol. 49 (March 2004), pp. 83–86. **9.** "How America's Top Railroad Learns to Fly," https://www.up.com, December 5, 2017; Eric Krell, "Budding Relationships," *HR Magazine*, vol. 50 (June 2005), pp. 114–118.

Employee Compensation and Benefits

10. "MillerCoors Hourly Pay," https://www.glassdoor.com, accessed February 8, 2018. **11.** Jacob Morgan, "The Top 10 Factors for On-the-Job Employee Happiness," *Forbes,* https://www.forbes.com, December 15, 2014.

The Labor Relations Process

12. Bureau of Labor Statistics, "Union Members Summary," https://www.bls.gov, January 19, 2018; Megan Dunn and James Walker, "Union Membership in the United States," U.S. Bureau of Labor Statistics, September 2016. **13.** Jill Lawrence, "Union's Break off from AFL-CIO," *USA Today*, July 26, 2005, pp. 5A and 6A. **14.** "About Us," http://www.changetowin.org, accessed February 8, 2018. **15.** Alisa Priddle and Brent Snavely, "UAW-Ford Deal Passes, and New Era Begins for Detroit 3," *Detroit Free Press,* https://www.freep.com, November 21, 2015.

Managing Grievances and Conflicts

16. Reuters, "Alcoa Locks Union Workers Out of Canada Smelter as Contract Expires," https://www.reuters.com, January 11, 2018.

Legal Environment of Human Resources and Labor Relations

17. Danielle Paquette, "The Gender Wage Gap Just Shrank for the First Time in a Decade," *The Washington Post,* https://www.washingtonpost.com, September 15, 2017; Barry Reece and Monique Reece, "Effective Human Relations: Interpersonal and Organizational Applications, 13e (Mason, OH: Cengage Learning, 2017), p.

356. **18.** Kristen Bialik, "7 Facts about Americans with Disabilities," *Pew Research Center,* http://www.pewresearch.org, July 27, 2017. **19.** Barry Reece and Monique Reece, *Effective Human Relations: Interpersonal and Organizational Applications,* 13e (Mason, OH: Cengage Learning, 2017), p. 362. **20.** Alexia Elejalde-Ruiz, "Ford Settles Sexual, Racial Harassment Claims at Chicago Plants for $10 Million," *Chicago Tribune,* http://www.chicagotribune.com, August 17, 2017.

Trends in Human Resource Management and Labor Relations

21. Taylor H. Cox and Stacy Blake, "Managing Cultural Diversity: Implications for Organizational Competitiveness," *Academy of Management Executive* 5(3): 45–56, 1991. **22.** United States Postal Service, "Workforce Diversity and Inclusiveness," https://about.usps.com, accessed February 8, 2018. **23.** Robert Steyer, "CBS Taps Fidelity Investments as Record Keeper for 401(k) Plan," *Pensions & Investments,* http://www.pionline.com, August 10, 2017. **24.** Ruth Umoh, "Want to Score a Job at Microsoft, Facebook, IBM or Amazon? Here Are Top Tips from Their HR Executives," *CNBC,* https://www.cnbc.com, November 29, 2017. **25.** "About SEIU," http://www.seiu.org, accessed February 8, 2018; Ira Boudway, "Union Booster Mary Kay Henry," *Bloomberg Businessweek,* https://www.bloomberg.com, October 19, 2016. **26.** Bureau of Labor Statistics, "Occupations with the Most Job Growth: 2016–2026," https://www.bls.gov, accessed February 8, 2018. **27.** "Victory! Hundreds of ResCare Workers Unionize to Join SEIU 721," https://www.seiu721.org, accessed February 8, 2018.

Maslow's Hierarchy of Needs

1. "Wegmans Food Markets #2," *Fortune,* http://fortune.com, accessed October 30, 2017; "20th Year in a Row: Fortune Names Wegmans One of 2017 Fortune 100 Best Companies to Work For, Ranking #2," https://www.wegmans.com, March 9, 2017; Claire Zillman, "Secrets from Best Companies All Stars," *Fortune,* http://fortune.com, March 9, 2017; Matthew Boyle, "The Wegmans Way," *Fortune,* January 24, 2005, pp. 62–68. **2.** Ibid.

McGregor's Theories X and Y

3. "Genencor Named One of America's Best Places to Work," *Dupont Industrial Biosciences,* http://biosciences.dupont.com, accessed October 30, 2017; Robert H. Mayer, https://relationshipscience.com, accessed October 30, 2017. **4.** "Sony Names Kazuo Hirai as President and CEO; Sir Howard Stringer to Become Chairman of the Board of Directors" (press release), https://www.sony.net, February 1, 2012; Brent Schlender, "Inside the Shakeup at Sony: The Surprising Selection of Howard Stringer as Sony's CEO was a Classic Boardroom Tale of Executive Intrigue and Dashed Ambitions," *Fortune,* April 4, 2005, p. 94.

Contemporary Views on Motivation

5. Michael Sasso, "Delivery Services Getting High Marks for the Holidays," *Boston Globe,* https://www.bostonglobe.com, December 28, 2017. **6.** Suzanna Kim, "Urban Outfitters Asks Employees to Volunteer for Weekend Shift in 'Team Building Activity,'" *ABC News,* http://abcnews.go.com, October 9, 2015.

From Motivation Theory to Application

7. Catey Hill, "6 Jobs Where Workers Get a Flexible Schedule—and Easily Make $100,000," *Moneyish,* https://moneyish.com, accessed January 12, 2018; "2017 Employee Benefits: Remaining Competitive in a Challenging Talent Marketplace," *Society for Human Resource Management,* https://www.shrm.org, accessed November 16, 2017. **8.** Ibid. **9.** "Piloting the Part-Time Team Initiative," https://www.amazon.jobs, accessed January 13, 2018; "2017 Employee Benefits," *Society for Human Resource Management,* https://www.shrm.org, accessed November 16, 2017; Karen Turner, "Amazon Is Piloting Teams with a 30-hour Workweek," *The Washington Post,* https://www.washingtonpost.com, accessed November 16, 2017; David Morris, "Amazon Tests 30-Hour Work Week," *Fortune,* http://fortune.com, accessed November 16, 2017; Theresa Agovino, "Is It Time to Kill the 40-Hour Workweek?," *Society for Human Resource Management,* https://www.shrm.org, accessed November 16, 2017; Stephan Aarstol, "What Happened When I Moved My Company to a 5-Hour

Workday," *Fast Company*, https://www.fastcompany.com, accessed November 16, 2017. **10.** Jacquelyn Pawela-Crew, https://www.linkedin.com, accessed October 30, 2017; Dan Enloe, https://www.linkedin.com, accessed October 30, 2017; Susan Caminiti, "A Champion of Change," *Fortune*, September 20, 2004, p. S10. **11.** Ibid. **12.** Ricardo Semler, "What Happens When You Run a Company with (Almost) No Rules?" *TED Radio Hour*, https://www.npr.org, accessed January 14, 2018; Mallen Baker, "Ricardo Semler: The Radical Boss Who Proved That Workplace Democracy Works," *Mallen Baker's Respectful Business Blog*, http://mallenbaker.net, accessed January 14, 2018; Stacy A. Teicher, "On the Frontier of Flexibility; Slowly, Companies Are Offering Flexible Schedules—a Key Demand of Workers," *The Christian Science Monitor*, June 7, 2004, p. 13. **13.** Maria Lamagna, "Job Sharing Might Be the Answer to Avoiding Burnout," *New York Post*, https://nypost.com, accessed January 14, 2018; Maria Lamagna, "Is Job-Sharing a Cop-Out or the Way to Avoid Burnout?" *MarketWatch*, https://www.marketwatch.com, accessed January 14, 2018; Vivian Wagner, "Take This Job and Share It," *AARP*, https://www.aarp.org, accessed January 14, 2018; "Work Muse in the News!" http://workmuse.com, accessed January 14, 2018. **14.** Paige Magarrey, "The Motley Fool's Awesome Employee Engagement Tactics," *Workopolis,* https://hiring.workopolis.com, accessed January 15, 2018; Ashley Bell, "33 Thoughtful Employee Recognition & Appreciation Ideas for 2018," *SnackNation,* http://www.snacknation.com, accessed January 15, 2018; Lindsay Tigar, "6 Job Perks that Actually Inspire Employee Happiness," *Ladders,* https://www.theladders.com, accessed January 15, 2018; "Our Mission: Helping the World Invest — Better," *The Motley Fool*, https://www.fool.com, accessed January 15, 2018. **15.** "Why Employees at Apple and Google Are More Productive," *Fast Company,* https://www.fastcompany.com, accessed January 15, 2018; Robert Shaw, "At Netflix, Autonomy above All Else," *Business Management Daily*, https://www.businessmanagementdaily.com, accessed January 15, 2018; Aimee Groth, "This Company Trusts Its Employees So Much It Has a 'No Limits' Expense Policy," *Quartz,* http://quartz.com, accessed January 15, 2018; Janko Roettgers, "How Netflix Ticks: Five Key Insights from the Company's New Corporate Culture Manifesto," *Variety*, http://variety.com, accessed January 15, 2018; Timothy Stenovec, "One Reason for Netflix's Success —It Treats Employees Like Grownups," *Huffington Post*, https://www.huffingtonpost.com, accessed January 15, 2018; "Netflix Culture," https://jobs.netflix.com/culture, accessed January 15, 2018. **16.** Alan Deutschman, "Can Google Stay Google?" *Fast Company*, https://www.fastcompany.com, accessed January 14, 2018; Joseph Blasi, "Tech Companies Are Shutting Employees Out of the Stock Market's Boom," *Fortune*, http://fortune.com, accessed January 14, 2018. **17.** Katie Hafner, "New Incentive for Google Employees: Awards Worth Millions," *The New York Times*, http://www.nytimes.com, accessed January 14, 2018; Paul Petrone, "Google Found Out That Giving Its Employees Trips to Hawaii Is Better Than $1M Awards," *LinkedIn Talent Blog*, https://business.linkedin.com, accessed January 14, 2018; Quentin Hardy, "Close to the Vest," *Forbes*, http://members.forbes.com, accessed January 14, 2018; Greg Linden, "Google Cuts Founders' Awards," *Geeking with Greg*, http://glinden.blogspot.com, accessed January 14, 2018; James E. McWhinney, "Raise vs. Bonus for Your Small Business Employees?" *Investopedia*, https://www.investopedia.com, accessed January 14, 2018; Jeff D. Opdyke, "Getting a Bonus Instead of a Raise: More Companies Link Pay to Performance for Broad Range of Employees," *The Wall Street Journal*, December 29, 2004, p. D1, D2. **18.** Paul Davidson, "Got a Small Raise? The Rest May Be in Your Bonus," *USA Today*, https://www.usatoday.com, accessed January 14, 2018. **19.** Jena McGregor, "Elon Musk's Pay Deal Could Be Worth $55.8 Billion—But He Could Also Get Nothing," *The Washington Post*, https://www.ndtv.com, January 28, 2018. **20.** "Despite Surge in Job Growth, Pay Raises and Bonuses for U.S. Workers Unlikely to Rise in 2018," *Aon Media Center*, http://www.aon.mediaroom.com, accessed January 14, 2018; Jena McGregor, "Your Chances of Getting a Bigger Raise or Bonus in 2018 Just Went Down," *The Washington Post*, https://www.washingtonpost.com, accessed January 14, 2018.

Trends in Employee Motivation

21. "A Statistical Profile of Employee Ownership," *National Center for Employee Ownership*, https://www.nceo.org, accessed January 15, 2018; "ESOPs by the Numbers," *National Center for Employee Ownership*, https://www.nceo.org, accessed January 15, 2018; OverHeadWatch Team, "What Is an ESOP? 3 Reasons Why You Should Consider It," http://overheadwatch.com, accessed January 20, 2018; "The Pros and Cons of Employee Stock Ownership Plans," http://www.dbd-law.com, accessed January 20, 2018. **22.** Ibid. **23.** "Research on Employee Ownership, Corporate Performance, and Employee Compensation," *National Center for Employee Ownership*, https://www.nceo.org, accessed January 15, 2018; "A Statistical Profile of Employee Ownership," *National Center for Employee Ownership*, https://www.nceo.org, accessed January 15, 2018; George Erb, "At Northwest Firms with ESOPs, Employees Act Like They Own the Place," *The Seattle Times*, https://www.seattletimes.com, accessed January 15, 2018; OverHeadWatch Team, "What Is an ESOP? 3 Reasons Why You Should Consider It," http://overheadwatch.com, accessed January 15, 2018. **24.** Tony Bartelme, "Stickin' with the Pig: A Tale of Loyalty and Loss," *The Post and Courier,* https://www.postandcourier.com, accessed January 14, 2018; "Piggly Wiggly Parent's Shares Virtually Worthless: Report," *Progressive Grocer,* https://progressivegrocer.com, accessed January 14, 2018; Warren L. Wise, "Judge Tosses Some Claims, Leaves Others in Piggly Wiggly Carolina Federal Lawsuit," *The Post and Courier,* https://www.postandcourier.com, accessed January 14, 2018; "Grapevine: Charleston Judge Tells Both Sides in Piggly Wiggly Suit to Sit Down, Talk It Out," *The Post and Courier,* https://www.postandcourier.com, accessed January 20, 2018; "Three Lessons from the Failure of Piggly Wiggly," https://www.nceo.org, accessed January 20, 2018; Loren Rodgers, "Former Employee Ownership 100 Company: Stock Now Essentially Worthless," https://www.nceo.org, accessed January 20, 2018; Warren L. Wise, "Former Piggly Wiggly Employees Told Stock Values Plummet to Near Zero," *The Post and Courier,* https://www.postandcourier.com, accessed January 14, 2018. **25.** Brena Swanson, "Are Employee Stock Ownership Plans the Key to Healthier Mortgage Finance Companies?" *HousingWire,* https://www.housingwire.com, accessed January 20, 2018; Rob Chrisman, "Jobs vs Rates; Zillow, CFPB, & RESPA in the Spotlight?" *Mortgage News Daily,* http://www.mortgagenewsdaily.com, accessed January 20, 2018; Loren Rodgers, "The Employee Ownership Update," https://www.nceo.org, accessed January 20, 2018; Rob Chrisman, "ESOP Ownership, Retail & Wholesale Jobs," http://www.robchrisman.com, accessed January 20, 2018; "Axia Home Loans Unveils Employee Stock Ownership Plan (ESOP)," https://www.mortgagecollaborative.com, accessed January 20, 2018; "ESOP Attracts Top Management," https://www.axiahomeloans.com, accessed January 20, 2018; Gellert Dornay, "ESOPs: An Attractive Exit Strategy," *Mortgage Banking* July 1, 2016. **26.** Ibid. **27.** David Burkus, "Research Shows That Organizations Benefit When Employees Take Sabbaticals," *Harvard Business Review,* https://hbr.org, accessed January 21, 2018; Jeanne Sahadi, "These Workplace Benefits Are Slowly Fading Away," *CNN Money,* http://money.cnn.com, accessed January 21, 2018; "2017 Employee Benefits Remaining Competitive in a Challenging Talent Marketplace," *Society for Human Resource Management,* https://www.shrm.org, accessed January 21, 2018; David Burkus, "The Surprising Benefit of Work Sabbaticals," *Forbes,* https://www.forbes.com, accessed January 21, 2018. **28.** Kathy Gurchiek, "4 Winning Workflex Strategies," *HR Magazine*, http://www.hrmagazine-digital.com, accessed January 21, 2018; "Morris Financial Concepts," http://www.whenworkworks.org, accessed January 21, 2018; Kathy Gurchiek, "Winning with Workflex," *HR Magazine,* http://www.hrmagazine-digital.com, accessed January 21, 2018; Cassidy Solis, "2017 When Work Works Award Winners Announced," https://www.shrm.org, accessed January 21, 2018; SHRM Online Staff, "When Work Works Winners Honored for Effective Workplace Practices," https://www.shrm.org, accessed January 21, 2018. **29.** Kathryn Vassal, "This Company Just Started Offering 6-Week Sabbaticals," *CNN Money,* http://money.cnn.com, accessed January 22, 2018; Valerie Bolden-Barrett, "Zillow to Offer Six-Week, Half-Paid Sabbaticals to Some Employees," *HR Dive,* https://www.hrdive.com, accessed January 22, 2018; Mary Shacklett, "Why More Tech Workers Should Take Sabbaticals," *TechRepublic,* https://www.techrepublic.com, accessed January 22, 2018; Kara Stiles, "Why Zillow Rewards Mid-Career Staff with Six-Week Sabbaticals," *Forbes,* https://www.forbes.com, accessed January 22, 2018; Amanda Pressner Kreuser, "One Underused Perk That Keeps Top Talent Happy and Productive at Work," *Inc.,* https://www.inc.com, accessed January 22,

2018. **30.** Kathy Gurchiek, "Fill Skills Gaps Using Learning Sabbaticals," https://www.shrm.org, accessed January 22, 2018; Hailley Griffis, "Why This Company Implemented a Learning Sabbatical for Its Employees," *Fast Company,* https://www.fastcompany.com, accessed January 22, 2018; Hailley Griffis, "Learning Sabbatical: How Existing Employees Are Developing New Skills for Different Roles," *Buffer,* https://open.buffer.com, accessed January 22, 2018. **31.** Bureau of Labor Statistics, "2017 Labor Force Statistics from the Current Population Survey," https://www.bls.gov, accessed January 23, 2018; "2016 Labor Force Statistics from the Current Population Survey," https://www.bls.gov, accessed January 23, 2018; Jean Folger, "The Causes and Costs of Absenteeism," *Investopedia,* https://www.investopedia.com, accessed January 23, 2018; Stephanie Martin Velez, "When Employees Call Off Work, You Lose Money (This is how much..)," *LinkedIn,* https://www.linkedin.com, accessed January 23, 2018; Ashley Handy, "The Cost of Absenteeism in the Workplace and How to Control It," https://www.dominionsystems.com, accessed January 23, 2018; Nettime Solutions Staff, "Minimize Employee Absenteeism with Time & Attendance Software," http://www.nettimesolutions.com, accessed January 23, 2018; Bill Cushard, "The Impact of Absenteeism," https://www.adp.com, accessed January 23, 2018; Caron Beesley, "Absenteeism in the Workplace: 7 Ways to Resolve This Bottom Line Killer," https://www.sba.gov, accessed January 23, 2018. **32.** Ibid. **33.** "Increased Number of Workers Calling in Sick When They Aren't, Finds CareerBuilder's Annual Survey," https://www.careerbuilder.com, accessed January 23, 2018; "CareerBuilder Survey: More Workers Calling in Sick When They Aren't," *Fox 5,* http://www.fox5dc.com, accessed January 23, 2018; Melissa Wylie, "More Staffers Calling in Sick—Even if They're Not," *Bizwomen*, https://www.bizjournals.com, accessed January 23, 2018; Aimee Picchi, "The Worst Excuses for Taking a Sick Day," *MoneyWatch*, https://www.cbsnews.com, accessed January 23, 2018. **34.** Folger, "The Causes and Costs of Absenteeism"; Martin Velez, "When Employees Call Off Work, You Lose Money"; "How to Reduce Absenteeism in the Workplace," *GTM Business Blog*, https://gtm.com, accessed January 23, 2018; "Absence Management: Three Ways to Reduce Employee Absenteeism," https://atstimecom.accu-time.com, accessed January 23, 2018; Patricia Lotich, "4 Tips for Reducing Absenteeism in the Workplace," *The Thriving Small Business,* https://thethrivingsmallbusiness.com, accessed January 23, 2018. **35.** Brandon Carter, "2017 Employee Engagement & Loyalty Statistics," *Access Perks Blog*, https://blog.accessperks.com, accessed January 24, 2018; "Job Seeking & Hiring Statistics," *Statistic Brain*, https://www.statisticbrain.com, accessed January 24, 2018; Brandon Carter, "Employee Engagement & Loyalty Statistics: The Ultimate Collection," *Access Perks Blog*, https://blog.accessperks.com, accessed January 24, 2018; Marcel Schwantes, "Why Do Employees Really Quit Their Jobs? Research Says It Comes Down to These Top 8 Reasons," *Inc.*, https://www.inc.com, accessed January 24, 2018. **36.** Bernard Marr, "Why Great Employees Quit," *CNBC,* https://www.cnbc.com, accessed January 24, 2018; Marcel Schwantes, "Why Do People Quit Their Jobs, Exactly? Here's the Entire Reason, Summed Up in 1 Sentence," *Inc.*, https://www.inc.com, accessed January 24, 2018; Jack Altman, "Don't Be Surprised When Your Employees Quit," *Forbes*, https://www.forbes.com, accessed January 24, 2018; "Why Employees Quit, According to New Glassdoor Economic Research," https://www.glassdoor.com, accessed January 24, 2018; Phil Albinus, "The Real Reason Employees Leave Their Employer," *Employee Benefit News (Online)*, https://www.benefitnews.com, accessed January 24, 2018; Joyce Maroney, "Stay or Go? Employees Say Job Satisfaction Matters Most," Workforce Institute, https://workforceinstitute.org, accessed January 24, 2018.

Location, Location, Location: Where Do We Make It?

1. Soyoung Kim, "New Water Bottling Plant in Los Lunas Brings Jobs, But Also Concerns," *KRQE News,* http://krqe.com, November 17, 2016. **2.** Brandon Loomis, "What drought? Nestle Plans $35 million plant to bottle water in Phoenix," *The Republic,* https://www.azcentral.com, May 19, 2016. **3.** Lydia DePillis, "Cities Try to Lure Amazon, But Want to Keep the Details Secret," *CNN*, http://money.cnn.com, October 19, 2017.

Pulling It Together: Resource Planning

4. Mike Colias and William Mauldin, "GM Expects to Move 600 Supplier Jobs from Mexico to Texas," *The Wall

Street Journal, https://www.wsj.com, June 16, 2017. **5.** Christian Davenport, "Is $48 Too Much for the Federal Government to Pay for a Hammer?" *The Washington Post,* https://www.washingtonpost.com, June 25, 2014. **6.** "Army Awards FedBid Contract to Provide Reverse Auction Acquisition Solution," *Business Wire,* https://www.businesswire.com, May 31, 2017. **7.** Aaron Huff, "Will Blockchain Extend or Disrupt Your Business?" *Commercial Carrier Journal,* https://www.ccjdigital.com, December 19, 2017.

Production and Operations Control
8. Claudia Infante,"Value Stream Mapping Boosts Productivity for Awning Maker," *Finance New Mexico,* https://financenewmexico.org, October 9, 2016.

Looking for a Better Way: Improving Production and Operations
9. "Best of the Best" Win U.S. National Excellence Honor: 2017 Baldrige Award Goes to 5 Outstanding Organizations," https://www.commerce.gov, November 16, 2017.

Trends in Production and Operations Management
10. National Association of Manufacturers, "Top 20 Facts About Manufacturing," http://www.nam.org, accessed February 20, 2018. **11.** Ibid. **12.** Matt Hourihan and David Parkes, "AAAS Appropriations Roundup," http://www.innovationtaskforce.org, September 16, 2016. **13.** World Bank, "High-Technology Exports," https://data.worldbank.org, accessed February 20, 2018. **14.** National Association of Manufacturers, "Manufacturers Strive to Close Skills Gap," https://www.nahad.org, accessed February 20, 2018. **15.** Benjamin Brandell, "What Is Business Process Management? A Really Simple Introduction," *Business 2 Community,* https://www.business2community.com, August 18, 2016. **16.** Dave Blanchard, "Dell Reinvents Its Supply Chain," *Industry Week,* http://www.industryweek.com, December 16, 2010. **17.** "Business Value of Process Standards," http://www.bpminstitute.org, accessed February 20, 2018.

The Marketing Concept
1. "Lexus Rises to the Top in Customer Satisfaction," *Automotive News,* http://www.autonews.com, August 25, 2015. **2.** "What Is Customer Retention?" *Customer Insight Group,* https://www.customerinsightgroup.com, April 20, 2017.

Creating a Marketing Strategy
3. Anna Nicolaou, "How Streaming Saved the Music Industry," *Financial Times,* https://www.ft.com, January 16, 2017.

Buyer Behavior
4. Catalin Zorzini, "Infographic: An Analysis of Online Shopping Habits of Men & Women," https://ecommerce-platforms.com, accessed October 8, 2017.

Market Segmentation
5. "Nielsen Announces Launch of National Television Out-of-Home Measurement Service," http://www.nielsen.com, October 24, 2016.

Creating Products That Deliver Value
6. Gary Hamel and Nancy Tenant, "The Five Requirements of a Truly Innovative Company," *Harvard Business Review,* https://hbr.org, April 27, 2015. **7.** Drake Baer and Jay Yarrow, "22 of the Most Epic Product Failures in History," *Business Insider,* http://www.businessinsider.com, July 31, 2014.

Trends in Developing Products and Pricing
8. Eugene Kim, "Amazon's Prime Membership Is Eating into Costco and Sam's Club's Territory," *Business Insider,* http://www.businessinsider.com, September 26, 2016. **9.** Glenn Taylor, "More than 90% of Consumers Use Smartphones While Shopping in Stores," *Retail Touch Points,* https://www.retailtouchpoints.com, August 20, 2015. **10.** Daniel Boffey, "Google Price Comparison Site to Compete with Rivals for Top Search Slot," *The*

Guardian, https://www.theguardian.com, September 27, 2017.

The Competitive World of Retailing
1. Jessica Dyer, "Albuquerque Lands a Big Catch in Retailing," *Albuquerque Journal,*
https://www.abqjournal.com, July 14, 2016; Stephen Singer, "Cabela's Touted as a Tourist Destination," *Deseret News*, https://www.deseretnews.com, October 28, 2007.

Promotion Strategy
2. Dan Orlando, "Kraft Heinz, Oprah Announce Retail Food Line," *Supermarket News*,
http://www.supermarketnews.com, August 11, 2017. **3.** "Stunt Marketing or No, Dominos Has Refurbished Their Brand," University of Maryland website, December 1, 2016, https://www.rhsmith.umd.edu/news/stunt-marketing-or-no-dominos-has-refurbished-its-brand **4.** Edmundas Jasinskas et al, "Impact of Hotel Service Quality on the Loyalty of Customers," *Economic Research,* 29(1): 559–572, 2016. **5.** "Low fares. Nothing to hide: Transfarency," www.southwest.com, accessed March 21, 2018; S. Carey, "Southwest Airlines Launches 'Transfarency' Campaign," *The Wall Street Journal,* https://www.wsj.com, October 8, 2015.

The Huge Impact of Advertising
6. Lucia Moses, "A Look at Kids' Exposure to Ads," *Ad Week*, http://www.adweek.com, March 11, 2014. **7.** "US Ad Spending: The eMarketer Forecast for 2017," *eMarketer*, https://www.emarketer.com, March 15, 2017. **8.** "Global Ad Spending Growth to Double This Year," *eMarketer*, https://www.emarketer.com, July 9, 2014. **9.** Lara O'Reilly, "These Are the 10 Companies that Spend the Most on Advertising," *Business Insider,* http://www.businessinsdier.com, July 6, 2015 **10.** "TV Universe Grows to 119.6 Million Homes for 2016-2017 Season," *Marketing Charts*, http://www.marketingcharts.com, August 29, 2017.

Sales Promotion
11. Jim Tincher, "Your Moment of Truth," *Customer Think*, http://customerthink.com, August 30, 2016. **12.** "Coupon Statistics: The Ultimate Collection," *Access Development*, http://blog.accessdevelopment.com, May 17, 2017. **13.** Drew Hendricks, "5 Ways to Enhance Your SEO Campaign with Online Coupons," *Forbes*, https://www.forbes.com, May 13, 2015 **14.** Laurent Muzellec, "James Bond, Dunder Mifflin, and the Future of Product Placement," *Harvard Business Review,* https://hbr.org, June 23, 2016. **15.** Josh Terry, "Unfunny Emoji Movie Is a Sad Echo of 2015's "Inside Out," *Deseret News*, http://www.deseretnews.com, July 31, 2017. **16.** Don Steinberg, "Science Affliction: Are Companies Cursed by Cameos in Blade Runner?" *The Wall Street Journal*, https://www.wsj.com, September 25, 2017.

Trends in Social Media
17. "Blog Posts Written Today," WorldoMeter, http://www.worldometer.info, accessed August 30, 2017; Tumblr website, https://www.tumblr.com, accessed August 30, 2017. **18.** Carly Botelho, "5 Impressive Brand Blogs and What They're Doing Right," *Business 2 Community,* http://www.business2community.com, March 21, 2014. **19.** Peter Kafka, "Podcast Network Gimlet Media Has Raised Another $5 Million—This Time from Ad Giant WPP," *Recode*, https://www.recode.net, September 6, 2017. **20.** "U.S. Pet Food Market Size & Share Is Expected to Reach USD 30.01 Billion in 2022: Zion Market Research," https://globenewswire.com, May 22, 2017; "How Purina Made Fetch Happen [Again]," *Medium.com,* https://medium.com, April 5, 2017.

Trends in E-Commerce
21. Stefany Zaroban and Fareeha Ali, "US Online Retail Posts Its Largest Gain in Five Years," *Internet Retailer,* https://www.digitalcommerce360.com, August 17, 2017. **22.** "Voice Echoes Outside the Warehouse," *DCVelocity,* http://dcvelocity.com, September 5, 2017. **23.** John Furth, "Amazon vs. Walmart Is Shaping Up to Be a Battle of the Mega-Retailers," *New York Daily News*, http://www.nydailynews.com, August 30, 2017.

Transforming Businesses through Information
1. Jason Compton, "Meet the Supercomputer Driving a Business Boom in the UK," *Forbes,*

https://www.forbes.com, Junes 14, 2016. **2.** Patrick Thibodeau, "U.S. To Have 200-Petaflop Supercomputer by Early 2018,"*Computer World*, https://www.computerworld.com, June 21, 2016. **3.** Thomas Friedman, *The World Is Flat* (New York: Farrar, Straus and Giroux, 2005) p. 8. **4.** Bhavan Jaipragas, "Free Trade for Minnows: How Alibaba Gave Malaysia's e-Hub Hopes a Boost," *This Week in Asia*, http://www.scmp.com, November 20, 2017.

Linking Up: Computer Networks

5. Jason Newton and Jesse Gosselin, "VA Looks to Install WiFi after News 8 Story," *WTNH News 8*, http://wtnh.com, February 20, 2017. **6.** Toby Ward, "Technology, the Intranet, and Employee Productivity," *Prescient Digital Media*, http://www.prescientdigital.com, accessed February 21, 2018. **7.** John Quain, "Alexa, What Happened to My Car?" *The New York Times*, https://www.nytimes.com, January 25, 2018. **8.** Michael Franco, "The Beginner's Guide to VPN's," *Life Hacker,* https://lifehacker.com, November 20, 2017. **9.** Chris Preimesberger, "Why Cloud Services Became the New Normal in 2017," *eWeek*, http://www.eweek.com, January 4, 2018. **10.** Bob Evans, "How Cloud Heavyweights Microsoft, Amazon and IBM Will Transform Cloud Computing in 2018," *Forbes,* January 3, 2018, https://www.forbes.com. **11.** "Global Managed IT Service Providers Market 2018-2021," *PR Newswire,* https://www.prnewswire.com, January 17, 2018.

Management Information Systems

12. Kathleen Hickey, "Data Warehouses Integrate Supply Chains," *World Trade*, February 1, 2006, p. 42.

Technology Management and Planning

13. Sami Barry, "The Strategic Role of a Chief Knowledge Officer," *Helbling and Associates, Inc. Insights*, https://www.helblingsearch.com, September 27, 2012. **14.** Milon Gupta, "How Strategic Leaders Use Storytelling," *Strategic Thinking*, http://www.strategicthinking.eu, November 2, 2015.

Protecting Computers and Information

15. Chris Low, "Information Security Policies Every Business Must Implement," *CIO*, https://www.cio.com, August 16, 2017. **16.** Steve Morgan, "Cyber Crime Costs Projected to Reach $2 Trillion by 2019," *Forbes*, https://www.forbes.com, January 17, 2016. **17.** Sean Michael Kerner, "IDC Analysts Identify IT Security Trends at RSA," *eWeek*, http://www.eweek.com, April 22, 2015. **18.** Ibid. **19.** Jack Cloherty and Pierre Thomas, "Trojan Horse Bug Lurking in Vital US Computers Since 2011," *ABC News*, http://abcnews.go.com, November 6, 2014. **20.** "Effective Planning and Preparation Can Reduce Impact of 2018 Cyber Security Attacks, Data Breaches," *Yahoo Finance*, https://finance.yahoo.com, January 30, 2018.

Trends in Information Technology

21. Patrick Watson, "Why Bitcoin Has Inflation Risk," *Equities.com,* https://www.equities.com, January 13, 2018. **22.** Kaveh Waddell, "CSI: Walmart," *The Atlantic,* https://www.theatlantic.com, April 3, 2017; Dave Smith, "Computer Fraud and Abuse Act 2013: New CFAA Draft Aims to Expand, Not Reform, the 'Worst Law in Technology'," *International Business Times*, http://www.ibtimes.com, March 28, 2013. **23.** "Remote Work is 'the New Normal,'" *Fast Company,* https://www.fastcompany.com, February 28, 2018. **24.** Michael Guta, "3.9 Million Americans—including Freelancers—Now Work from Home at Least Half the Week," *Small Business Trends,* https://smallbiztrends.com, April 2, 2018. **25.** Andrea Loubier, "Benefits of Telecommuting for the Future of Work," *Forbes*, https://www.forbes.com, July 20, 2017; Michelle Conlin, "The Easiest Commute of All," *Business Week*, December 12, 2005, p. 78. **26.** Paul Trujillo, "5 Reasons Small Businesses Need the Cloud," *B2C Community*, https://www.business2community.com, January 30, 2018.

Accounting: More than Numbers

1. Sneha Shah, "10 Biggest Recent Accounting Scandals in America," http://www.insidermonkey.com, March 27, 2017; Pat Wechsler, "This CEO Spent Nearly 7 Years in Jail. Now He's Helping Ex-Cons," *Fortune,* http://fortune.com, February 16, 2016; Joseph Ax, "Ex-Accounting Executive Avoids Prison in Madoff Fraud Case," *Reuters,* http://www.reuters.com, July 9, 2015; Scott Cohn, "Former Enron Executive Jeffrey Skilling

Moved to Minimum-Security Prison," *CNBC,* https://www.cnbc.com, January 9, 2014.

The Accounting Profession
2. "Accounting Industry in the U.S.," *Statista,* https://www.statista.com, accessed August 10, 2017; "Accountants and Auditors," *Occupational Outlook Handbook,* https://www.bls.gov, accessed August 10, 2017. **3.** Raymond Doherty, "Deloitte Overtakes PwC as World's Largest Firm," http://economia.icaew.com, accessed August 10, 2017. **4.** "About the AICPA," http://www.aicpa.org, accessed August 10, 2017. **5.** Eric Krell, "What Triggers Financial Restatements?" *Business Finance* magazine, http://businessfinancemag.com, accessed August 10, 2017. **6.** "A Guide to the Sarbanes-Oxley Act," http://www.soxlaw.com, accessed August 11, 2017; Ken Tysiac, "Companies Spending More Time on SOX Compliance," *Journal of Accountancy,* http://www.journalofaccountancy.com, June 12, 2017. **7.** "Fine-Tuning the SOX Compliance Process," https://www.protiviti.com, accessed August 11, 2017.

Trends in Accounting
8. "Key Developments in Standard-Setting for Private Companies," https://www.pwc.com, accessed August 10, 2017. **9.** Henry Bell, "6 Accounting Trends to Watch Out for in 2017 (And How to Make the Most of Then)," *The Receipt Bank Blog,* https://blog.receipt-bank.com, December 19, 2016; Samuel Edwards, "5 Trends Driving Disruption in the Accounting Industry," *Entrepreneur,* https://www.entrepreneur.com, September 23, 2016. **10.** Mary Ellen Biery, "3 Top Tech Trends for Public Accountants to Watch in 2017," https://www.accountingtoday.com, February 15, 2017. **11.** Sarah Ovaska-Few, "Technology Trends for Accounting Firm Leaders," *Journal of Accountancy,* http://www.journalofaccountancy.com, June 14, 2017.

Show Me the Money
1. "Currency in Circulation," https://fred.stlouisfed.org, accessed September 7, 2017. **2.** "Money Stock and Debt Measures—H.6 Release," https://www.federalreserve.gov, accessed September 7, 2017.

The Federal Reserve System
3. "The Federal Reserve Payments Study 2016," https://www.federalreserve.gov, accessed September 7, 2017; Brad Kvederis, "The Paper Check Lives: Why the Check Decline Slowed in 2016," http://fi.deluxe.com, January 19, 2017. **4.** "BLS Spotlight on Statistics: The Recession of 2007–2009," http://www.bls.gov/spotlight, accessed September 7, 2017. **5.** "Predatory Lending," *The Economist,* https://www.economist.com, accessed September 7, 2017; Steve Denning, "Lest We Forget: Why We Had a Financial Crisis," *Forbes,* http://www.forbes.com, November 22, 2011. **6.** Kimberly Amadeo, "What Is Too Big to Fail? With Examples of Banks," *The Balance,* https://www.thebalance.com, accessed September 7, 2017; John Maxfield, "A Timeline of Bear Stearns' Downfall," *The Motley Fool,* https://www.fool.com, accessed September 7, 2017. **7.** Chris Isidore, "Fed Made $9 Trillion in Emergency Overnight Loans," *CNN Money,* http://money.cnn.com, accessed September 7, 2017. **8.** Mark Koba, "Dodd-Frank Act: CNBC Explains," *CNBC,* https://www.cnbc.com, accessed September 7, 2017. **9.** James McBride, "The Role of the U.S. Federal Reserve," *Council on Foreign Relations,* https://www.cfr.org, accessed September 7, 2017; Donna Borak, "For the First Time, All U.S. Banks Pass Fed's Stress Tests," *CNN Money,* http://money.cnn.com, June 28, 2017.

U.S. Financial Institutions
10. "Statistics at a Glance as of June 30, 2017," https://www.fdic.gov, accessed September 7, 2017. **11.** "FDIC-Insured Savings Institutions," https://www5.fdic.gov, accessed September 7, 2017. **12.** "A Brief History of Credit Unions," and "Industry at a Glance as of 3/31/17," https://www.ncua.gov, accessed September 7, 2017. **13.** "U.S. Public Pension Assets Rise to $3.396 Trillion in Q4—Census," http://www.reuters.com, March 30, 2017.

Insuring Bank Deposits
14. "Who Is the FDIC?" https://www.fdic.gov, accessed September 7, 2017.

International Banking

15. James Passeri, "Citigroup Tops List of U.S. Banks with Exposure to China: Update," http://realmoney.thestreet.com, January 13, 2016. **16.** "Assets and Liabilities of U.S. Branches and Agencies of Foreign Banks," https://www.federalreserve.gov, accessed September 8, 2017. **17.** Thomas Colson, "At Least 12 Banks Are Moving Some Operations from London to Dublin after Brexit," *Business Insider,* http://www.businessinsider.com, June 30, 2017; Peter S. Goodman, "Europe's Economy, After 8-Year Detour, Is Fitfully Back on Track," *The New York Times,* https://www.nytimes.com, April 29, 2016.

Trends in Financial Institutions

18. Julie Conroy, "Top 10 Trends in Retail Banking & Payments, 2017: Data Analytics Differentiate," http://aitegroup.com, accessed September 7, 2017. **19.** Andre Bourque, "12 Top Fintech Companies to Watch," *Entrepreneur,* https://www.entrepreneur.com, February 28, 2017. **20.** Jim Marous, "Top 10 Retail Banking Trends and Predictions for 2017," *The Financial Brand,* https://thefinancialbrand.com, accessed September 7, 2017. **21.** Paul Maplesden, "8 PayPal Alternatives for Your Online Business," https://www.sitepoint.com, accessed September 7, 2017; "Pros and Cons of Mobile Check Deposit," *Consumer Reports,* https://www.consumerreports.org, accessed September 7, 2017.

Introduction

1. Danielle Kurtzleben, "While Trump Touts Stock Market, Many Americans Are Left Out of the Conversation," *NPR,* http://www.npr.org, March 1, 2017.

The Role of Finance and the Financial Manager

2. Gary P. Pisano, "You Need an Innovation Strategy," *Harvard Business Review,* https://hbr.org, accessed October 10, 2017. **3.** Panos Mourdoukoutas, "Corning Beats Apple," *Forbes,* https://www.forbes.com, July 9, 2017.

How Organizations Use Funds

4. Janis O'Dwyer, "5 Accounts Receivable & Collection Statistics That Should Scare You," https://www.yaypay.com, March 30, 2017. **5.** Susan Kelly, "Credit Management Technology Plays Catch-Up," *Treasury & Risk,* http://www.treasuryandrisk.com, March 20, 2017. **6.** Jason Bramwell, "CFOs More Likely to Outsource Accounting and Finance Projects," *Accounting Web,* https://www.accountingweb.com, accessed October 10, 2017. **7.** Joshua Kennon, "How to Calculate Inventory Turnover/Turns from the Balance Sheet," *The Balance,* https://www.thebalance.com, February 28, 2017.

Equity Financing

8. Peter McKay, "Why Going Public Doesn't Make Sense Right Now," *Fortune,* http://fortune.com, September 13, 2017; Brandon Kochkodin, "Blue Apron Is the IPO Bust of the Decade," *Bloomberg,* https://www.bloomberg.com, August 10, 2017. **9.** Chris Taylor, "The Best 11 Dividend Stocks for 2017," *Fortune,* http://fortune.com, December 2016. **10.** Jessica E. Vascellaro, "Apple Pads Investor Wallets," *The Wall Street Journal,* https://www.wsj.com, accessed October 10, 2017.

Securities Markets

11. Suzanne Woolley, "TD Ameritrade Jumps into Price War with Fidelity and Schwab," *Bloomberg,* http://www.bloomberg.com, February 27, 2017. **12.** "US Bond Trading Volume" and "2016 Year in Review," https://www.sifma.org, accessed October 10, 2017. **13.** "2016 Year in Review," https://www.sifma.org, accessed October 10, 2017. **14.** "US Bond Market Issuance & Outstanding," https://www.sifma.org, accessed October 10, 2017. **15.** "2016 Year in Review. **16.** "2017 Investment Company Fact Book," http://www.icifactbook.org, accessed October 11, 2017. **17.** Ibid.

Buying and Selling at Securities Exchanges

18. "Markets Diary: Closing Snapshot," *The Wall Street Journal,* http://www.wsj.com, accessed October 11, 2017;

"NYSE 2016 Year in Review," https://www.nyse.com, accessed October 11, 2017. **19.** "Non-U.S. Issuers Data," https://www.nyse.com, accessed October 11, 2017. **20.** John D'Antona, "The Reg NMS Debate Goes On and On," https://marketsmedia.com, June 23, 2017. **21.** "NASDAQ 2017/2016 Monthly Volumes," http://www.nasdaq.com, accessed October 11, 2017. **22.** "NASDAQ's Story," http://business.nasdaq.com, accessed October 12, 2017. **23.** "NASDAQ's Listing Markets," http://business.nasdaq.com, accessed October 12, 2017. **24.** Jeff Desjardins, "Here Are the 20 Biggest Stock Exchanges in the World," *Business Insider,* http://www.businessinsider.com, April 11, 2017; Jeff Desjardins, "All of the World's Stock Exchanges by Size," *Visual Capitalist,* http://money.visualcapitalist.com, February 16, 2016. **25.** "Indian Sensex Stock Market Index" and "Indian GDP Annual Growth Rate," https://tradingeconomics.com, accessed October 12, 2017. **26.** Zack Guzman and Mark Koba, "When Do Circuit Breakers Kick In? CNBC Explains," *CNBC,* https://www.cnbc.com, January 8, 2016.

Trends in Financial Management and Securities Markets

27. "The CFO's Evolving Role," https://home.kpmg.com, August 1, 2017; John Maxfield, "The Dodd-Frank Act Explained," *USA Today,* https://www.usatoday.com, February 3, 2017. **28.** Frank Chaparro, "A Merger Between 2 Stock Exchange Behemoths Makes a Lot of Sense," *Business Insider,* http://www.businessinsider.com, April 12, 2017.

Developing Interpersonal Skills Is Key to Your Success

1. Kristine Tucker, "The Importance of Interpersonal Skills in the Workplace," *Career Trend,* https://careertrend.com, July 5, 2017. **2.** Christina DesMarais, "How to Think on Your Feet Under Pressure: 6 Tips," *Inc.,* https://www.inc.com, accessed November 14, 2017. **3.** The Persuasion self-test was created by the authors and from the following sources: *Persuade Others to Follow Your Way of Thinking,* http://www.winstonbrill.com; *Six Unique Ways to Persuade Others,* http://www.micaworld.com; *Strategies of Influence and Persuasion,* Kendrick Cleveland, http://www.maxpersuasion.com; *Power Persuasion—How to Persuade People,* http://www.1000ventures.com; *How to Persuade and Influence People,* Wolf J. Rinke, Ph.D., CSP, #554 Innovative Leader, Volume 11, Number 6, June 2002, http://www.winstonbrill.com. **4.** The Office Politics scale was developed by the authors and from the following sources: *Don't Sabotage Your Success!—Make Office Politics Work,* Karen Ginsburg Wood, http://www.atlasbooks.com/markplc/00492.htm; *Play the Office Politics Game,* Cynthia A. Broderick, http://www.bankrate.com; *The Fairness of Office Politics . . . Integrity and Political Motivation!* Edward B. Toupin, http://hotlib.com; *Fly Under the Radar to Absorb Delicate Office Politics,* Peter Vogt, MonsterTRAK Career Coach, http://content.monstertrak.monster.com; *The New Office Politics: We've Seen the Enemy at Work, and Sometimes It's Us,* Audrey Edwards, *Essence*, March 2005, http://www.findarticles.com/p/articles/mi_ml264/is_11_35/ai_n11830673; *Assessment—Office Politics,* First Edition, http://www.course.com/downloads/courseilt/e-assessments/0619254394.pdf; and *Play Office Politics and Keep Your Soul,* http://www.createyourvision.com/playofficepolitics.htm. **5.** Alison Davis, "15 Questions You Should Ask Every Time You Start a Project," *Inc.,* https://www.inc.com, accessed November 19, 2017; Brett Harned, "10 Important Questions to Ask Your Client Before Your Project Starts," https://www.teamgantt.com, May 7, 2015.

Make Your Future Happen: Learn to Plan

6. The section on planning is adapted from: *Investing in Your Future* (Thomson South-Western, a part of The Thomson Corporation, 2007), pp. 1–10.

Going to College Is an Opportunity of a Lifetime—Never Drop Out

7. The material on Going to College is adapted from Abby Marks-Beale, *Success Skills: Strategies for Study and Lifelong Learning* (Thomson South-Western, a part of The Thomson Corporation, 2007). **8.** The Time Management scale was created by the authors and from the following sources: *Time Management Quiz,* http://www.nus.edu.sg/osa/guidance/quiz/timemgmtquiz.html; *Manage Your Time in Ten Steps,* http://www.familyeducation.com/article/0,1120,1-263,00.html; *Time Management Quiz,* http://tools.monster.com/quizzes/pareto; *Stress Management, Better Health Channel,* http://www.betterhealth.vic.gov.au/bhcv2/bhcsite.nsf/pages/quiz_manage_stress? *Stress Management Quiz,* http://www.betterhealth.vic.gov.au/bhcv2/bhcsite.nsf/pages/quiz_manage_stress?; *Time Management,* http://uwadmnweb.uwyo.edu/RanchRecr/handbook/time_management.htm; and *Time Management: Importance of Good Practice,* http://www.accel-team.com/techniques/time_management.html. **9.** The Ability to Manage Money scale was created by your authors from the following sources: *Quiz – Can You Manage Money?,* http://collegeanduniversity.net/collegeinfo/index.cfm?catid=20&pageid=2339&affid=75; *Boston.com/Business/ Your Money,* http://www.boston.com/business/personalfinance/articles/2005/04/ 03can_you_manage_your_own_month?mode=PF; *Psychology of Money Management,* http://www.uwec.edu/ counsel/pubs/Money.htm; *Managing Your Money,* http://www.nelliemae.com/managingmoney; *The Importance of Managing Money,* http://www.mtstcil.org/skills/budget-12.html; and *How Do You Rate as a Money Manager?,* http://cahe.nmsu.edu/pubs/_g/G-219.pdf. **10.** The self-quiz on How to Study was prepared by the authors and from the following sources: *EDinformatics – Education for the Information Age,* http://www.edinformatics.com/ education/howtostudy.htm; *The Manila Time*s, March 20, 2004, http://www.manilatimes.net/national/2004/ mar/20/yehey/life/20040320lif2.html; *Ten Traps of Studying—Improving Your Studying Skills—CAPS—UNC—Chapel Hill,* http://caps.unc.edu/TenTraps.html; and *Language Study Skills,* http://www.usingenglish.com/study-skills.html.

Get Your Career Off on the Right Track

11. Peter Jones, "5 Ways to Make Your Career Dreams Come True," *The Job Network,* https://www.thejobnetwork.com, accessed November 19, 2017; Julie Griffin Levitt. *Your Career: How to Make It Happen*, 5th edition (Thomson South-Western, a part of The Thomson Corporation, 2006), pp. 2–4. **12.** The Assertiveness test was prepared by the authors and from the following sources: *Test Your Assertive Level,* http://www.hodu.com/assertiveness-skills.shtml; *Assertive Action Plan,* http://www.headinjury.com/ assertplan.html; *Assertiveness,* http://www.coping.org/relations/assert.htm; *Perception of Assertiveness as a Function of Tag Questions,* http://www.ycp.edu/besc/Journal2002/paper%201.htm; and *Assertion Training,* http://front.csulb.edu/tstevens/assertion_training.htm. **13.** Brian Tracy, "Top 7 Qualities Employers Are Looking For in Candidates," *Undercover Recruiter,* https://theundercoverrecruiter.com, accessed November 19, 2017; Liz Ryan, "12 Qualities Employers Look for When They're Hiring," *Forbes,* https://www.forbes.com, March 2, 2016. **14.** "25 Best Cities for Jobs 2017," *Glassdoor,* https://www.glassdoor.com, accessed November 19, 2017; Tony Merevick, "Here Are the 25 Best Cities in America to Find a Job This Year," *Thrillist,* https://www.thrillist.com, September 15, 2017. **15.** "Entry Level Resume Information," https://collegegrad.com, accessed November 19, 2017. **16.** "How We Hire," https://careers.google.com, accessed November 19, 2017. **17.** "Top 15 Most Popular Job Websites: July 2017," *eBiz/MBA Guide*, http://www.ebizmba.com, accessed November 19, 2017. **18.** Mary Brandel, "Tech Resume Makeover: How to Add Multimedia," *CIO,* https://www.cio.com, accessed November 19, 2017. **19.** Alison Doyle, "Resume Keywords and Tips for Using Them," *The Balance,* https://www.thebalance.com, August 4, 2017. **20.** Ibid. **21.** Katharine Hansen, "College Students: You Simply Must Do an Internship (Better yet: Multiple Internships)!" *Live Career,* https://www.livecareer.com, accessed November 19, 2017. **22.** "17 Clever Ways to Interview Like a Pro," *Undercover Recruiter,* https://theundercoverrecruiter.com, accessed November 19, 2017; Alison Doyle, "Most Common Interview Mistakes," *The Balance,* https://www.thebalance.com, October 9, 2017. **23.** The Are You a Good Listener scale was created by the authors and from the following sources: *American Management Association – Self-Test: Are You a Good Listener,* http://www.amanet.org/ arc_center/archive/quiz_aug2003.htm; *How To Be an Active Listener,* http://techrepublic.com/ 5102-10878-5054191.html; *Are You a Good Listener?,* http://www.nidoqubein.com/article15.html; *Are You a Good Listener?,* http://www.lwvohio.org/members/postboard/june2004/Are_You_a_Good_Listener.pdf; *Productivity – Are You a Good Listener?,* http://www.effectivemeetings.com/productivity/communication/listener.asp; *Are You* *a Good Listener?—Listen and Profit,* Mike Kelly, http://www.simplysolo.com/kelly.htm; *Joan Lloyd at Work,* http://www.joanlloyd.com/articles/open.asp?art=026.htm; and *Humanities 2000—Listening Skills,* http://www.h2000.utoledo.edu/hs/clay/ListenSkills.html.

Understanding the Legal Environment
1. Lesley Fair, "Court Orders $280 Million from Dish Network, Largest Ever Do Not Call Penalty," https://www.ftc.gov, accessed June 23, 2017.

Index

CPSIA information can be obtained
at www.ICGtesting.com
Printed in the USA
BVHW021139080223
658059BV00011B/242